Readings in

CHILD
PSYCHOLOGY

SECOND EDITION

Readings in

CHILD PSYCHOLOGY

SECOND EDITION

Edited by

WAYNE DENNIS

Department of Psychology
Brooklyn College
of the City University of New York

Prentice-Hall, Inc.
ENGLEWOOD CLIFFS, N. J.

PRENTICE-HALL INTERNATIONAL, INC.
London • Tokyo • Sydney • Paris

PRENTICE-HALL OF CANADA, LTD.

PRENTICE-HALL DE MEXICO, S.A.

LIBRARY OF CONGRESS CATALOG NO.: 62-20092

PRINTED IN THE UNITED STATES OF AMERICA
75569-C

Fourth printing .... April, 1965

PREFACE

The first edition of this book appeared in 1951. The period since that time has been a very active one in child psychology. In slightly more than a decade much has happened to change the thinking of most child psychologists, including the editor of these readings. It is time, therefore, for a new edition.

Of the selections included in the new edition, one-third of these have appeared since the first edition was prepared. But in addition to incorporating many writings published since 1951, the new edition also includes some selections published earlier but not forming a part of the 1951 volume. The inclusion of a considerable amount of material not in the first edition has necessarily required the elimination of other material, some of which appears outdated at the present time and some of which has been superseded by better studies.

However, the editor has not abandoned important early contributions merely because of their age. Much excellent work was done in our field in the 1920's and the 1930's, and several classics from these periods and even earlier have been retained.

This edition, like the first edition, has made an eclectic choice of materials. Whatever the theoretical biases of the editor may be—and doubtless they show through—nevertheless he believes that readers should be exposed to a variety of points of view. For this reason he has deliberately included material from persons as different in viewpoint as Sigmund Freud, John B. Watson, Arnold Gesell, Kurt Lewin, and Jean Piaget. What this book proposes to do, therefore, is to supply to the reader a wealth of worthwhile materials.

The editor wishes to express his appreciation to the many authors and publishers who have been most generous in permitting the use of their publications. Specific acknowledgments will be found in connection with each selection.

WAYNE DENNIS

CONTENTS

I—PRENATAL AND NEONATAL BEHAVIOR

1 · The Development of Behavior in the Human Fetus

DAVENPORT HOOKER

This selection constitutes part of a lecture delivered at the University of Michigan and published by the University of Michigan in 1944 under the title *The Origin of Behavior*. It is reprinted (pages 19-35) by permission of Dr. Hooker. The illustrations are reprinted with Dr. Hooker's permission from A *Preliminary Atlas of Early Human Fetal Activity*, which was privately printed by Dr. Hooker in 1939.

The earliest human responses can be observed directly only on those relatively rare occasions when medical necessity requires the removal of the fetus. Over a period of many years Hooker had the cooperation of the medical profession in a large metropolitan center in making such fetuses available for observation. Hooker's series of cases is by far the most numerous yet reported, and his studies are likely to be the authoritative ones in this field for many years. In addition to the extensiveness of his series, Hooker had the further advantage, not shared by earlier investigators, of being able to record by means of the motion picture camera the fetal behavior that he studied. These records make it possible for unusual opportunities for observation to be shared permanently by other scientists. They will enable any researcher to observe the films repeatedly in order to arrive at a careful analysis and evaluation.

The behavior of the fetuses of infrahuman animals has been studied very extensively. If the student should wish to compare the human observations presented in this chapter with the methods and results of related animal studies, he may find a comprehensive survey of fetal behavior by Leonard Carmichael in his MANUAL OF CHILD PSYCHOLOGY, *2nd ed. Baltimore: John Wiley and Sons, Inc., 1954.*

Before giving you the data that I have gathered on the prenatal development of human behavior, it seems wise to discuss some of the conditions under which these human fetal observations were made and some of the methods used. These may give you an idea of some of the factors which might be considered as limiting the validity of observations on human fetuses. That such limitation exists is evident; that it constitutes seriously invalidating conditions may be doubted.

First, we may consider the question of age determination. For the time

1

being all that is necessary is to establish an approximate sequence according to age of the fetuses observed. No absolute accuracy may be claimed for the menstrual ages used in this presentation. They may differ from the true menstrual ages by a week or more in either direction. We have very few data which are reliable in regard to the actual menstrual histories of the fetuses. Although many other tables to determine menstrual age on length exist, those compiled by Streeter (1920) have been used in this work because they seem to fit best the type of population found in Pittsburg. In the main, it has been found that determination of menstrual age from the Streeter or almost any other tables causes the performance of the fetuses observed by us to fall into a definite sequence, with unexpectedly few exceptions. Age determination is important, but for the purpose of this discussion only relatively so, provided a sequence may be established.

Second comes the question of the nature of the stimulus. It soon became evident, in the course of the observations reported here, that it was necessary to refine the methods of stimulation if an attempt was to be made to secure responses to what was hoped would be tactile or touch stimulation. Thus, stimulators have been made from hairs roughly graded by what may be considered as the maximum pressure they could exert. Hairs just stiff enough to exert pressure balancing weights of 10, 25, 50, and 100 milligrams and 2, 5, and 10 grams were used. A small bead of Duco cement was placed on the tips of the hairs to prevent abrasion of the fetal skin.

Of course, no evidence whatever is available regarding the area of that part of the surface of the bead in contact with the surface of the fetus, which from a physicist's point of view is essential to determine pressure. However, the stimuli are applied in such a way that the pressure exerted by the hairs as they are used is much less than the maximum which they are capable of exerting.

CONDITIONS OF OBSERVATION

I wish now to note certain factors which introduce abnormal conditions into observations of this type. These factors are dependent upon the technics which must be employed. The majority of our material to the menstrual age of twenty-five weeks has been secured by hysterotomy. Such operations are performed only for carefully determined medical reasons and, of course, no member of our group has ever had any part in the decision.

When a fetus is removed from the uterus, the connection between the fetal and the maternal portions of the placenta is necessarily interrupted. In consequence, anoxemia or oxygen want begins at once and becomes progressively more severe. It has been impossible to overcome this by any means so far used. How damaging to the conclusions to be drawn this progressive oxygen want may be is a matter of dispute. We believe that the responses of even the youngest fetuses are true neuromotor responses in our series, an opinion based on a number of considerations.

Another abnormal factor is the release of the normal pressures exerted upon the fetus in the amniotic sac within the uterus. Furthermore, there is at least a temporary breakdown of environmental temperature control. Of course, a certain amount of physical insult is suffered by the immature fetus during operative procedures or during premature birth.

Many anesthetic drugs administered to the mother pass readily through the placenta and narcotize the fetus to varying degrees. In my experience, only novocaine, in its various forms, appears not to affect fetal movements when used either as a spinal or local anesthetic.

In examining a nonviable fetus our routine has been to transport the fetus as quickly as possible to the observation laboratory, place it in warmed saline or Tyrode's solution under the cameras and place the placenta in a separate jar under a moist atmosphere of oxygen. The time elapsed between beginning placental separation and the time of initial observation is in the neighborhood of one and a half to two minutes in most cases.

Spontaneously delivered premature infants (after twenty-five weeks of menstrual age) are resuscitated, if possible, placed in a heated "premature bed," supplied with oxygen and examined before being taken to the nursery.

We have used motion picture recording extensively in our studies. Motion pictures are objective records which can be examined repeatedly. A quick and intricate response, seen once in the fetus, is most difficult to analyze. When rechecked repeatedly on the films, its exact nature may be determined with a high degree of accuracy. For this reason, motion picture records are almost essential.

EARLIEST RESPONSES

The studies at Pittsburgh cover to date 98 individuals. These range from seven weeks of menstrual age to a postmature of forty-five weeks (forty weeks being the usual normal gestation period based on menstrual age). Before eight and one-half weeks, approximately, reactivity has been possibly observed in only one case. Stimulation of the region about the mouth resulted in a contralateral flexion of the neck, seemingly without participation of the upper extremities. Unfortunately, this response is not shown in the very poor motion pictures we secured.

Shortly after eight weeks of menstrual age, as determined by the Streeter tables, the reflexogenous area was found to lie over the upper lip and wings of the nose supplied by the maxillary division of the fifth cranial nerve, the trigeminal. Almost immediately thereafter the reflexogenous area extends to the upper lip, chin, and for a short distance onto the neck, supplied by the mandibular division of the same nerve.

The characteristic response at this age is of one type only and may be elicited by 10 milligram or stiffer hairs. It is a lateral flexion of the trunk and neck, usually contralateral, but sometimes ipsilateral, accompanied by slight but definite rotation of the pelvic region, in the same direction as the trunk flexure. The trunk flexure is also accompanied by an extension of the upper arms. The elbows, which are normally about half flexed at this age, do not participate, nor do the hands at the wrist, though the hands describe an arc as a result of the arm extension at the shoulder. The return to normal resting posture by the arms precedes that of neck, trunk, and rump, which maintain the reaction posture for an appreciable period of time before they also return to resting posture.

The response is stereotyped, that is to say, it is patterned and mechanical in nature. These fetuses (and I use the term fetus for all, rather than to distinguish between embryos and fetuses) are fairly active over the relatively short period of time during which they remain responsive to stimulation. However, each stimulation in the reflexogenous area evokes a response which, within the limits of ordinary biological variation, is identical with every other one secured. No "spontaneous" movements have been observed at this age. From my viewpoint, spontaneous movements occur in response to unknown stimulation, which may originate either within or without the organism.

At nine and one-half weeks, there has been no extension of the reflexogenous area. The response is similar to that secured at eight and one-half weeks, but is more marked. The characteristic response is again a lateral, usually contralateral, flexion of neck and trunk, with rump rotation and bilateral arm extension, but both lateral flexion and rump rotation are much more marked than at eight and one-half weeks. However, the responses are patterned and mechanical in nature, hence to that extent stereotyped. The fetuses of this age are active in responding, and exhibit spontaneous movements identical in character with response activity but occurring in rhythmic contractions of the body, first to one side, then to the other.

Two fetuses of nine and one-half weeks' menstrual age exhibited movements believed to be vestibular in origin. These movements occurred following rolling of the fetus to adjust it under the cameras. The vestibular apparatus appears sufficiently well developed at this age to justify the belief that the semicircular canals are functional.

Responses, clearly proprioceptive in nature (that is, originating from nerve endings in the muscles, tendons, or joints) have been secured for the first time at this age by stretching the forearm muscles in one instance and the biceps muscle in another.

At ten and ten and one-half weeks we have insufficient data for proper conclusions, but I would like to note that at ten weeks the eyelids are completely developed, though fused (as in a kitten at birth).

At eleven weeks, the reflexogenous areas have spread over a considerable additional portion of the body surface. As heretofore, the maxillary and mandibular areas of supply are functional, but now the ophthalmic division

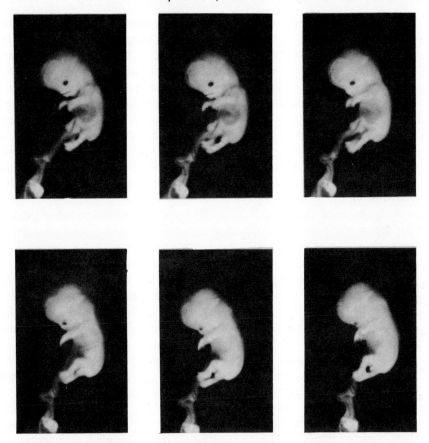

FIGURE 1. *Response to tactile stimulation of the face—eight and a half weeks. Stimulation was applied by stroking the integument lateral to the nose and mouth (A and B) with a fine hair. The response consisted of the following elements: (1) contralateral flexion of the trunk and neck, with barely discernible rotation of the rump (B and C); (2) backward movement of both arms and consequent caudal movement of the hands (B and C) without extension at the elbow; (3) return of body and upper extremities to normal fetal posture (F).*

of the trigeminal nerve, supplying the upper eyelids and forehead, exhibits capacity to function and the skin of the upper extremities, notably in the palms, also becomes reflexogenous. Only in the older fetuses, nearing eleven and one-half weeks, is the skin of the arms and forearms definitely reflexogenous. In the oldest classified at this age, a foot sole response was secured.

ELEVEN TO FOURTEEN WEEKS

At eleven weeks, extension of the trunk is beginning to be combined with, or substituted for, the lateral flexion hitherto present as the only response to stimulation in the facial reflexogenous area. All manner of combinations of extensions and lateral flexion may be present and the response to stimulation in the facial area may be segmental in character. In the segmental type of response, the upper part of the body is followed by the lower part in executing movements, as though a lag existed as the impulse passes caudally. Arm extension may or may not accompany the trunk extension. If lateral flexion is present, either as a component or as the sole response, arm extension is usually present. In general, the deeper oxygen want the greater is the tendency for the response to be largely or entirely a lateral flexion. This would seem to indicate that the older type of response tends to persist longer than the newer type as lack of oxygen progresses, though lateral flexion may be present at any time during the period when the fetus will respond to stimulation.

If the palm of the hand is stimulated with a relatively pliable hair at this age, a quick closure ensues. A study of the motion picture proves the finger closure to be only partial.

In the oldest fetus assigned to this age group, plantar stimulation caused plantar flexion of the toes. (Plantar flexion of the toes being their flexion toward the sole of the foot, dorsiflexion being their extension toward the dorsum of the foot.) Furthermore, forearm pronation followed stimulation over the arm, and stimulation of the eyelids caused a contraction of their muscles.

All of the responses at this age are mechanical in character and, hence, stereotyped. However, their stereotype is modified by the fact that a greater or less component of trunk and neck extension may be present.

In the eleven and one-half weeks menstrual age group, the reflexogenous areas have extended to include the entire face, the ventral neck, the upper chest, and the upper and lower extremities. Here, stimulation in the nose-mouth area evokes neck and trunk extension as a major component, though lateral flexion still is present. The arms rotate medially, so that the hands approach one another in front of the chest, as an accompaniment of trunk movements. In addition, movements involving thigh and leg extension, head rotation, arm abduction and rotation, or elbow and wrist flexion may occur as isolated responses or components of other more general bodily reactions. Finger closure is as yet incomplete. Stimulation of the sole of the foot may cause either plantar flexion or dorsiflexion of the toes, both types being present in one fetus at different stimulations and sometimes alternating with one another. There is no toe-fanning at this age. Toe responses are ordinarily accompanied by ankle, knee, and hip flexion. This response is still undeveloped, but presages the more complete plantar reflex as a stage in its progressive perfection.

At twelve weeks, there has been little further extension of the reflexogenous areas. Trunk and neck extension have become the characteristic response to stimulation in the nose-mouth area, with or without one or more of a wide variety of movements of the extremities. These movements of the extremities may occur as a result of flexion or extension at almost every joint. Digital closure is still only partial, but the foot-sole response is progressing toward completion, the toes plantar flexing or dorsiflexing with some fanning. Contraction of the eyelid muscle may be readily secured and, in one case where the highlights were suitable, movement of the eyeball behind the eyelids was indicated.

By thirteen weeks, the reflexogenous areas include practically the entire skin of the body, except the sides, back, and top of the head. Responses which may be secured involve a wide variety of movements at almost every joint of the body. However, stimulation in the nose-mouth area still evoked neck and trunk movements, chiefly extension. Thumb opposition, though only partial, has been observed when the other digits flexed. Swallowing, suspected but not proved in one case at twelve and one-half weeks, definitely occurred at thirteen weeks and thereafter on stimulation between the lips.

At thirteen and one-half weeks, the reflexogenous area includes the sides, but not the top or back of the head, a distribution found until birth. Very complicated combinations of specific reflexes are characteristic of fetuses from this age to birth. The more generalized type of neck and trunk responses hitherto observed are, at this age, only incidental, usually limited to fetuses suffering from quite marked oxygen want. Crossed reflexes appear at this time. Finger closure may be complete at this age. Lip closure follows stimulation of the lips and is often accompanied by tight closing of the eyelids and sometimes by scowling.

FOURTEEN TO TWENTY-FIVE WEEKS

Fourteen weeks is an important age landmark in the development of the fetus. The fetus is no longer marionette-like or mechanical in the character of its movements, which are now graceful and fluid, as they are in the newborn. A wide repertoire of specific reflexes may be elicited throughout the entire body and these activities are exhibited spontaneously. Stimulation in the mouth-nose area no longer causes a general trunk response, but evokes facial responses and a rotation of the head away from the stimulus.

Stimulation near the sides of the nose produces an elevation of the upper lip and wings of the nose resembling a sneer. Scowling and an avoiding movement of the head usually accompany the lip response. Stimulation of the tongue evokes its movement and, if repeated, swallowing.

At fourteen weeks, the fetus exhibits, in imperfect form at least, most of the reflexes of the neonate, except respiration, voice, grasp, suctorial response, tendon reflexes, and special sense responses. No tests of the special senses were made in these observations. From this age to birth, the character of the fetal activities remains much the same, with the emphasis on the specific reflexes. In consequence, I shall note only those activities which appear *de novo* or which reach important stages in their development.

By fifteen weeks, the abdominal reflex becomes definite in its appearance, though it is possible that it may be present earlier. If, at this age, a hair is drawn across the palm, the fingers not only close, but remain closed, particularly if the hair is left within the closed fingers. This seems to be the initial appearance of the grasping reflex though there is no effective clutching of the object within the palm.

By about sixteen weeks of age, an interesting change in the activity of the fetus has appeared. The younger fetuses observed have been active in their response to stimulation, but they now show a marked decrease in activity, becoming almost sluggish, although a few individuals have been observed which were still fairly active in their responses. Furthermore, where it may be accomplished, resuscitation causes disappearance of this inactivity and increase in threshold, otherwise rather characteristic of the period from about sixteen weeks to birth.

At seventeen weeks, stimulation of the lower lip causes lip closure, as heretofore, but stimulation of the upper lip evokes its marked protrusion. This is believed to be the initial phase of the developing suctorial response.

At eighteen weeks, stimulation of the chest wall has evoked thoracic contractions, interpreted as the first evidence (so far as these observations are concerned) of the ability of the chest wall to function in a respiratory manner.

At twenty weeks, both lips protrude when stimulated. By twenty-one weeks, the separation of the eyelids from one another, begun at about eighteen weeks, is usually completed, but the fetus rarely opens the eyes, either spontaneously or in response to stimulation, until later.

By twenty-two weeks, some fetuses are capable of briefly sustained respiration. That this is true inspiration and expiration of air is proved by the fact that, while it is respiring, the fetus is capable of making a thin crying noise on expiration. At this age, also, the lips are not only protruded but pursed, when a stimulating object touches both at the same time. There is, however, nothing which suggests sucking. Furthermore, the ability of the fetus to grasp an object has reached a point in the maturation of this reflex at which it is somewhat effective. It is sufficiently strong to enable the observer to move the upper extremity by pulling a grasped rod. It is interesting to note that the thumb plays no part in the grasping reflex.

At twenty-three weeks of menstrual age, a resuscitated fetus is capable of about a half-hour of self-sustained respiration and, at twenty-four weeks such respiration may continue for over three hours.

TWENTY-FIVE WEEKS TO NORMAL BIRTH

Twenty-five weeks of menstrual age marks another important landmark in the maturation of fetal reflex behavior. Self-sustained respiration, after resuscitation, may continue for more than twenty-four hours. Though I have not found any premature younger than twenty-seven weeks to be viable, even with the utmost care, cases have been reported of viable twenty-five weeks premature infants. Following resuscitation, certain tendon reflexes (knee-jerk, ankle clonus, and so on) can be elicited. The individual must, in my experience, have been respiring for nearly half an hour before any tendon reflexes can be secured. They have been sought in younger fetuses, but not found until this age, at which sustained respiration over a relatively long period is possible.

At twenty-five weeks, the eyes may be opened and closed spontaneously.

One twenty-five weeks premature, within a half-hour of birth, was gently lifted from the "premature bed" to change, for photographic purposes, the cloth on which it was lying. When this had been done, it was lowered suddenly into the bed. The response consisted of a rotary gyration of upper and lower extremities, fully abducted from the trunk, followed by the drawing of these extremities over the trunk. This is generally termed a Moro, or "startle" reflex. It is undoubtedly vestibular in origin.

At twenty-seven weeks of menstrual age, one fetus proved viable. This one exhibited a strong grasping reflex, sufficiently strong indeed to support almost its entire weight by one hand. During this grasp, the thumb was actively flexed but the weight was supported by the fingers, not by the thumb. It is not until after birth that the thumb plays an active role in grasping.

At twenty-nine weeks, an audible suctorial response was exhibited. At thirty-three weeks, when the lower lip alone was stimulated, the mouth was opened and the tip of the tongue "searched" the lower lip, following the stimulus.

NATURE OF FETAL DEVELOPMENT

The account given of the findings during the early phases of the development of overt behavior in man in the Pittsburgh studies should clearly set forth where I stand concerning the nature of this development. These earliest forms of response exhibited by man certainly constitute a total pattern, in Coghill's sense (1929). This total pattern expands to include additional elements of the neuromuscular apparatus as it develops. Following this, an individuation of specific reflexes or partial patterns occurs.

In these respects, the development of early overt behavior in man follows the basic principles discovered for *Amblystoma* by Coghill. However, the development of early overt behavior in man is not the same as that in *Amblystoma*, nor is it the same as that in the cat, the rat, the rabbit, or the sheep. Each animal form exhibits a sequence in the development of its early overt behavior which is entirely its own. In man, compared to some of the other mammals, this early sequence appears to be curiously telescoped in certain parts. However, the development of human fetal activity, as seen in our studies, is not only consistent with Coghill's principles, but no other interpretation seems justified.

In the course of the later development of human overt behavior, it might be suggested that the specific reflexes, once individualized as partial patterns from the total pattern, may be recombined into an almost infinite variety of action patterns which form the background of adult human behavior. This is probably true of all mammals, but I can speak with some degree of assurance only concerning man.

SUMMARY

In closing, permit me to review, once again, the steps in the development of human fetal overt behavior, as demonstrated by the work at Pittsburgh:

1. It begins at about seven and one-half to eight weeks of menstrual age as a lateral, almost uniformly contralateral, contraction of the upper trunk and neck musculature. Possibly the earliest form of this response does not include movement of the limbs, but these, particularly the upper extremities, are very early coordinated with the trunk.

2. The initial response quickly spreads to include the lower trunk and hips in the contralateral body flexion.

3. Beginning at ten and one-half to eleven weeks, specific reflexes of localized extent appear and the contralateral trunk flexure gives way to a trunk extension.

4. By thirteen to fourteen weeks, almost all the important movements of the fetus have the form of specific reflexes which have already begun to recombine into an amazing variety of complex activities.

5. From fourteen weeks to birth, some new components of activity appear. Among these are: the suctorial response, respiration and the use of the larynx, the grasping reflex, and so on. Otherwise, the development of the fetus during these six to seven lunar months is one of maturation of already existing reflexes and of their essential neuromuscular substrate.

6. These fetal activities are basic and integral parts of postnatal human behavior.

References

Coghill, G. E., *Anatomy and the Problem of Behavior*. Cambridge, Eng.: Cambridge University Press, and New York: The Macmillan Company, 1929, pp. x and 113.

Streeter, George L., "Weight, Sitting Height, Head Size, Foot Length and Menstrual Age of the Human Embryo," Carnegie Institute of Washington, *Publ. No. 274, Contributions to Embryology*, 11 (1920), 143-170.

2 · The Birth Equipment of the Human Being

JOHN B. WATSON

Abridged from *The Psychologies of 1925*, ed. C. Murchison, Worcester, Mass.: Clark University Press, 1925, pages 17-32, by permission of the publisher.

John B. Watson advocated the direct study of behavior by natural science methods without recourse to concepts such as instincts, motives, and conscious states. He illustrated the behavioristic method in his studies of animal and child behavior. In the chapter reproduced below, he summarizes his observations concerning the unlearned equipment of the young infant. By unlearned behavior he means responses which come about through growth alone, and do not require practice for their establishment.

Almost daily observation of several hundred infants from birth through the first thirty days of infancy and of a smaller number through the first years of childhood has given us the following set of (rough) facts on unlearned responses:

Sneezing. This apparently can begin in a full-fledged way from birth. The normal intraorganic stimulus calling out sneezing is not very well defined. Sometimes it occurs when the baby is taken from a cooler room into an overheated room. With some babies carrying them out into the sunshine apparently will produce sneezing.

Hiccoughing. This usually does not begin at birth but can be noticed in children from 7 days of age on with great ease. Over 50 cases have been observed carefully. The earliest noted case of hiccoughing was six hours after birth. The stimulus most commonly calling it out apparently is the pressure on the diaphragm coming from a full stomach.

Crying. The so-called birth cry takes place at the establishment of respiration. The lungs are not inflated until the stimulus of the air is present. As the air strikes the lungs and mucous membranes of the upper alimentary tract, the mechanism of breathing is gradually established. To establish breathing, the infant has sometimes to be plunged into icy water. Coincident with the plunge into the icy water, the cry appears. It usually appears during the vigorous rubbing and slapping of the infant's back and buttocks—a method employed to establish respiration. The birth cry itself differs markedly in different infants.

11

Hunger will bring out crying; noxious stimuli such as rough handling, circumcision, or the lancing and care of boils will bring out cries even in extremely young infants. When the baby suspends itself with either hand crying is usually elicited.

Numerous experiments have been carried out to see whether the crying of one infant in a nursery will serve as a stimulus to set off the rest of the children in the nursery. Our results are entirely negative. In order to more thoroughly control the conditions, we made phonographic records of a lusty crier. We could then reproduce this sound very close to the ear of, first, a sleeping infant, then a wakeful but quiet infant. The results again were wholly negative. Hunger contractions and noxious stimuli (also loud sounds) are unquestionably the unconditioned stimuli which call out crying.

Colic, bringing a set of noxious stimuli, may and usually does call out a cry and apparently one slightly different from other types. This is due to the pressure in the abdominal cavity caused by the formation of gas. The full set of muscles used in the hunger cry is thus not available for the colic cry. The cries of infants are so different that at night in a nursery of 25, it does not take very long to be able to name the child which is crying regardless of its location in the nursery.

Erection of Penis. This can occur at birth and from that time on throughout life. The complete set of stimuli calling out this response is not known. Apparently radiant heat, warm water, stroking of the sex organs, possibly pressure from the urine, are the main factors operative at birth.

Voiding of Urine. This occurs from birth. The unconditioned stimulus is unquestionably intra-organic due to the pressure of the fluid in bladder.

Defecation. This mechanism seems to be perfect from birth and in all probability the mechanism was perfected several weeks before birth. The stimulus probably is pressure in the lower colon. Pressing a clinical thermometer into the anus from birth often brings about the passage of faeces.

Early Eye Movements. Infants from birth when lying flat on their backs in a dark room with their heads held horizontally will slowly turn their eyes toward a faint light. Movements of the eyes are not very well coordinated at birth, but "cross-eyes" are not nearly so prevalent as most people seem to believe. Right and left coordinated movements of the eyes are the first to appear. Upward and downward movements of the eyes come at a slightly later period. Still later on a light can be followed when revolved in a circle over the baby's face.

Smiling. Smiling is due in all probability at first to the presence of kinesthetic and tactual stimuli. It appears as early as the fourth day. It can most often be seen after a full feeding. Light touching on parts of the body, blowing upon the body, touching the sex organs and sensitive zones of the skin are the unconditioned stimuli that will produce smiling. Tickling under the chin and a gentle jugging and rocking of the infant will often bring out smiling.

Turning the Head. A great many infants at birth, if placed stomach down with chin on the mattress, can swing their heads to right or left and lift their heads from the mattress. We have noticed these reactions from thirty minutes of age on. On one occasion fifteen babies were tested one at a time in succession. All except one could make these head reactions.

Holding Up Head When Infant Is Held in Upright Position. This seems to vary with the development of the head and neck musculature. Some newborn infants can support their heads for a few seconds. The infant is held in the experimenter's lap with stomach and back supported. There seems to be a rapid improvement in this response due apparently to the development of structure rather than to training factors.

Hand Movements at Birth. Marked hand movements in many children can be observed even at birth, such as closing the hand, opening it, spreading the fingers, stretching the fingers with one or both hands at the same time. Usually in these hand movements the thumb is folded inside the palm and takes no part in hand response.

Arm Movements. The slightest stimulation of the skin anywhere will usually bring out marked arm, wrist, hand, and shoulder responses. Apparently kinesthetic and organic stimuli may bring out these responses as well as tactual, auditory, and visual stimuli. The arms can be thrown up to to the face and even as far as the top of the head and down to the legs. Usually, however, the first movements of the arms, no matter where the stimulus is applied, is toward the chest and head. One of the ways of producing violent movements of arms and hands is to hold the nose. In a very few seconds one or the other or both arms fly upward until the hand actually comes in contact with the hand of the experimenter. If one hand is held, the other hand will go up just the same.

Leg and Foot Movements. Kicking is one of the most pronounced movements to be seen at birth. It can be brought out by touching the soles of the feet, by stimulation with hot or cold air, by contact with the skin, and directly through kinesthetic stimulation. One characteristic way of producing leg and foot movements is to pinch the skin over the knee.

Trunk, Leg, Foot, and Toe Movements. When an infant is suspending itself with either right or left hand, marked "climbing" motions in the trunk and hips are noticeable. There seems to be a wave of contraction pulling the trunk and legs upward followed by a relaxation period; then another wave of contraction sets in. Tickling of the foot, stimulating the foot with hot water, will produce marked movements in foot and toes. Usually if the bottom of the foot is stimulated with a match stick, the characteristic Babinski reflex appears in nearly all infants. This is a variable reflex. The usual pattern is an upward jump of the great toes (extension) and a drawing down of the other toes (flexion). Occasionally the Babinski takes the form merely of "fanning," that is, spreading of all the toes. The Babinski reflex usually disappears around the end of the first year although it may continue longer even in normal children. A wire or other small round object placed under the toes will often produce flexion, that is, a closing of the toes, but the slightest pressure will release the rod or wire.

Feeding Responses. Touching the face of a hungry baby at the corners of the mouth or on the cheek or on the chin will cause quick, jerky head movements which result in bringing the mouth near the source of stimulation. This has been observed many, many times from five hours of age onward. The lip or sucking reflex is another characteristic response. Tapping slightly with the tip of the finger below or above the corner of the mouth of a sleeping baby may bring the lips and tongue almost immediately into the nursing position. Sucking as such varies tremendously in young infants. It can be demonstrated in practically every infant within the first hour after birth. Occasionally when there is marked injury during birth suckling is retarded. The feeding response as such includes sucking, tongue, lip, and cheek movements, and swallowing. With most newborn infants this mechanism, unless there is birth injury, is fairly perfect.

Crawling. Crawling is an indeterminate kind of response. Many infants never crawl at all, and all of them exhibit different behavior in crawling. After many experiments I am inclined to believe that crawling comes largely as a result of a habit formation. When the infant is placed on its stomach, the contact and kinesthetic stimuli bring out very general bodily activity. Oftentimes one side of the body is more active than the opposite side; circular (circus) motions result. In one 9-months infant turning in a circle resulted for days but no forward progress could be observed. In this gradual twisting and turning of the body, the child sometimes moves right, sometimes left, sometimes forward, indeed, and sometimes backward. If, in these movements, it manages to reach and manipulate some object, we have practically a situation like that of the hungry rat in a maze that has food at its center. A habit of crawling toward objects results.

Standing and Walking. The whole complex mechanism of standing upright, first with support, then without support, then walking, then running, then jumping, is a very slowly developing one. The start of the whole mechanism seems to lie in the development of the so-called "extensor thrust." The extensor thrust is not usually present during the first few months of infancy. Some months after birth if the infant is gradually lifted up by the arms to nearly a standing position with a part of its feet in contact with the floor at all times, there comes, as weight falls on the feet, a stiffening of the muscles of both legs. Soon after the appearance of this reflex, the child begins to attempt to pull itself up. Between 7 and 8 months of age many infants can pull themselves up with very little help and can support themselves in a standing position holding on to some object for a short space of time. After this feat has been accomplished, the next stage in the general process is walking around holding on to an object. The final stage is the first step alone.

Grasping. With few exceptions infants at birth can support their full weight with either right or left hand. The method we use in testing them is to place a small rod about the diameter of a pencil in one or the other hand closing the fingers on the rod. This stimulus causes the grasping reflex to appear. It usually starts crying at the same time. Then fingers and hands clamp tightly on the rod. During the reaction the infant can be completely lifted from the pillow upon which it lies. An assistant places her two hands below the infant ready to catch it as it falls back to the pillow. The length of time the infant can support itself varies all the way from a fraction of a second to more than a minute. The time in a given case may vary considerably on different days.

The reaction is almost invariable from birth, until it begins to disappear around the 120th day.

Blinking. Any newborn infant will close the lids when the eye (cornea) is touched or when a current of air strikes the eye. But no infant at birth will "blink" when a shadow rapidly crosses the eye as when a pencil or piece of paper is passed rapidly across the whole field of vision.

SUMMARY OF UNLEARNED EQUIPMENT

Although our studies of man's birth equipment have only begun, we can get a fair picture of the type of activity to be seen and of the method of studying this equipment.

At birth or soon thereafter we find nearly all of the so-called clinical neurological signs or reflexes established, such as the reaction of the pupil to light, the patellar reflex, and many others.

We find the birth cry followed forever afterward by breathing, the heartbeat, and all circulatory phenomena, such as vasomotor constriction (decrease in diameter of vessels) and dilatation, pulse beat, etc. Beginning with the alimentary tract we find sucking, tongue movements, and swallowing. We find hunger contractions, digestion, necessitating glandular reactions in the whole alimentary tract, and elimination (defecation, urination, sweat). The acts of smiling, sneezing, and hiccoughing belong in part at least to the alimentary canal system. We find also erection of the penis.

We find general movements of the trunk, head, and neck. We can see the trunk at work in breathing, when the infant cries, during defecation and urination, when turning over, or when the head is raised or turned.

We find the arms, wrists, hands, and fingers in almost ceaseless activity (the thumb rarely taking part until later). In this activity especially are to be noted: Grasping, opening and closing hands repeatedly, "slashing" about of the whole arm, putting hand or fingers into mouth, throwing arm and fingers to face when nose is held.

We find the legs, ankles, feet, and fingers in almost ceaseless movement except in sleep and even during sleep if external (and internal) stimuli are present. The knee can be bent, leg moved at hip, ankle turned, toes spread, etc. If the bottom of the foot is touched there is a characteristic movement of the toes (Babinski reflex).

Other activities appear at a later stage—such as blinking, reaching, handling, handedness, crawling, standing, sitting up, walking, running, jumping. In the great majority of these later activities it is difficult to say how much of the act as a whole is due to training or conditioning. A considerable part is unquestionably due to the growth changes in structure, and the rest is due to training and conditioning.

3 · Changes in Activity Between Two Feeding Periods

ORVIS C. IRWIN

Abridged from an article entitled "The Distribution of the Amount of Motility in Young Infants Between Two Nursing Periods," *Journal of Comparative Psychology*, 14 (1932), 415-428, by permission of the author. Dr. Irwin kindly supplied the photograph that illustrates the type of experimental cabinet used.

The activities of the newborn infant may be studied by many methods. Several studies have been concerned with measuring the general activity of the young infant and with determining the effects of stimulating conditions and of physiological state. To accomplish these measurements, the infant is placed upon a platform that is sensitive to slight movements. The minute movements of the platform, which are caused by the infant's movements, are then recorded by pens writing upon a moving tape. This apparatus is called a "stabilimeter." In order to control the conditions surrounding the infant, the stabilimeter is enclosed in an experimental cabinet in which temperature, humidity, sound, light, and so on, can be regulated by the experimenter.

Irwin and his collaborators, using the apparatus described above, have contributed basic information concerning the activity of the child in the hospital period. The study that follows is concerned with the activity of the infant when no special external stimuli are applied. The infant is placed in the recording cabinet following one nursing period and remains there until the next feeding. The stimulus changes that occur during this time are, of course, primarily internal. The resulting activity is due primarily to the nutritional needs of the child.

SUBJECTS

The motility of 73 full-term infants was measured. With the exception of one infant thirty-two days old, the age range was from birth to sixteen days. Four of these infants were measured twice; the results, however, were considered as if they were those of different cases. The infants were born in the obstetrical department of the State University of Iowa General Hospital. They were fed at 2:00 and 6:00 P.M. The infants were placed on a stabilimeter at 2:30 P.M. and removed at 5:45 P.M., their motility being recorded continuously.

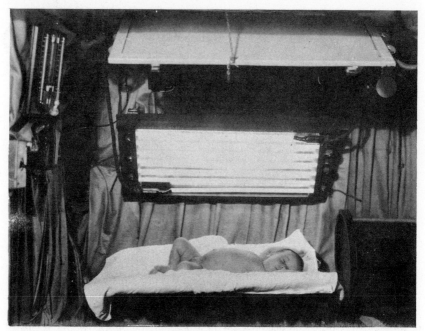

FIGURE 1. *A stabilimeter cabinet used by Irwin.*

DISTRIBUTION OF MOTILITY

The mean oscillations per minute for each of the thirteen 15-minute periods for all infants are given in Figure 2, which also shows graphically how motility is distributed between the two consecutive feedings. According to Figure 2, there is a fairly constant increase in motility from the first 15 minutes of the experimental period when motility amounts to 17.0 oscillations per minute to the last 15 minutes when it amounts to 49.1 oscillations per minute. Thus the increase in motility toward the end of the experimental period is not quite three times the amount at the beginning. This finding verifies the observation made previously by the author that motility in infants is greater just before nursing than immediately after. However, as will be pointed out, this principle which is based on mean values, does not hold true in 100 per cent of the cases.

In order to determine whether the increase in motility as revealed by Figure 2 is a true increment, the standard errors of the differences between the first, middle, and last 15-minute periods were determined. It was found that the difference of the means of the first and last 15-minute periods was more than four times greater than the standard error of the difference. Hence the increment is a true one. The differences between the first and middle, and the middle and last 15-minute periods are not as great as in the case of the first and last periods, but they are still indicative of a significant tendency to differ. It would seem, then, that the increment of about

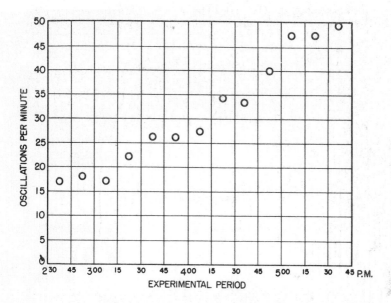

FIGURE 2. *Motility of 73 infants between two consecutive nursings.*

three times the initial motility for the group as a whole is statistically significant on the basis of 15-minute samplings.

The distribution of motility between the two consecutive nursings as indicated by Figure 2 represents mean values for the whole group of 73 infants. These means hide an important trend in the data. Not all of the individual subjects show an increase in motility at the end of the experimental period. This is shown by comparing the motility of each infant for the first hour with that of the last hour. It is, then, found that 67 per cent of the entire group show an increment, while 33 per cent show a decrement in the amount of motility.

However, the increment of the infants showing increased motility is 3.5 times greater than the decrement made by the 24 cases. The mean oscillations per minute during the first hour for the group of 49 cases are 16.2 and for the last hour, 66.4. The difference of these means is about 7.5 times the standard error of the difference. It is, therefore, certain that this increment is significant. Figure 3 gives the motility curve of the 49 cases showing increments in motility.

The amount of motility of both groups during the first hour of the experimental period is about the same. The difference, five oscillations per minute, is only 0.27 times the standard error of the difference. Thus this is not a real difference. Although both groups start the experimental period at about the same motility level, the difference in the amount of their motility at the end of the experimental period is a significant one. The

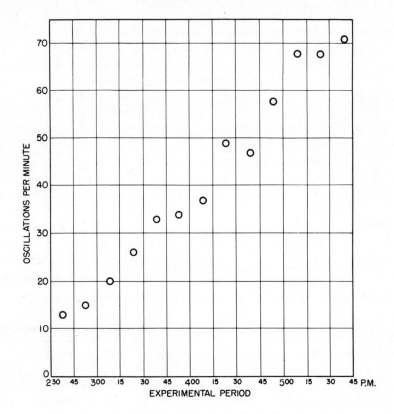

FIGURE 3. *Motility of 49 infants showing increment.*

value of this difference for the last hour is 59.5 oscillations per minute, which is 8.8 times the standard error of the difference. Thus the negative effect of some of the infants is not sufficient to offset the general tendency of the whole group.

It follows from these considerations that the increase at the end of the experimental period is statistically significant for the group as a whole, but that this increase is a resultant of a large increment made by two-thirds of the entire group and a lesser decrement by one-third of the group.

PER CENT OF INFANTS ASLEEP AND AWAKE

There are certain problems which our data can answer. These are: (1) What per cent of the infants is asleep during the experimental period, (2) how does the amount of motility distribute itself during waking and sleeping, and (3) is the waking state itself a condition of activity?

The answers to each of these questions are given by two groups of data and their similarity affords a test of their reliability. With one group of 31 infants judgments of sleep were made at 15-minute intervals. With 42 subjects judgments were made of 5-minute intervals.

The first of the three questions concerns the per cent of infants awake and asleep throughout the course of the experimental period. Figure 4 shows the per cent of 31 infants asleep during each of the thirteen 15-minute periods. During the first 15-minute period only 28 per cent of the subjects slept. Half or about 50 per cent of the infants slept during the last period. The largest number, 63 per cent, is asleep during the sixth 15-minute period. Thus the largest per cent of waking occurs at the beginning of the experimental period. This may be explained by the fact that at this time infants undergo handling. After being fed, they are carried from the mother to the nursery where they receive attention by the nurses. They are then brought to the experimental room, undressed, and placed on the stabilimeter in the experimental cabinet. The largest per cent of sleeping occurs about the middle of the experimental period. From this time to the end of the experimental period there is an increase in the number of infants who are awake.

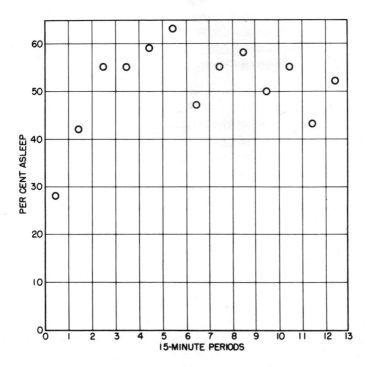

FIGURE 4. *Per cent of infants alseep during thirteen 15-minute periods (31 cases).*

Figure 5 shows the per cent of 42 infants asleep during each of thirty-nine 5-minute periods. Here again most of the sleeping occurs during the middle period. It will be noted that the distribution of sleep in these infants, in general, is similar to that of Figure 4. In other words, regardless of whether judgments of sleep are made at 5-minute intervals or at 15-minute intervals the curves of judgments approximate each other.

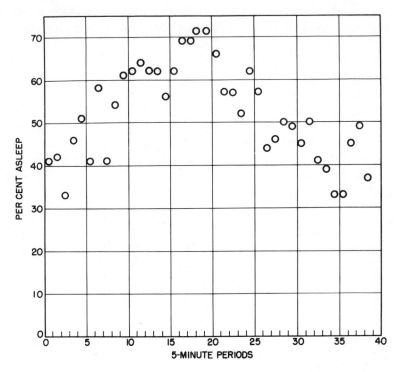

FIGURE 5. *Per cent of infants asleep during thirty-nine 5-minute periods (42 cases).*

DISTRIBUTION OF MOTILITY DURING WAKING TIME AND SLEEPING TIME

The second question concerns the amount of motility during the waking and sleeping time between feedings. How does activity distribute itself throughout the experimental period at such times as infants are judged to be asleep or awake?

Figure 6 answers this question. The circles represent the amount of motility during waking and the crosses show the amount of motility during sleep. In the latter case, the motility throughout the experimental period distributes itself, in general, as a straight line without any increment. This holds true whether the judgments of sleep were made at 5- or at 15-minute intervals. On the other hand, motility during waking, beginning at the first part of the experimental period at a level about equal to motility during sleep, increases markedly throughout the period until it ends at a level about 10 times greater than the value for sleep. Moreover, this result is consistent for both intervals of observations.

These findings throw light on a problem which has been the source of much difficulty in experimenting with infants and which perhaps explains the variation in results of different experimenters. The writer has suggested (1930) that the effect of internal stimulation, such as hunger, results in activity so great as to interfere with the experimental use of external stimuli,

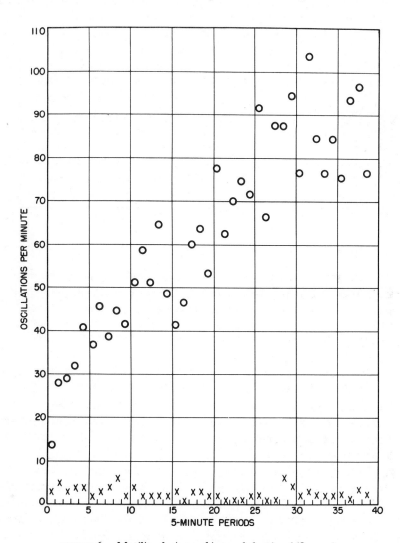

FIGURE 6. *Motility during waking and sleeping (42 cases)*.

such as sound, light, and so forth. It is important for the experimenter to know when the effect of internal factors is inoperative or at a minimum. In general, if inactivity in the overt behavior of the subject is a desideratum, these data show that the period following feeding is the best time to experiment on infants; if work on sleep is contemplated, the most suitable time for observation is the middle period.

IS THE WAKING STATE A CAUSE OF MOTILITY?

Since there is a striking difference in the amount of motility during the waking and sleeping states as revealed by Figure 6, the inference might seem justified that the waking condition itself may bear a causal relationship to motility. Nevertheless, this interpretation is not sustained when the results in this graph are considered in relation to those of Figures 4 and 5. For instance when Figure 6 is compared with Figure 4 it is found that 72 per cent of these infants are awake during the first 15-minute period, but that their motility amounts to only 20 oscillations per minute. During the last 15-minute period about half of the infants are awake, yet they account for 76 oscillations per minute. Although more infants are awake during the 15-minute period immediately following nursing, they show only a small amount of motility as compared to the motility of infants awake during the 15-minute period preceding nursing The conclusion seems justified, therefore, that the waking condition as such is hardly the cause of motility.

SUMMARY

The changes in the amount of motility of 73 young infants were measured between the hours of 2:30 P.M. and 5:45 P.M. by the stabilimeter-polygraph technique. Infants were fed at two o'clock and at six o'clock. The unit of measurement is the number of polygraph recording pen oscillations per minute.

The results of this study are as follows:

1. The motility of newborn infants varies from 17.0 oscillations per minute during the first 15-minute period after nursing to 45.0 oscillations per minute during the last 15 minutes of the experimental period.

2. An increment in motility was shown by 67 per cent of the subjects at the end of the experimental period.

3. Thirty-three per cent of the subjects show a decrement in motility at the end of the period amounting to 16.3 oscillations per minute.

4. Both groups at the beginning of the period show about the same level of motility.

5. The mean increment of motility for the entire group, is statistically significant.

6. When judgments of sleep are made at 15-minute intervals about 28

per cent of infants were asleep during the first 15 minutes of the experimental period, 63 per cent were asleep during the middle 15-minute period, and 52 per cent were asleep during the last 15 minutes.

7. When judgments are made at 5-minute intervals the largest number of infants were judged to be asleep during the middle third of the experimental period.

8. The amount of motility during sleeping varies little throughout the experimental period either when judgments are made at 5- or 15-minute intervals.

9. The amount of motility when waking during the first part of the experimental period is about the same as that when sleeping.

10. The amount of motility during waking increases throughout the experimental period until at the end of the period it is about nine or ten times its initial value.

Reference

Irwin, O. C., "The Amount and Nature of Activities of Newborn Infants under Constant External Stimulating Conditions During the First Ten Days of Life," *Genetic Psychology Monographs*, Vol. 8, No. 1 (1930), 1-92.

4 · Effects of Light and Sound Upon Neonatal Activity

LA BERTA WEISS

Abridged from "Studies in Infant Behavior," *University of Iowa Studies in Child Welfare*, Vol. 9, No. 4 (1934), 1-71, by permission of the publisher.

In the preceding section it was shown that if external conditions are kept constant, the activity of the infant when awake is at a minimum shortly after feeding and increases in successive periods of time thereafter. What happens if he is stimulated? Pain, loud noises, quick movements and many other kinds of sudden and intense stimulation will cause increased activity. But, as the present study shows, continuous mild stimulation has a soothing effect, causing a decrease in activity. The stimuli used in the present study were provided by moderate lights and tones. It seems likely, however, that many other forms of mild stimulation, such as carrying the infant, wrapping him snugly, swinging him, rocking him, stroking him, or singing to him will also reduce activity and crying.

The recording instrument used in the present study was a stabilimeter similar to that used in the preceding investigation.

GENERAL AIMS OF THE INVESTIGATION

The behavior of the normal newborn infant seems to be largely a reflection of his physiological condition. He sleeps when he is well fed. He cries and moves when he is hungry. His cries and his movements become increasingly intense and persistent as the feeding period draws near. Only when hunger is satisfied does he become quiet and go to sleep. Then the cycle begins again.

It is known, of course, from investigations with sensory stimuli, that under certain conditions the behavior of the newborn infant is affected by external factors. The conditions under which such effects have been noted, however, have been characterized by stimuli of very brief duration and of considerable intensity. Since it is the reverse of these two characteristics which typifies the everyday external environment, these investigations do not indicate whether the behavior of the newborn infant is at all affected by ordinary external stimuli.

The primary aim of the present investigation is to throw light on the above problem by determining whether mild auditory and visual stimuli may affect the behavior of the newborn infant (1) when these stimuli are presented over a continuous rather than a brief period, and (2) when behavior is measured in terms of amount of activity rather than in terms of specific reactions.

THE LIGHT EXPERIMENT

The present experiment consisted of submitting each infant to stimulation in each of three situations and recording its activity during stimulation by means of the stabilimeter-polygraph technique.

The three situations in which the behavior of the infants was studied in the visual experiment were minimal light, dim light, and moderate light.

Minimal light was secured by eliminating all sources of artificial light within the cabinet. Only a shaded bulb over the polygraph table was left burning in the experimental room. This bulb sent enough light rays into the cabinet to make the figure of the infant barely discernible after the experimenter had become adapted to the darkness. The light was too weak to give any reading on the Macbeth Illuminometer which was used to calibrate the intensities, but its strength was estimated by an experienced technician to be about .002 foot candle power.

Dim light was secured by the use of a 20 watt blue frosted bulb hung in the cabinet 6 inches back and 24 inches above the infant's head. The illuminometer reading for this light at the level of the subject's eyes was .02 foot candle power.

The light in the moderate situation was supplied by a 30 watt white frosted bulb suspended in the cabinet 9 inches back and 24 inches above the infant's head. The illuminometer reading was 3.9 foot candle power at the level of the infant's eyes. In both the moderate and the dim situation the shaded bulb on the polygraph table was left burning, so that its effects are included in the illuminometer readings.

Polygraph records were taken for five minutes under the dim period of stimulation and for six minutes under the other degrees of illumination. The activity of a given infant in each situation was then expressed as the number of oscillations of the pens per thirty seconds.

To compare the behavior of the newborn infant under different stimulus situations, it is essential that all other external conditions and physiological conditions remain constant.

The control of external conditions was relatively simple. The infant, when brought to the experimental room, was unclothed and placed on the stabilimeter in the experimental cabinet. The hygrometer and rheostat with which the cabinet was equipped made possible a control of temperature and humidity. During the present experiment the temperature was kept within the limits of 84 to 92 degrees, and the wet bulb reading within 64 to 68 degrees. The cabinet was located in a room free from sound other than the low hum of the motor-generator which ran the polygraph and which was itself placed in an adjoining room. The light in the room was furnished entirely by a bulb over the polygraph table during experimental periods.

The steps taken to insure constancy of physiological conditions in experimental procedure were:

1. The stimuli to be compared were presented consecutively with no time interval between.

2. A time limitation was set for the experimental period. The first step in this direction was an analysis of activity records taken continuously on eleven infants during the time elapsing between one feeding period and the next. The data indicate that it should be easy to find infants whose activity level remains relatively constant over a twenty-five minute period. The experiment was set up with this time limit in mind, no infant being kept on the stabilimeter for more than twenty minutes.

3. The experimental situations were presented in an alternated order. Except for the control period of dim light, which always came at the beginning of the experiment, the experimental situations were alternated in order of presentation from one subject to the next.

4. Experimental periods were equally distributed between feedings. The subjects of the experiment were fed every four hours and were available for experimentation about three hours of the time between feedings. The study was so conducted that the experiments were distributed evenly over this interval. For the purpose of evaluating the significance of the time factor, the three hour interval was divided into three periods—the A, B, and C periods designating, respectively, the first, second, and third hour elapsing since a feeding.

Further attempts to keep physiological conditions consisted of stopping the experiment whenever defecation or wetting occurred, just long enough to make the necessary change, and of discounting any record secured on the polygraph tape during such behavior.

Subjects

The subjects of the visual experiment were ninety newborn infants from the maternity ward of the State University of Iowa Hospital. Those infants who were available for study were state pay or partial state cases. For this reason, they probably represent a stratum of society somewhat below the average. Despite this fact all subjects used in the investigation were healthy and well nourished. Patients at the hospital are ordinarily dismissed on the tenth day after delivery. In the present study a few subjects were used who, for other reasons than those pertaining to health, remained in the hospital for more than the first ten days.

Results

Seventy-nine per cent of the ninety infants revealed a greater amount of activity under minimal than under moderate light conditions. The percentage is sufficiently high to indicate a marked consistency in the behavior of the group.

The mean activity of the infants in terms of oscillations per half minute was 27.5, 35.9, and 45.2 for the moderate, dim, and minimal situations respectively. From the following data it will be seen that each difference between mean scores has an appreciable statistical significance:

	Chances in 100 Difference Is Greater Than
Differences	Zero
Moderate vs. Dim	95
Minimal vs. Dim	94
Moderate vs. Minimal	100

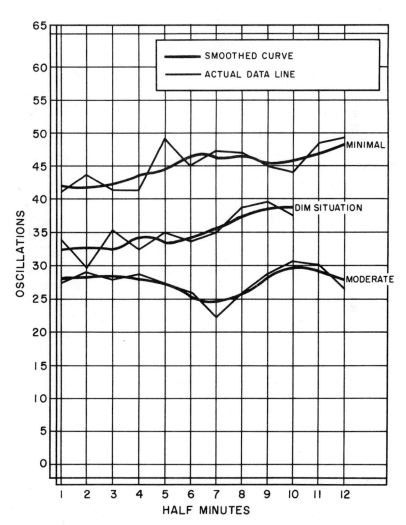

FIGURE 1. *Activity trends within each experimental situation in the visual experiment.*

To obtain a measure of activity trends within each experimental situation, the average activity of the group for each successive half minute of stimulation was determined for each situation. The results are pictured graphically in Figure 1. The activity in each situation begins at a point different from that of the other situations and maintains that difference throughout the period of stimulation.

THE SOUND-DARK EXPERIMENT

The purpose of the sound-dark experiment was to determine whether the relationship found between activity and stimulation in the former experiment holds when visual stimuli are replaced by auditory stimuli. The method and conditions of the experiment were exactly the same but the experiment was conducted in darkness.

In the present experiment, the control situation which was used as the basis for evaluating the effect of sound intensities was a five minute period of silence always given between the two sound stimuli. This order was maintained because the auditory stimuli seemed to have more possibilities of producing adaptation than did the stimuli of the visual experiment, and a five minute rest between stimuli seemed to offer greater chances of clear-cut results.

The sound stimuli themselves were two relatively pure tones produced by means of an audio-oscillator. Both tones had a frequency of 420 double vibrations. In other words, they were four-tenths of a whole tone below A_3 (the A above middle C). The intensity of the one tone was 50 decibels and that of the other, 75 decibels. Both intensities are well within the moderate range and are of strengths commonly met in the everyday environment. Thirty-nine newborn infants were subjects of the experiment.

The subjects of the sound-dark experiment reveal a marked tendency toward less activity in the sound situations than in the silent period. Seventy-one per cent were quieter in both sounds than in silence; 24 per cent were quieter in one of the sound situations than in silence; and only 5 per cent were quieter in silence than in either sound situation.

The cases also reveal a marked tendency toward less activity under 75 than under 50 decibels of stimulation; 74 per cent were quieter in the former situation than in the latter. The mean activity scores of the infants in the dark control, 50 decibel situation, and 75 decibel situation were respectively 50.3, 31.0, and 18.9 oscillations per half minute.

Figure 2 represents the average activity of the infants for each successive half minute of stimulation in each experimental situation. The figure reveals in a clear-cut manner the quieting effect of the sound stimuli, particularly of the 75 decibel tone. It also reveals, furthermore, a tendency for the activity of a given stimulus period to maintain a rather constant level after the first half minute of adjustment.

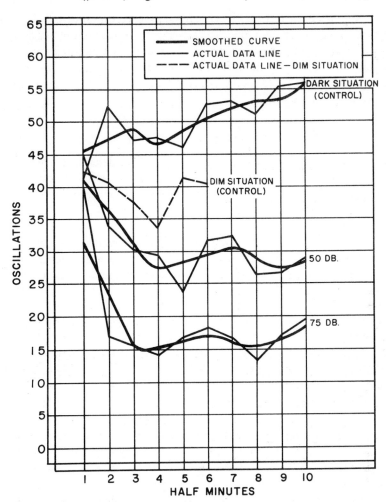

FIGURE 2. *Activity trends within each experimental situation in the sound-dark experiment.*

THE SOUND-LIGHT EXPERIMENT

The sound-light experiment was devised (1) to furnish a check on both of the previous experiments, and (2) to furnish information as to the effect of more than one sensory stimulus on the activity of the newborn infant. The experiment was conducted in exactly the same manner as the sound-dark experiment with the exception that the two sound situations and the control were run in moderate light (the same light as used in the visual experiment). Forty-two infants were used in the sound-light experiment.

The mean activity scores in the control, 50 decibel, and 75 decibel situations were 30.1, 18.6, and 8.7. All differences between these are significant at the 3 per cent level or above. It will be noted that with constant light activity was less in sound than in silence and less under 75 decibels of stimulation than under 50 decibels.

Figure 3 represents the activity of the forty-two infants of the sound-light experiment for each successive half minute of stimulation in each of the experimental situations. The curves are very similar to those for the

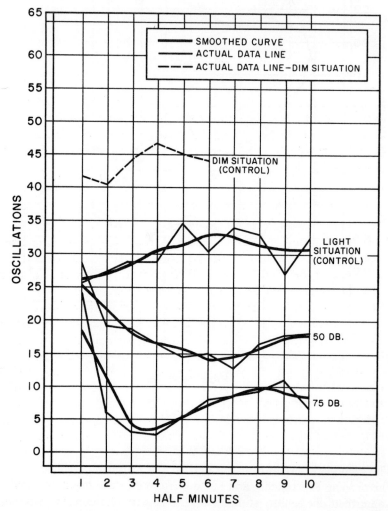

FIGURE 3. *Activity trends within each experimental situation in the sound-light experiment.*

sound-dark experiment; they reveal the quieting effect of the sound stimuli, and the tendency for activity of a given stimulus period to maintain a rather constant level after the initial period of adjustment.

It has been found that light alone is quieting and that sound alone is quieting. If these two stimuli are used together, is the effect greater than that occurring when either is used alone?

The mean activities of the infants in the three types of situations just listed are given below:

Situation	Mean Activity
Moderate light alone	27.5
50 Decibel stimulation alone	31.0
Moderate light and 50 decibel stimulation	18.6
75 Decibel stimulation alone	18.9
Moderate light and 75 decibel stimulation	8.7

All differences between the situations listed above are significant at the 3 per cent level or above. To find differences so clearly revealed is strong evidence that environmental factors affect the behavior of the infant even in the earliest days of life.

IMPLICATIONS OF THE INVESTIGATION

The present investigation has demonstrated repeatedly that mild auditory and visual stimuli reduce the activity of the newborn infant and that this reduction is proportional to the intensities of the stimuli used. It may be that the decreased activity was a direct effect of the stimuli, in which case the phenomena could be considered a type of inhibition.

The term inhibition is generally used to describe those situations in which the stimuli produce measurable reduction in an already existing activity but do not, on the basis of known techniques, produce measurable responses of their own. The phenomena which fit this definition have been widely investigated and have yielded many verifiable facts. Several of these facts have been found to hold in the present investigation. One of these pertains to the mildness of the experimental stimuli. This relation between mild stimulation and reduced activity is also demonstrated by our own everyday experiences. Faint or mild stimuli such as moderate warmth, soft tones, and dim lights lead to relaxation while intense heat, shrill tones, or glaring lights lead to violent reactions.

While the present study is of practical value (1) in suggesting a means for regulating the infant's activity and (2) in revealing a greater sensitivity to external stimuli than previously realized, its chief implications are of a research nature. From a research viewpoint the study makes two contributions: (1) It throws light on the problem of what constitutes a stimulus. (2) It opens a new type of investigation in the field of infant research.

The present study has emphasized the significance of the factor of stimulation. This factor may be of greater importance than has been formerly realized. Hence, it suggests that in future research the duration of stimulation as well as intensity should be considered.

The new phase of research which the present study opens is characterized by an interest in and a method for comparing the effects of different stimulus situations in a quantitative way.

5 · Effects of Cup, Bottle, and Breast Feeding Upon Newborn Infants

HERBERT V. DAVIS, ROBERT R. SEARS,

HERBERT C. MILLER, AND ARTHUR J. BRODBECK

Reprinted from *Pediatrics*, 3 (1948), 549-558, by permission of the publisher and the authors.

. *The belief that a newborn child should be fed in a particular way is often so strong that it is difficult to experiment with different forms of feeding. The present study, the only one of its kind, was made possible because a pediatrician was willing to try "cup" feeding. Dr. Robert Sears was the senior psychologist in the research team.*

The psychoanalytic theory that babies possess from birth a libidinal oral drive dominates much of the recent thinking and writing concerned with the emotional development of infants and children. In brief, the theory supposes that the baby not only has a sucking reflex but also a sucking drive, i.e., he gets satisfaction from sucking qua sucking, and wants to suck in the same sense that he wants to eat, evacuate, or be warm. The existence of such a drive is inferred from two kinds of behavior. One is the frequent occurrence of nonnutritional or "pleasure" sucking on such objects as the fists, thumbs, or bedclothes. The other is the group of frustration reactions (crying, thrashing, further effort) that commonly occur when someone interrupts the nonnutritive sucking.

There can be little doubt that a sucking drive does exist in most infants. Levy (1928, 1934) found that puppies which had little opportunity for vigorous nutritional sucking did more nonnutritional sucking, biting, and chewing than puppies that had greater opportunity, and that thumb-sucking in young children was associated with a history of infrequent or interrupted opportunities for sucking during early feeding. But whether the drive that causes such behavior is inborn is difficult to determine. The fact that feeding usually accompanies sucking during the first weeks of life means there is ample opportunity for the baby to learn a sucking drive if he does not already possess it. The necessary conditions for this would be the frequent occurrence of the act (sucking) followed by satisfaction of a primary drive (hunger). To determine whether the sucking drive is inborn or learned requires a comparison of the frequency of oral activities and frustration reactions in two groups of babies, one of which has had the experience of sucking followed by feeding, and the other of which has fed without sucking.

An opportunity to make this comparison was presented to us by a group of babies who were fed from birth from a cup. This method of feeding reduces nutritive sucking far below that which would occur among babies fed at the breast or from a bottle. According to the psychoanalytic theory, these babies would be expected to show more nonnutritional sucking and more emotional disturbance than babies fed from birth by bottle or breast. According to the learning theory, on the other hand, the cup fed babies should show less indication of a sucking drive than bottle or breast fed babies because they had less opportunity to associate sucking and feeding.

The present report is concerned with investigations made on 60 newborn infants divided into three groups of 20 each according to the method of feeding: cup, bottle, or breast. Daily measurements were made during the first 10 days of life on the strength of the sucking response, the frequency of nonnutritional oral movements, the amount of general body activity, the amount of crying, and the interest in food. The results obtained have been compared for the three groups.

EXPERIMENTAL CONDITIONS

Sixty full-term, healthy, newborn infants were used. No infants were included who failed to gain weight as normally expected, who became ill, or who were changed from one method of feeding to another. The decision to place an infant on the breast, bottle, or cup was made after prior consultation with the mother and in accordance with her wishes. The bottle and cup fed infants were fed by the nurses in the nursery of the University of Kansas Medical Center, except that in some instances the mothers took over the feeding on about the sixth day, using the same technic as the nurses. No feedings were given during the first 12 hours following birth; thereafter all infants were fed every four hours. No baby was allowed to feed more than 20 minutes at each feeding. The bottle and cup fed babies were limited to one ounce of milk each feeding on the first day, two ounces on the second day, and three ounces thereafter. All artificially fed infants received the same milk mixture, consisting of whole cow's milk to which was added 5 per cent cane sugar and 20 per cent water. Water was offered to all babies ad lib twice a day from the cup, at 10:30 A.M. and 3:00 P.M. Orange juice and cod liver oil were omitted during the experimental period. All infants were weighed before and after feedings at 10:00 A.M. and 2:00, 6:00 and 10:00 P.M. Throughout the study, the breast fed infants nursed a half hour later than the bottle fed babies in order to facilitate the routine of the nursing staff. All observations were made at standard intervals before or after the feedings and not according to the clock.

Feeding Methods. The significance of the obtained data, from a theoretical standpoint, rests on the differences between cup feeding and breast or bottle sucking. Cup feeding requires much less time than either of the other methods; although the nurse can govern the duration of cup feeding, the slowest cup feeder ordinarily has oral contact with the cup for a shorter length of time than the fastest bottle feeder, of the same age, has contact with the nipple. Bottle feeding, in turn, is faster than breast feeding. During feeding in the nursery, the cup fed baby is held like a bottle fed baby. He sits upright on the nurse's lap, supported by one hand at the back of his neck. He does not touch or lean against the breast. The cup is put against the lower lip and on top of the tongue, the milk being poured into the mouth as rapidly as the baby swallows. Reflex sucking is often stimulated by this procedure, but usually is considerably diminished, if not completely gone, by the tenth day. The baby's skill at swallowing improves markedly during the first ten days, and therefore the duration of oral stimulation at feeding time decreases daily.

In bottle feeding, the baby has more control over the rate of milk intake and the duration of a meal. Not only the rapidity of his swallowing, but also the strength of his sucking determines how fast the milk is taken. By resting or refusing to suck, he can prolong the period.

Bottle and breast feeding not only provide longer contacts, but the contacts are more extensive and are associated with vigorous manipulative activity. The cup touches only the lower lip and the tip of the tongue. A bottle nipple stimulates the lips, tongue, gums and palate, and the breast adds cheek and chin stimulation as well. This is of some importance because all these are sensitive areas for eliciting the sucking reflex.

The differences between the three types of feeding may be summarized as follows; in duration of oral stimulation, cup provides shortest, bottle considerable longer, and breast a little longer than bottle; in surface area stimulated, cup is much less than bottle, and breast is a little more than bottle; in vigor of sucking response, cup produces a minimal response that rapidly diminishes, bottle produces an active response that rapidly increases in strength and precision, and breast is similar to bottle except that it involves a more vigorous response because of the greater pressure required to secure milk.

Measurement. Observations were made of five kinds of behavior; (1) the response to a sucking test, (2) spontaneous oral activity, (3) general body activity, (4) crying, and (5) appetite. The observations were made by two investigators who practised the various types of measurement together before the study was begun. Each was responsible for the measurements taken at certain hours of the day, and the two sets of data have been combined for statistical analysis. The problem of observer agreement was important only in the observations of spontaneous oral activity and general body activity; the details of the test of agreement will be given below.

Sucking Test. The examiner gently inserted his finger, covered with a sterile rubber cot, between the baby's lips and into the mouth. If sucking did not occur within five seconds, a score of zero was recorded. If sucking started within five seconds, the duration of continuous sucking was measured in seconds by a stop watch. Values in Table I refer to "number of seconds."

The strength of the sucking response, measured by its duration, was tested twice daily. Measurements began two hours after the 6:00 A.M. and 2:00 P.M. feedings. Since there were rarely more than six experimental babies in the nursery at once, the testing required about 15 minutes. This point in the hunger cycle was chosen because the excitability of the response varies positively with degrees of hunger, (Pratt, Nelson, and Sun, 1930) and it was anticipated that fewer zero scores would be obtained at these times.

Table I

Median and Mean Durations in Seconds of Responses Obtained at Two Sucking Tests Daily with Each of the Three Groups (20 Infants in Each Group)

Group	Day: Means									
	1	2	3	4	5	6	7	8	9	10
Breast	2.3	5.2	7.0	8.8	7.7	7.5	7.8	5.2	7.0	13.6
Bottle	2.5	6.3	10.1	4.3	6.5	2.2	3.0	6.1	4.4	7.6
Cup	4.0	8.4	5.1	4.7	3.4	8.5	3.4	5.4	5.4	8.7

Group	Day: Medians									
	1	2	3	4	5	6	7	8	9	10
Breast	0	.2	.2	4.0	2.9	7.0	5.2	4.2	5.5	10.0
Bottle	1.1	2.2	5.5	3.0	5.0	1.5	1.0	4.0	2.0	1.5
Cup	1.0	3.4	5.8	2.5	.5	3.5	1.5	1.5	2.0	.6

Spontaneous Oral Activity. This was divided into three categories designated as (1) apparent effort to suck, (2) sucking of external object, and (3) intrinsic mouthing. Apparent effort to suck included mouthing movements which were accompanied by head turning and head seeking movements as seen in babies attempting to find the breast or bottle, and mouthing movements accompanied by attempts to bring the hand or some inanimate object to the mouth. Sucking of external object included the actual sucking of the fingers, hands, bedclothes, or other objects. Intrinsic mouthing were movements of the lips or tongue unassociated with body movements, such as sucking motions of the lips, protrusion of the tongue, tongue sucking, and licking of the lips. A fourth observational category was incidental movements of arms, legs, and head. This category was adopted in an attempt to get some measure of general body activity.

Each category was recorded during 10 consecutive periods of 10 seconds each four times a day, one hour before and two hours after the 10:00 A.M. and 2:00 P.M. feedings. The score for each category of oral behavior could, therefore, vary from zero (no movement in any 10-second period) to 10 (movement in every 10-second period). A daily score for each category of oral or incidental behavior could vary from zero to 40. This time-sampling technic has been shown by Olson (1929) to give a reliable measure of the total amount of non-nutritional activity.

The morning observations were usually made by one observer and the afternoon ones by the other, although occasionally the observers substituted for one another. On a test series before the investigation was begun, the observers independently but simultaneously recorded the activities of a group of children in the nursery. The agreement between the two records was 90 per cent, i.e., 90 per cent of the entries on the record blanks were identical. Repeated tests of this agreement were made during the investigation itself, and in every instance the agreement was 90 per cent or better for the three categories of oral activity. Agreement on incidental movements was poor toward the end of the investigation.

Crying. A time sampling procedure was used for measuring amount of crying. The babies were observed 30 minutes at a time three times daily, a total of 90 minutes. Each half-hour period was divided into 30 periods of one minute each, and a mark of one was given for any one-minute period in which crying occurred, regardless of volume. The crying score could vary from zero to 90 for each baby in any one day. The time samples of crying were done two hours after the 6:00 A.M. feeding and one hour after the 10:00 A.M. and 2:00 P.M. feedings.

Appetite. To evaluate the babies' enjoyment of their food, judgments of eagerness were made at the 10:00 A.M. and 2:00 P.M. feedings. The two observers practised with other newborns for some days before beginning their judgment of the experimental groups. A scale of three points was defined by the words eager, uninterested or casual, and rejecting. When the observers had agreed between themselves as to what kind of feeding reaction was meant by each of these three terms, they began judging the experimental babies.

RESULTS

Sucking Test. The results of the sucking test are shown in Table I. Both the median and mean duration of the response to the sucking test are given, since there were a number of zero scores each day and the distributions were therefore not always symmetrical. In any nonsymmetrical distribution of data containing several zero values or a few extremely high values, a median gives a somewhat more stable measure of the group's central tendency than does a mean score. The mean for a given day was calculated by averaging the two tests for each child and then averaging these values for all the children in the group. The medians were obtained by averaging each child's two tests and then calculating the median of these scores for the whole group.

On only one day was any difference between the means of the three groups significant by a *t*-test. On day 6 the bottle group was unusually low, for unknown reasons, and this mean is different from those for the cup fed and bottle fed groups to a level of confidence of .01.

A comparison of trends in the three groups, however, shows that there was an important difference between the breast fed group and the other two groups (Figure 1). Neither the bottle nor cup fed group showed any significant increase in median duration of response to the sucking test during the ten days. In contrast, the breast fed group, which started lower than they, increased until it was substantially higher during the last seven days.

This difference in trend is statistically reliable. A *t*-test comparison was made between the average duration for the first three days and for the

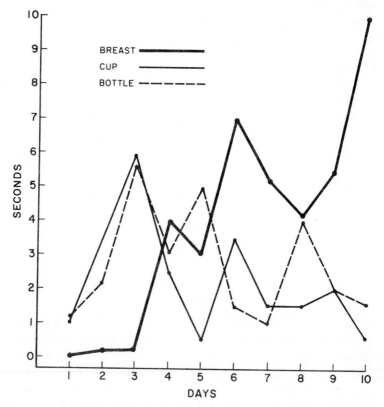

FIGURE 1. *Median duration of sucking response on first 10 days under three types of feeding.*

last seven days. For the first three days, there was not a reliable difference between the groups. For the last seven days, however, the level of confidence between cup and breast groups was $p = < .10$, and between bottle and breast groups, $p = < .01$. The difference between the first three and last seven days for the breast fed group had a reliability of $p = < .10$. None of the other differences were reliable.

Spontaneous Oral Activity. The results of the observations on the three categories of oral behavior are summarized in Tables II, III and IV.* There

Table II

Mean Frequency of 10-Second Periods Containing Apparent Efforts to Suck

Group	Day								
	1	2	3	4	5	6	7	8	9
Breast	2.2	1.4	2.6	2.5	3.2	3.4	1.6	3.1	4.6
Bottle	3.2	2.1	2.4	2.0	3.7	2.6	1.3	2.5	3.2
Cup	2.0	2.0	4.6	2.6	2.0	2.2	2.2	3.0	4.7

Table III

Mean Frequency of 10-Second Periods Containing Oral Movements Involving an Extrinsic Object

Group	Day								
	1	2	3	4	5	6	7	8	9
Breast	2.6	1.6	1.6	1.8	1.2	2.0	2.2	1.4	1.8
Bottle	1.9	2.0	1.4	.4	2.2	1.1	.8	.8	1.0
Cup	1.3	1.4	2.6	1.8	.2	1.0	.8	1.5	2.8

Table IV

Mean Frequency of 10-Second Periods Containing Intrinsic Mouthing Movements

Group	Day								
	1	2	3	4	5	6	7	8	9
Breast	11.8	7.5	7.5	6.1	7.5	8.6	6.3	7.4	6.8
Bottle	12.4	8.2	8.4	6.9	7.9	7.2	6.3	7.2	6.6
Cup	12.0	8.8	7.8	5.4	6.9	5.5	6.7	5.6	5.7

* The schedule for releasing babies from the nursery made it impossible to secure complete measures of any behavior except the sucking test on the tenth day. These tables, as well as those for crying and appetite, include data for the first nine days only.

was a definite decrease in the intrinsic mouthing movements in all three groups of infants during the first four days (Table IV), but there was no significant change thereafter. There were no significant differences among the three groups of infants in the apparent effort to suck (Table II) or in actual sucking of an extrinsic object (Table III). Both the latter types of oral behavior occurred too infrequently in all three groups of infants to determine whether or not significant differences were present.

Table V

Mean Frequency of 10-Second Periods Containing Incidental Body Movements (General Activity)

Group	Day								
	1	2	3	4	5	6	7	8	9
Breast	23.7	21.4	21.2	17.8	20.2	21.9	21.2	23.6	24.0
Bottle	21.4	23.2	21.4	17.9	20.0	16.8	16.5	21.4	19.3
Cup	22.5	19.4	20.8	16.5	17.4	13.3	15.2	19.1	17.9

Incidental Movement. The obtained values for incidental movement (general body activity) are shown in Table V. During the first four days, the three groups followed similar patterns, but beginning with the sixth day the amount of incidental movement among the breast fed group was greater. With one exception (the breast-bottle difference on day 8), all the daily differences between the breast fed and the other two groups are statistically significant to the .02 level of confidence, or better, during the last four days. Because of the low agreement on this category, between observers, toward the end of the study, the significance of this trend is questionable.

Crying. The results of the time-samples on the crying behavior are shown in Table VI. The behavior was much the same in all three groups. The amount of crying was consistently greater when the time-sampling was

Table VI

Mean Number of Minutes of Crying, During Each of Three 30-Minute Observation Periods, on the First Four and Last Five Days

Group	Day					
	1–4			5–9		
	8:00 A.M. 2 hr. A.C.	11:00 A.M. 1 hr. A.C.	3:00 P.M. 1 hr. A.C.	8:30 A.M. 2 hr. A.C.	11:00 A.M. 1 hr. A.C.	3:00 P.M. 1 hr. A.C.
Breast	5.4	2.4	3.4	8.4	2.6	3.5
Bottle	5.4	1.8	2.4	8.5	1.7	1.3
Cup	6.1	2.8	1.9	6.5	2.4	2.2

done two hours after the feeding, irrespective of the feeding method or the day of life. There appeared to be a general tendency for crying to increase in all three groups as they grow older, but although the breast fed group had slightly higher values than the other two groups during the last five days, none of the intergroup differences was statistically significant.

Appetite. The judgment of appetite showed that there was a significantly greater number of noneager feedings in the breast fed group than in the other two groups (Table VII). This difference occurred only in the first three days of life.

Table VII

Frequency of Noneager Feedings in First Nine Days; Two Feedings per Day Were Observed

Group	No. of Feedings Observed	No. of Noneager Feedings	Per cent Non-Eager
Breast	352	47	17%
Bottle	331	31	9%
Cup	343	21	6%

DISCUSSION

Although these three groups of newborn infants had substantially different sucking experiences in food-taking during the first 10 days, few significant differences in the measured forms of behavior were observed. The breast fed group showed a consistent increase in the sucking response to lip stimulation during the first ten days of life, while the response in the other two groups remained unchanged throughout this same period.

Halverson (1938) has shown that an infant at the breast needs to exert more physical strength in the sucking process than a baby who is fed from a bottle. It is a well recognized clinical observation that it is usually difficult to get a bottle fed baby to nurse at the breast successfully if the infant has been started on bottle feedings, presumably because of the greater ease with which milk is usually obtained from a bottle. From observations made during the study it was clear that many of the breast fed infants sucked the full 20 minutes allowed, while the bottle and cup fed infants usually consumed their feedings in about half the time. This rewarding of the more vigorous sucking among the breast fed infants, together with the greater number of rewarded sucks they necessarily had, very likely accounts for their increased response to the sucking test (greater habit strength) in the last seven days.

With a stronger response developing, it might be expected there would be more oral movements of the kind called intrinsic. The reason for this lies in the opportunity for a greater frequency of association of mouth movements with a greater variety of interoceptive and proprioceptive stimuli. The baby should learn to make mouth movements to a greater variety of stimuli. During periods between feedings, these random and nutritionally irrelevant stimuli, as well as hunger drive stimuli, would occur inside the child and then would evoke mouth movements. The data do not support this expectation; the breast fed group did not produce significantly more intrinsic movements.

There were more noneager feeders in the breast fed group than in the bottle or cup fed groups during the first three days, coinciding with a lesser response to lip stimulation on the sucking test. Breast milk does not flow as freely at first as later and the newborn baby has not developed much skill in getting it. Also, the breast feeding mother is less experienced than the pediatric nurse; the bottle and cup fed babies are approached with more confidence and skill than are the breast fed babies. It is not surprising that the latter infants showed less eagerness.

Parts of the data are relevant to the hypothesis concerning the development of an oral drive. According to the psychoanalytic view, this drive exists as a libidinal component from birth; it is a biologically inherent property of the organism. An alternative hypothesis has been suggested, however; namely, that the oral drive is in part a secondary drive, formed by virtue of the fact that sucking and oral stimulation commonly accompany primary drive reduction of hunger. According to the principles of learning (Miller and Dollard, 1941) any act that is instrumental in providing the gratification that comes with reducing one of the basic primary drives, such as hunger, thirst, temperature regulation, fatigue, etc., becomes gratfying in its own right. A secondary drive is formed, which can be satisfied only by performing this new secondary goal response.

If the first hypothesis is correct (i.e., that the oral drive is native), the cup fed group should show more signs of frustration and more seeking for stimulation than the other two groups. This would follow because the cup fed group got less opportunity at feeding times to satisfy the drive. There is no indication that the cup fed group showed either of these consequences. The breast fed group were more responsive, rather than less, to the sucking test; they did slightly, though not significantly, more crying toward the end of the period; and they showed more appetite disturbance during the first three days. The cup fed group showed less sign of frustration or unsatisfied oral drive than did the breast fed group.

On the other hand, according to the learning theory, the bottle fed babies should have shown behavior similar to that of the breast fed babies. They did not; they were similar to the cup fed group. Possibly this was caused by the use of very pliable nipples that required little vigor in sucking, but this factor was not measured.

The present study does not give any final solution to the problem of whether or not the oral drive is wholly inborn or entirely learned or a resultant of both influences. It does indicate the need for further study and open mind on this problem, on which so much has been written and so little has been done experimentally to evaluate the relevant factors involved.

SUMMARY

Sixty babies were divided into three groups of 20 each, one group being fed by cup, one by bottle, and one by breast during the first 10 days of life. The breast fed infants developed a stronger sucking reflex than either of the other two groups, which did not differ from one another. There were no statistically significant differences between the groups with respect to amount of spontaneous oral activity or amount of crying. The breast fed group showed slightly higher general body activity in the last five days and slightly poorer appetite on the first three days.

References

Halverson, H. M., "Infant Sucking and Tensional Behavior," *Journal of Genetic Psychology*, 53 (1938), 365.

Levy, D. M., "Fingersucking and Accessory Movements in Early Infancy," *American Journal of Psychiatry*, 7 (1928), 881.

——, "Experiments on Sucking Reflex and Social Behavior of Dogs," *American Journal of Orthopsychiatry*, 4 (1934), 203.

Miller, N. E., and J. Dollard, *Social Learning and Imitation*. New Haven, Conn.: Yale University Press, 1941, p. 341.

Olson, W. C., *Measurement of Nervous Habits in Normal Children*. Minneapolis: University of Minnesota Press, 1929, p. 97.

Pratt, K. C., A. K. Nelson, and K. H. Sun, *Behavior of Newborn Infant*. Columbus: Ohio State University Press, 1930, p. 237.

6 · Conditioning in the Neonate

DELOS D. WICKENS AND CAROL WICKENS

Reprinted from an article entitled "A Study of Conditioning in the Neonate," *Journal of Experimental Psychology*, 26 (1940), 94-102, by permission of the authors and The American Psychological Association.

When is a human being first capable of learning? The answer to this question depends in part upon one's definition of learning. One of the most studied types of learning is the classical or Pavlovian conditioned response. Several studies of newborn infants, and even studies of fetuses in utero, have apparently shown that the older fetus and the neonate can be conditioned to respond to previously ineffective stimuli. However, the following investigation shows that new stimuli may become effective even without the usual conditioning procedure. Some modification of behavior occurs but it does not fit the pattern of the classical conditioned response. We need to know much more about the ways in which the young infant's behavior can be modified and about the degree of permanence of these modifications before definitive statements concerning early learning can be made.

PROBLEM

The purpose of the present experiment was to investigate the problem of the conditionability of a withdrawal movement in the newborn infant, and, if positive results were obtained, to study other conditioning phenomena such as experimental extinction and spontaneous recovery in these subjects. This general problem has already been attacked in similar subjects by Marquis (1931), who used sucking as her unconditioned response, and by Wenger (1936), who employed lid closure and the withdrawal of the leg to shock in addition to sucking as a response. Although both of these studies obtained results which the writers interpreted as positive, neither of them is entirely conclusive and both have been subjected to criticism. Pratt (1930) and others (Wenger, 1936) have suggested that Marquis has not clearly shown that the response to the conditioned stimulus which she obtained after her training series might not have occurred without this training. Further, Wenger, using a procedure similar to that of Marquis, obtained negative results for this particular response. Wenger's own study, although careful and approaching objectivity, must be criticized because of the limited number of subjects used; in many groups only two or three infants were used and one important control group consisted of but four subjects. Since there is a considerable overlapping between the results of his control and his experimental group, this limitation in the number of subjects becomes a serious criticism. A further consideration of this point will be given in discussion of our results.

Because of these objections, it was felt that an additional experiment might clarify the question as to whether or not the newborn infant can become conditioned.

PROCEDURES

Subjects were under-ten-day infants born in the Ohio State University Hospital. Thirty-six infants in all were used in the actual experiment. These were full-term babies about equally divided as to sex. Approximately one-third of the subjects were of at least partial Negro parentage and the remainder were of white percentage. The infants were from three to five days old when they were brought in for the first experimental session, and, the study continuing for four days, the subjects were from seven to nine days of age at the last experimental period.

All experimentation was done with the infants inclosed in the sound-proof, thermostatic isolation cabinet, described by Dockeray and Valentine (1939).

Before the formal experimentation on the 36 final subjects was begun, various sorts of stimuli were administered to a number of other infants with a view to determining the optimal unconditioned stimulus. From these investigations it was concluded that the best type of stimulus for the study of conditioning of a withdrawal movement was a shock to the sole of the foot. To this stimulus the infant usually responds bilaterally with flexor movements of legs, feet, and toes, often followed by extensor movements. This response is usually more marked in the member receiving the shock than it is in the other member. Shock then was the conditioned stimulus. This was delivered from a Harvard inductorium, the current being derived from a 6 volt storage battery. The electrode consisted of two 4 by 36 bolt heads attached to the surface of a flexible rubber disc about the size of a penny. This was attached to the sole of the right foot by a strip of Sealtex tape. The conditioned stimulus was the sound of a muffled buzzer, placed in the cabinet about two feet from the infant's head. The buzzer and shock were administered by hand, with the buzzer (in the paired stimulation) preceding the shock by about a fourth of a second and continuing about a fourth a second more, along with the shock. This hand method of giving stimulations was, of course, necessarily subject to some variability. Stimulations were spaced one, two, three, or four minutes apart according to a varied and irregular pattern. An attempt was made to stimulate the infant only when his activity level corresponded with stages three to five of Wagner's criteria of sleep (1937), that is, when it was neither crying nor highly active and yet not in an extremely deep sleep. Since the babies did not always cooperate, the time intervals between the presentations of the paired stimuli occasionally ran over the one- to four-minute figures mentioned above. The same infant was always run at the same time on succeeding days, the times being directly following either the two or four o'clock feeding periods. The two experimenters observed and recorded the responses of the infants, one noting the movements of one limb and one the movements of the other. The responses were recorded upon form sheets in terms of flexor and extensor movements of the leg, foot, and toes.

Three separate groups, consisting of 12 infants each, were used—an experimental group and two controls. For all three groups items of initial procedure were the same. The infant was placed in the isolation cabinet, the electrode having been attached to the sole of the right foot. It was allowed about five minutes to become adjusted to the situation; then tests for responses to the buzzer alone were administered. Three different stimulations of the sound of the buzzer were given, and, if the infant responded by any movement of leg, foot, or toe, he was discarded and not used in any of the three groups. From this point on, the procedure for the different groups varied.

The experimental group received 36 paired stimulations of buzzer and shock, 12 each day for three consecutive days. At the end of the third day, the buzzer alone was sounded to test for the presence of conditioning, and these stimulations of the buzzer were administered until there were three consecutive failures to respond—the criterion of extinction in this experiment. On the fourth day, the buzzer alone was administered until the response was extinguished. This was done, of course, to test for the spontaneous recovery of the previously extinguished conditioned response.

In view of the possibility that positive results in the above group, if present, might be due to the effect of repeated presentations of shock, the unconditioned stimulus, rather than to the pairing of the buzzer and shock, the following control group was set up, which we shall call Control Group 1. Following the usual tests to the buzzer alone, the 12 infants of this group were given 36 shocks alone, 12 each day, for three consecutive days. Thus, they never received a paired stimulation of shock and buzzer. At the end of this period, on the third and fourth days, the buzzer alone was sounded, tests for extinction and spontaneous recovery of the response, if any, being administered just as in the experimental group.

Control Group 2 was run to check the possibility that any responses to the buzzer on the third day might be due solely to the factor of maturation rather than to training. The procedure for this group consisted in testing for responses to the buzzer alone on day 1; then, on day 3, after two days' delay, during which time no stimulations were given by the experimenters, administering a second test for responses to the buzzer alone.

RESULTS

The results for the experimental group are presented in Table I. Each baby is listed separately. Day 3 is, of course, the time of the test for

Table I

Showing the Number of Responses to the Buzzer Alone for the Experimental Group on the Third and Fourth Days of the Experiment, Day 3 Being the Original Test for the Presence of Conditioning, and Day 4 Being a Test for Spontaneous Recovery

Number of Responses	Subjects											
	He	Ca	De	Ch	Re	Mc	Bo	Jo	Ot	Fo	Gr	Ma
Day 3	2	2	4	0	3	1	5	2	0	1	0	3
Day 4	8	9	–	0	4	10	7	1	8	1	0	0

presence of the conditioned response, following the training series of 36 paired stimulations; day 4 was the day of tests for spontaneous recovery of the response which had been extinguished on the previous day. By number of responses is meant the number of times the infant responded to the buzzer alone by some movement of both limbs,* that is, gave a conditioned response. For example, subject He gave two conditioned responses on the third day and eight responses on the fourth day. It will be seen that 9 of the 12 infants in the experimental group gave conditioned responses to the buzzer alone on the third day. Only 11 of the 12 subjects were tested for spontaneous recovery. Of those who showed conditioning on the previous day, nine showed spontaneous recovery, and one infant, who gave no conditioned responses on the previous day, gave several such responses on the spontaneous-recovery day. In general, then, the results of the experimental group indicate that conditioning of the withdrawal response, its extinction, and the spontaneous recovery of the response on the following day, are obtainable in the under-ten-day-old infant.

The clearness of this picture is, however, clouded by the findings of the first control group, for the behavior of these subjects was practically identical with that of the experimental group, in spite of the fact that the subjects of Control Group 1 had never had a paired presentation of buzzer and shock. The results for Control Group 1 will be found in Table II, and may be read in the same manner as Table I. Ten out of the 12 infants responded to the buzzer, after the 36 shocks alone; all of these showed

---

* Movement of both limbs was demanded as a criterion of the conditioned response since this bilateral movement was typical of the response to the unconditioned stimulus.

Table II

Showing the Number of Responses to the Buzzer Alone for Control
Group 1 on the Third and Fourth Days of the Experiment

Number of Responses	Subjects											
	Hi	Al	Ad	Pa	Ja	Th	En	Sm	Am	Kl	Fj	Wi
Day 3	2	1	0	2	3	2	5	2	3	2	2	1
Day 4	2	10	0	9	3	2	3	–	5	–	2	1

extinction, and of the 10 babies who were tested on the fourth day, 8 showed spontaneous recovery. Needless to say, the slight differences between this control group and the experimental are not statistically significant. Conditioning, if you will, extinction, and spontaneous recovery are just as clearly demonstrated in this group as in the previous one.

It immediately occurred to the experimenters that these results might be due to faulty mechanics in the experimental setup. It might be possible that, although the infant was enclosed in a supposedly soundproof cabinet, he was able to react to the sound of the vibrator on the inductorium itself, and this might become a conditioned stimulus which could be easily generalized to the buzzer. That this was not true was proved by including checks brought about by activating the inductorium alone without the application of shock. In no cases were any responses made to these checks.

There still remained the possibility that the responses to the buzzer alone given on the third and fourth days were due simply to maturational factors (that is, increase in auditory acuity) rather than to any effects of the experimental routine. As will be recalled, Control Group 2 was designed to investigate this possibility. This group simply received two tests for responses to the buzzer, separated by two days. Of course, as in the other groups, no subject was included who responded to the buzzer on the first day. Only one out of the 12 subjects used gave any response to the buzzer on the second test. Applying the Chi Square formula we find that there is a statistically significant difference between this group and the experimental group and between this group and Control Group 1.

At this point it would perhaps be in order to consider the only other study we have found which investigated conditioning of the withdrawal movement in the under-ten-day-old infant, at the same time employing a control group similar to our Control Group 1. Wenger (1936), using five infants in his experimental group, concluded that the movement of withdrawal from shock in the infant could be conditioned to a tone. He ran a control of four subjects in which shock alone was given, followed by tests for responses to the tone (without any pairing of conditioned and unconditioned stimulus). This control group did give a number of responses to the tone alone. However, because the experimental group gave a few more such responses, Wenger concludes that there were essential differences between the two groups. An examination of his tables, however, indicates that this is not necessarily true, that there is no statistically significant difference between his experimental and control groups, and that his results are actually in accord with ours. Whatever differences there exist between the two groups may be attributed to sampling errors.

DISCUSSION

There seems, then, to be an essential similarity between our experimental group and our first control group, both of them showing evidences of "conditioning," extinction of the conditioned response, and spontaneous recovery, even though the situation for the control group was not a conventional conditioning situation. This similarity seems not to be due to artifacts of the experimental setup, or to any maturational effects. There remains the problem of accounting for it. Two possible interpretations present themselves. These are highly speculative, neither proved nor disproved by the extant experimental evidence. However, they are perhaps worthy of consideration with a view to further investigation.

1. Perhaps the continued stimulation which results in the leg movement characteristic response to shock serves to sensitize and make this response prepotent. The muscles involved in the response are, then, in a state of readiness, and may be tripped off at almost any stimulation. Highly analogous to this in the field of infant behavior are the findings of Pratt, Nelson, and Sun (1930), Jensen (1932), and others, which indicate that nearly any stimulus will set off the sucking response, supposedly a prepotent response in the neonate. Possibly analogous in the field of adult conditioning is the phenomenon of sensitization (Bernstein, 1934). If this interpretation of sensitization is accepted, it would seem that our infants are not showing conditioning in the ordinary meaning of the term. However, before sensitization can become a complete explanation, we must know more concerning the nature of this phenomenon. The fact that spontaneous recovery existed—that these withdrawal responses to the buzzer appeared as late as 24 hours after the last shock, sometimes indeed with greater frequency than in the tests immediately following shock—certainly implies that sensitization is a relatively long-lasting thing.

2. Perhaps conditioning in the ordinary sense is operating after all, but we, as experimenters, are not clearly recognizing the nature of the conditioned stimulus. Perhaps the infant, in responding to the conditioned stimulus, is not responding to the sound of the buzzer as such, but merely to the buzzer's characteristic of being a sudden change in the environment. If we analyze the nature of the shock, we may see how the

infant has become so conditioned, that is, conditioned to respond to a sudden change in the environment. The shock has two characteristics: it is not alone a pain-giving and response-producing stimulus, but it also possesses the character of being a sudden, sharp change in the environment. That is, first there is no shock; then, suddenly, there is shock. This sudden change in the environment is the conditioned stimulus, and it is always followed by pain, the unconditioned stimulus. Thus, the organism becomes conditioned to a change in the environment, and the buzzer, which is also a change in the environment, may now act as a conditioned stimulus. If this were true, we would expect many other stimuli which are effective to the infant also to set off the conditioned response, and this, of course, could easily be attacked experimentally. The interpretation implies that the infant does not easily make discriminations between specific stimuli, and reacts instead to major changes and characteristics—a view which is also supported by the findings of Pratt, Nelson, and Sun (1930).

These theoretical interpretations may be of some value in suggesting problems for future attack. In any case, our data seem to have reopened the question of conditionability of the newborn infant. The results would indicate that, without further experimentation, it cannot be stated that the withdrawal movement in the neonate can be conditioned, in the ordinary sense of that term. Modifiability, however, is clearly shown, and conditioning of some sort may be operating. The investigation points incidentally to the need for adequate controls in conditioning experiments, especially in those which use lower organisms as subjects.

SUMMARY

To investigate the problem of conditionability of the neonate, three groups, consisting of 12 under-ten-day-old infants, were studied, the conditioned stimulus being the sound of a buzzer, the unconditioned stimulus a shock to the sole of the foot.

Members of the experimental group received 12 paired stimulations a day for three consecutive days. They were then tested for conditioned responses to the buzzer alone, the responses were extinguished, and on the following day tests for spontaneous recovery were made. Members of Control Group 1 received 12 shocks alone per day for three consecutive days. Like members of the experimental group, they were tested for responses to the buzzer alone at the end of the third day and on the fourth day. Members of Control Group 2 were tested for responses to the buzzer alone on the first day; then, two days later, during which time no stimulations were given, they were again tested for responses to the buzzer alone.

Results showed that the experimental group gave evidence of conditioning, extinction, and spontaneous recovery. Control Group 1 gave almost identical results, although members of this group had never had a paired presentation of conditioned and unconditioned stimulus. Only one subject in Control Group 2 responded to the buzzer alone on the third day.

Conditionability (in the ordinary sense of the term) of the neonate, and incidentally also of the fetus, is thus not unequivocably supported. Two possible theoretical interpretations are advanced.

References

Bernstein, A. L., "Temporal Factors in the Formation of Conditioned Eyelid Reactions in Human Subjects," *Journal of Genetic Psychology*, 10 (1934), 173-197.

Dockeray, F. C., and W. L. Valentine, "A New Isolation Cabinet for Infant Research," *Journal of Experimental Psychology*, 24 (1939), 211-214.

Jensen, K., "Differential Reactions to Taste and Temperature Stimuli in Newborn Infants," *Genetic Psychology Monographs*, Vol. 12, Nos. 5-6 (1932).

Marquis, D. P., "Can Conditional Responses Be Established in the Newborn Infant?" *Journal of Genetic Psychology*, 39 (1931), 479-492.

Pratt, K. C., "The Neonate," in Carl Murchison, ed., *A Handbook of Child Psychology*, 2nd ed. rev. Worcester, Mass.: Clark University Press, 1930.

———, A. K. Nelson, and K. H. Sun, *The Behavior of the Newborn Infant.* Columbus: Ohio State University Press, 1930.

Wagner, I. F., "The Establishment of a Criterion of Depth of Sleep in the Newborn Infant," *Journal of Genetic Psychology*, 51 (1937), 17-59.

Wenger, M. A., "An Investigation of Conditioned Responses in Human Infants," *University of Iowa Studies in Child Welfare*, Vol. 12, No. 1 (1936), 9-90.

II—PERCEPTUAL–MOTOR DEVELOPMENT

1 · Fetal Reactivity to Sound

JACK BERNARD AND LESTER W. SONTAG

Reprinted from the *Journal of Genetic Psychology*, 70 (1947), 205-210, by permission of the senior author and the Journal Press.

While the fetus is cut off from visual stimulation and no doubt from many other environmental events, the present study shows that external sounds of considerable intensity can reach and stimulate the ears of the fetus.

In 1925 Peiper (1925), using a "loud and shrill" automobile horn as the stimulus and fetal movement as the index of reactivity, obtained some fetal responses, but cautiously concluded that the results of his experiment were ambiguous. More recently Sontag and Wallace (1934, 1936) and Sontag and Richards (1938) have produced evidence that the fetus in utero is responsive to a 120-cycle vibratory stimulation applied to the maternal abdomen, responding by cardio-acceleration and by muscular activity in a way which is suggestive of a fetal startle pattern.

In this connection, it is pertinent to consider the fact that infants born prematurely are responsive to sound stimulation. It may be assumed, therefore, that the seven- or eight-month fetus possesses the necessary equipment for hearing. But, within the uterine environment, does the fetus hear?

The possibility that the human fetus in utero is capable of receiving and responding to stimulation, which outside of the mother's abdomen is perceived as sound, opens an intriguing field of inquiry. When the vibratory stimulus used is evaluated as sound stimulation and calibrated for its qualities, such as tonal range and intensity, do we detect a differential response in the fetus in utero? Are sounds in the everyday external environment, such as music, the dropping of heavy objects, the sound of automobile horns, and so on, perceived by the fetus? How does the fetus' sensitivity to vibratory stimulation change with age? Another crucial question—and one which previous studies involving vibratory stimulation have failed to settle—is this: To be effective in arousing fetal response, must vibratory stimulation be applied directly to the mother's abdomen, that is, contiguous to the tissue of the mother's body? Or will vibration transmitted through air space be further transmitted through the mother's body to the fetus?

In an attempt to answer some of these questions, the following procedures were initiated.

PROCEDURE

Our experimental procedure involved the weekly presentation of tonal stimulation during the last two and a half months of pregnancy. The tones, relatively pure in character, were generated by a Jackson Audio Frequency Oscillator, amplified by a Setchell-Carlson Amplifier Model 13-B, and brought to the maternal abdomen through a Utah G8P speaker resting on a rubber baffle centered over the head region of the fetus. Thus any vibratory stimulus reaching the fetus would have to pass through an air space and could not be interpreted as being conducted through physical contact with the mother's body.

Fetal cardiac change was used as an index of fetal reactivity. Fetal heart sounds were picked up by means of a Brush microphone strapped to the maternal abdomen at the point where the sound was loudest, suitably amplified, and recorded by means of an ink-writer on a moving tape. A switch broke the microphone circuit as it made the speaker circuit, thus avoiding damage to the recording equipment.

During the weekly experimental sessions, each of which involved the presentation of approximately 10 tonal stimulations, the subjects rested in bed in a relatively soundproof room which the experimenter entered only for the purpose of adjusting the microphone. The frequencies used ranged from 20 to 12,000 dv/sec, and were varied systematically. Each stimulation lasted five seconds and was preceded by a warning about three seconds before. In the earliest work this warning was verbal; later a small signal lamp was substituted. In the present analysis, we shall consider only frequencies of 6,000 dv/sec and lower, as intensity fell off rapidly above that point with our present apparatus.

RESULTS

Ten-beat intervals were marked off on the records in both directions from the stimulation, measured as to length, and converted by means of a table to beats per minute. This analysis is therefore in terms of beats per minute of 10-beat samples. The 10-beat periods were continuous.

Figure 1 presents three individual curves for Subjects F, H, and I, and a composite curve for 73 stimulations conducted on these three subjects plus a few observations on a fourth subject, Subject J, who had too few stimulation sessions to permit treating her individual data statistically. It will be seen in each of these curves that a high fetal cardiac rate obtains shortly after stimulation. The critical ratio of the difference between the means of the five consecutive 10-beat prestimulation intervals and the three consecutive poststimulation intervals (when the effect of the stimulation was at its height) was highly significant in the case of each subject.

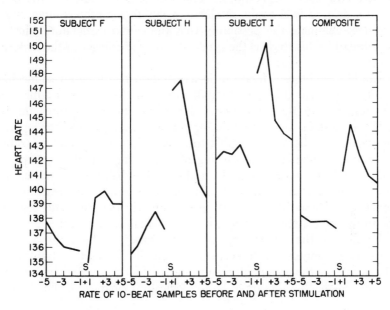

FIGURE 1. *Fetal heart rate in three individual subjects and as a group before and after tone stimulation.*

DISCUSSION

Four explanations of the phenomenon of cardio-acceleration visible in each of the curves appear plausible. We shall discuss each of these in turn.

1. Could the observed cardio-acceleratory response of the fetus be due to maternal stimulation with resultant humoral changes in the mother, which are then passed on through the placenta to the fetus to serve as a secondary stimulus? The four graphs in Figure 1 show that the cardio-acceleratory effect of the stimulation reaches maximum in the second 10-beat period following stimulation, or about 11 seconds after the onset of stimulation. The rapidity of this response eliminates the possibility of its being a maternal stimulus transmitted secondarily to the fetus through passage of newly liberated blood components into the fetal circulation. Any endocrine or other products released into the mother's blood stream as a response to stimulation could not possibly be circulated to the placenta and through the fetal circulation in so little time.

2. If the mother knew far enough in advance just when the stimulation was coming, is it conceivable that her emotional response might occur early enough to permit humoral changes to reach the fetal circulation? To

test this possibility, we used suggestion of stimulation during 15 of the experimental sessions. On these occasions warning of impending stimulation was given, but no tone sounded. There was no significant change in fetal heart rate after such "suggestions." This fact does not rule out the possibility of a *delayed* fetal cardio-acceleration due to the process cited above, but it does eliminate the possibility that the cardio-acceleratory effect as demonstrated in this study is the result of humoral changes in the maternal organism.

3. Could the observed fetal cardio-acceleration be the result of mechanical stimulation caused by tensing abdominal muscles as part of a maternal startle response to the stimulation? No overt startle responses on the part of the mothers were noted during the study, and no mother reported being startled by the sound. Ample time was allowed to permit relaxation before each stimulation, and warning of impending stimulation kept the sound from being unexpected. In addition, the baffle concentrated the sound on the maternal abdomen and reduced the intensity reaching the maternal ear. These facts make it appear unlikely that the fetal response stems from *any* maternal reaction, either physical or chemical.

4. Finally, is the cardio-acceleratory response of the fetus a direct response to a stimulus which, evaluated externally as sound, is transmitted to the fetus via the maternal tissues and/or fluids? In the light of the above discussion, this appears to be the logical explanation of the observed results.

The cardio-acceleratory effect shown in the curves is distributed over the full range of frequencies used, and is not the property of any narrow band. The problem of mapping the limits of fetal tonal sensitivity is therefore opened for future investigation.

By referring to Figure 1 it will be seen that the cardio-deceleration precedes cardio-acceleration for Subject *F*. This is in contrast to the direct acceleration in the other curves and is worth comment. Sontag and Richards (1938, p. 49) have interpreted fetal cardio-acceleration following vibratory stimulation as an aspect of a fetal startle response. It is well known that the cardiac response in the human adult startle pattern involves a momentary deceleration followed by acceleration. It is possible that the same pattern obtains in the fetus, the deceleration in Subjects *H* and *I* taking place during the five-second stimulation period and thus not visible in our records, while for some reason not now apparent the deceleration in Subject *F* lasted beyond the stimulation period. This is a point which requires further investigation.

CONCLUSION

The experimental data presented here indicate that the human fetus in utero is capable of perceiving a wide range of tones. This tone sensitivity is such that tones produced by an amplifier loud-speaker arrangement and transmitted through the air to the mother's abdomen elicit a fetal response. Whether such tonal perception is accomplished by means of the fetal auditory apparatus or represents a vibratory perception sense of other parts of the body, has not been established. It may or may not be proper to speak of "fetal hearing." Response to tonal stimulation is expressed in sharp body movements and cardiac acceleration.

References

Peiper, A., "Sinnesempfindungen des Kindes vor seiner Geburt," *Monatschrift für Kinderheilkunde*, 29 (1925), 236-241.

Sontag, L. W., and R. I. Wallace, "Preliminary Report of the Fels Fund: A Study of Fetal Activity," *American Journal of Diseases of Children*, 48 (1934), 1050-1057.

————, and R. I. Wallace, "Changes in the Heart Rate of the Human Fetal Heart in Response to Vibratory Stimuli," *American Journal of Diseases of Children*, 51 (1936), 583-589.

————, and T. W. Richards, "Studies in Fetal Behavior: I. Fetal Heart Rate as a Behavioral Indicator," *Child Development Monographs*, Vol. 3, No. 4 (1938).

2 · Color Vision in Infants

WILTON P. CHASE

Abridged from the *Journal of Experimental Psychology*, 20 (1937), 203-222, by permission of the author and publisher.

While no one has tried to train newborn infants to respond to differences in color, studies with older children show that learned responses to specific colors are difficult to establish. Yet the newborn infant is not color blind. To establish this fact, Dr. Chase made use of an unlearned response, namely, following a moving object with the eyes. The description of Dr. Chase's apparatus, which is quite technical, has been omitted, but the general principles involved are presented in nontechnical terms.

HISTORICAL AND THEORETICAL INTRODUCTION

Color vision in adults has been very extensively investigated. The problem of the nature of color vision in children first arose in 1877 when Darwin, from observations upon his own children, concluded that color vision in children is a rather late chronological development. However, there is a notable lack of knowledge concerning the color vision of very young infants. So far, certain evidence merely suggests that they have color vision. There has been no direct evidence that very young infants can discriminate between colors, due to the fact that suitable methods for investigating the problem have been lacking.

The following experiment will attempt to show that color discrimination is present in infants as young as fifteen days of age.

METHOD, APPARATUS, AND SUBJECTS

All normal infants will follow moving objects with their eyes from birth. This is, then, the simplest reaction to utilize in examining color vision. A situation must be devised which will stimulate moving of the eyes only if the infant is able to discriminate between colors. Two colors must be presented simultaneously. In order to be sure that the infant must respond to color to make the discrimination between the two, they must be perceptually equal in brightness. The colors must be equated upon photopic values for daylight adaptation to assure equal intensities for the infants. The two colors presented must be arranged so that one can be moved while the other remains stationary. If the infant can discriminate between the two colors which have been equated for brightness he will see the moving color and will watch it move. The present experiment has attempted to fulfill the requirements outlined above.

The procedure was to combine color filters in such a form that they could be projected upon a screen placed above the infant so that one color would be in the center of the screen, completely surrounded by another color. All of the surrounding filter was not used for projection at any one time. It therefore could be moved back and forth in the projection machine, keeping the screen always flooded with color. Thus, the center color alone appeared to move because the outside color never went off the screen. The resulting effect was that the center color appeared to move within the field of the other color.

An experimental situation, therefore, was established in which, if the infant was able to discriminate between colors, the movement of the center could be followed. If he could not discriminate between colors, no movement would be apparent.

The infant to be tested was placed on his back upon a platform. His head was held in position so that his eyes were directly under the center color in its stationary position on the screen. A simple device, adjustable to the infant's head, held it still so that eye movements could be observed without the complication of frequent turning of the infant's head to obscure them. When the infant was in this position, it was about fifteen inches from his eyes to the screen directly above.

The whole housing of the structure, built on top of an ordinary table was made of Masonite board. The dimensions of it were built to conform to the measurements of the screen. A heavy curtain over the opening at the top fitted tightly around the objective lenses of the projection machine and served to keep out any extraneous light. The light emanating from the projection machine was the only light which reached the screen. Two sides of the compartment in which the baby was placed were of the Masonite material. One end was covered with a large piece of cardboard with a small observation opening near the top. The other end was hung with heavy black cambric to serve as a curtain. The child was thus cut off from outside light and disturbances when he was in the compartment.

When observing the infant's reactions to the moving stimulus the observer stood at the head of the table looking through the observation opening in the cardboard screen. He held his head in such a position that the moving stimulus and the infant's eyes could be watched simultaneously.

The experimental procedure was the following. The colors were projected upon the screen with the center color in the center of the screen. The baby was then laid upon the platform. His head was clamped into position and the curtain was lowered. A control period of one minute allowed the experimenter to observe the eye-movements of the baby while the stimulus was stationary in order to later contrast them to eye-movements in relation to the moving stimulus. At the end of the control period, the experimenter started the color moving. He then carefully watched for following of the infant's eyes in relation to the moving stimulus.

The length of the observation period was set for five minutes at the beginning of the experiment. It was found, however, that it was not necessary to hold to the full length of the period for all infants. Following of the stimulus, sufficient to show the presence of color discrimination, occurred early in the period in most cases. When no following could be observed, the infant was dismissed at the end of five minutes. All children were observed for at least one minute.

When no observation could be made because of crying or sleepiness, the infant was dismissed at the end of one minute. In some cases, it was possible to make observations while the infant was crying or was sleepy, as will be indicated later.

The criterion for judging whether or not the infant followed the moving stimulus during the experimental period was as follows. If at any time during the period the infant definitely followed the moving stimulus at the same rate at which it was moving it was counted as following.

The experimenter had to adjust the speed of the moving stimulus to the rate at which the infant could follow best in order to determine more accurately whether the eye-movements were moving in relation to the stimulus. Each infant seemed to have a rate at which he could best follow, and the rate of movement could be quickly adjusted to that rate at each observation.

The experiment was made with 24 infants, 13 girls and 11 boys, at the Harriet Walker Maternity Hospital in Minneapolis. They ranged in age from 15 days to 70 days on the first day they participated in the experiment. The average age was 43 days. The group was divided into three experimental groups. The first had 8 babies, the second, 12 babies, and the third, 9 babies, 5 of them continuing from the second experimental group and 4 of them new.

Each infant in the group being tested was observed each day of the experiment. One filter combination per day was presented to each infant.

With the third experimental group of 9 babies a second observer observed simultaneously with the experimenter in order to test the reliability of obtaining judgments of following under the experimental conditions employed. He observed the baby from the foot of the table while the experimenter observed from his accustomed stand at the head of the table. Each observer made his judgments of when the infant was following the moving stimulus independently of the other. The observer at the foot of the table pushed the button provided at that end when he noted a period of following, and the observer at the head of the table did likewise, a button being placed at his end of the table. The degree of correspondence of judgment could then be determined by the number of concurrent marks upon a polygraph record.

The second observer and the experimenter observed together for 53 observation periods. In 41 of these periods the experimenter judged that the infant followed the moving stimulus. The second observer agreed with the experimenter in judging that the infant followed the stimulus in the same 41 periods. In only one observation period did the second observer judge that the infant followed when the experimenter did not, and there were no such instances when the experimenter judged that the infant followed when the second observer did not. Since this is the basis upon which the results are presented below, it shows that the method of making judgments is one where high agreement between two observers can be obtained.

To further show the reliability of the method used, the following computations show that two observers can agree upon specific "periods of following" during observation periods. When the infant followed the stimulus across the screen without interruption, either with one long pursuit movement of the eyes or with saccadic movements, it was counted as a "period of following," or, if at any time in its course across the screen, the infant followed the moving stimulus in definitely separated intervals, each such interval was also considered a "period of following." The total number of "periods of following" recorded by the second observer was 327, and by the experimenter, 365. The two records corresponded 249 times. The experimenter agreed with the second observer upon 75 per cent of the latter's judgments, and the second observer agreed with 68 per cent of the experimenter's judgments.

RESULTS

Tables I, II, and III give the complete results from the observations upon the infants. The first and second groups had two opportunities to observe each color combination. Since there was but one filter which had the YG and BG combination, this filter was used twice in the experimental series. There were but two children who did not respond by following all color combinations, both failing to follow the filters with the YG and G combination due to crying each time they were presented.

Summarizing the results, excluding infants W through Z, 100 per cent of the children responded to the R and G combination; 100 per cent to the R and YG combination; 100 per cent to the R and BG combination; 90 per cent to the YG and G combination; 100 per cent to the YG and BG combination; and 100 per cent to the G and BG combination. None of the children responded either to the red control filter, the neutral tint filter

Table I

Results from First Experimental Group

Infant	Sex	Age in Days at Start of Experiment	Colors in Order of Presentation																
			Outside Color	R	YG	R	R	YG	BG	G	BG	YG	G	G	YG	R	GR	BG
			Inside Color	G	G	BG	YG	BG	G	YG	R	R	BG	R	BG	R	25% Darker	24% Darker
			No. of Days Increase in Age	0	1	2	4	5	6	7	8	9	11	13	14	15	16	16
A*	M	70		F†	F	F	F	F	F	F	F	F	F	F	F	N	N	
B	F	68		F	C	C	F	F	F	F	F	F	F	F	F	N	N	
C	F	67		F	F	F	F	F	C-F	C	C-F	C-F	F	C-F	F	C-N	C-N	
D	F	66		F	C	F	F	C	F	F	F	F	F	F	F	N	N	
E	F	64		F	F	F	F	N	F	F	N	F	F	F	F	C-N		C-N
F	F	56		F	F	F	F	F	F	F	F	F	F	F	F	N	N	N
G	F	54		F	F	F	F	F	F	F	F	F	F	F	F	N	N	N
H	F	53		F	C-F	F	F	C	C	F	F	F	F	F	F	N	N	N

* Premature infant.

† Explanation of symbols: F, following; C, crying, fussing, or fretting, no following; N, no response; C-F, crying, fussing, or fretting, but with eyes open and following; C-N, crying, fussing, or fretting, but with eyes open and no following; S-F, sleepy, but occasional awakenings with following. R, red; YG, yellow-green; BG, blue-green; G, green.

with the 25 per cent darker spot in the center, or to the BG filter with the 24 per cent darker spot in the center. Four of the eight babies in the first experimental group were presented with the neutral tint filter. The remaining were tested with the BG filter. With these control filters the movement upon the screen was almost imperceptible and was not sufficient to attract the infant's attention. Throughout each period the experimenter and a second observer watched carefully to detect any following but observed no response in any case. It is, therefore, evident that the difference in color of the color combination filters was the factor which attracted the infant's attention to the moving filter.

All of the cases where no response to color combinations are indicated in Tables I, II, and III can be accounted for by the fact that the infant's attention was not centered upon the moving stimulus. For example, Baby E's eyes were fixed upon the observer's eyes at the observation opening throughout both the control and the experimental period when the YG-BG and BG-R combinations were presented to her. The observer tried to overcome this difficulty by putting a piece of paper over the opening and moving it aside just enough to permit him to make his observations. This was fairly successful but she would suddenly stop following the moving

Table II

Results from Second Experimental Group

Infant	Sex	Age in Days at Start of Experiment	Colors in Order of Presentation		Response of Infants													
				Outside Color	YG	R	R	YG	R	G	YG	G	G	BG	BG	YG	R	BG
				Inside Color	G	BG	G	BG	YG	BG	R	R	YG	R	G	BG	R	24% Darker
			No. of Days Increase in Age		0	2	3	4	5	7	9	10	11	12	14	16	17	18
J	M	25			F*	F	C-F	C	F	F	C-F	F	F	F	C	F	C-N	C
K	M	19			C	F	F	C-F	F	F	S	S	F	S	F	F	N	N
L	M	27			C	S	C-F	C-F	C	F	F	F	C	F	F	F	C-N	C
M	F	33			C	C	C-F	C	N	C-F	F	F	F	C-F	F	C-F	C-N	N
N	M	35			F	C-F	F	F	C	C-F	F	F	F	F	S	F	N	N
O	M	40			C-F	F	C-F	C	C-F	F	F	C-F	F	F	F	F	C	N
P	F	43			F	C-F	F	F	F	F	F	F	F	C-F	F	C-F	C-N	N
Q	F	45			C	C	C-F	C-F	C	C-F	C-F	F	C	C-F	C	F	C-N	N
R	M	47			F	F	F	C-F	F	F	C-F	F	F	F	F	F	N	N
T	M	55			C	C	F	C-F	C-F	F	F	F	S-F	F	F	F	N	N
U	M	57			S	C-F	F	C-F	F	F	F	S-F	F	F	F	C-F	N	C
V	M	17			F	C-F	S-F	F	F	F	F	F	C	F	C	C-F	C	N

* For explanation of symbols see Table I.

Table III

Results from Third Experimental Group

Infant	Sex	Age in Days at Start of Experiment	Colors in Order of Presentation		Responses of Infants					
				Outside Color	R	BG	G	G	G	YG
				Inside Color	YG	R	YG	R	BG	BG
			No. of Days Increase in Age		0	2	4	5	6	7
K	M	38			F*	F	F	F	F	F
R	M	66			C	C	N	F	N	F
T	M	74			F	F	F	F	C-F	F
U	M	76			N	F	F	F	F	F
V	M	36			F	F	F	F	F	F
W	F	15			F	F	F	F	C	C-F
X	F	26			C	S-F	C-F	S	F	F
Y	M	22			C	S	C	C-F	F	F
Z	F	21			C	F	C	C-F	F	C

* For explanation of symbols see Table I.

stimulus on other occasions to look up toward the opening, and if the observer's eyes were there she would fixate upon them every time.

Baby M's failure to react to the R-YG combination was due to the fact that she was quite active on that day and had slipped down upon the platform so that her head was out of position and not centered under the screen. The moving stimulus was beyond the top of her head where she could not see it. The experimenter attempted to place her back into position but she commenced to cry and had to be dismissed.

In the third experimental group the introduction of a second observer who looked through the side of the curtain at the foot was a distraction to Baby R on presentation of the G-YG and the G-BG combinations, and to Baby U on the presentation of the R-YG combination. Their eyes were focused upon him and never were centered upon the screen above.

CONCLUSION

It has been demonstrated in this experiment that infants are able to discriminate between colors employed, as evidenced by the fact that they followed the movement of each color within the field of another. They were not making the discrimination upon the basis of a brightness difference or of some mechanical aspect of the experimental situation. This was shown by the use of adequately controlled situations involving only these conditions, and no following occurred.

The present experimental conditions were not designed to discover hereditary color-blindness. When congenital color blindness occurs, the relative luminosity values for daylight adaptation do not conform to those for normal color vision. A congenitally color-blind infant, therefore, being tested under the experimental conditions used in this experiment, might be able to follow the moving stimulus on the basis of a difference in intensity. Since only 8 per cent of males and 1 per cent of females are classed as dichromats, with 11 males and 13 female infant subjects in this experiment, the chances of obtaining in this group even one dichromat would be very small. The chances of having a total monochromat would be exceedingly small indeed, and the chance of having a blue-blind infant would still be very much smaller. The chance that all 24 infants would have one or another of these congenitally color-blind conditions is practically impossible. Because of this, it is possible to assume that probably all of the infants used in this experiment had normal vision.

It therefore follows, in conclusion, that the infants used in this experiment, except for the rare possibility of a congenitally color-blind infant, were discriminating between red and yellow-green, red and green, red and blue-green, yellow-green and blue-green, and green and blue-green.

3 · Visual Depth Perception in Infants

RICHARD D. WALK AND ELEANOR J. GIBSON

Abridged from *Psychological Monographs*, 75 (1961), pages 1, 2, 6, 8, 23, 24, 25, by permission of the authors and of the American Psychological Association.

Here is another "natural" test of visual perception. However, since the test requires locomotion, and no child can creep until he is several months of age, the test does not reveal whether or not the child is born with depth perception or has learned to perceive depth in the period between birth and the onset of creeping.

One of man's strongest fears is the fear of high places and falling. The paratrooper standing in the door of his airplane waiting to jump and the steel worker on the girders of a rising skyscraper are dramatic cases of fearful situations. Nearly all adults have felt apprehensive of height when looking down from a tall building or into a gorge, when balanced at the top of a high ladder or preparing to jump from a high diving board.

The problem with which this monograph is concerned is the discrimination, by vision alone, of depth downward at an edge. Some of the questions to be answered are the following: When is the discrimination present in children? Can it be detected by tendency to avoid a drop-off? What conditions or cues are actually operative in making the discrimination? And what is the role of visual experience in promoting the discrimination?

The apparatus designed for the present experiments, which we named the "visual cliff," uses the principle of a drop-off or graduated heights, but gives the child a *choice* between a short drop-off on one side of a center board and a long drop-off on the other side. A child, if it detected the difference, should prefer the short drop-off at a safe depth to the long drop-off at a dangerous depth. To eliminate nonvisual cues that might permit detection of the difference, such as auditory, olfactory, or temperature differentials from near or distant surfaces, a sheet of glass was inserted under the center board where the organism was placed, so as to extend outward across both the shallow ("safe") drop and the deep ("dangerous") one. The glass was placed over the shallow side as well as the deep side to equate stimulation produced by the glass itself, if any (e.g., reflections), and to equalize tactual cues for locomotion.

Patterned material (wallpaper, linoleum, etc.) could be placed directly under the glass on the shallow side and on the floor below, at any desired distance, on the deep side. Information in the light coming to the eye from the patterns on either side, in combination with stimulation produced by the child's own motion and ocular equipment constituted the stimulus basis for visually differentiating the two sides. Figure 1 shows diagrammatically the situation created by the apparatus.

APPARATUS AND PROCEDURE

This model of the visual cliff was designed to test larger animals and human infants. A table was constructed of 2″ × 4″ pine, measuring 8′ long, 6′ wide, and 40″ high. Supporting legs were placed at each corner and in the middle of each long side where an additional supporting cross beam was also used. Two large pieces of Herculite glass 4′ × 6′ × 3/8″ formed the surface of the table. Under the shallow side a 46″ × 68½″ × 3/4″ piece of composition plywood 1/4″ below the glass was placed to support a textured surface, an irregular green and white pattern of linoleum tile that matched the floor. The same tile pattern was laid over the center board which measured 6′ × 11½″ × 1″.

The cliff table was entirely surrounded by an 8″ high board of 3/4″ pine to protect the subject from accidentally falling off the cliff.

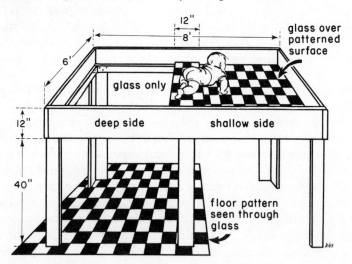

FIGURE 1. *Drawing of the visual cliff, Model III. An infant is starting from the center board toward the shallow side. The entire floor of the room is covered with the checkered linoleum identical with that on the cliff.*

Illumination was supplied by fluorescent lighting directly over the apparatus. The fluorescent lights were covered with brown wrapping paper to diffuse the lighting more evenly over the ceiling and to minimize reflection of the lights from the glass.

The standardized procedure evolved was as follows: The mother stood twice at each side, alternating, some mothers starting at the shallow side, some at the deep. The mother stood for 2 minutes at each side unless the child got off the board and reached a lure. If this happened, the child was put back on the board and the mother switched sides. An experimenter stood at each end of the board so as not to influence the way the infant crawled. If the child crawled away from the mother the experimenter went toward the infant to safeguard him.

RESULTS

The use of this standardized procedure clearly showed that the babies discriminated depth. They crawled toward the mother when she stood at the shallow side and refused to cross the glass to her when she stood at the deep side. Many infants crawled to the shallow side when the mother stood at the deep side and urged him to come to her. Eleven subjects did this; no subject crawled away from the mother across the deep side when she stood at the shallow. Some of the babies cried when the mother stood at the deep side and would not go to her. In such cases, the 2-minute observation period from the deep side was usually terminated at 1 minute.

Once the procedure was standardized, from Subject 10 on, the infants tended to behave very consistently. They crawled to the shallow side twice; in only two cases did the child go but once to the shallow side. The three negative cases, all boy infants, were also consistent; each child crawled twice to the mother across the deep side, twice to her at the shallow side.

When 30 subjects had been run, there were five subjects in the youngest (6-7 month) age group. Of these infants, three had not moved from the center board, one had gone to the shallow side only and one to both sides. Even though two cases is not a large sample, one of the two had crawled across the deep side and it seemed possible, a trend that had to be checked, that very young infants could not discriminate depth as adequately as older ones. Consequently telephone calls were made to mothers in the city with infants 6-7½ months old. Very few of these infants were crawling, but five subjects were added to the youngest group. Of these five children, two remained on the shallow side. The indication was, therefore, that younger infants have as adequate depth perception, if they can be tested, as the older ones.

The results on the first 36 subjects run are shown in Table I. The only age trend is the inadequate locomotor ability of the younger subjects. They evidently crawled at home but not in a strange place. One must recognize that Table I is not a random sample of babies at the indicated ages, but a sample of infants whose mothers say they crawl. It is probably slightly skewed toward younger developers in the 6-7 months old group.

There is much interesting behavior to be observed in this situation. The babies were attracted by the lure and when they reached it, played with it eagerly. They peered down through the glass, sometimes patted it or leaned on it with their faces, yet refused to cross. Some used the deep side for support with one knee, others *backed* partly out across it (in first locomotion in the human infant the child often goes in reverse when he means to go forward), yet they still refused to cross. It was as if the infant could not recognize the consequences of his own actions, since he had already been where he now refused to go. The attitudes of the mothers were interesting as well. The predominant impression among mothers seemed to be that the child had failed the "test" because he did not have enough sense to realize the glass was safe to crawl over. The glass on the deep side was banged with hands and fists; cigarette boxes, lipsticks, purses, crumpled bits of paper, and other releasers of infant approach behavior were proffered—but the babies still refused to go across the glass of the deep side.

Table I

Behavior of Human Infants on the Visual Cliff

Response of S	Age of infant (months)				Total	%
	6–7	8–9	10–11	12–14		
Did not move off center board	5	2	1	1	9	25
To shallow side only	4	7	8	5	24	67
To deep side only	0	0	0	0	0	0
To both sides	1	1	1	0	3	8
Total	10	10	10	6	36	100

Reproduced below are two protocols from the experiment. The first one illustrates the youngest negative case, and the second the normal behavior of an older infant.

S_{17}. Male, 6½ months. (Mother at shallow.)—baby looks at both lures, turns toward mother and crawls to her after 60 seconds. (Mother at deep.) —turns to her at 15 seconds, starts to her at 20 seconds, and gets there in 50 seconds. (Mother at shallow.)—goes to her at once, gets there in 15 seconds. (Mother at deep.)—baby starts toward shallow side; mother goes toward him; he goes back toward her, reaches her at deep in 60 seconds; then looks down through glass and starts back to center board.

S_{30}. Male, 11 months. (Mother at deep.)—he looks both ways and at experimenter; whimpers; looks other way, whimpers (2 minutes). (Mother at shallow.)—goes instantly to shallow side. (Mother at deep.)—baby goes other way (to shallow) at once, cries, starts toward mother, cries. (Experiment terminated here at 1 minute.) (Mother at shallow.)—gets to mother in 3 seconds.

These data show that the average human infant discriminates depth as soon as it can crawl. By the time that locomotion is adequate, which is the time when depth discrimination is necessary for survival, the infant can discriminate depth. In this the human infant fits with other late maturing species we have studied, the rat and the cat. But the human infant does not have quite the same marked apprehension of depth as the goat or the sheep, and a few crawled across the deep side. One also notes the relative clumsiness of the human infant at this age. Despite adequate depth discrimination many babies would have fallen but for the glass on the deep side to protect them.

But there is no evidence from these data that apprehension of height is learned from prior experience with falling. The avoidance and apprehension of height seems in general to be present as soon as an infant has adequate locomotion.

4 · The Motor Sequence

MARY M. SHIRLEY

Abridged from pages 4-8, 34-46, of Volume 2 of *The First Two Years*. Minneapolis: University of Minnesota Press, 1933, by permission of the publisher.

Information concerning when a given response begins or ends can come only from continuous or repeated observations of the same individual. Shirley's study, conducted at the Institute of Child Welfare at the University of Minnesota, was the first investigation to apply uniform methods of recording to a sizable group of children over a period of two years. The findings presented here represent only a small part of her results. This longitudinal approach is now being used at many child research centers. In some instances, data on the same individuals from birth to maturity are now available.

METHODS

Whatever contributions this study may make to our knowledge of infancy will be largely attributable to the method used. Certain fundamental problems of development have only one avenue of approach, that of long continued, or frequently repeated, observations of the same individual. A view of the child as a whole and an understanding of the detailed course of child development, its continuity and its rate, are the rewards of pursuing this route.

Thus far the longitudinal road has been sparingly traveled by students of child development, the reason being, of course, that one can progress much faster and much further toward an understanding of many fundamental principles by taking a short cut that crosses the lives of many children at the same time than by following a few babies down the long lanes of the months and years. For many years interested parents and relatives were the only ones to undertake such long journeys, the obvious reason being that they were perhaps the only persons who had continuous and easy access to the child over long periods. With all their obvious faults and defects, the contributions of these biographies of children kept by parents and relatives are of inestimable value to the modern student of child development. From them one not only gets an impression of the continuous onsweep of developmental processes, but he also feels intimately acquainted with the child as a person.

72

The growth of the intelligence-testing movement and the theoretical problem of the constancy of the IQ that it has raised has resulted in the practice of making "follow-up" studies, whereby individuals tested or measured at an early age are examined again at a later age. Perhaps the largest and most completely organized follow-up work has been done by Terman and his co-authors in their *Genetic Studies of Genius*. Indeed, so comprehensive is the study and so continuous is the contact that it might be called the first of the "follow-through" studies, if we may designate as follow-through studies those in which the contact is maintained over a long period and observations are made at repeated intervals. These are in contrast to the "follow-up" studies, in which the contact may be broken and re-established once or oftener during the individual's childhood. In the field of follow-up work Gesell has retested enough children to enable him to draw up developmental curves.

The present study is, so far as the author is aware, the first of the follow-through studies of babyhood. A few months after it was begun, a similar study was initiated at the University of California, where Bayley and Wolff made repeated monthly examinations of a group of 60 babies. The Minnesota study does not include so many subjects, but the deficiency in that respect is perhaps offset by the greater frequency of the examinations and by the fact that the study was conducted in the homes instead of being confined to the laboratory.

In brief, the general procedure consisted of observations of a sizable group of babies in the hospital and in the homes from the day of birth. Examinations were made daily during the first week of the hospital period and every two days during the second week. During the remainder of the first year the babies were observed at weekly intervals in their homes and at biweekly intervals during the second year. At the age of two years two of the children became regular attendants at the Institute nursery school and entered into the regular program of observations and tests carried out by Institute workers. The remaining 17 children were visited four times a year for the collection of anthropometric data and twice for psychological data, and once a year they were brought to the Institute for a mental test. The weekly examinations of the first year were supplemented by the mothers' daily records of food intake and habits of sleep and by their summaries of elimination, developmental items, and general behavior.

By virtue of its follow-through character this study for the most part treats the order of development without respect to age. Conducting the observations in the home introduced considerable informality into the examining situation, and the systematic record that was kept of incidental reactions in addition to responses to the tests greatly increases the value of the data as an index to the ordinary course of behavior development. In view of the similarity of this approach to that of the biographical studies, it is not surprising that there are similarities in the results. The course of development, as will appear later, is so consistent from baby to baby that it may be studied more effectively by the careful, continuous observation of one baby than by a cross-section survey of many babies at widely spaced age intervals.

Similarity of the two methods may account likewise for the high consistency of this study with that of Bühler. Her method was to observe constantly for an entire day and night the activities of a small group of babies on each monthly birthday. The observations were made without artificial stimulation; the observer merely sat near the infant, watching and recording his spontaneous behavior in his usual daily environment. The present study differs from Bühler's in that simple tests were planned in the hope of tapping the baby's entire repertoire of acts in a brief half hour of examination each week. However, the examining situation soon became a usual part of the baby's routine, and the mother's presence and the familiar home environment completely robbed the examination of all strangeness. The tests themselves closely duplicated the parents' play stimulation and were appropriate for calling forth the babies' abilities and interests. Responses to the tests were recorded in descriptive terms rather than in terms of arbitrary standards of behavior, and the records of incidental behavior and the mothers' records adequately supplemented the test data. For all these reasons it is likely that this material is almost as free from the unfavorable influences of artificial stimulation as is that of Bühler. It presents the additional advantages, moreover, of being somewhat more controlled and of including a larger number of babies of each age than Bühler's. The qualitative descriptions of infant behavior obtained by the two methods are strikingly similar.

Before we attempt to say just what the present study has added to our knowledge of motor development let us consider briefly the things it has not added. Only with a clear understanding of the scope of a piece of scientific work may its contributions be evaluated and allocated among the existing body of facts.

There are four or more courses that a student of motor development in infancy might follow. He might set up age norms of development by means of a study of large numbers of babies; he might measure the degree of motor skill possessed by the individual baby; he might devote his attention to the modification of given motor items after they were established and determine the conditions that led to modification; or he might interest himself in the sequence of motor development. In this study the fourth course was followed; a few minor facts relating to the other three were gathered, but they were only incidental to the main objective.

The reason for rejecting the first three methods may be briefly stated. In the first place, age standards of development derived from so small and so selected a group of babies as entered into this study would be valueless for future comparisons. It cannot be stressed too often that the age figures given in this work apply to this group alone and are not to be used as criteria for other groups. Far better norms have already been established by Gesell, Jones, and others, and therefore there is no great need for a normative study at the present time.

A study of the degree of motor skill possessed by each baby could be conducted only if accurate ways of measuring the skill could be devised. This is not beyond the limits of possibility, but it is not an easy task. The difficulty of even estimating degrees of head control and the skill involved in sitting alone and other motor accomplishments is baffling. Although the investigator is able to judge the degree of skill in an older child by putting him through a strict set of performance tests, it is likely that he would have to limit the items in his tests of babies to the things they do spontaneously in order to insure their wholehearted cooperation. Such a study would entail the establishment of standards of degree of skill. Worthwhile as the investigation would be, it could be carried out only with the aid of better controlled experimental conditions and more refined examining techniques than were possible in this investigation.

Likewise, a study of the nature and degree of modification that motor skills undergo from their earliest manifestation to their perfection would require more time and more elaborate treatment than was possible in this study. One phase of motor development, walking, has been fairly adequately studied in this way, but techniques for similar studies of other aspects of motor development were not available, so they were not attempted.

There remains the developmental order, or motor sequence, the only aspect of motor development on which this study offers new and reasonably complete data. Before entering upon a description of the sequence and a discussion of its importance it is necessary to make clear two distinctions: first, the difference between motor activity and motor control, and, second, the difference between ability and proficiency in the performance of motor acts.

Motor Activity Versus Motor Control

In centering attention on the order of motor development the observer did not fail to take cognizance of the profuse and varied activity present in the babies at birth. It is difficult to define this activity in such a way that the differences between it and the controlled acts that developed later may be readily apparent. The early activities of kicking, waving, and squirming were not uncoordinated, nor were they altogether random and spontaneous. Perhaps the most characteristic earmark of the activity of this period was that it "didn't get the baby anywhere"; it apparently was directed toward no goal, or if it was it did not effect an adjustment to the environment. Controlled motor acts, on the other hand, were successful responses to definite stimuli, and with the development of motor control the baby began to manipulate and manage his environment to a considerable degree. The motor sequence represents only the development of motor control and not the manifestation of undirected motor activity.

Ability Versus Proficiency

The reader must also remember that there is a great difference between ability to do and excellency in the doing of motor acts. The motor sequence takes into account only the former. It represents the order in which the babies were first able to watch, to reach, to sit alone, and so forth; it is not concerned with the proficiency with which they performed each act. It goes without saying that the babies differed in proficiency at the onset of each new phase of motor development even though the degree of difference could not be measured, and that proficiency increased in individual babies at different rates and to different degrees. But the transition from the inability to reach, creep, or walk to the ability, however feeble, to perform these acts is well marked. The order of these transitions from uncontrolled generalized activity to successfully controlled motor acts comprises the motor sequence.

Sequence Not a By-Product of the Motor Tests

The reader may question whether the motor sequence is not merely a product of the motor tests. That possibility was safeguarded against in two ways; first, by the recording method, by which the observer wrote down in consistent descriptive terms exactly what the baby did in response to each motor test instead of marking them passed or failed; and, second, by including in the sequence items that were not tested for but that occurred spontaneously. The consistency with which the items of motor play fit into the sequence is a strong argument against its artificiality.

SEQUENCE OF MOTOR DEVELOPMENT

Much has been made of the point that motor development in the first two years follows a definite sequence, at least when its various phases—postural control, locomotion, and manipulation—are considered separately. It remains to be seen whether the sequence holds when these different aspects of development are thrown together into one series. Under such treatment the sequence might conceivably break down; granting that the sequence comes about by virtue of the fact that coordinations acquired through the perfection of one motor item are essential components of the item next developed, then the sequence of these items would be a logical necessity. Undoubtedly this is true in such a sequence as that of reaching, touching, grasping, and retaining; it is mechanically impossible for the baby to grasp a toy without having first reached and touched it, although it is not quite clear why the ability to do these three acts does

FIGURE 1. *The motor sequence.*

77

not appear simultaneously instead of at intervals of one or two weeks. It is a little less obvious but still well within reason that chest up succeeds chin up, rolling succeeds swimming movements, and creeping succeeds scooting backward, because coordinations acquired in preceding acts are used in the ones following. If this explanation fully accounts for the sequence within any given phase of development, such as manipulation or assumption of an upright posture, one might expect to find no sequence from one type of motor performance to another where the coordinations acquired in the first motor act seemingly play no part, or an obscure and minor one, in the second. One would not expect that head control would precede reaching in the lying posture, or that reaching, grasping, and holding would precede sitting alone, nor would the sequence of the play reactions of scratching, playing with the toes, bouncing, and rocking be an obvious inference.

When all the motor items are thrown together, however, the sequence is just as well defined as when each motor phase is considered separately. To be sure, some items of the manipulatory phase develop simultaneously with items of the locomotor and postural phases, but simultaneity of items does not impair the fundamental sequence. For the most part, the items of one phase dovetail with those of the others. The extent of simultaneity and of dovetailing in the sequence may be seen in Table I. In Figure 1 the items have been made to appear equally spaced for the sake of a more diagrammatic effect, but since the order of the items rather than the expansion or contraction of their spacing is of most interest, the equality of the spacing does not distort the facts.

Consistency of the Sequence

The table and the figure depict only the order of the medians. To show that the sequence does not break down when it is applied to the progress of an individual baby the data on individual comparisons will be given. There were 42 motor items developed between the median ages of four days and forty-seven weeks; during this period the items were naturally spaced at frequent intervals, and there were only three intervals of three weeks or more during which no new motor item was developed.

In order to obtain a measure of the extent to which individual babies adhered to the sequence, each item was paired with another having a different median, and the number of babies in which the order of the medians was reversed was obtained. With 42 items it would have been possible to compare 861 pairs of items, but items at the extremes would have been separated by an age range so great that there would have been no overlapping. Consequently a range of 6 weeks was arbitrarily chosen as the limit for comparisons. In all there were 224 pairs of items separated by a median range of 6 weeks or less; items with identical medians were not compared. The average separation of the medians of these items was 3.66

Table I

Median Ages and Parts of the Body Controlled in Various Reactions in the Motor Sequence

Median Age in Weeks	Eye Coordination	Locomotion	Fine Motor Reactions	Motor Play	Parts of Body Controlled
6 da.	Follow light				
2.0	Watch person				
3.0		Chin up			Eyes, head, and neck
5.0	Follow tape H				
9.0	Follow tape V	Chest up			
10.0	Follow tape C			Smile at person	
14.0		Adjust for lifting	Reach and touch		
15.0		Sit on lap	Grasp object	Play with hands	Arm and upper trunk
18.0			Retain object (thumb opposition)		
21.0			Grasp dangling object	Object to mouth	
25.0		Sit alone momentarily	Transfer object from hand to hand	Play with toes	
28.5		Roll		Pat toy	Hands and lower trunk
30.5		Sit alone 1 minute		Rock, shake head	
31.5		Stand with help		Suspension bridge	
38.0		Some progress on stomach		Pat-a-cake	
41.0		Scoot backward		Peeka-boo	
42.0		Stand holding to furniture	Point with index finger		
45.0		Creep			Pelvic region, legs, and fingers
45.0		Walk when led			
47.0		Pull to stand by furniture	Open simple boxes		
56.0–62.0				Put fingers in holes	
62.0		Stand alone			
66.0		Walk alone		Run, climb	

79

weeks. These 224 pairs embraced a total of 5,019 case comparisons, of which 4,294 were consistent with the order of the median. Thus the number of reversals was 725, or 14.45 per cent.

Generally speaking, the reversals were more frequent on those items that were difficult to define and for which the criteria were somewhat vague, such as tensing to be lifted, early stepping, and straightening the knees in the standing posture, and on those items that were not tested for but were noted when they spontaneously occurred, such as scratching, transferring the object from hand to hand, playing with the toes, ringing the bell, and pointing with the index finger. A partial explanation is that there is less likelihood that spontaneous items occurred in the examiners' presence during the same week the babies were first capable of performing them than that the items tested for were called forth and observed as soon as the capacity developed. Moreover, examinations were occasionally missed; if several new motor items appeared simultaneously at the next examination the observer might fail to note all of them, and thus the possibility of reversals would be increased. Considering all these possibilities for error, the wonder is not that reversals in the sequence are so many but that they are so few.

The sequence was further tested for consistency by running rank order correlations between the order of items for each baby and the order of the medians. These correlations, which are given in Table II, all lie between .93 and .98, and 60 per cent of them are .97 or above. The consistency of the correlations adds much to their significance, since it shows conclusively that the sequence is as representative of individuals as it is of the group as a whole. From baby to baby the sequence holds with far greater consistency than could be accounted for by chance.

Table II

Individual Correlations with the Motor Sequence

Baby	r	Baby	r
Winifred	.95 ± .010	Martin	.93 ± .012
Fred	.98 ± .009	Quentin	.97 ± .009
Carol	.96 ± .010	Virginia Ruth	.96 ± .010
Doris	.94 ± .010	Sibyl	.93 ± .012
David	.95 ± .010	Maurice	.95 ± .010
Donovan	.97 ± .009	Torey	.98 ± .009
Harvey	.97 ± .009	Judy	.97 ± .009
James D.	.97 ± .009	Peter	.98 ± .009
Irene May	.97 ± .009	Patricia	.97 ± .009
Larry	.97 ± .009	Walley	.97 ± .009

Harmony with Anatomical Laws

There is a well-known anatomical law of developmental direction which may be stated briefly as the law that the growth wave which sweeps over the body begins at the head and travels toward the feet.

From a study of Table I it would appear that not postural development alone but the entire motor sequence is in harmony with this fundamental law of growth. The eye muscles come under control first; a little later control of the facial muscles for smiling and of the neck muscles for head-lifting and head-turning is achieved. Gradually motor control creeps downward to the arm and upper trunk region; with the advent of sitting alone it has migrated down to the lower trunk; and when thumb opposition appears, it has advanced to the forearm and hand. Finally the leg muscles come under control, first for standing erect with help, somewhat later for locomotion in the creeping posture, and still later for walking alone.

Not only is the order of development in harmony with the law of developmental direction, but the speed of development also seems to be graduated from the head downward. Control of eyes, head, neck, upper trunk, and arms follow each other in rapid succession. About the time the ability to sit alone is achieved, however, the rate becomes noticeably slower. Whereas the attainment of a new motor item was a matter of days at the outset, it now becomes a matter of months. These differences in the rate of assuming motor control suggest that the growth gradient that makes for different rates of growth in different parts of the body is also operative, or at least has a counterpart in the development of functional control.

A second interesting feature of the sequence is that postural control of a given part always precedes controlled movements of that part. The baby holds his head erect before he turns it; he sits alone before he sways and rocks in this posture; and he stands before he climbs or walks. This is probably just a matter of body mechanics; it would be impossible to execute coordinated movements in a given posture before the posture itself could be maintained. The progress from flexion to extension in babyhood is, however, worthy of note. In the newborn baby the dominance of the flexor muscles over the extensors is so great that arms, hands, and legs can hardly be stretched out for measuring. Gradually the extensors begin to oppose this state of flexion, and the early flexed lying posture gives way to more extended postures. It is largely the extensor muscles that are involved in the maintenance of upright postures. Investigators are still pretty much in the dark as to the nervous mechanism of postural control, but whatever the mechanism, it is logical for extensor muscles to come under control for posture before they work together with the flexors to execute directed acts involving a rapid losing and regaining of postural equilibrium.

Maturation as an Explanation of the Motor Sequence

In order to prevent misunderstandings that might lead to controversy, the term "maturation" must be rigidly defined. In this study it is used to connote the sum total of the growth processes. It is not used in the more restricted sense of the development or maturing of the nervous system alone.

Maturation, defined in this way, appears to be the most satisfactory way of accounting for the motor sequence. The number of items included in the sequence and the closeness of their spacing certainly precludes the possibility of a consistent order being established by chance; the consistency of the sequence from baby to baby, not only in the motor functions tested but also in spontaneous play reactions, casts doubt upon the learning hypothesis as an explanatory principle. Finally, the harmony of the sequence with the fundamental law of anatomical growth is a strong argument for the acceptance of the maturation hypothesis.

How Maturation Functions

In accepting the maturation hypothesis it is not necessary to settle the question as to whether the motor sequence is a function of growth or whether it is merely a manifestation of growth. It may be that the relationship between body growth and motor development is one of cause and effect, or it may be that the two are merely parallels, the one being the manifestation of growth in body structure and the other the manifestation of growth in body function. But in either case maturation is at work.

The present study does not enable us to say what matures or how maturation operates in bringing about the motor sequence. No doubt the fact that motor control begins at the head and moves toward the feet is partly a matter of body mechanics; to a certain extent it is true that outlying muscles are incapable of making adequate adjustment to peripheral stimuli until the larger, proximal muscles work to bring them directly in contact with the stimuli. It is also true that motor development consists largely of the differentiation of specific movements from generalized mass activity. Neither of these possibilities, however, weakens the sequence itself nor precludes the interpretation of it by the maturation hypothesis, since neither of them is adequate to completely account for a sequence of such remarkable length and detail. The consistency of the sequence from baby to baby speaks well for its reliability, and its harmony with the accepted laws of growth attests to its validity as a maturing process.

SUMMARY

Progress in motor control follows an orderly sequence beginning at the head and traveling toward the feet. The sequence as determined from the medians of the group holds for individual babies, and it includes, in addition to items specifically tested for, items of motor play that occurred spontaneously. Hence it is unlikely that the sequence is merely the byproduct of the tests. The sequence of development strongly supports the maturation theory of motor development. It appears that maturation gives ability to do motor acts and that subsequent practice gives proficiency in doing them.

5 · Environmental Influences Upon Motor Development

WAYNE DENNIS

Reprinted from an article entitled "Causes of Retardation among Institutional Children: Iran" appearing in the *Journal of Genetic Psychology*, 96 (1960), 47-59, by permission of The Journal Press.

While it can scarcely be doubted that, as Shirley has argued, stages of maturation of the nervous system and of other bodily structures beyond the neonatal level are prerequisite for the appearance of "the motor sequence," the present study appears to show that maturation alone is not sufficient. Certain opportunities for learning motor skills also must be present. The study further shows that under some environmental conditions the motor sequence itself is changed; in this instance, scooting replacing creeping.

INTRODUCTION

Considerable interest has recently been shown in the fact that in some institutions for children there occurs a decided retardation in behavioral development. The observations of Spitz (1945, 1946a, 1946b) in particular have received much notice, chiefly because of the interpretations which Spitz has placed upon his data. In our opinion, the primary importance of these observations lies in their challenge to the theory that infant development consists largely of the maturation of a motor sequence which is little affected by learning.

Aside from the investigations of Spitz, studies of behavioral retardation among institutional children have been few in number. The scarcity of such studies is due in large part to the fact that institutions in which conditions comparable to those described by Spitz can be found are not numerous. In many countries institutional care has been replaced by other methods of caring for dependent children. However, institutions in which behavioral development is retarded can still be found in countries which are "underdeveloped" not only in regard to modern technology but also in respect to newer methods for the care of foundlings and other homeless infants.

The present paper reports studies of development in three institutions in Tehran, the capital of Iran. In two of these institutions, children are exceedingly retarded in their motor development. In the third little retardation is present. It is believed that comparisons of child care in these institutions, and of behavioral development in them, will throw considerable light upon the nature of the environmental factors which influence motor development. This paper supplements a recent report on behavioral retardation in a Lebanese institution by Dennis and Najarian (1957). In the earlier report attention was directed primarily to motor development in the first year of life, whereas in the present instance the period from one year to four years of age is the one with which we are mainly concerned. Preliminary observations indicated that development during the first year in the two Iranian institutions in which retardation occurs is essentially the same as in the Lebanese institution described in the previous paper. For this reason in the present study attention is given chiefly to the age period to which little attention was directed in the earlier report.

DESCRIPTION OF THE INSTITUTIONS

The two institutions in which marked retardation occurs, which will be called Institutions I and II, are supported chiefly by public funds; the third institution, to be labeled III, is supported by private funds. Several other children's institutions both public and private, exist in Tehran. The present report should not be taken to imply that retardation prevails in the majority of Iranian institutions.

It is worthy of note that the number of children to be found in institutions in Tehran is quite large. This number is explained by several factors. For one thing, Tehran is a large city, having approximately two million inhabitants. The recent growth of Tehran has taken place in the main through migration from villages. This has led to a considerable amount of social disorganization which has increased the number of illegitimate children, foundlings, abandoned children, orphans, and half-orphans. Furthermore in Tehran at the present time, provisions for the care of dependent children, other than by institutionalization, are quite inadequate. Consequently, almost all children not living with parents or relatives are to be found in institutions.

Institution I

Institution I feels obligated to accept all foundlings and all abandoned children under three years of age who are brought to it. The population of the institution varies from day to day because of departures and admissions. During the time of the present study (September, 1958) the average daily population was about 600; of these about 275 were between birth and one year of age, 135 were between one and two years of age, and about 110 were between two and three years of age. While children above three years are generally transferred to other institutions, a few remain in Institution I beyond this age.

The excess of younger children over older children in Institution I may be due to several causes, including an increased intake rate in recent years, a higher death rate during the first year than in later years, return of older children to relatives, and transfer of older children to other institutions. The data at our disposal do not permit an assignment of relative weights to these factors.

More than nine-tenths of the children in Institution I are recorded as having been under one month of age at the time of their admission. When the actual date of birth is not known, an estimate of age at admission, based on weight, size, and appearance is made and placed in the child's record.

The mother never accompanies the child to Institution I nor sees him after admission.

In general children are placed in individual cribs, although at times, because of overcrowding, two infants temporarily occupy the same crib. In such instances, the heads of the two babies are placed at opposite ends of the bed.

A child is bathed on alternate days. Except when being bathed, the younger children spend practically their entire time in their cribs. They are given milk and other liquids while lying in bed, the bottle being supported by a small pillow. When semi-solid foods are introduced, infants are sometimes held by an attendant and sometimes fed in bed. The children are placed in bed in the supine position. They are never placed prone and seldom get themselves into this position.

The paucity of handling is due primarily to the attendant-child ratio. On the average there were eight children per attendant. In addition to feeding the children, bathing them, and changing clothing and diapers, the attendants are also responsible for changing the bed-linen and cleaning the rooms, and have some responsibilities for preparing food. Each attendant is on duty 12 hours per day. In general there are 32 children and four attendants to a room, although this varies somewhat according to the size of the room. There is no assignment of attendants to particular children. The attendants have no special training for their work and are poorly paid. The emphasis on the part of the supervisors seems to be on neatness in the appearance of the rooms, with little attention to behavioral development.

In his crib the child is not propped up, and is given no toys. The child who can pull himself to sitting, and hence is in some danger of falling from his shallow crib, is placed, when awake, on a piece of linoleum on the composition stone floor of the room. Until he himself achieves the sitting position he remains in bed. In two rooms some of the children who can sit are seated in a row on a bench which has a bar across the front to prevent falling. Aside from these two benches and the frames for the cribs, the rooms have no children's furniture and no play equipment of any kind.

Institution II

This institution accepts children over three years of age. The children in this institution come mainly from Institution I. Child care practices in II are a continuation of the practices existing in I, but sanitation and cleanliness are poorer and the appearance of the children suggests that nutrition and health are poorer. However, in neither I nor II are there any records of growth in height or weight, and it was not possible for us to obtain any objective assessment of nutritional status.

Institution III

Institution III was established only one year prior to the present study. It was started primarily to demonstrate improved methods of institutional care. The children in III come from Institution I but are selected for transfer in the early months of life. It seems likely that those sent to Institution III are chosen from among the more retarded children. They remain in III until three years of age unless adopted before that date. The number of children per attendant is 3-4. Children are held in arms while being fed, are regularly placed prone during part of the time they are in their cribs, are propped up in a sitting position in their cribs at times, and are placed in play pens on the floor daily when above four months of age. Numerous toys are provided. Attendants are coached in methods of child care, and supervisors emphasize behavioral development as well as nutrition and health.

Individual growth charts are available for each child in Institution III and show without exception that these children are much below prevailing weight norms on arrival but attain normal weight within a few months.

TYPES OF BEHAVIORAL DATA

Quantitative observations on the behavioral status of the groups described above were made only with regard to motor coordinations. Some general observations on social and emotional behavior will be presented after motor behavior has been discussed.

In respect to motor development, each child who was a subject of this study was classified with regard to his ability to meet each of the following behavioral criteria:

1. *Sit alone.* The child was placed in a sitting position on the floor. He was scored as sitting alone if he maintained this position for one minute. However, if a child could maintain this position at all he ordinarily could maintain it indefinitely.

2. *Creep or Scoot.* The child was placed sitting on the floor and was encouraged to locomote by having the attendant hold a cookie, or extend her arms, toward the child at a distance of about six feet. He was scored

as passing the test if he covered the distance in any manner. If he loco-moted, his mode of progression was recorded. The modes of locomotion will be discussed at a later point.

3. *Stand by holding.* The child was held under the arms and placed adjacent to the horizontal bars of a child's bed. It was observed whether or not he grasped the bars and maintained a standing position.

4. *Walk by holding.* The child who could stand by holding was observed for some minutes to determine whether he took steps while holding. He was urged to walk by the attendant.

5. *Walk alone.* The child who could walk by holding objects was placed standing without support and was encouraged to walk to the outstretched arms of the attendant. The child was scored as walking alone if he took at least two steps without support.

In the above tests one of the attendants with whom the child was familiar was coached to make the tests while the experimenter remained at a distance of six feet or more from the child and somewhat behind him. This procedure was followed because it was found that the child's unfamiliarity with the experimenter often inhibited the child's behavior if he was tested by the examiner himself. Communication between the attendant and the examiner was conducted via an Iranian interpreter. Tests were conducted among the children of a given room only after the experimenter and the interpreter had made several visits to the room and some-what decreased the children's shyness. If a child failed a test, the attend-ant was asked whether or not he could usually perform the required re-sponse. If the answer was positive, renewed efforts were made to elicit a successful performance. The experimenter is convinced that subjects who were scored as failing a test were actually unable to perform the required task.

The numbers of children tested at each age level in each institution are shown in Table I. In Institutions I and II the total number of children tested was 123. In selecting children to provide this sample, the children of appropriate ages were selected at random from each of several rooms,

Table I

Per Cent of Each Group Passing Each Test

Institutions	I	I	II	III	III
N	50	40	33	20	31
Age in years	1.0-1.99	2.0-2.99	3.0-3.99	1.0-1.99	2.0-2.99
Sit alone	42	95	97	90	100
Creep or Scoot	14	75	97	75	100
Stand holding	4	45	90	70	100
Walk holding	2	40	63	60	100
Walk alone	0	8	15	15	94

the rooms so far as we could determine not being unusual in any respect. However, we excluded from testing any child who had sensory or motor defects, who was ill, or who had recently been ill. In Institution III all children between age one and three were tested. They totaled 51.

RESULTS OF TESTS

Table I shows the per cent of each group which passed each test. The reader is asked to direct his attention first to the retardation which is evident in Institutions I and II. Among those children in Institution I who were between 1.0-1.9 years of age, fewer than half could sit alone and none could walk alone. In normative studies, of home-reared children, such as those conducted by Jones (1926), Gesell (1928), Dennis and Dennis (1937) and others, it has been found that by nine months of age all normal noninstitutional American children can sit alone. By two years of age nearly all can walk alone. A majority of the children of Institution I cannot perform these responses at ages at which almost all home-reared children can perform them. It will be noted that even between 2.0-2.9 years of age only 8 per cent of the children in Institution I are able to walk alone and only 15 per cent of those children in Institution II who are 3.0-3.9 years of age are able to walk alone. We are not aware that any groups so retarded as Groups I and II have previously been reported.

In Institution III the picture is different. Of those children between 2.0-2.9 years of age nearly every child is able to walk unaided. While these children do not equal the performance of home-reared children, their motor behavior is much superior to that of children in Institutions I and II. In other words it is not institutionalization per se which handicaps Groups I and II since Group III children who are also institutionalized are but slightly retarded in motor development. The records of Group III also show that motor retardation is not a general characteristic of Tehran children.

Of special note is the difference in types of pre-walking locomotion between Institutions I and II on the one hand and Institution III on the other.

Of the 67 children in Institutions I and II who engaged in creeping or scooting, only 10 did so by creeping, i.e., going on hands and knees or on hands and feet. All others progressed by "scooting," i.e., their locomotion took place in the sitting position, the body being propelled forward by pushing with the arms aided by propulsion from the legs. Many children who could not walk were quite adept at scooting.

Since tests for creeping or scooting were made when the child was in a sitting position, it might seem that the frequency of scooting was due to the nature of the starting position. To test the effect of starting position, many subjects who were "scooters" were placed prone and offered a cookie at some distance, a powerful incentive for locomotion in these children. In each case the child first pushed himself to a sitting position and then scooted. Scooting was definitely the preferred mode of locomotion even when the child was placed prone. So far as we could determine, the majority of the scooters were completely unfamiliar with creeping.

In Institution III, the reverse situation prevailed. Of 15 children who were observed to creep or scoot, all progressed by creeping. No scooting whatsoever was seen in this institution, yet tests were made from the sitting position as with Groups I and II. When placed sitting and encouraged to locomote, the children leaned forward, got themselves on hands and knees, and crept.

INTERPRETATIVE COMMENTS ON MOTOR DEVELOPMENT

Let us examine now the probable reasons why the children in Institutions I and II were so severely retarded relative to home-reared children and why they were so much more retarded than children in Institution III. Several different possibilities need to be considered.

Attention should first be directed to malnutrition as a possible cause of retarded motor development. As noted earlier there can be no doubt that many of the children in Group I were much smaller and lighter than non-institutional children and children of the same age in Group III. There can be no doubt, too, that malnutrition can be so severe as to interfere with motor performance and motor progress. But the question at stake is not whether malnutrition can affect motor functions but whether malnutrition was in fact a major cause of the retardation of Groups I and II.

We are inclined to think that undernourishment was not the major factor. The following considerations have led us to this interpretation: In the first place, Groups I and II were not entirely listless and inactive. In this connection we need to bring out a fact that we have not noted in earlier sections, namely that these children engaged to a considerable extent in automatisms such as head shaking and rocking back and forth. In many cases, these actions were quite vigorous. These activities tend to indicate that these children were not slow in motor development simply because of motor weakness.

The second consideration is somewhat similar to the first, namely, that the locomotor activities in which the children in Groups I and II engaged seem to require as much as or more energy than the locomotor activities which are usual at their respective ages, but in which they did not engage. For example, while few two-year-olds in Group I walked, three-fourths of them locomoted, chiefly by scooting. No physiological data are available, but it seems likely that the metabolic cost of covering a certain distance by scooting is as great as, or even greater than, the effort required to go the same distance by walking. Certainly this would be true for an adult, but of course one cannot argue from the adult to the child. At any rate the possibility exists that the reason that these children scooted was because this was the only form of locomotor skill which they had learned, not that they were too weak to walk.

This interpretation seems to be borne out by the fact that the pre-walking methods of locomotion were different in different groups. The retarded groups scooted. It is difficult to believe that malnutrition can lead to scooting rather than creeping. It is far from obvious that scooting is "easier" than creeping. If it is, why should not all children choose the easier method? In other words, the differences between groups seem to us to be due to the outcome of different learning situations rather than to differences in nutritional status.

What were the differences in the situations faced by Groups I and II and Group III which may account for the development of two different types of locomotion and different degrees of retardation? We suggest the following:

In Group III and in many homes infants are propped up in a sitting position, or held in a sitting position. In this position the child can raise his head and can partially raise his shoulders for short periods and can relax these efforts without falling. He can thus practice some elements of sitting. On the other hand, the child who remains on his back has no such opportunities to learn to sit. In some respects it is surprising that children who are never propped up or held on the lap are able to learn to sit at all. But it will be remembered that in Groups I and II some children could not sit until they were more than two years of age. Until they could sit alone, all forms of locomotion were impossible for them, because they were not placed in a position in which creeping was possible.

This is not true in Group III. In this group and in many homes, the child is frequently placed prone in bed or on the floor. In this position he can raise his head from the surface, push with his arms, raise his chest, pull his arms and legs beneath his body—in other words, he can practice acts which are employed in creeping. The child who lies on his back nearly every moment of the day is denied such practice. Thus one specific item of child care, i.e., occasionally placing the child face downward, may well contribute to the development of creeping in most children and its absence may account for the lack of creeping in Groups I and II.

The question may be raised as to why children in Institutions I and II did not get themselves into the prone position in their cribs. Repeated observations of these infants in their cribs showed that few ever attained the prone position. The probable reasons are the small size of the cribs and the softness of the beds, both of which made turning over very difficult.

It is likely that this item, i.e., absence of placement in the prone position, may lead to delayed development not only in regard to creeping but also in respect to walking. The child who can creep can go to a piece of furniture, grasp it, and pull to his knees. This may lead to walking on his knees while holding furniture. Many children go from knee walking to walking by holding to furniture and thence to walking alone. In contrast to the child who creeps, the child who scoots to a piece of furniture is sitting when he arrives at his goal and can attain a higher position only by lifting his entire weight by his arms. In our opinion, the lack of creeping accounts in large measure for the retardation in walking of Groups I and II.

We are well-aware that some persons have interpreted the behavioral retardation of institutional infants to emotional factors rather than to a paucity of learning opportunities. Some have even suggested that under certain conditions institutional infants simply "waste away" from psychological, not from medical causes, a process called marasmus.

If marasmus actually exists, it has somehow been escaped by several hundred children in Iranian institutions living under conditions which are supposed to foster it. Although the prevailing emotional tone of children in Institutions I and II is dysphoric, it is difficult to conceive of mechanisms whereby their unhappiness retards their motor development and causes them to scoot rather than to creep.

There remains the necessity of relating the results of the present study to certain findings reported earlier by the present author. We refer to a study which found no apparent effect of cradling upon the motor development of Hopi children (Dennis, 1940) and a study which indicated that infant development can proceed normally under conditions described as "minimal social stimulation" (Dennis, 1941). On the surface these results seem contradictory to those here reported, because the former studies found that environmental deprivations had but little effect whereas the present study reports that major consequences can ensue from them. In fact, however, the studies are not contradictory but complementary. To bring the results of these studies into harmony, one needs only to examine the kinds of deprivation which were involved and their severity. Certain differences among these studies seem to us to be crucial. The Hopi children were limited in regard to learning opportunities only *while on the cradleboard.* As we pointed out in our original report, they were on the cradleboard chiefly during these sleeping hours, when in any case little learning is expected to occur. When awake they were handled, held upright against the mother, placed sitting on her lap, and placed prone. Their deprivation of learning opportunities was much less than that encountered by the children in Institution I who 24 hours per day for many months remained in a supine position.

A similar contrast exists between Rey and Del, the subjects of an experiment in environmental deprivation, and children in Institutions I and II.

Rey and Del were not deprived to the same degree nor in the same manner as the institutional children described above. As the original report shows (Dennis, 1941), Del and Rey, beginning at nine months, were regularly placed in a prone position on a pad on the floor. After it was found that they could not sit alone they were given special practice in sitting. Del and Rey were also given special training in supporting their weight when held upright. Such training was not given in Institutions I and II.

These experiences with special training given to Del and Rey suggest that the retardation of the institutional children could be fairly rapidly remedied if intensive specialized practice were given them. Unfortunately it was not possible for us to undertake such experiments while we were in Tehran. The speed with which delayed skills can be developed remains an important problem for future researches with institutional children.

So far as the permanency of motor deficiencies is concerned it should be noted that Institution II had many children between ages 6 and 15 years who presumably were as retarded at ages two and three as were the children whose behavior was described above. Yet these children were attending school, playing games, doing chores, and being trained in difficult skills, such as the weaving of Persian rugs. There was nothing in their general behavior to suggest that any permanent consequences issued from the extreme retardation in motor development during the early years. To be sure, we have no direct evidence that these children were retarded at two and three years of age, but so far as we could ascertain there has been no change in the child care offered by Institutions I and II and no reason to suppose that their early development was different from that of their counterparts in the present study.

Finally let us note that the results of the present study challenge the widely held view that motor development consists in the emergence of a behavioral sequence based primarily upon maturation. Shirley's chart of the motor sequence is a textbook favorite. It show. s. 'ting alone at seven months, creeping at 10 months, and walking alone at 15 months. The present study shows that these norms are met only under favorable environmental conditions. Among the children of Institution I not only was sitting alone greatly retarded but in many cases creeping did not occur. Instead, an alternate form of locomotion was employed. These facts seem to indicate clearly that experience affects not only the ages at which motor items appear but also their very form. No doubt the maturation of certain structures, which as yet cannot be identified, is necessary before certain responses can be learned, but learning also is necessary. Maturation alone is insufficient to bring about most postnatal developments in behavior. This is also the conclusion which we reached in the Del-Rey experiment, but the present study supports this position more dramatically because the limitations of learning in Institutions I and II are more drastic and more long-continued than were those in the Del-Rey study.

SOCIAL AND EMOTIONAL BEHAVIOR

Only incidental observations were made relative to social and emotional behavior. Several of these had to do with the infants' reactions to visitors.

In the weeks preceding our tests, it appears that Institution I seldom had visitors. The children of Institution II formerly had few visitors but several weeks before our arrival a volunteer social service group, aware of the isolation of these children, began to make periodic visits to them, taking them from their beds, holding them, and carrying them about. Institution III also had several visitors, partly because of the demonstration nature of this orphanage.

Children in Institution I, probably because of their unfamiliarity with visitors, were somewhat afraid of us during our first visit. They did not smile with us and, in most cases, would cry if we picked them up. On repeated visits, however, they became more friendly, smiled at us, and before our work was completed some of them would hold out their arms to be carried.

Most of the children in Institution II were positive to visitors at the beginning of our work. Several employed attention-seeking devices before visitors and cried if other children were selected for attention. In contrast in Group III, probably because of the greater time spent with attendants and because of their familiarity with visitors, there was little fear of strangers and only limited attention seeking.

Eagerness for food appeared to be greatest in Institution II. In this institution there was much crying before meal time. Children of this group handled cups and spoons quite well. In general there was very little wasting of food on the part of these children. Cups of milk were reached for eagerly, handled carefully, and drunk rapidly. There were attempts, sometimes successful, on the part of those who had finished eating to obtain the food of others, and hitting, pinching, and biting were sometimes the outcomes of such clashes. Children who could not walk could nevertheless manage to attack others and to defend themselves with considerable skill. After feeding they became much more jovial and nearly every child could be made to smile or laugh by an adult who shook him lightly or tickled him.

SUMMARY

This paper has presented data concerning behavioral development among 174 children, aged one year to four years, in three Iranian institutions. In Institutions I and II infant development was greatly retarded. The behavioral progress of children in the third institution was much less retarded. The interpretations offered for these differences in behavior among the children of different institutions are as follows: the extreme retardation in Institutions I and II was probably due to the paucity of handling, including the failure of attendants to place the children in the sitting position and the prone position. The absence of experience in these positions is believed to have retarded the children in regard to sitting alone and also in regard to the onset of locomotion. The lack of experience in the prone positions seems in most cases to have prevented children from learning to creep; instead of creeping, the majority of the children in Institutions I and II, prior to walking, locomoted by scooting. In Institution III, in which children were frequently handled, propped in the sitting position, and placed prone, motor development resembled that of most home-reared children. The retardation of subjects in Institutions I and II is believed to be due to the restriction of specific kinds of learning opportunities. This interpretation was found to be congruent with the results of other studies in environmental deprivation. In the light of these findings, the explanation of retardation as being due primarily to emotional factors is believed to be untenable. The data here reported also show that behavioral development cannot be fully accounted for in terms of the maturation hypothesis. The important contributions of experience to the development of infant behavior must be acknowledged.

References

Dennis, W., "Infant Development Under Conditions of Restricted Practice and of Minimum Social Stimulation," *Genetic Psychology Monographs*, 23 (1941), 143-189.

———, and M. G. Dennis, "Behavioral Development in the First Year as Shown by Forty Biographies," *Psychological Record*, 1 (1937), 349-361.

———, "The Effect of Cradling Practices upon the Onset of Walking in Hopi Children," *Journal of Genetic Psychology*, 56 (1940), 77-86.

———, and P. Najarian, "Infant Development Under Environmental Handicap," *Psychological Monographs*, 71 (1957), 1-13.

Gesell, A., *Infancy and Human Growth*. New York: The Macmillan Company, 1928.

Jones, M. C., "The Development of Early Behavior Patterns in Young Children," *Pedagogical Seminary*, 33 (1926), 537-585.

Shirley, M. M., "The First Two Years: Vol. I. Postural and Locomotor Development," *Institute of Child Welfare Monograph Series*, No. 6. Minneapolis: University of Minnesota Press, 1933.

Spitz, R. A., "Hospitalism, an Inquiry into the Genesis of Psychiatric Conditions in Early Childhood," *Psychoanalytical Studies of the Child*, 1 (1945), 53-74.

———, "Hospitalism: A Follow-Up Report," *Psychoanalytical Studies of the Child*, 2 (1946a), 113-117.

———, "Anaclitic Depression," *Psychoanalytical Studies of the Child*, 2 (1946b), 313-342.

III—EMOTIONAL DEVELOPMENT

1 • The Interpretation of Emotional Responses

MANDEL SHERMAN

Abridged from an article entitled "The Differentiation of Emotional Responses," *Journal of Comparative Psychology*, 7 (1927), 265-284, by permission of the author.

This study shows how difficult it is for observers to know what is causing them to perceive as they do. Sherman's observers thought they were observing the infants' emotions, but the research results indicate that they were judging the responses primarily in terms of the stimuli. It seems likely that at the neonatal level all strong stimuli produce essentially the same response.

This paper deals with one phase of the work on the differentiation of emotional responses in infants and is concerned with the ability of various observers to name and differentiate the reactions of infants below twelve days of age to stimuli which presumably elicit distinctive emotional responses.

The specific problems were whether the observers could agree as to the emotional characteristics of these responses, whether the judgments were based upon observable differences in the infants' responses or upon the knowledge of the stimuli employed, and whether the previous training and experience of the observers were factors in the judgments made.

PROCEDURE

Four types of stimuli were employed: hunger, dropping suddenly, restraint of the head and face, and sticking with a needle. For the hunger response the infants were observed about 15 minutes past the proper feeding time (the infants had not been fed). For the second type of response the infants were dropped suddenly for a distance of from two to three feet toward the table. For restraint, the head and face were held down on the table with fairly firm pressure. For the fourth reaction the infants were given six successive stimuli on the cheek with a needle. The various stimuli were given at different times of the day so as to obviate any possible "running over" of the stimuli or of the reactions.

The judgments of the various observers were obtained under the following conditions. (1) A group of observers were presented with motion picture views of the stimulating circumstances and the ensuing responses, and the observers were asked to write down the name of the emotions.

95

In the case of the hunger reaction the observers were informed of the nature of the stimulating circumstances. (2) With a second group of subjects the stimulating conditions were deleted from the pictures, and the observers were asked to name the emotion when only the responses were observed. They were also asked to give a judgment as to the nature of the stimuli used to bring out the various reactions. (3) With a third group of observers the stimuli and responses were transposed in the film, and the subjects were required to name the emotional character of each response when it was presented with a stimulus different from that which aroused it. (4) The infants were stimulated behind a screen, which was immediately removed, and the subjects were required to name the emotion on the basis of direct observation of the infants' responses. This method of presentation gave a number of additional sensory data, such as flushing of the face, and the character of the cry.

For the motion picture views the infants were photographed in a light room, the light being just strong enough for the photography but not of sufficient strength to cause any perceptible reaction in the infants. The infants were undressed except for the abdominal bandage and were placed upon a well-padded table. For the hunger response the infants were photographed 15 minutes past the proper feeding period, and no attempt was made to elicit any other type of response within five hours. The method of presentation of the film was as follows. The film contained about 15 feet of views of the infant in its normal resting state, followed by the stimulating condition, the reaction of the infant, and an interval of opaque leader during which the observers gave their judgments in writing. The rest of the film then followed in the same order. In the experiments with the observers who were not shown the stimuli the parts of the film showing the stimulating circumstances were replaced by opaque leader film. Since the hunger stimulus could not be shown on the film, about 15 feet of opaque leader was used, the experimenter explaining that it denoted the missing of a meal.

The observers of the motion picture views were given small slips of paper on which were typed the numbers 1 to 4 under each of which were written the words Emotion and Stimulus. After each reaction of the infant was shown the room was lighted and the observers asked to write the name of the emotion and the probable stimulus for each reaction when the stimulating conditions were not shown. After all of the film was shown the observers were asked to write on a separate sheet of paper the reasons for their differentiation between the various reactions of the infants.

SUBJECTS

The infants employed were normal and full-term, and only those whose nursing charts showed them to be progressing normally were used. For the motion picture photography two infants were used, R., age seventy-four hours, and M., one hundred and forty-five hours of age. For the actual presentation in the nursery the infants were picked at random, and only one type of stimulus was given each infant when shown to a group of observers. The hunger reaction was not attempted when the infants were shown to the observers, because of the conditions in the nursery and the confusion which the inclusion of this reaction would create.

RESULTS

1. The judgments of a group of graduate students in psychology to the motion picture views when the stimuli were not shown are given in Table I. The list of judgments are tabulated in the first vertical column, and the numerical data indicate the number of each of these judgments that were given for each of the stimulating conditions. For example, the judgment of anger was most frequently given; 11 times to the hunger reaction, 14 times to the reaction following dropping, 13 times to restraint, and 8 times to the response to sticking with a needle.

It is seen, then, that although a fairly large percentage of the students named anger to the reaction following restraint, a greater number named anger to the reaction following "dropping," and an almost equal number gave the same name to the reaction following the missing of a meal. A similar dispersion is seen in naming the emotion in the other reactions; 9 observers named fear to the reaction following sticking with a needle, 7 to that following the delay in feeding, and only 5 students named fear to the reaction following "dropping." To the reaction following restraint 8 different "emotions" were named, 7 were named to the reaction following the delay in feeding, to sticking with a needle 8 "emotions" were named, and 8 "emotions" to that following restraint.

It is seen that the graduate students in psychology showed no agreement in naming the emotions shown by the infants' reactions when the stimuli for those reactions were not included in the motion picture presentation. Out of a total of 119 answers anger was the most frequent named, 46 judgments of "anger" being made. No definite relationship is noted between the answers given by the students and those which are generally expected of observers who are shown the reactions of infants to such stimuli as were employed in this experiment. The judgments of hunger, anger, fear, and pain included 101 of the total of 119 answers. Although this may at first indicate that the judgments made corresponded with the answers generally expected two factors must be considered in explaining the frequency of these answers. First, as was pointed out above, there was no correspondence between the emotion named and the answer expected, the emotions named being dispersed widely. Second, in the vocabulary of the average student the names of hunger, anger, fear, and pain stand out prominently, and it may be that the frequency of these answers is due to this factor of vocabulary.

Table I

Judgments of Graduate Students in Psychology to Motion Pictures of the Reactions of Infants When the Stimuli Were Not Shown

Judgments	Stimuli Calling Out the Reactions				Total
	"Hunger"	Dropping	Restraint	Sticking with needle	
	Number of students naming the emotion				
Hunger	7	6	2	2	17
Anger	11	14	13	8	46
Fear	7	5	5	9	26
Pain	3	3	4	2	12
Grief	1	1		1	3
Hurt				1	1
Rage	2	1	3	1	7
Discomfort		1			1
Sleepy			1		1
None				1	1
Consternation	1	1			2
Nausea		1			1
Physical discomfort ..			1		1
Total*	32	32	30	25	119

* The totals are not the same because not all observers made judgments to every reaction shown.

2. In order to study the influence of more sense data than can be shown in the motion picture views, a group of third-year medical students were shown the reactions of the infants in the nursery. In this way the observers noted in addition the crying, the rush of blood, and so on, which were not as clearly evident in the motion pictures.

Several infants were picked at random, all of ages between one hundred and twelve and one hundred and sixty hours. The same stimuli and method of experimentation were used as in the photography experiments. About 50 medical students who were finishing their third year in the medical school were the observers. During the course of instruction in neuropsychiatry in the clinic the various emotions were discussed especially with emphasis upon their differentiation according to psychological criteria. The students were not told beforehand, however, that they were to be required to observe the emotional responses of infants.

The method of showing the reactions of the infants to this group of students was as follows. The students were taken in small groups to the nursery and grouped behind a screen which hid the experimenter and the infant. Immediately after the stimulus was given the screen was pulled aside and the students observed the reaction until the infant was quiet again. The screen was then replaced and another infant stimulated for another type of response and the students again observed the reaction.

They wrote the name of the emotion and the probable cause for the reaction during the periods between the various reactions.

Table II lists the responses of the medical students to the various reactions of the infants. It should be noted that only three types of stimuli were given since the method of experimentation when the observers actually saw the infants made it impossible to show the hunger reaction to the students in the nursery.

It is seen that eight different "emotions" were named to the three reactions shown the students. The most frequently named was "colic," then in order of frequency "anger," "fear," "organic brain emotion," "awakened from sleep," "hunger," and so on. To the reaction following dropping of the infant there were 11 judgments of "awakened from sleep," 11 of "colic," 7 of "anger," and 6 of "hunger." A similar variety of answers was given to the reactions of the infant following restraint and sticking with a needle. The greatest confusion was evident in the students' attempt to differentiate the reaction following dropping from that following restraint.

No agreement is noted in the judgments of the medical students. The answers to the three reactions of the infants show a wide dispersion, and show no definite relation to names of the emotions generally expected as a result of the stimuli given. The medical students who were shown the infants in the nursery and who had all the data possible did "no better" than the graduate students in psychology who were shown the motion pictures.

Table II

Judgments of the Medical Students to Actual Observation When the Stimuli Were Not Shown

Emotion Named	Stimuli Calling Out the Reactions			
	Dropping	Restraint	Sticking with Needle	Total
	Number of students making the response			
Hunger	6	3	3	12
Pain	3	1	6	10
Fear	2	11		13
Anger	7	3	6	16
Colic	11	6	4	21
Awakened from sleep	11			11
Bandage tight	1	3	2	6
Organic brain emotion ...	1	7	3	11
Total*	42	34	24	100

* The totals are not the same because not all observers made judgments to every reaction shown.

The comparison of Tables I and II shows an interesting difference in the types of responses given by graduate students in psychology and by medical students and this fact indicates that many of the answers were due to differences in the interests and attitudes of the two groups of students. It may be repeated that both groups presumably knew of the work of previous investigators of the emotional development of infants, although the graduate students in psychology were more familiar with the subject matter of psychology. The graduate students in psychology named 13 "emotions" while the medical students named 9. The graduate students named anger, fear, and hunger most often while the medical students named colic, anger, fear, and awakened from sleep most frequently. The difference between the two groups in naming the emotion and in stating the probable cause of the reactions indicates that the particular interests of the individuals were often the deciding factor in their decisions.

3. Because of the lack of agreement of the graduate students in psychology and of the medical students in naming the emotions when the reactions of the infants were shown without presenting the stimuli, a group of graduate students were shown the motion pictures of the reactions together with the stimuli calling out those reactions. This group consisted of graduate students and instructors in psychology. The general observers were told beforehand about the nature of the stimulus to each of the reactions which were to be shown. Each part of the film was shown in the same manner and order that it was shown to the previous group of graduate students except that the stimuli were included in this demonstration. For the stimulus to the first reaction the opaque leader film was explained as denoting a period of 15 minutes past the proper feeding period, the infant not having been fed. This group was also requested to observe carefully the various manifestations of the infants' reactions, such as the arm, leg, and body movements, facial expression, duration and character of the cry, and so on. When the film was finished they were asked to write the reasons for their naming and differentiating the emotional responses.

Table III shows the responses of this group of observers. Twenty-four different names were given, the greatest number being anger, fear, pain, hunger, and discomfort in the order of frequency. To the "hunger" reaction 13 different "emotions" were named, the most frequent being anger. To the reaction following dropping of the infant 10 different "emotions" were named, the most frequent being fear, and to the reaction following restraint 13 names were given, the most frequent being anger. Of the 40 observers 27 answered "fear" to the dropping, 24 named "anger" to the restraint reaction, 13 answered "pain" to the sticking with a needle, and 7 named "hunger" to the reaction of the infant when it missed a meal.

The analysis given by this group of students for naming the emotions and differentiating between the various reactions of the infants is of significance in accounting for the answers. Eighteen of the observers stated that they named the various emotions as they did because they were either directly influenced by seeing the stimuli being given or because they were influenced by previous work in which it was found that certain stimuli give rise to certain definite emotional responses. Five students stated "I named anger, fear, and so on because I knew that those emotions would result from the stimuli given." Three observers stated "I named the emotions because I would feel the same if those stimuli were given to me." Several stated "the child looked angry," and several that the child appeared afraid.

Table III

Judgments of Graduate Students in Psychology to Moving Picture Views of the Infants When the Stimuli Were Shown

Answers	Stimuli Calling Out the Reactions				Total
	Delay in Feeding	Dropping	Restraint	Sticking with Needle	
	Number of students naming the emotion				
Fear		27	4	7	38
Mad		1			1
Discontented	2		1		3
Rage			1		1
Pain	2	2	1	13	18
Negative emotion	1	1	1	1	4
Hunger	7				7
Anger	14	4	24	13	55
Discomfort	6				6
Irritation	1		1		2
Excitement		1			1
Anger or pain	1		1	3	5
Disgusted or weary ...	1				1
Pain with fear		1			1
Anger with fear		4	1	1	6
Rage	1	1	3		5
Surprise		1			1
Resistance to restraint			1		1
Anxiety				1	1
Hate	1				1
Restiveness	1				1
Repulsion				1	1
Suffocating			1		1
No emotion	2				2
Emotion doubtful		1	1	1	3
Total*	40	43	42	41	166

* The totals are not the same because not all observers made judgments to every reaction shown.

Comparison of Tables I and III indicates the possible influences of a knowledge of the stimuli in the ability of the students to differentiate the emotional responses of the infants, since both groups of students are comparable in regard to psychological knowledge, interests, attitudes, and the like. It is seen that of the students who did not see the stimuli 15 per cent of those who responded to the reaction of the infant after dropping named "fear," while in the group who saw the stimuli 64 per cent of the students who made a decision as to the same reaction named "fear." To the reaction following restraint about 45 per cent of the first group named "anger" while 60 per cent of the second group gave a judgment "anger" to the reaction.

4. The previous experiments had indicated that when the observers knew the stimulus causing the reactions of the infants they showed much more agreement in their differentiation of the emotional responses than the groups of observers who were not shown the stimuli. For that reason it was decided to show the motion pictures to two groups of medical students allowing them to see the stimuli, but with the stimuli transposed.

Table IV

Responses of Medical Students to Motion Picture Views When the Stimuli Were Shown but Transposed

Answers	Stimuli Calling Out the Reaction				Total
	"Hunger"	Dropping	Restraint	Sticking with Needle	
	Stimuli Shown to Students				
	Sticking with pin	Restraint	Dropping	"Hunger"	
Fear		4	10		14
Pain	15	3			18
Anger	6	13	7		26
Discomfort		2		3	5
Hunger				17	17
Pain or anger		2	1		3
Intestinal colic				1	1
Terror	2		4		6
Gastric pain				2	2
Pain or fear	1	1	2		4
Irritation	1	3			4
Grief		1			1
Surprise			1		1
Resistance		1			1
Total*	25	30	25	23	103

* The totals are not the same because not all observers made judgments to every reaction shown.

The procedure in showing the film was essentially similar to that used with the graduate students in psychology, that is, the film was shown in separate sections, an interval of about one minute being allowed for the observers to write the name of the emotion. The difference in the film was as follows: The order of stimuli was the reverse of that of the original experiments, that is, the pain stimulus was shown preceding the hunger reaction, the restraint stimulus preceded the "fear" reaction, dropping the infant preceded the "anger" reaction, and the leader portion of the film preceded the "pain" reaction. The students were instructed to note carefully the activity of the infants, such as movements of the arms, legs, and body, movements of the head, duration and apparent intensity of the crying, manner of breathing, and so on, and to give their true opinion of the emotion manifested by the infant upon the basis of objective signs.

Table IV shows a relationship between the stimulus shown and the emotions named. For example, 15 out of 25 students, or 60 per cent, named "pain" to the first reaction which was preceded by the stimulus of sticking with a needle. Thirteen out of 29 students named "anger" to the second reaction, restraint being the stimulus shown. Forty per cent named "fear" to the third reaction, an "anger" reaction preceded by the stimulus of dropping. Seventeen out of 23, or about 74 per cent named "hunger" to the reaction which was presumably pain, the stimulus shown being the leader film denoting a missed meal.

It is seen that the most frequent name of the emotion given by both groups of students was governed not by the actual reaction of the infant but by the stimulus shown preceding that reaction.

SUMMARY

In differentiating and naming the reactions of infants below twelve days of age to stimuli presumably eliciting a particular and definite emotional response, a considerable lack of agreement was apparent in undergraduate and graduate students in psychology and medical students, not only when shown motion picture views of the infants, but also upon actual observation of the infants in the nursery. For the four possible types of reactions shown, namely, hunger, fear, anger, and pain, students in psychology named from 12 to 25 different emotions, when shown motion pictures. When medical students were shown three possible types of reactions in the nursery, namely, fear, anger, and pain, medical students named eight different emotions. The graduate students in psychology had no better success in naming the emotions than the medical students. The difference in the number of emotions named by students in psychology and medical students may possibly be due to the difference in the vocabulary of the two groups. Apparently a knowledge of psychology and of the previous work on the emotions of infants did not aid the graduate students in differentiating between the various emotional reactions. The emotions named by students of psychology differed from those named by the medical students to some extent. This fact is significant in indicating that the emotion designated for a certain reaction depends to some extent upon the interests and attitudes of the observers.

When the stimuli causing the reactions of the infants were shown to the observers the degree of "success" in naming and differentiating between the various emotions was much greater than when the stimuli were not shown. This fact indicates that the knowledge of the stimuli used was an important factor in the observers' decisions.

The reasons given by the two groups of observers for their differentiation between the various emotional reactions indicated that for the most part the differentiation was strongly influenced by the knowledge of the stimulus. This was shown by the fact that the majority of graduate students who were successful in making the differentiation stated that the knowledge of the stimulus influenced them in their decisions or that they knew that no other emotional response would result from a certain stimulus.

The dependence upon the stimuli in naming and differentiating the emotions is clearly brought out by the responses of the group of medical students when the stimuli were transposed. The results indicate that the stimulus preceding the reaction shown was usually the deciding factor in the name given to the reaction.

2 · Conditioned Emotional Reactions

JOHN B. WATSON AND ROSALIE RAYNER WATSON

Abridged from the *Journal of Experimental Psychology*, 3 (1920), 1-14.

Almost any infant can be made to cry by presenting very loud sounds; indeed, nearly any form of stimulation—cold, heat, hunger, pain—will cause crying if the stimulus is very intense. Contrariwise, weak or mild stimuli will not ordinarily cause crying.

The Watsons, in the article which follows, show how a previously ineffective stimulus can be made effective through conditioning.

In recent literature various speculations have been entered into concerning the possibility of conditioning various types of emotional response, but direct experimental evidence in support of such a view has been lacking. If the theory advanced by Watson and Morgan to the effect that in infancy the original emotional reaction patterns are few is correct, then there must be some simple method by means of which the range of stimuli which can call out these emotions and their compounds is greatly increased. Otherwise, complexity in adult response could not be accounted for. These authors without adequate experimental evidence advanced the view that this range was increased by means of conditioned reflex factors. It was suggested there that the early home life of the child furnishes a laboratory situation for establishing conditioned emotional responses. The present authors have recently put the whole matter to an experimental test.

Experimental work has been done so far on only one child, Albert B. This infant was reared almost from birth in a hospital environment; his mother was a wet nurse in the Harriet Lane Home for Invalid Children. Albert's life was normal: He was healthy from birth and one of the best developed youngsters ever brought to the hospital, weighing twenty-one pounds at nine months of age. He was on the whole stolid and unemotional. His stability was one of the principal reasons for using him as a subject in this test. We felt we could do him relatively little harm by carrying out such experiments as those outlined below.

At approximately nine months of age we ran him through the emotional tests that have become a part of our regular routine. In brief, the infant was confronted suddenly and for the first time successively with a white rat, a rabbit, a dog, a monkey, with masks with and without hair, cotton wool, burning newspapers, etc. A permanent record of Albert's reactions to these objects and situations has been preserved in a motion picture study. Manipulation was the most usual reaction called out. *At no time did this infant ever show fear in any situation.* These experimental records were confirmed by the casual observations of the mother and hospital attendants. No one had ever seen him in a state of fear and rage. The infant practically never cried.

Up to approximately nine months of age we had not tested him with loud sounds. The test to determine whether a fear reaction could be called out by a loud sound was made when he was eight months, twenty-six days of age. The sound was that made by striking a hammer upon a suspended steel bar four feet in length and three-fourths of an inch in diameter. The laboratory notes are as follows:

> One of the two experimenters caused the child to turn its head and fixate her moving hand; the other, stationed back of the child, struck the steel bar a sharp blow. The child started violently, his breathing was checked and the arms were raised in a characteristic manner. On the second stimulation the same thing occurred, and in addition the lips began to pucker and tremble. On the third stimulation the child broke into a sudden crying fit. This is the first time an emotional situation in the laboratory has produced any fear or even crying in Albert.

The sound stimulus, thus, at nine months of age, gives us the means of testing several important factors. (1) Can we condition fear of an animal, e.g., a white rat, by visually presenting it and simultaneously striking a steel bar? (2) If such a conditioned emotional response can be established, will there be a transfer to other animals or other objects? (3) What is the effect of time upon such conditional emotional responses? (4) If after a reasonable period such emotional responses have not died out, what laboratory methods can be devised for their removal?

(1) *The establishment of conditioned emotional responses.* At first there was considerable hesitation on our part in making the attempt to set up fear reactions experimentally. A certain responsibility attaches to such a procedure. We decided finally to make the attempt, comforting ourselves by the reflection that such attachments would arise anyway as soon as the child left the sheltered environment of the nursery for the rough and tumble of the home. We did not begin this work until Albert was eleven months, three days of age. Before attempting to set up a conditioned response we, as before, put him through all of the regular emotional tests. *Not the slightest sign of a fear response was obtained in any situation.*

The steps taken to condition emotional responses are shown in our laboratory notes.

11 Months 3 Days

1. White rat suddenly taken from the basket and presented to Albert. He began to reach for rat with left hand. Just as his hand touched the animal the bar was struck immediately behind his head. The infant jumped violently and fell forward, burying his face in the mattress. He did not cry, however.

2. Just as the right hand touched the rat the bar was again struck. Again the infant jumped violently, fell forward, and began to whimper.

In order not to disturb the child too seriously no further tests were given for one week.

11 Months 10 Days

1. Rat presented suddenly without sound. There was steady fixation but no tendency at first to reach for it. The rat was then placed nearer, whereupon tentative reaching movements began with the right hand. When the rat nosed the infant's left hand, the hand was immediately withdrawn. He started to reach for the head of the animal with the forefinger of the left hand, but withdrew it suddenly before contact. It is thus seen that the two joint stimulations given the previous week were not without effect. He was tested with his blocks immediately afterwards to see if they shared in the process of conditioning. He began immediately to pick them up, dropping them, pounding them, etc. In the remainder of the tests the blocks were given frequently to quiet him and to test his general emotional state. They were always removed from sight when the process of conditioning was under way.

2. Joint stimulation with rat and sound. Started, then fell over immediately to right side. No crying.

3. Joint stimulation. Fell to right side and rested upon hands, with head turned away from rat. No crying.

4. Joint stimulation. Same reaction.

5. Rat suddenly presented alone. Puckered face, whimpered, and withdrew body sharply to the left.

6. Joint stimulation. Fell over immediately to right side and began to whimper.

7. Joint stimulation. Started violently and cried, but did not fall over.

8. Rat alone. *The instant the rat was shown the baby began to cry. Almost instantly he turned sharply to the left, fell over on left side, raised himself on all fours and began to crawl away so rapidly that he was caught with difficulty before reaching the edge of the table.*

This was as convincing a case of a completely conditioned fear response as could have been theoretically pictured. In all, seven joint stimulations were given to bring about the complete reaction. It is not unlikely had the sound been of greater intensity or of a more complex clang character that the number of joint stimulations might have been materially reduced. Experiments designed to define the nature of the sounds that will serve best as emotional stimuli are under way.

(2) *When a conditioned emotional response has been established for one object, is there a transfer?* Five days later Albert was again brought back into the laboratory and tested as follows:

11 Months 15 Days

1. Tested first with blocks. He reached readily for them, playing with them as usual. This shows that there has been no general transfer to the room, table, blocks, etc.

2. Rat alone. Whimpered immediately, withdrew right hand, and turned head and trunk away.

3. Blocks again offered. Played readily with them, smiling and gurgling.

4. Rat alone. Leaned over to the left side as far away from the rat as possible, then fell over, getting up on all fours and scurrying away as rapidly as possible.

5. Blocks again offered. Reached immediately for them, smiling and laughing as before.

The above preliminary tests show that the conditioned response to the rat had carried over completely for the five days in which no tests were given. The question as to whether or not there is a transfer was next taken up.

6. Rabbit alone. The rabbit was suddenly placed on the mattress in front of him. The reaction was pronounced. Negative responses began at once. He leaned as far away from the animal as possible, whimpered, then burst into tears. When the rabbit was placed in contact with him he buried his face in the mattress, then got up on all fours and crawled away, crying as he went. This was a most convincing test.

7. The blocks were next given him, after an interval. He played with them as before. It was observed by four people that he played far more energetically with them than ever before. The blocks were raised high over his head and slammed down with a great deal of force.

8. Dog alone. The dog did not produce as violent a reaction as the rabbit. The moment fixation occurred the child shrank back and as the animal came nearer he attempted to get on all fours but did not cry at first. As soon as the dog passed out of his range of vision he became quiet. The dog was then made to approach the infant's head (he was lying down at the moment). Albert straightened up immediately, fell over to the opposite side and turned his head away. He then began to cry.

9. The blocks were again presented. He began immediately to play with them.

10. Fur coat (seal). Withdrew immediately to the left side and began to fret. Coat put close to him on the left side, he turned immediately, began to cry, and tried to crawl away on all fours.

11. Cotton wool. The wool was presented in a paper package. At the end the cotton was not covered by the paper. It was placed first on his feet. He kicked it away but did not touch it with his hands. When his hand was laid on the wool he immediately withdrew it but did not show the shock that the animals or fur coat produced in him. He then began to play with the paper, avoiding contact with the wool itself. He finally, under the impulse of the manipulative interest, lost some of his negativism to the wool.

12. Just in play W. put his head down to see if Albert would play with

his hair. Albert was completely negative. Two other observers did the same thing. He began immediately to play with their hair. W. then brought the Santa Claus mask and presented it to Albert. He was again pronouncedly negative.

From the above results it would seem that emotional transfers do take place. Furthermore it would seem that the number of transfers resulting from an experimentally produced conditioned emotional reaction may be very large. In our observations we had no means of testing the complete number of transfers which may have resulted.

(3) *The effect of time upon conditioned emotional responses.* We have already shown that the conditioned emotional response will continue for a period of one week. It was desired to make the time test longer. In view of the imminence of Albert's departure from the hospital we could not make the interval longer than one month. Accordingly no further emotional experimentation was entered into for thirty-one days after the above test. During the month, however, Albert was brought weekly to the laboratory for tests upon right- and left-handedness, imitation, general development, etc. No emotional tests whatever were given and during the whole month his regular nursery routine was maintained in the Harriet Lane Home. The notes on the test given at the end of this period are as follows:

1 Year 21 Days

1. Santa Claus mask. Withdrawal, gurgling, then slapped at it without touching. When his hand was forced to touch it, he whimpered and cried. His hand was forced to touch it two more times. He whimpered and cried on both tests. He finally cried at the mere visual stimulus of the mask.

2. Fur coat. Wrinkled his nose and withdrew both hands, drew back his whole body, and began to whimper as the coat was put nearer. Again there was the strife between withdrawal and the tendency to manipulate. Reached tentatively with left hand but drew back before contact had been made. In moving his body to one side his hand accidentally touched the coat. He began to cry at once, nodding his head in a very peculiar manner (this reaction was an entirely new one). Both hands were withdrawn as far as possible from the coat. The coat was then laid on his lap and he continued nodding his head and whimpering, withdrawing his body as far as possible, pushing the while at the coat with his feet but never touching it with his hands.

3. Fur coat. The coat was taken out of his sight and presented again at the end of a minute. He began immediately to fret, withdrawing his body and nodding his head as before.

4. Blocks. He began to play with them as usual.

5. The rat. He allowed the rat to crawl toward him without withdrawing. He sat very still and fixated it intently. Rat then touched his hand. Albert withdrew it immediately, then leaned back as far as possible but did not cry. When the rat was placed on his arm he withdrew his body and began to fret, nodding his head. The rat was then allowed to crawl against his chest. He first began to fret and then covered his eyes with both hands.

6. Blocks. Reaction normal.

7. The rabbit. The animal was placed directly in front of him. It was very quiet. Albert showed no avoiding reactions at first. After a few seconds he puckered up his face, began to nod his head and to look intently at the experimenter. He next began to push the rabbit away with his feet, withdrawing his body at the same time. Then as the rabbit came nearer he began pulling his feet away, nodding his head, and wailing "da da." After about a minute he reached out tentatively and slowly and touched the rabbit's ear with his right hand, finally manipulating it. The rabbit was again placed in his lap. Again he began to fret and withdrew his hands. He reached out tentatively with his left hand and touched the animal, shuddered, and withdrew the whole body. The experimenter then took hold of his left hand and laid it on the rabbit's back. Albert immediately withdrew his hand and began to suck his thumb. Again the rabbit was laid in his lap. He began to cry, covering his face with both hands.

8. Dog. The dog was very active. Albert fixated it intensely for a few seconds, sitting very still. He began to cry but did not fall over backwards as on his last contact with the dog. When the dog was pushed closer to him he at first sat motionless, then began to cry, putting both hands over his face.

These experiments would seem to show conclusively that directly conditioned emotional responses as well as those conditioned by transfer persist, although with a certain loss in the intensity of the reaction, for a longer period than one month. It should be recalled again that Albert was of an extremely phlegmatic type. Had he been emotionally unstable probably both the directly conditioned response and those transferred would have persisted throughout the month unchanged in form.

3 · Fear of Snakes

HAROLD E. JONES AND MARY COVER JONES

Reprinted from "A Study of Fear" by Harold E. Jones and Mary Cover Jones, from *Childhood Education*, 5 (1928), 136-143, by permission of Mary Cover Jones and the Association for Childhood Education International, 3615 Wisconsin Ave., N.W., Washington 16, D. C.

We are prone to suppose that the child has native fears of specific objects, such as snakes. The following study points out how the child's reaction to snakes is not a specific fear but results from his general ability to perceive danger and strangeness.

WHAT DO CHILDREN FEAR?

As children grow older, they begin to show differences in the number and kinds of things of which they are afraid. The only general statement which seems to cover all the cases of fear which we have observed in children is that children tend to be afraid of things that require them to make a sudden and unexpected adjustment. Stimuli which are startlingly strange, which are presented without due preparation, or which are painful or excessively intense, belong in this category. For example, in our study of the reactions of pre-school children to flashlights, darkness, false-faces, snakes, rabbits, frogs, and the like, it was found that the animal which most often caused fear was the frog, the fear not usually appearing at first sight of the frog, but at sight of the frog suddenly jumping. Likewise, a child was often afraid of a jack-in-the-box. A species of beetle which suddenly snaps up in the air when placed on its back was fairly efficient in arousing alarm, while caterpillars and earthworms produced no more than a mild curiosity in the younger children.

While traces of these childhood fears may last throughout life, affecting adult behavior profoundly, the overt expression of fear is apt to be less marked as childhood is outgrown—partly because the adult meets fewer unfamiliar situations (encounters fewer stimuli for which his action system contains no ready adjustment) and partly because he has learned to mask and repress the more conspicuous symptoms of emotion. From watching individuals of different ages in similar test situations, it is evident that the effectiveness of a stimulus and the type of emotional response are greatly

111

affected by maturity. From the diffuse responsiveness of the infant, to the blunted and inhibited reaction of the blasé adult, the variety of unpredictable behavior in fear-producing situations provides a rich field for research.

How does the sight of a snake affect a baby, a toddler, a youth, a grandfather? A few cases, chosen from our laboratory notes, show an interesting developmental sequence.

EXPERIMENTS WITH YOUNG CHILDREN

Experimental Situation

A pen 8 by 10 feet by 6 inches high was built on the nursery floor. Within this a number of blocks and toys were scattered, and two black suitcases were placed flat on the floor near the wall. The suitcases could be opened easily by a child; one contained a familiar mechanical toy, the other contained a snake of a harmless variety (*Spilotes corais*) about six feet in length and slightly under four inches in girth at the middle of the body. When free in the pen, the snake glided actively about, showing a powerful and agile type of movement, and frequently protruding a black forked tongue about an inch in length. If the child did not open the suitcase containing the snake, an observer was able to do so from a concealed position behind a screen, by pulling a string attached to the lid of the case.

Subject 1. Irving, age 1 year 3 months.
Irving sat in the pen, playing idly with the ball and blocks. After being released, the snake glided slowly toward Irving, whipping up his head and deflecting his course when within 12 inches of the infant. Irving watched unconcerned, fixating the snake's head or the middle of his body, and letting his gaze wander frequently to other objects in the pen. The snake furnished only a mild incentive to his attention.

Subject 3. Enid, age 1 year 7 months.
Enid sat passively in the pen, playing with blocks in an unsystematic fashion. The snake was released and moved fairly rapidly about the pen. Enid showed no interest, giving the snake only casual glances and continuing to play with her blocks when it was within two feet of her. When (later) the snake was held by the observer directly in front of her face, she showed no changes in facial expression, but presently reached out her hand and grasped the snake tightly about the neck.

Subject 8. Sol, age 2 years 3 months
When the snake began moving about the pen, Sol watched closely, holding his ground when the snake came near, but making no effort to touch it. He resisted when an attempt was made to have him pick up the snake (this was the same guarded reaction that he had shown previously with the rabbit and white rat). He stood unmoved when the snake was thrust toward him, and showed no overt response, save an attempt to follow visually, when the head of the animal was swung in front and in

back of him, neck writhing and tongue darting. After the snake was returned to the suitcase he went to it again and lifted the lid, looked within, and then closed it in a business-like manner.

Subject 11. Laurel, age 3 years 8 months.
Laurel opened the suitcase, picking out two blocks which were lying against the snake's body. The snake was immobile and she evidently had no differential reaction to it. The snake was taken out. Laurel: "I don't want it." Avertive reactions, moved off, then stood up and started to leave the pen, although without apparent stir or excitement. Experimenter: "Let's put him back in the box." Laurel: "I don't want it." Experimenter: "Come and help me put him back." After slight urging she came over and assisted, using both hands in picking up the snake and dropping him quickly when she reached the suitcase.

Subject 12. Edward, age 4 years 2 months.
Edward sat down in the pen and began playing constructively with the blocks. At sight of the snake he asked: "Can it drink water?" Experimenter: "Do you know what it is?" Edward: "It's a fish." He puckered his brows and made slight avertive reactions when the snake was swung within a foot of him, but this was overcome through adaptation in three trials. When encouraged to touch the snake he did so, tentatively, but soon grasped it without hesitation at the neck and body.

Subject 15. Ely, age 6 years 7 months.
On opening the suitcase he smiled and looked within for nearly a minute, making no effort to reach, and dropping the cover quickly when the snake moved. The snake thrust the lid up with his head, and glided out into the room. Ely took up a post of observation outside the pen. Experimenter: "Do you like him?" Ely nodded in the affirmative and smiled. Experimenter: "Touch him like this." Ely very hesitatingly touched his back, and withdrew his hand quickly, later consenting to stroke him. He asked: "Does he have teeth?" a reasonable enough inquiry. When the snake moved in his direction he drew away and looked distressed, but was persuaded to help pick him up and to put him back in the suitcase.

Of 15 children, 7 showed complete absence of fear indications; their age range was from 14 to 27 months, with a median of 20 months. Eight individuals showed "guarded" reactions, 2 of these revealing distinct fear, and 2 showing marked avertive responses when the snake gave the appearance of aggression; the other four being classified as "unafraid but wary." The age range of the "guarded" group was from 26 to 79 months, with a median of 44 months. The only case of a child under three years showing fear was Doris, age 26 months, and her reaction changed markedly the following day, as indicated by the report of the group response:
The suitcase was taken into the nursery when 9 children were present. Most of them recognized it, and one of the older children said, "There's an animal in there." Several of the children moved forward to touch it

as soon as the snake was released; Doris who had been afraid the day before now showed no fear, crowding close and attempting to hit the snake's head with a wooden boat. The two oldest children in the group remained cautious: Lawrence, age five years seven months, climbed up on a table, and John, age five years ten months, retained hold of the experimenter's hand, and refused to come near. After a few minutes of play, the experimenter said, "Now everyone has touched it except John and Lawrence." Both of these now came forward and touched the snake's back, social pressure being evidently effective in encouraging a more positive response.

EXPERIMENTS WITH OLDER CHILDREN

The following results were obtained in a group of 36 school children, with an age range of from about six to ten years.

The children were sitting on low chairs in a circle about 20 feet in diameter. The experimenter placed the suitcase containing the snake in the middle of the circle, asking, "Who wants to open the suitcase?" Harry, eight years of age, opened it, and took the snake out when requested. The snake glided about the floor, passing between the feet of one of the boys; no disturbance was shown. The experimenter now asked, "Who wants to touch the snake?" holding the snake's head so that the children had to reach past it, and walking slowly around the inside of the circle. The first 11 children touched the snake with no hesitancy. Four boys about ten years of age hesitated, one withdrawing markedly, another falling over backward in his chair. (This was due to an emotional heightening, arising partly from fear and partly from a desire to show off.) Two girls refused to touch the snake, but jumped up and ran around behind the circle, following the experimenter and watching closely. An undercurrent of reassurance was constantly heard, "He won't let it hurt you. Go ahead, touch it, it won't bite."

Only 9 of the 26 children showed definitely resistive behavior, and these were chiefly boys and chiefly the oldest in the group.

EXPERIMENTS WITH COLLEGE STUDENTS

How do adults behave, when presented with a similar situation?

In several classes of undergraduate and graduate students, a snake was introduced as "a perfectly harmless animal; the skin of this reptile has a smooth and pleasant feeling, and we guarantee that in touching him no one runs the slightest risk." In some classes the same reptile was used as in the preceding experiments; in others the snake was a boa constrictor, somewhat smaller and of a less "dangerous" appearance than the *Spilotes*. Of about 90 students nearly one-third refused to have the snake brought near; one-third touched him, with obvious hesitation and dislike, while the remainder (including as many women as men) reached forward with apparently complete freedom from any emotional disturbance. Several of the women obviously regarded the presence of a snake in the room as an almost unbearable ordeal, and several of the men solved the problem of emotional conflict by retiring to a neighboring room until the experiment was concluded.

With some of our adult subjects, we noted that while they stroked the snake in an apparently composed fashion, the subject's face and palms were nevertheless covered with beads of perspiration, indicating a marked degree of emotional tension. With young children such repressions are less likely to occur: The emotion is more superficial, and expresses itself readily and frankly in external symptoms. In studying the elimination of a fear, however, we should bear in mind the possibility that an attitude of tolerance and self-assurance may be merely a mask for an internal emotional upset; methods of elimination which "cure" the external signs may sometimes fail to reduce, and may even increase, the actual emotional intensity.

It should be pointed out that experiments of this character should not be attempted except by workers who are accustomed to handling both animals and children. A snake should not be used until he has been adequately tamed and has established a record of reacting well to handling. Some nonpoisonous species are likely to be dangerous because of vicious and unpredictable tempers. The situation must always be kept in control, so that a nervous child is not overfrightened; a slight degree of fear, which he later recognizes as groundless, may be of hygienic value, but a marked emotional upset is never hygienic, and the experimenter must take care to avoid traumatic episodes. In regions where poisonous snakes are common, it may be undesirable to train young children in emotional tolerance. The subjects used in our experiments were city children who had never before seen a snake of any kind, and who would be unlikely to encounter a poisonous snake in the course of a lifetime. Even in infested districts, it would seem desirable to cultivate a reaction of intelligent caution, in place of the blinding and tumultuous fear which was shown in so many of our adult subjects.

THE NATURE OF FEAR

In our group of 51 children and about 90 adults, children up to the age of two years showed no fear of a snake; by three or three and a half, caution reactions were common; children of this age paid closer attention to the snake's movements, and were somewhat tentative in approaching and touching it. Definite fear behavior occurred more often after the age of four years, and was more pronounced in adults than in children. No sex differences were observed. This "maturing" of a specific fear may be interpreted in at least three ways: (1) as the result of conditioning, (2) as the result of the ripening of an innate fear of snakes, (3) as the result of a general maturation of behavior, which leads to greater sensitiveness and more discriminatory responses.

The first explanation does not seem to be applicable to our group. Our children were developing in a common environment in an institution, and had no opportunity to be conditioned against snakes, either through pictures, stories, or from encounters with live specimens. When first seen in our experiments, the snake was as novel to them as a unicorn, and their response to it must be regarded as a novel and unpracticed adjustment. If the response changed from the age of two to the age of three years, this development cannot be interpreted in terms of *specific* training.

The second explanation we are also inclined to reject: It assumes an instinctive fear of snakes, a reaction which is latent and immature at birth, and which develops by a special process of innate growth; such a belief is related to the doctrine of innate ideas and the inheritance of acquired characters, and is not in keeping with present-day theory. It is possible to understand the inheritance and ripening of a general disposition, such as sex, for here we are dealing with a definite internal source of stimulation, and with a glandular basis which is subject to growth. It is possible to understand the inheritance and ripening of a specific simple pattern of response, such as a startle response to loss of support, which may be dependent upon a structural development in the semicircular canals or in the vestibular nerves. But the fear of a visual object, such as a snake, involves an emotional response to a complex and variable perception, differentiated out of a total situation. The perception will vary according to the size and other characteristics of the snake, according to its behavior and its distance from the perceiver. It appears very unlikely that a complex and many-faceted perceptual-emotional disposition can be inherited, or that it can develop by innate ripening.

We are left, then, with the third interpretation, which is in agreement with the theory of fear discussed on an earlier page. Fear may be regarded as a response to certain changes in a total situation—changes requiring a sudden new adjustment which the individual is unprepared to make. The arousal of fear depends not only upon situational changes, but also upon the individual's *general* level of development. With a young infant, perhaps the only changes which are fear-producing are those which substitute loud sounds for quiet, pain for comfort, or loss of support for a previous state of bodily balance. As a child develops, his intelligence innately matures, and his perceptions become enriched through experience. New things startle him because of his keener perception of the fact that they *are new and unusual.* We have an old saying, "They who know nothing fear nothing." It would be equally true to say, "They who know everything fear nothing."

4 · Infant Reactions
to Restraint

WAYNE DENNIS

Abridged from the publication in the *Transactions of the New York Academy of Science*, Series II, Vol. 2 (1940), 202-217, by permission of the Academy.

Although the infant in the new born stage may be rightly thought of as having specific unlearned reactions, such as crying, blinking, and sucking, as he grows older his behavior can be understood only in relation to his experience. His interest in the human face is not an attraction to faces per se *but represents his reaction to the agency that ministers to his wants. A face covered by a beard or a veil if it alleviated his needs, would call forth the same smiling and cooing as does the American mother. His fears, likewise, are relative to his experience. If he is reared in a typical American home, he will be afraid of a veiled Mohammedan or a bearded Sikh. But we may be sure that the Mohammedan and Sikh babies develop no such fears. The child of nine to twelve months is afraid of no absolute stimulus but is afraid of unfamiliar stimuli.*

The paper that follows attempts to show that the same sort of principle prevails in respect to reaction to restraint.

WATSON'S THEORY

At the outset, I shall discuss briefly one of Watson's hypothesized native emotions; namely, that rage is a response to restraint (Watson and Morgan, 1917).

The stimuli which Watson employed to restrain the infant were numerous. They included holding the head of the infant between the experimenter's hands or between pads of cotton, holding the nose, pressing the arms to the sides, and holding the legs tightly together. Watson repeatedly stated that the essential stimulus to rage was the "hampering of the infant's movements." He claimed that in no case was the pressure which was exerted sufficient to cause real pain, although this is a point concerning which only the baby could have had immediate knowledge. It is interesting to note the behaviorist taking such liberties with the infantile consciousness.

FINDINGS OF OTHER INVESTIGATORS

After Watson, the next experimenters who made use of similar stimuli administered to the newborn infant were Sherman and Sherman in 1925

(1925). These investigators applied pressure to the chins of 83 infants. They found that diffuse arm reactions occurred; but the Shermans were more interested in the fact that in older infants the movements were better coordinated than they were in the fact that the reactions, as described by them, were somewhat similar to those which had been reported by Watson.

The later reports of Mandel Sherman (1927) are widely known and frequently are cited in partial refutation of Watson's findings. Sherman, in a part of his experiments, exhibited to judges babies which had been stimulated in ways unknown to the judges. He also exhibited movies of infants reacting to stimuli which had been deleted from the films. One of his forms of stimulation consisted in holding the infant's head on the table "with fairly firm pressure." The point which was emphasized by Sherman was the fact that the observers did not designate with much correctness the causes of the reactions which they saw. This, of course, tells as much about the observers as it does about the infants. We do not know whether the reaction patterns of the infants or the perceptual patterns of the observers were loosely organized. However, when the infants were restrained, the observers almost invariably described the reaction as being of a vigorous character, and reported it as anger, fear, pain, or colic so that it can be gathered that Sherman's restraint, like Watson's, resulted in pronounced reactions.

Next comes the monograph of Pratt, Nelson, and Sun (1930). A section of this publication deals with reaction to restraint. In one experiment the investigators "held the (infant's) arms pressed firmly against the body and held them there against whatever energy the infant would exert." However, in a tabular statement of the ensuing reactions one finds that sometimes the "arms immediately flexed to the original posture" and that sometimes the "arms did not remain at the sides of the body." One must conclude that the infant occasionally overpowered Pratt, Nelson, and Sun, or that these remarks refer only to what happened after the child was released. If that is the case, then the experimenters failed to state what happened while the infants were being held.

The only condition under which a sufficiently large number of subjects were stimulated by Pratt, Nelson, and Sun was the state described as "asleep and dry." Watson, on the other hand, worked only with wide awake babies, and it is likely that he did not intend his observations to apply to sleeping children.

In another part of their work, Pratt and his collaborators held the infant's nose between the thumb and forefinger with gentle pressure in such a way as to close off the nostrils. In some experiments this was done for 6 seconds, in others the stimulation was continued for 15 seconds. However, if the infant cried, the stimulation was immediately discontinued. In their typical style, these investigators report their results as follows: To 234 experiments on infants who were asleep and dry, there occurred 197 movements of the extremities, 134 of drawing back of the head, and 70 of arching of the spine. These experiments are often cited as being somewhat contrary to the theory of Watson. If, however, it be conceded that Pratt, Nelson, and Sun probably stimulated the subjects less vigorously than did Watson, if it is borne in mind that the condition of the infant when it was stimulated was different in the two investigations, if it is recalled that the duration of the stimulation was not the same, and finally, if one is reminded of the different manner in which the results were reported, it will seen that there cannot be a contradiction between the two, since the second study scarcely in any sense was a repetition of Watson's. The most reasonable conclusion from Pratt, Nelson, and Sun's work would seem to be that less severe stimuli cause less vigorous reactions.

Taylor's research (1934) comes nearer to duplicating Watson's conditions for rage, but in this experiment, too, many of the infants were asleep. Furthermore, the stimulations, which consisted in cutting off inhalation by holding the nose between the experimenter's thumb and forefinger, or in holding the arms at the sides, lasted for only 20 seconds, whereas Watson, in personal correspondence with Taylor after Taylor's experiment was completed, suggested that a duration of one minute should have been used. In Taylor's investigation each of 40 infants was stimulated once by each of the two methods listed above. To nose stimulation, 6 subjects stiffened the body, 11 slashed with the arms, 30 abducted the head, and 21 arched the back. To arm stimulation, 15 stiffened the body and 8 gave vigorous limb reactions. While Taylor concluded that he did not observe Watson's rage pattern, the correctness of this conclusion hinges upon what one means by a pattern. The responses which Taylor observed most frequently were a part of Watson's "pattern" but the pattern did not occur in its entirety at each stimulation.

I wish to report next some experiments which Mrs. Dennis and I performed upon a set of nonidentical twins. Other researches upon these subjects have been described elsewhere (Dennis, 1935a, 1935b, 1938, 1941), but the following observations have not been previously reported. When the infants were about two months old, they were presented with certain stimuli and their responses to these were recorded by motion picture camera. A series of stimuli was presented each day for 18 days. The stimulations included holding the head between the experimenter's hands, so that it could not be moved, and pressing the nose of the subject with the experimenter's forefinger. The amount of pressure involved in these two forms of stimulation was not measured objectively, but I can say that it was vigorous, since it was desired to obtain some responses to each stimulation.

In any form of experimentation one expects some variation in response from stimulation to stimulation, and this variation Watson's reports tended to ignore. In our records, the variability of the response is marked.

Nevertheless, in approximately two-thirds of the stimulations, the movie records show behavior which may be characterized as struggling, thrashing about, or crying. This is not very different from Watson's so-called rage pattern.

But we not only stimulated the infants by holding the nose and by restraining the arms, but also by strong taste stimuli—a saturated salt solution, a very bitter quinine solution, and by dilute citric acid. So far as we were able to determine, the limb reactions to these stimuli were not distinguishable from those which followed the stimulation by restraint. Let me call them by the neutral title of restlessness and crying. It is my belief that many strong and persistent stimuli will cause roughly the same sort of infant reaction.

Was Watson correct in assuming that it was *restraint of movement* which caused the restlessness and crying which he observed or was it caused by intense stimulation? Watson was not a gentle experimenter as anyone will attest who has seen Watson's research film which portrays his methods of infant investigation. He did not merely hold the infant's head and arms; he exerted pressure upon them. Pratt, Nelson, and Sun and Taylor, who merely restrained the movements of their subjects did not obtain such vigorous responses as did Watson.

FETAL RESPONSES

In addition to the observations of the experimenters just mentioned, several other considerations suggest that restraint of movement of itself does not cause restlessness and crying. One of these considerations arises from the situation of the infant in utero. Here, if anywhere, is to be found a profound hampering of movements. The head, the arms, the legs, the trunk, all are restrained. There is no free space in which to move. The arms cannot be extended, the feet meet resistance in kicking, the head cannot be lifted from the chest. Yet the evidence indicates that the mature fetus moves only occasionally. From Watson's theory, one would expect the unborn child to be in a permanent state of violent rage. There is no indication that this is the case, and no indication that the prenatal responses which do occur are the result of restraint. Watson seems never to have faced the question as to why the infant immediately after birth should react emotionally to a condition very similar to that in which it exists for several months in relative quiescence.

If we consider the effective element in Watson's stimulation to have been the intensity of the stimulation rather than its hampering character, no such contradictions in interpretation are met. Intrauterine pressure is not great, and, since the fetus is in a fluid medium, the pressure is approximately equal upon all parts of the body. Each part is subjected only to a very gentle pressure.

SWADDLING AND CRADLING

No psychological theory ever revealed so clearly the need of psychology for an historical and cultural perspective as did Watson's hypothesis of a negative reaction to restraint in early infancy. Had Watson appeared upon the scene of Western civilization prior to 1750, he could not have formulated such a view, nor, in his own time, could he have done so if he had considered the methods of infant care prevalent before the modern era. The theory should have been forestalled by a knowledge of the widespread practice of swaddling and binding the infant. An adequate history of swaddling, so far as I can ascertain, has not been written. We know that swaddling clothes were employed by the Jews, the Greeks, and the Romans before the Christian era, and were used throughout the medieval period in all European countries. Swaddling did not begin to disappear in England until 1750, following a severe criticism of its detrimental effect upon infant health by an influential physician, Cadogan (1750). Swaddling is practiced by the Lapps of today. I am told that it persists in some Italian peasant districts, and I have no doubt it is to be found in other parts of Europe as well. The Albanian custom is known through the study of Danzinger and Frankl (1934).

In its most extreme form, swaddling involved wrapping the infant round and round with long strips of cloth in a manner such that the arms were held extended along the sides and the legs were bound together. Furthermore, at times, the head was fastened to some sort of a stay in order to prevent it from wobbling. The general idea underlying swaddling practices was that of straightening the infant and of protecting him from injury. While the general nature of swaddling in Europe is clear from works of art and from casual references to it, I have nowhere been able to find a very adequate description of how it was actually done, or of how tightly the infant was bound. Salzman (1926) states that the infant was able to move only its head; Crump (1929) gives some description of the practice as does Buffon (1812). The condition of the swaddled infant was such that, according to Watson's theory, the infant continually should have expressed rage. It has not been possible to find a single statement concerning the newborn infant's reaction to the swaddling process. Tiedeman, it is true, mentions a slight repugnance to swaddling on the part of his son, but this was when his son was several months of age. If children had uniformly cried during most of the time that they were swaddled that fact could hardly have escaped observation, nor, I think, could the practice have endured for centuries.

But we are not dependent upon European sources for information concerning reactions to swaddling. The binding of infants occurs in many parts of the world other than Europe. It was practically universal on the continent of North America at the time of its settlement by white men. The early explorers frequently mentioned the binding of the American Indian infant, probably because it differed in one or more respects from European binding. One of these differences consisted in the fact that whereas the European child was swaddled and then lain in a crib or on a bed, the swaddling of the Indian infant bound him to a rigid or semi-rigid cradleboard. The Indian infant was more restrained than was the European child. The accounts of various travelers, explorers, missionaries do not indicate that the Indian infants objected to this treatment. In fact, many observers commented on the good behavior of infants when thus bound.

In some sections of America, many aboriginal customs still persist, and one can observe at the present time the reaction of the Indian infant to his bindings. I have been interested in making such observations among the Hopi and Navaho Indians of Arizona and New Mexico. Since these observations have been published in detail elsewhere (Dennis, 1940a and 1940b) they need be mentioned only briefly here. They show beyond doubt that the young Indian infant does not cry when bound, although his limb movements and bodily movements are very greatly restricted.

In the Southwestern culture area, the head of the infant remains free to move. But among some Indian groups, in the past, even the head of the infant was fixed. This condition was imposed as a part of the process of head-molding or head flattening, which was most prominent along the Northwest Coast, particularly among the Chinook. The procedure made the head completely immobile. At the same time, the limbs were encased by bindings. The flattening of the forehead, so as to make the head more or less wedge-shaped, was achieved by placing on the forehead a hard pad, which was pressed against the forehead by means of the thongs which passed through the floor of the cradle and were tied. The thongs were kept tightened to what was considered to be just the right degree, the adjustment of them often being entrusted to skilled and experienced individuals. The resulting head shape was a mark of high social station and was considered to lend beauty. The process began shortly after birth and was continued, almost without interruption, for several months, often from eight to ten months. The head-molding technique has been described for various Northwest Coast groups by Kane (1859), Swan (1857), Cox (1832), and Gunther (1927). It is not followed at the present time.

Most of the writers cited above have said nothing about the behavior of the infant who is being subjected to this treatment. This, in itself, would suggest that the infant's behavior was not unusual. Bancroft (1882) and Cox (1832), however, stated that the infants seemed to feel no pain, and Kane (1859) observed, "I have never heard the infants crying or moaning. . . ." Kane's interpretation, however, was that the infants may have been partially stupefied by the procedure. The eyes are described as bulging as a result of the intracranial pressure. The fact may be, however, that this pressure, although great, caused no pain. One can readily demonstrate to himself that pressure applied to the *forehead* does not hurt, where as pressure applied to the sides of the head, where it was administered by Watson and others, is quite painful. The temporal regions of the head are particularly sensitive to compression.

The argument up to this point may be summarized as follows: The newborn and slightly older infant has no unique pattern of reaction to restraint. He reacts to all strong and persistent stimuli with restlessness and crying, a crude pattern of activity which is similar for all sorts of intense and enduring stimuli. The effective aspect of the stimulations employed by Watson, Sherman, Taylor, and ourselves was probably strong pressure or pain. On the other hand, methods which achieve restraint of movement without steep gradients of pressure—such as the conditions which are found in utero, in swaddling, and in binding to a cradleboard— do not produce restlessness and crying. These statements, I believe, will harmonize all the seemingly contradictory evidence which has been presented.

Let us turn now to a consideration of the older infant. In Watson's theory, the negative reaction to restraint is characteristic not merely of the neonatal period but it is a permanent part of the human makeup. In *Psychological Care of Infant and Child* he stated that no amount of training will ever completely eliminate the response.

THWARTING

In later infancy, everyone knows that "thwarting" of various sorts will lead to something which may be called rage. The early baby biographies are full of instances of reaction to frustration. For example, it was recorded that one baby cried because he was not permitted to pull his grandfather's beard. Such stimulation is "restraint" only in a metaphorical sense. It is likely that Watson knew that such responses occurred, and his research may be interpreted as an attempt to find an instinctive basis for the responses to frustration. We have seen that he was probably wrong in tracing them back to the neonatal level. Rage, I believe, is a reaction which is not present until purposeful behavior has been developed and is foiled in attaining its end. It is unlearned in this sense, that when the child has developed a purposive sequence of behavior which can be interfered with, he will exhibit "rage" on the first occasion on which this interference occurs.

It was possible to observe early reactions to thwarting in the case of the two infant subjects previously referred to, since they lived under controlled conditions which made it possible for us to know when a particular activity first suffered interference. As soon as the infants became accustomed to playing with a rattle, which was not offered them until the eleventh month, each twin cried when her rattle was taken away. Another type of thwarting arose as follows: When we picked up the infants, it was usually for the purpose of feeding them or bathing them or experimenting with them. But occasionally we picked up an infant who was quiet and contented and returned her to the crib without further ministrations. In these circumstances she invariably cried. Furthermore, if we failed to experiment with either child at the usual time of day, she became restless. This may also be looked upon as a form of frustration, or at least as an interference with the usual routine.

Of course, physical restraint of movement may be employed as *one* means of frustrating the older infant. When our twin subjects were several months of age we restrained their arms by removing the arms from the sleeves of their garments, and buttoning the clothing over the arms so that they could not be employed as usual. This did not exert pressure but it made it impossible for the subjects to carry out their ordinary manual activities. This situation, of course, led to restlessness and crying.

Some Pueblo Indian infants at several months of age (Dennis, 1940a) begin to object to being placed on the cradleboard. But it is important to note that the Indian infant of this age has been off the cradleboard each day for an interval sufficient to accustom him to manual play and to other activities. The negative reaction to the cradleboard which sometimes occurs in older infants may be due not merely to restraint but to the prevention of customary activities.

Physical restraint of movement does not *always* cause negative reactions in the older infant. In the case of the two infant subjects to which I have already referred several times, attempts were made to test reaction to restraint in the tenth month by repeating the head and nose stimulations which had been employed in the third month. No such stimulations had been presented during the interval. But, while Mrs. Dennis and I had not restrained the infants during this period, we had stimulated them in innumerable other ways. Not only had we fed, bathed, dried, and clothed the subjects but we had plied them with odors, tastes, sights, and sounds, as parts of experimental tests. To most of these they had reacted favorably. In consequence, when one of us leaned over the crib and held the head of either subject very firmly between our hands, her reaction was to quietly look up and *smile*. For several minutes no negative reaction occurred. Eventually the child became tired of the stimulation, but no sooner than did we. It was sometimes necessary to hold a subject's head immobile for a full five minutes before she became restless and began to fret. I feel certain that it was discomfort rather than restraint which occasioned the final fretting.

It must be emphasized that the head and nose stimulations, in this situation, were not frustrating or thwarting in character. The infants were lying on their backs in their cribs, without toys, unoccupied. Their behavior indicated that they definitely wanted us to come near them. Any attention on our part, so long as it was not painful, they welcomed. Under the circumstances, their positive reactions to the head and nose stimulations were a form of positive social reaction. In other circumstances, holding the head or pressing on the nose might have been a pronounced form of thwarting, and might have led to different results.

Such considerations show the probable futility of attempts to test for "instincts" or native emotional stimuli after the very early months of life. Every stimulus which is presented, even if it has never before been employed, bears some relationship to the experience of the child. This is a fact which has general importance beyond the bounds of the mere topic of reaction to restraint. The child's reaction tendencies with respect to any test situation, like his reaction to restraint, can be stated, not absolutely, but only in terms of the relationship which the test situation bears to past situations and to the behavior repertoire. The child of several months of age does not react to a piece of fur, a snake, a loud noise, or a pinching of the nose as a unique stimulus, as a thing-in-itself, but he seems to place each situation into some category of stimulation. A stimulation is a playful approach, a firm oral administration, a strange object, or a frustrating circumstance. The same absolute stimulating situation may be any one of these things depending upon the history of the child. Reaction tendencies beyond the first few months cannot be said to have absolute stimuli, such as loud noises or restraint of movement but instead they have relative stimuli, such as strange objects and frustrating situations (1941). What is strange and what is frustrating necessarily depends upon the stimulation history of the child.

It has been seen that reaction to frustration involves the prior acquisition of the responses which is to be thwarted. Therefore, this reaction does not correspond to Watson's notion of an instinct; that is, a native response pattern elicited by certain native stimuli. The stimuli which will elicit rage are not determined solely by the structure of the individual but in part by the child's experience. In other words, a certain kind of learning is involved in reaction to frustration.

I would caution, however, that this does not mean that this reaction is learned in the same sense that language is learned. In the past the gap between instinct and learning has been made too large. It has been customary simply to classify all behavioral phenomena with reference to this dichotomy, without attempting an analysis of the intermediate modes of development.

I believe a useful subclassification of the learned aspects of behavior can be attained by distinguishing between those things which the individual learns by himself without the aid or direction of others, and those things, like language, which are socially transmitted. The former I have called autogenous, the latter, sociogenous behavior (Dennis, 1941). It must be said that this division still is a crude one, but it is adequate for our present purposes.

Often we have been led by our terminology to place whatever is not totally instinctive into the class of socially transmitted phenomena. As we have accumulated evidence which indicates that stereotyped response patterns with predetermined stimuli are fewer than we had supposed, we have put a great deal of emphasis upon the *social* determination of behavior. Today, no one will deny that a very large part of the behavior of the human *adult* is socially determined. But, in my opinion, we should not conclude that behavior during the first year of life also is socially determined. Most of the infant's repertoire, like his reaction to frustration, is attained through maturation plus the infant's individual experience, and does not require the intervention of other persons (Dennis, 1941).

For it is true that the reaction to thwarting may come about autogenously. Our two infant subjects were under observation from the age of five weeks onward. In no sense can it be said that we trained them to cry when thwarted, or that we provided an example. Yet this response appeared without trial and error on the initial occurrence of each of several situations. In other words it was not a sociogenous response. To the contrary, the experiment proved it to be autogenous.

SUMMARY

In closing, I may say that I have attempted to demonstrate the following points:

1. At birth, the infant reacts with crying and restlessness to any form of intense and enduring stimulation, of which rough restraint may be one form.

2. Restraint of movement achieved without the use of intense stimulation does not cause negative reactions in the newborn.

3. At a later age, the infant will react also with crying and restlessness when some customary sequence of events meets interference.

4. Whether or not restraint of movement will cause negative reactions in the older infant depends upon whether or not the restraint interferes with customary sequences which have been built up. What is thwarting to the infant is not predetermined but depends upon postnatal events.

5. Interference with behavior sequences gives rise to negative reactions in the absence of any social transmission of this phenomenon.

Finally, I have suggested a terminology, by which some of these views may be expressed as follows: Reaction to frustration is not congenital or instinctive but it is autogenous.

References

Bancroft, H. H., *The Works of Hubert Howe Bancroft*, Vol. 1. San Francisco: A. L. Bancroft & Co., 1882.

Buffon, Count de., *Natural History, General and Particular*, Vol. III, trans. W. Wood. London: Codell and Davies, 1812, 120-121.

Cadogan, W., *An Essay upon Nursing and the Management of Children from Their Birth to Three Years of Age*, 4th ed. London: J. Roberts, 1750.

Cox, R., *Adventures on the Columbia River*. New York: Harper & Row, Publishers, 1832.

Crump, L., *Nursery Life 300 Years Ago*. London: George Routledge & Sons, Ltd., 1929.

Danzinger, L., and L. Frankl, "Zum Problem der Funktionsreifung," *Zeitschrift fur Kinderforschung*, 43 (1934), 219-254.

Dennis, W., "An Experimental Test of Two Theories of Social Smiling," *Journal of Social Psychology*, 6 (1935a), 214-223.

———, "The Effect of Restricted Practice upon the Reaching, Sitting, and Standing of Two Infants," *Journal of Genetic Psychology*, 47 (1935b), 17-32.

———, "Infant Development under Conditions of Restricted Practice and of Minimum Social Stimulation: A Preliminary Report," *Journal of Genetic Psychology*, 53 (1938), 149-158.

———, *The Hopi Child*. New York: Appleton-Century-Crofts Inc., 1940a.

———, "Infant Development under Conditions of Restricted Practice and of Minimum Social Stimulation," *Genetic Psychology Monographs*, 23 (1941), 143-189.

———, "Does Culture Appreciably Affect Patterns of Infant Behavior?" *Journal of Social Psychology*, 17 (1940b), 305-317.

Gunther, E., *Klallam Ethnography, University Washington Publication Anthropology*, 1 (1927), 173-314.

Kane, P., *Wanderings of an Artist among the Indians of North America*. London: Longmans, Green & Company, 1859.

Pratt, K. C., A. K. Nelson and K. H. Sun, *The Behavior of the Newborn Infant*. Columbus: Ohio State University Press, 1930.

Salzman, L. F., *English Life in the Middle Ages*. London: Humphrey Milford, 1926.

Sherman, M., "The Differentiation of Emotional Responses in Infants. I. Judgments of Emotional Responses from Motion Picture Views and from Actual Observation," *Journal of Comparative Psychology*, 7 (1927), 265-284.

———, and I. C. Sherman, "Sensori-motor Responses in Infants," *Journal of Comparative Psychology*, 5 (1925), 53-68.

Swan, J. G., *The Northeast Coast or Three Years' Residence in Washington Territory*. New York: Harper & Row, Publishers, 1857.

Taylor, J. H., "Innate Emotional Responses in Infants, in *Studies of Infant Behavior*. Columbus: Ohio State University Press, 1934.

Watson, J. B., and J. J. B. Morgan, "Emotional Reactions and Psychological Experimentation," *American Journal of Psychology*, 28 (1917), 163-174.

5 · The Effects of Sudden Weaning on Zulu Children

RONALD C. ALBINO AND V. J. THOMPSON

Abridged from the *British Journal of Medical Psychology*, 29 (1956), 178-210, by permission of the publisher and the authors.

As the authors indicate, there have been many speculations concerning the effects of weaning and several retrospective studies of weaning, but only a few investigations have reported direct observations of the behavior which occurs before, during, and after the weaning process. The present study, therefore, stands almost alone. It is particularly interesting because the ages of the children at weaning (15 to 24 months) and the methods of weaning differ greatly from those with which most readers of this selection are familiar.

It has been said that ". . . however long a child is fed at his mother's breast he will always be left with the conviction after he is weaned that his feeding was too short and too little" (Freud, 1940). Similar assertions that weaning is a major frustration are found elsewhere in psychoanalytic and psychiatric literature. Spock and Huschka (1938) believe weaning to be life's first major frustrating experience, while according to Schmideberg (1933) weaning from the breast may be equated with leaving the mother entirely. Bergler (1934) states that the child never resigns himself to the loss of the breast, and Klein (1940) believes that the infant reacts to weaning with a depression approaching melancholia in intensity. All these workers base their conclusions on indirect evidence obtained from the study either of adult phantasy or children's play.

Other workers have attempted to confirm the effects of weaning in indirect ways by testing the predicted correlations between various weaning practices and specific types of adult personality. The anthropological work of Erikson (1945), Mead (1935), Ritchie (1943) and Money-Kyrle (1939) exemplify this type of investigation. Other workers have attempted to show by more rigorous methods than those used by the anthropologists similar correlations between weaning practices and adult personality traits. Goldman (1948a, b), Childers and Hamil (1932), Maslow and Smilagyi (1946) and Hill (1937) found a positive relationship between the duration of breast feeding and later personality characteristics. On the other hand, Thurston and Mussen (1951) and Peterson and Spano (1946) found no such relationship.

As the studies quoted start from the initial assumption that weaning does affect the organism and are directed to testing this assumption, it is surprising that so few workers have adopted the more direct method of investigating the immediate effects of weaning. The literature on this question is more or less restricted to reports of individual cases and lacks systematic studies. For example, Bjerre (1924) reports a child weaned at six months who cried, kicked, refused the bottle, and had to be forcibly fed to prevent starvation. Grulee (1924) states that often at the time of weaning he encountered severe anorexia nervosa. Ribble (1944) studied the overt behavior of 600 infants during the nursing and weaning periods, but was less concerned with the specific effects of weaning than with the deprivation of maternal care in general and with the value of suckling for the young infant.

The study of weaning presented in this paper was prompted by the lack of information on what is, in psychoanalytic theory and in the opinion of many workers, an important procedure in the treatment of the infant. It is a preliminary survey of the material and is not quantitative except in the crudest sense. It should be noted, however, that we studied the effect of a standardized form of sudden weaning at a given age on a fairly homogeneous group of children, and in these respects our findings have greater value than isolated observations of various children weaned at various ages by different methods. The study is more or less restricted to behavioral changes and a minimum of interpretation has been made.

THE SAMPLE

(1) Experimental Group

The cases were drawn from the Polela reserve in the Bulwer district of Natal, South Africa. The people in this area form a fairly homogeneous group; they belong to the same language group, are mostly Christian and live under similar geographic, climatic, and economic conditions. A Health Center serves the area, and it was on the information of the nurses in this center responsible for the care of mothers and children that the first cases were approached. The mothers of these first cases told us of other children about to be weaned in the neighborhood, and some mothers, hearing of the project, presented themselves. This method of selection (the only possible one) resulted in our sample being drawn from two main areas with a few instances from more remote districts. However, though the sample is in no sense random, it has the advantage of being homogeneous in the sense that families living in a neighborhood are more likely to be similar than those living in different neighborhoods.

There were sixteen children in the sample, two of these being twins (10a and 10b in Table I). The sample is analyzed in Table I. The families from which the children came were virtually fatherless; the father was either away from home for long periods, or the child was illegitimate. How-

Table I

Composition of Sample

Child	Age at weaning (months)	Sex
1	22	M
2	15	M
3	15	F
4	15	M
5	16	M
6	18	F
7	19	M
8	19	F
9	17	M
10 a	21	M
10 b	21	F
11	22	F
12	18	F
13	21	F
14	24	M
15	21	M

Experimental group:
Number of cases: 16 (9 males, 7 females)
Mean age: 18.9 months
Age range of females: 15–24 months
Age range of males: 15–24 months
(Cases 10a and 10b were twins)

ever, this did not mean that the mother and child lived alone. In all but three homes at least one other adult was permanently present, and in all but one there were siblings.

The sample is small largely because of the difficulties of the terrain. The area is mountainous, poorly served by roads and most homes were a considerable distance from the health center. Because of these difficulties, as much—or perhaps more—time was spent in reaching the homes as in interviewing the parents.

(2) The Nutritional Status of the Children

In Polela, as in most of Africa, malnutrition is commonly observed. The most widespread syndrome is *kwashiorkor* (Brock and Autret, 1952). As this condition is reported to be accompanied by marked mental changes, it was essential for the nutrition of the sample to be controlled.

Each child was given a full nutritional examination before he was weaned and twice after weaning. No member of the sample was found to be markedly malnourished, and neither did the level of nutrition appear to change from the first to the last examination (which were usually separated by a period of three weeks). Nevertheless, all the children displayed some of the stigmata of mild malnutrition.

The mental changes to be expected as a result of incipient *kwashiorkor* are not discussed in the literature, but Clark (1951) has described the symptoms characteristic of the established disease. He asserts these to be more constant, characteristic, and important than the skin changes, and it may, therefore, be the case that such symptoms are to be observed early in the condition. "A child," writes Clark, "with kwashiorkor is dull, apathetic and miserable. It rarely screams or cries: a low miserable whimper is the only sign of its wretchedness. We are all familiar with the African child, who, terrified by the European doctor, fights and resists to the limit of its strength. Not so the kwashiorkor child; it will rarely, if ever, resist examination in the least degree, and will never fight or scream—its apathy being too great. Children with kwashiorkor are so dull and apathetic that if put to sit in one place they will remain sitting there until lifted up again. They never, as do so many other children, go wandering off down the road to investigate matters for themselves. If one can get a smile out of a child with kwashiorkor, one assumes it is well on the way to being cured."

Only one child (No. 1) showed any symptoms of this kind. The remainder were active and curious during all the time we observed them. Even those children who showed an apathetic immediate response to weaning were, most of the time, lively, their apathy only appearing in particular situations. The one exception (No. 1) who was markedly apathetic before weaning did not show any more marked signs of malnutrition than the others. He did, however, come from a family with an epileptic history, and it was noticed that he had frequent spells of apathy and immobility accompanied by a fixed gaze which pointed to a diagnosis of *petit mal* rather than *kwashiorkor*.

We are reasonably sure that no marked malnutrition existed in the sample and, what is more important, that no mental symptoms attributable to *kwashiorkor* were to be seen.

The Effects to be Expected from Recovery from Malnutrition

The observed results of malnutrition are apathy, and it would be expected that recovery from the disorder would be accompanied by a greater liveliness and activity. All the children in our sample showed an increasing activity, spontaneity, and aggressiveness following weaning. If the children were originally malnourished, then our findings could be explained as being due merely to improved nutrition following the administration of dried milk.

It is unlikely that this is entirely the case. The changes occurred suddenly, immediately following weaning, whereas, had they been due to improved nutrition, they would have occurred gradually. Also, no child appeared to have mental symptoms of *kwashiorkor* before weaning. It is therefore probable that the changes observed in this study were the result of weaning, but it would be unwise to assume that some of the changes of behavior may not have been partly the result of better nutrition.

The Effect of Loss of Breast Milk

Some of the effects of weaning, and especially those occurring within the first few days, may have been the result of nutritional disturbance following on the loss of breast milk. It is unlikely that this is the case, because the flow of milk is very poor by the time the child is weaned and it is also of low nutritive value. The child has also been on a diet of solid food for some months prior to weaning and the breast is more of a comforter and a supplement to the diet than a major part. Lastly, the ration of dried milk would have been sufficient to replace the breast milk lost at weaning. It is, therefore, probable that the weaning is more a psychological than a nutritional deprivation.

METHODS

(1) The Interview

The greater part of the information was obtained by means of unstructured interviews with the mothers in their own homes. Care was taken to establish good rapport with the families in the first few interviews, which was not difficult as the study was conducted from a health center with great prestige in the district. Frequent visits of workers from the center to the homes had removed all suspicion of strangers. The success of the rapport is indicated by the number of mothers who requested interviews, by the fact that mothers were very disappointed when a visit had to be canceled, and by the amount of intimate family data which occurs in the records. These interviews began approximately two weeks before weaning and continued for a further seven weeks.

At the first interview the mother was told the purpose of the study and any questions she asked were answered as fully as possible. From this point the interviews were undirected but, because the parent was aware that her child was being studied, most conversation was about that child. In later interviews a number of specific questions were asked, and these tended to become more frequent as knowledge of the child's behavior accumulated. The aim of the interview was first to obtain a broad picture of the child's behavior and later to concentrate on those aspects which appeared to have been markedly affected as a result of weaning.

The interviews were conducted through an interpreter who was a nurse and had been born in the district. Though the investigator could not speak Zulu she could understand it, and was well able to estimate how far the interpreter distorted questions and the replies to them. In both instances distortion appeared minimal.

Apart from simple distortion there are two great dangers in the use of an interpreter. Good rapport may not be established, and subtle forms of behavior may pass unobserved because the linguistic forms of a language which refer to behavior peculiar to the society, or having a special meaning for its members, cannot be translated easily into another language, or even comprehended by a foreigner. There was no doubt that rapport in all our cases were excellent. Subtle behavior may have passed unobserved, but that must merely be counted a loss. The behavior we did observe was gross, would be describable in any language and was of a kind found universally.

The interviews were conducted in the open in front of the home or, in wet weather, inside the hut. Each interview was recorded in English in longhand as nearly verbatim as possible, and the record typed within at most two days from the interview, but usually on the same night. The interviews were about an hour long. Near to, and including the day of weaning they would last up to three hours, and might be as short as fifteen minutes at the end of the period of investigation.

(2) Observations of the Child

During lulls in conversation the child's behavior was noted. This crude form of time sampling provided a fairly adequate description of the child's predominant behavioral characteristics.

(3) Photographs

Photographs were taken at frequent intervals. This did not in any way disturb the child or its family, the members of the latter appearing to be indifferent to the camera at all times.

(4) The Protocols

The final protocol on each child consists of a written verbatim record of the interview interspersed with descriptions of the child's behavior and photographs.

During the interview the investigator would often feel, without adequate evidence, that some remark or behavior had a special significance and meaning. Such interpretations were recorded, but were distinguished from records of fact. The data are thus a combination of observations of the child, reports on the child given by the parent, material on the psychological history of the family, and the investigator's impressions.

(5) Treatment of the Protocol

The protocols are all of considerable length and contain unordered information on many topics. To reduce and order this data it was tabulated thus:

(i) A topic was chosen for tabulation. The choice was determined by our judgment of what had seemed important in the behavior of the weaned children.

(ii) Each protocol was carefully studied for statements relating to behavior of the kind chosen for investigation, and all such statements were marked.

(iii) These statements were entered verbatim in a table in which a column was devoted to each day of observation and a row to each child.

(iv) This first table was further reduced by abstracting the entries into a smaller similar table. This latter table is the one on which the findings are based.

(6) The Status of the Data

The entries in any table consist of material of various kinds. In some instances they are reports made by the mother on behavior, in others they consist of direct observation.

Which type of data predominates in the tables covering one topic is normally evident from the discussion of that topic. However, it must be remarked that all the data are very variable in their reliability, and for this reason we do not claim more than preliminary validity for our findings. Every topic requires further detailed and rigorous investigation before its exact characteristics can be said to have been established.

(7) Developmental Investigation

The children were tested one day before, one day after, and one week after weaning on a modified Gesell Developmental Schedule. The following tests were used: Nos. 8-12, 18, 19-24, 26-30, 32, 33, 38-40, 42, 43, 46, 53, 54. (Gesell and Armatruda, 1941). The instructions were given to the child in its own language, and testing began only when good rapport had been established.

RESULTS

A. THE WEANING

(1) The Pre-Weaning Suckling Methods

The infants in the community studied are allowed almost unlimited access to the breast before weaning, and mothers use suckling as a method of comforting and reassuring a disturbed child. The breast is usually given to the child on demand. He may ask for it, approach the mother and open her dress, or may sit fingering the covered breast. In the latter case the mother almost immediately offers the breast to the child. She rarely allows him to whimper for any time. The child is suckled as soon as he wakes, when the mother returns after an absence, when he is crying after a fight, when he is hurt, and on any other occasion when he may need comforting. Once the breast has been given to a child he usually continues sucking until he is satisfied. Only rarely does a mother disturb a child while he is at the breast.

(2) The Method of Weaning

No detailed description of weaning is to be found in the literature. Bryant (1949), Krige (1950), and Hellmann (1948) all agree that the nursing period is lengthy. Krige puts the age of weaning at two to three years, and Bryant remarks that nursing may continue into the fourth year. Hellmann mentions that urban mothers may limit nursing to the first year. Hellmann (1948), Bryant (1949) and Doke and Vilakazi (1948) all report the use of bitter aloes (*umhlaba*) to make the breast repugnant to the child. Krige (1950) does not mention the aloes but describes a bitter medicine (called by the mothers in our sample *imFingo* medicine) mixed with "a species of fly" which is tied round the child's neck and smeared on the breast.

Table I shows the mean age of weaning in our sample to be 18.9 months; this is nearer to Hellmann's urban group than to the rural groups reported by Krige and others. It is, perhaps, the penetration of urban influences into an area as remote as Polela that is responsible for this lowering of the age of weaning. Children over three are rarely found at the breast in Polela, unless they have been suckled by a grandmother after being weaned for some extraordinary reason at an early age from the mother.

(3) Stated Reasons for Weaning

It is traditional for the paternal grandmother to decide on the time and mode of weaning. This is still true in the case of the firstborn, but less so for later siblings. In the latter case the grandmother is usually consulted on the advisability of weaning, while the mother fixes the actual date. Three of our cases were firstborn and the weaning date was fixed by the grandmother.

Each family told us that the child was being weaned because "he was old enough." On inquiry this was found to mean that it could walk, could talk well enough to be understood when demanding food, that it could obtain its own food from the pot if hungry, and could compete successfully with siblings.

(4) The Weaning Procedure

In every case the breast was smeared with the bitter juice of the aloe in the presence of the child, and it was offered to him at intervals during the remainder of the day. In all but one case a charm was tied round the child's neck to encourage the child to forget the breast and to overcome the troublesome effects of weaning. The contents of the charm and the associated magical practices (which were observed in some homes) were variable. In fourteen cases the *imFingo* medicine was used, in twelve a fly, in ten the child's saliva, in five the mother's breast milk, in one a cockroach, and in one the child's tears. The charm always contained two or more of these substances. It seems as if some are intended to work by sympathetic magic; the large appetite of the cockroach would ensure a healthy appetite for the child, and the inability of a fly to cry would prevent the child from crying. The breast milk, *imFingo*, and tears were said to make the child forget the breast. It is interesting that three homes rejected the fly as a useful charm on the grounds that it remained awake at night and might encourage the child to do the same. In two homes a "weaning specialist" who was not a diviner was called in. She performed an elaborate ritual which need not be detailed here.

In all homes weaning was considered a serious event. The approximate date is fixed some months ahead and the mother will spend the whole day of weaning at home, even during the very busy reaping season. In every case a "substitute" for the breast was provided, usually a chicken or some delicacy such as meat, bread, or sweets.

When directly questioned mothers deny weaning has any unpleasant effect on the child; an attitude contradicting strangely with their obvious anxiety and the magical precautions they observe to prevent presumed ill effects.

B. THE EFFECTS OF WEANING

(1) Reaction to Application of Aloe to the Breast

All the children were disturbed by the application of the aloe to the breast. None cried markedly for any length of time nor did they speak, all of them appearing more bewildered or afraid than excited. Two forms of disturbance were observed: an apathetic one in which the child remained quietly near to its mother with an expression of bewilderment, and an escape reaction in which the child ran away in apparent fear and remained at some distance from its mother.

(2) Behavior During the First Few Hours After Weaning

Only one child accepted the breast more than once after weaning, and this was probably because very little aloe had been used. Of the remaining cases nine accepted the breast once but refused it subsequently, and the other six refused to take the breast at any time during the interview, even though they had no experience of the bitter taste of the aloe. All but two children (both of whom refused to approach the mother when her breasts were exposed) manipulated the breasts, either touching them in a tentative way, exploring them, or holding them. Two children applied more aloe to the breast and one poked the breast with the spine of an aloe as if to injure it.

During the first two hours after weaning children were observed to become negativistic, aggressive, and fretful, and they might begin to suck their fingers or other objects more frequently than they had appeared to immediately before weaning. Some children performed stereotyped activities repetitively, and a few ignored their mothers, acting as if she did not exist. Table II lists these early reactions to weaning.

Table II

Frequency of Early Reactions to Weaning

(x = present; 0 = absent)

	Child															
Reaction	1	2	3	4	5	6	7	8	9	10a	10b	11	12	13	14	15	
Negativistic behavior (refusal to respond to mother)	x	x	x	x	x	x	x	x	x	x	x	x	0	x	x	x	15
Aggressive (attacks on mother)	0	x	0	0	x	x	x	x	x	x	x	0	0	0	x	x	10
Oral behavior (sucking of objects)	0	x	0	0	0	x	0	x	0	0	0	x		x	0	0	0	5
Repetitive behavior (repeated performance of stereotyped movements)	0	x	x	x	x	0	x	0	0	x	x	0		x	0	0	0	8
Fretfulness (whimpering and crying)	x	x	x	x	x	0	x	x	0	x	x	x	0	x	0	x	12
Apathetic (A) or escape reactions (E)	E	E	A	E	E	A	E	E	E	E	E	A	A	E	E	A	A:5 E:11

(3) Behavior Changes Subsequent to the Day of Weaning

The observed changes can be classified into those of affective behavior, aggressive behavior, social, and developmental. The child also begins to perform acts which, while not easily falling into any of these categories, are regarded by the parents with disapproval. These acts have been termed "naughty."

(4) Disturbances of Social Behavior

(*a*) *Relations with other people.* Every child showed a change in his relationship to others in the home. However, as the family constellation differs from home to home, it is not possible easily to systematize the changes which were observed.

(*b*) *Relations with mother.* Of all relationships that of the child with its mother is most disturbed. In ten children it is possible to isolate three distinct stages in which the relationship to the mother as taking a specific form. The length of the stages and their order, however, varied from case to case.

(i) A period of alternate attacking and ignoring mother, the attacks occurring mainly at night and usually being directed towards obtaining the breast. In this stage the previous close attachment to the mother appears to have been destroyed—the child rarely sitting with his mother as he did before weaning and spending little time with her. In most cases he becomes attached to another person in the household; a sibling, nursemaid, or grandmother. This stage may continue for a few days or up to as long as three weeks.

(ii) A stage in which the child makes positive attempts to gain his mother's care and attention. He becomes irritable and fretful and is described as behaving as if he were ill. He constantly demands to be nursed on his mother's back and will not allow her out of his sight. This behavior may be very marked or intermittent, alternating with features of the first stage. The duration of this stage may be from a day up to one week.

(iii) A period of increasing independence of the mother. The child begins to spend more time with others and rarely takes notice of his mother at all. He shows no anger toward her as he did in the first stage and appears to be less disturbed than he was in that stage. This independence may begin suddenly or gradually. During this period the attachment he made in the first stage to another person may continue, or he may renounce it and become fully independent.

The following four cases did not demonstrate this pattern:

Cases 1 and 2. Both children showed a gradually decreasing attachment to mother which progressed until the end of the period of observation.

Case 7. In the first week following weaning this child combined the behavior of stages (i) and (ii) above, appearing very attached to his mother but frequently attacking her and demanding the breast. By the fifth day the attachment and aggression had lessened. From then until the end of the period of observation the child became increasingly independent of his mother.

Case 8. For the first five weeks following weaning this child gradually lost her attachment to her mother and became closely attached to a sibling. In the sixth week, by which time the child appeared independent, she suddenly began to make attempts to gain her mother's attention; attempts which the mother described as "trying to be good." This behavior was still present in the seventh week.

Only in three cases was a close relationship to the mother observed at the end of the seventh week.

(c) *Changes in behavior toward others in the household.* Besides the disturbed relationship to its mother, the child also shows marked changes in its relationship to others in the household. In all but two cases the pre-weaning relationship of the child to its mother is replaced by an attachment to some other member of the family such as a nurse or a sibling. However, during the period of demanding behavior [stage (ii)] described above, this attachment becomes less intense and may be renounced altogether, but is ultimately restored again. By the seventh week only four cases remained unattached.

The increasing aggressiveness of the child also affects its relationships with other people. At first it is the mother who suffers most, but later the whole environment is attacked. In eleven cases aggression was also specifically directed at one sibling with whom the child refused to play. These aggressive attacks were provoked whenever there was a positive relation between this sibling and the mother.

(5) Increased Maturity of Behavior

Most children in the sample suddenly developed forms of behavior normally expected only of older children, such as helping in the household tasks, an increased facility in speech, and a greater independence of the support of adults. Some mothers referred to this by asserting that the child had "grown up" even though not all could state exactly what they meant by this phrase.

Twelve children began to help in the home by sweeping the floor, washing dishes, fetching water and wood, and carrying out instructions more promptly and effectively than previously. Eleven children began to imitate the behavior of other people in the home. Seven began to use new words and to talk more distinctly. Their mothers described them as trying "to talk and to name everything." In four cases this increased facility in speech was reported as early as the fifth day after weaning, in the remainder it was reported after the thirteenth day. The latter cases may obviously have been the result of maturation, but it is difficult to escape the impression that the former cases were a direct result of weaning.

Five children left home more frequently than before, going to other homes, to the river, or to herd goats and cattle, and there did not appear to be any social compulsion on the child to do these things at this particular age.

Four children suddenly began to show concern for the investigator following weaning. They offered her mats to sit on and brought her food and drinking water, all forms of behavior which were not observed before weaning.

(6) Changes in Affective Behavior

During the first week three main kinds of affective behavior which could be attributed to weaning were observed: apathy, fretfulness, or combinations of the two. The apathetic reaction was found in seven children, fretfulness in four, and five cases exhibited a combination of the two reactions.

The apathetic children became quieter than normal, sat apart from the others in the home and were reported by their mothers to be "unhappy." The reaction persisted for from three to six days. The fretful cases constantly cried or whimpered and demanded their mother's attention. The remaining children were alternately fretful and quiet.

During the remainder of the seven-week period of observation these changes in mood gradually disappeared in twelve children. The child became apparently normal so far as his mood was concerned, both as could be judged from his appearance and in the opinion of his mother. The four remaining cases continued to be described as fretful, cheeky, and bad tempered up until the end of the period of observation.

In addition to these changes of mood, it was also noticed that six children became very noisy after the first week. They talked loudly, shouted and often sang during play. In only two cases did this noisiness persist until the end of the investigation.

(7) Aggressive Behavior

Every child showed an increase in aggressive behavior following weaning, the most usual pattern taking the form of a gradual increase in extent and intensity which continued in some cases up to the end of the investigation.

In eleven cases aggression began with attacks on the mother during the first night after weaning. In seven of these children these attacks took the form of incessant fighting in which they screamed, bit, scratched, and kicked their mothers and demanded the breast. These attacks were sufficient to prevent the mother from sleeping.

Five children did not attack their mothers during the first night after weaning. Two of these slept with the grandmother, two were described as "quiet and unhappy," sitting quietly during the evening and sleeping all night. One child woke and cried a great deal during the night but did not attack his mother.

After the first night the child's aggression gradually extends to the whole family, and in one group continued until the end of the seven-week period of study, but in another it disappeared before that time.

(8) Incidence of Behavior Disapproved of by Mother

(a) Use of the term "naughty." Before weaning the mothers spoke of certain behavior as being "naughty" in the sense that it was troublesome to them. After weaning, similar behavior was considered naughty, but new troublesome behavior, for example, fighting and fretfulness, was included in the same category. It is convenient to discuss "naughty" behavior separately from such new behavior however. The main reasons for doing so are that "naughty" behavior of the kind present before weaning has a special meaning for the mothers in that it is not approved nor regarded as a pathological matter, and because it is not included in any of the other categories of behavior discussed.

Behavior which the mothers described as "naughty" can best be discussed in terms of specific acts performed by the children. These may be grouped as follows:

Play with water. Play with water was the first example of naughty behavior to be quoted by every mother. (It is not difficult to understand why water is of such importance in the home. Rivers and streams are very often far away and the fetching and carrying of water is a difficult daily task.) This includes: playing with and spilling water, and deliberately pouring it on the floor; dirtying the water by dropping dirty utensils, soil, food, and other impurities into the water bucket.

Play with fire. This includes: play with ashes; extinquishing the fire (by pouring water on it, or by removing the firewood); play with matches (upsetting the box, striking matches, or throwing them on the fire); throwing clothing, cutlery, utensils, and other valuables on to the fire.

Messing. This includes: deliberate spilling of food and water, overturning dishes containing food or freshly ground mealie-meal; mixing sand and water inside the hut, as well as any other dirty play with soil carried on inside (though not outside); throwing soil on food or dirtying food in other ways.

(b) *Methods of scoring naughty behavior.* The sixteen cases in the sample fell naturally into five grades:

(1) Children who seldom showed naughty behavior and who rarely or never needed to be punished.

(2) Children who indulged in naughty behavior and had to be reproved but who were not constantly troublesome, and who listened when reproved.

(3) Children who performed many naughty acts and often had to be punished, but who also listened when reproved.

(4) Children who had to be watched constantly and prevented from naughty behavior. These children did not listen when reproved.

(5) Children who were excessively naughty. When prevented from completing one naughty act they proceeded to be troublesome in some other way. Mothers found these children extremely difficult; punishment had no effect and the children became aggressive when reproved. (This behavior was only observed after weaning.)

(c) *Naughty behavior in the sample before weaning.* The rating of cases according to naughty behavior before weaning showed ten cases falling into grades 1 and 2, the remaining six cases being divided between grades 3 and 4. The sample is therefore composed mainly of children who were mildly naughty before weaning.

(d) *Changes in naughty behavior after weaning.* The changes in naughty behavior can be discussed conveniently in two parts, viz., (i) the day on which the change in naughty behavior was observed; and (ii) the development of naughty behavior during the seven-week post-weaning period.

(i) *The day on which the change was observed.* In every case an increase in naughty behavior was observed after weaning. This increase does not appear immediately after weaning, but usually on about the fourth or fifth day after. By the sixth day twelve cases showed an increase; only two cases showed an increase during the third week, and only one case during the sixth week after weaning.

In three cases (nos. 2, 4, 14) the children were at some stage of the seven-week post-weaning period described as "too unhappy to be naughty." This statement may provide an explanation of the relatively late appearance of the increase in naughty behavior.

In every case a marked increase in naughty behavior was observed. In eight cases this increase persists until the seventh week after weaning. In the remaining five cases observed for the full seven weeks, four have returned to their pre-weaning behavior, and one has become considerably less naughty than before weaning, being described as "trying to be good."

(9) Disturbances During the Nights Following Weaning

(a) *Disturbed sleep.* All children, except one who slept with her grandmother and took her breast, were disturbed on the night following weaning, although all had previously slept well.

In regard to subsequent nights, half the children were sleeping normally by the end of the observation period (seven weeks), but in the fifth week ten were still disturbed.

The mean intensity of the disturbance, rated on a five-point scale, for all children was greatest on the first night and decreased until the eighth day, beginning to rise again on the ninth night and reaching a second maximum in the second, third, and fourth weeks. By the end of the observational period it was at a minimum.

(b) *Changes in the normal routine of waking and going to sleep.* All children except three went to sleep later on the night after weaning than was usual for them. In one child this continued, with one night in which he went to sleep earlier than usual, until the fifth week. In most cases our information is not adequate for making any specific statements about the duration of this disturbance, but most children had several nights during the first week in which they went to sleep late.

There was not sufficient information in the records to determine whether there was any change in the time of waking.

(c) *Alterations in customary sleep posture.* Every child had a well-defined sleep posture before weaning and every child but two had changed this posture by the end of the first week after weaning, the new posture persisting until the end of the observation period (seven weeks). In most cases the change was from sleeping facing mother to sleeping turned away from her.

(d) *Changes in individual child sleeps with.* Five children who normally did not sleep with their mothers refused to sleep with their customary partner on the first night after weaning. The remainder stayed with mother with whom they normally slept. One child who had slept with a sibling went to its mother and remained with her until the end of the observational period.

(e) *Night terrors and fears.* Only two children were reported as being afraid at night before weaning, but neither showed any fears after weaning. Six children, who had not previously had either fears at night or night terrors, developed one or the other within the first week after weaning.

(f) *Dreams (excluding night terrors).* Every child dreamt at some time during the observational period, irrespective of whether it had dreamed before weaning or not, and eight children dreamed within the first week after weaning. However, there is no indication in the data of a marked increase of dreaming during the post-weaning period, though it is possible that there was a slight increase.

(g) *Changes in the attitude of the child to the breast.* The attitude of the child to the breast during the nights after weaning showed great individual variations and many different attitudes were demonstrated. Twelve children demanded the breast on the first night and cried a great deal. One child ignored the breast on the first and every other night, one refused the offered breast, and one was allowed free access to the grandmother's breast.

All cases, except one, who was given the grandmother's breast every night after weaning, had periods in which the breast was ignored. The length of the periods varied from one night to seven weeks, and did not seem to have occurred at any particular time after weaning.

The other observed reactions do not occur in any constant pattern:

(h) *Bed-wetting.* There are no obvious changes in the frequency of bed-wetting after weaning, the children continuing after weaning with the behavior which was reported of them before.

(10) Appetite Following Weaning

Eleven children were reported to have increased appetite in the first week, three showed no change, and one showed a decrease. The appetite remained greater and tended to increase up to, or beyond, the fourth week in seven children, or to the point at which reports ceased.

By the fourteenth day all children except one were reported to have an increased appetite. The one exception, which showed no change in the first week, had an increased appetite by the nineteenth day.

In some cases the increase was very marked, the child stealing food and taking it from siblings, and the mother remarking that she was unable to satisfy the child. The increase was at first more marked in the morning, the child often waking very early and demanding food.

(a) *Changes in eating pattern.* Various changes in eating pattern were observed. Some children refused to be fed by their mothers and threw tantrums if she attempted to do so; others demanded to be fed by mother.

Instead of eating in its accustomed manner with its siblings, the child would often eat on its own away from them. Most children developed a preference for meat and milk rather than the usual diet of porridge.

(b) *Demand for food and drink every night.* Every child after weaning woke frequently during the night and demanded food or drink, whereas they were not reported as having done so before weaning.

(c) *Probability of these effects being simply due to deprivation of breast milk.* The increased appetite at weaning might possibly be simply physiological due to deprivation of breast milk and not a psychological effect of deprivation of the breast.

This is unlikely, for the child's main diet has been solid food for some months prior to weaning and the amount of milk given by the mother is very little. One fact that supports the view that it is psychological is that the increase becomes more marked as time passes. If it were simply physiological, one would expect the appetite first to increase up to the level necessary to make up for the loss of breast milk and then to remain constant. However, without a careful determination of the amount of milk fed to a child in the few weeks prior to weaning it cannot definitely be stated that the increased appetite is psychologically caused, although it is our impression that the latter is the case.

(11) The Developmental Schedule

Only eleven children could be tested on the modified Gesell Schedule. No changes in developmental level were observed in any child.

(12) Reactions of Children Weaned Earlier than Usual

In the course of the investigation we collected reports from nurses and mothers of the effect of early weaning on children. The number of cases that were reported fully were few, and it is not advisable to discuss the results systematically. However, it appears that the earlier the weaning occurs the more marked are the aggressive symptoms. Children show intense temper tantrums and destructiveness, cry a great deal, and do not sleep at night. It is in the case of early weanings that mothers have been known to leave home temporarily and to leave the child in charge of another person, being themselves unable to tolerate the greatly disturbed child.

DISCUSSION

There is little doubt, in view of our previous arguments, that weaning in our sample is mainly psychological and that, therefore, its observed effects are not due to nutritional disturbance. It is important, also, to note that in addition to the weaning there is a rejection of the child by its mother, and that she may be the source of the observed effects.

Because of the difficulty of making inferences from behavior to psychological states in an alien group, on account of linguistic and other obstacles, we have restricted ourselves almost entirely to a discussion of observed behavior. We have not, as a result, been able to confirm the psychoanalytic views on the psychological effects of weaning, which refer specifically to states of mind. Our findings do, however, in a general way, confirm the general hypothesis of the psychoanalysts that weaning is disturbing and that the intensity of the effect is proportional to age.

The reaction to weaning varies from child to child in form and intensity. Every child was disturbed, but the disturbance could be a transitory upset lasting only a week or so, or a gross change in the personality of the child which was still present at the end of seven weeks after weaning. The constancy of the weaning procedure implies that the variability is due largely to the previous history and constitution of the child, and we must assume that the effects of weaning cannot be considered without reference to those factors.

It is also evident that the immediate gross disturbance from weaning is usually short-lived. Most of the children in our sample were normal in the sense of being fairly well, though not fully, adapted members of their society seven weeks after weaning.

If any permanent changes do occur as a result of weaning they are not due to the persistent effect of immediate reactions, such as aggression, but are rather the readjustments of the organism to the effects of weaning. The event of weaning seems to force upon the child the necessity of altering his behavior in certain ways. That this is so is clear in the case of the child's personal relationships. In all the children the mother comes to be regarded in a different way, the previous close attachment to her, which has existed from birth, being replaced by an apparent indifference which lasts for some weeks. Also, the child develops new relationships of both a positive and negative kind with siblings which in many instances persist and, together with the new attitude to the mother, form a new matrix for the child's social behavior.

The particular manner in which the relationship becomes reorganized varies from child to child. So far as the mother is concerned, the child in some cases not only renounces her but is at some time very hostile towards her, although in some the child apparently merely renounces his mother; in others it is difficult for him to renounce her altogether and he makes attempts to regain her affection.

Most children were ambivalent, being alternatively hostile and affectionate towards their mothers. Together with the ambivalence, and perhaps being part of it, are attempts to overcome the hostility. Child No. 8, for example, who, the mother asserted, was "trying to be good," showed this clearly. Further evidence of ambivalence is seen in the fact that all but five children continued to sleep with their mothers after weaning, though they tended to sleep facing away from her. One child, who had previously slept with a sibling, went to its mother on the night of weaning.

It is interesting to note that the aggressiveness towards the mother spreads into the environment. In this respect again weaning must be regarded as not merely affecting the child as an isolated organism, but as an event which disturbs both it and all of the small society in which it lives.

Thus, it seems that weaning is an event which produces great changes in the child's social relationships. The important question is how permanent are these changes. For the majority of our sample the change towards the mother is permanent in its form—the child never again recovering the close pre-weaning attachment to her. And their permanence is also seen in the changed relationships to the siblings.

After this readjustment of family relationships, the most interesting finding is the increased maturity of the child. The independence, greater facility in the use of language, and the appearance of concern for strangers, all of which persist, give the impression (which the mothers also have and which they seem to expect) that the child has grown up and is no longer an infant. It would seem as if weaning, far from being a merely disorganizing experience at this age, is also a socializing and maturing influence. In earlier weanings, so far as can be inferred from our few reports, this does not appear to be the case. In them the disorganization of behavior is very gross and would appear to outweigh any socializing influences. Also, these early cases do not appear to be able to adjust so easily to the loss of the mother as the later cases, for they continue to be greatly disturbed for a longer period.

If one looks at the nature of the socialization and of the changed social relationships of the child, it appears that they are the result of two factors. A replacement of the mother as a love object by others in the environment (there is perhaps also an aggressiveness towards any object that is identified with the mother, as we observed in twelve cases). That is, the attitudes to the mother are displaced to the environment. The second factor is the isolation of the child from the environment. He sits alone and goes off on expeditions of his own and also takes note of strangers who previously were not part of the family. It would seem as if the child has given up his close dependence upon others and on the family as a result of his mother's rejection and has been forced, by his hostility, to isolate himself and to become an independent being. It may be, if this interpretation is true, that the child in adapting to the effects of weaning undergoes a sudden increase of ego development. That is, he becomes more aware of himself as an independent entity separated from this environment, and takes active steps to adapt himself to this environment, and it to him.

The one symptom which showed the greatest tendency to continue was the aggressiveness. Taken in conjunction with the increased maturity of the child, it implies that weaning produces an individual both more mature and more inclined to make active demands upon his environment than the unweaned child.

The two immediate reactions of apathy or of "excitement" are interesting in that they appear very similar to reactions observed by Ribble in children deprived of maternal support and which Bowlby (personal communication) has also observed in deprived children. The determinants of the two reactions are not evident from our data, and neither is it clear whether the later behavior of children showing the two reactions differs. The variability of pre- and post-weaning behavior within the two groups is as great as that between them, and with such a small sample using qualitative methods it is impossible to be definite. It seems, however, that these two reactions are fundamental in the reaction of infants to deprivation, and it would be worth investigating whether there might not be genetic as well as environmental factors present.

Aggressiveness, besides being the most persistent of all the immediate reactions, seems to tend to increase rather than to diminish and may, or may not, be accompanied by an increased naughtiness. It begins very soon after weaning, usually on the first night, and may be considered the most immediate reaction to weaning. It is, also, the most disturbing reaction, as it is the main cause of the disturbances in the child's social relationships, and especially of his relationship with his mother. Its continuance and its frequency both seem to imply that it is of very great importance. Naughtiness, on the other hand, appears later than aggression and must be regarded as a secondary effect resulting from an organized attempt to control the situation. One may, perhaps, interpret the aggressiveness as a nonspecific reaction directed at first against the mother and then the environment and the naughtiness as a more specific and controlled direction of the aggression. If this is the case, then we again have evidence that weaning intensifies, after an initial disorganization, the controlling mechanisms in behavior. The undifferentiated and more primitive aggression gives place to the performance of acts with an aggressive aim, but of a kind which are known by the child to cause greater disturbance in the family. (It will be noted that all the naughty acts are highly directed in that the child chooses just those forms of behavior, such as spilling water, which are very disturbing in the society in which he finds himself.) There may be a further reason for the persistence of aggression. It seems that so far as the aggression is not directed to the mother and does not disorganize the social relationships of the child or its own activities it may be regarded as a socially useful form of behavior, for it enables the child to gain its own ends. This, and the fact that a certain amount of aggression is encouraged and tolerated in Zulu society, may be the reason why this change persists; as well as being the main initiator of the changes, aggression may eventually become a valuable result of weaning, once it is directed in a socially approved manner.

The changes tend to show a cyclic character which is particularly evident in the relationship of the child to its mother. We have already noticed that he may, after a period of attacking his mother, change his behavior to a more demanding form. This is replaced later by attacks, and the alternation continues for a period, when, in most cases, the child gives up these responses to its mother. This alternation, which was characteristic of all the behavior we observed, makes it seem as if the child is attempting, in an active way, to adapt himself to the situation of being rejected by his mother. He does not merely react by frustrated behavior, but undertakes various activities which may be regarded as attempts, first, to restore the mother to her original position and, later, to exist without her support. Again, it seems as if the child is compelled by the weaning to become a mature and independent person, and achieves this only after a period of readjustment involving several trial solutions; for example, demanding the mother, trying to please her, attaching himself to another person, aggressively trying to influence his mother by naughty behavior. The immediate reaction seems to be one of attack and aggression which, in the face of the frustration received, is to be expected. It is only after this preliminary disorganized form of behavior that the attempt at adaptation occurs. It is important to emphasize here that weaning does not appear to be simply a disturbance in response to frustration which gradually settles down, but that it involves, after a preliminary disturbance, a series of active adaptive changes in the organism, and may, at the age of about eighteen months, be a most powerful stimulus to ego development.

References

Bergler, E., *Imago*, 20 (1934), 330-376.

Bjerre, P., *Psychoanalytical Review*, 11 (1924), 1-27.

Brock, J. E., and M. Autret, *Kwashiorkor in Africa*. Geneva: World Health Organization, 1952.

Bryant, A. T., *The Zulu People*, Pietermaritzburg, S. Africa: Shuter and Shooter, 1949.

Childers, A. T., and B. M. Hamil, *American Journal of Orthopsychiatry*, 2 (1932), 134-142.

Clark, M., *East Africa Medical Journal*, 28 (1951), 229.

Doke, C. M., and W. Vilakazi, *Zulu-English Dictionary*. Johannesburg: Witwatersrand University Press, 1948.

Erikson, E. H., *Psychoanalytical Study of the Child*, 1 (1945), 319-350.

Freud, S., *International Journal of Psychoanalysis*, 21 (1940), 27-84.

Gesell, A., and C. S. Amatruda, *Developmental Diagnosis*. New York: Harper & Row, Publishers, 1941.

Goldman, F., *Journal of Personality*, 17 (1948a), 83-103.

————, *Journal of Personality*, 19 (1948b), 189-196.

Grulee, C. G., *International Archives of Pediatrics*, 3 (1924), 363-364.

Hellmann, E., *Rooiyard: A Sociological Survey of an Urban Slum Yard*. London: Oxford University Press.

Hill, J., *Psychiatric Quarterly*, 2 (1937), 356-382.

Klein, M., *International Journal of Psychoanalysis*, 21, (1940), 125-153.

Krige, E. J., *The Social System of the Zulus*. Pietermaritzburg, S. Africa: Shuter and Shooter, 1950.

Maslow, A. H., and K. Smilagyi, *Journal of Abnormal and Social Psychology*, 41 (1946), 83-85.

Mead, M., *Sex and Temperament*. New York: William Morrow & Co., Inc., 1935.

Money-Kyrle, R., *Superstition and Society*. London: Hogarth Press, 1939.

Peterson, C., and F. Spano, *Character and Personality*, 10 (1941), 62-66.

Ribble, M. A., in J. McV. Hunt, ed., *Personality and the Behavior Disorders*. New York: The Ronald Press Company, 1944.

Ritchie, J. E., "The African as Suckling and as Adult," *Rhodes-Livingstone Paper* No. 9, 1943.

Schmideberg, M., *British Journal of Medical Psychology*, 13 (1933), 313-327.

Spock, B., and M. Huschka, in G. Blumer, ed., *Practitioner's Library of Medicine and Surgery*, Vol. 13, 757-779. New York: Appleton-Century-Crofts, Inc., 1938.

Thurston, J. R., and P. H. Mussen, *Journal of Personality*, Vol. 19, No. 4 (1951).

IV—LANGUAGE DEVELOPMENT

1 · The Expressive Nature of Early Vocalizations

M. M. LEWIS

Reprinted from pages 26-37 of *Infant Speech*, 1936, by permission of Humanities Press Inc. and Routledge & Kegan Paul Ltd.

Is infant vocalization simply random behavior? Are sounds produced in an unpredictable and meaningless way? Lewis thinks not and presents a coherent theory of early speech.

In describing infant sounds, Lewis uses the symbols of the International Phonetic Alphabet. A description of this may be found in Webster's New International Dictionary. Many of the symbols used refer to sounds which are frequently designated by the same letters in English. However, some of the symbols of the International Phonetic Alphabet refer to sounds that do not occur in English.

The newborn child in a state of discomfort utters vowel-like cries, ranging from e to ɑ, and frequently nasalized. Soon the semiconsonant ŭ intervenes, followed by h, l, and ŋ. Finally the nasal front consonants m and n appear. Contrasting with these are the sounds he utters when comfortable. At first these are non-nasalized vowels, of indeterminate quality, interspersed with the back consonants g, g, x, k, and r. Then front consonants appear, mainly non-nasal, p, b, t, and d, together with the corresponding nasals m and n.

What light does this analysis throw upon the expressive character of the child's early sounds? The answer lies in considering their phonetic nature, that is, in noticing which movements of the vocal organs are required to make them.

PHONETIC FEATURES OF THE CHILD'S EARLIEST SOUNDS

We may first of all be allowed to recall that phonetically there is no clear line of division between vowels and consonants. If in the course of utterance we contract some part of the vocal apparatus so that complete or partial closure results, the sound produced has the quality of a consonant; in the absence of such closure the sound has the quality of a vowel. Evidently there will be instances of sounds which will seem partly vocalic, partly consonantal, in character. For example, if when uttering the vowel

149

u we contract the lips still further, the sound takes on the quality of a consonant (ŭ); in this way we may speak of the child's ŭ and ŭe as semi-vocalic.

The child's earliest sounds, as we have seen, are vocalic; consonants begin to appear in his utterance when the contractions at different points of the vocal apparatus become more definite. We may regard this as one instance of that increase in definiteness which marks all the child's motor activities. During a period, therefore, which extends over several months, it is not always easy to decide whether a given sound is vocalic or consonantal.

With this reservation, we may examine the phonetic characteristics of the child's utterance, and consider the relation between the specific sounds and the effective states which they express.

THE EARLIER DISCOMFORT CRIES

We begin with the principle that there is an innate tendency for a child to vocalize when in discomfort. If he were merely to open his mouth widely and phonate, the sound would be heard as a and this does occasionally occur. We might call this the primary open vowel, for when we produce this sound a, the tongue is in a more or less relaxed position, resting on the floor of the mouth, and the lips are also in a medium position between the extreme rounding which occurs in u and the extreme stretching which occurs in i.

But many of the earliest cries of the child are not simply produced by opening the mouth as widely as possible. He is in discomfort, and as Darwin has pointed out (1873) the mouth of a child in such circumstances tends to take on "an oblong, almost squarish outline," the upper lip being raised by the contraction of the muscles round the eye—a reflex mechanism, as he thought, to protect the eyeball from becoming engorged by the increase of blood pressure in the head and face. Darwin himself was not inclined to lay much stress on this explanation, but of the accuracy of the observation there can be no doubt—clear instances are given in the photographs of crying children in his book.

Let us notice what happens to the open sound a when the mouth is drawn into this oblong shape; it evitably changes its quality and becomes a —precisely the sound which is most characteristic of the child's earliest cries. This possibility, that the shape of the mouth—itself due to expressive muscular contractions—might give rise to expressive differences of speech, occurred to Darwin, although he did not attempt to apply it to the cry of the child. Following up the clue given by him, we can say that the characteristic form of the child's cry a may certainly be called expressive, for it is the direct vocal manifestation of the contractions which occur in a state of discomfort.

We are not saying here that the muscular contractions are the "cause" and the sound a the "effect." What we are pointing out rather is this: that specific contractions are the innate accompaniment of a state of discomfort, that vocalization is another accompaniment of this state, and that when vocalization and the contractions occur simultaneously, we hear the sound a.

With this clue before us, let us now look at the other sounds which we have found to be characteristic of the child's earliest cries. First we have the further narrowing of the primary open sound a in the direction of ε and e. Now it is interesting to notice that these sounds may be produced if the *pitch* of the voice is raised while uttering a.* And, as we are again reminded by Darwin, shrillness is an expressive characteristic of the cries of animals when in pain. Thus e and ε may also be regarded as expressive in nature: They are the vocalic modifications which result from the expressive raising of pitch during a state of discomfort.

A further marked characteristic of utterance at this stage is nasalization. This too we may show to have an expressive basis. For nasalization in speech occurs very frequently when we wish to produce a greater volume of sound; it is well known that some public speakers tend unconsciously to nasalize their speech in the effort to increase its carrying power. The volume of sound is certainly increased by nasalization: Paget, working with his artificial resonators, found that the addition of a nasal cavity (the equivalent of nasalization in human speech) invariably had this effect.

We may reasonably suppose that nasalization occurs in the child's utterance, as he tries to scream his loudest under the stress of hunger or other discomfort. If this is so, nasalization may well be regarded as expressive in the Darwinian sense, in that it is a quality taken on by the child's cries as he tries—unconsciously—to increase their volume. This is a point of some importance when we come to consider the nasal consonants which appear later.

We pass now to the group of sounds ŭ, l, ŋ, h which commonly occur interspersed among the child's early vocalic cries: ŭ and h from the outset, the others later. Phonetically, these four sounds may all be characterized in this way: They occur during the utterance of a vowel if the vocal organs are momentarily either allowed to relax or to contract. The child does not utter one prolonged vowel; he produces a series of rhythmical cries: for instance, ŭe-ŭe-ŭe . . . or le-le-le . . . , the one vowel e in fact being broken up into a series of cries, as the mouth partially contracts for a moment before letting out the next bellow. The contraction however is not usually sharp enough to produce the effect of a definite consonant.

Now there are, roughly speaking, four points in the vocal apparatus at which a vocalic cry might be modified: the lips, the front of the tongue

---

* This has been demonstrated experimentally by Engelhardt and Gehrcke (1930) by means of gramophone records played at varying speeds.

against the hard palate, the back of the tongue against the soft palate, and the vocal chords. The first of these modifications would give the quality of ŭ, the second that of l, the third that of g, or with nasalization ŋ, the fourth that of h. For if the lips partially contract while a vowel is being uttered, the semiconsonantal ŭ will tend to appear; the vowel a or e or whatever it may be, takes on for the moment the character of ŭ. Again, if the tip or blade of the tongue happens to touch the hard palate— while the sides of the tongue are still lowered to allow the breath to pass out—l results. This may happen during the utterance of any vowel, the main part of the tongue being still in position for that vowel. Again, during the utterance of the nasalized vowels which tend to appear in crying, the back of the tongue is raised and the uvula correspondirgly relaxed so that the breath may pass out through the nasal passage. If now the back of the tongue is contracted further toward the soft palate, ŋ results. Finally, if the vocal chords, which are being held close together during the production of a vowel, are relaxed for a moment, h appears; to cite Jones (1927), "h is the fricative sound heard as the air passes through the open glottis, the other organs being in position for the following vowel." In other words, h is the sound heard if the voice is momentarily withheld in the act of uttering any vowel.

Each of these four semiconsonants is therefore expressive. The child's vocal organs function rhythmically; as Wundt points out (1924), we may regard this as an instance of the rhythm which characterizes the utterance of all animals. The child, in fact, utters not one prolonged cry, but a series of cries, and as the vocal apparatus is contracted or relaxed at the beginning of each successive cry, the listener hears a modified sound which is consonantal in quality. Then, according to the place at which the modification takes place, it is heard as something approaching ŭ, l, ŋ, or h.

Thus we are able to show that all the chief characteristics of the child's discomfort cries—vocalic and consonantal—are expressive, in the accepted Darwinian sense of this term.

THE EARLIER COMFORT SOUNDS

Let us pass to the comfort sounds. Here again we begin with the principle that there is an innate tendency for the child to vocalize when in a state of comfort, although this vocalization makes its appearance only when the expression of discomfort is already well established. But why should the sounds uttered in comfort take the form of the back consonants, g, x, g, k, and "guttural" r?

The first point to notice is that all these five consonants are produced at the same spot in the mouth—by raising the back of the tongue so that it comes into contact with, or approaches, the soft palate (velum). The difference between the pair of spirants, **g** and **x**, and the corresponding stops g, **k** is merely that the former pair is uttered during narrowing by a continuous emission of breath, the latter pair by a full closure followed by an explosion of breath. Further, in the first pair, **x** differs from **g** only in being unvoiced, that is, there is little or no vibration of the vocal chords in its production; in the second pair, **k** differs from g precisely in the same way. And "guttural" **r** is produced at the same point of the mouth, or slightly farther back, by a rapid series of broken contacts between the back of the tongue and the termination of the soft palate— the uvula. In the case of the child, this **r** may be regarded as a rolled form of the sound **g.**

This voiced spirant **g** is the most characteristic sound of the group. It is a sound which—as made by the child—does not happen to occur in any European language, with the result that different observers have resorted to different signs in recording its occurrence in children's cries. It is the sound indicated by Stern (1922) as *rr* in *erre,* for he tells us of this, that it resembles both guttural *r* and *ch* as in *doch*—a good description of the spirant **g.** This is the sound, he adds, that is the earliest comfort sound to be noted by the majority of observers—the sound recorded by Preyer (1889) in *örrö, arra.* To this we may add further that from Hoyer's account (1924) it must be the sound recorded by him as ̇g.

Why should the raising of the back of the tongue toward the soft palate occur in a state of comfort? One answer—that of Grégoire (1933)— is that when the child is lying comfortably on his back, his tongue naturally lolls against his soft palate, producing the characteristic sounds. But we can perhaps suggest a more exact answer. Under what conditions do these sounds appear? On this point, observers are fully agreed. The normal child during his first weeks, manifests pleasure, if at all, mainly after feeding: when he is lying satisfied in his mother's arms. It is then that "smiles" and gurgling noises appear, not very easily distinguishable at first from belchings, gruntings, and signs of "wind." In the case of K, observed by me, the first certain instance of **g** occurred when he was just six weeks old, lying on his back very comfortable after a feed. A few faint utterances of this sound appeared interspersed among grunting noises, accompanied by those face and lip movements which are regarded as signs of "wind."

This is a possible clue to the origin of back consonants in states of comfort. The movements which take place in the back of the child's mouth as he expels "wind" are, if accompanied by phonation, heard by us as guttural grunting, some of which approximate **g.**

There is, however, a further condition which determines the child's utterance in a state of comfort after a feed. Some swallowing movements are likely to occur, partly because of the excess of saliva which will have remained in the mouth, partly perhaps as the persistence of reflex movements of those organs which have been working rhythmically throughout the period of feeding. Now the movement of swallowing involves just that approximation of the back of the tongue to the soft palate which, if made during phonation, would be heard as sounds of the g-type.

It is clear then that the production of this back consonant g probably arises directly out of the movements intimately connected with the business of feeding in which the child has just been engaged. If we are willing to accept the principle that there is an innate tendency in the child to utter a cry expressive of his state of satisfaction, then the facts we have mentioned help to show why the cry should take on the form of this specific back consonant g. It is the vocal manifestation of the fact that the child is making guttural movements expressive of satiety while uttering a cry of satisfaction. As for the sounds x, k, g, and uvular r, these are all either voiced or unvoiced variations of g, and have the same expressive origin; they arise as movements inherently connected with the state of satiety which they manifest.

Do these back consonants express other states of comfort in addition to satiety? On this point the published records are not quite clear, the observer usually indicating no more than the fact that the child was making the sounds in a state of comfort. In my own observations I certainly noticed that throughout the child's earlier months, whenever he used back consonants with the characteristic intonation expressing comfort, it was immediately after a feed. But Preyer, Stern, and Hoyer all give cases of the occurrence of these consonants as expressive of contentment without mentioning definitely that this was a state of satiety: and a curious instance of the wider function of the expressive back consonants occurs in an early account of the blind deaf-mute Laura Bridgman given by Lieber (1851). "Frequently I have heard Laura expressing a feeling of satisfaction by a subdued tone, somewhat between chuckling and a slight groaning." He adds quaintly, "I would have said *grunting,* as more accurately expressing the sound, had I not felt reluctant to use this word in connexion with that amiable and delicate being."

It is clear that a transition of this kind might readily occur, so that sounds expressive of satiety would ultimately become expressive of other states of satisfaction. In the child's earliest weeks, as Charlotte Bühler points out (1930), the *only* time when he expresses satisfaction at all is when he is satiated, immediately after feeding; when he is not asleep, he is either crying, taking food, or resting peacefully after feeding: Only in this last state does he express satisfaction. As time goes on, the periods of waking satiety grow longer: The child begins to notice—with apparent pleasure—the things about him, and then to play. And because these periods of contentment are extensions of his states of satiety, the guttural sounds which expressed his satisfaction after feeding will tend to become expressive of his comfort in general.

THE FRONT CONSONANTS

We come finally to those consonants which are so important in relation to the first "words" uttered by the child: the nasals m, n, the dentals t, d, and the labials p, b. What are the physiological conditions of their formation; are they to be regarded as expressive?

The first point to notice is that m falls into a group with the labials p, b; n into a group with the dentals t, d. The three consonants of each group are formed by contact at the same part of the mouth. In the labial group, m, p, b, the lips are brought together; but for m the uvula is lowered towards the back of the tongue so that the breath passes out through the nose in a continuous stream, the difference between p and b being only that the former is unvoiced. In the same way, in the dental group, all three consonants n, t, d are formed by contact of the fore part of the tongue against the upper gum ridge. For n again, the lowering of the uvula allows the nasal emission of breath, while the difference between t and d is once more only of voice. Thus we have a labial group m, p, b, and a dental group n, t, d; the nasal member of each group being characteristic of a state of discomfort.

The connection between these labial and linguo-dental movements and those involved in sucking is obvious at once. It has often been mentioned in a general way, as for instance by Wundt (1924) and Jesperson (1923). But no attempt has, I think, hitherto been made to analyze the phonetic basis of this similarity.

If we observe the movements made by the lips and tongue in sucking, we find that it is essential for the lips to be brought together, while simultaneously, or immediately afterwards, the front of the tongue is pressed against the upper gum ridge. The former of these movements is precisely that involved in saying m, p, or b; the latter in saying n, t, or d. How then do these consonants become expressive of discomfort or comfort?

FRONT CONSONANTS EXPRESSIVE OF DISCOMFORT

A common observation helps us here; at a very early age the child is found to be making anticipatory sucking movements when he is hungry or expects to be fed. Darwin (1877) noticed it long ago in the case of his own child, thirty-two days old; and the fact has been repeatedly corroborated by careful observers such as Bühler and Hetzer (1928) who noticed it of children in their second month. Curti also (1930) reports some Russian observations which go to show that if the child, in the third or fourth week, is merely held in the normal feeding position, this will be sufficient to evoke sucking movements, in the absence of any other stimulus.

In the case of K, these sucking movements were very marked. From his first days he was accustomed to having a bib tied under his chin before being given his food. After his thirty-fifth day, when the bib was tied at feeding time he definitely pursed his lips into the sucking position, before he was brought within reach of the food. Nine days later, at the time of his evening feed, this reaction was most definite. "He was crying lustily. His mother put the bib under his chin. His cries gradually lessened, and ceased within about 30 seconds. Then he very definitely began to make sucking movements. His lips were pursed, and the tip of his tongue slightly protruded."

We are here introducing a third factor into our discussion—that of training or conditioning—in addition to our two principles of Darwinian expression and the differentiation of affective states. But it is a factor that is certainly not in dispute. We may take it as a generally accepted principle that when an organism has experienced a pattern of events, the recurrence of any salient item of this pattern will tend to cause the organism to behave as though the rest of the pattern were present. Here the child when hungry has felt the bib being tied under his chin, and this followed by feeding; sooner or later the touch of the bib when he is hungry, or the mere sight of preparations for food, will evoke sucking movements appropriate to feeding.

It is evident that if the child phonates while making these anticipatory sucking movements, the sounds produced will approximate to the labial and dental consonants. If, further, he is in a state of discomfort such as hunger, and phonates *nasally*—as we have seen he does—then the consonants produced will inevitably be m and n. Many observers have noticed that these nasal consonants appear when the child is hungry, but I do not think that they have been shown to arise out of anticipatory sucking movements made during nasal phonation.

The occurrence of these front consonants is so marked—they are indeed the first definite sounds that a casual observer of a child notices—that their origin has sometimes been ascribed to imitation. Wundt, for instance reminds us that mothers commonly make a sound like *mum-mum* when coaxing their infants to take food, and obviously this might have some influence upon the child's own utterance. But it is clear that imitation can at most be only a secondary factor in the production of these front consonants. For neither blindness nor deafness in children seems to prevent their occurrence. Wundt himself cites the case of a deaf-mute aged nineteen who habitually used *mum* to signify food. Jespersen doubting the influence of imitation on the production of the front consonants, suggests that we should find that they regularly occur in blind children also. Since the publication of his work a case has been described by Bean (1932); the child, who was afflicted with congenital cataract in both eyes, nevertheless uttered ŭa, ŭa in states of discomfort soon after birth, and *mmuh* at the age of 0-3, 2, when hungry.

There can be little doubt that the origin of the nasals, m, n, is that they are expressive of hunger; that is, they are the audible manifestation of the mouth movements which are bound up with that state. And because the expression of hunger is the most important function of the child's utterance during his earliest months, these nasal sounds become one of the chief means by which the child enters into linguistic communication with those about him.

FRONT CONSONANTS EXPRESSIVE OF COMFORT

The appearance of front consonants—**p, b, t, d,** sometimes **m** and **n**—in a state of comfort is not so easy to observe as the consonants expressive of discomfort. The child when contented does not articulate with the same definiteness as when moved by the urgency of discomfort. Yet if one listens carefully, one hears sooner or later, emerging from the welter of semiarticulate guttural sounds, consonants which approximate to the labials and dentals.

They occur when the child is contented; chiefly, that is, either after a feed or when he delightedly perceives his food already before him. If we bear in mind this fact of their appearance, their expressive nature is at once evident. They are the vocal manifestation of sucking movements, made usually without nasal urgency, the child uttering them while phonating contentedly on seeing food, or while continuing to make sucking movements after a feed. And, just in the same way as the back consonants are expressive of satiety, these front consonants may ultimately become expressive of other states of contentment.

One tendency will clearly bring all the child's early consonants into the stream of contented utterance—the rise of babbling or vocal play. And an important feature of this activity, we shall show, is that even consonants which are primarily expressive of discomfort may become transformed into play, and so appear in a state of contentment.

RESULTS

Our phonetic analysis of the child's earliest utterance has enabled us to demonstrate its expressive character, in the Darwinian sense. In particular, we have found that the origin of the earlier back consonants and of the latter front consonants lies almost entirely in the expression of hunger and of its satisfaction. This is not surprising, for by far the greatest part of the child's life in his earliest months is taken up by food and sleep. And it is inevitable that any utterance made by the child in connection with feeding should become shaped by the movements of feeding; in discussing the nature of language we cannot evade the fact that the organs of utterance are also the organs of sucking.

We have shown also that some order and regularity may be found in what has often been regarded as the chance and chaotic occurrence of the child's earliest sounds. We have shown that they fall into groups which may be explained by referring to three generally accepted factors— the principle of Darwinian expression, the differentiation of affective states, and the occurrence of behavior anticipatory of a sequence of events.

References

Bean, C. H., "An Unusual Opportunity to Investigate the Psychology of Language," *Journal of Genetic Psychology,* 40 (1932), 181-202.

Bühler, C., *The First Year of Life.* New York: The John Day Company, Inc., 1930.

————, and H. Hetzer, "Das erste Verstandnis der Ausdruck im ersten Lebensjahr," *Zeitschrift fur Psychologie,* 107 (1928), 50-61.

Curti, M. W., *Child Psychology.* New York: Longmans, Green & Company, 1930.

Darwin, C., "The Biography of an Infant," *Mind* 2 (1877), 285-294.

————, *The Expression of the Emotions.* New York: Appleton-Century-Crofts, Inc., 1873.

Engelhardt, V., and E. Gehrcke, "Uber die Abhändigkeit der Vokale von der absoluten Tonhohe," *Zeitschrift fur Psychologie,* 115 (1930).

Grégoire, A., "L'apprentissage de la parole pendant les deux premières annees de l'enfance," *Journal de Psychologie,* 30 (1933), 375-389.

Hoyer, A., and G. Hoyer, "Uber die Lallsprache eines Kindes," *Zeitschrift fur Angewandte Psychologie,* 24 (1924), 363-384.

Jespersen, O., *Language, Its Nature, Development and Origin.* New York: Henry Holt & Company, Inc., 1923.

Jones, D., *The Pronunciation of English,* (2nd ed.), 1927.

Lieber, F., "On the Vocal Sounds of Laura Bridgman," *Smithsonian Contributions to Knowledge,* 2 (1851).

Preyer, W., *The Mind of the Child,* Vol. II. "The Development of the Intellect." New York: Appleton-Century-Crofts, Inc., 1889.

Stern, C., and W. *Die Kindersprache.* Leipzig: Borth, 1922.

Wundt, W., *Völkerpsychologie.* Leipzig: Krones, 1924.

2 · Social Conditioning of Vocalizations

HARRIET L. RHEINGOLD, JACOB L. GEWIRTZ, AND HELEN
W. ROSS

Reprinted from the *Journal of Comparative and Physiological Psychology*, 52 (1959), 68-73, by permission of the authors and publisher.

In Skinner's terms, the "reinforcing" of a response is the standard way of conditioning an instrumental response. The present study shows that the vocal responses of three-month-old infants can be conditioned in this manner. Differences in the amount of social conditioning which is received by different groups of children may explain why speech development differs greatly between socio-economic classes, between home-reared and institutionalized children, and between twins and singletons (see selection IV-4).

By three months of age the infant gives a well-defined social response to the appearance of adults. He looks at them intently, smiles, becomes active, and vocalizes. This behavior is repeated again and again in sequence. Adults often respond to these acts of the infant; they may only look at the child, but they may also smile at him, touch or caress him, or vocalize in return. Frequently one observes "answering" social and, in particular, vocal play between mother and child. The adults' responses may therefore play an important part in maintaining and developing social responsiveness in the child (Rheingold, 1956). The principles of operant conditioning (Skinner, 1953) suggest that some of these adult responses, functioning as reinforcers, may affect the development of the child's social behavior (Gewirtz, 1956). Thus, smiling in the infant has been shown to respond to conditioning (Brackbill, 1958).

The present study was an attempt to condition vocalizations in infants. Vocalizations were selected for study because they seem to provide an index of the whole social response (Rheingold, 1956). The reinforcing stimulus was a complex of social acts which resembled those an attentive adult might naturally make when a child vocalizes. If temporal contiguity between the infant's vocalization and the reinforcing stimulus, which follows it, brings about an increase in the vocalizations, conditioning may be said to have occurred. The possibility that the reinforcing stimulus may also have functioned as an arouser of vocalizations will be considered. In any case, the results of the study should provide further understanding about the development of social responsiveness, as well as of speech.

METHOD

Two parallel experiments were carried out in sequence. In the first, 11 babies (Ss) were studied, with one experimenter (E) and one observer-recorder (O), both women. In the second, 10 other Ss and one S from Experiment I were studied with the E and O of the first experiment exchanging roles. An experiment was composed of three successive units in each of which three or four Ss were studied at one time.

Subjects

The Ss were 21 infants, all residents almost from birth in the same institution. Their median age was 3.0 months; three-quarters of them were no more than three days older or younger than the median. In each experiment six Ss were male, five were female. Age was the main criterion for selection. Four possible Ss were rejected: one seemed immature, two had a very high rate of vocalizing during the first baseline measure, and one was markedly fussy.

The institution offers excellent care and, as is characteristic of institutions, there are multiple caretakers. In general, the Ss were well developed, healthy, alert, and socially responsive. The Es asked for no modifications in the usual caretaking routines. The caretakers knew that the Es were observing the development of social behavior, but they did not know the details of the experiment. The caretakers' usual behavior toward the Ss appeared not to be modified by the conditions of the experiment.

Experimental Conditions

Baseline. In experimental Days 1 and 2 (first and second Baseline days) E leaned over the crib with her face about 15 in. above S's and looked at him with an expressionless face, while O tallied vocalizations, out of S's sight. The E moved her head as necessary to remain in S's line of vision, a condition which obtained throughout the experiments.

Conditioning. During experimental Days 3 and 4 (first and second Conditioning days), E again leaned over the crib with an expressionless face except that when S vocalized, E made an immediate response and then resumed the expressionless face until the next vocalization. The response, or *reinforcing stimulus*, consisted of three acts executed by E simultaneously, quickly, and smoothly. They were a broad smile, three "tsk" sounds, and a light touch applied to the infant's abdomen with thumb and fingers of the hand opposed. No more than a second of time was required to administer the reinforcer.

At the beginning of the conditioning periods each vocalization was reinforced. Sometimes, as the rate of vocalizing increased, only every second, and later, every third, vocalization was reinforced. In Experiment I, 72% of the reinforcers occurred after *each* vocalization; in Experiment II, 94%. Less frequent reinforcing seemed to depress the rate, at least initially, and, because of the rather severe time restrictions, was abandoned altogether by the end of the study.

Extinction. Experimental Days 5 and 6 (first and second Extinction days) were the same as Days 1 and 2; *E* leaned over the crib with an expressionless face and made no response to *S*'s vocalizations.

The Vocal Response

Every discrete, voiced sound produced by *S* was counted as a *vocalization.* A number of other sounds characteristically made by very young infants, e.g., straining sounds and coughs, and the whistles, squeaks, and snorts of noisy breathing, were not counted as vocalizations. Sounds falling under the categories of protests, fusses, and cries (see Emotional Behavior below) were recorded separately. No attempt was made to record the phonetic characteristics of any of the sounds or their duration.

Observer agreement. Agreement between two *O*s on the number of vocalizations produced by *S*s in 3-min. periods was high. Counts for 27 periods, using 13 different *S*s, yielded a median percentage agreement of 96 (range, 67 to 100). About half of these reliability measures were obtained at the *S*s' cribs, and the rest from tape recordings made during the experiment. These two techniques yielded similar percentages of observer agreement.

The unit of measurement. The unit for statistical analysis was the number of vocalizations an *S* gave in a 3-min. period. The counts were recorded by half-minutes and these were summed to give the score for the 3-min. period. After a rest period of 2 min., in which both *E* and *O* walked away from the baby's crib, another 3-min. count was made. After a second rest period a third count was made.

In each day nine such 3-min. counts were planned, distributed thus: one block of three in the first part of the morning, the second block of three in the late morning, and the third block of three after the midday meal. The minimum amount of time between blocks was 10 min., although usually an hour or more elapsed.

Actually, nine periods of observations were obtained during only 80% of the 132 subject-days (22 *S*s × 6 experimental days). Since three or four *S*s were studied at a time, it was not always possible to find nine periods in a day when each was awake, alert, and content. Further, because the experiments were carried out in the nursery which the *S*s shared with 12 other infants, the presence and activities of these other babies, and of the caretakers in carrying out their routines, sometimes made it impossible to obtain the desired number of periods.

Emotional Behavior

A number of responses which seemed to be "emotional" were recorded during the observation periods. These were: "protests," discrete sounds of a whining nature; "fusses," a series of sounds separated by a catch in the voice, whimpering; "cries," continuous loud, wailing sounds; "persistent looking away from E," rolling of the head from side to side or staring to one side or the other of E; and "marked hand activity," hand play, finger sucking, or face or head rubbing. The last two activities seemed to be attempts to avoid E. Measures of observer-agreement in the recording of these responses were not made.

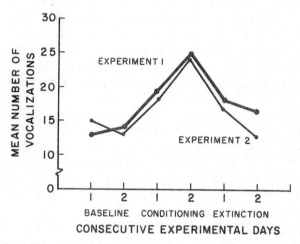

FIGURE 1. *Mean number of vocalizations on consecutive experimental days.*

Each of these responses was given a credit of one for each half-minute in which it occurred. From the sum for each S a mean score was obtained for each experimental day.

RESULTS

Similarity Between Experiments

Figure 1 presents the means of both experiments for the six experimental days. Each point represents the mean of 11 individual means. It was expected that the effect of the experimental conditions would be similar from experiment to experiment, but the extent to which the slopes of the curves would be congruent was not predicted.

The amount of similarity between the two experiments was estimated by an analysis of variance, using Lindquist's Type VI design (1953). The analysis reveals no evidence of a difference between Experiments. Further, no source of variation involving Experiments is significant. (The difference between the two experiments in second Extinction day means is not significant; it suggests, however, that the less frequent reinforcement in Experiment I may have made the behavior more resistant to extinction.)

Three conclusions may be drawn from such close agreement in the results of two parallel experiments, each using different Ss and different Es: first, we are dealing with some relatively stable characteristics of three-month-old infants; second, the results may be accepted with confidence; and third, the results of the separate experiments may be pooled for all remaining analyses.

Effect of Experimental Conditions

Statistical analysis shows that there was a difference in the effect of the three two-day experimental conditions ($p < .001$), and, also, in the effect of successive days within conditions ($p < .001$). These effects were assessed by t tests (for paired data) on the amount of change from one day to another in the mean number of vocalizations given by individual Ss. The error term was derived only from the scores for the two days being compared. The tests on the pooled sample show that:

1. There was no statistically significant difference in the mean number of vocalizations given in a 3-min. period from the first to the second Baseline day ($t = 0.87, p > .30$).

2. The mean number of vocalizations increased from the second Baseline day to the first Conditioning day ($t = 2.69, p < .01$).

3. A further increase occurred from the first to the second Conditioning day ($t = 3.61, p < .001$).

4. On the first Extinction day, vocalizations decreased ($t = 3.19, p < .0025$).

5. The mean number of vocalizations on the second Extinction day was smaller than on the first Extinction day, but the difference was not reliable ($t = 1.35, p < .10$).

6. There was no statistically significant difference between the mean number of vocalizations given on the second Extinction day and on the second Baseline day ($t = 1.20, p > .20$).

If final days within conditions are compared, the differences are more marked: the mean for the second Conditioning day is higher than that of the second Baseline day at $p < .0005$ ($t = 4.80$), and the second Extinction day mean is lower than the second Conditioning day mean at $p < .0005$ ($t = 4.08$). Similar differences occur between the means of experimental conditions, obtained by averaging the first- and second-day results for each condition.

Amount of Change in Number of Vocalizations

Under baseline conditions the three-month-old infants gave about 13 to 14 vocalizations in a 3-min. period. Individual differences were wide and ranged from 3 to 37 vocalizations. Using the social reinforcer for one day raised the rate to 18 vocalizations, an increase of 39%. A second day of conditioning elevated the rate to 25, a further increase of 34%. In all, conditioning brought about an increase of 86%. Removing the reinforcer depressed the rate to 17 during the first and to 15 during the second day, the latter approaching very closely the level of baseline performance.

Emotional Behavior

Emotional behavior, while striking when it occurred, was observed infrequently. The largest mean for any day in both experiments was 3.0, the smallest was 1.9. The order of the means by experimental days was identical in the two experiments. It was: first Extinction day, second Extinction day, second Baseline day, second Conditioning day, first Conditioning day, and first Baseline day. The greater number of emotional responses during Extinction agrees with the findings of others (e.g., Brackbill, 1958; Skinner, 1953; Verplanck, 1955). Because the responses labeled emotional occurred so infrequently and because observer-agreement measures were not made, no further statistical analysis seemed warranted.

Additional Findings

Performance of successive groups. It will be recalled that in any one experimental week the Ss were studied in groups of three or four. Inspection of the results suggests that in each successive group of each experiment an increasing number of Ss conformed to expectation, showing an increase in vocalizations during Conditioning and a decrease during Extinction. The Es apparently became more adept in executing the reinforcer as each experiment progressed.

Performance of individual subjects. Although differences between experimental conditions have been demonstrated for the Ss as a group, the performance of individual Ss is of interest. Of the 22 Ss, 19 showed an increase in vocalizations under Conditioning. For 14 of these 19 the increase was significant at the .05 level, according to the Mann-Whitney Test (1947). Under Extinction, 16 of the 22 Ss showed some decrease, and for 10 of these 16 the decrease was significant at the .05 level.

Three Ss departed widely from the group pattern. For two, not only did Conditioning depress the rate of vocalizing, but Extinction restored it to its Baseline rate. The first chewed her thumb more during Conditioning than before or after. The second strained (in an apparent effort to defecate) during Conditioning whenever anyone, E or the nurse, leaned over his crib. Both activities precluded vocalizing. Both babies were very active, and it is possible, therefore, that in the very first Conditioning period E may have inadvertently reinforced these activities. For the third S, in Experiment I the experimental conditions appeared not to affect the frequency of vocalizations. Developmental immaturity seemed the most likely reason, for two weeks later he was studied again in Experiment II (the only *S* to be used in both experiments) with satisfactory results.

Effect of Baseline performance upon Conditioning. The *Ss* tended to maintain their relative positions under Baseline and Conditioning. The rank-order coefficient of correlation (R) was .66, $p < .0005$. Further, the amount of gain under Conditioning was not correlated with original position (R $= .24, p > .05$).

Sex differences. The 12 male *Ss* gave slightly more vocalizations during Baseline and gained more under Conditioning than the 10 female *Ss*, but the differences were not reliable.

DISCUSSION

The results of these experiments suggest that:

1. Infants' vocal behavior in a social situation can be brought under experimental control; that is, it appears to be conditionable.

2. A social event composed of an everyday complex of acts, performed by an adult who is not a caretaker, can function as a reinforcing stimulus.

3. The incidence of such behavior can be very quickly modified in as young an organism as the three-month-old infant.

Alternative Explanation

The question raised in the introduction may now be considered. Did the reinforcing stimulus function as an arouser of vocalizations? Would infants have vocalized more often because of the stimulation it provided, even if it had *not* been made contingent upon the infant's behavior? Or, did some part of the reinforcing stimulus (say, the smile) act as a social "releaser"? The findings appear to be compatible with the conclusion that conditioning occurred: The rate of vocalizing continued to rise on the second day of Conditioning; the rate did not fall to the Baseline level on the first day of Extinction; it continued to fall on the second day of Extinction; and *Ss* with low Baseline rates of vocalizing gained under Conditioning, although for them there was often a relatively long time interval (30 sec. or more) between the reinforcing stimulus and the occurrence of the next vocalization. Still, the decisive answer to the question must await an experiment in which the reinforcing stimulus is administered with equal frequency, but never directly after the infant vocalizes.

Nature of the Reinforcer

The results seem to show that some everyday behavior of adults can function as a reinforcing stimulus for an infant. One would like to know from what sources its reinforcing properties arise. In the simplest case, the smiles, sounds, and caresses of adults may be reinforcing only because they provide a change in stimulation. Further information on this matter could be obtained by working with the separate parts of the reinforcing stimulus, one by one; by substituting for them lights or sounds dispensed by a machine; or by using a reinforcer of a less "affectionate" nature than the one used here appears to be. On the other hand, even for the three-month-old infant the smiles, sounds, and caresses of the adults may function as conditioned reinforcers because of their past association with caretaking acts.

It is possible that the Ss of this study, living in an institution, may have had a less rich experience with adults. Institutional babies were used as Ss only because they were more readily available, because more of them could be studied at one time, and because the complicating variable of differences in maternal care could be bypassed. They did not appear however to be "starved" for attention or affection. Indeed, the attendants were often observed responding to babies when they vocalized. While it is possible that mothers would respond more often, in the absence of a comparative study we believe that infants in general would respond as these infants did.

Relation of Results to Theories of Speech

Since this study was limited to the vocalizing of infants in a social situation, attempts to reconcile the results with theories which account for all classes of prelinguistic utterances (babbling is the class frequently mentioned) cannot be complete. Thus, nothing in the findings of this study is incompatible with, for example, Holt's theory (1931) that the sound which the child hears himself make has reinforcing properties; with Lewis' theory (1951) that the adult's speech calls forth the infant's speech (a kind of imitation); or with Piaget's theory (1952) that vocalizing is perpetuated for its own sake by the processes of assimilation and accommodation. These may be labeled circular theories, for they do not postulate the necessity for any class of events prior to the moment when the infant responds to his own or another's vocalization. The theories of Miller and Dollard (1941) and of Mowrer (1950), on the other hand, are based upon the infant's associating the gratification of his needs and the accompanying vocalizations of the caretaker. Again, the results do not contradict this possibility.

The present study, however, does demonstrate the operation of still another principle: that the speech of the infant, if only in a social situation, can be modified by a response from the environment which is contingent upon his vocalizing. Hence, what happens *after* the infant vocalizes has been shown to be important.

Significance of Results

On the basis of the results of these experiments it is seen that responses of adults which do not involve caretaking can affect the vocalizing of the young in a social setting. If the results can be extended to life situations, then mothers might be able to increase or decrease the vocal output of their children by the responses they make when the children vocalize. Other kinds of social behavior in addition to vocalizing behavior should respond similarly to conditioning. Brackbill (1958) has shown that smiling in the four-month-old infant may be increased when followed by a social response from an adult. It is likely that still other kinds of social behavior in babies, such as showing an interest in people, reaching out to them or turning away, perhaps even fear of the stranger, may also be affected by the responses adults make to them.

SUMMARY

Infants often vocalize as part of the response they give to the appearance of an adult. The central question of this study is: Can the frequency of vocalizing be increased if the adult makes a social response contingent upon it?

The Ss were 21 normal infants, three months of age, living in an institution. Eleven of them were studied in Experiment I with one E; 10 different Ss and one S from Experiment I were studied in Experiment II with a different E.

During the first and second Baseline days E leaned over S with an expressionless face, and the number of vocalizations was tallied. During the next two days, the first and second Conditioning days, E reinforced vocalizations by simultaneously smiling, clucking, and touching S's abdomen. During the last two days, the first and second Extinction days, E returned to Baseline conditions.

The results indicated that: (1) there was no difference between Experiments, (2) Conditioning raised the rate of vocalizing above the Baseline level, (3) while Extinction lowered it until it approached the Baseline level.

The results suggest that the social vocalizing of infants and, more generally, their social responsiveness may be modified by the responses adults make to them.

References

Brackbill, Y., "Extinction of the Smiling Responses in Infants as a Function of Reinforcement Schedule," *Child Development,* 29 (1958), 115-124.

Gewirtz, J. L., "A Program of Research on the Dimensions and Antecedents of Emotional Dependence," *Child Development* (1956), 205-221.

Holt, E. B., *Animal Drive.* London: Williams & Norgate, Ltd., 1931.

Lewis, M. M., *Infant Speech: A Study of the Beginnings of Language,* 2nd ed. New York: Humanities Press Inc., 1951.

Lindquist, E. F., *Design and Analysis of Experiments in Psychology and Education.* Boston: Houghton Mifflin Company, 1953.

Mann, H. B., and D. R. Whitney, "On a Test of Whether One of Two Random Variables is Stochastically Larger than the Other," *Annals of Mathematical Statistics,* 18 (1947), 50-60.

Miller, N. E., & J. Dollard, *Social Learning and Imitation*. New Haven: Yale University Press, 1941.

Mowrer, O. H., *Learning Theory and Personality Dynamics*. New York: The Ronald Press Company, 1950.

Piaget, J., *The Origins of Intelligence in Children*. New York: International Universities Press, Inc., 1952.

Rheingold, H. L., "The Modification of Social Responsiveness in Institutional Babies," *Monographs of Social Research in Child Development*, Vol. 21, No. 63 (No. 2) (1956).

Skinner, B. F., *Science and Human Behavior*. New York: The Macmillan Company, 1953.

Verplanck, W. S., "The Control of the Content of Conversation: Reinforcement of Statements of Opinion," *Journal of Abnormal and Social Psychology*, 51, (1955), 668-676.

3 · The Expansion of Meaning

M. M. LEWIS

Reprinted from pages 189-199 of *Infant Speech*, 1936, by permission of Humanities Press Inc. and Routledge & Kegan Paul, Ltd.

Once a sound is used in a specific context, how is it extended to other situations? This is the problem that Lewis discusses in the following section.

We have used only two short selections from Lewis' book Infant Speech. *The student interested in language will find the entire book very stimulating and informative. A very extensive survey of the writings on language development in Children is McCarthy's chapter in* Manual of Child Psychology, *edited by Leonard Carmichael.*

A marked characteristic of children's early use of words is that both in response and in utterance they will apply a word to a wide range of situations extending far beyond those in which it was first acquired. K, for instance, came to respond to "Where's ballie?" (0-10+27) by holding up a large colored ball in place of the original small one; and—in the development of an uttered word—he grew to say *tittit* (1-8+28) on seeing the church clock, having previously used this word for his father's watch.

Such extensions are so striking and obviously so important that they have never failed to obtain a good deal of attention. Perhaps the best known case is that reported by Romanes of a child in his first year who having learnt the word *quack* for a duck, applied it to the figure of an eagle seen on a coin, and then to coins in general. The Chamberlains (1904) tell us of their daughter that having at 1-7 learnt the word *mooi* with reference to the moon, she proceeded to apply it to cakes, round marks on the window, writing on the window, writing on paper, "round things in books," tooling on books, faces, postmarks, and the letter O. Lindner (1882) records that his wife had made a sledge (*schlitten*) out of a postcard for the daughter at 2-0. A month later, when the toy had long been destroyed, the child said *mama litten* on seeing a postcard delivered at the house, and some months after this again *litten* on seeing a letter. Numerous other instances of this kind of extension occur in the records of a host of observers.

The records of most of these observers consist of a list of the various meanings which have been given by a child to one and the same word. Observations of this kind, valuable as they may be as illustrations, do not throw much light on the actual process of extension. For this we need a fuller statement; we need to know in some detail how the child behaved in using or responding to the word on successive occasions. Records of this kind are rarer; the only ones in fact at all full enough for this purpose are those published by Ament (1899) and Idelberger (1903). To these I venture to add some of my own observations of K.

EXTENSION AS THE GROWTH OF GENERALIZATION

How are we to explain this wide use of words? The most obvious view is that the child has begun abstraction and generalization; abstracting from diverse situations some features which they have in common, and thus grouping all these situations into the same class. Most of the things, for instance, named *mooi* by the Chamberlains' (1904) little daughter were circular in shape. The child extends the use of the word from the situation in which it was first acquired—seeing the moon—to other situations more or less like it.

There is obviously some truth in the view that here we have a clear step in the development of conceptual thinking—and this is a point which has been fully recognized, from the time of the early observers—Sigismund, Taine, Darwin, and Romanes—right up to our own day. But no one today would, I think, be satisfied with this as a full explanation. At least three other factors must be taken into consideration. First we must recognize that this broad use of words does not begin at the moment when the child acquires conventional speech: it is a gradual development of his earlier linguistic activity. Secondly, it is not enough to speak of the objective similarity of situations for the child, neglecting the affective responses they arouse in him and their functions in his behavior. Thirdly, we must not forget that the word itself is an instrument for the child, a tool, and that this certainly determines the manner in which it is used.

In these three ways we have to supplement the account given even by Stern (1928). For although he refers to other factors, on the whole he confines himself to a summary of those kinds of *objective* similarity in diverse situations which will cause a child to extend a word from one to the rest.

THE EARLY WIDE USE OF SOUNDS

To take full account of the process it will not do to begin at the point where the child first acquires conventional words from the adult language. We must go further back into his linguistic history. If, for instance, we find Stern's daughter Hilde in her twelfth month applying *puppe*—used first for her doll—to any one of a large number of her toys, we have to consider the possible connection between this behavior and the sounds which she made while playing with these toys before she learned their conventional names. For our study of children's language leads us to assert that its development is continuous, not—as some writers such as Bühler (1926) have maintained—a series of sudden steps. The history even of the child's first conventional words does not begin at the moment when he acquires them; they have their root in his earlier use of sounds. In a real sense we can say that no word used by the child can be totally new to him; every word has affinities with his earlier linguistic experience.

With a record of observations such as those of K, it is not difficult to trace the changes in the child's use of sounds, preceding his adoption of conventional words. We find that even at the outset the child's sounds are used in a wide rather than a limited way. This is true both of his utterance of language and of his response to it. As for his response to language, we found that when he hears a particular pattern of intonation and sound he will respond at first not always with the same movement but with any of a number of movements—all expressive of the same affective state. And in the development of his utterance, we find that a particular sound such as a is called forth at first not by a particular situation, but by any one of a number—again alike in this, that they arouse the same affective state.

In tracing the development of such a sound we were able to observe these stages: First its use with varied intonations to express different affective states; second; the increase of reference to a situation in the use of the same sound; third; the adoption of a conventional substitute for the sound, such as **fa** (flower), or **pei** (airplane), this bringing with it a further increase of objective reference.

The next stage of development is that which particularly interests us here: The child extends the use of the conventional word to situations other than those in which it has been acquired. Thus K, having at 1-6+14 begun to use the word **fa** on seeing some hyacinths, used the same word on the following day for tulips, six days after this for irises, and again six days later (1-6+27) on being wheeled beneath a flowering cherry. Four months later, at 1-10+26, he said the same word on seeing a biscuit decorated with a flower in sugar, and again on seeing embroidered flowers on a pair of slippers.

A similar development took place in the case of the word **pei**, which the child used for the first time at 1-9+27 on seeing an airplane, in place of his customary **e e**. Next day he repeated the word on seeing not an airplane, but a child's kite.

Now the important point that emerges from these series of records is that it clearly is not possible to draw a hard-and-fast line at any particular moment in the child's development and say: Here the extended use of sounds begins. For while the child is still in the stage of uttering his own primitive sounds he already uses them in an extended fashion. K, for instance, used a a at 1-4+8 on smelling a handkerchief and again at 1-4+12 on smelling jonquils. Similarly, he used **e e** at 1-1+26 while reaching out for milk, at 1-4+1 for cake, and up to 1-8+16 for butter; again he used the same sound at 1-8+10 for shoe, and at 1-9+15 for airplane. About all these cases we could say, if we wished, that the child was extending his use of a sound in an extraordinary and striking manner: to mean two different pleasant smells, or to mean milk, cake, and butter, or to mean airplane and shoe; and this is in fact what such an observer as Idelberger says of his son's varied uses of the sound ɑ, a list which is cited by Lorimer (1928) as an instance of the unstable character of early "nominal relationships."

But if we trace the child's development as I have done here it is clear that a sound such as ɑ or e is not a name for any one object, subsequently extended to another. It is simply a differentiation of the child's earlier use of a sound to express an affective state, a use which gradually becomes more definitely directed to the situation with which he is dealing, without however being attached to any one particular situation. And if we accept this, then it also becomes clear that when the child begins to use a conventional word such as fa for flower instead of his own primitive sounds, he is at first likely to use it just in the same extended manner as he has been using his own sounds. This point needs to be stressed, because when we find a child using adult words it is only too natural for us to imagine that he is using them as names for particular objects; but more careful observation makes it clear that he is using them not very differently from the way in which he was using his own primitive sounds not long since.

For instance, if we heard a child who has been accustomed to say ɑ on seeing flowers, say this the first time he sees a branch of flowering cherry, we should probably regard this simply as an expression of the child's delight at seeing the beautiful thing, and of his desire to touch and smell it. It would hardly occur to us to say that the child has made a generalization, extending the name ɑ from its use for tulips and applying it now to cherry-blossom. But let us suppose that this happens at a time when—as in the case of K—he was already using the word fa; at once we feel that the child has shown himself capable of generalization, that he has realized the similarity between the tulips and the cherry-blossom, and therefore uses the same name for them both.

Clearly we can easily overestimate the difference between these two stages—before and after the child adopts the conventional word. It is true that there has been some development: The word fa, because it has been adopted from the adult name for the flower, is rather more closely attached to that object than the child's own sound ɑ had been. But even so, the use of a word, first for tulips and then for cherry-blossom, cannot be accepted purely as a case of objective reference to one thing, followed by extension of the name to another thing on a basis of objective similarity. For in neither case is the child using the word simply as a means of naming a thing, as a label to be attached to an object. Just as when the child said ɑ he was at the same moment drawing attention to the flower, expressing his delight at seeing it and possibly his wish to smell it, so now when he uses the learnt word **fa,** this new utterance must retain something of the new functions of the earlier sound which it replaces.

Further, it is also brought home to us that this extension of the use of a word to apply to a new situation is something more than the evocation of a sound from a passive child. It is the child's own activity which brings about the extension. The flower which he sees is something to be grasped and smelt. And the word he utters is a means by which the attention of others may be drawn to this desirable thing (the declarative use), or their help secured in obtaining it (the manipulative use). Of course, it need hardly be said that I am not suggesting that the child will be aware of these functions; only that they are likely to be present in a more or less rudimentary form. What I *am* suggesting is that because the word and the new situation each plays a part in the child's behavior he will broaden his use of the word to apply to the situation.

Thus in tracing the course of the child's development preceding his adoption of conventional words, we see that objective extension is not to be regarded as beginning with this adoption, but that it is based upon the early use of a sound to express an affective state, first in a wide range of situations, and then with an increase of objective reference to these situations. This use develops under the stress of the child's need to bring other human beings into the situation, to obtain their help, or at least their company. Then, by the intervention of these other human beings, the original widely functioning sound-group is replaced, in one situation after another, by a specific conventional sound-group. We next have to consider which features of these situations are likely to give rise to wide applications of words.

THE KINDS OF SIMILARITY AMONG SITUATIONS

Objective Similarity

Stern (1928) gives a comprehensive summary of the objective conditions under which the application of a word will be extended. He classifies the conditions of similarity between situations into three groups. First, the situations may be similar as a whole; second, there may be similarity of particular features; third, the child's attention may shift from feature to feature, so that a word is applied to a new situation which has no resemblance at all to the original situation, but has some point of likeness to an intermediate situation.

1. *Similarity of the Situation as a Whole.* In Stern's first group of cases a word is applied from a customary situation to another one which as a whole objectively resembles it; for instance, **pei** for an airplane and then for a kite, **mooi** for the moon and then for any round object. Many other instances could easily be given.

2. *Similarity of Particular Features.* Stern's second group of cases are

those in which the likeness is said to exist only in particular features of the situations. This may be illustrated by two cases from my own observations. The first is K's use of the word **kotibaiz.**

At 2-2+14 he was given a large toy abacus; immediately on seeing it he said **kotibaiz.** It was impossible to tell whether the use of this word was due to a memory of a cot in which he had last slept more than a year since, and which had one or two rows of beads, or whether he was referring to the parallel wires of the abacus which resembled the parallel bars of his own cot. Two months later, at 2-4+12, he used the same word **kotibaiz** for two other objects: on first seeing a toast-rack (with parallel bars), and again for a picture of a building with fluted columns.

In the second case, having learnt to say **fi:** (sea) for the seashore, K subsequently said it on seeing a railway track; there was certainly a resemblance between the slope of the grassy sand banks by the sea and the slope of the railway embankment.

3. *Shifting from Feature to Feature.* Stern's third group of cases are those in which the extended application of a word is due to particular features similar to those present in an earlier situation. Here Stern cites the instance from Romanes which we have already mentioned, where the word *quack* first used for a duck, ultimately came to be used for a coin. Similar cases are recorded by Idelberger (1903); the child, having used **wauwau** on seeing a dog or hearing the animal bark, later said it at the sight of a fur collar with a dog's head, then for a fur collar without a head, finally for buttons; presumably he had seen buttons on the fur collars. It was the same child who used the word **baba** both for his father and for the sound of a bell; the route this time being from his father to his father's trousers hanging on a hook, then for his father's portrait, then for an electric bell which his father had repaired, finally for the sound of any bell.

This threefold classification of Stern's certainly helps us to understand what we may call the objective side of the process—the various kinds of objective similarity among situations which may help to bring about the application of a word from one to another. But when we come to examine both Stern's own cases and others more closely, we find that this analysis is inadequate.

THE AFFECTIVE ASPECT OF EXTENSION

In the first place, Stern hardly lays sufficient emphasis upon the part played by the child's affective responses. It is true that he mentions affect as a factor which is likely to permeate all the varied applications of a word, but he makes no further reference to it in his detailed analysis. This neglect seems strange in the light of the importance that has been given to affect as one of the chief factors in determining the influence of past upon present experience, not only by the psychoanalysts but by English writers such as Ward, Stout, and Bartlett; and all the more strange since Meumann—to whom Stern constantly refers—paid special attention to this point in his account of children's wide applications of words.

Meumann's view is this (1903): That in cases where situations are only very slightly similar objectively, extension of a word may take place because the situations arouse in the child similar feelings and similar strivings. To apply this, for instance, to a case given by Stern; his daughter Hilde at 0-11 extended the word **puppe** from her doll, to a toy rabbit and other playthings. Stern suggests from this that a general similarity of the most superficial kind may be enough to bring about extension; but if we follow Meumann here we should say that the sight of a toy rabbit aroused the same feeling of delight and desire to play as the original doll had aroused; and it was this affective-conational similarity which was powerful in bringing about the extension.

The truth is perhaps that Stern, making a somewhat conservative summary, is still mainly concerned with the cognitive factors in the process of extension, and sees this process mainly as a step in the development of abstract thinking; but there is no doubt that Meumann was right: The more we pay attention to the conditions in which the wide applications of words take place, the more certain does the place of affect become. It plays an important part, as we have seen, while the child is still using his own primitive sounds, and it retains this function when he comes to replace them by conventional words. When, for instance, K said fi: for the first time it was not a mere indication of the sea or sandhills; the child had been awakened by the thunderstorm and called out the newly learnt word to express his terror at what he thought was the roaring of the sea. In the same way when he said **pei,** first for an airplane and then for a kite, it was surely partly because he felt the same delight (or perhaps fear or wonder) at them both. A few weeks earlier he would have said e e on seeing the new thing; now he uses the learnt word **pei** which, whatever else it may do, expresses his affective reaction just as his earlier sounds had done. Again, when he said fɑ on seeing the cherry-blossom, this must have expressed the peculiar pleasure aroused in him by the sight of a flower. Observations of this kind make it certain that effective similarity may be a very powerful factor in determining the wide use of words.

FUNCTIONAL SMIILARITY

If affective similarity has been neglected, this is even truer of functional similarity. Yet it is more than 40 years ago that Dewey first drew attention to its importance, in his usual vigorous fashion (1894).

> The tendency to apply the same term to a large number of objects ("ball" to ball, orange, moon, lamp-globe, and so on) can be understood,

I think, only if we keep in mind the extent to which the formal noun "ball" has really an active sense. "Ball" is "to throw" just as much as it is the round thing. I do not believe that the child either confuses the moon with his ball, or abstracts the roundness of it; the roundness suggests to him something which he has thrown, so that the moon is something to throw—if he could only get hold of it.

In a word, Dewey insists upon the importance of functional similarity in the situations for the child, that they do not merely exist statically for him, but are bound up with his activity. To this we shall have to add that they are also frequently bound up with the activity of those around him. Functional similarity of either kind may determine the wide use of words.

THE FUNCTION OF THE SITUATION IN THE CHILD'S OWN ACTIVITY

This point is not absolutely neglected by Stern; he does note in passing what he calls an exceptional instance where the function of the situation becomes a factor in bringing about the wider use of a word. Hilde, he tells us, used *Nase* at 1-7 for the toe of a shoe, because she found she could pull this in the same way as she would playfully pull someone's nose. But we have to go further than Stern and point out that this is by no means an exceptional instance; functional similarity is as constant a factor as objective or affective similarity.

Take, for instance, Hilde's use of **puppe** for a wide range of playthings, including a doll, a toy rabbit, and a toy cat; Stern recognizes that these things are objectively unlike each other, and urges therefore that extension will occur when only a very superficial resemblance is present. But the fact is that a stuffed cat is really very unlike a doll, unless we remember that a child *plays* with both of them. Again, to go back to K's use of **fa** for tulips as well as cherry-blossom; the resemblance is certainly very superficial unless we remember that when he saw a flower he was usually invited to *smell* it.

It is equally necessary to emphasize this functional factor in these cases where the likeness is said to lie not in the situations as wholes, but in particular features of them. When K used **fi:** for the railway track after having used it for the seashore, there can be no doubt that the word was evoked not only by the resemblance between the two slopes, but also by the fact that the child had enjoyed climbing the sandbank and that here was something else to climb. That this view is justified is shown by an observation of mine in this connection; a few days after the episode of the railway track the child was taken near a grassy bank; this time he said **ʌpi fi:**, using again the word **ʌpi** that he had constantly used when he wished to be taken over the sandbanks by the sea.

It is interesting to notice that in some cases, the wide application of a word seems to rest almost entirely upon the existence of this functional similarity. Take, for instance, K's use of the word **da** (from the word *down*; at 1-6+8) he said the word before climbing *down* from his mother's knee; a few days later he began to use the word frequently to indicate that he wished to go *up* stairs (1-6+16-26). Here the circumstances show that the point of similarity was not a matter of direction, up or down, but that there was climbing to be done in both cases.

THE FUNCTION OF THE SITUATION IN THE ACTIVITY OF OTHERS

In a further group of instances we have to take a broader view of this notion of functional similarity; where the situations have a similar function, not in the child's own activity, but in the activity of some other person. For instance, among the extraordinary uses made by Idelberger's son of the word **wauwau** were those which included, first, a sewing table and secondly a bathroom thermometer. Now the only possible point of resemblance between these two objects is this, that they are instruments used by someone. Again, Guillaume tells us (1927) that at 1-2 his son learned the word **ato** (*marteau*) for hammer, and in a short time was applying it to a large variety of objects: button-hook, hand-mirror, comb, handbag, saucepan, hairpin, wooden spade, key, gun, box, belt, purse, ruler, puttees, basin, safety pin, candlestick, coffee-mill, plate, spoon. Guillaume adds that it was never used for people, animals or food, but seemed to be equivalent to *machin* or *chose*, that is to say, an instrument used by some person.

No interpretation which relies upon the evocation of a word by the similarity of objective features can cover a case of this kind. We are bound to say that the word is the child's way of dealing with a complex situation, the similarity of which with another situation is now mainly this, that in each case someone is using something, a person manipulating an instrument.

It is clear that to Stern's emphasis upon objective similarity we have to add the two other features emphasized by Meumann and by Dewey—affective and functional similarity. Together these three views give us a comprehensive view of the similarities of the *situations* among which a child may extend the use of a word. Now if we look at this summary two very interesting points stand out. The first is that while the traditional account emphasized by Stern gives a picture of a somewhat passive child from whom a word is wrung on successive occasions by similar situations, both Meumann and Dewey emphasize the place of the situation in the child's activity. And secondly, that all these three views alike deal only with one side of the process—the nature of the situations—and neglect the other side—the nature of the instrument which is applied to those situations, that is to say, the function of the word used.

References

Ament, W., *Die Entwicklung von Sprechen und Denken beim Kinde*. Leipzig: Vunderlich, 1899.

Bühler, K., "Les lois generales d'evolution dans le langage de l'enfant," *Journal de Psychologie*, 23 (1926), 597-607.

Chamberlain, A. F. and I. C. "Studies of a Child," *Pedagogical Seminary,* 11 (1904).

Dewey, J., "Psychology of Infant Language," *Psychological Review,* 1 (1894), 63-66.

Guillaume P., "Les débuts de la phrase chez l'enfant," *Journal de Psychologie,* 24 (1927), 26-77.

Idelberger, H., "Hauptproblemen der kindlichen Sprachentwicklung," *Zeitschrift für Psychologie.* (1903).

Lindner, G., "Beobachtungen, und Bemerkungen über die Entwicklung der Sprache des Kindes," *Kosmos* 9 (1882), 321-430.

Lorimer, F., *The Growth of Reason.* New York: Harcourt, Brace & Company, Inc., 1928.

Meumann, E., *Die Sprache des Kindes.* 1903.

Stern, C. and W., *Die Kindersprache.* Leipzig: Barth, 1928.

4 · The Development of Language in Twins

ELLA J. DAY

Abridged from the article in *Child Development*, 3 (1932), 179-199, by permission of the Society for Research in Child Development.

Early studies of language development were naturalistic. The child's vocalizations were described, his progress was charted, but seldom did the investigator introduce any experimental factor to determine its influence upon the child's language.

In the study described in this section, there is an experimental factor—twinning. There is no reason to believe that twins in general differ in heredity from singletons in general. Differences between twins and singletons in language may therefore be attributed to the unusual social situation created by the presence of two children of the same age.

INTRODUCTION

In the year 1886, Horatio Hale (Romanes, 1889) in a paper published in the Proceedings of the American Association for the Advancement of Science, reported the case of a pair of twin boys who were so retarded in speech that members of the family could not understand them. These children lived in Boston in 1860. According to the report of an aunt, who visited them frequently, they developed a twin language so unlike English that they could not be sent to school because no one could understand them. Observation of the occasional development of such a special language by twins, suggested the problem of research undertaken here. The twin situation is, from an environmental point of view, quite unlike that of single children and it seemed possible that this might be a factor of considerable significance in the development of language.

McCarthy's (1930) investigation *The Language Development of the Preschool Child* provided an excellent basis for comparison. This study was completed in the summer of 1928 at the Institute of Child Welfare of the University of Minnesota. Dr. McCarthy selected 140 children (20 at each six-months-age-level from eighteen to fifty-four months) on the basis of sex and socio-economic status. She visited them and recorded 50 consecutive responses made by each child while he played with a group of toys that she presented to stimulate speech. These data were then analyzed in four different ways: by mean length of response; according to the Piaget (1928) functional analysis; by the grammatical construction of the sentence; and a word analysis by parts of speech. In brief the results indicated the developmental changes with age in agreement with other studies, as well as sex differences in favor of the girls. Differences in favor of the upper occupational groups were indicated also in each method of analysis. In the foreword to this study Dr. John E. Anderson says, "On the basis of the number of controls utilized in the selecting of subjects and the care and thoroughness with which the data are analyzed, this monograph stands out as one of the best studies of the development of language which has yet appeared." The present investigation was planned to repeat the McCarthy technique using twins.

PURPOSE

The purpose of this investigation was to compare the development of language in twins with that of singletons of the same ages, sex, and socio-economic status.

SELECTION OF CASES

Through the courtesy of the Minneapolis and St. Paul Departments of Health, the writer had access to the birth registrations. The date of birth, sex, place of birth, name of physician attending the birth, and the father's name, address, and occupation were all recorded on the registration cards.

SUBJECTS

Age and Sex

After consideration of the findings of the McCarthy study, it was decided to select 80 pairs of twins, 20 pairs at each of four age levels, two, three, four, and five years. Since McCarthy reports that 74 per cent of the responses of the eighteen-month-old children were incomprehensible, it seemed adequate from the standpoint of the methods of analysis to be used, to begin with the two year age group. The wisdom of carrying the group on through the fifth year was not so apparent at the time the selection was made as the results now show it to be. An equal number of boys and girls at each age were selected except at age four (see Table I) where there are 19 boys and 21 girls. These age groups are discrete because the records were taken within one month of the birthday. With the exception of one case where the records of the two children were not taken on the same day, the greatest deviation from the birthday was 38 days and the mean deviation for the whole group was 19.69 days. The one exception referred to deviated 99 days from the birthday.

Socio-Economic Status

The importance of securing a representative sampling of the population is clearly brought out in such studies as the McCarthy study and the Goodenough (1928) evaluation of the Kuhlman-Binet tests for children of preschool ages. The sampling was made according to the Goodenough (1931) classification of the Minneapolis population which was based on the application of the Barr Scale for Occupational Intelligence and the Taussig industrial classification to the 1920 census report of the occupations of males in Minneapolis between the ages of twenty and forty-five years. The occupational levels are grouped into sixfold classification. Group I consists of the professional vocations; group II the managerial occupations; group III the retailers, salesmen, and skilled workmen; group IV the semiskilled workmen; group V the drivers, helpers, and the like; group VI the day laborers. Table 1 shows the percentage of each occupational class found in the Minneapolis population and the percentages represented by twins and singletons.

The distribution of the sexes is not equal at each occupational class but is equal in the upper three and lower three classes at each age, except at age four.

METHOD OF OBSERVATION

The Language Record

Just as the selection of cases was made on a basis similar to that used in the McCarthy study, the technique of obtaining the language record was carried out as it was with the singletons. A group of toys consisting of two linenette picture books, one of familiar animals and one of Mother Goose, a very small automobile, a rubber ball, a pasteboard cat that meowed when squeezed, a telephone with a bell, and a small music box were shown to the children to stimulate speech. In so far as possible, McCarthy's toys were duplicated exactly. The examiner requested to see each child alone but this was not always possible. The children were permitted to open the suitcase and look at the toys as they wished. The examiner remained out of the situation as much as possible because spontaneous responses were desired. Some conversations between the examiner and the child however always occurred. When members of the family insisted upon remaining in the room, they sometimes facilitated spontaneous speech on the part of the twin and sometimes interfered with obtaining an accurate record.

Fifty consecutive verbal responses were recorded and the time noted. The responses were recorded exactly as they sounded to the examiner. A response was denoted as complete when a distinct pause occurred. A complete sentence was always considered as a single response, although a single

Table I

Distribution of Cases by Age, Sex, and Occupational Class

Occupational Class	2 Years Boys	2 Years Girls	3 Years Boys	3 Years Girls	4 Years Boys	4 Years Girls	5 Years Boys	5 Years Girls	All (number of pairs)	Twins	Minneapolis Population	McCarthy Singletons
I	1	1	2	0	0	2	1	1	4	5.0%	5.4%	5.0%
II	2	0	1	1	0	2	0	2	4	5.0	6.3	6.4
III	7	9	8	8	10	6	9	7	32	40.0	37.3	35.7
IV	6	4	4	6	4	6	3	5	19	23.8	24.3	25.7
V	2	4	3	3	1	5	3	5	13	16.2	14.9	15.7
VI	2	2	2	2	4	0	4	0	8	10.0	11.8	11.4
Total	20	20	20	20	19	21	20	20	80	100.0%	100.0%	100.0%

182

response might be either a complete or incomplete sentence. The mean time for obtaining such a record was 14.9 minutes for the twins as compared with 19.3 minutes for the singletons. The shorter time required by the twins is probably due to two factors. In the first place, they said considerably fewer words in the 50 responses. In the second place, the examiner was in the home anywhere from one to two and a half hours and at least one of the children had a somewhat greater opportunity to become adjusted to the presence of a stranger. The examiner practiced taking such records with a group of children attending the nursery school at the University of Minnesota, preliminary to taking any records with the twins. She also had the advantage of being able to talk with Dr. McCarthy frequently and so check on minor differences in procedure.

The Intelligence Tests

The Goodenough (1926) drawing test of intelligence was given by the examiner to all the twins. This test consists merely in having the child draw a man. It is nonverbal and very simple to give. The results however were not usable since such a large percentage of the twins had not manipulated pencil and paper before and therefore they only scribbled.

The department of mental testing of the Institute of Child Welfare volunteered to give the twins the Minnesota Preschool Scale (Goodenough, 1932), which at this time was in the process of standardization. This test was devised by Goodenough and is a revision, for the most part, of the tests for these ages in the Kuhlman-Binet and the Stanford-Binet tests. Test results were obtained on 123 of the 160 children.

METHOD OF ANALYSIS

McCarthy's methods of analysis were duplicated exactly. A total of 7,836 responses were made and of these 7,156 or 90 per cent were comprehensible and 780 or 10 per cent were classed as semicomprehensible or incomprehensible.

RELIABILITY

Method of Observation

In order to get some estimate of the degree of accuracy in recording such a verbal record, Dr. McCarthy, the examiner, and one other observer took records simultaneously, 25 responses in length, on 10 two- to five-year-old children from a settlement house.

Table II shows the coefficients of reliability found between each two observers. The examiner first analyzed the language records as to length of response, the functional classification, and the construction of sentence category, just as the original data had been treated. The Spearman method

Table II

Reliability Coefficients on the Method of Recording

	Observation			
	1 and 2	1 and 3	2 and 3	Mean of All
	p	p	p	p
Mean length of response	.98	.99	.99	.99
Naming	.90	.99	.94	.94
Remarks about immediate situation	.95	.87	.94	.92
Functionally complete but structurally incomplete	.92	.91	.99	.94
Simple sentences	.32	.69	.72	.57
Incomplete sentences	.65	.40	.87	.64

of rank differences was used to determine the coefficients of reliability. In length of response the mean for each child according to each observer was used for the correlation and in the other analyses the percentage of whatever item was being correlated was used.

These coefficients seem sufficiently high to indicate reliability of the method of recording.

Methods of Analysis

The reliability of the various methods of analysis used in treating the language records was not determined in this investigation since McCarthy had determined this and found it to be high.

COMPARISON OF DATA ON LENGTH OF RESPONSE:
TWINS AND SINGLETONS CHRONOLOGICAL AGE

Figure 1 shows a surprising difference in rate of language development for twins and singletons. At two years the difference is small but appears to become increasingly greater with age and is consistently in favor of the singletons. The mean length of response for the five-year-old twins is slightly below that of the three-year-old singletons. A retardation of two years in language development, one would think, was a serious handicap since contacts with our fellowmen depend so largely upon our ability to make ourselves understood verbally.

Critical ratios D/σ_D, computed for each age level were high and increased with age. At two years the ratio was 4.9; at three, 11.6; and at four, 15.3. Hence the superiority of singletons to twins in language development is highly significant statistically.

Smith's investigation (1926) of the development of the sentence and the extent of vocabulary in young children agrees very closely with the

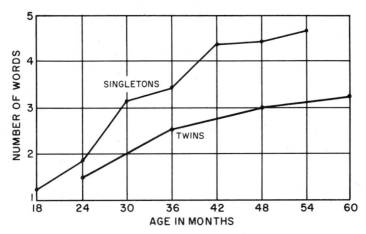

FIGURE 1. *Mean length of response of singletons and twins by chronological age.*

McCarthy results, and so only further emphasizes the handicap of the twins. The most rapid gain in length of response is made between two and three years by both twins and singletons. Although twins gain only one word in the entire year, singletons gain more than one word in the first half of the year. This difference in rate of development remains relatively the same up to five years. Smith feels that the relatively little gain in length of sentence after four or four and one-half years indicates that the sentence length has little value as a measure of sentence development after this age.

The question immediately arises as to when the curve of development for the twins turns and reaches the level of that of the singletons. Does the greater contact with other children, which occurs upon entrance in school, at or soon after the fifth year, stimulate language development sufficiently to give the twins this needed spurt? Does the twin situation so limit the child's environment in the early years of rapid development that he is always at a disadvantage? What is responsible for the retardation, heredity or environment, or both?

All of these questions and many more are as yet unanswered. Nevertheless the author has attempted to get what evidence she could to throw light on the problem.

Attention may be called at this time to the fact that the mental ability as well as the language development of the twin group appears to be below average. The mean IQ for the whole group is 94. This is based upon the results of the Minnesota Preschool Scale. The singletons, with whom the twins are compared, have a mean IQ of 103.3, after the correction recommended by Goodenough has been applied. This correction is a subtraction due to Goodenough's observation that the Kuhlman-Binet test (the test used for the singletons) tended to score too high at the early ages. The singletons then appear to have been a group slightly superior even though they were so carefully selected. Had they been an average group the differences would be slightly decreased. That the twin group deviates even farther from normal is quite true although the evidence seems to be that this is a normal phenomenon rather than a matter of selection.

SEX DIFFERENCES

In agreement with the findings of McCarthy, Nice (1925), Gale (1902), Mead (1913), Terman (1925), and Doran (1907), our data show differences in favor of the girls. (See Figure 2.) These differences are less

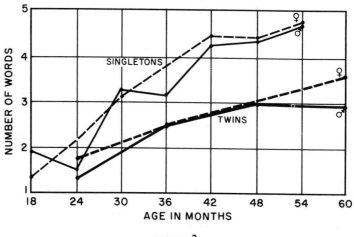

FIGURE 2.

marked than in the group of singletons at every age except four years, but are consistently in the same direction. It may be noted that at two years the twin girls are slightly superior to the single boys. The twin boys make a greater gain between two and three years than do twin girls but gain less thereafter. The differences between twin boys and girls at five years is greater than at any other age, while the greatest differences between the sexes in singletons was found at two and three years. Smith does not report a consistent sex difference.

PATERNAL OCCUPATION

Because of the unequal number of cases in each of the six occupational classes the differences between occupational classes is most fairly shown by dividing the age groups into the upper three and lower three occupational classes. By so doing an equal number of cases and an equal number of each sex appears in each group. Figure 3 shows the expected differences between these groups. In comparing these results with the McCarthy results it must be noted that the age groups are not strictly comparable. The singletons were so grouped in reporting these findings that the age groups become eighteen, twenty-seven, thirty-nine, and fifty-one months, rather than at the exact year levels of the twins. The differences between twins and singletons are even more striking when based upon distribution by occupational class. That the singletons of the lower occupational groups are consistently above the twins of the upper groups presents

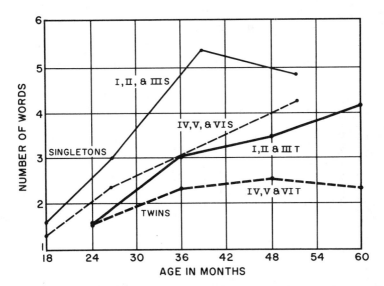

FIGURE 3. *Mean length of response of singletons and twins by upper and lower occupational groups and chronological age.*

a surprising picture of retardation. The mean of the differences at each age between upper and lower groups is .90 words for the singletons, .85 words for the twins, so that the differences between upper and lower groups remain relatively the same. The fanning out of curves of the upper and lower group twins indicates that the difference increases with age, which suggests that environment plays a role in this.

COMPARISON OF DATA ON FUNCTIONAL ANALYSIS: TWINS AND SINGLETONS

The percentage of responses of the functional classification were worked out both inclusive and exclusive of the incomprehensible responses. Figure 4 shows the percentages of this classification based on all responses, including the incomprehensible responses.

When considered from the standpoint of age groups, the incomprehensible responses, though somewhat fewer for twins at two years are slightly greater at three and four years and are still in evidence at five years. With the marked retardation in language development indicated by the differences in mean length of response of twins and single children, one might expect a very much greater percentage of incomprehensible responses on the part of the twin. Such responses do seem to persist for a longer time in the twins, however, which is suggestive of a slower development. Two factors in the twin situation may have acted to reduce somewhat the per-

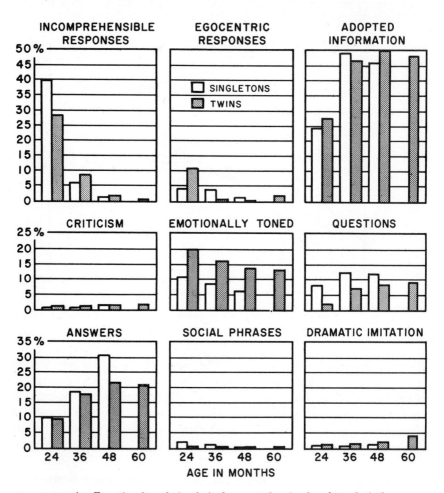

FIGURE 4. *Functional analysis of singletons and twins by chronological age.*

centage of incomprehensible responses. It may be easier to understand short statements as compared with long ones and the twin data are composed of many more single word responses. Also, the examiner had had, just previous to making this study, two and one-half years' nursery school experience and was quite accustomed to interpreting the speech of young children. Dr. McCarthy on the other hand had had only the contact any adult may have with children previous to collecting her data.

The 780 incomprehensible responses include 83 semicomprehensible responses. Of 697 responses actually incomprehensible 287 or 41 per cent were single syllables, 121 or 17 per cent repetition of the same syllable, and 289 or 42 per cent a series of different syllables. At two and three years the single syllables slightly exceed the others in number. At four and five years the series of different syllables is in the lead; in fact, at five years, it is the only one represented. This type of incomprehensible response is no doubt a poor attempt at adult speech but the single syllables and repetition of the same syllable may be the voice play similar to that practiced by the young infant.

The three types of egocentric responses described by Piaget are grouped together because each one appears to such a small extent. The twins, though they show more of this type of speech than the singletons at two years, show considerable less at three and four years, with an increase at five years. The twin situation of constant companionship, one might expect, would not be conducive to extensive egocentric speech but rather to socialized forms of speech.

The different types of socialized speech are best presented in Figure 5 where adapted information is divided into its subheads of naming, remarks about the immediate situation, remarks associated with the situation, and irrelevant remarks. Here too all percentages appear slightly increased since they are based upon comprehensible responses only.

Though as a whole adapted information shows increase with age and percentages in fairly close agreement with the singletons, when the four types of adapted information are considered separately, differences between twins and singletons show up. Naming, the first type, scarcely shows any decrease while with the singletons there is a marked decrease. That this function of language, typical of the two-year-old singletons but not so much so of the four-year-olds, persists through five years in the twins is indicative of maintenance of early language habits after they should have been dropped.

Remarks about the immediate situation increase with age but are present in greater numbers in twins than in singletons, whereas remarks associated with the situation are very few in number as compared with singletons, show relatively no increase with age, and do not appear at all until three years. In consideration of these two differences, one may wonder whether the limitations of the twin environment may account for these differences.

The percentages of irrelevant remarks are comparatively insignificant. The singletons show a slight increase with age, however, which the twins do not show.

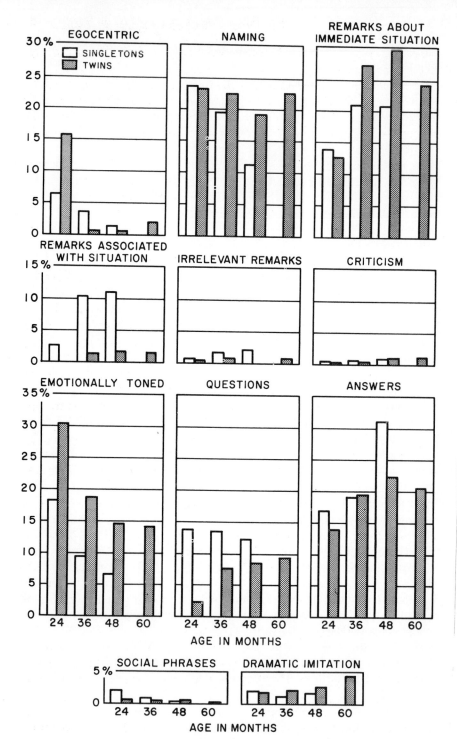

FIGURE 5. *Functional analysis of singletons and twins by chronological age (based on comprehensible responses).*

190

Criticism shows close agreement between twins and singletons and does increase with age.

The emotionally toned responses show one of the most striking differences between the two groups. Twins have almost double the per cent of the singletons at every age. Both show a decrease with age. This, like naming, is suggestive perhaps of persistence of infantile habits of language.

Questions increase with age in the twins but even at five years have not attained the per cent shown by singletons at two years. This no doubt is somewhat indicative of the retarded language development as well as of a high degree of satisfaction from companionship rather than from investigation of the environment.

Answers also increase with age but neither increase as much nor are present to so great an extent as with single children. This cannot be attributed entirely to retarded development, however, since the extent to which the examiner asked the child questions determined to a considerable extent the percentage of answers given.

Social phrases, though very much less at two years, are slightly less at three years for twins than for singletons and greater at four years. Close companionship may be a factor here in reducing the need for such phrases.

Dramatic imitation increases very much with age and appears to be of greater significance in twins than in singletons. The social advantages of the twins through their companionship may bring this out somewhat more.

In considering the functional analysis as a whole it may be pointed out that the twins show retardation in those phases of the analysis which show the greatest developmental changes with age such as naming, emotionally toned responses, and questions. In egocentric responses and dramatic imitation, however, they appear in advance of the singletons. These last two phases may easily be the result of close companionship.

As with the singletons, girl twins show some superiority over the boys in those items which make the greatest change with age. Comprehensive tables for these items are too detailed for publication. A large difference between boy and girl twins in incomprehensible responses at two years puts the girls quite in advance of the boys. At three and four years the girls have a slightly greater percentage of incomprehensible responses, and at five they have less, but these differences are so slight and the total percentage at three, four, and five years so small that the reversion is probably due to selection of cases.

The girls also show less egocentric speech at every age except five years. The differences are small, however, except at two years, which is the most significant age from the standpoint of total percentage of this type of response.

In naming, the boy twins increase slightly while the girls decrease from the second to fourth year and then increase at five years. Girls have somewhat greater proportion of remarks about the situation and both boys and girls increase with age to four years then drop a bit at five years.

Girls increase more and are superior at all ages in remarks associated with the situation.

Emotionally toned responses are decidedly greater for the girls except at age three where a difference of only 1 per cent is in favor of the boys. The greatest differences in percentage of questions occurs at two years and is in favor of the girls. The other phases of the functional analysis though they show some differences between the sexes show no striking or consistent trends.

The chief phases of analysis which showed marked differences between the upper three and lower three occupational classes are incomprehensible responses, egocentric speech, questions, and remarks about the immediate situation. The great differences in incomprehensible responses is at two years where the upper class twins show about one-half as great a proportion as the lower class. Just the reverse situation is found in egocentric speech. The lower group have slightly less than twice as much as the upper group at two years, and have none at all at the other ages. This was also the case with the singletons, except at thirty-nine months, where the lower group exceeded the upper group by quite a large proportion. Perhaps the sampling is not sufficient for these differences to mean a great deal since the percentage at any age is not very great. In both questions and remarks about the immediate situation the differences are not so marked at two and three years but become increasingly so at four and five years. The lower group shows a smaller proportion of these than the upper groups. A similar situation was found with singletons in regard to questions but not in regard to the other phase.

COMPARISON OF DATA ON CONSTRUCTION ANALYSIS: TWINS AND SINGLETONS

Chronological Age

Figure 6 again shows that twins are retarded in language development as compared with singletons. Since they were found so retarded when measured by length of response one could scarcely expect to find them using many of the more complex forms of the sentence. It may be said, however, that in general the same tendencies with age are indicated in both the twins and singletons.

The functionally complete and structurally incomplete responses though they decrease with age are present to a somewhat greater extent in twins than in singletons. This group, as has been stated, consists very largely of the single-word responses. Although such responses appear rather commonly in adult speech they appear there largely in conservational usage while the young children employ them in other ways. For instance, in looking through the picture books it was not uncommon for the children to point at and name objects, and use no sentence at all. Twins evidently maintain

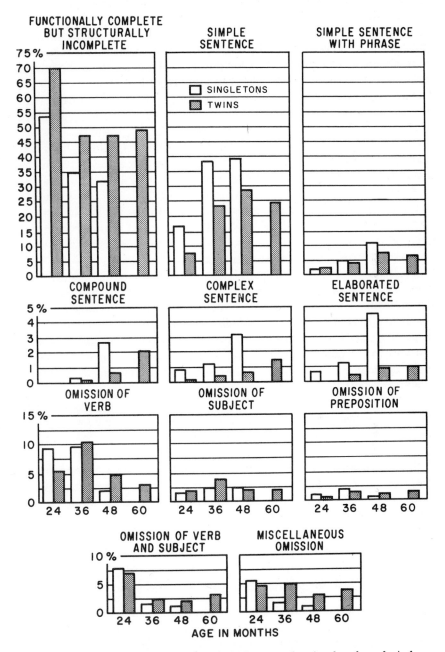

FIGURE 6. *Construction analysis of singletons and twins by chronological age (exclusive of incomprehensible responses).*

this rather infantile manner of talking about what they see longer than do single children.

The simple sentence and all other forms of complete sentences increase with age but at every age are present to a considerably less extent than they are in singletons. The more complex the form of the sentence the greater the relative differences between twins and singletons become.

Incomplete sentences while not always present to a greater extent than in singletons do not drop off as rapidly. This again indicates persistence of early modes of talking or of rather infantile language habits.

The sex differences in sentence structure are not as marked for twins as singletons. There is no consistent trend in the differences between the boy and the girl twins in any of the items of the classification. It may be noted, however, that the girls do show all the forms of the complete sentence earlier and in larger proportion than the boys. Probably these items show the most important developmental changes with age and thus the girls may be considered in advance of the boys since they are using the more complex forms of the sentence earlier.

In relation to the singletons both boy and girl twins are retarded. In fact, as in the length of response, the girl twins rank below the boy singletons in practically all classifications of construction. Both sexes show the continuance of the functionally complete but structurally incomplete responses in much greater proportion than do singletons of the same age and sex.

When the responses are considered from the point of view of occupational class and construction of the sentence the differences are again found in favor of the upper groups.

The functionally complete but structurally incomplete responses are maintained in larger proportion through the fifth year by the lower groups and seem to indicate, as has been pointed out before, the continuance of a somewhat infantile habit of speech. All of the more complex forms of the sentence are present to a greater extent in twins from the upper groups than those from the lower groups. But as in the other analyses the upper group of twins is frequently below the lower group of singletons. In the comparison of two groups, however, it must be remembered that the singletons are so grouped that the age falls three months in advance of the age of the twins.

COMPARISON OF WORD ANALYSIS: TWINS AND SINGLETONS

These data were treated in two ways. Both the total number of words used by each child and the number of different words used by each child and each age group were separated into the parts of speech.

Figure 7 shows the percentage of each part of speech of the total words used. Nouns show close agreement for twins and singletons both in the total percentage used and in the marked drop in percentage from two to three years. The percentage of verbs in which singletons show a gradual increase, from two to four years, is relatively much less at two years in twins, equal to the singletons at three years, and constant thereafter. Adjectives increase from approximately 2 per cent at two years to 8 per cent at five years, in twins. Singletons do not show this marked increase but even at two years have 10 per cent of adjectives, which exceeds the twin five-year-old percentage. Adverbs, except for a slight use at three years, are constant throughout and slightly greater in percentage in twins than in singletons. Pronouns increase with age to a greater extent in twins than singletons. They are, at every age, somewhat fewer in proportion. Conjunctions are late in appearing. Girl singletons show a small per cent at eighteen months and the boys show none until thirty months. A smaller per cent (.9) appears at three years in the twins, and at five years the proportion is still smaller than that for singletons. Prepositions, although they show a greater increase with age in twins than in singletons, at two are much less in proportion, the same at four years, and drop some at five years. Although interjections decrease with age markedly, the twins show a very much greater proportion at all ages, especially at two years, than do singletons. This, no doubt, is related to the large proportion of emotionally

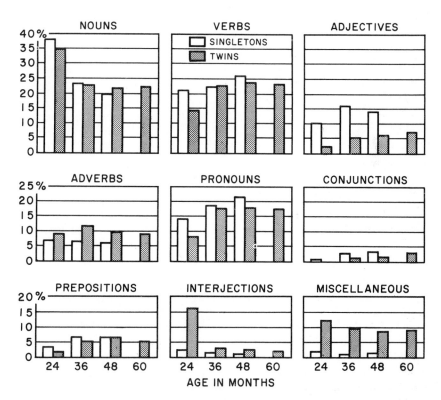

FIGURE 7. *Percentage of parts of speech used by chronological age (based on total words used).*

toned responses which the twins showed in the functional analysis, and like it, is somewhat indicative of maintenance of infantile language. The miscellaneous parts of speech include words which were difficult to classify more positively, such as "uhm-uh," "uh-uhm" used so frequently for "yes" and "no." These appear to be used to a considerably greater extent by twins than by singletons. This then seems to show a tendency to attain adult standards more slowly.

Table III shows the mean number of total words used by both singletons and twins. This shows differences similar to those in the mean length of response. The singletons have but a slight advantage at two years, but show an increasing advantage with age. The 158 words attained by the twins at five years are equaled in number by the singletons between thirty and thirty-six months. The retardation at five years is equivalent to approximately two years.

Table III

Mean Number of Words Used by C. A. and Sex

Chrono-logical Age	Mean Number of Total Words					
	Singletons (McCarthy)			Twins		
	Boy	Girl	All	Boy	Girl	All
Months						
24	36.8	87.1	66.0	40.11	70.9	55.90
36	164.4	176.2	170.3	116.80	112.45	114.63
48	213.4	218.5	216.3	146.31	146.00	146.15
60				143.30	173.20	158.25

The percentage of different words of each part of speech used by each age group are presented in Figure 8. It may be observed that the changes with age are not the same when considered from the standpoint of percentage of different words used. For instance, the percentage of nouns remains relatively constant rather than decreasing with age. The child's vocabulary of nouns is actually increasing with age. The percentage of verbs remains relatively constant. Twins show a smaller percentage of verbs than singletons at all ages. Adjectives increase in percentage slightly with age in both groups. The percentage of adverbs increases with age more in the singleton group than in the twin group. Pronouns decrease in percentage with age although the actual number after three years remains about constant. Conjunctions increase in percentage a little in both groups and agree closely in total percentages. The percentage of prepositions decreases with age in twins and remains constant in singletons. Interjections decrease in percentage with age. The twins, however, show even at five years a percentage almost equal to the two-year-old singleton. The miscellaneous words decrease with age and are higher in percentage for the twin group than for the singleton group.

The chief differences between singletons and twins in percentage of parts of speech used are in verbs, adjectives, pronouns, conjunctions, and interjections. The twins differ from the singletons in showing a smaller percentage of verbs at two years, a smaller percentage of adjectives, pronouns, and conjunctions at all ages, and a greater percentage of interjections at all ages. In the percentages of parts of speech of the different words, adjectives, pronouns, and conjunctions do not show great differences in proportion between twins and singletons. Adverbs, interjections, and verbs continue to show distinct differences. Twins show a greater percentage of adverbs and interjections and a smaller percentage of verbs.

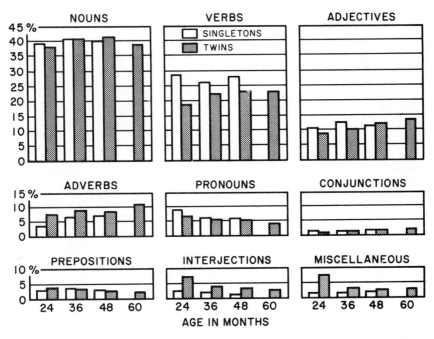

FIGURE 8. *Percentage of parts of speech used by chronological age (based on different words used at each age group).*

The sex differences in percentage of parts of speech, of the total words used, are of the same order as in the singleton group although they are less in magnitude in most instances. Girls are in advance. The greatest differences appear at two years, indicating, perhaps the earlier linguistic maturity of the girls.

The total number of words used also favors the girls. As in the mean length of responses, the boy and girl twins do not differ at three and four years although they show striking differences at two and five years. In the number of different words used (Table IV) girls are superior at every age except three years, when the boys exceed by a slight amount.

Table IV

Mean Number of Different Words Used by Twins and Singletons

Years	Singletons (McCarthy)						Twins					
	No cases	Boys	No cases	Girls	No cases	All	No cases	Boys	No cases	Girls	No cases	All
2	8	16.6	12	37.3	20	29.1	19	16.4	20	24.2	39	20.4
3	10	60.1	10	66.0	20	62.8	20	45.4	20	45.1	40	45.3
4	9	91.1	11	93.8	20	92.6	19	59.1	21	56.1	40	56.5
5							20	61.3	20	69.4	40	65.3

The twin group, when divided into the upper and lower occupational classes, shows differences similar to those found in the singletons. The upper group shows a superiority which is most marked at two years in those parts of speech of greatest developmental significance. This may indicate an earlier linguistic maturity of twins from the upper occupational classes.

Descoeudres (1921), Drever (1919), Gesell and Lord (1927), Hetzer and Reindorf (1928), Smith (1926) and McCarthy (1930) all have obtained results which agree in showing a positive relationship between linguistic development and socio-economic status. Stern (1924) in reworking the Descoeudres data estimated the difference between educated and working class children to be equivalent to about 8 months in age.

SUMMARY

1. As compared to single children twins are retarded in language development, as measured by each of the methods of analysis used.

2. This language retardation increases with age, within the age period covered (two to five years), and is most clearly shown in the comparison of the findings of mean length of response.

3. Both in the analysis according to the structure of the sentence and in the word analysis, twins show the greatest retardation in those phases which make the greatest change with age.

4. This is also true in the functional analysis with the exception of two phases. Egocentric responses and dramatic imitation, which are both affected, probably by the social advantage of the twin situation, show a superior development in twins as compared with singletons.

5. A small sex difference in favor of the girls appears in all methods of

analysis. These sex differences are not as great as in the case of singletons, due possibly to the operation of the social factor.

6. Twins of the upper three occupational classes are superior in all methods of analysis to the twins of the lower three occupational classes.

7. Singletons of the lower three occupational classes are superior in mean length of response to the twins of the upper three occupational classes. They are frequently superior in the phases of the other analyses.

8. The twins in this study were found to be approximately 10 points below the IQ of the slightly superior group of singletons with whom they were compared.

If in the twin situation each child has the other for a model in speech a large proportion of the time, rather than adults or older children as in the case of singletons, perhaps we may expect slower progress with a poorer model. Nothing in the situation prevents two children from listening simultaneously to what adults say, although the time spent in practicing speech might be limited and considerably reduced. In the first place only one person can talk at a time and in the second place perhaps the activities or even the presence of a twin provide some of the satisfaction otherwise obtained from conversation. Whatever the factors may be however, the evidence is clear that during the preschool years twins progress toward adult use of language at a relatively slow rate.

References

Descoeudres, A., *Le Développement de L'Enfant de Deux à Sept Ans*. Neuchâtel and Paris: Delachaux et Niestle, 1921.

Dewey, J., "The Psychology of Infant Language," *Psychological Review*, 1 (1894), 63-66.

Doran, E., "A Study of Vocabularies," *Pedagogical Seminary*, 14 (1907), 401-438.

Drever, J., "The Vocabulary of a Free Kindergarten Child," *Journal of Experimental Pedagogy*, 5 (1919), 28-37.

Gale, M. C. and H., "The Vocabularies of Three Children in One Family at Two and Three Years of Age," *Pedagogical Seminary*, 9 (1902), 422-435.

Gesell, A., and E. Lord, "A Psychological Comparison of Nursery-School Children from Homes of Low and High Economic Status," *Pedagogical Seminary*, 35 (1927), 339-356.

Goodenough, F. L., *Measurement of Intelligence by Drawings*. Yonkers, New York: World Book Company, 1926.

———, *The Kuhlman-Binet Tests for Children of Preschool Age. A Critical Study and Evaluation*. Minneapolis: University of Minnesota Press, 1928.

———, and J. E. Anderson, *Experimental Child Study*. New York: Century Company, 1931.

———, J. C. Foster, and M. J. Van Wagenen, *Minnesota Pre-School Scale*. Minneapolis, Minn.: Educational Test Bureau, Inc., 1932.

Hetzer, H., and B. Reindorf, "Sprachentwicklung und soziales Milieu," *Zeitschrift für Angewandte Psychologie*, 29 (1928), 449-462.

McCarthy, D. A., *The Language Development of the Preschool Child*. Institute of Child Welfare Monograph Series No. 4. Minneapolis: University of Minnesota Press, 1930.

Mead, C. D., "The Age of Walking and Talking in Relation to General Intelligence," *Pedagogical Seminary*, 2, (1913), 460-484.

Nice, M. M., "Length of Sentence as a Criterion of a Child's Progress in Speech," *Journal of Educational Psychology*, 16 (1925), 370-379.

Piaget, J., *The Language and Thought of the Child*, trans. M. Warden. New York: Harcourt, Brace Company, Inc., 1928.

Romanes, G. J., *Mental Evolution in Man*. New York: Appleton-Century-Crofts, Inc., 1889.

Smith, M. E., "An Investigation of the Development of the Sentence and the Extent of Vocabulary in Young Children," *University of Iowa Studies in Child Welfare*, Vol. 3, No. 5 (1926).

Stern, W., *Psychology of Early Childhood up to the Sixth Year*, trans. A. Barwell from 3rd ed. New York: Henry Holt & Company, Inc., 1924.

Terman, L. M., and others, *Genetic Studies of Genius*. Stanford: University of California Press, 1925.

5 · Learning to Speak After Years of Silence

MARIE K. MASON

Reprinted from the *Journal of Speech and Hearing Disorders*, 7 (1942), 295-304, by permission of the publisher.

It is frequently believed that if a child fails to acquire an important human attribute, such as affection or speech, at the "proper" time, he may never acquire it. Seldom does life produce a natural experiment which tests such a theory. The present case is therefore most unusual and, from a scientific point of view, most illuminating.

INTRODUCTION

History records many cases of children, who, for various reasons, have not learned to speak at the time when speech is normally acquired. Deafness, auditory aphasia, neuro-muscular articulatory incoordination, negativism, and mental deficiency are possible impeding factors in normal speech development. The clinical procedure in each of these types of delayed speech varies with the case. Clinical records show the results of the therapeutic measures effective in speech rehabilitation. There are but few cases in clinical pathology in which such environmental factors as isolation, imprisonment, and the almost total absence of normal life experiences are alone responsible for a child's inability to talk.

The case here discussed is that of a child, Isabelle (fictitious), who, because of her imprisonment with a mute and uneducated mother, did not learn to speak until she was six and a half years old. The purpose of this paper is to discuss briefly the introductory educational technique which the speaker developed in eliciting the child's first speech and language concepts.

SIGNIFICANT HISTORICAL ASPECTS

The mother of the child had, at the age of two, sustained an injury which destroyed the sight of the right eye. Her subsequent failure to develop speech was diagnosed by the physician in charge as a lesion in the association center of the cerebral cortex (Broca's area). She was wholly uneducated. She could neither talk, nor read, nor write, but communicated with her family by means of crude gestures of her own origination. She occupied herself in performing simple household tasks. She was not allowed to leave home unaccompanied. The advent of a child to this unwed mother of twenty-two was a surprise to the family, and the paternity has not yet been established.

During the period of pregnancy, and for six and a half years after the child's birth, mother and child had apparently been locked in a room behind drawn shades. Lack of sunshine, fresh air, and proper nourishment had developed in the child a rachitic condition which produced such extreme bowing of both legs as to make locomotion almost impossible. Carrying her six and a half year old child, Isabelle, the mother finally escaped and was brought to the attention of proper authorities who obtained Isabelle's admittance to Children's Hospital, Columbus, Ohio, on November 16, 1938, for orthopoedic surgery and physiotherapy.

Isabelle spent the first two days of her hospitalization in tears. As Assistant Director of the Speech Clinic of the Hospital, I was called in to see what could be done toward orienting the child to her new and strange environment. "We can't get her to talk; see what you can do," the hospital attaches told me. My entrance into the ward where Isabelle lay was greeted by a gesture of repulsion from the wan-looking, distraught child whose face bore the marks of grief and fear.

Sensing that any direct approach which I might make would not only be of no immediate avail but might disastrously affect any future confidence, I pretended absorption in a doll brought to me by Jane, another child in the same ward. Covertly watching Isabelle, I chose a chair close to her bed and drew Jane and the doll to my lap. I glanced up casually to find Isabelle watching me. I gave her a friendly smile but made no attempt to engage her attention. Soon her attitude of repulsion gave way to one of curiosity. She made a gesture with the palm of her hand first raised to me and then to the child in my lap. This I interpreted as her desire to discover the relationship between Jane and myself. I felt that she wanted to know whether the child belonged to me. Fearing to lose by denial what seemed to be Isabelle's first indication of interest or response to anyone, I smilingly nodded my head and, with an affectionate gesture, drew Jane more closely to me. Thereupon Isabelle immediately shook her head negatively and again made her gesture of repulsion, which seemed to me an indication that she disliked my attention to Jane.

Following this lead, I allowed Jane to slip off my lap. As I did so, the following method of approach occurred to me: I held my wrist watch to Jane's ear, "Do you hear it tick?" I asked. Jane listened and said, "Yes!" In pantomime, holding my watch to my own ear and with a questioning look on my face intended as an invitation to Isabelle to listen to my watch, I held it to her ear. Isabelle studied me for a moment, reached out her forefinger guardedly, and touched the watch. Then, of her own accord, she touched the ring I was wearing on the same hand, lifted the finger, and placed the ring to her ear. Holding the ring to my own ear and again to hers, I shook my head to indicate that the ring made no sound. Then pointing to the watch and holding it again to my ear, I nodded my head affirmatively, placed the watch to her ear, and indicated that the watch made a sound but that the ring did not. Then I smiled confidentially at her, gave her a reassuring pat on the hand, and, fearing to mar this first friendly contact, I left her, waving my hand as I left the room. What lay behind the child's silence? This was a problem, the solution of which, for the time being, could be one of mere conjecture.

My first successful attempt at winning the child's confidence encouraged me to make a second visit the following day. Taking with me a toy wrist watch, a ring, and a doll, I entered the room, pausing to smile at her and to wave a greeting before advancing to her bedside. Since her first gesture was again one of repulsion, I began to talk to the other children in the room. In a moment Isabelle made a gesture of interest toward the package I had brought. I smiled reassuringly and handed her the doll. She looked at it, smiled, and immediately pulled off its stocking. This was plainly an experience with which she was familiar: i.e., putting on and taking off her own stockings. Then she pointed with her forefinger to the doll's eye and looked at me questioningly. I said, "Eye, the doll's eye." Pointing to my eye and to Isabelle's, I repeated the word, "Eye." A moment later I playfully pointed to the doll's nose and said. "Nose." Tapping Isabelle's nose lightly, I repeated the word. She showed amusement but made no attempt at response.

When interest in the doll lagged, she remembered the other packages and pointed questioningly to them. I handed her the package containing the toy watch. She immediately thrust forward her wrist in pantomimic gesture and indicated that she wanted me to put it on. When I had clasped it on her wrist, she admired it for a moment, examined it carefully, and looking up quickly, pointed with the index finger of one hand to the ring finger of the other, as if to ask. "Where is the ring?" I handed her the box containing the ring. This time she thrust her ring finger forward and I slipped it on. She studied the watch and ring intently, now plainly her own possessions, again looked at me with a question in her eyes, and pointed to the wrist and ring finger of the other hand. It was clear to me that she wanted to know if I had brought her a watch and ring for that hand also. I hastily showed her that I was not wearing a watch and ring on both hands. She seemed to consider my gestured explanation satisfactory.

Following this, I pointed to the watch on her wrist and said, "Watch"; and, using the same gesture which she had used the day before to establish the idea of possession, I placed the upright palm of my hand close to her and said. "Your watch." Over and over I repeated the gesture and, each time, accompanied it with the words, "Ring, your ring; watch, your watch." Then, placing my hand palm to my chest, I said, "My ring, my watch"; repeating the same procedure with the concepts, doll, eye, nose, etc. Despite my constant repetition, she made no attempt to reproduce these concepts orally. However, through gesture, she distinctly indicated a comprehension of their meaning.

All this had been accomplished while I was alone in the room with her. Upon the nurse's entrance with her supper tray, Isabelle refused to eat and motioned her away with that same characteristic gesture of repulsion. I suggested to the nurse that Isabelle be removed from her bed to a chair before a small table on which her tray could be placed. She watched the other children as they ate their soup, but made no attempt to eat. I offered her a spoonful of soup which she took, and a moment later Isabelle drank some milk from her cup; then, ignoring the empty space on her tray, she replaced the cup in a plate of mashed potatoes. I offered her some of the food on her plate; she ate a small quantity. This was her first acceptance of any food other than the milk and crackers which she had allowed the nurse to feed her.

Subsequent visits established a greater rapport, and because of the child's confidence in me the consulting psychologist invited me to assist in the first perfunctory intelligence test of mother and child. I use the term "test" ill-advisedly, since at this time no accurate estimate of either sensory or cortical reactions could be made. It was impossible to tell whether the child's inability to speak was due to the fact that she could not hear; or, hearing what was said to her, she failed to comprehend its purport; or, hearing and comprehending, she was unable to form the motor coordinations necessary to speech.

An initial and perfunctory test of hearing given simultaneously with the attempted psychological test seemed to give evidence that the mother suffered a serious loss of hearing and that Isabelle heard either wholly or at least to a substantial degree. Audiometric tests of the mother could not be made because of her inability to comprehend spoken or written directions. She made no response to a vocal sound in her right ear, but seemed to feel a slight auditory sensation in the left ear. Deafness, therefore, occurring as a result of the accident when she was two years old, would seem to account for the mother's failure to develop speech rather than any destruction of the cerebral speech center, which, according to the family, had been the physician's early diagnosis. This makes apparent the fact that Isabelle's mother should have been educated in a school for the deaf where she could have been taught speech and lip-reading. She might thus have become educationally and economically independent, instead of the pathetic creature she now is: grown to a woman's maturity, but, for lack of instruction, attaining only a child's educational status.

The fact that Isabelle heard was further substantiated as she learned to listen. Words were, at first, meaningless to her, and, therefore, evoked no response. Thus deafness as a casual factor of Isabelle's speechlessness could be definitely eliminated.

With hearing ability established, the possibility of auditory aphasia or word deafness could likewise be eliminated. The circumstances of Isabelle's isolation and the fact that she did not hear spoken language during the long confinement with her mute mother would tend to rule out the possibility that she was unable to comprehend and reproduce in speech words which were said to her.

This lack of speech and language, together with her inferior response to simple tests of performance skill, suggested the possibility of amentia, or definite feeble-mindedness. The report of the first phychological test revealed the performance of a three-year-old child with complete failure on any test involving linguistic skill.

Conflicting opinions of psychologists, physicians, pediatricians, and other authorities rested upon these assumptions:

1. That her inability to speak suggested mental deficiency.
2. That, if of normal intelligence and if her inability to speak were the result of long isolation with her mute mother, the transfer to normal speech environment would affect the acquisition of speech and language skill.

The general impression was that she was wholly uneducable and that any attempt to teach her to speak, after so long a period of silence, would meet with failure. In spite of this I decided to make the attempt on my own assumption that Isabelle's failure to speak was due to the six and a half years of isolation with a mute and deaf mother; that, in spite of her hearing acuity, she had either heard speech not at all or at such distance and with such indistinctness as to have established no auditory impressions of speech or language forms.

The first important problem to confront me in my endeavor to teach Isabelle to speak was the choice of some satisfactory method of procedure. Gesture was her only mode of expression. In her characteristic descriptive motions with which she tried to make clear what she wanted, I noted a similarity to the sign language used by deaf children. She seemed to have had no acquaintance with simple childhood toys. She was apparently utterly unaware of relationships of any kind. When presented with a ball for the first time, she held it in the palm of her hand, then reached out and stroked my face with it. Such behavior is comparable to that of a child of six months. She made no attempt to squeeze it, to throw it, or to bounce it. These observations prompted me, therefore, to adopt an educational approach combining gesture, facial expression, pantomine, dramatization, and imitation.

Isabelle made her first attempt at vocalization one week after my first visit to her. I sat with her at a small table on which I had placed a ball, a toy automobile, a horn, and a bell. She seemed interested in each object as I presented it, but their spoken symbols seemed to make no impression on her. In the form of play, I held up the ball and said, "Ball," close to her ear. This seemed a pleasurable sensation, but she gave no response other than a smile. Repeating the performance and again saying "Ball," I placed my ear close to her mouth and in pantomime indicated that I wished her to make a vocal response, whereupon she gleefully said "Buh" (ba),* making the labial approximation for the consonant "b," and the laryngeal adjustment which produced the neutral vowel "uh" (a). Her joy in successful performance was similar to that of a baby whose first "coo" elicits his parents' surprise and approval. My praise of her attempt immediately prompted her to say "Ah," in response to my word, "Car." Thus Isabelle's first imitative utterances were made. While apparently proud of her first vocal sounds, Isabelle seemed disinclined to repeat the attempt on the following day, and it was only after many repetitions that these two words were correctly spoken and became for her the verbal symbols of the objects represented.

Thus began my laborious task of devising resources to assist her in establishing relationships between symbolization and concrete objects. Independent word concepts were introduced at first, and Isabelle was taught to make individual oral responses. The habit of silence was so ingrained that the mere fact that she could speak a word was not a sufficient stimulus to motivate its spontaneous and automatic reproduction.

Simultaneous with her attainment of independent word concepts, phrases and short sentences were used in addressing her, but with no expectation of demanding that she reproduce them. Nouns were naturally the first concepts introduced. Verbs were represented in the form of action and dramatization. This was limited to certain activities because of her difficulty in walking as a result of the bowed leg condition and also to the postoperative cast on both legs which held her bedfast from December 13, 1938 until March 13, 1939.

Isabelle's first language concepts were developed exclusively through experience with actual objects. Whenever this was impossible, brightly colored pictures, sketches, and diagrams of various types were utilized. Action games, such as throwing a ball, holding up an object as its name was spoken, were begun as early as November 26, 1938, and similar games involving more complicated dramatic action grew out of these as Isabelle's vocabulary increased. By December 1939, Isabelle participated in the dramatization of many of the nursery rhymes and children's songs involving both the spoken word and pantomimic or imitative action.

Music was first introduced on December 5, 1938. Hoping to encourage her newly acquired word concepts, I used them in little home-made songs for which I improvised piano accompaniment. Victrola records were next

* Symbols used are those of the international phonetic alphabet.

introduced, and Isabelle was taught to clap her hands to the music. On February 4, 1939, she had her first experience in beating the rhythmic tempo of a musical selection, using percussion instruments, such as tambourines, bells, triangles, drums, etc. Soon after March 13, 1939, when the removal of the plaster casts allowed free motor leg and foot activities, skipping, hopping, marching, and dancing were performed to music, in order to develop in Isabelle a rhythmic response to motor stimuli in preparation for stress and accent in speech and for continuity of articulation and modulation in phonation. Isabelle's love of music was further fostered by teaching her to play some simple melodies.

Other educative materials such as those used in pre-school classes, kindergarten, and first grade, were utilized in order to build up Isabelle's speech vocabulary and to prepare her for future reading, writing, and numerical accomplishment. Attractive pictures to be colored, cut out, and the printed name pasted under it were used as early as March 9, 1939. The use of a clock, calendars, and geographical maps gave Isabelle an idea of temporal and spatial relations.

Isabelle's acquisition of speech seemed to pass through successive developmental changes. While it is true that her earliest vocal utterances, at the age of six and a half, were those of a child of a year and a half or two years, it is also true that she passed through each successive stage more rapidly than the normal child whose speech maturation begins at two or before and extends over a longer period of time.

Some idea of the progress of these successive stages, together with the lapse of time from one to the other, may be gained from the following excerpts from detailed chronological records of her speech education covering the period from November 19, 1938 to September 10, 1940.

11-16-38: Admittance to Children's Hospital, Columbus, Ohio.

11-17, 18-38: Cried almost continuously; would not partake of food except milk and crackers; showed either recoil, disinterest, or fear of everyone with whom she came in contact.

11-19-38: My first visit, described above.

11-20-38: My second visit. Isabelle showed interest in the watch, ring, and doll which I brought her. Partook of some food when seated at a small table.

11-22-38: Gesture communication between mother and child before and during psychological examination. No attempt at vocalization.

11-25-38: First vocalization. Attempt to say the words "ball" and "car" and "bye" (good-bye). Described above.

11-26-38: Repeated the words "baby" and "dirty" in imitation of words spoken to her in the form of play. "Baby" was the most distinct articulation to date.

11-30-38: Said flower, one, two. Jabbered succession of nonsense syllables in imitation of my rather lengthy explanation to Jane that she should not appropriate Isabelle's toys.

12- 3-38: Isabelle began to associate the word with its object; does not associate individuals with their names, but recognizes her own name when spoken.

12- 5-38: Said voluntarily the words "mama," "fat," "pretty," "hot"; used "bye" spontaneously to everyone.

12- 8-38: Said watch, ring, blue, car, ball, lady, bell, bow-wow, dog, hot, cold, warm, one, two, three, red, dirty, pretty, baby.

12-13-38: Surgical operation.

1- 4-39: Repeated for student teacher (J. H.), dog, baby, pretty, hair, one, two, three, Jane, good-bye, girl, boy, paper, cut, locket.

1-13-39: Repeated: house, eye, red, green, yellow, purple. Distinguished yellow from the other colors and said "yellow" voluntarily.

1-31-39: Said for student teacher (B. O.), penny, purse, dime, open, all right, come again.

2- 8-39: Says the following sentences voluntarily: That's my baby; I love my baby; open your eyes; close your eyes; I don't know; I don't want; that's funny; 'top it—'at's mine (when another child attempted to take one of her toys).

2-11-39: New words: milk, soup, coat, fur. Sentences: I want the scissors; I want a balloon; want some soup; Pick it up, Dorothy—indicating something that had fallen on the floor. She now associates people with names.

2-18-39: Says, "Give me a penny."

3- 2-39: Isabelle said, "Say please," when I asked her to hand me something. Later she said, "I'm sorry," when she accidentally hurt another child's finger.

3- 4-39: Isabelle said, "I love you, Miss Mason."

3- 9-39: Identified printed form of the words, blue and yellow, and matched the word with the color.

3-10-39: Isabelle matched the printed forms of cow, sheep, dog, and cat with corresponding pictures.

3-11-39: "Stay, I don't want you to go home."

3-13-39: Isabelle pointed to pictures in her book, saying: "This is a boy; This is a baby," etc. Said, "I'm sleepy."

3-22-39: Said, "I see a purple flower; I see a pretty flower."

3-27-39: Isabelle voluntarily sang, "I see you, tra la, la-la, la-la."

4- 1-39: Isabelle goes about humming nursery rhymes, "Here we go round the mulberry bush," and "baa, baa, black sheep."

5- 2-39: Isabelle gets first formal lesson in reading in a book called "Play and Read"; said "Where's my book?"

The above citations give the reader an idea of the development of some of Isabelle's first language concepts. Since space will not permit a further detailed synopsis of her progress to date, some excerpts follow which are contained in my summary of her educational achievement down to December 1939, after one year of effort:

1. Isabelle has shown considerable progress in word recognition in preparation for reading readiness. She identifies the printed forms of many words and of whole sentences.

2. Her speech has improved noticeably. Her vocabulary is much increased. However, in expressing herself, unless cautioned, she is likely to run her

words together. This may be accounted for by her inability to form all of her sentences correctly from the standpoint of grammatical construction and, in her attempt to speak her thoughts, her mental reaction out-speeds her motor speech reactions and a resultant jabber is noticeable.

3. Isabelle's writing has taken on splendid form. She writes with a steadiness and character which might do credit to an older child.
4. She now comprehends numerical concepts, which, at first, were extremely difficult for her. She counts to 20, readily; sometimes, beyond. She has acquired a knowledge of addition to 10.
5. Isabelle listens attentively while a story is read to her. She retells the story in her own limited vocabulary, bringing out the main points.
6. She is much interested in her rhythmic activities. She can interpret the tempo of a musical selection in various ways, and she can march and dance. Isabelle is anxious for Santa Claus to come. She says she wants a bicycle and a "real baby" and "Jingle Bells."

A summary dated June 1940, after a year and a half training, including items from my own notes and those of five student teachers, may give the reader an idea of Isabelle's vocabulary of nouns, adjectives, verbs, etc., and her use of question forms:

1. Vocabulary between 1,500 and 2,000 words. (Lists of five student teachers.)
2. Questions asked by Isabelle: (student teacher, B. J.)
Why do crayons break? Why does the hand move around the clock? Why does the paste come out if one upsets the jar? Do you go to Miss Mason's school at the University? Are you going to Church tomorrow? Does your dog sleep in your bed? What did Miss Mason say when you told her I cleaned my classroom?
3. Isabelle now tells in detail the story of Little Black Sambo. (D. B., student teacher.)
4. Isabelle recited Baa, Baa, Black Sheep. (M. V., student teacher.)
5. Isabelle made up a story, using it in a puppet show. (I. S., student teacher.)

Summarizing the twenty-two months of Isabelle's speech and linguistic development, we find that she has progressed from her first spoken word to full length sentences, intelligent questioning, recitation of nursery rhymes, story-telling, and songs. She has a reading readiness vocabulary of words and sentences; she counts to a hundred; identifies coins; recognizes their numerical values; and performs arithmetical computations to ten. She has a well-defined sense of form in manuscript writing and evidences taste and discrimination in crayon work and painting.

She is aggressive, often to the point of stubbornness; under certain conditions she shows extreme negativism. She has an excellent sense of humor and is an inveterate tease; she is given to temporization which she utilizes to delay an undesirable task, to divert attention from her mistakes or lack of knowledge, or to enjoy in others the exasperation which her actions provoke.

She is highly imaginative and has an acute sense of the dramatic. She is very affectionate and lovable. Her first unsocial behavior which betrayed itself in antagonistic and often animalistic reaction, in the richness of her newly acquired experiences, has changed to one capable of making adjustments in social situations.

Here is a little girl now eight years old, who, in a period of less than two years, has made striking social adjustments to a living and hearing world after six years in a world of silence, fear, and isolation; a child who can communicate with others in speech after six and a half years of primitive gesturing to a mute and deaf mother; a child who, at six and a half years, bearing the semblance of a mental defective, after two years of changed environment, enriched experience, unremitting instruction, improved physical condition and appearance, is, at eight years, considered a child of normal intelligence.

6 · Communication Between Children

JEAN PIAGET

Reprinted from pages 80, 82, 83, 85-87, 94, 99, 101-103, *Language and Thought of the Child*, 1926, by permission of Humanities Press Inc. and Routledge & Kegan Paul Ltd.

Communication between two adults is frequently subject to error, but Piaget indicates that communication between young children is even more defective unless the ideas to be communicated are already well-known to both children.

The matter can be introduced as an amusement or a competition: "Are you good at telling stories? Very well then, we'll send your little friend out of the room, and while he is standing outside the door, we'll tell you a story. You must listen very carefully. When you have listened to it all, we'll make your friend come back, and then you will tell him the same story. We shall see which of you is best at telling stories. You understand? You must listen well, and then tell the same thing . . ." and so on. Repeat the instructions as often as necessary, and stress the need for a faithful rendering.

Then one of the subjects is sent out of the room, and the set piece is read to the other. The more complicated passages are repeated, everything is done to make the subject listen, but the text is not altered. Then one or the other of the following methods is adopted: (They have been used alternately, the one serving as a test of the other.) Either the child who has been waiting outside in the passage, and whom we shall call the *reproducer*, is sent for, and everything that the other child (whom we shall call the *explainer*) says to him is taken down in *extenso*; or else the explainer is asked to tell us a story in the first instance, and is then sent to tell the same story to the reproducer out in the lobby or in the garden, that is, in our absence, and with the injunction to take as much time as he likes. In both cases the story, as told by the reproducer, is taken down verbatim.

When the experiment is over, the two children exchange parts; the explainer is sent out of the room and becomes the reproducer in this second test, a new story is told to the former reproducer who now becomes explainer, and everything is done as in the previous case.

We have carried out with these methods some hundred experiments on 30 children from seven to eight, taken in pairs (that is, 15 couples with 4 experiments per couple, say 2 explanations and 2 stories), and on 20 children from six to seven (10 couples with 4 experiments per couple).

Here are the stories which were used:

> *Story I.* Epaminondas is a little Negro boy and he lives in a country where it is very hot. His mother once said to him: "Go and take this short-bread cake to your granny, but don't break it." Epaminondas put the shortbread under his arm, and when he got to his grandmother's the short-bread was in crumbs. His granny gave him a pat of butter to take back to his mother. This time Epaminondas thought to himself: "I shall be very careful." And he put the pat of butter on his head. The sun was shining hard, and when he got home the butter had all melted. "You are a silly," said his mother, "you should have put the butter in a leaf, then it would have arrived whole."

> *Story II.* Once upon a time, there was a lady who was called Niobe, and who had 12 sons and 12 daughters. She met a fairy who had only one son and no daughter. Then the lady laughed at the fairy because the fairy only had one boy. Then the fairy was very angry and fastened the lady to a rock. The lady cried for ten years. In the end she turned into a rock, and her tears made a stream which still runs today.

> *Story III.* Once upon a time, there was a castle, and in it were a king and queen who had three sons and one daughter. Near the castle was a wicked fairy who did not like children. She took the king and queen's children to the seashore, and changed them into four beautiful white swans. As their children had not come home, the king and queen went to look for them everywhere, and they came right down to the seashore. There they saw four beautiful swans, who told them that they were their children. The swans stayed on the sea for a very long time, and then they went away to a very cold country. After many years they came back to where their castle was. There was no castle there any longer, and their parents were dead. The swans went into a church and they were changed into three little old men and one little old woman.

So far, then, the method is quite simple. You read one of the stories to the explainer, but you must not appear to be reading, and you must talk in the most natural manner possible. The explainer then tells the story to the reproducer, who finally serves it up to you again.

But this is not all. Once the reproducer's story has been obtained and taken down in its entirety, the explainer is taken aside for a few moments, and the reproducer is asked a certain number of questions on the points that have been omitted, so as to ascertain whether he has really failed to understand them. He may either have forgotten them or he may not know how to express them. In order to judge of the child's degree of understanding these factors must at all costs be eliminated, so as to clear the ground for a more searching investigation. If in the story of Niobe, for example, the end is forgotten, the child is asked whether there is nothing about a stream. Thus by means of questions, vague at first and then more and more precise, and with the help of that division into points which we shall give in the next paragraph, the reproducer's degree of understanding can be properly put to the test. When this has been done, the explainer is questioned in the same manner, to see whether he has really understood the points which appear doubtful.

We have divided each of our set pieces into a certain number of points, a̍ done in the sifting of evidence, so as to see which of these points have been reproduced or omitted by the subjects, and instead of choosing a large number all bearing on questions of detail, we have restricted ourselves to a small number of rubrics connected solely with the understanding of the story. In estimating the correctness of each point, moreover, we have taken no notice in parceling out the material of the factors that were not essential to the understanding of the story. Thus in the tale of Niobe the name of Niobe plays no part whatsoever; it is sufficient if mention is made of "a lady" or even "a fairy." Similarly, "12 boys and 12 girls" can be changed into "many children" or "3 children," and the like, provided a difference is made between the number of children belonging to "the lady" and that of those belonging to the fairy.

Here, in detail, are the points taken into consideration in story II:

(1) Once there was a lady (or a fairy, and so on). (2) She had children (provided they outnumber those of the other fairy). (3) She met a fairy (or a girl). (4) This fairy had few children (or none at all, provided their number is inferior to the first lot). (5) The lady laughed at the fairy. (6) Because the fairy had so few children. (7) The fairy was angry. (8) The fairy fastened the lady (to a rock, a tree, to the shore). (9) The lady cried. (10) She turned into a rock. (11) Her tears made a stream. (12) Which flows to this day.

It is obvious that each of these points except point (7), which can easily be taken for granted, and points (9) and (12) which are supplementary to the body of the story, are necessary to the comprehension of the story. It will be seen, moreover, that we are very generous in our estimates, since any alternation of detail is tolerated.

The stories of Epaminondas and of the four swans were parceled out according to exactly the same principles.

[Piaget here presents numerical data to show that in general a child does not understand another child's account at all well, whereas the original stories were quite well comprehended.]

Conversation between children is therefore not sufficient at first to take the speakers out of their egocentrism, because each child, whether he is trying to explain his own thoughts or to understand those of others, is shut up in his own point of view. This phenomenon occurs, it is true, among adults. But these have had at least some practice in argument or conversation, and they know their faults. They make an effort to understand and be understood, unless indeed distrust or anger reduces them to a childish state, because experience has shown them the appalling density of the human mind. Children have no suspicion of all this.

If children fail to understand one another, it is because they think that they do understand one another. The explainer believes from the start that the reproducer will grasp everything, will almost know beforehand all that should be known, and will interpret every subtlety. Children are perpetually surrounded by adults who not only know much more than they do, but who also do everything in their power to understand them, who even anticipate their thoughts and their desires. Children, therefore, whether they work or not, whether they express wishes or feel guilty, are perpetually under the impression that people can read their thoughts, and in extreme cases, can steal their thoughts away. It is obviously owing to this mentality that children do not take the trouble to express themselves clearly, do not even take the trouble to talk, convinced as they are that the other person knows as much or more than they do, and that he will immediately understand what is the matter.

These habits of thought account, in the first place, for the remarkable lack of precision in childish style. Pronouns, personal and demonstrative adjectives, "he, she" or "that, the, him," and so on, are used right and left, without any indication of what they refer to. The other person is supposed to understand. Here is an example:

> GIO tells the story of Niobe in the role of explainer: "Once upon a time there was a lady who had 12 boys and 12 girls, and then a fairy a boy and a girl. And then Niobe wanted to have some more sons than the fairy. (Gio means by this that Niobe competed with the fairy, as was told in the text. But it will be seen how elliptical is his way of expressing it.) Then she (who?) was angry. She (who?) fastened her (whom?) to a stone. He (who?) turned into a rock, and then his tears (whose?) made a stream which is still running today."

From this account it looks as though Gio had understood nothing. As a matter of fact he had grasped nearly everything, and his understanding in relation to us was high. He knew for instance that the fairy was angry "because she (N.) wanted to have more children than the fairy." The pronouns distributed at random are therefore a characteristic of the style, and not a proof of lack of understanding. Gio knows perfectly well that it was the fairy who fastened N. to the rock and not *vice versa*.

It is easy to forsee the results of such a style. The reproducer, Ri, begins by taking N. for the fairy, and by thinking that it is N. who fastens the lady. After being put right on this point, he reproduces the story as follows:

> There was a lady once, she had 12 boys and 12 girls. She goes for a walk and she meets a fairy who had a boy and a girl and who didn't want to have 12 children. 12 and 12 make 24. She didn't want to have 24 children. She fastened N. to a stone, she became a rock, and so on.

V—INTELLECTUAL DEVELOPMENT

1 · Binet's Method of Measuring Intelligence

LEWIS M. TERMAN

Reprinted from *The Measurement of Intelligence*. Boston: Houghton Mifflin Company, 1916, pages 36-42, by permission of the publisher.

Beginning about 1890, there were several attempts to measure intelligence by psychological tests. The early attempts failed because the measures tried consisted of relatively simple functions: memory span, reaction time, size estimation, speed of association, and so on. Binet, a noted French psychologist, and Simon, a collaborating physician, constructed the first successful intelligence scale in 1905. It was first developed for use with the feeble-minded but was extended for use with the normal and the gifted. Binet and Simon included in their scale a diverse array of items, including knowledge of common objects and words, and tests of memory and judgment. The account of the Binet-Simon tests given below was written by Terman, whose own contributions to the measurement of intelligence were very substantial.

DESCRIPTION OF THE BINET-SIMON METHOD

Essential Nature of the Scale

The Binet scale is made up of an extended series of tests in the nature of "stunts," or problems, success in which demands the exercise of intelligence. As left by Binet, the scale consists of 54 tests, so graded in difficulty that the easiest lie well within the range of normal 3-year-old children, while the hardest tax the intelligence of the average adult. The problems are designed primarily to test native intelligence, not school knowledge or home training. They try to answer the question, "How intelligent is this child?" How much the child has learned is of significance only in so far as it throws light on his ability to learn more.

Binet fully appreciated the fact that intelligence is not homogeneous, that it has many aspects, and that no one kind of test will display it adequately. He therefore assembled for his intelligence scale tests of many different types, some of them designed to display differences of memory, others differences in power to reason, ability to compare, power of comprehension, time orientation, facility in the use of number concepts, power

215

to combine ideas into a meaningful whole, the maturity of apperception, wealth of ideas, knowledge of common objects, etc.

How the Scale Was Derived

The tests were arranged in order of difficulty, as found by trying them upon some 200 normal children of different ages from 3 to 15 years. It was found, for illustration, that a certain test was passed by only a very small proportion of the younger children, say the 5-year-olds, and that the number passing this test increased rapidly in the succeeding years until by the age of 7 or 8 years, let us say, practically all the children were successful. If, in our supposed case, the test was passed by about two-thirds to three-fourths of the normal children aged 7 years, it was considered by Binet a test of 7-year intelligence. In like manner, a test passed by 65 to 75 per cent of the normal 9-year-olds was considered a test of 9-year intelligence, and so on. By trying out many different tests in this way it was possible to secure five tests to represent each age from 3 to 10 years (excepting age 4, which has only four tests), five for age 12, five for 15, and five for adults, making 54 tests in all.

List of Tests

The following is the list of tests as arranged by Binet in 1911, shortly before his untimely death:—

Age 3:
1. Points to nose, eyes, and mouth.
2. Repeats two digits.
3. Enumerates objects in a picture.
4. Gives family name.
5. Repeats a sentence of six syllables.

Age 4:
1. Gives his sex.
2. Names key, knife, and penny.
3. Repeats three digits.
4. Compares two lines.

Age 5:
1. Compares two weights.
2. Copies a square.
3. Repeats a sentence of ten syllables.
4. Counts four pennies.
5. Unites the halves of a divided rectangle.

Age 6:
1. Distinguishes between morning and afternoon.
2. Defines familiar words in terms of use.
3. Copies a diamond.
4. Counts thirteen pennies.
5. Distinguishes pictures of ugly and pretty faces.

Age 7:
1. Shows right hand and left ear.
2. Describes a picture.
3. Executes three commissions, given simultaneously.
4. Counts the value of six sous, three of which are double.
5. Names four cardinal colors.

Age 8:
1. Compares two objects from memory.
2. Counts from 20 to 0.
3. Notes omissions from pictures.
4. Gives day and date.
5. Repeats five digits.

Age 9:
1. Gives change from twenty sous.
2. Defines familiar words in terms superior to use.
3. Recognizes all the pieces of money.
4. Names the months of the year, in order.
5. Answers easy "comprehension questions."

Age 10:
1. Arranges five blocks in order of weight.
2. Copies drawings from memory.
3. Criticizes absurd statements.
4. Answers difficult "comprehension questions."
5. Uses three given words in not more than two sentences.

Age 12:
1. Resists suggestion.
2. Composes one sentence containing three given words.
3. Names sixty words in three minutes.
4. Defines certain abstract words.
5. Discovers the sense of a disarranged sentence.

Age 15:
1. Repeats seven digits.
2. Finds three rhymes for a given word.
3. Repeats a sentence of twenty-six syllables.
4. Interprets pictures.
5. Interprets given facts.

Adult:
1. Solves the paper-cutting test.
2. Rearranges a triangle in imagination.
3. Gives differences between pairs of abstract terms.
4. Gives three differences between a president and a king.
5. Gives the main thought of a selection which he has heard read.

It should be emphasized that merely to name the tests in this way gives little idea of their nature and meaning, and tells nothing about Binet's method of conducting the 54 experiments. In order to use the tests intelligently it is necessary to acquaint one's self thoroughly with the purpose of each test, its correct procedure, and the psychological interpretation of different types of response.

In fairness to Binet, it should also be borne in mind that the scale of tests was only a rough approximation to the ideal which the author had set himself to realize. Had his life been spared a few years longer, he would doubtless have carried the method much nearer perfection.

How the Scale Is Used

By means of the Binet tests we can judge the intelligence of a given individual by comparison with standards of intellectual performance for normal children of different ages. In order to make the comparison it is only necessary to begin the examination of the subject at a point in the scale where all the tests are passed successfully, and to continue up the scale until no more successes are possible. Then we compare our subject's performances with the standard for normal children of the same age, and note the amount of acceleration or retardation.

Let us suppose the subject being tested is 9 years of age. If he goes as far in the tests as normal 9-year-old children ordinarily go, we can say that the child has a "mental age" of 9 years, which in this case is normal (our child being 9 years of age). If he goes only as far as normal 8-year-old children ordinarily go, we say that his "mental age" is 8 years. In like manner, a mentally defective child of 9 years may have a "mental age" of only 4 years, or a young genius of 9 years may have a mental age of 12 or 13 years.

Special Characteristics of the Binet-Simon Method

Psychologists had experimented with intelligence tests for at least twenty years before the Binet scale made its appearance. The question naturally suggests itself why Binet should have been successful in a field where previous efforts had been for the most part futile. The answer to this question is found in three essential differences between Binet's method and those formerly employed.

1. *The use of age standards.* Binet was the first to utilize the idea of age standards, or norms, in the measurement of intelligence. It will be understood, of course, that Binet did not set out to invent tests of 10-year intelligence, 6-year intelligence, etc. Instead, as already explained, he began with a series of tests ranging from very easy to very difficult, and by trying these tests on children of different ages and noting the percentages of successes in the various years, he was able to locate them (approximately) in the years where they belonged.

This plan has the great advantage of giving us standards which are easily grasped. To say, for illustration, that a given subject has a grade of intelligence equal to that of the average child of 8 years is a statement whose general import does not need to be explained. Previous investigators had worked with subjects the degree of whose intelligence was unknown, and with tests the difficulty of which was equally unknown. An immense amount of ingenuity was spent in devising tests which were used in such a way as to preclude any very meaningful interpretation of the responses.

The Binet method enables us to characterize the intelligence of a child in a far more definite way than had hitherto been possible. Current descriptive terms like "bright," "moderately bright," "dull," "very dull," "feeble-minded," etc., have had no universally accepted meaning. A child who is designated by one person as "moderately bright" may be called "very bright" by another person. The degree of intelligence which one calls "moderate dullness," another may call "extreme dullness," etc. But every one knows what is meant by the term 8-year mentality, 4-year mentality, etc., even if he is not able to define these grades of intelligence in psychological terms; and by ascertaining experimentally what intellectual tasks children of different ages can perform, we are, of course, able to make our age standards as definite as we please.

Why should a device so simple have waited so long for a discoverer? We do not know. It is of a class with many other unaccountable mysteries in the development of scientific method. Apparently the idea of an age-grade method, as this is called, did not come to Binet himself until he had experimented with intelligence tests for some fifteen years. At least his first provisional scale, published in 1905, was not made up according to the age-grade plan. It consisted merely of 30 tests, arranged roughly in order of difficulty. Although Binet nowhere gives any account of the steps by which this crude and ungraded scale was transformed into the relatively complete age-grade scale of 1908, we can infer that the original and ingenious idea of utilizing age norms was suggested by the data collected with the 1905 scale. However the discovery was made, it ranks, perhaps, from the practical point of view, as the most important in all the history of psychology.

2. *The kind of mental functions brought into play.* In the second place, the Binet tests differ from most of the earlier attempts in that they are designed to test the higher and more complex mental processes, instead of the simpler and more elementary ones. Hence they set problems for the reasoning powers and ingenuity, provoke judgments about abstract matters, etc., instead of attempting to measure sensory discrimination, mere retentiveness, rapidity of reaction, and the like. Psychologists had generally considered the higher processes too complex to be measured directly, and accordingly sought to get at them indirectly by correlating supposed intelligence with simpler processes which could readily be measured, such as reaction time, rapidity of tapping, discrimination of tones and colors, etc. While they were disputing over their contradictory findings in this line of exploration, Binet went directly to the point and succeeded where they had failed.

It is now generally admitted by psychologists that higher intelligence is little concerned in such elementary processes as those mentioned above. Many of the animals have keen sensory discrimination. Feeble-minded children, unless of very low grade, do not differ very markedly from normal children in sensitivity of the skin, visual acuity, simple reaction time, type of imagery, etc. But in power of comprehension, abstraction, and ability to direct thought, in the nature of the associative processes, in amount of information possessed, and in spontaneity of attention, they differ enormously.

3. *Binet would test "general intelligence."* Finally, Binet's success was largely due to his abandonment of the older "faculty psychology" which, far from being defunct, had really given direction to most of the earlier work with mental tests. Where others had attempted to measure memory, attention, sense discrimination, etc., as separate faculties or functions, Binet undertook to ascertain the *general level* of intelligence. Others had thought the task easier of accomplishment by measuring each division or aspect of intelligence separately, and summating the results. Binet, too, began in this way, and it was only after years of experimentation by the usual methods that he finally broke away from them and undertook, so to speak, to triangulate the height of his tower without first getting the dimensions of the individual stones which made it up.

The assumption that it is easier to measure a part, or one aspect, of intelligence than all of it, is fallacious in that the parts are not separate parts and cannot be separated by any refinement of experiment. They are interwoven and intertwined. Each ramifies everywhere and appears in all other functions. The analogy of the stones of the tower does not really apply. Memory, for example, cannot be tested separately from attention, or sense-discrimination separately from the associative processes. After many vain attempts to disentangle the various intellective functions, Binet decided to test their combined functional capacity without any pretense of measuring the exact contribution of each to the total product. It is hardly too much to say that intelligence tests have been successful just to the extent to which they have been guided by this aim.

Memory, attention, imagination, etc., are terms of "structural psychology." Binet's psychology is dynamic. He conceives intelligence as the sum total of those thought processes which consist in mental adaptation. This adaptation is not explicable in terms of the old mental "faculties." No one of these can explain a single thought process, for such process always involves the participation of many functions whose separate roles are impossible to distinguish accurately. Instead of measuring the intensity of various mental states (psycho-physics), it is more enlightening to measure their combined effect on adaptation. Using a biological comparison, Binet says the old "faculties" correspond to the separate tissues of an animal or plant, while his own "scheme of thought" corresponds to the functioning organ itself. For Binet, psychology is the science of behavior.

Binet's Conception of General Intelligence

In devising tests of intelligence it is, of course, necessary to be guided by some assumption, or assumptions, regarding the nature of intelligence. To adopt any other course is to depend for success upon happy chance.

However, it is impossible to arrive at a final definition of intelligence on the basis of a priori considerations alone. To demand, as critics of the Binet method have sometimes done, that one who would measure intelligence should first present a complete definition of it, is quite unreasonable. As Stern points out, electrical currents were measured long before their nature was well understood. Similar illustrations could be drawn from the processes involved in chemistry, physiology, and other sciences. In the case of intelligence it may be truthfully said that no adequate definition can possibly be framed which is not based primarily on the symptoms empirically brought to light by the test method. The best that can be done in advance of such data is to make tentative assumptions as to the probable nature of intelligence, and then to subject these assumptions to tests which will show their correctness or incorrectness. New hypotheses can then be framed for further trial, and thus gradually we shall be led to a conception of intelligence which will be meaningful and in harmony with all the ascertainable facts.

Such was the method of Binet. Only those unacquainted with Binet's more than fifteen years of labor preceding the publication of his intelligence scale would think of accusing him of making no effort to analyze the mental processes which his tests bring into play. It is true that many of Binet's earlier assumptions proved untenable, and in this event he was always ready, with exceptional candor and intellectual plasticity, to acknowledge his error and to plan a new line of attack.

Binet's conception of intelligence emphasizes three characteristics of the thought process: (1) Its tendency to take and maintain a definite direction; (2) the capacity to make adaptations for the purpose of attaining a desired end; and (3) the power of auto-criticism.

How these three aspects of intelligence enter into the performances with various tests of the scale is set forth from time to time in our directions for giving and interpreting the individual tests. An illustration which may be given here is that of the "patience test," or uniting the disarranged parts of a divided rectangle. As described by Binet, this operation has the following elements: "(1) to keep in mind the end to be attained, that is to say, the figure to be formed; (2) to try different combinations under the influence of this directing idea, which guides the efforts of the subject even though he may not be conscious of the fact; and (3) to judge the combination which has been made, to compare it with the model, and to decide whether it is the correct one."

Much the same processes are called for in many other of the Binet tests, particularly those of arranging weights, rearranging dissected sentences, drawing a diamond or square from copy, finding a sentence containing three given words, counting backwards, etc.

However, an examination of the scale will show that the choice of tests was not guided entirely by any single formula as to the nature of intelligence. Binet's approach was a many-sided one. The scale includes tests of time orientation, of three or four kinds of memory, of apperception, of language comprehension, of knowledge about common objects, of free association, of number mastery, of constructive imagination, and of ability to compare concepts, to see contradictions, to combine fragments into a unitary whole, to comprehend abstract terms, and to meet novel situations.

2 · The Stability of Mental Test Performance Between Two and Eighteen Years

M. P. HONZIK, J. W. MACFARLANE, AND L. ALLEN

Abridged from the *Journal of Experimental Education*, 17 (1948), 309-324, by permission of the authors and the publisher.

Since behavior changes with age the relationship between behavior in infancy and behavior in later life often is slight. Many studies reveal a tendency for the behavior of the child to become more stable as he becomes older. This study supports this generalization with regard to "general intelligence" scores.

In an earlier study, the constancy of mental test performance was reported for a group of normal children during their preschool years (Honzik and Jones, 1939). These children are now young adults, and it is possible to show the relative stability or lability of their mental test scores over the entire period of testing, 21 months to 18 years, inclusive. The contribution of the present study lies in the fact of repeated individual tests given at specified ages over a 16-year period to more than 150 children; and, second, in the fact that this group of children was selected so as to be a representative sample of the children born in an urban community during the late 1920's. Furthermore, since the Guidance Study has as its primary purpose the study of personality development and associated factors, it has been possible to note the relation of fluctuations or stability in rate of mental growth to physical ills, unusual environmental strains or supports, and to evidences of tension or serenity within the individual child.

THE SAMPLE

The Guidance Study has been described in detail in previous publications (Macfarlane, 1938, 1939, and 1943). Suffice it to say here that the two groups, which are referred to as the Guidance and Control Groups, constitute representative subsamples of the Berkeley Survey. The names of every third child born in Berkeley between January 1, 1928, and June 30, 1929, were included in the Berkeley Survey (Welch, 1928-1929). A total of 252 children from the Berkeley Survey Group were asked to come to the Institute for their first mental test at the age of 21 months. At this age level, the group of 252 children was divided into two matched subsamples of 126

223

children on the basis of socio-economic factors (parents' national derivation, income, father's occupation, socio-economic rating, neighborhood, and mother's age and education). One of these subsamples (of the Berkeley Survey) has been called the "Guidance Group" because of the program of intensive interviews had with the parents and children; the second group, which has had physical examinations and mental tests but fewer and less intensive interviews and these at a much later age of the child, has been called the "Control Group." The children in both groups were given mental tests at the age of 21 months. At ages 2 and 2½ years, only the children in the Guidance Group were tested. Thereafter, the testing program was the same for the two groups.

Every effort was made to test the children as nearly as possible on or near their birthdays. Actually, from 72 to 95 per cent of the children were tested within one month of their birthdates at the various ages up to and including 8 years (Honzik and Jones, 1939).

As was to be expected in a longitudinal study, a number of children were unable to come in for one or more of the mental tests. The most frequent cause of a missed test was the family being "out of town." However, a number of families lost interest or became uncooperative as their children grew older; one child was killed in an automobile accident. Table II shows the number of children tested at each age level. It will be seen that at 18 years 153 of the 252 children were tested on the Wechsler-Bellevue. The reasons that the remaining 99 did not come in for a test are listed in the following table:

	Guidance	Control
	n	n
"Out of town"	24	26
Uncooperative	17	16
Died	—	1
Case closed early, cause unknown	—	6
Missed 18-year test (due to changes in staff, illness, or transportation difficulties)	5	4
	46	53

The reasons for lack of cooperation on the part of the parents and children are many and varied. Three children were embarrassed by the physical examinations. One father objected to his daughter having a physical examination. Two children objected to taking mental tests (their I.Q.'s were 101 and 110, respectively, at 15 years). One uncooperative family was in legal difficulties and did not want to discuss their affairs. A rough method of evaluating the selectiveness of the sample not tested at 18 years is to compare the education of their parents with that of the children who were tested at 18 years:

Education of Parents	Tested at 18 years	Not Tested at 18 years
	%	%
College	40	33
High School	40	46
Grammar School	20	21
	100	100

This comparison shows that more of the parents of children who were tested at 18 years were college trained; fewer had a high school education, and the same proportion had a grammar school education, as was true of the group as a whole. These differences may modify but do not invalidate our conclusions.

THE TESTING PROGRAM

The testing program followed in the Guidance Study is summarized in the following table:

Ages	Test
21 months-5 years	California Preschool Schedule I or II
6 and 7 years	Stanford-Binet, 1916 Revision
8 years	Stanford Revision, Form L
9-15 years	Stanford Revision (either Form L or M; see Table I)
18 years	Wechsler-Bellevue

During the preschool years, 21 months to 5 years, inclusive, each child was tested at successive age levels on the same test, either the California Preschool Schedule I or California Preschool Schedule II.* Beginning at

* The published California Preschool Scale Form A (Jaffa, 1934) is composed largely of items from the California Preschool Schedule I, together with a few items from the California Preschool Schedule II. The test items for the California Schedules I and II include selections made by Dr. Adele S. Jaffa from several standardized tests, together with some original items first validated at the Institute. These scales have been normed by the Thurstone method of absolute scaling.

age 9, a program of test alternation was begun which was designed to show the effects of a change in the form of the test on mental test constancy (see Table I). As may be seen in this table, all the children in both groups were tested on either Form L or Form M of the Stanford Revision at age 9 years. But at ages 12 and 14 years, only two-thirds of the groups were given mental tests; the remaining third of the groups was tested at ages 13 and 15 years. In presenting group results, the scores for ages 12 and 13 years have been considered together, as have scores for ages 14 and 15 years.

The I.Q.'s obtained on the Stanford tests and the Wechsler-Bellevue were converted into sigma or standard scores so that they would be in comparable form to the mental test sigma scores obtained between 21 months and 5 years.

Although these children were selected as a representative sample of urban children, their scores are considerably above the test norms. The average I.Q. on the Stanford-Binet at ages 6 and 7 years and on the Stanford Revision, Form L, at 8 years varied from 118.3 to 118.7. During the age period 9 to 13 years, the average I.Q. was approximately 120. The highest average I.Q. of 123 was obtained for the test period of 14 and 15 years; and the lowest I.Q. average (118.2) was earned on the Wechsler-Bellevue at 18 years.

The percentage distributions of I.Q.'s are relatively normal at all ages at which the Stanford-Binet or Form L or M of the Stanford Revision were the tests given. But at 18 years, the distribution of I.Q.'s on the

Table I

Test Alternation Plan in the Guidance Study

Age Level in Years	Group	Tests Given to Children Whose Birthdates Occur in:		
		Jan.-June, 1928	July-Dec., 1928	Jan.-June, 1929
9	Guidance	Stanf. Form L	Stanf. Form M	Stanf. Form M
	Control	Stanf. Form L	Stanf. Form L	Stanf. Form M
10	Guidance	Stanf. Form M	Stanf. Form L	Stanf. Form L
	Control	Stanf. Form M	Stanf. Form M	Stanf. Form L
12	Guidance	—	Stanf. Form L	Stanf. Form M
	Control	—	Stanf. Form L	Stanf. Form L
13	Guidance	Stanf. Form M	—	—
	Control	Stanf. Form L	—	—
14	Guidance	—	Stanf. Form M	Stanf. Form L
	Control	—	Stanf. Form L	Stanf. Form M
15	Guidance	Stanf. Form M	—	—
	Control	Stanf. Form M	—	—

Wechsler-Bellevue suggests that this test lacks "top" or at least does not differentiate between the children earning the highest scores at the earlier ages.* Bayley (1948) has another explanation for the decreased variability at maturity. She suggests that variability is greatest during the age periods when the children are acquiring the functions being tested and that variability becomes restricted with the approach to maturity of the particular processes being measured.

GROUP TRENDS IN MENTAL TEST STABILITY

Pearsonian coefficients of correlation between test scores earned at specified ages between 21 months and 18 years are shown in Table II. These correlation coefficients are based on the scores of the children in the combined Guidance and Control Groups for all but two age levels (2 and 2½ years) when only the children in the Guidance Group were tested.

Correlations for adjacent ages indicate a fair degree of mental test constancy when the interval between tests is at a minimum. The range of correlations for adjacent ages varies from $r = .71$ (between ages 21 months x 2 years; 2 x 2½ years; 3 x 3½ years; and 5 x 6 years) to $r = .92$ for the ages 12 x 14 years on the Stanford Revision, Form L. However, the correlations decrease markedly with the interval between tests but tend to increase with the age of the children when tested.

Comparison of the correlation coefficients for three-year intervals shows clearly the increase in mental test constancy with age:

2 x 5	years	$r = .32$
3 x 6	years	$r = .57$
4 x 7	years	$r = .59$
5 x 8	years	$r = .70$
7 x 10	years	$r = .78$
9 x 12 or 13	years	$r = .85$
14 or 15 x 18	years	$r = .79$

The correlation between tests given at 2 and at 5 years ($r = +.32$) suggests a prediction which is not much better than chance, but the magnitude of the test-retest correlation increases markedly with age.

The importance of both age and interval between tests on the test-retest correlation is shown by the relation of these r's (of Table II) to the age ratio (age at first test/age at second test), $= .85$ (Honzik and Jones, 1937).

The relation of test scores earned at four specified ages (21 months, 3

* J. H. Ranzoni and R. D. Tuddenham are preparing a more detailed evaluation of the scores earned by these children on the Wechsler-Bellevue in contrast to their scores on earlier tests.

years, 6 years, and 18 years) to test scores earned at all other ages may be seen in Chart 1. In the upper left quadrant of this Chart is shown the correlation of the 21 month test with scores at later age levels. We note a marked decrease in the size of these correlation coefficients with age, especially during the preschool years. However, the correlation between the 21-month and 2-year test ($r = .71$) indicates that the first test given the children at the age of 21 months was fairly reliable.

The results of the upper right quadrant, showing the correlation of the 3-year mental test scores with scores at other ages, should be compared with those of the upper left quadrant. The correlations of the 3-year test with scores at the adjacent ages 2½ and 3½ years are fairly high (r's are .71 and .73) but decrease to values which indicate poor prediction by 9 years ($r = .43$).

Since Stanford tests are frequently given to children in the first grade, the results given in the lower left quadrant should be of interest to educators. The 6-year I.Q.'s are fairly constant, but the correlation coefficients are not sufficiently high so that the possibility of marked changes in the I.Q.'s of individual children is precluded.

The fourth quadrant of this chart shows the increasing prediction with age of success on the Wechsler-Bellevue at 18 years. The writers are concerned that the correlations with the Wechsler-Bellevue are not higher. Restricted variability, regardless of its cause, is probably a contributing factor. Another factor may be the differences in the types of test items included in the Stanford and Wechsler-Bellevue tests.

EFFECT OF CHANGE OF FORM OF TEST ON MENTAL TEST CONSTANCY

The correlation between the 8- and 9-year tests for children tested on the same form of the Stanford (Form L) is .91; but the correlation is even higher for the remainder of the group who were tested on Form L at 8 years and Form M at 9 years ($r = .93$). Comparison of the effect of change of form on the test-retest correlations is made for six age periods. In all of these comparisons, the difference between the test-retest coefficients, when the same or different forms of the Stanford test were used, was negligible. Bayley obtained similar results in the Berkeley Growth Study (1948).

CHANGES IN SCORES OVER CERTAIN AGE PERIODS

The correlation coefficients in Table II indicate the group trends with respect to the constancy of mental test performance. It is also of interest to know the extent of the changes in sigma scores or I.Q. which are occurring in individual children. Furthermore, the question arises as to whether the correlation between mental test scores is largely determined by a relatively small proportion of the cases or by the group as a whole. In a previous study (Honzik and Jones, 1937), we published the distribution of

Table II

Correlations Between Test Scores Given at Different Ages

Column groups — *California Preschool Schedule I or II* (ages 2–7); *Stanford-Binet*; *Stanford Revision Forms* (L 8; L/M 9; L/M 10; L 12; L/M 12 or 13; L/M 14 or 15); *W-B* (18).

Test	Age	n	2	2½	3	3½	4	5	6	7	Stanford-Binet	L 8	L 9	M 9	L 10	M 10	L 12	L (12 or 13)	M (12 or 13)	L (14 or 15)	M (14 or 15)	W-B 18
California Preschool Schedule I or II	1¾	234	.71	.62	.52	.48	.38	.39	.27	.29		.27	.26	.17	.22	.19		.19	.13	.07	.21	.07
	2	113		.71	.69	.60	.46	.32	.47	.46		.43	.45	.29	.37	.37	.49		.26	.21	.34	.31
	2½	114			.73	.64	.57	.46	.37	.38		.37		.32	.36					.26	.31	.24
	3	229				.71	.58	.57	.57	.55		.49	.53	.32	.36	.55		.36	.42	.35	.37	.35
	3½	215					.76	.71	.64	.60		.50	.59	.49	.59	.60		.51	.52	.49	.46	.42
	4	211						.72	.62	.59		.61	.59	.60	.66	.62		.48	.63	.54	.44	.42
									.71	.73		.70	.68	.71	.75	.67		.62	.68	.61	.62	.56
Stanford-Binet	6	214									.82	.77	.80	.67	.71	.76		.74	.65	.67	.70	.61
	7	208										.83	.82	.80	.77	.78		.71	.82	.73	.76	.71
Stanford Revision Forms: L	8	199											.91	.93	.88	.88	.85	.85	.82	.85	.81	.70
L	9	90													.90		.90			.87		.76
M	9	104														.88			.79		.91	.66
L	10	107															.87	.87		.85		.70
M	10	83																	.91		.87	.76
L	12	92																		.92		.76
L	(12 or 13)	120																		.89		.78
M	(12 or 13)	71																			.88	.84
L	14	51																				.73
M	(14 or 15)	117																				.79

changes in sigma scores which occurred between the 6- and 7-year tests ($r = .82$) for these children. This distribution was normal, with 80 per cent of the group showing sigma score changes of .5 or less. However, there were six children whose scores differed on these two tests by 1.5 sigma (approximately 20 I.Q. points since the standard deviation for ages 6 and 7 years is approximately 13) or more. The average change in score between 6 and 7 years was .5 of a sigma (6.5 I.Q. points).

If changes in I.Q. of 20 points can occur between the 6- and 7-year tests, it would be reasonable to expect rather marked changes in scores over the entire test period, 21 months to 18 years. We have, therefore, prepared distributions of the range of sigma score changes for the entire 16-year period of testing. We find that the scores of three children have increased between 4 and 4½ sigma (roughly between 70 and 79 I.Q. points, assuming an approximate standard deviation of 17.5 I.Q. points); and the scores of two children have decreased a similar amount. The most interesting

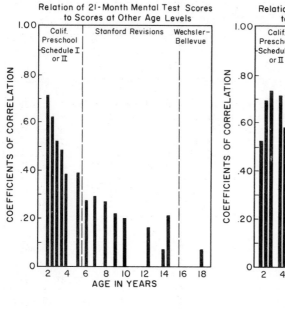

Relation of 21-Month Mental Test Scores to Scores at Other Age Levels

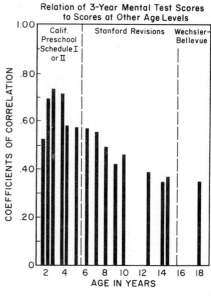

Relation of 3-Year Mental Test Scores to Scores at Other Age Levels

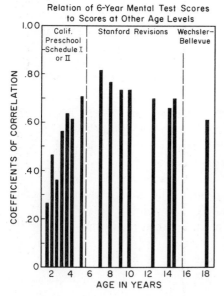

Relation of 6-Year Mental Test Scores to Scores at Other Age Levels

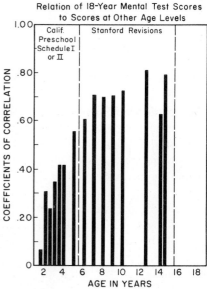

Relation of 18-Year Mental Test Scores to Scores at Other Age Levels

CHART I.

aspect of these tremendous changes in scores is the fact that the changes are not made abruptly but consistently over a long period of time. However, the greatest changes do occur on the preschool tests. We have, therefore, prepared distributions showing the range of changes in sigma scores and I.Q.'s between 6 and 18 years. No child's sigma score changes as much as 4 sigma during the school years. But the scores of one child changes 3 sigma; and those of four others between 2.5 and 2.9 sigma.

Since educators and clinical workers use I.Q.'s rather than standard scores, we have prepared a distribution of the range of changes in I.Q. during the 12-year period 6 to 18 years for the two groups, Guidance and Control:

I.Q. Changes Be-tween 6 and 18 years	Guidance n=114 %	Control n=108 %	Total n=222 %
50 or more I.Q. pts.	1	–	.5
30 or more I.Q. pts.	9	10	9
20 or more I.Q. pts.	32	42	35
15 or more I.Q. pts.	58	60	58
10 or more I.Q. pts.	87	83	85
9 or less I.Q. pts.	13	17	15

Although it is extremely important to point out the possibility of marked changes in scores in individual cases, it is equally important to emphasize that the scores of many children change only slightly with respect to the group from one age period to the next. And it is only when the changes are consistently in one direction, or the other, over a period of years that the range of variation becomes as great as 3 or 4 sigma (or over 50 I.Q. points).

SUMMARY AND CONCLUSIONS

A group of 252 children, who comprise a representative sample of the children living in an urban community, were given mental tests at specified ages between 21 months and 18 years. These data have been analyzed to show the extent of the stability of mental test performance for this age period. The results may be summarized as follows:

1. Mental test constancy for the age period 21 months to 18 years is markedly dependent upon the age at testing and the interval between tests. That is, group prediction is good over short age periods, and mental test scores become increasingly predictive after the preschool years.

2. Test-retest correlations are as high for children tested on different forms (L or M) of the 1937 Stanford Revision as for children tested on the same form over the same age periods.

3. Distributions of the extent of the changes in I.Q. for the age period 6 to 18 years show that the I.Q.'s of almost 60 per cent of the group change

15 or more points; the I.Q.'s of a third of the group change 20 or more points; and the I.Q.'s of 9 per cent of the group change 30 or more points. The I.Q.'s of 15 per cent of the group change *less* than 10 points of I.Q. The group averages, on the other hand, show a maximum shift in I.Q. over this age period of from 118 to 123.

In conclusion, it should be re-emphasized that, whereas the results for the group suggest mental test stability between 6 and 18 years, the observed fluctuations in the scores of individual children indicate the need for the utmost caution in the predictive use of a single test score, or even two such scores. This finding seems of especial importance since many plans for individual children are made by schools, juvenile courts, and mental hygiene clinics on the basis of a single mental test score. Specifically, it could be noted that a prediction based on a 6-year test would be wrong to the extent of 20 I.Q. points for one out of three children by the age of 18 years, and to the extent of 15 I.Q. points for approximately six out of ten children.

References

Bayley, Nancy, "Consistency and Variability in the Growth of Intelligence from Birth to Eighteen years," *Journal of Genetic Psychology* (1948).

Honzik, M. P., and H. E. Jones, "Mental-Physical Relationships During the Preschool Period," *Journal of Experimental Education*, VI (December 1937), 139-146.

Jaffa, A. S., *The California Preschool Mental Scale (Form A)*. Syllabus Series No. 251 (Los Angeles: University of California, 1934), p. 66.

Macfarlane, J. W., "Studies in Child Guidance, I. Methodology of Data Collection and Organization," *Monograph Society for Research in Child Development*, III (1938), 1-254.

———, "The Guidance Study," *Sociometry*, II (1939).

———, "Study of Personality Development," from *Child Behavior and Development*, Barber, Hounin, and Wright, eds. New York: McGraw-Hill Book Co., 1943.

Welch, F. M., *The Berkeley Survey: A Study of the Socio-Economic Status of Four Hundred Berkeley Families in Years 1928-1929*. Manuscript (Berkeley, California: Institute of Child Welfare, University of California).

3 · The Development of Parent-Child Resemblance in Intelligence.

MARJORIE P. HONZIK

Abridged from *Child Development*, 28 (1957), 215-224, by permission of the author and the Society for Research in Child Development.

Under ordinary circumstances, there are appreciable resemblances between parents and children in psychological as well as in physical traits. These are difficult to interpret in terms of heredity and environment, since usually parents and children share not only common genes but also a common environment. The present study is remarkable for having found data which appear to attribute much of the parent-child resemblance in intelligence in American society to an hereditary basis. This, of course, does not contradict studies which show that intelligence is also affected by environment.

A number of developmental studies have reported that the mental test scores of children under two years have little or no relationship to parental ability as measured by the number of years of schooling, ratings of intelligence, or test scores (Bayley, 1954; Honzik, 1940 and 1948). When these same children are retested at later ages, their mental test scores are found to be significantly correlated with parental ability. A crucial question is the extent to which these age changes in relationship are due to environmental factors, or to intrinsic differences in the patterns of mental growth. One way in which this increasing resemblance can be evaluated is by comparing the age changes in the correlations which occur among children reared by their own parents in contrast to those reared apart from their parents.

In this report we shall compare the age changes in relationship for two distinct groups, each of over 100 children, who were tested at various ages between 21 months and 16 years, and then contrast this trend with that reported by Skodak and Skeels (1949) for 100 adopted children who were tested four times between their second and fourteenth year.

In the Guidance Study at the University of California Institute of Child Welfare, a sample of 252 children who were representative of those born in Berkeley during an 18-month period were divided into equivalent subsamples called the "Guidance" and "Control" groups. This division of the main sample was made on the basis of certain socio-economic variables before the mental testing program was begun (Macfarlane, 1938). The children in the two groups were first brought to the Institute for mental tests at the age of 21 months. The tests used at this age level and at the subsequent testings during the preschool years were the California Pre-school Schedules (see Table I). Beginning at six years, the 1916 Stanford Revision of the Binet Scale was the test used, with a shift to the 1937 Revision at age eight. The parents were not given intelligence tests but the number of years of schooling is known for both parents. In addition, in the Guidance group, ratings (on a seven-point scale) of the mothers' intelligence were made when the children were between 3½ and 4½ years

Table I

Correlations of the Children's Mental Test Scores with the Mothers' Education and Ratings of Her Intelligence

G = Guidance Group   C = Control Group

								RELATION OF THE CHILDREN'S MENTAL TEST SCORES X
Age in Years	Mental Test Given Children	Number of Cases			Mother's Education			Ratings of Mother's Intelligence
		G	C	G+C	G	C	G+C	G
					r	r	r	r
1¾	Calif. Preschool	117	117	234	.13	00	.06	.11
2	Calif. Preschool	113	...	113	.07	..	.07	.08
2½	Calif. Preschool	114	...	114	.10	..	.10	.06
3	Calif. Preschool	116	113	229	.10	.08	.09	.17
3½	Calif. Preschool	107	108	215	.27**	.25**	.26**	.39**
4	Calif. Preschool	105	106	211	.22*	.25**	.23**	.38**
5	Calif. Preschool	104	106	210	.45**	.25**	.35**	.53**
6	Stanf.-Binet (1916 Rev.)	109	102	211	.27**	.37**	.32**	.40**
7	Stanf.-Binet (1916 Rev.)	104	104	208	.35**	.33**	.33**	.51**
8	Stanf., Form L	100	98	198	.34**	.32**	.33**	.54**
10	Stanf., Form L or M ..	105	92	197	.33**	.34**	.34**	.52**
12 or 13	Stanf., Form L or M ..	98	94	192	.38**	.38**	.38**	.54**
14 or 15	Stanf., Form L or M ..	90	78	168	.39**	.30**	.35**	.59**

* Significant at the 5 per cent level.
** Significant at the 1 per cent level.

by staff members who had had many hours of discussion with the mothers. The correlation between these ratings of the mothers' intelligence and the number of years of schooling of the mothers is +.73. In fact, in this study all measures which reflect the ability of the parents were intercorrelated to about the same extent (socio-economic status correlates with both mothers' and fathers' schooling +.73; mothers' and fathers' schooling correlate +.74).

The correlation between the education of the mothers and the children's mental test scores at 21 months was negligible but between 3 and 3½ years, the relationship became significant (see Table I). To check the validity of this age trend, correlations were computed separately for the

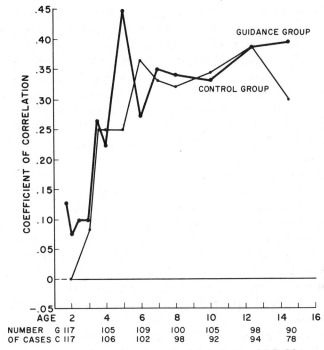

FIGURE 1. *Education of mother in relation to child's IQ.*

two subsamples of the total Guidance Study sample. The results of this comparison are shown in Table I and Figure 1. The finding that these subsamples exhibit essentially the same age changes in relationship suggests that the trend is a valid one and would be duplicated in comparable developmental studies; in fact, Bayley (1954) has reported a similar trend in the Berkeley Growth Study.

In a study of 100 adopted children, Skodak and Skeels (1949) report that adopted children whose true mothers tested quite low in intelligence earned mental test scores which were substantially higher than those of their mothers. In addition, these authors report the relation of various indices of ability of the true mothers to the mental test scores of their children at four successive age levels. It is these correlations which interest us and which we wish to compare with the relationships obtained in the Guidance Study for children reared by their own mothers.

Regardless of the index used (IQ or number of years of schooling), Skodak and Skeels found that the correlation between the *true* mother's ability and her child's mental test scores at approximately two years of age is insignificant. By the time the adopted children reached four years on the average, the correlations between their IQ's and the true mothers' education and intelligence are +.31 and +.28, respectively. These correlations are significant at the 5 per cent level. In contrast these authors found *no* relationship at any age between the mental test scores of these same children, who were adopted in the first months of life, and their *foster*, or adopting, mothers' education. These highly significant results are especially interesting when compared with the findings for the groups of children who have always lived with their own parents (Bayley, 1954; Honzik, 1940).

In Figure 2, the mother-child correlations for the total Guidance Study sample (combined Guidance and Control groups) are compared with those reported by Skodak and Skeels for the adopted children. It will be noted that the true mother-child correlational age trends in their study and ours are as alike as those shown in Figure 1 for the two subsamples of our group. The similarity in the changing relationships with age for the Guidance Study group who always lived with their parents as compared with the Skodak-Skeels group who never lived with their parents is impressive. However, the final correlations between the index of maternal ability (number of years of schooling) and the children's mental test scores is only +.35 for the children reared by their true parents, and +.32 for the children not reared by their true parents, indicating that less than 15 per cent of the variance in the children's scores can be accounted for by this very rough index of the true mother's ability.

The fact that the individual differences in the adopted children's mental test scores are not related to the foster mothers' education at any age is also shown in Figure 2. This finding is surprising since the average IQ of the adopted children at 13½ years was 106, while the average IQ of their true mothers was reported as only 86. A regression upward toward the mean is to be expected but not beyond the mean. Our interpretation of these findings is that the educational level of the true mother roughly indicates her intellectual capacity and this capacity is at least somewhat determined by genetic factors which she, in turn, transmits to her children. The difference in the level of ability of the adopted children and their true mothers may be due in part to systematic undermeasurement of the true mothers' intelligence and in part to the generally favorable environment provided by the foster families. It is conceivable, and it seems to us probable, that in this sample certain unmeasured family variables such as the affection and emotional support given the foster children were as important as purely intellectual stimulation in nurturing the mental growth and performance of these foster children.

A better indication of the age changes in the mother-child resemblance would probably have been obtained if optimal test scores had been available for the mothers in these two studies. In the Skodak-Skeels investigation, 63 of the mothers were given individual mental tests but these mothers were tested shortly after the babies' births, "usually after the mother had decided to release the baby for adoption." The authors note that "these IQ's were consistent with other evidence of the mental ade-

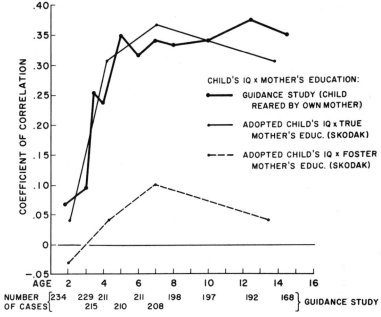

FIGURE 2.   *Education of mother in relation to child's IQ.*

quacy of the mothers" and the "tests were never given when the mother was ill or obviously upset," but it is unlikely that these IQ's reflect the optimum performance of which these mothers might have been capable under more favorable conditions. However, even these IQ's showed age trends in relationship to the mental test scores of the children which were similar but tended to run a little higher than those obtained for the mothers' education. The mother-child correlations in the Guidance Study are higher when based on ratings of the mother's intelligence than when education is used as an index of the mother's ability (Table I). They are, in the former instance, comparable with the correlation of .49 reported by Jones (1928) in a study in which testing procedures for both parents and children were carefully controlled.

In Figure 3, the age change in mother-child resemblance in intelligence reported by Skodak and Skeels for 63 of the adopted children is compared with the findings for the Guidance group where the measure of maternal intelligence was an averaged rating. The correlations obtained in the Guidance group are higher than those reported for the adopted children. This latter difference may be due to differential environmental stimulation by the more intelligent mothers in the Guidance group but there is also the likelihood in the Skodak-Skeels study of an unequal effect of stress on the mothers' IQ's. These findings certainly suggest that the variations in the magnitude of the correlations depend somewhat on the sensitivity of

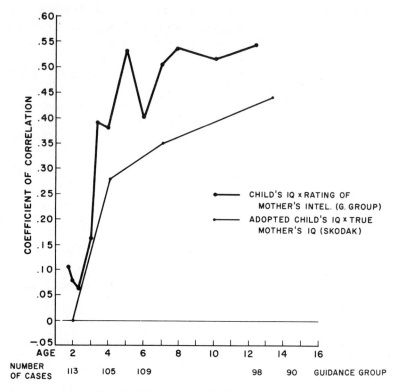

FIGURE 3.   *Intelligence of mother in relation to child's IQ.*

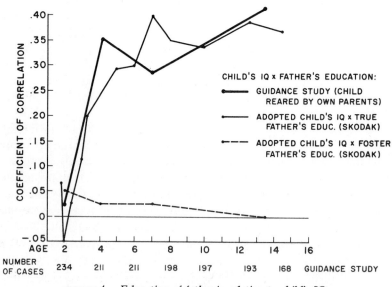

FIGURE 4.   *Education of father in relation to child's IQ.*

238

the measures of maternal intelligence, but the question of whether the differences in the correlations shown in Figure 3 are entirely attributable to differences in the validity of the measures of mothers' intelligence cannot be answered by these studies.

The correlations between the number of years of schooling of the father and the children's mental test scores at successive ages are compared with the findings for adopted children in relation to the education of their true fathers in Figure 4. The impressive fact shown by Figure 4 is that the trend in relationships for the adopted children resembles so closely that found for the children reared by their own parents. Since the relationships obtained in the Guidance Study are no higher than those found for the adopted children, we may infer that the more highly educated fathers do not offer differentially more stimulating environments to their children. This inference is confirmed by the findings for the foster fathers shown in Table II.

Table II

Correlations Between the Children's Mental Test Scores and the Fathers' Education (Skodak-Skeels)

Average Age of Adopted Children in Years	Mental Test Given Children	True Father's Education × Child's IQ N = 60	Foster Father's Education × Child's IQ N = 100
		r	r
2-2	Kuhlman or 1916 Stanford-Binet	+.03	+.05
4-3	Stanford-Binet (1916 Rev.)	+.36*	+.03
7-1	Stanford-Binet (1916 Rev.)	+.28*	+.03
13-6	Stanford, 1937 Revision	+.42*	+.00

* Significant at the 1 per cent level.

SUMMARY AND CONCLUSIONS

The increasing parent-child resemblance in mental ability found for two groups of children reared by their own parents has been compared and found to be similar to that reported for a group of children reared from early infancy by foster parents (Skodak and Skeels, 1949). The ability measures used in both studies were, for the children, individually administered intelligence tests, and for the parents, the number of years of schooling; and additionally for the mother, test scores and ratings. The finding that the parent-child resemblance in ability follows the same age changes in the two studies, even though the true parents did not rear the children in the Skodak-Skeels group, suggests that the existing relationship is largely due to genetic factors which tend to become manifest in the child during the later preschool years. Although the group age trends in relationship for both the adopted and nonadopted children are similar, the extent of the relationship is of low predictive value.

The fact that the parent-child resemblance is no greater for children reared by their own parents and the further fact reported by Skodak-Skeels of no relationship between the children's mental test performance and the foster parents' ability suggest that the education of the parents per se is not an environmentally important factor and that the obtained parent-child correlations reflect individual differences which are largely genetically determined.

References

Bayley, Nancy, "Some Increasing Parent-Child Similarities During the Growth of Children," *Journal of Educational Psychology*, 45 (1954), 1-21.

Honzik, Marjorie P., "Age Changes in Relationship Between Certain Environmental Variables and Children's Intelligence," *Yearbook of the National Society for the Study of Education*, II, 39 (1949), 185-205.

————, Jean W. Macfarlane, and Lucile Allen, "The Stability of Mental Test Performance Between Two and Eighteen Years," *Journal of Experimental Education*, 17 (1948), 309-324.

Jones, H. E., "A First Study of Parent-Child Resemblance in Intelligence," *Yearbook of the National Society for the Study of Education*, I, 27 (1928), 61-72.

Macfarlane, Jean W., "Studies in Child Guidance. I. Methodology of Data Collection and Organization," *Monographs of the Society for Research in Child Development*, Vol. 3, No. 6 (1938).

Skodak, Marie, and H. M. Skeels, "A Final Follow-up Study of One Hundred Adopted Children," *Journal of Genetic Psychology*, 75 (1949), 85-125.

4 · Children's Ideas

JEAN PIAGET

Reproduced from a chapter entitled "Children's Philosophies" in the *Handbook of Child Psychology*, ed. C. Murchison. Worcester, Mass.: Clark University Press, 1931, pages 377-391, by permission of the author and the publisher.

Jean Piaget, of the University of Geneva, Switzerland, has been an outstanding contributor to our knowledge of children's thinking. The present selection, written early in his career, exemplifies his approach and foreshadows much of his later work.

However unconnected and incoherent the spontaneous remarks of children concerning the phenomena of nature, of the mind, and of the origin of things may be, we are able to discern in them some constant tendencies, reappearing with each new effort of reflection (Piaget, 1929).

I should like to emphasize three aspects of these "children's ideas," *realism, animism,* and *artificialism.* The intellectual tendencies of the child are very marked in the uncivilized adult, the so-called "primitive." But even with us, if the superficial coating which education has left on our minds be scratched ever so little, we find the same characteristics, at least in the matter of mental orientation.

Child *realism,* in fact all realism, may be defined as a sort of confusion between the inner and outer, or the tendency to fix in objects something which is the result of the activity of the thinking subject. We know how slow to develop is the consciousness of self in a small child. Everything he feels, knows, and sees seems to him common to the whole world and part of external reality. For him nothing is inner and subjective. It is this phenomenon, which continues much later than is supposed, which we shall call child realism.

The first manifestation of child realism is what we might call the confusion of psychic and physical, which J. M. Baldwin (1906, 1908) emphasizes in his *Genetic Logic* and on which Sully (1896) makes some curious observations. Small children have no notion of thought as distinct from material activity. Stern (1930) noticed that his four-year-old daughter confused thought with the voice. She said expressly that we think with the mouth and tongue. This spontaneous remark of a child gave us the idea for

241

a systematic inquiry on this point. We asked sixty children between the ages of four and twelve what one thinks with, and whether one can see and touch thought. The results of this inquiry were very clear. All the children under about seven answered, like Stern's little girl, "We think with our mouths." "As for animals," said a little boy of six, "they think with their mouths, too, all except the horse, and he thinks with his ears, because he hears when you speak to him but he doesn't talk himself." "But," we objected, "you can think with your mouth shut?" "No." "Shut your mouth and think of your mother. Can you?" "Yes." "Well, what did you think with?" "*With my mouth.*"

During the next stage, which lasts from about seven to ten, or eleven, grown-up influence is felt. The child answers that we think with our heads, because that is the current social belief. But, under these words, the child's conception remains spontaneous and in complete continuity with the answers of the first stage. We think with "*a little voice inside our heads,*" says a boy of nine, with "*a little mouth*"; "*we hear inside our heads,*" says another child. Thought is "*what we make happen.*" You cannot touch or see it, but you can feel it with your finger when it comes out of your mouth, etc.

We see how little the distinction of psychic and physical is innate. You may say, it is true, that "voice" is something immaterial to the child. But the following remarks disprove this. "*Can we touch thought?*" we ask a youngster who believes he thinks with his mouth. "*No, it's made of air.*" "Where are your thoughts?" "*Everywhere.*" And this from a boy of seven: "Can we see it?" "*Yes; you see the wind making the trees and grasses wave; that's thought.*"

These explanations are, of course, not spontaneous. Let us pass now to a phenomenon which has struck all children and forced them to explain it to themselves spontaneously: dreams and nightmares. This study not only confirms the foregoing, but proves the existence among children of another confusion or "adualism," as Baldwin calls the confusion between inner and outer things.

Ask a child these three questions: Where do dreams come from? Where is the dream while you are dreaming? What do you dream with? The questions are not chosen at random, but after careful observation. Sully mentions a little girl who would not go into a certain room because "*it's full of dreams.*"

The children's replies can be classed in three stages. Up to seven or eight, children think of dreams as coming from outside and fluttering round the bed during the night. "*They're little pictures,*" "*little lamps,*" "*they're lights,*" says the children; "*the moon sends them,*" or "*the street lamps,*" "*the clouds, the sun, the wind,*" etc. These are the usual formulae. The dream is conceived sometimes as light, in which case some source of light is thought of as explaining it, sometimes as smoke, black air, night, etc. To the question, "where are your dreams?" children at this stage invariably answer, *"in the room,"* or *"on the bed,"* or *"in front of me."* There is a very interesting realism here. The child is not taken in by the dream. He soon knows that a dream ship cannot take him on the lake. The dream is conceived as illusory, but he believes it to consist of real pictures—as fairytale pictures are real—and to be in the room. We have tried telling these children that the dream is in their heads or in them. They answer, *"If it were in my head I shouldn't see it."* One boy of five gave this remarkable answer: *"I'm in the dream. The dream isn't in me."*

The answers in the stage from seven to nine or ten are stronger still. At this age the child is learning that he thinks with his head. He answers that the dream comes from us, from our heads; a dream is *"when we're thinking of something."* He seems to have understood it all. Not a bit of it: he goes on admitting that the dream is in the room; he places it on the bed, a few inches from his eyes. He thinks it is made of air, wind, smoke, or light. One boy said straight away: *"When I'm awake the dream is in my head. When I go to sleep, it comes out."* Naturally we always ask, "Does the dream only seem to be in the room, or is it really there?" Children at this stage are convinced that a material image is in the room.

We must avoid interpreting these facts according to our adult logic. They are specific. They are due simply to the child's inability to conceive the dualism of inner and outer. All thought, even false and illusory, belongs to the outside world. It is only towards the ages of ten and eleven that children grow out of this realism and say, "The dream *seems* to be in front of me. It is *as if I saw* something. But there is nothing there."

These ideas of children about dreams confirm what we have said of the realism of thought. But what is this realism itself? Clearly it is a confusion of the symbol and the things signified. As Delacroix has recently shown, all thought is symbolic, and all symbols, to begin with, remain attached to the things they signify. With children this phenomenon is very clear. Ask children how the names of things originated, and they say that the names came from the things themselves, or that the names were made with the things: whoever made the sun gave it its name once for all. You object, "But how did people know that the sun was called that?" The child answers: *"They saw it was called sun, because they could see it was round and hot." "They saw that the clouds were called clouds, because they could see they were all gray,"* etc.

If now you ask the children where the names are, the older ones, from ten upwards, say *"in my head, in my mouth when I'm speaking,"* but the little ones say *"in the things."* The sun's name is *"in the sun."* The child does not maintain that it is written on the sun. He simply thinks that this name is part of the essence of the sun: it is in the sun *"because the sun is bright."* The color, shape, place, and name of the sun are all in the same perspective.

A fourth form of realism is the confusion of perspective proper with the real movements of things. The child thinks that the sun and moon follow him, the clouds, the whole sky goes with him. Here realism sometimes engenders magic.

We ask a boy of four what makes the sun move: *"I do, when I walk,"* he answers. Another boy says, *"It's we who make it move."* Whence can such strange ideas come? Almost all children discover at the age of three or four years that the sun and moon advance when they advance, stop when they stop. Rasmussen and others noted this in their own children. In Geneva we have found this belief to be general. Here is an example:

Jac (aged 6): "Does the sun move?" *"Yes, when I walk it comes too. When I turn, it turns too. Doesn't it ever follow you?"* "Why does it move?" *"Because when I walk, it walks."* "Why does it walk?" *"To hear what I say."* "Is it alive?" *"Oh, rather! or it couldn't come after me, and it couldn't shine."* After a minute: "Does the moon move?" *"Yes, when I walk, and more than the sun, because when I run she runs too, and when I run, the sun only walks. Because the moon's stronger than the sun is, she goes faster. The sun can't ever catch her up."* (It is true that the impression is much clearer with the moon than with the sun.) "And when you stop?" *"The moon stops. But when I stop, someone else starts running."* "If you run and one of your friends runs the other way, what happens?" *"She goes with him."* After a lot of questions on the cause of movements in general: "How is the sun moving today?" *"It isn't moving, because we're not walking. Oh, yes, it must be moving; because I can hear a cart."*

It is the same with clouds, but naturally the illusion is not so strong in this case.

Beliefs like this comprise two elements. With small children they verge on magic: the child believes that he is making the sun and moon and clouds move, and amuses himself by using his power. With older children the totality is more animist than magic: he thinks the stars follow him in spite of himself, by virtue of their own will. This brings us to the study of animism in the child.

Without wishing to pronounce on the nature of animism among primitive peoples or to enter into the discussion which Lévy-Bruhl has opened on the theories of the English anthropological school, we shall call animism the tendency among children to consider things as living and conscious.

Child animism is much disputed. Some hold that children endow everything with a personality and intentions; others, among them Durkheim, that child animism has nothing to do with the animism of primitives, being much more make-believe than real. For our own part, we have tried to contribute some precise data, taking care, as far as possible, to avoid prejudices and preconceived ideas.

We named a number of objects to the children: a table, a dog, the sun, a stone, the wind, clouds, rivers, etc., asking if each one were living or not, if it knew what it was doing or not, if it could feel a prick or not, etc. This was done to find out to what extent children believe things to have consciousness and intention.

In spite of the obvious drawbacks of this method, it has given some results systematic enough to be noted. Let us begin by studying the child's definitions of the word "alive."

For children between four and six everything active is alive. But as activity is taken to consist in usefulness to man, and as children of this age are anthropocentric, everything is, in fact, considered as alive. The sun is alive because it gives light, the wind because it moves the trees, stones are alive because you can throw them, the lake because it carries boats, the stove because it cooks the dinner, etc.

The generality of these answers would rob them of interest if an essential distinction did not appear in the second stage. Children of six and seven call what moves "alive" in contrast to what is inert. So the sun and moon, clouds, wind, water, fire, motor cars, and engines are alive, while tables, mountains, and stones are not alive. *"To be alive,"* children tell us, *"means that we move."* A boy of six saw some dead leaves on the ground and asked if they were alive. "No," he was told; *"But,"* he retorted, *"they're moving in the wind."* All movement, even induced from without, is a sign of life.

From eight to ten years a new distinction arises, that of original and acquired movement. To be alive is "to move of oneself." Sun and moon and wind are alive, but not the clouds, because the wind pushes them, machines are not, because man sets them in motion, etc.

Finally, at about eleven the child reserves life to animals and plants, or even to animals alone.

It is interesting to note that the replies of children about the consciousness of things develop in just the same way. Everything endowed with consciousness, consciousness restricted to moving bodies, to self-moving bodies, and finally to animals, are the four stages of the process. We need not give examples from all four. Here are a few from children restricting consciousness to things which move of themselves. We ask a boy of nine if the clouds know they are going forward. "No," he says *"because the wind is pushing them."* "And does the wind know it is going forward, or not?" *"It knows, because it's blowing."* Another child said of the moon: *"Of course she knows she's moving, else she couldn't come back every night."* "Does the sun know he's called sun?" we asked a boy. *"Of course, because it's he that makes the sunshine."* All these answers are alike; things that move of themselves necessarily have consciousness and intention.

We now see that child animism is the result of a confusion or rather lack of differentiation between the psychic and the physical. Just as we saw with realism that the self is very slowly differentiated from things, in the same way things are long endowed with the idea of intention, voluntary effort, living, and spontaneous activity by simple indifferentiation. Child animism, therefore, presents no problem. The real problem is to know how the differentiation is made and how the child gradually grows out of his initial animism. This will be shown by an analysis of the ideas of the cause of movement (Piaget, 1930).

We may say that up to seven or eight the real cause of movement in nature, for the child, is a moral one. Natural law is still the social law. In its most primitive form this phenomenon partakes at the same time of magic and artificialism. The clouds are thought to move because of us; we make them move by walking. Or else people make them come because it must rain. The moon comes back every night because we must be able to see. Streams and rivers run because we must have water. If the child has noticed that they always run in the same direction, he says it is because there must be water in the lake. Moral obligation is enough to explain the movement. If we show surprise at this explanation and make the child be more precise about this power of man over things, he invents myths. He says that a man throws the sun and moon, so as to make them move, or that men send the rivers on with the oars of their boats.

Of course, these explanations imply animism. They imply that the things obey, that the moon knows when she must come back, that the streams know where the lake is to which they must run.

During a slightly more developed stage of these moral explanations, the artificialism is transferred to the things themselves. The child's explanation at first appears to be mechanical. He declares that the clouds send the sun or moon along, that the pebbles send the stream along, that the clouds move because of the moon, or the rain, or the night, etc. But if we examine these explanations a little more closely, we find that they are all quite finalistic, or even moral.

When the child believes that the sun and moon move because of the clouds, he admits a kind of struggle between good and bad weather; the sun must go when the clouds come, and the clouds must go when the sun comes back. The cause of the movement is still moral. Or when he says it is the night that makes the clouds move, he simply thinks that the clouds must come so as to make the night. In fact, for children, as for the early Greek thinkers before Empedocles, night is a black vapor, a great black cloud which fills the atmosphere. To say that the clouds come on because of the night is to say that they have the moral obligation to come, so that little children can go to sleep.

When the child says that the stream advances because of the pebbles, the explanation is more curious still. He has seen that stones sticking up to the surface of the water produces waves and rapids; from this he concludes that the water "takes a run" to get over the stone. The stone is the obstacle which excites it. If there were no stone, says the child, there would be no stream. The stone is the cause of the stream of water as the hurdle is the cause of the horse's jump. The spontaneous questions of small children reveal this tendency of their thoughts at once. A boy of four asked one day, "*Auntie B., how do the streams take a run to start with?*"

We see how, in these primitive stages, movement remains spontaneous and close to life itself. During a second stage the child arrives at the idea of the need of an exterior physical cause or transmitter of movement. Actual physical cause thus succeeds the moral cause. But an interesting thing is that this physical cause does not begin with simple forms. With children it takes on the complicated appearance which characterizes the physics of Aristotle, and which Meyerson has called the scheme of "surrounding activity."

We know how Aristotle explained the movement of projectiles. The motive force, he said, is itself motor. In moving it moves the surrounding air which flows back behind the moving object and pushes it forward. It is this kind of reciprocal action or the shock and return of the air current which is called "surrounding activity."

Bizarre as it may seem, this is exactly how children between the ages of seven and nine explain movement to themselves, that is to say, when they are making their first attempts at physical explanations.

The phenomenon is clearest in the case of clouds. The clouds, says the child of eight, move forward because of the breeze they make. Here are some examples. One boy told us, "*It's the wind that drives the clouds along.*" "But where does the wind come from?" "*From the clouds. They make a wind.*" "How?" "*By moving.*" And a little girl: "*It's the wind that pushes them.*" "Where does the wind come from?" "*From the clouds.*" In the most primitive cases the child believes that the wind comes out of the clouds as though from the sack of Æolus, and that this wind sends the clouds along. But in the most developed cases the child says plainly that the clouds make a wind "*by their movement*" and that the wind pushes them.

It is the same with the sun and moon, but not so frequently. Children have said to us that the sun and moon make a wind as they move, and that this wind moves them along. The same is true in the case of streams and waves. The stream of water is thought to produce a stream of air, which is believed to cause the movement of the water.

To understand these curious facts one must know that for the child the cause of the wind is the thing which, to our minds, is moved by the wind. If you ask a child of five or six point-blank, "Where does the wind come from?" he answers, "*From the trees,*" thinking that the trees sway to make a wind, or he says it comes from the clouds, the waves, or even from the dust. Sully had noted this fact, which our investigations have shown to be quite general.

We had the curiosity to lay before children of from eight to ten the problem which preoccupied Aristotle, that of projectiles. "Why," we asked, "when you throw a ball does it go on, instead of falling on the ground at once?" Strangely enough the children thought of Aristotle's explanation. *"The ball goes on because of the wind,"* and this wind is caused *"by the movement of the ball."*

It is only at nine or ten that the child discovers the real cause of the movement of streams; then, too, he leaves off applying the theory of "surrounding reaction" to the sun and moon.

Our last problem is that of the origin of things and child artificialism.

We know how interested children are in the problems of origin. "Who makes the sun?" asks a boy of two years nine months. "Who made the air? the earth?" "How is thunder made in the sky? Are there all the things to make fires in the sky?" "Where do stones come from? glass? wood?" "Who made the birds?" These questions abound with children between four and five years old.

Often these questions arise from curiosity about birth itself. "Mummy, where was I before I was born?" "Where do babies come from?" "How are ladies made?" "And people, how are they made?" A few questions from among the hundreds published.

To understand the spontaneous thought of the child it is most important to know what these questions really mean, and what are the child's ideas on the origin of things. To solve this problem, we asked some hundreds of children between four and twelve years of age questions such as, "How did mountains and rivers begin?" "Where do clouds come from?" "Where does rain come from?" "How did the sun begin?" etc.

Some of these questions may seem strange; to ask children how the sun and moon began may seem a psychologist's mistake. We felt this so strongly that it was not without timidity that we at first ventured on them, expecting the children to laugh at us. But, as a matter of fact, the more primitive the mentality, the less it feels the difficulties of the problems. The children had no more difficulty with questions of cosmogony than with those treated up to now. Moreover, the answers were very uniform and advanced progressively with the age. This is a double guarantee that the method is well founded.

The explanations of the origin of things offer two stages of development. The first is artificialist or theological; for the child, man made nature. The other tends to become natural: things derive from each other by generation, which comes nearer and nearer to causality by identification.

The first stage, up to seven or eight years, is extraordinarily fertile in artificialist myths, the details of which are all more or less fabulous. The child believes, for example, that the sun and moon are great balls which men have made, lit, and thrown into the sky. One boy of six told us: *"The sun began when life began."* "What do you mean?" *"When we began to be alive."* "But how did the sun begin?" *"By a match."* Another boy said that the sun was a big round stone that a gentleman had lit. "But how does it stay in the air?" "*Because the gentleman threw it into the sky.*" As for the moon, she is continually being remade. Children take her quarters to be so many new moons. "*A gentleman made half of her first, and then the rest.*"

These answers give the impression that the children are telling stories without believing them themselves. But let us remember William James' examples of the childhood recollections of deaf-mutes. The deaf-mute D'Estrella, after puzzling over the origin of the sun, had a sudden revelation on seeing some boys playing at throwing lighted torches into the air. Then he imagined a great strong man standing behind the hills of San Francisco, who for fun threw a lighted ball into the air every morning and caught it every night.

Child artificialism and animism are, moreover, allied here quite naturally. Sun and moon are for the child both fabricated and alive. The same children who talk of the sun being made believe that it follows and watches them. The children who think the quarters of the moon are moons that are being made speak of the moon as pushing. A boy of six said, for example, "*We have to be babies before we can grow up, so the moon begins by being quite little, and afterwards she gets big.*" A boy of nine who declared that the moon pushed so as to get bigger was quite troubled when we asked him how the moon began. At last he got very red and said that she came from the person who made her, and that the person who made her was a gentleman. Obviously he was a child who had been forbidden to talk about birth and was as embarrassed in talking of the birth of the moon as of that of any small animal.

This shows how the ideas of birth and fabrication are primitively linked for the child. It is therefore not surprising to find that all the bodies which the children have just spoken of as living and conscious are now considered to have been made by men.

The wind, for example, is caused by fans or bicycle-pumps. Or "*there was a gentleman who has blown a lot.*" The clouds were made by masons out of earth or stone. Then, when the child realizes that they must be light, he thinks they are made of smoke coming from the chimneys. If there were no houses there would be no clouds, and the sky would be always blue. The sky itself is a great dome made by men, and if it is blue it is because it has been painted. Rain comes from pipes and taps situated above this dome. Rivers, lakes, and seas were dug by men, and water put in them. The mountains were built, or rather, hills were built and then went on growing by themselves. Stones are made of earth pressed together, and earth of pebbles crushed into powder. Trees come from seeds which shopmen make, and there is red, blue, or green, etc., put into these seeds for the flowers and leaves.

We will not insist too much on the varieties of these conceptions, for the flourishes are naturally open to the suspicion of invention. But let us separate the roots of this artificialism. These roots are essentially two in number. On the one hand, there is child egocentricity and the complete finalism to which it leads. It is well known, since Binet and Simon, that children define everything "by its use." The sun for them is "to warm us," the moon "to make a light at night," the mountains "to go for walks on," the rain "to water the garden," "to wash the streets," the wind "to push the ships," "to make the clouds come," etc. Therefore, if all nature is made for us, if it shares in all human activities and purposes, it is natural that questions of origin should be solved by the child in an artificialist sense. Nature is made by man to the extent that it is made for man.

There is a further point. Bovet (1925) has shown, in his penetrating studies, that there exists among children, at least among the very little ones, a spontaneous religion: the religion of parents. Parents are omniscient, all-powerful, eternal. From this to the idea that man made the universe is only a step. The conviction that his parents have organized the best possible world for him leads the child to conceive all nature as organized according to a plan and constructed by man himself.

What then produces the decline of these artificialistic beliefs? The child will seek to explain nature by himself, without the aid of human activity, but these artificialist tendencies are too strong to be eliminated all at once. Artificialism will then still partially exist but will be transferred to different things. Along with the survivals of animism, this inherent artificialism by two investigators who practised the various types of measurement to- will thus give birth, in children from the age of about seven to eight years, to a type *sui generis* of explanation, which leads us towards causality for identification and which we shall call the causality by generation. The child of eight to nine years, in reality, conceives the various objects of nature as issuing one from another without so much as stopping to consider whether they are living.

Take the stars, for example. The sun and the moon, the boys of nine tell us, are in the clouds. They are the little red clouds which press close together and make themselves into a ball. The reasons these children give are very interesting. Sometimes they point out the golden clouds that one sees at sunset and which to them appear to be made of the same substance as the sun. Sometimes they remark that the moon when seen by day looks like a very thin white cloud. Other children consider the stars are like pressed and ignited air; others consider them as smoke which has once more become fire.

We realize how interesting these explanations are from the historical point of view. Indeed, they intimately recall the conceptions of Anaximandre, Anaximène, and other pre-Socratics.

Still further: At this age the children explain the clouds as being air which is pressed together, as air becoming water and changing itself into rain. They explain rock as being earth made hard and the pebbles as being

formed of all the little twigs. One sees how very readily the law of identification recalls the law of condensation and rarefaction belonging to the pre-
Socratic school.

At this juncture it may be well to make certain experiments on the
genesis of the principles of conservation in the child's natural philosophy.
We show the child two pellets of clay or plasticine having the same form,
the same dimensions, and the same weight. In full view of the child we
then make one of these into a long sausage, leaving the other in its original
shape. We thereupon ask the child whether the two lumps of clay have
the same weight. If the child doubts it, we should then ask him whether
they still consist of the same amount of clay or not.

The results of the experiment are very clear. Before the age of seven
years the child believes that the sausage is not so heavy as the ball and that
it contains less clay. The child then has neither the idea of preservation
of material nor that of preservation of weight. From seven to ten years,
the child still declares that the sausage is lighter than the ball, but he
thinks that it contains the same amount of clay. The idea of preservation
of material has then made its appearance, but not that of preservation of
weight. On the other hand, the law of condensation has appeared: at this
age the child declares that a pebble is heavier than a piece of wood of
equal volume, because, he says, the pebble is more *pressed* or more *full*.

Instead of contenting ourselves with having wholly verbal conversations
with the child, we may institute little physical experiments on which he
is questioned. The most simple experiments are, in this respect, the best.
The very general result that we have obtained is that the child's thought
proceeds from dynamism or from substantialism to a mechanism more and
more founded on logical relations.

Here is a first example. We show the child a glass three-quarters full of
water. We also show the child a stone and ask him what the water will do
when we drop the stone into it. We suit action to words and ask the child
to explain the result. Strange as it may seem, it is only from nine to ten
years of age that children are capable of giving a correct explanation, that
is to say, of understanding that the level of the water rises because the
stone is large and takes up space. The youngest children, on the contrary,
have recourse at the outset to a dynamic explanation. They pretend that
the water rises because the stone is heavy, and that, being heavy, it weighs
down the water and produces a current, this explains why the water rises.
In that, there is not only a verbal shade of meaning. These children believe,
for example, that a little nail will make the water rise higher than a block
of wood because the nail is heavy. Moreover, they suppose that a stone
immersed but held by a thread so that it does not touch the bottom will
not make the water rise. For them it is the pressure of the stone on the
bottom of the glass which produces the current.

This direction of dynamic thought is very clear in the case of the floating of boats or the suspension of clouds. For children of four to nine years, the boats float, not because they are light, but because they go quickly. If they stopped they would sink and if they are able to stop for a short while it is because they have enough "go" for that. It is a case of a gliding flight, as it were. In the same way, if the clouds remain suspended in the air, it is not because they are light. On the contrary, they are considered as being heavy. It is because they go fast enough to be held in position by their own movement. They fly. It is only at about the age of nine to ten years that the ideas of weight and relative weight appear and permit of correct explanations. In following this evolution, we can clearly distinguish two aspects. On the one hand, from the logical point of view, weight is less and less considered as an absolute; it is progressively connected with volume. On the other hand, from the physical point of view, the mechanical explanation gives way, little by little, to an animistic dynamism.

Another striking example is that of shadows. With the hand or a book we cast a shadow on the table in front of the child, and ask him to explain what he sees. We also ask the child to foretell from which side the shadow will be produced in relation to the source of light. Here, again, the evolution of the responses comes very clearly from dynamic substantialism or from mechanical relativism. We can distinguish four stages in these replies.

The first stage is characterized by a sort of reasoning by participation, akin to the manner of the primitives. The child declares, for example, that the shadow produced on the table comes from under the trees or from the sky, that is to say, from night, or from the depths of the room. In other words, for him there is not only identity of substance between the shadow produced and all the other shadows in the universe, but also direct action one with the others. It is sufficient to put a book above the table for a piece of the sky or a fragment of shade hanging under the trees to rush to take up a place under the book.

During the second stage, the child renounces these participations, but, for all that, does not abandon the idea that shadow is a substance and that this substance moves about by itself. For the child the shadow comes from the hand, or from the book, and it can take its place on either side, no matter which. The relation between the shadow and the source of light is not understood at all.

During the third stage, this relation is, on the contrary, distinctly perceived. The child realizes that the shade is always on the side away from the window or the lamp. But the child still continues to believe that the shadow is a substance issuing from the book or from the hand. If this substance makes for the side away from the daylight it is because the shadow is black and flees from the day.

It is only during the fourth stage, that is to say at about nine to ten years, that the shadow is clearly understood as an absence of light, and that the object, the cause of the shadow, is considered as a simple screen. We thus see how these various actions converge to show the progressive abandonment of dynamism in favor of rational and mechanical explanation.

References

Baldwin, J. M., *Thoughts and Things, or Genetic Logic:* Vol. 1, *Functional Logic, or Genetic Theory of Knowledge;* Vol. 2, *Experimental Logic, or Genetic Theory of Thought.* New York: The Macmillan Company; London: Swan, Sonnenschein, 1906, 1908; Vol. 3 *Interest and Art.* New York: The Macmillan Company; London: George Allen & Unwin, Ltd., 1911.

Bovet, P., *Le sentiment religieux et la psychologie de l'enfant.* Neuchâtel and Paris: Delzchaux and Niestlé, 1925.

Piaget, J., *La représentation du monde chez l'enfant.* Paris: Alcan, 1926.
The Child's Conception of the World, trans. J. and A. Tomlinson. New York: Harcourt, Brace & Company, Inc.; London: Kegan Paul, Trench, Trubnes & Co., Ltd., 1929.

————, *La causalité physique chez l'enfant.* Paris: Alcan, 1927.
The Child's Conception of Physical Causality, trans. M. Gabain. New York: Harcourt, Brace & Company, Inc.; London: Kegan Paul, Trench, Trubnes & Co., Ltd., 1930.

Stern, W., *Psychologie der frühen Kindheit, bis zum sechsten Lebensjahre.* Leipzig: Quelle & Meyer, 1914; 6th ed., rev., 1930.
Psychology of Early Childhood; up to the Sixth Year of Age, trans. from the 3rd German ed. by A. Barwell. New York: Henry Holt & Company, Inc.; London: George Allen & Unwin, Ltd., 1924; 2nd ed., rev., 1930.

Sully, J., *Studies of Childhood.* London and New York: Appleton-Century-Crofts, Inc., 1896; new ed., 1908.

5 · Experiments in Productive Thinking

MAX WERTHEIMER

Reprinted from *Productive Thinking*. New York: Harper & Row, Publishers, 1945, pages 89-95, 101-102, by permission of the publisher.

Wertheimer, one of the leaders of the Gestalt school of psychology, points out that solution of a problem by blind obedience to rules prevents real understanding of the problem and forestalls the formulation of a genuine and original solution.

First a question to the reader:

A staircase is being built along the wall in the hall of a new house. It has 19 steps. The side away from the wall is to be faced with square carved panels of the size of the ends of the steps. The carpenter tells his apprentice to fetch them from the shop. The apprentice asks, "How many panels shall I bring?" "Find out for yourself," rejoins the carpenter. The apprentice starts counting: $1 + 2 = 3; + 3 = 6; + 4 = 10; + 5 = \ldots$.

The carpenter laughs. "Why don't you think? Must you count them out, one by one?"

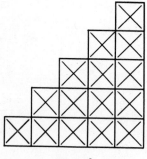

FIGURE 1.

Dear reader, if you were the apprentice, what would you do?

If you do not succeed in finding a better way, I will ask: "What if the staircase were not along the wall and required the square wooden panels on both sides? Would it help if I suggested thinking of the patterns of the two sides cut out of paper?"

The foregoing are some of the various experimental questions by which I studied features in the range of problems involved in the Gauss task.

Now I shall tell the story of young Gauss, the famous mathematician. It runs about as follows: He was a boy of six, attending grammar school in a little town. The teacher gave a test in arithmetic and said to the class: "Which of you will be first to get the sum of $1 + 2 + 3 + 4 + 5 + 6 + 7 + 8 + 9 + 10$?" Very soon, while the others were still busy

254

figuring, young Gauss raised his hand. "Ligget se," he said, which means "Here it is."

"How the devil did you get it so quickly?" exclaimed the surprised teacher. Young Gauss answered—of course we do not know exactly what he did answer, but on the basis of experience in experiments I think it may have been about like this: "Had I done it by adding 1 and 2, then 3 to the sum, then 4 to the new result, and so on, it would have taken very long; and, trying to do it quickly, I would very likely have made mistakes. But you see, 1 and 10 make eleven, 2 and 9 are again—must be—11! And so on! There are 5 such pairs; 5 times 11 makes 55." The boy had discovered the gist of an important theorem.* In diagram:

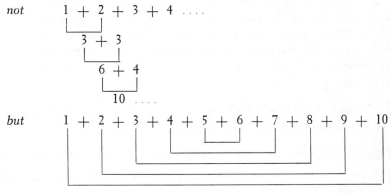

FIGURE 2.

As the teacher had put the problem to the class, I put it to many subjects, including children of various ages, to see whether a good solution would be found, and what helps, what conditions, might bring it about. In order to study the steps and the features involved, I employed systematic variations some of which I shall describe later. Sometimes I gave very long series. I said directly: "Solve the problem without using the cumbersome additions," or I simply waited for reactions.

Here are the best types of genuine processes that I found.

1. At first no way was seen of dealing with the problem. Then: "If a sequence of numbers is to be added, it is certainly correct to add them as they come—but tiresome." Suddenly: "This is not just any sequence; the numbers increase consistently, one by one—this fact may . . . it must have something to do with the sum. But how the two hang together—the form of the sequence and its sum—what the inner relation is between them—is dark, unclear; I feel it somehow but I cannot clarify it."

After a while: "The series has direction in its increase. A sum has no direction. Now: The *increase* from left to right involves a corre-

* $Sn = (n + 1)\dfrac{n}{2}$

sponding *decrease* from right to left! This *has* to do with the sum. —————→ more and more; ←————— less and less; in the same amount. If I go from left to right, from the first number to the second, there is an increase of one; if I go from right to left, from the last number at the right to the next preceding, there is a decrease of one. Hence the sum of the first and the last numbers must be the same as the sum of the next inner pair. And this must be true throughout!

"There remains only the question; how many pairs are there? Obviously the number of pairs is one-half of all the numbers; hence of the last number."

Essentially there is involved the regrouping, the reorganization of the series in the light of the problem. This is no blind regrouping; it comes about reasonably as the subject seeks to grasp the inner relation between the sum of the series and its structure. In the process the various items clearly gain a new meaning; they appear functionally determined in a new way. Nine is no longer viewed as 8 plus 1, it has become 10 minus 1, and so on.

If one gets the general formula $Sn = (n + 1)\frac{n}{2}$ in some such way, then one understands its terms in the light of this structure: $(n + 1)$ represents the value of a pair, $\frac{n}{2}$ the number of pairs. But many know only the formula, in a completely blind way. To them all forms $(n + 1)\ \frac{n}{2}$, or $\frac{n+1}{2}\ n$, or $\frac{n(n+1)}{2}$, or $\frac{n^2 + n}{2}$ are simply equivalent. The two n's seem to them to stand for the same item. They do not realize that, in the first formula, n in the expression $n + 1$ is one member of a pair, while n in $\frac{n}{2}$ stands for the number of terms in the series, determining the number of pairs. Of course the four formulas give the same end-result and are in a way equivalent, but not psychologically. In reality they are logically different too if one views them with regard to their form and function, and not solely in terms of external equivalence. Of course it is a matter of logic only if one does not exclude from logic the functional meaning of terms, the genetic question, the question of the approach to the formula—finding or understanding the formula sensibly.

The formula applies equally when the series ends with an uneven number, e.g., 1 2 3 4 5 6 7. Here the grouping described sometimes

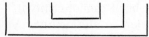

produces hesitation: What is to be done with the number in the middle which cannot be paired? A further step is required in this kind of procedure. Looking at the single number there comes a sudden discovery: "This must be half a pair, $\dfrac{n+1}{2}$!" And after some deliberation it is found that this does not change the formula: There are 3 pairs and there is the remainder in the middle, now understood as half a pair.

There are other ways of proceeding productively and sensibly. The following procedure by an 11-year-old boy is in line with what I have just described. After I had simply put the question to him: "What is $1 + 2 + 3 + 4 + 5 + 6 + 7 + 8 + 9$?" he asked, not too well pleased, "Should I count them?" "No," I answered. Suddenly smiling, he said, "There at the end is 9. Eight with the 1 in the beginning is also 9, and so must be the other pairs . . . ," then he stated the result.

2. Another way found by a 12-year-old boy started out differently. The task was: $1 + 2 + 3 + 4 + 5 + 6 + 7$.

Told not to do it by counting step by step, he said slowly: "The numbers ascend consistently . . ." And then, suddenly happy, "Oh, I have an idea! I simply take this number in the center and multiply it by the number of terms in the series—which is of course equal to the end number." It was clearly a discovery for him. Asked to show what he meant, he took the middle number, 4, and multiplied it by 7. Given a series ending with 8, he took the middle value between 4 and 5, viz., 4½.

In terms of a general formula, this means

$$c \cdot n \text{ (central value times } n\text{), or } \frac{n+1}{2} \cdot n$$

The formula is structurally different from the first in which $n + 1$ was the sum of each pair, and $\dfrac{n}{2}$ the number of pairs.

I wanted to become clearer as to what he meant and how he had reached his solution. He was not able to give any clear-cut mathematical formulations, but what he said was: "The numbers ascend consistently. This means that for the sum the central value is significant. The numbers increase to the right of it; and they decrease in the same way to the left of it. So what is added on the right is just what is lacking on the left." In diagram

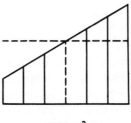

FIGURE 3.

3. The following was a structurally different procedure: Realizing the consistently ascending character of the series, the subject viewed finding the sum as: "Very troublesome because of the jagged edge." "But"—and

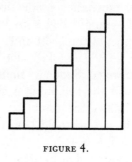

FIGURE 4.

here the subject's face lit up—"I can easily make this trouble disappear. If I combine this staircase with another, inverted one, they will have to fit and give a clear figure without any trouble. The sum is clearly base times height, $n \cdot (n + 1)$; half of it."

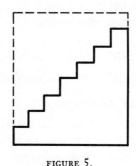

FIGURE 5.

This provides a sensible foundation for the well-known procedure in which the teacher says, "To get the sum of such a series, write it out, then just write it below in the opposite order and add each vertical pair. They are equal."

$$
\begin{array}{cccccccc}
1 + & 2 + & 3 + & 4 & \ldots\ldots\ldots\ldots & + 58 + & 59 + & 60 \\
60 + & 59 + & 58 + & 57 & \ldots\ldots\ldots\ldots & + \ 3 + & 2 + & 1 \\
61 + & 61 + & 61 + & 61 & \ldots\ldots\ldots\ldots & + 61 + & 61 + & 61
\end{array}
$$

I found a number of persons who gave this procedure as the solution. They said they had learned it that way in school. Asked why they wrote the series twice, and in this inverted fashion, all were puzzled, did not know what to answer. When I insisted, "What I want is the sum of the series; why find twice the sum first?" for the most part I got the answer, "Well, it leads to the solution in the end." They were unable to say how the idea of doubling might have originated. I confess that I myself was for a long time at a loss to see how one could reasonably have come to the idea of doubling. It had looked to me like a trick, as it does to many, like a chance discovery.

When I showed these results to a mathematician, he said, "Why do you bother about what you call 'functional differences,' 'differences in the meaning of terms'? What matters is the formula, which is identical in all cases."

This attitude is certainly justified if nothing matters but the correctness and validity of the final result. But the moment one tries to get at the psychological process in productive thinking, one *has* to investigate, to view the terms in their functional meanings. These bring about the solution in the sensible, productive processes; they constitute the basic difference between finding the formula in a sensible way and finding it by blind learning or by chance trial and error.

Confronted with the problem of the sum of a series, and given no help, many fail to find the Gauss solution. Why? What makes the task so difficult for many? What does it mean when one says, "It took the genius of young Gauss to do it"? Or why was it that the young boys in the examples mentioned, did it, and did it consistently and easily? What is at the bottom of these achievements psychologically?

The Gauss tasks involve structural difficulties. To overcome them, really to see one's way in spite of them, requires something. On the basis of my experiences, I would say that the essential features in genuine solving are:

Not to be bound, blinded by habits;
Not merely to repeat slavishly what one has been taught;
Not to proceed in a mechanized state of mind,
    in a piecemeal attitude,
    with piecemeal attention,
    by piecemeal operations;
But to look at the situation freely, open-mindedly, viewing the whole,
    trying to discover, to realize how the problem and the situation are related,
    trying to penetrate, to realize and to trace out the inner relation between form and task; in the finest cases getting at the roots of the situation, illuminating and making transparent essential structural features of regular series, in spite of the difficulties.

VI—PERSONALITY DEVELOPMENT

1 · Desires Expressed in Children's Dreams

SIGMUND FREUD

Reprinted from *The Interpretation of Dreams*. London: George Allen & Unwin Ltd., 1913, pages 109-112, by permission of the publisher.

Any important key to the understanding of the child is a knowledge of his wishes, goals, desires; in short, his motivation. Freud held that all behaviors, except reflexes, are motivated. In this selection, Freud argues that the child's desires or wishes tend to be fulfilled in his dreams.

The most simple dreams of all, I suppose, are to be expected in the case of children, whose psychic activities are certainly less complicated than those of adults. The psychology of children, in my opinion, is to be called upon for services similar to those which a study of the anatomy and development of the lower animals renders to the investigation of the structure of the highest classes of animals. Until now only a few conscious efforts have been made to take advantage of the psychology of children for such a purpose.

The dreams of little children are simple fulfillments of wishes, and as compared, therefore, with the dreams of adults, are not at all interesting. They present no problem to be solved, but are naturally invaluable as affording proof that the dream in its essence signifies the fulfillment of a wish. I have been able to collect several examples of such dreams from the material furnished by my own children.

For two dreams, one of my daughter, at that time eight and half years old, the other of a boy five and a quarter years of age, I am indebted to an excursion to the beautiful Hallstatt in the summer of 1896. I must make the preliminary statement that during this summer we were living on a hill near Aussee, from which, when the weather was good, we enjoyed a splendid view of the Dachstein from the roof of our house. The Simony Hut could easily be recognized with a telescope. The little ones often tried to see it through the telescope—I do not know with what success. Before the excursion I had told the children that Hallstatt lay at the foot of the Dachstein. They looked forward to the day with great joy. From Hallstatt we entered the valley of Eschern, which highly pleased the children with

262 · SIGMUND FREUD

its varying aspects. One of them, however, the boy of five, gradually became discontented. As often as a mountain came in view, he would ask: "Is that the Dachstein?" whereupon I would have to answer: "No, only a foot-hill." After this question had been repeated several times, he became altogether silent; and he was quite unwilling to come along on the flight of steps to the waterfall. I thought he was tired out. But the next morning, he approached me radiant with joy, and said: "Last night I dreamt that we were at Simony Hut." I understood him now; he had expected, as I was speaking of the Dachstein, that on the excursion to Hallstatt, he would ascend the mountain and would come face to face with the hut, about which there had been so much discussion at the telescope. When he learned that he was expected to be regaled with foot-hills and a waterfall, he was disappointed and became discontented. The dream compensated him for this. I tried to learn some details of the dream; they were scanty. "Steps must be climbed for six hours," as he had heard.

On this excursion wishes, destined to be satisfied only in dreams, had arisen also in the mind of the girl of eight and a half years. We had taken with us to Hallstatt the twelve-year-old boy of our neighbor—an accomplished cavalier, who, it seems to me, already enjoyed the full sympathy of the little woman. The next morning, then, she related the following dream: "Just think, I dreamt that Emil was one of us, that he said papa and mamma to you, and slept at our house in the big room like our boys. Then mamma came into the room and threw a large handful of chocolate bars under our beds." The brothers of the girl, who evidently had not inherited a familiarity with dream interpretation, declared just like many authors: "That dream is nonsense." The girl defended at least a part of the dream, and it is worth while, from the point of view of the theory of neuroses, to know which part: "That about Emil belonging to us is nonsense, but that about the bars of chocolate is not." It was just this latter part that was obscure to me. For this mamma furnished me the explanation. On the way home from the railway station the children had stopped in front of a slot machine, and had desired exactly such chocolate bars wrapped in paper with a metallic lustre, as the machine, according to their experience, had for sale. But the mother had rightly thought that the day had brought enough wish-fulfillment, and had left this wish to be satisfied in dreams. This little scene had escaped me. I at once understood that portion of the dream which had been condemned by my daughter. I had myself heard the well-behaved guest enjoining the children to wait until papa or mamma had come up. For the little one the dream made a lasting adoption based on this temporary relation of the boy to us. Her tender nature was as yet unacquainted with any form of being together except those mentioned in the dream, which are taken from her brothers. Why the chocolate bars were thrown under the bed could not, of course, be explained without questioning the child.

From a friend I have learnt of a dream very similar to that of my boy. It concerned an eight-year-old girl. The father had undertaken a walk to Dornbach with the children, intending to visit the Rohrerhütte, but turned back because it had grown too late, and promised the children to make up for their disappointment some other time. On the way back, they passed a sign which showed the way to the Hameau. The children now asked to be taken to that place also, but had to be content, for the same reason, with a postponement to another day. The next morning, the eight-year-old girl came to the father, satisfied, saying: "Papa, I dreamt last night that you were with us at the Rohrerhütte and on the Hameau." Her impatience had thus in the dream anticipated the fulfillment of the promise made by her father.

Another dream, which the picturesque beauty of the Aussee inspired in my daughter, at that time three and a quarter years old, is equally straightforward. The little one had crossed the lake for the first time, and the trip had passed too quickly for her. She did not want to leave the boat at the landing, and cried bitterly. The next morning she told us: "Last night I was sailing on the lake." Let us hope that the duration of this dream ride was more satisfactory to her.

My eldest boy, at that time eight years of age, was already dreaming of the realization of his fancies. He had been riding in a chariot with Achilles, with Diomed as charioteer. He had, of course, on the previous day shown a lively interest in the *Myths of Greece*, which had been given to his elder sister.

If it be granted that the talking of children in sleep likewise belongs to the category of dreaming, I may report the following as one of the most recent dreams in my collection. My youngest girl, at that time nineteen months old, had vomited one morning, and had therefore been kept without food throughout the day. During the night which followed upon this day of hunger, she was heard to call excitedly in her sleep: "Ann Freud, strawberry, huckleberry, omelette, pap!" She used her name in this way in order to express her idea of property; the menu must have included about everything which would seem to her a desirable meal; the fact that berries appeared in it twice was a demonstration against the domestic sanitary regulations, and was based on the circumstance, by no means overlooked by her, that the nurse ascribed her indisposition to an overplentiful consumption of strawberries; she thus in the dream took revenge for this opinion which was distasteful to her.

If we call childhood happy because it does not yet know sexual desire, we must not forget how abundant a source of disappointment and self-denial, and thus of dream stimulation, the other of the great life-impulses may become for it. Here is a second example showing this. My nephew of twenty-two months had been given the task of congratulating me upon my birthday, and of handing me, as a present, a little basket of cherries, which at that time of the year were not yet in season. It seemed difficult for him, for he repeated again and again: "Cherries in it," and could not be induced to let the little basket go out of his hands. But he knew how to secure his compensation. He had, until now, been in the habit of telling his mother every morning that he had dreamt of the "white soldier," an officer of the guard in a white cloak, whom he had once admired on the street. On the day after the birthday, he awakened joyfully with the information which could have had its origin only in a dream: "He(r)man eat up all the cherries!"

What animals dream of I do not know. A proverb for which I am indebted to one of my readers claims to know, for it raises the question: "What does the goose dream of?" the answer being: "Of corn!" The whole theory that the dream is the fulfillment of a wish is contained in these sentences.

2 · Values Expressed in Children's Drawings

WAYNE DENNIS

This selection constitutes part of a Falk Foundation lecture presented at the Carnegie Institute of Technology, in 1961, and here published for the first time.

The author is not a supporter of all Freud's theories, but the expression of wished-for qualities in children's drawings has an obvious relationship to the fulfillment of wishes in children's dreams discussed in the preceding section.

It has been proposed that human figure drawings reveal a variety of things, including what has been called the total personality. These claims have been made on slight evidence or on no evidence at all. The proposal made in the present paper is a more modest one.

The primary hypothesis which is proposed is that the child reveals in his drawings of people what he admires or wishes to possess in respect to racial features, hair style, clothing, adornment, accoutrements, and other evidences of status or affiliation, and thus reveals his values in so far as they can be indicated by visible signs.

First I shall present some evidence to support this hypothesis. Later a theoretical justification of the hypothesis will be presented, followed by studies of additional groups.

In explaining drawings, it has been said that a child draws what he knows. Certainly a person must know an object in order to draw it, but he does not draw all that he knows. He shows selectivity, and it is here proposed that within the compass of his knowledge he draws what he likes, admires, and approves of, i.e., what he values.

In this connection the Hassidim are an instructive group. Even though an Hassidic boy lives in the midst of Brooklyn and moves about in this city of three million non-Hassidim he believes that the ideal man is not the typical American but the pious Hassidic. He wishes to be and to look Hassidic. The essentials of the appearance of an Hassidic male are as follows: His hair is cropped close to the head, except for a small area above each ear. The hair of these spots grows long, is curled, and hangs in front of the ears. All men and young boys wear these curls. Men wear a black-rimmed hat. Boys wear a similar hat or a skull cap. A full beard is grown at the earliest possible age.

It is important from the point of view of this paper that while there is a traditional appearance on the part of the Hassidim, there is *no* traditional way of drawing this appearance, human representations being proscribed because they are conceived as coming under the Talmudic prohibition against the making of graven images.

Because of this taboo no photographs are taken or possessed by Hassidim, no paintings or sculptures are in their homes, and the watching of movies and TV programs is condemned. However, the Hassidic boy in passing newsstands, placards, billboards, and movie houses cannot avoid seeing American representations of the human figure. Even the secular textbooks used in the Hassidic schools contain pictures, because no textbooks without pictures are available. In other words, the Hassidic boy is familiar with American art and no other.

Despite the interdiction of drawings of a man by the Hassidim, through a cooperative teacher I was able to obtain drawings from a class of Hassidic boys. A few members of the class refused to draw. Many who did draw said they had never previously drawn a man. It has also been possible to obtain drawings of a man from Hassidic children in Israel, many of whom came from Yemen.

In general, the drawings are primitive, but even though primitive, most of them represent a man with curls before his ears, or with a broad-rimmed hat, or with a beard, or some combination of these characteristics. No drawing represents hair, other than the traditional curls. Many drawings which portray curls, hat, or beard do not portray ears, hands, trousers, or feet. The explanation seems to be that the Hassidic boy, when asked to draw a man, within the limits of his proficiency represents the most important aspects of the Hassidic male.

The Amish are a Christian group somewhat similar to the Jewish Hassidim, but they are rural rather than urban, and have no taboo against representational art. All are farmers. Most of the children attend one-room rural schools located near their homes, schools attended almost exclusively by the Amish. Education above the elementary grades is not approved of by the Amish.

The distinguishing marks of a married Amish man are a broad-rimmed flat-topped hat, plain clothing, suspenders, and a beard. Boys and unmarried men have the same appearance, except for the beard.

The Amish boy is familiar with the appearance of non-Amish men, because he necessarily sees mailmen, road workers, truck drivers, delivery men, telephone men, salesmen, etc. His teachers are non-Amish, his classroom contains pictures, and his textbooks contain the usual American textbook illustrations.

Drawings of a man were obtained from 90 Amish children attending three elementary schools near Lancaster, Pa. Many of the drawings clearly represent an Amish man, identified by his hat or his suspenders or both. However, few of the men drawn wore beards. This suggests that school-age boys and girls among the Amish admire younger rather than older people, but no independent evidence on this point has yet been gathered.

Only a few of the pupils tested were beyond age 12. Of these several drew men who were typically American rather than Amish. This suggests a breaking away from Amish ideals among the present teen-agers, but again no independent evidence was obtained, since the drawings were gathered before the present hypotheses were developed.

The results obtained from the Hassidim and from the Amish are subject to the interpretation that the majority of any group, when drawing a man, will depict a man of their own group. But this interpretation is negated by results obtained from a large section of our population, the American Negroes.

Results have been obtained from both Northern and Southern Negroes, ranging in education from the first grade to college seniors. The total number of drawings collected exceeds seven hundred. Only a few show a dark face or kinky hair, a broad nose or thick lips. Nearly all show a white face, straight hair, a straight nose, and thin lips.

I have asked each of several psychologists who are quite familiar with human drawings to examine samples of this collection "blindly," and to tell me what ethnic group made the drawings. None guessed that the drawings were made by Negroes.

We are familiar with the efforts made by Negroes to straighten the hair, to lighten the complexion, and otherwise to simulate a Caucasian appearance. Many studies show that the American Negro wishes to avoid a Negro appearance and thinks he is handsome to the extent to which he approaches the appearance of the white. Any perusal of current Negro magazines supports this interpretation. It appears that the American Negro draws a man who has the appearance he admires, which is not the appearance of a Negro.

The only interpretation I can suggest which encompasses the results from the Hassidim, the Amish, and the Negro is that which was suggested earlier, namely, that the contents of drawings reflect the values of the artist who may or may not approve of the appearance of his group.

The manner in which one accounts for the representation of values in drawings will depend upon one's preferences among psychological theories. I prefer an eclectic approach. It has been recognized for a long time that acts which are followed by consequences which may be called rewards or positive reinforcements tend to be repeated. The Hassidic boy finds that growing a beard is reinforced, the Amish boy that wearing suspenders is praised, the Negro child that "looking white" brings rewards. Each tries to obtain the pleasant effects which accompany their respective reinforcements.

According to association theory, something which is associated with a pleasurable experience will in some degree revive the pleasure. Visual representations early become associated with the real objects and events which they represent. It is to be expected therefore that making a drawing of an event or of physical features or of kinds of clothing which have been praised will be pleasurable and will lead to repeating such a drawing.

In other words, the human being, unlike most animals, can reward himself by creating images of rewarded features, clothing, or behavior. Of course, he can do this with actions and sounds as well as with pencil and paper. The pleasure which the child shows in engaging in make-believe, in talking, and in drawing supports this principle. It is a corollary of this principle that all spontaneous activities of children reflect their values.

Now that a principle has been derived which appears to harmonize the findings from three diverse groups, and a tentative theoretical interpretation has been offered, let us examine the data from several other groups with a view to determining whether or not they too are in accord with this principle.

First let us consider the occupational status of the persons drawn. Behavioral scientists agree that there is a hierarchy of occupational prestige which is fairly uniform in Western societies. Numerous studies show that the professional group is most respected, other white-collar workers rank next, and that manual laborers and service workers are low in prestige. As would be expected on the basis of interpretation that has been presented, few drawings of American children represent persons in manual labor or service occupations. Milkmen, farmers, garbage men, waiters, cooks, plumbers, and other kinds of working men whose occupations are recognizable by their working costumes or their instruments of work are almost never drawn. Of all of the blue-shirted proletariat, the cowboy is most often depicted. He has a special prestige of his own, not based on his being a laborer.

Reflection of preferred social status and of high occupational prestige in drawings occurs outside of America. I have a large collection of children's drawings from the Middle East, particularly from Lebanon and Egypt. In Lebanon a common article of dress consists of home-made trousers, made of thin cotton cloth, very full in the waist and seat, tied about the waist by a draw-string, but fitting tightly at the knee and calf. These baggy pants are familiar to children in all parts of Lebanon, but they are worn by laborers and farmers and not by business and professional men. As one would expect on the basis of the theory here proposed, these trousers are almost never drawn by children, whatever their social class.

Another Middle Eastern example of the effect of social prestige on drawings involves headgear. In several Middle Eastern countries, a common form of head covering is the kafia, a cloth held by a cord around the head and allowed to cover the neck and shoulders. This was formerly a widespread article of dress, but has been largely abandoned by the more well-to-do. It is still worn by the poor and by persons in the least modernized areas. As a consequence, children, even poor children, seldom depict this form of headgear.

Another traditional Middle Eastern hat is the fez or trabush, a truncated red felt cone with a tassel. This hat was traditionally worn by the more well-to-do, and is still frequently worn by them except in Turkey, where it was outlawed by Ataturk in his modernization program. It appears on Turkish statues and in old portraits but is not worn at present. Needless to say, the fez is frequently drawn by children in Lebanon and Egypt, but not by children in Turkey.

In Egypt men of modest means wear western trousers and shirts. The quite poor, however, wear a long single garment called a galabia, which reaches from the shoulders to the ankles and resembles a nightgown. In conformity with the theory here presented, Egyptian children, well-to-do or poor, seldom draw the galabia. Once again it is seen that the social prestige of an article of clothing has a powerful effect upon its presence in drawings.

Permit me to present one more instance of the effect of prestige symbols. Japan has been undergoing westernization for some time but the speed of change has been particularly great in the postwar years. At the present time practically all middle-class urban Japanese men wear western street clothes. Through the kind offices of Professor Koji Sato of Kyoto University I have obtained a collection of drawings from the public schools of Kyoto, which is a modern city. The majority of these drawings represent men in modern dress.

At an earlier point it was indicated that white Americans draw Caucasian features and that the drawings of American Negroes represent Caucasians. What about the racial features drawn by other groups?

While many Japanese drawings represent Western clothing, they give little indication of admiration for Caucasian features. Many drawings clearly represent Japanese, others are so schematic as to be nonracial, few represent such exclusively Caucasian features as curly hair, prominent jaws, and long noses.

Drawings have been obtained from Cambodia in southeast Asia. The majority of the drawings by Cambodian children are clearly drawings representing native persons, who comprise a portion of the yellow race. This is true, even though these children are acquainted with Frenchmen and Americans. In other words, there appears to be no universal preference for Caucasian features. It should be noted that traditional art in southeast Asia and Japan depicts Oriental features.

Permit me to return for a few moments to Negro art. Negroes draw Caucasians, presumably because they admire the Caucasian appearance. It follows that if a Negro admires Negro racial characteristics he should make Negroid drawings. Is this the case? Unfortunately with respect to present-day Negroes, little evidence is available on this point. The attitudes of present-day Negroes concerning their racial features have been studied very little except in the United States, and few drawings of Negroes have been collected except in America. We know, however, that aboriginal

Negro art depicts Negroes. For example, in the traditional African sculptures and masks black wood was used or other wood was stained black. It seems reasonable to suppose that before white military and cultural superiority was imposed upon the Negro he valued his own appearance. There seems to be no reason to doubt that the principle that art reflects values applies universally to physical features as well as to indicators of social status.

In a previous paper I have hypothesized that societies which are technologically and educationally primitive will show higher sustentative and religious values, and lower hedonistic values, than do modern societies. Are these generalizations, which were supported by the data on uses also supported by data on art?

It is assumed that sustentative values (which stress subsistence and survival) will be shown in drawings by the depiction of men engaged in breadwinning activities, such as hunters, fishermen, shepherds, and farmers, and that religious values will be shown by representations of religious activities or of men whose appearance indicates their religious duties or affiliation. Hedonistic values should be represented by games, recreational activities, and appropriate costumes.

I have referred to drawings obtained from a school in an agricultural community in Cambodia. Several of these show men engaged in agricultural pursuits. But none depicts Buddhist monks or religious statues with whom all of the children are presumably familiar. However, all the children tested are receiving secular education. The lack of religious figures in their drawings may be a valid indicator of religious indifference.

In Japan drawings were obtained not only in a modern city but in two villages which are among those least touched by modern influences. The children of these villages drew many men engaged in sustentative activities, such as farmers, gardeners, porters, and miners, occupations seldom represented by urban children. However, in a large number of village and urban drawings no religious figures were represented. It should be noted, however, that secular education is universal in Japan, including the remote villages.

Turning now to groups which have been more influenced by modern technology and education than those just reviewed, it will be found that their drawings show little interest in sustentative and religious activities. It has been noted previously that in the Middle East, in Japan, and in the United States urban children almost never draw men engaged in basic productive activities, choosing instead to draw men of greater occupational prestige. It remains to comment on the absence of religious figures in the drawings obtained from modern urban groups.

In many religious groups, the clergy can be recognized by their dress. This is true among Roman Catholics, Greek Catholics, Moslems, and Buddhists, and in some Protestant and Jewish groups. Among thousands of drawings from the United States, Lebanon, Egypt, Syria, and Israel, no distinguishing dress of a religious sort appears except among the very conservative Jews of Israel and Brooklyn. In this connection it is worthy of note that while many Christians wear a cross, this does not appear in drawings. This suggests that it does not have a deep significance for the wearer, such as the skull cap has for the orthodox Jew or the black hat has for the Hassidim and the Amish.

3 · Personality and Play Therapy

VIRGINIA M. AXLINE

Reprinted from the article in *Journal of Abnormal and Social Psychology*, 43 (1948), 300-310, by permission of the author and the American Psychological Association.

Free play situations are employed both to reveal personality and to assist in bringing about better adjustment. The following description of a permissive play group illustrates how a concern with racial discrimination revealed itself and was, to some extent, ameliorated by play therapy technique.

There seems to be a growing interest on the part of many people today to explore more fully and objectively the dynamics of group behavior in an attempt to determine better methods of meeting the issues that sometimes arise in the areas of human relations. Certainly the race issue is one that provokes further investigation and study. And as one sees examples of individuals becoming involved in race issues, with the scatter and spread and clash of the generated emotionalized attitudes that are often a part of this issue, many questions arise that might throw some additional light on this problem if they could be answered in such a manner that a constructive way of meeting the problems would be forthcoming.

In this article there is a brief account of some experimental work done in group play therapy with six-, seven-, and eight-year-old children. The primary purpose of the study was to determine the effectiveness of play therapy for small groups of children who were having difficulty adjusting to other children. The children who were selected for participation in the group therapy experience were either extremely withdrawn or aggressively antisocial. There were four groups of children from four different classrooms—and four children in each group, two girls and two boys.

The plan for the therapy was as follows. Each group would meet with the play therapist for one 40-minute period each week for 10 meetings. At the conclusion of the tenth meeting the groupings would become transitory, mixed groupings. In other words, the eleventh meeting of the grouping would be composed of four children, one from each class room represented in the study. The next four meetings would continue on this pattern so that each time there would be a group of children who had never been together in the play group before. The purpose of this procedure was to study the children's adjustability to new group experiences.

A study of the data of this experiment revealed some interesting material on the problem of racial conflict among young children and the results of the group experience for these children. In this article only that material related to the race issue will be included.

This material is presented here for consideration as a possible means of studying the dynamics of group behavior, and the generation and dissipation of the children's emotionalized attitudes. It is presented with these questions: Does this type of verbatim descriptive material seem to lend itself to a scientific study of the "race issue"? And does this therapeutic procedure seem to be an effective way of resolving racial conflict among children?

These play contacts were not directed by the therapist. The children were in a free play situation where they could express any attitudes and feelings that they wished to express. In this type of experience we often see the child's real self in spontaneous expression. Consequently, it seems that such material might offer rich resources for a detailed study. These excerpts, lifted out of the complete context of the record of the children's play, are presented only as examples of the type of behavior that is available for further study and analysis. Brief as they are, however, it seems to me that they suggest a way of studying the race issue from the inner frame of reference of the child. It seems as though a more detailed collection of data, a more rigorous analysis of the material, and a more systematic procedure might yield some very significant studies of the race issue.

In the nondirective play therapy sessions no attempt is made to bring out any specific type of material. Consequently, the examples offered, coming as a completely spontaneous expression on the part of these children, seem to be more valuable because of that very spontaneity.

When the complete record of this play group is studied one notes that these children are not always "race-conscious" children. Nor does the issue loom up after every clash of personalities. One might ask: Why does it become an issue at one time and remain completely out of the picture at another time? The play experiences of these children ran the gamut of the usual group therapy play with all shades of interaction and self-expression coming out. In only five brief incidents was there any obvious awareness of the race issue on the part of these children. So, when studying these children's behavior and emotional reactions, it seems well to keep this in mind so that they are seen in more accurate perspective.

In the first group mentioned are four seven-year-old children. There is June, a Negro. Her teacher describes her behavior as "aggressive, quarrelsome, sulky. The children do not like her because she is always starting trouble." Beverly's teacher describes her as "wild, rough, loud, aggressive, destructive, and *naturally* not liked by the other children." Jackie is described as a "very quiet, dreamy, child, who will not participate in group activities, but who always clings to any adult in the group." The children do not dislike Jackie, according to his teacher, but he rejects any overture from them to include him in the group. Pete is described as "*impossibly* aggressive, *highly* emotional, *extremely* quarrelsome."

This constitutes the membership of the first group. The first and second meetings were stormy ones—with the children frequently arguing over the toys—usually playing alone. Jackie, true to his reputation, assumed the role of kibitzer most of the time. During *the third meeting* of this group the following incident occurred.

June's opening remark as she enters the room is to the effect that she had gotten sand in her hair the last time she had come to the group meeting and her mother had said that she was not to get sand in it again. Beverly, who is loud, active, aggressive, jeers at June. "So what if you do get sand in your hair? You know what our rules are. We can throw sand in this half of the room. And if you come over that line you risk getting sand in your hair. And if you don't like it you should stay over there on that side and not come over here and try and bring the rules for that side of the line over here on this side of the line."

Jackie is a quiet, gentle dreamer who talks a great deal to the therapist but has up to now stayed out of any active group participation—other than calling across an observation to one of the other children.

Pete is active, excitable, and aggressive. He wants to run the show. When things do not go as he wants them to go he quickly doubles up his fists and asks belligerently, "Do I have to *show* you I mean business?"

June and Beverly went into the puppet theater—June crossing the line and squealing out, "Don't throw the sand on me!" and the boys throwing it because she stepped over the line. Finally they settled down. The girls idly manipulated the puppets. The boys played in the sand. Then the girls went over to the easel and began to paint. Pete commented that he didn't see why they couldn't do absolutely everything they wanted to do in this place even to killing off one another and demolishing the room. He had experienced the limitations only when he had in previous contacts made an attempt to strike someone in the group and when he had not been permitted to throw paint on the walls or to dig off the plaster. He had accepted the limitations but was still verbally growling about it. The therapist accepted his feelings of wanting to do these things, but held the limitations firmly in place.

Suddenly the two boys whispered together, then quickly jumped out of the sand box and proceeded·to wreck the collapsible doll house. This was an acceptable play of destructiveness, the house having been constructed for that purpose. They screamed and yelled.

Pete: "Tear down the house. Wreck it."

Jackie: "The morons will completely demolish this dump."

Pete: "Off with the roof. Off with the walls. I hate—hate—hate this miserable house. The walls close in on them all. Bang, goes the roof smack down on them."

Jackie: "Did they get killed? Did they? Did they?"

Pete: "Of *course* they got killed. They died *horrible* deaths. And their blood ran like rivers down the street."

The two girls were watching the boys. Beverly picked up her brush, dipped it into the red paint, and swiped it across the picture.

"Blood—blood—blood!" she yelled with vigor. "All over everybody and everything. Come on, June. Let's let them throw the sand at us."

"All right—all right!" June cried—and they leaped quite happily across the "safety" line. Immediately the boys grabbed up handfuls of sand and threw it at the girls. Immediately June reverted to her usual protest and Beverly as usual pointed out to June that she could not come over the line unless she would take the consequences. It was all so noisy and moved so rapidly that the therapist said nothing until a remark was addressed to her. "People are so very funny," Jackie said to the therapist. "They pretend they do not want the thing they want the most. June *wants* us to throw sand at her. She yells when we do. I *say* I don't like noise and fights and I could scream all day long and stick knives in people."

"People don't always behave the way they feel, hm?" said the therapist. "You act and say one thing and sometimes mean another?"

"Yes," Jackie said. "Quite often I do. But I never tell how I *really* feel. I *pretend—pretend* all the time."

June and Beverly lay down on the floor and rolled. Pete dumped large boxes of sand on them. They laughed and picked up handfuls and threw it back at the boys.

Then June got in the sand box. There was an immediate protest. Both boys declared the sand box was their territory and called the girls invaders.

The girls retreated to the puppet theater and put on a play. The boys watched. All the boy puppets were beaten up by the girls—declared "incompetent, feeble-minded, and morons." Beverly then announced that she *really* loved boys and wished she was a boy. Jackie said he *loved* girls and wished he was a girl. Pete said he was happy just the way he was—but wished he was a king and that everyone *had* to obey him. June said nothing. She withdrew to the easel. Beverly's loud voice demanded that June, too, should say how she felt about herself. June turned her back to the others. Beverly continued to demand an answer. June turned defiantly and said, "I will *not* tell you. And you *white folks* went ahead and got sand in my hair *again*. And I *told* you not to."

"It was your own fault," Beverly shouted. "You got over the line."

Angrily June stepped across the line again. "I'll come across the line again," she declared, "and again and again and I'll tell my mother you *white folks* did this to me."

Because she was across the line, the "white folks" again threw the sand at her. The therapist reflected the attitudes all the children expressed. She did not attempt to restrain the sand-throwing because June was over the line. When June got back in the safety zone and Beverly threw more sand for good measure, then the therapist entered in with a limitation. "This is the safety zone. No sand over here."

June sulked. She returned to the easel and stirred the paints without much interest in what she was doing.

Suddenly June turned toward the others, who had quieted down and were now playing together in the sand box.

"Look at you three together," she cried. "You awful three! You white trash!"

Beverly sprang up. "Don't you call me that—you—you—" She looked furtively at the therapist.

"You want to call her a name because she called you one, don't you?" the therapist said.

"Yes," Beverly replied.

But Jackie, the young philosopher, said, "Be kind to her, Beverly. Her feelings *must* be hurt." He dug quietly in the sand—looked up at Beverly and said, "You really wanted to call her a nigger, didn't you?"

Beverly hung her head. She did not reply. June looked at them with hot eyes.

"Do you want to come in here and play with us?" Jackie invited June.

"No," June said.

"Come on," Jackie said.

"Well," said June.

"You can have my place," Jackie said, jumping out, "and I'll paint."

June gingerly took Jackie's place. Beverly handed her a shovel and a little bucket. Pete retreated to a corner in the sand box with his back to the girls. Jackie painted a piece of paper solid black. Then he placed a thick gob of red finger-paint in the middle. He came over to the therapist and whispered:

"Guess what it is?"

"I don't know," said the therapist. "Do you want to tell me?"

Jackie grinned wickedly. "It's got something to do with June," he whispered, "and it *looks* like she got hurt."

Beverly and June started to play together and soon Pete joined them. Finally Jackie came over and sat on the edge of the sand box.

"Do you like us better now?" he asked June.

She smiled at him quite happily. "Uh-huh!" she said.

Jackie went over to the easel and tore down his painting and threw it in the waste basket. He looked at June.

"What color do you like the best?" he said.

"Pink," she said.

Jackie carefully mixed some red in the pan of white paint. He tried it out on the paper.

"This pink?" he asked.

"Yes," she said and settled back to watch him. He painted a row of pink flowers, added green stems and green leaves.

"There," he said as he finished it. "This is for you, June."

"Make me one! Make me one!" called Beverly.

"No, that's all I want to do today," Jackie said.

"Our time is up for today," said the therapist.

June chose that minute to pour a handful of sand on Beverly's hair, as she jumped out of the sand box. There was a squabble and a flare-up. Finally they quieted down and left together to return to their class at school.

This is the kind of data that seems to contain valuable material for a study of attitudes and behavior of children. A few of the significant things that stand out are the comments of Jackie, implying he does one thing, feels another, "pretends, pretends all the time." The way June reacts when they ask her how she feels about herself is interesting. The injection of racial feelings and the way in which the group meets this challenge seems important. Does this seem to be significant material for a study in attacking the problems related to social issues?

Following this meeting it was necessary to place June in another group. This was due to the fact that she was transferred to another classroom and the teacher's reading schedule conflicted with the time of the group meeting. June was placed in Group 2. *This was the fourth meeting* of this group, the fourth group therapy meeting for June, but her first meeting with these children. The children were well acquainted, however, outside of the group.

These children are also seven years old. They were referred for the group therapy experience for the following reasons, as stated by their teachers:

Louise is very quiet, very withdrawn. She seldom plays with the group— seldom asserts herself.

Perry is inclined to be domineering and bossy. He always likes to have his way. He is excitable and nervous. He does not get along with other children—does not seem to want to.

Rollin is moody—at times very withdrawn and again very aggressive. He is a lone wolf most of the time.

Louise did not live up to her teacher's description at any time during the therapy. Perry and Rollin behaved more or less as they had been described.

June was the only Negro in this class at school. An excerpt from the group which June joined illustrates a little more how the child sometimes expresses significant attitudes in his play—and how these attitudes are influenced by other children in the group.

Rollin, June, Louise, and Perry are playing together in the sand for the first few minutes. Then the group splits up. Rollin and June play at the doll house. Perry and Louise paint. The play at the doll house centers around the dolls going to the toilet.

"Look at him. He's on the toilet," Rollin says.

"Shame! Shame!" June cries.

"Why?" Rollin asks.

"I don't know," June says.

Then they set the table and begin to play house.

"We're eating breakfast. This is fun," June cries.

They play around. June bumps into the table and knocks it over.

"These children are bad girls!" Rollin shouts.

"They are *not* bad," June shouts in reply.

"You *dope!*" Rollin yells.

"Who says I'm a dope? I'm *not* a dope. You're a dope yourself!"

"You—you *red head* you!" Rollin screams.

"Red head yourself!" screams June.

"You should go away to the nuthead house!" Rollin says. "Come on, let's fix this so the people won't have any home to live in."

June and Rollin yell and scream and wreck the house.

June grabs up the baby doll and swings it around by the leg. Then she says, "Oh let's play right. Let's don't be so wild."

"Okay, okay," says Rollin. "Let's use this big doll." He tosses it in the sand box. "I'm going to put all the people in the attic and I'll lock 'em up there and they will never in the world get out again."

The other two children continue to paint—talking quietly. Perry asks for more paper. He looks at the therapist.

"What is your real name?" he asks. She tells him her name. As he tries to tack up the paper he sticks his finger. "Look," he says, "I'll need first aid. I'll wash it off." He spills some water on the floor.

"Oh, I *am* sorry," he says.

"Why did you say you were sorry?" Louise asks.

"Well, it was an accident," Perry comments.

"I daresay you won't need to say 'I'm sorry' in here," Louise observes.

"Then that is why I will say it in here. I get so tired of saying what I'm *supposed* to say."

"Is anyone interested in modern art?" Louise asks with a giggle. "I think I've just done some very, very modern art."

Perry holds up the brown paint water. "Nice whiskey," he says.

June turns and holds up a small table from the doll house. "This is a cocktail table." As she reaches over she jars Rollin's arm and he spills the tray on which he was carrying "the drinks."

"Oh, for Christ sake," he shouts, "you Goddam nigger. You *spilled* the tray! This makes me so Goddam mad I could spit on you!"

June draws back. Her face clouds over. "I am *not* a nigger!" she shouts. "What are you then?" Rollin demands.

June looks about her unhappily. "I—I—I am a *person!*" she says.

There is absolute silence in the playroom. All three children turn and look at June.

"Oh," says Rollin. There is another silence. Rollin looks down at the floor. He goes over and sits down on the edge of the sand box. He puts his hand down in the sand, idly sifts it through his fingers. June stands still in the middle of the room, staring at Rollin. He looks up at her again. "I'm sorry, June," he says finally.

"That's all right," June says. There is once more quietness in the room. June turns her back to the others—goes over to the doll house things and sorts through them until she finds a little Negro doll. She holds it in her hand and looks at it. Rollin still sits on the edge of the sand box watching June with an odd expression on his face.

June picks up a white doll, holds the white doll and the Negro doll side by side, looks at them for a long time. She picks up one of the doll house beds and places the white doll in it very carefully. Then she glares at the Negro doll. She lays it on the table, grabs the wooden hammer and pounds the doll viciously.

"Get rid of the old nigger!" she shouts. "Dirty old nigger. Black, hateful old nigger."

Rollin stands up quickly and looks at her. "June!" he says, "June! She is a *person!*"

"Oh," says June in a tone of distress, "I'm sorry." She picks up the Negro doll. She looks at Rollin again. "Could I—" she asks, then hesitates.

"What!" Rollin asks.

"Could I put her in the same bed with the—the *pretty* doll?"

Rollin comes over and looks at the white doll in the little bed and at the Negro doll in June's little brown hand. He considers it for a long time. Perry and Louise leave their painting and come over, too. They all gather around June, who is still holding the little black doll.

"Is there—is there another bed?" Perry asks. "Everyone should sleep in a bed of his own. No two people should *ever* sleep together."

"I sleep with my sister," Louise says, "and that's all right!"

Rollin stoops down and sorts through the toy furniture. He finds another bed. June watches him silently. There are tears in her eyes. They are not doing this to the doll. They are doing this to her. The therapist stays out of it at this point—watching this stark drama unfold slowly and with intense meaning for all these children.

"Here is another bed," Rollin says to June. She stretches the doll out toward him. Rollin does not touch the doll.

Perry reaches out a hand to take the bed. Rollin pulls it out of his reach. He glares at Perry. "You keep outa this," he says roughly.

Then he looks at June and asks her very gently, "Where does she want to sleep, June? Does she want a bed all her own? Or does she want to sleep with the white girl?"

June will not commit herself. She blinks back her tears and continues to hold the Negro doll out to Rollin. Finally he takes it, places it in the bed alone, quickly removes it, throws the empty bed across the room with violence and places the Negro doll in the bed with the white one. June smiles radiantly.

"Why did you do *that?*" Perry asks.

"I know why," Louise says. "I'm glad you did, Rollin."

"Why *did* you?" Perry demands again.

Rollin shrugs his shoulders and sits down on the edge of the sand box.

"I know why he did," Louise says. "You didn't want June to cry. Isn't that why?"

"No," Rollin says, shaking his head.

"Well, I think you're crazy," Perry says, and goes after the other doll bed. He brings it back and reaches for the Negro doll. Rollin grabs his arm.

"You let that alone!" he yells. "You keep your hands off."

"They should each have their own bed!" Perry shouts.

"Let them alone," Rollin shouts. "Let them alone!"

The group splits up again. Rollin crawls into the sand box and sits with his back to the others. June sits down at the table and rolls a ball of clay in her hands. Louise and Perry return to their painting. None of the children speaks. When it is time to go they leave quietly. June walks back to the schoolroom with Perry and Louise and they talk happily together. Rollin walks back alone—hanging his head. What is he thinking? Why did he react like that? Rollin is only eight. He is a Jew. Does this suggest that there is value in such a group for the handling of social conflicts? Does this suggest that the attitudes of even young children soon are influenced by prejudice and discrimination?

I believe that this little experience and many other group experiences will shed some light on the issue of social therapy—or social education, call it what you will. I believe this is of special significance to teachers as well as therapists.

June attended six more meetings with this group. And three more times some aspect of the race problem was brought into focus.

The causes of the race question's being brought into the group play seem to be significant. In the first excerpt quoted here it is a bit difficult to pin down the exact cause of June's withdrawal from the group and then her attack upon them. One might speculate that she withdrew when asked to state her wish because it pointed up a difference between herself and the others—a difference which she was reluctant to face; and consequently she met it with an attack upon the other members of the group. In the second example the race issue was injected as a result of Rollin's anger. It was the climax of milder name-calling. At no time after this incident did Rollin ever bring out any attack upon June's race. However, Perry and Louise did.

The other three incidents will now be cited:

At the fifth meeting of the second group the children were playing quietly—each one pursuing his own interests. Rollin was playing in the sand. Perry was modeling an animal out of clay. Louise was painting. June was playing with the large rag doll. Suddenly June threw down the doll and sat down at the table across from Perry. He did not pay any attention to her. She reached over and took a piece of his clay. Immediately Perry sprang to his feet screaming, "Give me back my clay!"

"I want it!" June said, hugging it tightly.

"Give me it! Give me it!" yelled Perry angrily.

He reached across and snatched at it. June held it in her hands, sat down on the chair, bent over so that Perry could not get the clay out of her hands.

Perry was beside himself with anger. The therapist reflected the attitudes the children were expressing—June's desire to keep the clay and Perry's anger at the act. June grinned at the therapist. "He's sure mad!" she said gleefully. "Look at his face. He gets so red in the face when he gets mad," she giggled. "I *like* to make his face change color!"

Perry glared at her and said coldly, "I'd like to make *your* face change color. I'd like to make it *white* so you wouldn't be so mean!"

The therapist said, "You would *both* like to change the color of the other's face?"

June stood up and hurled the clay down on the floor as hard as she could. "Don't you call me names!" she yelled at Perry.

"June doesn't like to have someone call her names," said the therapist.

Perry looked angrily at the therapist.

"She is a mean, nasty—"

"I am *not!* I am *not!*" screamed June and tears rolled down her face.

"Look," Perry said, suddenly speaking in a very calm voice, "I didn't *like* it, June, when you jerked away my clay. Why did you do it to me?"

"I dunno," June said meekly. She hung her head, wiped her eyes with her fists.

Louise came up to June. "Do you want to play with one of us?" she asked. June nodded.

"Want to paint with me?" June nodded.

Louise looked at June and suddenly reached out and laid her hand on June's hair.

"Your hair feels funny," Louise said. June put her hand up to her hair. She looked at Louise suspiciously. Then she reached out and touched Louise's hair.

"*Your* hair feels funny," June said belligerently. But Louise was not making fun of June. She was interested in June's hair and touched it gently with both hands.

"Your hair is *different*," Louise said.

"*No!*" June protested, burying her hands not so gently in Louise's hair. "*No!* It's your hair that's different."

"You've *both* got *different* kinds of hair," said the therapist.

Rollin got out of the sand and came over and touched June's hair very gently.

"I think your hair is *nice*, June," he said.

Perry stuck his hand on June's hair, then on Louise's hair, then on his own hair, then on Rollin's hair.

"Your hair is sort of like June's," he said to Rollin.

"Is it?" June asked. She felt Rollin's hair. He shook off her hand and got back in the sand box and kept his back to the others.

"Each one of you has hair that is a little different from one another," said the therapist.

June laughed. Louise laughed. Perry laughed.

"But it *all* grows on our heads!" Perry said. He sat down at the table. "Here's some clay if you want it," he said. June sat down and played with the clay.

Here again we note the attack, the anger, the hurt feelings when June is made to feel "different." Here again we see the dissipation of the feeling when June does not feel alone in her "differences." The exploratory interest all the children displayed as they studied the differences in the texture of their hair brought with it the calm of a shared interest. Perry's generalization that they all had one thing in common—it grew on their heads— seemed to dissolve the last shred of tension between them.

At the sixth meeting of the group Louise was painting a picture of a "princess." It was a very good picture for a seven-year-old child to draw. June watched Louise. Rollin came over and looked at it. "That's pretty," he said, with genuine appreciation of Louise's art.

"I don't think it is," June said. Rollin walked away from the easel. June picked up a brush, dipped it in the brown paint, and smeared it across the face of the "princess." Louise turned on her angrily. "You look what you've done!" she cried. "You've made my beautiful princess into an ugly nigger!"

June glared at Louise.

"Louise is angry because June *painted on her* picture," the therapist said.

June stood still and looked at the painting, then at Louise, then at the therapist.

"She called me a nigger," she said, but her voice was quiet.

"I did *not* call *you* a nigger," Louise said, "I said you spoiled my picture by putting that paint on it."

June looked again at the picture and then at the therapist.

"I guess I *did* spoil the picture," she said, "I'm sorry."

In this incident June for the first time seemed to realize that she was partly responsible for the attacks she drew upon herself. The fact that June had used brown paint and had smeared it on the face of Louise's "princess" seemed to have suggested the accusation Louise hurled at June. Why did June use the brown paint and smear it over the face? I don't know. The therapist's statement seemed to point out to June the fact that it was the *paint on the picture* to which Louise was reacting, rather than the color of June's skin.

During the seventh meeting the fifth and last incident in which the race issue was brought out in this play group occurred in a very interesting manner. Rollin was finger-painting. Three of the children were playing "house." Perry said he would be the "father" and Louise would be the "mother" and June would be their "baby." Thus they started their play.

Suddenly, without any obvious reason for his change in attitude, Perry announced that June could not be their baby any more. She would have to be the maid.

"Here, Black Girl," he said, "go get—"

That was all that it took to set June off.

"I am *not* a black girl," she yelled.

"I didn't mean to make you mad," Perry said. "*I* wouldn't get mad if you called *me White Boy*."

June looked at him, bewildered by what Perry had said.

"But she isn't *black*," Louise said. She went over to the table where Rollin was finger-painting. She brought back the jar of brown finger-paint and took off the lid.

"Look," she said, "This is just the color of June." She dug out some of the paint and held it toward June's arm. At first June drew back, then, noting that Louise was not attacking her or making fun of her, she looked in the jar. Then Louise rubbed the brown finger-paint on her own hands and arms. Perry, rising to the occasion, rubbed it on his hands and arms and face. Then Louise put some on her face. They were all laughing. June reached in the jar and rubbed the paint on her arms and hands and face.

"Look!" Perry shouted. "It *matches* exactly."

Rollin stopped his finger-painting and sat there grinning at them. Suddenly he joined the others and smeared the brown paint on his hands, arms, and face.

"This is fun! This is fun!" they cried dancing around the room.

"Where's some *white* finger-paint?" June asked. They all stopped and looked around for the white finger-paint.

"There isn't any white finger-paint," said the therapist.

"We're all *alike* now," Louise said. "June and Perry and Rollin and me!"

And the children danced around smearing the paint on themselves for the remaining ten minutes of the play period. When it was time to leave they all washed their hands and arms and faces and left together in a happy, cheerful mood.

After this session there were no other incidents that referred to June as a Negro—or as anyone differing from the group. They all seemed to have accepted one another. This also carried over in the classroom situation. The teacher's report states that June has become "more sociable, more cooperative, more friendly, with a definite decrease in her former aggressiveness." The report also notes that June was accepted in her classroom by the other three children in her therapy group—and gradually by the other children in the class.

The report in regard to the other three children mentions the following changes:

> Louise has changed more than any of the other children in the group. She is now definitely a leader of a group and gets along well with the other children.
>
> Perry is much more agreeable. He still likes to boss the others around but does not react unfavorably when put in his place by one of the others. He plays more with the other children.
>
> Rollin is still moody—but seems to have more *ups* than downs. He seems quieter, more relaxed, less tense. He plays quite a bit with his "play group."

These children made interesting adjustments to the last series of group meetings. There was a tendency to participate in the group meetings with an awareness of the rights of others. There was a marked tendency to plan what they would do at the beginning of the meetings and the plans were usually carried out.

Since this occurred in all the meetings, it seems that one could infer that these children had learned how to adjust to others in a free play situation so that the rights of others were considered. Any clashes that did occur were gotten out in the open immediately and some satisfactory solution was arrived at by the children. Sometimes they each played alone, but most of the time they played together. There was a considerable lessening of destructive, aggressive play as the time passed. Finally, and certainly important, at no time during these last five meetings did the race problem become an issue. It seems to have disappeared from the attitudes and feelings of these children.

These children seem to have been able to get beneath the surface and to have achieved a respect for the personality of one another, an acceptance of their differences, and a perception of a common bond between them.

When one provides a situation wherein the children are given an opportunity to be themselves—and an opportunity to interact in a very permissive situation, then it seems that they can more readily come to terms with their own attitudes and emotions; and in a face-to-face situation where their free expression is *not* checked, they *can* and *do* assume responsibility for their attitudes and can experience the effect that the emotional expression of those attitudes can have upon themselves and others.

So it seems that these small group experiences had special significance for these children and enabled them to offer emotional hospitality and understanding to one another that seem to be necessary for us if we are ever to achieve a togetherness of effort and a unity of civilized thought.

4 · Aggression in Doll Play

HARRY LEVIN AND ROBERT R. SEARS

Reprinted from *Child Development*, 27 (1956), 135-153, by permission of the authors and the Society for Research in Child Development.

In the editor's opinion, this study is one of the most carefully planned and executed, and one of the most convincing, relative to the influence of parental behavior upon child behavior.

A major problem in the study of personality development is to discover behavior variables that not only are relevant to the more important motivational systems of the child but which also permit precise measurement and some degree of experimental control. The so-called projective techniques have seemed promising in these respects. They provide responses belonging to significant motivational categories such as sex, aggression, dependency, and achievement, and may be elicited safely and conveniently under controlled conditions. Projective responses have no special virtues other than these; they are not, in themselves, "true" measures of any "deep motives," nor do they have any unique validity as measures of personality qualities. They are simply acts that have presumably discoverable antecedents and that bear regular relationships to other acts. Fantasy behavior, in other words, is no different from any other behavior in its logical status as a reference event to be accounted for by principles of learning and action.

Experimental doll play has been rather widely used for the study of fantasy aggression in preschool children, both because this method requires less verbal skill than the visual-perceptual projective techniques and because it seems to be peculiarly effective in eliciting aggressive activity. Doll play offers an opportunity for measurement of three aspects of fantasy aggression: (1) the *amount*, as indicated either by frequency of aggressive behavior units or by proportion of time devoted to aggression, (2) the *agents and objects* of aggression, i.e., who attacks whom, in thematic play with doll characters, and (3) the *quality* of the aggression in terms of such categories as directness, intensity, verbal or physical expression, and pro- or contrasocial quality. These various attributes of aggression can be measured by the use of appropriate recording categories, and the resulting quantitative "scores" can then be used as standard reference events for which correlates can be sought. While these fantasy events are of considerable interest in their own right, they have added importance that comes from their, as yet, largely undiscovered relationships to comparable aspects of overt social aggressive behavior, and their inhibiting or facilitating influence on nonaggressive activity.

Previous researchers have discovered some of the factors that influence these doll play measures. We will limit our consideration here to those that have been found to be related to the *amount* of aggression, since this is the measure with which the present study is concerned.

There are several aspects of the methods used for doll play that are relevant (R. R. Sears, 1947). Among these are (1) the amount and kind of interaction between the child and the experimenter, with a high level of interaction initiated by the latter being positively related to frequency of aggressive response; (2) the realistic quality of the doll house materials, the more realistic being favorable to aggression; (3) the duration of the play session, with a 20-minute session producing a relatively greater amount of aggression than a full hour session, which tends to elicit a good deal of tangential behavior; and (4) degree of organization of the doll house and furniture, the more organized setup providing higher average aggression scores.

The actual handling of the child during his play session is also important. Experimental doll play is customarily done under conditions of high permissiveness for aggression, the experimenter adopting an interested but neutral attitude toward the child's behavior. With this procedure there is usually an increase in frequency of aggressive acts from the beginning of a session to its end, and also from session to session. When this permissiveness is replaced by what is perhaps a socially more customary attitude, one that involves reproof or disapproval for thematic aggression, the frequency of this kind of act decreases at once (Hollenberg, 1951). It appears that the permissive attitude is anxiety reducing: it eliminates the constraint that the usual social control by adults ordinarily imposes on the child's aggressive activity, whether reality-oriented or fantasy. In sum, these methodological factors provide variations in the immediate instigating conditions.

There are other sources of influence, however, that are not subject to the experimenter's control. These are the child's relatively stable response potentialities that have developed either from his past experiences or are characteristic of his constitution. Some children are more aggressive than others in the doll play situation. In general, boys have been found to be more aggressive than girls (Pintler, 1946; P. S. Sears, 1951), accident-prone boys more so than nonaccident-prone ones (Krall, 1953), and boys with their fathers living at home more so than those with their fathers absent from home (P. S. Sears, 1951; R. R. Sears *et al.*, 1946).

While it is probable that constitutional factors have some influence on these aggressive response potentials, our present concern is with the effects of differences in child-rearing experiences. The studies just mentioned are of some value in this respect, for they refer to groups which have been or could be examined with respect to the kinds of child training used by the children's mothers. For example, as has been shown elsewhere (R. R. Sears *et al.*, 1957), there are important differences in the treatment accorded boys' and girls' aggression in early life, and these differences are relevant to the sex differences in expression of fantasy aggression.

There are many other differences between boys and girls, however, and it is difficult to assess the exact influence of all of them on doll play aggression. A more direct approach can be made by holding constant such gross sources of influence as sex of child, and searching for the effects of specific child-rearing practices as these are revealed in interviews with the mothers of children whose fantasy aggression is measured. This was the procedure used in an earlier investigation (R. R. Sears *et al.*, 1953), which provided a crude assessment of the effects of one child-rearing variable on amount of fantasy aggression, and suggested the hypotheses that have been tested in the present research.

PREVIOUS FINDINGS

In the earlier study (R. R. Sears *et al.*, 1953), 40 mothers of preschool children were interviewed about their child-rearing methods. From these reports, the mothers were rated on a scale that described the dimension *severity of punishment for the expression of aggression.* Their children were tested with two 20-minute sessions of doll play. Severity of punishment proved to be positively related to the amount (frequency) of doll play aggression. For the girls, the correlations were +.41 and +.46 for the first and second sessions respectively; for the boys, +.46 and +.23.

It is evident, of course, that this one child-training dimension was not accounting for a very substantial proportion of the total variance of the fantasy aggression scores. Another finding from the same study drew attention to the possible influence of *identification with parents.* The children were also observed in preschool, and measures were obtained of the amount of overt social aggression exhibited there. For the boys, the correlation of this measure with severity of punishment was +.56. But for the girls, the relation was curvilinear, with both high and low punishment associated with low overt aggression. It was as if the girls had been more severely punished on the average, although the ratings did not show this, and the highest punished ones had become inhibited and passive in their social expression of aggression. The hypothesis was suggested that girls, being more highly identified with their mothers, suffered more inhibitory effects from a given degree of severity of punishment.

HYPOTHESES ABOUT IDENTIFICATION

Our attention having been brought to the identification process, we considered what possible effects it might have on expressions of fantasy aggression. Its relevance seemed to lie, possibly, in the character of doll play as a situation that permits a child to play the role of whichever family-member he wishes. There is a presumption that he identifies in some degree with all the persons who both reward him and place demands on him; this includes all the members of his family, but pre-eminently the parents. In doll play he can perform these identified-with roles, and do the kinds of things that he understands those roles require. Thus, the higher the identification a child has with a parent, the more his doll-play behavior should be like the behavior that the child believes is characteristic of that parent.

In the present context, we will assume that aggressiveness is a quality in a parent's behavior that a child can recognize, and that the child can discriminate whether the parent shows much or little aggression in relation to other (nonaggressive) forms of action. Thus, if we also assume, as suggested above, that in doll play a child adopts the role of his most-identified-with parent and acts out that parent's characteristics, we arrive at our first hypothesis:

1. The more strongly a child is identified with a given parent, the more nearly will he approximate in doll play the level of aggression he perceives as characterizing that parent. This means that if a boy is strongly identified with his father, and the father is very aggressive, the boy will display a high level of aggression in doll play. Conversely, if the father is relatively nonaggressive, the boy will be also. If, however, the boy's identification is weak, the father's level of aggressiveness should have little or no influence.

But with which parent does a child identify? By the age of five years, most children may be assumed to have developed their strongest identification with the same-sexed parent. This development is not the same for the two sexes, because the conditions for establishing primary identification are such that the mother is the initial identificand for both boys and girls. Only as the boy begins to perceive himself as a male, "like" his father and "unlike" his mother, can he begin to shift his identificand from mother to father. Hence, identification is more straightforward in the girl, and she develops a stable sex-typing more rapidly in this respect than the boy.

This latter assertion is supported by two findings from previous studies of doll play. If we accept the assumption that the doll most frequently chosen as agent of an act is the fantasy representative of the chief identificand, we can examine frequency of choice by children of both sexes. P. S. Sears reported (1953) that the five-year-old girls of the present study used the mother doll most frequently for neutral positive (nonaggressive) acts, whereas boys used the mother and father dolls almost equally in the first session and used the father more only in the second session.

Another type of comparison was made by Johnson (1951). She compared the relative frequency of prosocial and contrasocial aggressive acts in five- and eight-year-old children of both sexes. The prosocial acts were chiefly disciplinary ones that represented *adult quality* of behavior. Both sexes increased sharply in this type of aggression from five to eight years of age, but the girls were very much higher than the boys at both ages, and the five-year-old girls were almost as high as the eight-year-old boys.

We can conclude from these findings that the chief identificand for a child at five to six years of age is most commonly the parent of the same sex, though the relative strength of such an object choice for identificand is greater for girls than for boys. This leads to our second hypothesis:

2. The father's level of aggression will be most influential in determining the boy's frequency of aggressive doll acts, and the mother's level will be most influential for the girl's.

But what determines the child's perception of his same-sexed parent's aggressiveness? There appear to be two types of experience that are important, and their interaction produces a curious and complex difference between the sexes with respect to what child-training variables influence the frequency of doll play aggression.

The first of these two factors is perception of sex role. Characteristically the male is more aggressive. Among adults, there are more suicides, homocides, and street fights by men. War has always been a male preoccupation. Rough contact games are mainly for males. Even in nursery school the sex difference is evident, in both overt and fantasy expression. The boy may be expected to perceive his father as a representative of males in general, and hence as relatively aggressive.

The other factor is the child's own *personal experience of parental aggression*. Even though a boy recognizes the aggressiveness of the male role, his own father may be relatively mild. The opposite variation can occur for a girl. For most children, it seems likely, the clearest measure of parental aggressiveness is derived from the severity with which the parents punish the child for his aggressive actions toward them. If his aggressive acts are met with vigorous counter-aggression—i.e., parental actions that the parents themselves view as punishment—the child will perceive parents as more aggressive than if his acts met with only mild punishment. The important aspect of this experience lies in the distinctiveness of the cues it provides the child. Presumably, when the chief punisher is the parent with whom the child identifies more strongly, the cues will be more distinctive. Hence we get the following hypotheses:

3. The frequency of doll play aggression will be greater in boys than in girls (because of the male role perception). This hypothesis has been verified by a number of studies (Bach, 1945; Pintler, 1946; P. S. Sears, 1951).

4. The frequency will be greater when punishment for aggression is severe than when it is mild. This was found to be the case in one previous study, mentioned earlier (R. R. Sears, 1953).

5. Given severe punishment for aggression, the frequency of doll play aggression will be greater when the parent of the same sex is the chief disciplinarian.

If we now convert these five hypotheses to statements of what child-training antecedents will contribute to the frequency of children's doll play aggression, we find that the factors are different for the two sexes. For boys, we would expect the following for the reasons indicated: (1) *degree of identification* with parents, because the male role is an aggressive one, (2) *severity of punishment*, because this adds information for the boy's perception of his identificand's level of aggressiveness, and (3) *the father is the chief disciplinarian*, because this increases the distinctiveness of cues and spells out unmistakably to the boy that males are aggressive. In all likelihood, too, this increases the severity of frustration the boy suffers, because the punishment comes from the identificand, and hence adds to the boy's motivation for aggressive counteractions.

For girls, the factors are different. Since the female role is *not* an aggressive one, the girl's identification with her mother should not in itself be a significant antecedent except as it may be associated with a mother who is a very aggressive person.

The antecedents should be (1) *degree of identification*, but only when there is high punishment, that is, the girl is provided with an atypical female model, (2) *severity of punishment*, because this provides an aggressive role model, but only when (3) *the mother is the chief disciplinarian*.

METHOD

The testing of these hypotheses required measurement of four variables. One was the criterion, or consequent, variable of frequency of aggressive acts in the doll play of five-year-old children of both sexes. The second was the degree of identification of these children with their parents. The third was the severity of punishment for aggression that the parents used on the children, and the fourth, an indication of which parent was the chief punisher of the child.

In connection with an extended study of the origins of identification in a group of 379 five-year-old children, these four measures were obtained. The last three were secured through interviews with the children's mothers. The children were all enrolled in public school kindergartens in two suburbs of a New England metropolitan area. There were 202 boys and 177 girls, of various ordinal positions, and the families were fairly evenly spread from upper lower socio-economic status to upper middle. The mean age of the subjects was 5-7, the range 4-11 to 6-7, with a standard deviation of 4.4 months. The details of this sample have been described elsewhere by Maccoby and Gibbs (1954).

Doll Play

Each child was given two 20-minute sessions of doll play, never on consecutive days, but always within a five-day period. The play was scored in terms of behavior units with but two categories, aggression and neutral positive acts. Aggression was defined as an action that had the intent to irritate, hurt, injure, punish, frustrate, or destroy a doll or equipment. It ranged in intensity from innocuous mischief (the girl sneaks out of bed) to severe accidents, fights, and catastrophes (the father spanks the boy, the father has half his head sliced off, a bomb falls on the house and kills everybody). Verbal aggression such as scolding, threats, and uncooperativeness were included, as were instances in which discomfort was attributed to a doll (the boy is sick, sad, lost, etc.). The doll agent of each act was also recorded. The measure used in the present study is the "per cent aggression" for each session separately. This value is obtained by dividing the frequency of aggressive behavior units in a session by the total number of units of play. Nine experimenters collected these data. They had been trained to an adequate degree of comparability in their scoring, so their data have been combined. A full account of this doll play procedure is presented elsewhere (P. S. Sears, 1951).

Mother Interviews

The children's mothers were interviewed in their own homes by women interviewers who had been trained to use a standardized set of questions that covered the major areas of child rearing. This interview, which has been described elsewhere (R. R. Sears, 1957), consisted of 72 main questions and appropriate probe questions to assure that the necessary information would be obtained on each topic. The interviews were recorded and then were transcribed to typescript. They averaged between two and two and a half hours in length, and approximately 50 pages in single-spaced typed form. A series of rating scales and category codes was used for quantifying the interview information. Each interview was rated on every scale by two raters working independently. The reliabilities of the ratings were calculated by correlations between these independent judgments. The final score used for each scale on an interview was the pooled rating of the two raters; when the two ratings were seriously discrepant, the judges re-examined the interview and attempted to reach a closer agreement. Reliability coefficients were calculated *before* any such discussions.

From the interviews, measures were obtained of the three variables that were required for the present analysis. These, together with their Spearman-Brown corrected reliability coefficients, were (1) degree of identification with parental role that was displayed by the child ($r = .77$), (2) the severity of punishment given the child for expressing aggression toward the parents ($r = .77$), and (3) which parent was the usual punisher ($r = .95$). Some comments are needed to clarify the bases on which ratings on these three scales were made.

Identification

The rating of the child's degree of identification was based on the mother's replies to the following questions:

1. We'd like to get some idea of how X acts when he's naughty . . . when he has deliberately done something he knows you don't want him to do, when your back is turned; how does he act?
2. Does he ever come and tell you about it without your having to ask him?
3. When you ask him about something he has done that he knows he's not supposed to do, does he usually admit it or deny it?
4. What do you do about it if he denies something you are pretty sure he has done?

We reasoned that the identification process is necessary to the formation of super-ego, or conscience, and that the amount of identification the child has with parental roles can be estimated from the stage of development he has reached in internalized control. These four interview questions were designed to bring out the mother's observations of her child's behavior that were relevant to this matter.

The rating scale was labelled *evidence of superego in child,* and the raters were instructed to take into account the following: "High superego is inferred from confession of deviation, acting guilty, and feeling bad over deviations, admitting rather than denying a fault. Hiding and other evidences of fear should be taken as evidence of *low* superego. The making of reparations is evidence of *high* superego. If any of the indicators of high superego are explicitly stated to have occurred because of fear, however, they should be discounted. For example, if child admits rather than denies because he has been severely punished for denying, admitting is less direct evidence of superego."

The following descriptive statements were used to define the five points on the rating scale; the per cent of children rated at each point is also given.

1. No evidence of superego. Child denies, hides, doesn't seem unhappy when naughty.   13%
2. Slight superego.   28
3. Moderate superego. May not confess directly, but looks sheepish; seldom denies.   38
4. Considerable superego. May come and express affection to mother when he has been naughty; tries to repair damages.   17
5. High superego. Feels miserable when naughty; always confesses, never denies; strong need for forgiveness.   3
   Not ascertained.   1

   Total   100%

The following example will indicate the type of report that was rated toward the high end of the the super-ego scale:

I: We'd like to get some idea of how Ed acts when he's naughty; when he deliberately does something he knows you don't want him to do your back is turned, how does he act?

S: Very seldom does that. But a few times he has done something that he shouldn't do, that I don't know anything about, if I'm in the other room, he just can't hold it in very long and finally comes in to me and he says, "Mother," and I'll say, "What?" "I did something I shouldn't have done." Instead of leaving it and getting away with it he usually comes over and tells me what he's done. He usually comes, I mean, and it's not very long after he's done it. He can hardly hold it in to himself, you see.

One anecdote that was volunteered by a mother, although not necessarily an example of high superego, suggests the way in which a child can display adult attitudes and play the adult role; it shows how a highly identified child takes over some normally parental behavior:

S: I've taught him never to touch a medicine cabinet. I showed my little boy bottles—medicine bottles—and I've told him—he was sick, oh, about a year ago, in the hospital; and he's never forgotten it, and I don't think he ever will. He's told his brothers about it plenty of times. And I told him, "If you took your medicine bottle, you're going to get sick like you did then." He won't go near that medicine cabinet. And if he sees one of his brothers going to touch it, he'll tell him, "You'll go to the hospital, and you'll stay in the hospital for a long, long time; and you won't see Mommie or Daddy. And you won't have no toys to play with—just lay in bed all the time and get needles." And now none of them will go up there. I think he's really the one that broke them of going to the medicine cabinet.

Severity of Punishment for Aggression Toward Parents

An extended report of this scale and of the influence of such punishment on overt aggressive behavior in the home is published elsewhere (R. R. Sears *et al.*, 1957). The scale was a five-point one that took account of how severe the punishment was that the child actually received, regardless of who did the punishing.

Which Parent Was the Usual Punisher

The mother was asked, "Who usually diciplines, you or your husband?" The replies were categorized as "husband," "wife," or "about equal." Of the 379 cases, 108 were judged to fall in this last category, and 11 could not be evaluated. Since the hypotheses with which we are concerned here relate only to the condition in which the preponderance of punishment is by one parent or the other, we have limited the data analysis to the 260 children whose mothers reported either "husband" or "wife" as the usual punisher.

Since there were a few cases which could not be evaluated on the *identification* and *severity of punishment* scales, the total number of children actually utilized for the present analysis was 241, of whom 126 were boys and 115 were girls.

The various hypotheses outlined above offered certain predictions as to what combinations of the three mother interview variables would be associated with high or low frequency of doll play aggressive acts. These predictions have been tested by a triple classification analysis of variance, separately for the sexes. Except for *who usually punishes,* which contained two mutually exclusive categories, the variables were continual; it was necessary, therefore, to break each distribution into as nearly equal halves as possible for the analysis of variance. It was impossible to secure exactly equal numbers of cases in the eight required cells, however, and hence the correction for unequal cells as given by Walker and Lev (1953) was used. The analysis was done separately for each of the two doll play sessions.

Boys

The analysis for boys is shown in Table I, which gives the mean per cent Aggression scores for the eight groups of children representing the eight possible combinations of the three antecedent variables. The table also shows that in both sessions there were two major sources of variation in the per cent Aggression scores. One of these was *identification* and the other an interaction between *identification* and *agent of punishment.* The influence of these sources of variation is clearly shown in the means; the two highest means for the first session are "Father punishes, High Identification." On the second session, two of the three highest were in the same category.

Table I

Mean Per Cent Aggression for Two Doll Play Sessions, (Boys Only)

| | High Identification | | | | Low Identification | | | |
| | Severe Punishment | | Mild Punishment | | Severe Punishment | | Mild Punishment | |
	Father	Mother	Father	Mother	Father	Mother	Father	Mother
Session I	18.6	13.9	23.0	13.8	5.8	12.1	10.2	13.6
Session II	28.8	20.1	25.9	26.7	12.4	23.9	18.7	23.4
N	18	11	18	13	14	18	14	20

The effects of these two variables can be more easily seen when the data are regrouped, as in Table II. When the mother punished, the degree of identification had no influence on the amount of aggression displayed, but when the father punished, high identification produced high aggression. These findings confirm the hypotheses that place emphasis on the boys' identification with an aggressive male role model as a determinant of the frequency of aggression in doll play.

Table II

Mean Per Cent Aggression in Two Doll Play Sessions According to the
Degree of Identification and the Agent to Punishment (Boys Only)

| | High Identification | | Low Identification | |
	Father Punishes	Mother Punishes	Father Punishes	Mother Punishes
Session I ...	20.8	13.8	8.0	12.9
Session II ..	27.3	23.7	15.6	23.6
N	36	24	28	38

One hypothesis is not supported, however. The severity of punishment
for aggression proved to have no influence on doll play aggression. This
finding is in contrast to that from the earlier investigation, although in
that one the correlation of this variable with second session doll play
aggression was quite small in boys (.23), while the girls' was larger (.46).
Since neither *identification* nor *agent of punishment* was measured in that
study, it is possible that the small positive correlation was a product of
some unknown correlation with these variables.

We have no certain explanation for the lack of influence of severity of
punishment, on boys, in the present study. One possible reason may be
that, by the age of five years, most boys have been so much exposed to aggressive male models that the added experience of observing the father's
being aggressive has little or no added effect. Possibly boys get enough
training in male role aggressiveness that the only factors required for making them behave aggressively themselves are a strong identification with the
adult role and the clear cues that derive from paternal punishment.

Girls

The case is quite different with girls as Table III shows. The data are
rearranged in Table IV. When the mother was the punisher and the
punishment was severe, the fantasy aggression was greater than under any
other combination of variables.

This finding supports the prediction that exposing girls to an aggressive
role model increases their doll play aggression. It is to be noted that the

Table III

Mean Per Cent Aggression for Two Doll Play Sessions (Girls Only)

| | High Identification | | | | Low Identification | | | |
| | Severe Punishment | | Mild Punishment | | Severe Punishment | | Mild Punishment | |
	Father	Mother	Father	Mother	Father	Mother	Father	Mother
Session I	8.8	13.2	11.0	5.7	5.2	9.5	8.1	7.8
Session II	15.4	20.1	12.3	8.5	7.7	11.3	13.6	10.4
N	9	18	9	24	11	13	11	20

Table IV

Mean Per Cent Aggression in Two Doll Play Sessions According to the Severity of Punishment for Aggression and Agent of Punishment (Girls Only)

| | Severe Punishment | | Mild Punishment | |
	Father Punishes	Mother Punishes	Father Punishes	Mother Punishes
Session I ...	6.8	11.7	9.4	6.6
Session II ...	11.2	16.4	13.0	9.4
N	20	31	20	44

converse holds true as well; when the mother was the punisher, but punishment was mild, doll play aggression was least. In other words, the mothers who did not punish severely permitted their daughters to take over the socially modal nonaggressive female pattern. Severely punitive mothers erected potential barriers against their daughters' copying of at least this one aspect of approved femininity.

The role of identification appears to have been of some importance in this connection. In the second doll play session, there was a significant interaction between identification and severity of punishment. The data are regrouped in Table V to show the joint effects of these two predictor variables. Girls who were both highly identified and severely punished exhibited more aggression than the girls falling in the other three combinations. These latter did not differ from one another, on the average, since the remaining influential variable (agent of punishment) varied randomly among the groups.

Table V

Mean Per Cent Aggression in the Second Doll Play Session According to the Degree of Identification and the Severity of Punishment for Aggression (Girls Only)

| | High Identification | | Low Identification | |
	Severe Punishment	Mild Punishment	Severe Punishment	Mild Punishment
Session II ...	18.5	9.5	9.6	11.5
N	27	33	24	31

This finding adds further support to the prediction that identification will lead to much aggression for girls only when it is associated with an atypically aggressive female role model, as exemplified in a severely punishing mother.

Comparison of the Sexes

There are two striking sex differences in the antecedents of doll play aggression frequency. One is with respect to identification and the other to severity of punishment. In boys, identification is a significant positive influence, both alone and in interaction with other variables. In girls, it is apparently less so. There are two possible explanatory factors to be considered. One is that the measure of identification is of less discriminating value with girls than with boys, because girls are developmentally farther along in the process. As was mentioned earlier, boys presumably develop identification with their mothers first and then must shift to fathers for the appropriate role model. Girls, in other words, may have reached an asymptotic level of identification in their sixth year, while the boys of this age are strung out along a fairly wide range of identification. Thus this variable would assume greater significance for boys.

The other factor has to do with severity of punishment. The male role is an aggressive one, and the actual day-to-day demonstration of this fact by the father's use of severe punishment may add little or nothing to the boy's understanding of how he should behave. It is more important for the boy that he have high identification with the role. For girls, however, the appropriate sex role model is normally nonaggressive. Only when the particular model most visible to the girl (her mother) is especially aggressive does the girl adopt an aggressive way of behaving.

There is one further hypothesis we might suggest for further research on this problem of sex differences. Among the children in this sample, the boys were subjected to more *physical punishment*, according to the mothers' reports (R. R. Sears, 1957). If the aggressive behavior in doll play were scored as to whether it was physical or verbal in content, we would therefore expect that the boys would show more physical and the girls more verbal expressions. This sex difference was found in studies by P. S. Sears (1951) and by Bach (1945), but no child training antecedent measures were available. In the present study, the differentiation of content was not scored.

Identification with the Aggressor

Extended clinical study of children led Anna Freud (1937) to the discovery of a defense mechanism she has termed identification with the aggressor. This mechanism is a technique by which a child can reduce his fear of an aggressor, perhaps a punitive parent, by identifying with that person and adopting his aggressive behavior.

The findings of the present study are fairly well in accord with what one would predict from this mechanism if one assumes that frequency of doll play aggression is a measure of the aggressive motivation derived from that identification process. It is the girls who have most to fear from their mothers, i.e., the daughters of severe punishers, who show the highest aggression. The same does not hold for the boys, but for both sexes it is the children who are ordinarily punished by the *parent of the same sex* who show greatest aggression. The connection between the measure of identification and amount of aggression may equally well be interpreted either as evidence that identification with the aggressor had taken place or, as we have done above, as an indication of the requirement of identification in order that agent of punishment be effective. In other words, the rating of high identification in those children (especially boys) who showed high aggression could be viewed as an *effect* as well as *a cause*.

We are inclined to rely on the interpretation we presented in the introduction to this paper rather than on the conception of identification with aggressor because we do not have any way of determining, from the present data, whether the fantasy aggressions had anxiety-reducing effect. This is an essential assumption underlying an interpretation in terms of this defense mechanism. As the data stand, however, there is no factual reason why the doll play aggressive acts cannot be interpreted as evidence of the operation of this mechanism.

NORMATIVE FINDINGS

Since standardized doll play as used in this study is a common method of research with children, it is useful to catalog norms of such behavior. An analysis of the influence of sex, age, ordinal position and father's absence on doll play aggression has been reported by P. S. Sears (1951). The present results, where applicable, will be compared with hers.

Sex Differences

As has been stated earlier, the boys devoted significantly more of their actions to aggression in both doll play sessions than did the girls (Table VI). This confirms other findings (Bach, 1945; Johnson, 1951; Pintler, 1946; P. S. Sears, 1951) and may be taken as a reasonably stable characteristic of doll play behavior.

Session Changes

For both sexes, there was a significant session-to-session increase in the proportion of aggression units (Table VI). This finding is also in line with previous studies (Hollenberg, 1951; P. S. Sears, 1951) and has been interpreted to mean that the deliberate permissiveness of the experimental procedure progressively acts to reduce the inhibitions about aggression that the child has heretofore acquired.

Table VI

Mean Per Cent Aggression for Two Doll Play Sessions, with Correlations and Differences Between Sessions and Sexes

	N	Session I	Session II	r	t
Boys	202	14.28	21.84	.61**	3.30**
Girls	177	8.64	12.76	.69**	2.25**
t between sexes		4.32**	4.95**		

** Significant at p < .01.

Although there was a session-to-session increase in the mean per cent Aggression scores, there was a correlation between sessions of .61 for boys and .69 for girls. P. S. Sears (1951, p. 35) reported session-to-session correlations of .74 for five-year-old boys and .53 for five-year-old girls, with 25 cases in each category.

Ordinal Position

P. S. Sears (1951, p. 24) found that, for both sexes, children who were "youngest" in their family or who were "only" children showed more aggression than "oldest" children. In the present study, four ordinal positions were analyzed: (1) *only* children, (2) *oldest* of two or more children, (3) *youngest* of two or more children, and (4) *middle* of three or more children. The results are presented in Table VII.

Table VII

Mean Per Cent Aggression for Two Doll Play Sessions According to the Sex and Ordinal Position of Subjects

	BOYS			GIRLS		
	N	Session I	Session II	N	Session I	Session II
Only	33	19.36	30.64	19	8.88	13.76
Oldest	59	13.08	19.32	50	8.76	12.84
Youngest	62	14.68	18.72	51	8.48	13.36
Middle	48	13.28	22.84	57	7.84	11.76

The present findings only partially replicate the earlier ones. In both doll play sessions, "only" boys exhibited the most fantasy aggression, but among the girls, there are no sizeable mean differences in per cent Aggression which are attributable to ordinal position.

Descriptive categories such as ordinal position or socio-economic status are useful in understanding behavior insofar as they lead the researcher to investigate the particular patterns of experiences which people occupying such categories have had. Other analyses of the child-training data upon which the present study is based indicate that "only" children were judged more strongly identified with their parents, as measured by the superego rating, than were children of other sibling statuses (R. R. Sears, 1957). This finding, together with the effect of identification on aggression for boys as reported above, makes reasonable the result that the "only" boys were most aggressive. One can speculate that P. S. Sears may have had some highly identified boys in her "younger" group, but the evidence is not available.

Socio-Economic Status (SES)

Previous studies of doll play aggression have utilized children from widely differing social class groups. Those done in university (Bach, 1945; Hollenberg, 1951; Pintler, 1946; R. R. Sears, 1953) or private preschools

(Johnson, 1951) have drawn subjects from mainly middle-class populations. P. S. Sears (1951 and 1946) reported that her group represented "a predominantly upper-lower and lower-middle class position." Yarrow (1948) had a definitely lower-class group. In the absence of any direct comparison of the aggressiveness of children from the different SES levels, it has been difficult to know how widely the results of the various studies could be generalized.

The present sample was chosen to represent a wide range of SES. Warner's Index of Status Characteristics was computed for each family on the basis of the father's income and occupational status. Maccoby and Gibbs (1954) have reported in detail the rationale and computation of the score, and the SES characteristics of the present sample. For our purposes the sample was divided into two groups which may be described as "working class" and "middle class." As may be seen from Table VIII, there were no differences in mean per cent Aggression scores attributable to SES in either doll play session.

Table VIII

Mean Per Cent Aggression: The Influence of Socio-Economic Status

	BOYS			GIRLS		
	N	Session I	Session II	N	Session I	Session II
Middle Class	117	13.76	22.36	86	8.80	12.58
Working Class ..	82	15.28	22.48	88	8.76	13.88

SUMMARY

A test was made of the hypothesis that the frequency of five-year-old children's fantasy aggression is in part a function of the children's identification with aggressive role models. The frequency of aggression was measured in two sessions of doll play with each of 241 children, 126 boys and 115 girls. The degree of the children's identification with their parents, the severity with which the parents punished aggression, and an indication of which parent usually did the punishing were ascertained from interviews with the children's mothers.

As was predicted, boys who were highly identified, and who had the distinctive cues for male aggressiveness provided by being usually punished by their fathers, showed the highest frequency of aggression. Identification was related to high aggression in the girls only when it was associated with severe punishment by mothers who usually did the punishing, i.e., when the girl was identified with an aggressive role model.

The present study replicated several earlier reports in finding that, in both doll play sessions, boys were more aggressive than girls, and that, for both sexes, there was an increase in the amount of aggression from the first to the second session. "Only" boys were more aggressive than boys of other ordinal positions, but there were no ordinal position differences for girls. The difference for boys was related to differences in child training practices by the parents of the "only" children. No differences in aggression were attributable to the socio-economic status of the children's families.

References

Bach, G. R., "Young Children's Play Fantasies," *Psychological Monographs*, Vol. 59, No. 2 (1945).

Freud, Anna, *The Ego and Mechanisms of Defense*. London: Hogarth Press, Ltd., 1937.

Hollenberg, Eleanor, and Margaret Sperry, "Some Antecedents of Aggression and Effects of Frustration in Doll Play," *Personality*, 1 (1951), 32-43.

Johnson, Elizabeth Z., "Attitudes of Children Toward Authority as Projected in Their Doll Play at Two Age Levels." Unpublished doctor's dissertation, Harvard University, 1951.

Krall, Vita, "Personality Characteristics of Accident Repeating Children," *Journal of Abnormal and Social Psychology*, 48 (1953), 99-107.

Maccoby, Eleanor, and Patricia Gibbs, "Methods of Child-Rearing in Two Social Classes," in W. E. Martin and Celia B. Stendler, eds., *Readings in Child Development*. New York: Harcourt, Brace & Company, Inc., 1954.

Pintler, Margaret H., Ruth Phillips, and R. R. Sears, "Sex Differences in the Projective Doll Play of Preschool Children," *Journal of Psychology*, 21 (1946), 73-80.

Sears, Pauline S., "Doll Play Aggression in Normal Young Children: Influence of Sex, Age, Sibling Status, Father's Absence," *Psychological Monographs*, Vol. 65, No. 6 (1951).

———, "Child-Rearing Factors Related to Playing of Sex-Typed Roles," *American Psychologist*, 8 (1953), 431 (Abstract).

Sears, R. R., "Influence of Methodological Factors on Doll Play Performance," *Child Development*, 18 (1947), 190-197.

———, Eleanor Maccoby, and H. Levin, *Patterns of Child Rearing*. Evanston, Ill.: Row, Peterson & Company, 1957.

———, Margaret H. Pintler, and Pauline S. Sears, "Effect of Father Separation on Preschool Children's Doll Play Aggression," *Child Development*, 17 (1946), 219-243.

———, J. W. M. Whiting, V. Nowlis, and Pauline S. Sears, "Some Child Rearing Antecedents of Aggression and Dependency in Young Children," *Genetic Psychology Monographs*, 47 (1953), 135-234.

Walker, Helen, and J. Lev, *Statistical Inference*. New York: Henry Holt & Company, Inc., 1953.

Yarrow, L. J., "The Effect of Antecedent Frustration on Projective Play," *Psychological Monographs*, Vol. 62, No. 6 (1948).

5 · Personality Organization in Children

JOHN E. ANDERSON

Abridged from the article in *American Psychologist*, 3 (1948), 409-416, by permission of the author and the American Psychological Association.

There are many divergent views concerning the role of childhood experiences in the formation of personality. Anderson, for many years director of the Institute of Child Welfare at the University of Minnesota, presents an over-all evaluation of this problem.

It is my purpose to examine some of the current conceptions of the personality of young children in the light of modern research, and more particularly, the implications of erroneous conceptions that have far-reaching effects in determining policy and practice with children.

Many discussions of child personality found in textbooks in general, abnormal, and social psychology are written from an adult point of view by persons who have had little contact with children. Many of the statements made seem to be projections backward upon the child of concepts that seem necessary for the author's conception of adult behavior. In the main, the impression given is that the young child is passive, delicate, unusually subject to shock and trauma, and responsive to all possible stimuli. For instance, some advocates of the frustration-aggression hypothesis picture the child as a passive person who reacts when he is blocked and who expends energy in proportion to the amount of frustration. So far so good. But when it is assumed that all aggressive activity in young children is the outcome of frustration, the active display of energy which is the most fundamental characteristic of a living organism is denied, and docility and passivity are attributed to the young child as normal.

This is also the purport of much of the psychoanalytic teaching about children. The adult is what he is, not because of inadequacy in his makeup or training, but because of a traumatic experience. Since this experience cannot be found in the present, it is pushed back into an earlier period. When it cannot be found there, it is pushed still further back. Thus, the trauma of adolescence moves back into late childhood, then into early childhood, then into infancy, then to birth, and then into the fetal period. The only place left for trauma is conception.

The analytic and case history writings abound with instances of traumatic and dramatic episodes that are presumed to affect later development. But if the data do not support this view, there is an easy out since such episodes can be repressed and still function if it is assumed that the child remembers everything. Thus, Symonds (1946) in citing the Landis study (1940) reports correctly when he says: "Little children who are the recipients of sexual advances from adults usually have no memory of them," and quotes Landis in a footnote to the effect that only 3 out of 295 individuals reported such incidents as occurring before five years. But Symonds (1946) goes on to say:

> They become deeply repressed. However they may later cause personality disturbances and grievous conflicts which are difficult to manage. Likewise almost any traumatic or painful experience of childhood is rapidly forgotten, which means it is repressed. Children seldom remember the extreme dangers encountered in early childhood, the extreme punishments which they received, the accidents which befell them. Where such memories persist these are not usually the really dangerous, harmful, painful experiences; it has been found that they represent screen memories which protect one from the memories of really traumatic events.

Recently Ribble (1943) in her book on *The Rights of Infants* has emphasized the infant's need for security and affection and traces almost every type of mental and physical disturbance in infancy and early childhood back to lack of affection. So extreme are her statements that almost every review in scientific journals has pointed out many misinterpretations of established fact. For the understanding of children, Ribble would substitute love and affection. Such conclusions make little difference if read only by scientific workers competent to judge the evidence for themselves; unfortunately, however, the book has become a Gospel among social workers who in one instance took the children out of home management houses by citing the Ribble generalizations, even though all the objective evidence obtained by medical examinations and the case histories of the former children showed excellent health and good adjustment as did also the scientific studies published on this problem. Policies of many years' standing with demonstrated successful outcomes in terms of child behavior went by the board almost without protest. Not long ago a social agency discussed seriously whether or not infants should be kept temporarily in an institution for several months for examination and study prior to adoption, on the ground that life in an institution for one or two months would make the infant insecure and cause later personality difficulties. No one seemed aware of the fact that in ordinary homes children are sometimes away from loved ones for months without serious consequences and that adoption itself forces new emotional attachments which are readily made by infants.

In the otherwise excellent study of children's paintings by Alschuler and Hattwick (1947), an example of another error is found. In the first volume, many adult characteristics are read into children's paintings by making symbolic interpretations in terms of adult values. Thus, it is said that the child's use of browns and reds and yellows which are "smeary" indicate his concern with eliminative processes, and a little later on a somewhat similar statement is made about the child's use of green. When the statistical material in the second volume is examined for validation of these generalizations, no attempt to check the use of various colors against the children's eliminative habits is reported.

Various generalizations on the personality of the infant and young child which follow from these impressions and interpretations can be made: (1) Infants and young children are essentially passive recipients of stimulation who display little energy or activity on their own; (2) are very delicate and tender, and have little capacity to resist or survive and are especially sensitive to lack of affection to which they cannot adapt for even short periods; (3) are unusually susceptible to, and carry the effects of, traumatic episodes indefinitely; (4) carry forward all their memories and experiences, which later come out to plague them; (5) in their behavior and the products resulting, are subject to all the implications and values that inhere in adult reactions in similar situations.

In contrast to these views of child nature, scientific findings which lead to a more accurate picture may be considered. These can be grouped under several heads: the child as an energy system with high capacity for self-repair and selectivity; the child as a persistent personality system with high capacity to resist deformation, stress, and trauma; and the child as a mechanism that meets life not as a storehouse or filing cabinet, but as an active system engaged in transforming input into outgo.

In living animals with their capacity to move about, life and activity are closely related phenomena. The inactive organism is dead. A live animal is an active center for transforming food into energy and stimulation into activity. The young organism is more active than the older one, and expends energy at a higher rate. Given normal conditions of health, high motility and activity characterize the waking hours. To produce inactivity, it is only necessary to cut down the food intake for a period long enough to outlast the first increase in motivation. When intake is thus cut, children adjust by becoming lethargic and inactive. When normal food levels are restored, energy expenditure increases.

Insight into the child's effectiveness as an energy system can be gained from a study of the energy maintenance process in both animals and humans. Brody (1945) in his book on *Bio-energetics and Growth* has brought much of this material together. With increase in size, maintenance cost in terms of energy becomes greater, because more effort is necessary to push the weight around. In younger children with low body weight and slight mass in comparison with the mechanism available for motion, energy can be expended at a very high rate at a low cost to the organism. Thus, as size increases, more energy is needed for maintenance and less is available for both growth and work. While no studies over a long span of years under comparable conditions have been made of the activity level of humans, the animal studies indicate that with growth and increase in body size, total activity lessens. Casual observations together with informal checks covering all activities in the attempt to measure total energy output make it seem clear that as an energy expending mechanism the infant and young child are very efficient. But if measurement is made in terms of direction of output, that is, effectiveness in accomplishing a particular piece of work, the results are not so favorable to the child. The child's energy expenditure is essentially unstructured, whereas that of the older workers is highly disciplined. In fact, skill consists largely in doing more with less effort. Thus in terms of the energy available, the young child is not tender or delicate. He is so lively and active that he tends to wear out the inferior adult. As adults we look upon growth as gain. But in terms of total energy growth is loss. Efficiency seems to be gained at the cost of energy.

As an energy system the child is composed of many interrelated parts which work together as a functional unit. Within the system as a whole, and even within the parts of which it is composed, there is much opportunity for compensation and adjustment in order to meet external stress and strain. This principle can be readily demonstrated for the body as a whole and for any of the great organ systems as well; it is one of the basic devices by means of which life is maintained in the face of an environment.

Not only is there capacity for compensation and adjustment, but also tremendous capacity for self-repair when damage occurs. Within limits, this is also a property of all living systems. Evidence indicates that this capacity for self-repair decreases with age. For example, in the deNouy (1937) investigations of the rate at which cuts heal, it was found that in the ten-year-old child cuts heal twice as fast as in the twenty-year-old, in whom they heal three times as fast as in the sixty-year-old. Thus, in the ten-year-old child the healing rate is six times that of the sixty-year-old. If these results can be generalized to other processes and extrapolated, it would appear that a physical shock or trauma to produce the same amount of deformation in a ten-year-old would have to be twice as severe as that for the adult, and six times that for the sixty-year-old.

As evidence against this view, the great sensitivity of the young child to drugs and toxic substances of various types might be cited. This, however, seems to be much more a function of the mass of the body than of its reactiveness as is shown by its variation with differences in weight in species and individuals and in the use of simple linear conversion formulae. Infants and young children, however, show very quick recovery rates from the drugs given in doses appropriate to their weight. Similarly, they recover quickly from toxic effects and from illness.

Students of the physical effects of birth, while emphasizing the rigor of the birth process for the child, also stress the tremendous capacity of the infant to withstand the shock. It has been said that for the normal infant, the physical shock of being born is about the equivalent to an adult being thrown out of a third-story window. Yet normal infants take this shock in their stride, without serious aftereffects or bodily difficulties.

Being prematurely born should constitute a trauma of the first magnitude, not perhaps physically, but certainly psychologically if generalizations of the type made by Ribble and the psychoanalysts are correct, because of the forced separation of the infant from its mother well in advance of the appropriate time. Yet a substantial amount of writings in anatomy, physiology, and psychology shows that prematures cannot be distinguished by any criteria whatever from full-term infants after nine months in most cases, and after eighteen months in all cases.

Another characteristic of a living system is the selective character of its reactions to the environment, that is, the manner in which it preserves its essential unity by choosing that which fits the system, and neglecting or rejecting that which is not congruent. This is also a protective device that enables the child to insulate himself against unwanted stimulation and to resist shock and trauma.

Are the infant and young child more or less delicate than older persons? If this problem, thus far studied to only a limited degree, were analyzed in terms of healing times, repair rates, recovery from illness, and the rapidity with which lost function is regained, in my opinion the results would be very favorable to the infant and young child, not quite so favorable to the adult, and much less so to the old person. Children have an amazing capacity to survive in the face of the various demands made upon them. By and large, most life processes look toward the preservation of the young in preference to the older organisms.

But there is also a more direct answer to this question. What do the scientific studies, carried on over a span of years, reveal with respect to the persistence or nonpersistence of personality traits? If the personality of the infant and young child is so delicate, it should be modified easily and show great change from year to year and over a period of years; if it is a system that resists deformation and maintains its integrity, it should show less change with time, and the changes, when and if they occur, should be consistent with the original personality.

With the cumulation of data on children as a result of many years' observation in modern centers, this problem is being attacked for a wide variety of traits and trait patterns, in addition to the many studies of the persistence of intelligence which on the whole support the view of stability.

Baby biographers of the older days (Hogan, 1901; Shinn, 1900) noted the emergence of individuality in infancy and emphasized the persistence of temperamental or personality traits. Woolley (1925) described Agnes, a little girl who showed the same personality pattern of aggressive behavior from ages two to five. Studies on groups of children are found in more recent writings. Cushing (1929) found persistence in perseveration, Washburn (1929) in smiling, Brackett (1935) in laughter, and Bayley (1932) in crying. Green (1933) found persistence for group play and Loomis (1931) for social contacts. Jersild and Markey (1933, 1935) found conflict behavior similar over a year's time. Stutsman (1935) studying 140 preschool children for 3 consecutive years found high consistency in ratings on traits and in profile patterns. In the McGraw study (1939), Johnny and Jimmy maintained personality differences as long as they were studied. Allport (1937), studying his own son, found that the prognosis of personality development at four months of age tended to be borne out at two later ages. Gesell (1939) showed movies of five children at ages one and five to trained observers who ranked the children on 15 behavior traits, including energy, demeanor, ascendance, social responsiveness, and the like. Out of 75 rankings, 48 coincided, 21 were displaced by only one rank, 5 by two ranks, and 1 by three ranks. He concludes that this shows the prophetic character of the first year's behavior traits.

In the study by Sanford, and others (1943), a restricted sample of children was studied over a three-year period on an unusually wide variety of personality variables. To quote:

> The results analyzed indicate that, in general, subjects do tend to be consistent in their behavioral manifestations over the three-year period to a degree that approaches statistical significance (average r equals .33). Subjects who rate high, as compared to their fellows, on one of the variables present in 1937 also rate high in 1938 and in 1939. On the other hand, the present coefficients of consistency are not large, and it is clear that subjects vary considerably, in standing on the different variables, from one year to another. How much of this variation is due to the fact that subjects actually change and how much is due to the unreliability of the measures cannot be determined from our data. (p. 236)

Roberts and Fleming (1943) analyzed the persistence and change in personality patterns in the precollege, college, and postcollege periods for 25 women whose life histories were obtained through four years of contact with a college advisory service. In each case, some nucleus of traits persisted throughout the whole period of observation. In each there was also some fluctuation in traits. Although the whole persistence was greater than fluctuation, the amount varied from case to case. At one extreme, one woman showed 85 per cent persistent traits, whereas at the other, one woman had only 26 per cent persistent traits. For the group as a whole the percentage of persisting and fluctuating traits was in the ratio of 3:2. Of the 25 women, 16 showed more, 6 showed an equal amount, and 3 showed less persistence than fluctuation.

It is one of the paradoxes of our modern discussions of personality that those who are most insistent upon the responsiveness of the personality to shock and trauma are also those who believe most strongly that the individual is a vast storehouse of persistent memories which underlie his subsequent behavior. How the contradiction between changing personality and permanent memories is to be resolved is not clear. Let us turn to the material on memory and learning in young children.

The studies of learning and memory in young children show results that are similar to those obtained on older persons (Anderson, 1941), namely, a rapid forgetting rate unless there is restimulation and overlearning. Young children show tremendous repetitive activity and much overlearning rather than marked superiority in retention itself. Some superiority in young children might be expected from priority in learning and lack of interference. But results show that memory for both nonsense and meaningful material increases with age.

Pertinent to the problem of retention is the amount of experience young children have. Although most adults assume relatively slight amounts of stimulation and response, the evidence obtained in studies of young children is quite the reverse. The mass of impressions crowding in, and the number of specific responses made within a single day, and the number of potential memories created even in a short period is tremendous. For instance, studies on language development show that four-year-olds speak as many as 10,000 words per day, which multiplied by 365 for the year begins to reach astronomical figures. Studies of social contacts of young children reveal hundreds of teacher-child and child-child contacts within a relatively short period of time. In a reasonably stimulating environment, the sheer quantity of interrelations tends to be overpowering and raises a question how, out of such a mass of materials, specific items can be retained.

Not often considered in connection with child memories and traumatic episodes is the information on the learning of skills, in which control groups and checks for retention have been used. On the whole, most of these studies have yielded negative results for continuation of skill at the terminal practice level. Even within a short time there is substantial loss. These results have been somewhat discouraging, particularly to those who expect to train and find an intact result years later. Unless there is occasional practice to keep a particular skill or activity alive by occasional practice, it tends to regress or drop to a low level. In those instances, such as the Jersild and Bienstock (1935) experiment on the persistence of musical skill after an interval of two years, a theory in terms of sensitization and implicit practice as a result of musical stimulation in the environment is developed to account for the differences in the two groups. In actual life in contrast to experimental situations, the child who learns to swim early tends to swim much more than the child who learns late and thus maintains superiority. The learning material not only indicates the child's enormous capacity to forget, but also shows that much forgetting is quite complete.

Additional light is thrown on the problem of the persistence of personality traits by a whole group of studies not often considered in connection with the problem of personality organization. These also show failure to retain new modes of behavior and adjustment in which training has been given. I refer to the follow-up studies of delinquent behavior, of which the most striking example is that of Glueck and Glueck (1940), who found extraordinarily high proportions of recidivists when every case that had been through guidance clinics and juvenile court treatment was followed up. This discouraging result, however, should only give us pause; on the whole, after their curative and remedial treatment, these children had to return to their old environments in which all the factors which produced the original delinquency were still operative.

While many stimulating and brilliant researches have shown the possibilities of modifying social behavior by measuring the child's responsiveness to his group, giving intensive training apart from it, and then measuring his responsiveness on his return, few checks for retention are seldom made. Hence, no one knows how long, subsequent to training, such modifications will persist without reinforcement. If the personality is a selective system operating on its environment in accordance with a principle of congruence, care must be taken in interpreting the effects of such experimental or training procedures.

The implications of the foregoing view are reasonably clear. Instead of being a passive and receptive organism, the young child is a personality system that functions as a unit in its present environment. Available in the present is an energy mechanism which, because of some degree of organization, is selective in relation to its environment. Of the countless experiences in an almost continuous round of stimulation and response, some are retained and incorporated into the system, while very many are lost and lost permanently.

How, then, are the temporary experiences distinguished from those which are transformed from the situation into the internal system of the individual? How is the developmental stream of personality manifestation modified? For temporary experiences, the response is related quite directly to the stimulus and is determined by the valences within the situation. With more permanent modifications, the effects produced within the organism or by the organism on the external environment may have little or no relation whatever to the intensity of stimulus or the immediate valences which function merely as cues to set off a response which thenceforth goes on its own course. Thus, the personality achieves a type of inner organization which becomes more and more powerful with the passage of time, and which frees the personality to a greater and greater degree from the dominance of the situation.

If this principle holds, a traumatic experience is not really an episode but an event which modifies the stream of organism-environment relations. The factors which make an experience traumatic for one child and not for another are precisely those which determine the permanence or impermanence of memories. In order to modify the stream of organism-environment relations there must be reiteration; that is, a mechanism similar to that which produces overlearning in the case of a skill or memory must be present. It then becomes important to examine the environment for recurring stimulation and the individual for manifestations of an internal process that can exercise a "carrier" function, which operating again and again, will keep alive the subsystems of response which are crucial in personality organization. Such an internal mechanism is found in speech and the symbolic processes which are universally used by those responsible for children to control and educate them and by the person himself either overtly or implicitly to fix and control his own behavior. While some research has been done on these controlling functions, when used on others little has been done on the devices by means of which the individual controls himself.

In my opinion, promising opportunities for future research lie in the analysis of the organism-environment relation in terms of the repetitive and reiterative phenomena occurring within the constant stream of stimulation and response that serve to keep skills, experiences, and memories alive and which make of certain experiences, traumatic episodes. The following suggestions as to possible devices may be made.

1. *The family story.* Many of the young child's experiences occur under conditions in which they are observed by others and become the occasion of family stories. Thus, in one family one child behaved bravely and another in cowardly fashion in the face of a fearsome situation. The story of Mary's fear and Johnny's bravery was told again and again in their presence; in fact, the children came in time to ask that the story be told. Here is not only a reinforcing mechanism but also one that sets up an expectancy with regard to future behavior.

2. *Consistent presentation of attitudes and roles.* In the study by Child and others (1946) of children's textbooks and personality development, an environmental factor that involves reiteration was located. By analyzing a large number of school readers available to children, it was found that characteristic attitudes were consistently presented. Thus, the school readers regularly presented the boy as active, seeking adventure, and achieving, and the girls as sociable, kind, timid, and relatively uncreative. Although no similar analysis of consistent emphasis and values which parents and associates put upon certain types of stimulation and behavior has been made, it seems clear that such analysis would reveal similar factors operating.

3. *Attention-getting devices.* Another type of reiteration may be found in the child's accounts of his own experiences in order to secure attention. In a brief moment of high excitement all others turned to him. Why not recapture it by retelling? If the audience responds, all well and good, if not,

the child blocked from overt expression can turn to silent speech and fantasy. Here again will come reinforcement and expectancy.

4. *Return again and again to experiences because of their incompleteness.* Actions cutting the child's experience short may bring an experience out of its background and cause its repetitive behavior. The mother's unsatisfying answer to a question about sex in comparison to her direct answer to other questions may cause the child to return again and again to the question. A child told not to touch a gas stove could hardly keep away from it, while another shown how to operate the valves, quickly lost interest.

5. *Persistent problem of adjustment.* In the Alschuler and Hattwick study of *Painting and Personality,* Aileen who had a continuing adjustment problem, made paintings for many years with a common element, which apparently had a symbolic relation to the problem.

6. *Group expectancies and roles.* Within a group of children, roles are assumed by individuals who thereafter are expected by the group to take these roles on subsequent occasions. In time persistent patterns of behavior in terms of group expectancies emerge. Here are reiterative relations which force conformity because of their recurrence and which mold personality.

SUMMARY

The personality of young children is frequently misrepresented because of views based on adult behavior which project back upon the child adult characteristics. Common types of misrepresentation are: (1) the child is passive and responds to all the stimulation to which he is exposed without action or selection on his part; (2) the child is so delicate and tender that he must be protected at all costs, and must have exceptional amounts of love, affection, and security; (3) the child carries forward all his memories and experiences to later behavior, and is particularly affected by so-called "traumatic" episodes or single intense experiences.

In contrast to these, the following picture of the child as a personality system is presented: (1) The child is an active energy system that responds selectively to its environment and neglects as well as takes in many stimuli; (2) the child has substantial capacity to withstand stress and strain, and recovers quickly from deformation and has great capacity for self-repair and readjustment; (3) the child lives in the moment rather than in the past or future. What affects him must somehow or other get into the field of forces in which he is reacting; (4) the child forgets much of what he experiences and carries forward as mental and behavior equipment only that part of his experience which, because of reiteration, has received unusual emphasis; and (5) because the stream of stimulation and reaction in the normal young child is tremendous, the quantity of experience had within even a short time far exceeds that which persists.

Personality becomes organized around certain nodal points or experiences which have received particular emphasis and much reiteration. As examples of reiterated factors that give particular experiences significance were mentioned: (1) the oft-repeated family story which fixes behavior and creates expectancies; (2) repeated environmental simulation consistent in attitude and role; (3) accounts of experiences which because they attract the attention of others are repeated either aloud or silently; (4) the return again and again to incomplete and unsatisfactory experiences; (5) persistent problems of adjustment which force symbolization; (6) group expectancies which create roles that are assumed again and again.

The child, then, is not a simple passive creature molded exclusively by external forces; he is very much a creature in his own right, moving through his own experiences and creating his own world. This is not to deny the value of nurture in creating the best possible world for children, but to plead for a study of the child as he is rather than to use him as a convenient locus for images which fit adult conceptions and convenience.

What I have said might be interpreted as indicating that personality traits are unmodifiable, and to deny the value of good nurture. Such is not my view at all. What we need, it seems to me, is a much more complete approach to the problem of persistent and fluctuating traits and characteristics with an analysis of all our data in terms of a span of time. When this is done we will locate the factors that produce modifications and find that change is orderly and consistent. We will move away from emphasis upon the traumatic episode, which is but another instance of what E. B. Holt called the "great white flame" theory of behavior. By locating in the stream of stimulation and response the recurring factors which are subject to control, we will be able to guide the process of growth and development more effectively and improve the adjustment of all children. We not only need to know how *to create* a good environment for children; once created, we need to know how *to maintain it*.

References

Allport, G. W., *Personality: A Psychological Interpretation.* New York: Henry Holt & Company, 1937.

Alschuler, R. H., and L. W. Hattwick, *Painting and Personality*, Vols. I and II. Chicago: University of Chicago Press, 1947.

Anderson, J. E., "Child Development. Relation of Learning Capacity to Age," in *Encyclopedia of Educational Research.* New York: The Macmillan Company, 1941.

Bayley, N., "A Study of the Crying of Infants During Mental and Physical Tests," *Journal of Genetic Psychology*, 40 (1932), 306-329.

Brackett, C. W., "Laughing and Crying of Preschool Children," *Journal of Experimental Education*, 2 (1935), 119-126.

Brody, S., *Bio-energetics and Growth.* New York: Reinhold Publishing Corporation, 1945.

314 · JOHN E. ANDERSON

Child, I. L., and others, "Children's Textbooks and Personality Development: An Exploration in the Social Psychology of Education," *Psychological Monographs*, Vol. 60, No. 3 (1946).

Cushing, H. M., "A Perseverative Tendency in Preschool Children: A Study in Personality Differences," *Archives of Psychology*, No. 108 (1929).

Gesell, A., and others, *Biographies of Child Development*. New York: Harper & Row, Publishers, 1939.

Glueck, S. and E. T., *Juvenile Delinquents Grown Up*. New York: Commonwealth Fund, 1940.

Green, E. H., "Friendships and Quarrels Among Preschool Children," *Child Development*, 4 (1933), 237-252.

Hogan, L., *A Study of a Child*. New York: Harper & Row, Publishers, 1900.

Jersild, A. T., "The Constancy of Certain Behavior Patterns in Young Children," *American Journal of Psychology*, 45 (1933), 125-129.

———, and S. F. Bienstock, "A Study of the Development of Children's Ability to Sing," *Journal of Educational Psychology*, 25 (1934), 481-503.

———, and E. V. Markey, "Conflicts Between Preschool Children," *Child Development Monographs*, No. 21. New York: Bureau of Publications, Teachers College, Columbia University, 1935.

Landis, C., and M. N. Bolles, *Sex in Development*. New York: Paul B. Hoeber, 1940.

Loomis, A. M., *A Technique for Observing the Social Behavior of Nursery School Children*. New York: Columbia University Press, 1931.

McGraw, M. B., "Later Development of Children Specially Trained," *Child Development*, 10 (1939), 1-19.

deNouy, P., *Biological Time*. New York: The Macmillan Company, 1937.

Ribble, M. A., *Rights of Infants*. New York: Columbia University Press, 1943.

Roberts, K. E., and V. V. Fleming, "Persistence and Changes in Personality Patterns," *Monographs of the Society for Research in Child Development*, Vol. 8, No. 3 (1943).

Sanford, R. N., and others, "Physique, Personality, and Scholarship. A Cooperative Study of School Children," *Monographs for the Society for Research in Child Development*, Vol. 8, No. 1 (1943).

Shinn, M. W., *The Biography of a Baby*. Boston: Houghton Mifflin Company, 1900.

Stutsman, R., "Consistency in Personality Trends," *Psychological Bulletin*, 32 (1935), 701-702.

Symonds, P., *The Dynamics of Human Adjustment*. New York: Appleton-Century-Crofts, Inc., 1946.

Washburn, R. W., "A Study of the Smiling and Laughing of Infants in the First Year of Life," *Genetic Psychology Monographs*, 6 (1929), 403-537.

Woolley, H. T., "Agnes: A Dominant Personality in the Making," *Journal of Genetic Psychology*, 32 (1925), 459-498.

VII—DURATION OF THE EFFECTS
OF EARLY EXPERIENCES

1 · Development Under Environmental
Handicap

WAYNE DENNIS AND PERGROUHI NAJARIAN

Reprinted from *Psychological Monographs*, Vol. 71, No. 7
(1957), by permission of the American Psychological Association.

*Child psychology resembles a pie, in that it can be cut in many different
ways. In this book the editor, as a convenience to students, has attempted to
serve pieces of approximately equal size. It is obvious, however, that the serving
called "effects of early experience" could assume major proportions. Some segments which could be placed under this heading have appeared in several of
the preceding chapters.*

*One of the primary difficulties in evaluating the effects of early experiences
as contrasted to the effects of later experiences is that experiences at different
ages are usually congruent. For example, in the Levin-Sears study (VI-4), the
fathers who were severe in punishment at one age were probably severe in
punishment at other ages as well, so that the effects of having a severe father
at any early period cannot be separated from the results of later experiences of
the same kind.*

*What distinguishes the selections in the present chapter from those in other
chapters is that they are among the relatively few studies in which certain
environmental conditions were present at an early period but did not continue
to be present throughout childhood. For this reason, they make it possible to
assess the influence of those early experiences which are of relatively short duration.*

Ribble (1943, 1944) and Spitz (1945, 1946a, 1946b, 1949, 1951) have
proposed that if certain stimulus deprivations occur in early childhood the
consequences are drastic and enduring. These views have arisen largely
from observation of infants in institutions. The supporting evidence has
consisted in part of scores of institutional subjects on infant tests and in
part upon general impressions of the emotional states of the children.

This report is concerned with behavioral development in an institution
whose care of infants is in some respects identical with, and in some respects quite different from, that described in other studies.

The data were obtained in a foundling home in Beirut, Lebanon, which,
because of inadequate financial support, is able to provide little more than

essential physical care. We will report upon the developmental status of two age-groups of children in this institution: those between 2 months and 12 months of age, and those between 4½ and 6 years of age. After describing the environmental conditions and presenting the data we will discuss the relationship of this study to previous studies, and to theories of child development.

THE CRECHE

The institution in which the study was conducted will be called the Creche, although this is not the formal name of the home. The Creche is a home for infants and young children operated by a religious order (of nuns). All children in the Creche are received shortly after birth. They arrive via two routes. The majority come from a maternity hospital operated by the religious order referred to previously. An unmarried woman being attended by this hospital may arrange to have her infant taken to the Creche. In so doing she relinquishes claim to the infant and may not see or visit it thereafter. The remainder of the Creche population consists of infants left upon the doorstep of the institution. Nothing is known definitely concerning their parents, but it is likely that the majority of these infants, too, are illegitimate.

The Creche is nearly 30 years old but it has a new building which was completed in the spring of 1955, and for which the order is still indebted. The building is an excellent one, being fireproof, sunny, and airy. The infant beds and other pieces of equipment are new and modern. The appearance of the institution fails to reveal that it exists month after month upon inadequate and uncertain contributions. The feeding, clothing, and housing of the children have the first claim upon the Creche's meager income. The most stringent economy must be exercised in regard to expenditures for personnel. For this reason the number of persons taking care of the children is extremely limited. Understaffing is the direct cause of whatever deficiencies may characterize the child-care practices to be described later.

Naturally the number of children in the institution varies from time to time with the advent of new arrivals, and departures due to deaths, or to transfer to other institutions to which the children are sent at about six years of age. The size of the staff, too, is subject to some variations. However, estimates made at two periods separated by five months agree in showing that for each person directly concerned with the care of the children—i.e., those who feed the children, change diapers, bathe and clothe them, change their beds, nurse them when they are ill, supervise their play, and teach them—there are 10 children. This ratio of 1 to 10 includes those on night duty as well as on day duty. It does not, however, include personnel who work in the kitchen, laundry, and mending room, nor those who do the cleaning. It does not include the four nuns who constitute the administrative staff and who frequently assist in direct care. Clearly this is an extremely limited staff. The essential functions can be accomplished only by means of hurried procedures and long hours of work.

From birth to one year there is no assignment of individual children to particular attendants. Rather, a room of children is assigned jointly to several caretakers and observation showed no consistent relationships between attendants and children. At later ages, each group of children is assigned most of the day to a supervisor and an assistant.

During the first two months of life the infant is taken out of his crib only for his daily bath and change of clothes. He is given his bottle while lying on his back in his crib, because ordinarily no one has time to hold it. The nipple is placed in his mouth and the bottle is propped up by a small pillow. Bathing and dressing are done with a maximum of dispatch and a minimum of mothering.

In conformity with a widespread Near Eastern practice, the infant is swaddled from birth. Figure 1 illustrates the type of swaddling used. The baby has his arms as well as his legs enclosed in tight wrappings, and hence the scope of his movements is greatly restricted. During the early weeks the infant is bound as depicted except when being bathed and dressed. No fixed schedule is followed in regard to freedom from swaddling, but in general the hands are freed at about two months of age, and swaddling is ended at about four months. Swaddling is continued for a longer period during the winter months than during the remainder of the year because the wrappings of the child serve to keep him warm.

As shown in Figure 2, each crib has a covering around the sides. This is present to protect the child from drafts, but as a consequence the child can see only the ceiling and the adults who occasionally come near him.

The adults seldom approach him except at feeding times. When they feed him they do not usually speak to him or caress him. When two or three persons are feeding twenty infants, many of them crying, there is no tendency to dally.

At about four months of age the child is removed to a room for older infants. He is placed in a larger crib, but for several further months his care remains much the same as it has been. A typical scene in the room is shown in Figure 2. A toy is usually placed in each crib, but it soon becomes lodged in a place inaccessible to the child and remains there. The child remains in this second crib until he begins to pull to the edge of the crib and faces some danger of falling out. At this point, he is usually placed during his waking hours with one or two other children in a play pen. This situation is illustrated in Figure 3. Sometimes he is placed in a canvas-bottomed baby chair, as shown in Figure 4, but this is usually done only for short periods of time. The older child takes his daytime naps in the play pens. He is returned to his crib at night and tightly tucked in. The child graduates from room two to another room at one year of age or slightly thereafter. Some description of the care of older children will be given on later pages.

Until about four months of age the infant's food consists of milk, supplemented by vitamins. The feedings during this time are on a schedule of six feedings per day at daytime intervals of three hours. After four months bottle feeding is gradually reduced in frequency. It ceases at about twelve months.

The introduction of cooked cereals begins at four months, and fruit juices, crushed bananas, apple sauce, and vegetables are begun at five months. Depending upon the preferences of an attendant a child is sometimes given these supplementary foods held in arms, sometimes while sitting in chairs, and sometimes lying down. Beginning at eight months, eggs

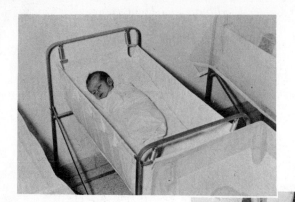

FIGURE 1.

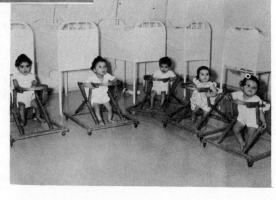

FIGURE 2.

FIGURE 3.

FIGURE 4.

318

and chopped meat are occasionally given. Feeding times are reduced to five times per day at four months and to four times per day at one year. Toilet training is begun between 10 and 12 months.

Children are weighed at weekly intervals. Serious efforts are made to give special feeding to infants who are not gaining properly but again staff limitations make it difficult for an attendant to spend much time with any one child. The average weight during the first six months, based on records of the infants which we tested, is appreciably below what is ordinarily considered desirable (see Table I). Comparable data are not available for other Lebanese children. No data are available on children beyond six months of age at the Creche.

From about one year to about three years the children spend much of the day in play groups of about twenty children with a supervisor and an assistant. Equipment is limited to a few balls, wagons, and swings. From three to four years of age much of the day is spent seated at small tables. The children are occupied in a desultory way with slates, beads, and sewing boards. At about four years they are placed in kindergarten within the Creche where training in naming objects and pictures, writing, reading, and numbers is begun. Instruction is given in both Arabic and French.

Diet and medical care are under the supervision of a physician who devotes, gratis, about one hour per day to the Creche, whose population is about 140 children. During the winter months colds are common, and pneumonia occasionally occurs. The usual childhood illnesses occur. When a contagious disease enters the Creche it is likely to become widespread since there are no facilities for isolation of infectious cases. We do not have adequate statistics on mortality. It is our impression that it is high in the first three months of life, but not particularly high thereafter. Mortality seems especially high among those infants who are found on the doorstep, many of whom are suffering from malnutrition, exposure, or disease upon admission. In evaluating institutional mortality it should be noted that in some areas of Lebanon the crude death rate in the first year among children in homes is as high as 375 per 1000 (Khamis and Powers, 1955).

Table I

Average Weights of Creche Infants

Statistic	Boys						
	Birth	1 mo.*	2 mos.	3 mos.	4 mos.	5 mos.	6 mos.
Average weight in grams	2926	3233	3746	4365	4926	5555	5984
Number of cases	28	28	28	27	23	18	16
	Girls						
	Birth	1 mo.	2 mos.	3 mos.	4 mos.	5 mos.	6 mos.
Average weight in grams	2727	2985	3353	3858	4436	4910	5463
Number of cases	13	12	13	13	11	10	8

* In computing this average, for each child the record of weight taken nearest age 1.0 month was employed. A similar procedure was used at other ages.

For comparison with behavioral records of the Creche infants, data were obtained from children brought to the Well Baby Clinic of the American University of Beirut Hospital. All well babies of appropriate age who were brought to the clinic on certain days were tested. They were from among the poorer, but not the poorest, segments of the Beirut population.

> All children tested were living at home and were brought to the clinic by their mothers. The majority were being breast fed. We did not obtain detailed data on swaddling, but typically the younger babies were brought in swaddled and the older ones unswaddled. It is our impression that swaddling customs among the poorer half of the Beirut population approximate those of the Creche. This conclusion is supported by a study by Wakim (1956). Other comparison data were provided by American norms and certain Lebanese norms to be described later.

THE TESTING PROGRAM

For the subjects under one year of age the Cattell (1940) infant scale was employed. This scale was selected because among available tests it seemed to offer the most objective procedures for administration and scoring. It provides five items for each month from two to 12 months of age, with one or two alternate items at each age level.

The procedures described in the test manual were carefully followed. They call for testing each infant at a level at which he passes all tests, at a level he fails all tests, and at all intermediate levels.

Several items on the test were not applicable to the Creche group because they require the examiner to obtain information from the mother or other caretaker. Among such items are babbles, anticipates feeding, inspects fingers, says "dada," etc. Attendants at the Creche could not supply the information required by these items. For this reason, "alternate" items provided by Cattell and based on direct observation were regularly substituted for these items. In the case of the comparison infants, all age-appropriate items, including all alternates, were administered; but in computing developmental scores for comparative purposes identical items were used for the Creche and the comparison groups.

At the 4½-to-6-year level the tests used were the Goodenough draw-a-man test, the Knox cube test, and the Porteus maze test. These were chosen because it was judged that they might be but little affected by the environmental handicaps of the Creche children. They have the further advantage of requiring a minimum of verbal instructions.

In giving and scoring the draw-a-man test, Goodenough procedures (1926) were followed. For the other two tests the procedures and norms employed were those given in the Grace Arthur Scale of Performance Tests, Revised Form II (1947).

We tested all subjects who fell into our age categories upon two series of testing dates. The only exceptions consisted of children who were ill or who had just undergone serious illness. The infant tests were given to 49 Creche infants and the 41 comparison cases. Since rather few of the Creche infants were above six months of age at the time of our first period of testing, during our second testing period we tested all infants who were six months of age and over even though this meant retesting in 13 cases. For this reason the number of *test scores* for the 49 Creche infants is 62.

In the 4½-to-6-year group, Goodenough tests were given to 30 subjects, and the Knox cube test and the Porteus maze test were each given to 25 subjects. None was retested.

For the infants, Table II indicates by age levels the score earned on each test. The Creche scores are shown by O-symbols, the comparison scores by X-symbols. Scores are grouped by step intervals of ten points. Thus, examining the figure by beginning at the top of column one, one finds that between 2.0 and 2.9 months of age one comparison infant had a developmental quotient between 140 and 149, two comparison infants had quotients between 130 and 139, etc.

Examination of Table II shows that at the two-months age level there is little if any difference between the two groups. The mean of the Creche group is 97, that of the comparison group 107. These means, each based on only 8 cases, are not significantly different from each other or from the American norms. However, at all ages beyond 3.0 months the Creche infants score definitely lower than either the comparison or the normative groups, whose records are indistinguishable.

If all scores from 2 to 12 months are averaged, the Creche mean is 68, the comparison mean 102. For the 3-to-12-month period the mean of the Creche scores is 63, (SD 13), that of the comparison group 101 (SD 15), a difference of 38 points. This is a very large and highly significant difference ($P < .001$). In this age range all of the comparison infants tested above the mean of the Creche subjects and all of the Creche subjects were below the mean of the comparison group. No Creche baby between 3 and 12 months had a DQ above 95.

Before discussing the results of the infant tests we turn now to the tests given to Creche children between 4.5 and 6 years of age. We note first that there are reasons to believe that the subjects tested at 4.5 to 6.0 years of age performed, as infants, at the same level as did the children whose test results have just been presented. Because procedures of admission to the Creche have not changed in recent years the two groups of infants can be assumed to be genetically similar. Since practically all infants who enter the Creche remain for six years, there are no selective influences between admission and six years. The only qualification of this statement regards infant mortality, whose selective action so far as psychological tests

Table II

Individual Infant Scores by Age*

Scores	Age in Months										
	2	3	4	5	6	7	8	9	10	11
140–149	X										
130–139	XX		X								
120–129	X	X					X				
110–119	OO		X		XX	XX		X			
100–109	OOXX	XXXX	X	XX		X	XX	X	XX		
90–99	OO	O		XX		OX					
80–89	OOX	OX	XXXXX			O		O		O	
70–79		OO	OOX		OO			O	OO		
60–69		O	OOOOOO	OOOOO	O	X	O	O	O	O	
50–59	X	OO	OOO	OO	O	O			OO	OO	
40–49			O		OO	OOO		OO	O		

* Creche infant scores are indicated by O; comparison infants by X.

are concerned is unknown, here as elsewhere. According to the supervisory staff there have been no changes in child care within the past six years.

The results of the performance tests are shown in Table III. It will be noted that the data there reported agree remarkably well in showing that on these tests the development of the Creche children is only about 10 per cent below the norms of American home-reared children. In a separate report (Dennis, 1957) it has been shown that on the Goodenough test Lebanese children at the five-year level make scores equivalent to the American norms. No Lebanese norms are available for the Knox cube or

Table III

Results of Performance Tests

Test	Various "DQ" Scores				
	N	Range	Median	Mean	SD
Goodenough	30	58–136	93	93	20
Porteus maze*	25	69–150	89	95	20
Knox cube†	25		100		

* Four children earned fewer than 4 points, which is the minimum score for which Arthur gives a mental age. Since the lowest MA given by Arthur is 4.5, these children were arbitrarily given a mental age of 4 years and DQ's were computed accordingly. Obviously these scores affect the mean and SD but not the median.

† On this test, 11 of the 25 subjects scored below the 4.5 MA, the lowest age for which Arthur gives norms. Because of the large number below 4.5 no arbitrary scores were given. Of the 14 subjects who earned MA's of 4.5 and above, one had a DQ of 80 and two of 100. The remaining scores ranged from 101 to 165. The median of 100 seems representative.

Porteus maze tests but there is no reason to believe that they would be higher than the published standards. In other words, there is evidence that the environment of the Creche produces only a slight retardation among four- and five-year-olds on these tests.

In summary, the data show that, with respect to behavioral development, children in the Creche are normal during the second month of age, are greatly retarded from 3 to 12 months of age, and almost normal on certain performance tests between 4.5 and 6 years of age.

INTERPRETATIVE DISCUSSION

To a reader acquainted with the numerous and often divergent opinions concerning the effects of early environment, the results just reported may, on the surface, only serve to confuse further the already unclear picture. We believe, however, that we can show that these data and others can be fitted into a coherent view.

Early Normality of Creche Infants

The fact that the Creche subjects had DQ's of approximately 100 during the second month, and presumably during the first month also, should not be surprising. It has not been shown that any stimulus deprivation will affect infant behavioral development during the first two months. The twins reared under experimental conditions by Dennis and Dennis (1951) made normal progress during this period. The infants tested by Spitz (1945) had a mean developmental quotient of 130 during the second month. The super-normality of this score was probably due to the inadequacy of test norms rather than to institutional influence.

If it is true that restricted stimulation has little or no effect upon early behavioral development, this can be due to at least two different causes. One explanation would be in terms of maturation. Perhaps growth of the nervous system, apart from sensory stimulation, is alone responsible for postnatal behavioral growth during the first two months. A second explanation lies in the possibility that sensory experience is essential, but that for the tests presented to him the infant even when swaddled hand and foot and lying on his back obtains sufficient stimulation.

> For the Cattell infant tests the second interpretation is not altogether unreasonable. Of the five tests which we employed at the two-months level, four are given to the infant while lying on his back and the responses required are visual. These are "inspects environment," "follows moving person," "follows moving ring vertically," and "follows moving ring horizontally." Since the infants spend nearly 24 hours per day in a supine position in a well-lighted room, and some movement occurs near them, there is considerable opportunity to practice visual pursuit movements.
>
> The fifth item among the two-month tests is lifting head when prone. The Creche infants are placed on the abdomen for a short time daily while being bathed, dried, and dressed. For this reason, lifting the head

while in this position can be practiced and direct observation shows that it is practiced. Possibly the Creche infants respond normally to the items given them at two months because the required responses are well practiced. However, the possibility that maturation alone is sufficient for the development of the items is not ruled out.

Retardation Between Three and Twelve Months of Age

Beyond the two-months level the majority of items on the Cattell scale require that the infant be tested in a sitting position while being held on the lap of an adult. Sitting is a position to which the Creche infants under about ten months of age are relatively unaccustomed. They are not propped up in their beds or placed in chairs before that age. The first occasion for placing the infants in a sitting position may come with the introduction of semisolid foods, but we have noted that some of the infants are given these while lying down. Perhaps as a consequence of inexperience in being held upright the infants as a group make a poor record on the test item which involves holding the head erect and steady. This unsteadiness of the head, plus general unfamiliarity with sitting, may account in part for the low scores earned on certain purely visual items. These are "regards cube," "regards spoon," "follows ball," and "regards pellet."

Many of the remaining items involve not only sitting but in addition manual skills directed by vision. Among the items are "picks up spoon," "picks up cube," "grasps pellet," "grasps string," "lifts cup," "takes two cubes," "exploits paper," "pulls out peg," etc. Between ages five and seven months, the age placement given these items, the infants have little opportunity to practice visuo-manual coordinations in a sitting position and, further, visuo-manual coordinations are not required or encouraged even in a lying position.

Analysis of other items whose placement is between three and twelve months reveals that practically all of them require manual skills and require adjustment to visually presented objects. It is suggested that the relationship between the items and the environmental restrictions experienced by the children account for the low scores made by the Creche subjects.

We examined the records made by the Creche children aged 3 months and above on each item, expecting that one or two items might be found in regard to which their performance is normal. We were able to find none. But we were also unable to find an item in this age range on which the subjects were judged to receive a normal amount of relevant experience.

It is interesting to note two items on which the subjects are very deficient even though the motor component of the item is clearly present. These involve turning to sound. In one of these items, the child, sitting on the lap of an adult, is required to turn toward the experimenter who stands by the shoulder of the seated adult, and calls the infant's name. The second item is similar but a small hand-bell is used instead of the voice. The first item has an age placement of four months, the second, five months. Of 36 children tested between 4.0 and 10.0 months of age only one turned to the voice and only 4 turned to the bell.

Now all of the children turned to and followed a moving person in the field of view. The difficulty of the item apparently lies in the subject's lack of associations with sounds. We have noted that in approaching a child or providing services for a child the attendants seldom speak to him. This seems to be due partly to the fact that the attendants are too busy. A second relevant fact is that, with 20 children in a room, and the windows open to rooms containing 100 additional children, it is seldom quiet enough at feeding times and bathing times to encourage verbal greetings. So far as we could determine no event which happens to a Creche baby is consistently preceded by a sound signal. These conditions seem to explain the finding that the infants seldom turned to a voice or a ringing bell only a few inches from their ears.

From the preceding discussion it will be obvious that we tend to attribute the retardation of Creche subjects between 3 and 12 months of age to a lack of learning opportunities relative to the Cattell test items.

Relationship of the 3-to-12-Month Retardation to the Findings of Other Studies

There seems to be a superficial, if not a basic, disagreement between the results here reported, and those of other studies, particularly those of Dennis and Dennis (1951) and those of Spitz (1945, 1946a, 1946b, 1949). We wish to comment on the apparent divergences and to indicate how they can be reconciled.

In a study of a pair of twins named Del and Rey who were reared under experimentally controlled conditions until thirteen months of age, Dennis and Dennis found that, while the subjects were retarded beyond the range of ordinary subjects in regard to the appearance of a few responses, the subjects' development in general equalled that of home-reared infants. The few specific retardations occurred on items in respect to which the infants could not engage in self-directed practice, namely, visually directed reaching, sitting without support, and supporting self with the feet. These retardations seem consonant with the behavior of the Creche subjects. However, the prevailing normality of Del and Rey seems at variance with the Creche findings.

To begin with, certain differences between the environmental conditions of the subjects in the two studies should be noted. For one thing, the adult-child ratios in the two studies were very different. In the Del-Rey study there were two subjects and two experimenters, a one-to-one ratio. In the Creche, the adult-child ratio is one to ten, a greatly different situation. In the Del-Rey study the environmental restrictions in regard to learning were rather severe in the beginning, but were gradually relaxed as desired data were obtained. In the Creche, very limited opportunities for learning and practicing responses continue throughout the first year.

Certain specific contrasts may be mentioned: Del and Rey were kept in larger and deeper cribs, were less restrained by clothing, and consequently probably had more opportunities for motor experimentation than did the Creche infants. Further, Del and Rey may have received more handling and more varied exposure to stimuli than did the Creche infants. However, there can be no doubt that in several respects Del and Rey suffered as much a restriction of experience as did the Creche infants. Speech was not directed to Del and Rey nor did adults smile in their presence until they were six months of age. No toys were provided until the twelfth month. They were not placed in a sitting position until they were over eight months of age.

But it is our belief that the difference between the normality of Del and Rey and the retardation of the Creche infants is due to the use of different indices of behavioral development rather than to real differences in behavior. In the Del-Rey study no general scale of infant development was administered. The majority of the developmental data reported for Del and Rey consisted of noting when each of a number of common infant responses first appeared. That is, the observers recorded when each subject first brought hand to mouth, first laughed, etc. The initial date of occurrence of such responses cannot be determined by testing. The Del-Rey data are longitudinal and the Del-Rey records were found to be normal when compared with similar data obtained in other observational studies.

Now since observation in the Del-Rey study was directed primarily toward responses which could occur at any time and did not require the introduction of test conditions, it follows that poverty of environmental stimulation would not be expected to yield much evidence of retardation. The child left to his own devices on his back in his crib can bring his hand to his mouth, grasp his bed clothes, vocalize, observe his own hands, grasp his own hands, grasp his own foot, bring foot to mouth, etc. These are the items which were observed. One of the major findings of the Del-Rey study was that the untutored infant does do these things, and does them within the usual age range of home-reared babies.

In regard to such responses it *may* be that the Creche babies are normal. The relevant facts can be discovered only by observers each spending full time observing a few infants. If all Creche infants were to be observed it would necessitate the presence of many additional observers or caretakers. The reader is reminded that the Del-Rey investigation, involving only two infants, took a major part of the time of the two observers for one year. To devote one year, or even one month to observing each Creche subject cannot be proposed in an institution which has severe limitations of caretaker personnel. In contrast to the requirements of an observational study of development, the testing time in the Creche study was only 10 to 30 minutes per subject.

If we cannot compare Del and Rey with the Creche babies in terms of observational data, it is likewise not possible to compare them in terms of test data. It is impossible to estimate in retrospect with any degree of confidence how Del and Rey would have scored at various times during the first year on the Cattell Infant Scale. We arrive, therefore, at the following conclusion: It is likely infants with restricted learning opportunities are normal on "observational" items but retarded on "test" items. It is believed that the latter, but not the former, are influenced by environmental limitations. If this is a correct interpretation, the Del-Rey study and the Creche study are two sides of the same coin. However, to establish that this is the case appears to be a very difficult research assignment.

We consider next the work of Spitz. The observations by Spitz which seem most closely related to the present study concern the institution called Foundling Home. Here, as at the Creche, there was a shortage of personnel. Although the mothers were present in the institution for several months, they seem to have had little contact with their children aside from breast-feeding them. Pinneau (1955) points out that Spitz does not explain why this was the case. Despite the presence of the mothers in the institution the adult-child ratio in the nursery is reported to be about 1 to 8. The children spent most of their time for many months on their backs in their cribs, as did the Creche infants. At one point Spitz reports that a hollow worn in their mattresses restrained their activity. This, however, was definitely not true of the Creche infants.

Since Spitz's studies have been extensively reviewed and criticized by Pinneau, only a limited amount of space will be devoted to them here. Spitz used some form of the Hetzer-Wolf baby tests. There is no doubt that their standardization leaves much to be desired. Spitz reports scores for the Foundling Home group and a control group of 17 home-reared infants. In the second month both groups had mean DQ's between 130 and 140. The private home group remained at that level but the mean of the Foundling Home group dropped precipitously to 76 by the sixth month and to 72 by the end of the first year. Spitz believes that this decline in DQ was due to the emotional consequences of separation from the mother, but Pinneau has pointed out that most of the decline took place prior to the prevalent age of separation. Pinneau indicates further that at least some of the decline is probably due to inadequate test standardization.

We compare our data with those of Spitz with considerable hesitation because the two sets of data were obtained by tests whose comparability is unknown. In numerical terms the results of the two studies in the second half of the first year seem to agree fairly well, Spitz's mean for this period being about 74 and ours 63. But the findings for the first half-year present some apparent differences. Our subjects drop from a mean of 97 to a mean of 72 between the second and third months, and drop only ten additional points thereafter. Spitz's group starts higher and declines for a longer period.

Spitz's data and ours agree in finding that environmental conditions can depress infant test scores after the second month of life. We disagree with Spitz in regard to the interpretation of the cause of the decline. He believes it to have been due, in the case of his subjects, to a break of the emotional attachment to the mother. This could not have been the cause of the decline of the Creche infants. Since the conditions for the formation of an emotional tie to a specific individual were never present, no breach of attachment could have occurred. We have noted above Pinneau's demonstration that even Spitz's own data do not support his interpretation. We believe that Spitz's data as well as ours are satisfactorily interpreted in terms of restricted learning opportunities. We suggest that an analysis of the relationship between test items and the conditions prevailing in the Foundling Home would reveal that retardation could readily be explained in terms of restriction of learning opportunities. But such restriction is not inherent in institutional care. Klackenberg has presented a study (1956) of infant development in a Swedish institution, in which the adult-child ratio was 1 to 2 or 3, in which no retardation was found.

Discussion of the Creche Four- and Five-Year Olds

We have no doubt that on many tests the Creche four- and five-year-olds (and also two- and three-year-olds) would be retarded, perhaps to a marked degree. We think this would be particularly true in regard to tests involving more than a very modest amount of language comprehension and language usage. The language handicap of institutional children with limited adult contact has been sufficiently demonstrated (McCarthy, 1951).

It is likely that on some performance tests the Creche children also would score below available norms. On the Healy Picture Form Board, for example, most of the incidents represented are outside the experience of Creche children. We assume that the older Creche children are retarded on some tests, but we wish to determine whether retardation is general or whether it is related to specific environmental handicaps.

We chose the draw-a-man test, the Knox cube test, and the Porteus maze test because it was thought that the Creche environment might affect these tests less than other tests. So far as the Knox cubes are concerned, it is difficult to imagine how one can deprive a child of the experience of visually remembering just-touched objects, except through loss of sight. So far as the Goodenough is concerned, both human beings and two-dimensional representations of them were familiar to the subjects. They were also familiar with the idea of drawing and with the use of pencils. Knowledge of the use of pencils may also play a part in the Porteus maze test. It is uncertain what other experience may play a role in this test.

The results show clearly that on these tests the Creche children approximated the performance of children in normal environments. In other words, the retardation which was found to exist between 3 and 12 months of age did not produce a general and permanent intellectual deficit. It is possible for infants who have been retarded through limitations of experience at an early age level to perform normally, at least in some respects, at later age periods. The assumption that early retardation produces permanent retardation does not receive support from our data.

Emotional and Personality Effects

No doubt many readers would like to know the emotional and personality consequences of the Creche regime. So would we. But to the best of our knowledge no objective and standardized procedures with adequate norms are available which would enable us to compare the Creche infants with other groups of children in these respects. This is equally true of studies conducted earlier.

> In the absence of objective techniques, we can only report a few impressions. The Creche infants were readily approachable and were interested in the tests. Very few testing sessions were postponed because of crying, from whatever cause. There was very little shyness or fear of strangers, perhaps because each infant saw several different adults. In the cribs there was very little if any crying that did not seem attributable to hunger or discomfort. However, some of the older babies developed automatisms such as arching the back strongly, or hitting some part of the body with the hand, which may have represented a type of "stimulation hunger." It was almost always possible to get the infants over two months of age to smile by stroking their chins or cheeks or by shaking them slightly. The older children, like the infants, were friendly and approachable. However, such observations are not meant to imply that other personality consequences could not be found if adequate techniques existed.

SUMMARY AND CONCLUSIONS

This study has been concerned with the development of children in an institution in Beirut, Lebanon, called the Creche, in which "mothering" and all other forms of adult-child interaction are at a minimum because the institution is seriously understaffed. The children come to the institution shortly after birth and remain until six years of age. Contact with the mother ceases upon the child's entrance to the institution and contact with mother-substitutes is slight because the adult-child ratio is 1 to 10.

Opportunity for developing infant skills through practice is very slight. In the early months the infants are swaddled. For many months the infant lies on his back, and is even fed in a supine position. He is not propped up, carried about, or provided with the means of practicing many activities.

Data on behavioral development were obtained by giving the Cattell infant scale to all infants between two and twelve months of age and the Goodenough draw-a-man test, the Knox cube test, and the Porteus maze test to all children between 4½ and 6 years of age. Comparison data were available from American norms and from certain groups of Lebanese subjects.

It was found that in terms of developmental quotients, the mean quotient at two months was approximately 100. Between three and twelve months the mean was 63. In the tests given at the four- and five-year level, the mean scores were roughly 90.

Possible interpretations of these data have been discussed at some length. Our conclusions may be summarized as follows:

1. It is uncertain whether the normality of behavior at two months shows that maturation plays a major role in early development, or whether experience, limited as it was, provided the essential requirements for learning the responses which were tested.

2. The retardation prevailing between three and twelve months of age seems to be due to lack of learning opportunities in situations comparable to the test situations. It is possible that an observational approach in the day-by-day situation might reveal that some behaviors developed normally.

3. The infants did not undergo loss of an emotional attachment. There is nothing to suggest that emotional shock, or lack of mothering or other emotion-arousing conditions, were responsible for behavioral retardation.

4. Retardation in the last 9 months of the first year to the extent of a mean DQ of 65 does not result in a generally poor performance at 4½ to 6 years, even when the child remains in a relatively restricted environment. The study therefore does not support the doctrine of the permanency of early environmental effects.

5. It is believed that the objective data of other studies, as well as this one, can be interpreted in terms of the effects of specific kinds of restrictions upon infant learning.

References

Arthur, Grace, A *Point Scale of Performance Tests*, rev., Form II. New York: Psychological Corp., 1947.

Cattell, Psyche, *The Measurement of Intelligence of Infants and Young Children*. New York: Psychological Corp., 1940.

Dennis, W., "Performance of Near Eastern Children on the Draw-a-Man Test," *Child Development*, 28 (1957), 427-430.

———, and M. G. Dennis, "Development Under Controlled Environmental Conditions," in W. Dennis, ed., *Readings in Child Psychology*. Englewood Cliffs: Prentice-Hall, Inc., 1951, pp. 104-131.

Goodenough, Florence, *The Measurement of Intelligence by Drawings*. New York: World Book Company, 1926.

Khamis, S. H., and L. E. Powers, *Report on Infant Mortality Survey of Rural Lebanon*. Mimeographed report, American University of Beirut, June 1955.

Klackenberg, G., "Studies in Maternal Deprivation in Infants' Homes," *Acta Pediatrics*, 45 (1956), 1-12.

McCarthy, Dorothea, "Children's Speech," in Carmichael, ed., *Manual of Child Psychology*, 2nd rev. ed. New York: John Wiley & Sons, Inc., 1951.

Pinneau, S. R., "The Infantile Disorders of Hospitalism and Anaclitic Depression," *Psychological Bulletin*, 52 (1955), 429-452.

Ribble, Margaret, *The Rights of Infants.* New York: Columbia University Press, 1943.

————, "Infantile Experience in Relation to Personality Development," in J. McV. Hunt, ed., *Personality and the Behavior Disorders,* Vol. 2. New York: Ronald Press, 1944, pp. 621-651.

Spitz, R. A., "Hospitalism. An Inquiry into the Genesis of Psychiatric Conditions in Early Childhood," *Psychoanalytical Studies of the Child,* 1. New York: International University Press, 1945, pp. 53-74.

————, "Hospitalism: A Follow-up Report," *Psychoanalytical Studies of the Child,* 2. New York: University Press, 1946a, pp. 113-117.

————, "Anaclitc Depression," *Psychoanalytical Studies of the Child, 2.* New York: International University Press, 1946b, pp. 313-342.

————, and Katherine M. Wolf, "Autoerotism. Some Empirical Findings and Hypotheses on Three of Its Manifestations in the First Year of Life," *Psychoanalytical Studies of the Child,* 3-4. New York: International University Press, 1949, pp. 85-120.

————, "The Psychogenic Diseases in Infancy: An Attempt at Their Etiologic Classification," *Psychoanalytical Studies of the Child,* 6. New York: International University Press, 1951, pp. 255-275.

Wakim, S. "Child Care in Mieh-Mieh." M.A. Thesis, Library of the American University of Beirut, June 1956.

2 · Development After Noncontinuous Mothering

D. BRUCE GARDNER, GLENN R. HAWKES, AND LEE G.
BURCHINAL

Reprinted from *Child Development*, 32 (1961), 225-234, by
permission of the senior author and the Society for Research in
Child Development.

As the reader will have noted from some of the preceding selections, several authors have proposed that adverse consequences result if the young child is not almost continuously under the care of the same adult, who, of course, is usually the mother. The present study represents one of the few direct investigations of this hypothesis.

On the strength of assertions which have been made about the effects of inadequate mothering, it might be hypothesized that, if maternal deprivation does occur, the children who experience it should reveal the results of that inadequacy in discriminable variations in personality structure and content. In the absence of such observable, discriminable variations in personality, any assumption of maternal deprivation seems unwarranted, regardless of the fact that unusual mothering conditions may actually have occurred.

In an earlier report (Pease and Gardner, 1958) a research design was described, the central objective of which was to ascertain both short-term and long-range effects on children of an unusual, noncontinuous mothering experience during infancy. The major condition of that unusual mothering experience was residence in a home management house on a university campus, prior to being placed in private adoptive homes. During the period of residence in the home management house, each infant's care was provided by many different mother figures, each having responsibility for the baby for a few days at a time.

At the same time as the longitudinal study of these subjects has been going on, efforts have been made to locate children who resided in the home management houses over the past few years and to evaluate their present status in comparison with children who did not experience such an unusual mothering situation in infancy. One purpose for including this group of subjects in the over-all study is to make more meaningful any findings obtained with the younger, longitudinal group. In general, the condition of older children who were exposed, as infants, to such unusual mothering should help us to formulate clearer and more significant hypotheses about the future development of the larger group under investigation.

The purpose of this report, then, is to present information on a smaller group of older children who lived for a period of time during infancy in a home management house and who were subsequently adopted into private homes.

PROCEDURE

The subjects for investigation were selected through the cooperation of the Iowa Children's Home Society. That agency was responsible for the adoption proceedings for each home management house baby at Iowa State University since 1940. Their records indicated that there were 62 children who had lived in a home management house and had subsequently been adopted into families in Iowa.

Of that number, however, only 29 were still residing in Iowa and available for the investigation. Their ages ranged from 8 to 17, and their school grade placement from third through twelfth. Data summarizing the experiences of these children prior to being adopted are presented in Table I.

Table I

Preadoption Data on Home Management House Subjects

	Mean	SD	Range
Age on admission to H. M. H.*	5.0	3.1	0.5–14.0
Length of residence at H. M. H.	5.1	3.1	0.8–12.0
Age at adoption†	12.1	5.6	3.0–23.0
Number of changes in residence	3.4	1.4	1.0– 7.0

* Age data reported in months.
† Refers to age at which child was first placed in adoptive family.

A group of comparison subjects were selected on a matched-pair basis. That is, a child of the same age and sex who had lived with his own biological family from birth was matched with each adopted child.* The matching procedure was carried out in the following manner:

All children in the school class in which the group A child was located were given the Otis Mental Ability Test and were asked to complete a family data sheet. This data sheet provided information about parents' ages, education, occupation, and number of children in the family. In addition, the children completed items from the Gough Social Status Inventory (1949), an index of socio economic status.

From the classmates of each group A child, between one and three

---

* For convenience in the discussion which follows, children who had lived in a home management house and, subsequently, in an adoptive family, are designated group A; those who had lived only in their own biological families are referred to as group B.

potential group B children were selected. Factors considered in this selection were: sex, age, Otis IQ, family socio-economic status, age of parents, parents' educational level, and father's occupation. The families of all children were intact and living together. Because of the selection procedure, each group B child was from the same community, grade level, and class as his mate in group A.

Inasmuch as no one "B" child could represent a perfect match with respect to all of the criteria, the final selection was made by a panel of three judges, working together, who agreed on the one "B" subject who most closely approximated the "A" child when all factors were considered.

Table II reveals, in part, the extent to which this matching procedure was successful. Variables for which continuous data were available are listed in the left-hand column. The Wilcoxon matched-pairs signed-ranks test (Siegel, 1956) was used to determine whether significant differences remained between the pairs of children. In this nonparametric technique, N refers to the number of pairs in which differences occurred. The Z score is based on standard deviation scoring units. Probabilities of differences as great as those observed between pairs are shown in the last column.

Table II

Partial Results of Matching Procedure

Matching Variable	N	Z	P
Otis IQ	29	1.93	.052
Age of children	27	1.22	.222
Age of father	25	3.49	$< .001$
Age of mother	25	4.07	$< .001$
Economic status	29	2.62	$< .01$

With respect to sex, the matching was perfect; hence, no test was made. With respect to age, the differences were insignificant. With respect to age of fathers and age of mothers, there were highly significant differences between pairs. Although average scores for groups are not pertinent to the Wilcoxon procedure, they are of interest in interpreting the differences found between pairs. The mean age of fathers in group A (48.4) was considerably higher than that for fathers in group B (41.1). Similarly for mothers, the mean age in group A (45.3) exceeded that for group B (37.7).

Differences between pairs with respect to socio-economic status favored the adopted children. The absolute differences were small, but consistent enough to be highly reliable.

In spite of the careful efforts to match the pairs on the basis of intelligence, the data in Table II indicate that there may be some question about their comparability. The p value of .052 approaches the 5 per cent level, which had been arbitrarily established in advance as the criterion for rejecting the null hypothesis. The mean scores favor the group B children (108.3) over group A (105.6). The differences are certainly not large, and it seems unlikely that such small differences in performance on the Otis examination would be of great significance. We are evidently dealing with the same general range of intellectual functioning for both groups. Thus, it was concluded that the matching procedure had been at least relatively successful with respect to intelligence.

The remaining matching variables included number of children in the family, educational level of fathers and mothers, and father's occupational classification. The occupational classification was based on the six major categories described by North and Hatt (1957): (1) professional, (2) proprietary, (3) clerical, (4) craftsmen, (5) operatives, and (6) farmers. Of the 29 pairs, 13 were in agreement with respect to occupational groups. For eight additional pairs, the occupational group of the "B" father was in the next higher or lower classification, adjacent to that of the "A" father. In the remaining eight pairs the two fathers were separated by one or more occupational categories. All of the six occupational categories were represented in both groups, and there was no tendency for one group to rank higher than the other.

Comparison of educational level of parents was accomplished by establishing three broad educational categories: (1) completion of grade school only, (2) completion of high school, and (3) completion of college. Of the 29 pairs, there were 16 agreements and 13 disagreements for fathers, and there were 13 agreements and 16 disagreements for mothers. However, when the subjects were considered as groups rather than as pairs, the proportions in each of the three categories were almost identical, both for fathers and for mothers.

With respect to number of children in the family, the difficulty of maintaining absolute control in matching became even more apparent. Since the "A" children were all adopted and since it is unusual for parents to adopt more than one or two children, it might be expected that important discrepancies would be found here. Nevertheless, of the 29 pairs, 16 were in agreement on the number of children in the family. Another 10 pairs had only one more child in the "B" than in the "A" family, and in just three pairs was there a difference of two in the number of children.

To summarize the results of the matching procedure, the pairs of subjects were perfectly matched with respect to age, sex, educational level, community, and criterion of living in a complete (unbroken) family. Matching on the basis of intelligence was at least relatively successful; although differences between pairs approaching a level of significance were observed, in favor of group B, the average difference between pairs was so small as to warrant the conclusion that we were dealing with the same range of intellectual functioning. Matching of the pairs was less perfect with respect to the factors of size of family, educational level of parents, socio-economic status of family, father's occupation, and age of parents.

In addition to the forms and tests described above, the subjects completed a number of procedures designed to get at some aspects of personality and adjustment. These tests included the California Test of Personality, the Children's Form of the Manifest Anxiety Scale, and the Rosenzweig Picture-Frustration Study. In addition, data were available for 18 of the pairs for the Iowa Every-Pupil Test of Basic Skills, a widely used test of general school achievement.

With the exception of the Rosenzweig P-F Study, which was administered individually, the tests were given in the classroom group, with all children participating. Thus, the subjects were not aware of the special nature of our interests. All of the tests, excepting the achievement tests, were administered by one of the authors.

Statistical comparisons of the 29 pairs were made with respect to the variables measured by these tests, and the results are presented in the following section.

RESULTS

Subjects were compared in the three major scoring categories of the California Test of Personality: Personal Adjustment, Social Adjustment, and Total Adjustment, the latter representing a favorable balance of elements of the other two. Results, shown in Table III, indicate that there were no significant differences between pairs in any of these scores. These figures are based on the Wilcoxon procedure, previously described. It will be noted, however, that in the case of the Personal Adjustment scores, the

Table III

Significance of Differences Between Pairs: Dependent Variables

Variable	N	Z	p
California Test of Personality			
Personal Adjustment	28	1.81	.07
Social Adjustment	28	1.39	.16
Total Adjustment	27	1.55	.12
Children's Form, Manifest Anxiety Scale			
Anxiety Score	28	.06	.95
"L" Score	28	.41	.68
Iowa Every-Pupil Test of Basic Skills			
Composite Score	18	.20	.84

Z value of 1.81 and corresponding p value of .07 approach the 5 per cent probability level.

The differences favor group B, whose mean score was 60, in comparison with group A, whose mean score was 56. While the statistics do not allow us to reject the null hypothesis, it should be remembered that criteria for rejection, in this case, the .05 level, are always arbitrarily established. Thus, on the basis of this one finding alone, the possibility of there being real differences in personal adjustment between the two groups should not be overlooked.

For the Children's Form of the Manifest Anxiety Scale, no differences attributable to experiences of the group A subjects were observed. This scale provides an index of the level of anxiety of the subject and also an "L" score which indicates the tendency of the subject to falsify his responses to the anxiety items in the scale.

In school achievement, complete test data were available for only 18 of the pairs. For this small group, the test was not analyzed by subscores. When the composite scores were compared, no differences were observed between pairs.

Protocols for the Rosenzweig P-F Study were analyzed along somewhat different lines, since the primary justification for use of this instrument was to enable us to get at larger, more complex units of personality than could easily be subjected to a relatively simple numerical scoring. It was also desirable to have the initial scoring and analysis of the subjects' record done by someone not involved in nor familiar with the matched pair arrangement. For this reason, the Rosenzweig protocols were submitted to an independent consulting psychologist,* particularly trained in the use of this instrument, for scoring and analysis. The consultant prepared a scoring summary and a brief written report of each subject's tendencies in response to frustration situations.

The written summaries were next presented to the consulting psychologist in pairs, without identification, and she was asked to rate each pair with respect to which child's record revealed a more "mature," more "integrated," or more "healthy" response to frustration situations. Of the 29 pairs, 12 of the ratings favored group A children, while 17 favored those in group B.

Under the null hypothesis, we would predict that half of the ratings would favor each group. A simple test was used to determine the probability of variations as large as those observed. Since we did not predict the direction of differences, a two-tailed test of significance was in order. The probability of variations as great as those observed was found to be .45; thus, there was no basis for rejection of the null hypothesis.

A more detailed analytical approach to the Rosenzweig scoring summaries was next undertaken in an effort to ascertain whether the written reports, necessarily brief and somewhat general, were masking real differences between pairs. Such differences might take the form of specific variations in one or more of the nine scoring factors described in detail by Rosenzweig (1948). Briefly, the protocol is scored for each of three directions in which aggressive reactions are made (extrapunitive, intrapunitive, and impunitive) and for each of three types of reaction (obstacle-dominant, ego-defensive, and need-persistent). It is the possible combinations of reaction types with directions of aggression which results in the nine possible scoring factors.

* We should like to express grateful appreciation to Janet Hirsch for her cooperation and assistance in this study.

The form of our data, with protocols available on a matched-pair basis, suggested the possibility of a kind of analysis which would allow us to examine the interaction effects of groups, reaction types, and directions of aggression simultaneously. The basic question we sought to answer through such an analysis was, of course, whether reaction types and direction of aggression are in any way affected by variation between the two groups of subjects.

A form of the chi square technique was employed for this analysis, results of which are summarized in Table IV. In that table, "Rows" refers to the three directions of aggression, "Columns" refers to the three reaction types, and "Groups" refers to the groups of subjects. It may be inferred from the table that neither the reaction type nor the direction of aggression was in any way affected by the presence of the two groups on a matched-pair basis.

Table IV

Summary of Analysis of Rosenzweig Picture-Frustration Study Protocols

Variable Combinations*	x^2	df	p
Rows × Groups	3.96	2	≅ .15
Columns × Groups	1.64	2	≅ .45
Rows × Columns	91.35	4	< .001
Rows × Columns × Groups	4.43	4	≅ .35
Total	101.38	12	

* In the computation of chi square, "Rows" refers to the three directions of aggression (extrapunitive, intropunitive, impunitive); "Columns" refers to the three reaction types (obstacle-dominance, ego-defense, need persistent); and "Groups" refers to the two groups of children.

An interesting sidelight is the highly significant dependence of direction of aggression and reaction type (Rows × Columns) on each other. In general, this dependence seemed to have the form of relatively more impunitive behavior on the part of the obstacle-dominant reaction type, with relatively more extrapunitive behavior on the part of the ego-defensive and need-persistent reaction types. This finding was not pursued, however, since our major concern was with the groups of children both of which showed such trends in about equal degree.

Another type of rating is also obtained on the Rosenzweig data. It is called the "Group Conformity Rating" and indicates the tendency to give more or less popular responses to frustration situations. There were no differences between the two groups with respect to that rating.

DISCUSSION

In this study, scores in the tests of achievement and personality generally favored the control children. In only one case, the Personal Adjustment score of the California Test of Personality, did the difference approach the

.05 probability criterion. It would be hazardous to try to explain this only or even largely on the basis of the "experimental" variables. It is conceivable that scores in the California test are in some way associated with one or more, or a combination of, the matching variables in which we achieved limited success. It would be of more than theoretical interest in the professional field of adoption work to determine, for example, the effects of age of adoptive parents on the personality development of children.

For purposes of this presentation, the "unusual mothering conditions" described at the outset could be assumed to include the early discontinuities associated with being placed in a home management house, being cared for there by from 20 to 30 mother figures for a period averaging over five months, then being placed briefly in a foster home, and finally being adopted into a private family. In addition, however, it seems reasonable to assume some further discontinuities in the over-all development of a sense of personal identity, based on the fact of adoption *per se*. One of the obvious limitations of this study is that it does not differentiate between these two types of discontinuities.

For practical purposes at the moment, this may be a somewhat academic question since it has not been demonstrated that real influences on personality are associated with the complex of experiences in the home management house and later adoption. However, the type of control exercised in this study, where no major differences were found to exist, leads us to question whether the same thing would hold true had control subjects been selected during infancy. Presumably, if there are basically distorting or handicapping effects resulting from maternal deprivation, these might well manifest themselves in some of the very things which were used here as criteria for selection of comparison subjects. The most pertinent of these factors, probably, is intelligence. It might be argued that the procedure we have followed, since it meant selecting subjects for comparison whose intelligence was limited to the same level of functioning as that of the respective partner in the adoptive group, might have had an important leveling effect on other aspects of personality, such as those measured by the California Test of Personality, the Manifest Anxiety Scale, and the Rosenzweig P-F Study.

It would seem that the only real answer to that question would have to come from longitudinal studies beginning with the facts of discontinuities in infancy, following subjects over significant periods of development and making comparisons at critical stages with control subjects. One such study (Pease and Gardner, 1958) is currently in progress.

SUMMARY

Maternal deprivation in infancy should reveal itself in discriminable variations in personality during later childhood, as well as when the unusual mothering occurs. This study was concerned with the long-range effects of an unusual, noncontinuous mothering experience during infancy, a kind of mother-child relation which departs radically from the normal familial patterns of our culture for the first year of life. The problem is whether this constitutes a form of deprivation.

Subjects were 29 children, ages 8 to 17, who had lived in a college home management house during infancy and were subsequently adopted. In the home management house they had been cared for by a large number of mother figures, in serial fashion, experiencing a marked discontinuity in mother-child relations during the first year.

Subjects were paired with children from the same communities, attending the same schools and in the same classes. Pairs were also matched individually on sex, age, and intelligence. Matching for age and education level of parents, family economic level, occupation of father, and number of children in the family was only partially successful.

Subjects completed the California Test of Personality, the Children's Form of the Manifest Anxiety Scale, the Rosenzweig P-F Study, and Iowa Every-Pupil Test of Basic Skills. Statistical comparisons were made, in keeping with the matched-pair design.

The Personal Adjustment score in the California test favored the children who had not been subjected to unusual mothering. Statistically, the difference approached significance. However, this trend was not supported by other findings.

In selecting the tests used, attempts were made to focus on a variety of dimensions of personality processes: school achievement, personal and social adjustment, anxiety level, and response to frustration. In none of these variables could differences be attributed to the factor of discontinuity of mothering in early childhood.

References

Gough, H. G., "A Short Social Status Inventory," *Journal of Educational Psychology*, 40 (1949), 52-56.

North, C. C., and P. K. Hatt, "North-Hatt Scale to Determine Relative Occupational Prestige," *Opinion News*, 9 (1947), 3-13.

Pease, D., and D. B. Gardner, "Research on the Effects of Noncontinuous Mothering, *Child Development*, 29 (1958), 141-148.

Rosenzweig, S., E. Fleming, and L. Rosenzweig, "The Children's Form of the Rosenzweig Picture-Frustration Study," *Journal of Psychology*, 26 (1948), 141-191.

Siegel, S., *Nonparametric Statistics for the Behavioral Sciences*. McGraw-Hill Book Company, Inc., 1956.

3 · The Retention of Early Memories

HAROLD E. BURTT

Abridged from articles in the *Journal of Genetic Psychology*, 40 (1932), 287-295; 50 (1937), 187-192; 58 (1941), 435-439, by permission of the author and of The Journal Press.

Few experiments on the effects of early experiences cover a period of 18 years. Here is a truly heroic one which does.

If one hears Greek in the cradle does he retain it in college? This might be said to be the problem which is investigated.

INTRODUCTION

There have been numerous reports as well as informal collection of data regarding the earliest period in life which a person can remember. The data usually take the form of memory for some particular event which can later be placed chronologically by other criteria. The obvious difficulty is that actual memory for the event may be confused with memory of accounts of the event which have been related by the child's parents. A crucial experiment necessitates the use of material which can be checked objectively in such a way as to eliminate all possibility of others coaching the subject. The general program of the present experiment was to present nonsense material to the subject in infancy and early childhood and later conduct learning experiments with this material as contrasted with other material of similar character which had not been presented in infancy. If the material which had been presented at the outset was relearned more readily than the new material was learned this would indicate some memory effect produced by the first presentation.

MATERIAL

Passages from Sophocles' *Oedipus Tyrannus* in the original Greek were used as material. This was tantamount to nonsense material for the subject. Furthermore, no members of the family or relatives who might overhear the experiment had any knowledge of Greek so that there would be little opportunity for anyone subsequently to coach the subject deliberately or inadvertently. The material being in the same meter and dialogue form was presumably fairly uniform in difficulty throughout. Selections were taken from scattered points throughout the play. No choruses were used, but merely dialogue portions, all in iambic hexameter. Each selection involved approximately 20 lines, 240 syllables. Occasionally there were a few syllables more or less than that due to the inclusion of more than two syllables in a measure. Moreover, a slightly longer cue was necessary at the beginning of some selections because several of them were rather similar in the first words. In one or two instances slight variations in length were made in order to preserve the unity of the selection. On the average, however, the actual number of syllables learned in the original passages and the new passages differed by only three syllables—less than 1 per cent.

METHOD

The subject was a boy with an IQ of approximately 130 based on the average of periodic Binet examination. Twenty-one passages similar to those above described were selected for the original presentation. Beginning at the age of 15 months three of these passages were read once daily to the subject for a period of three months, a total of 90 repetitions. The reading was at as uniform a rate as possible, approximately 2 seconds per line. At the age of 18 months these three passages were dropped and three more read daily for three months. This procedure was continued until the subject was three years old.

The subject was always kept in a situation as conducive as possible to maximal attention to the reading. No toys or playthings were permitted and no activity such as running about was allowed, although minor squirming and restlessness could not be controlled. In the later portions of the original reading, of course, the subject began to take the procedure as a matter of course and called it his "Greek lesson."

LEARNING AT EIGHT AND ONE-HALF YEARS

After the subject reached the age of three years, the entire matter was dropped until he was eight years and six months of age. No one else had heard enough of the material to be able to recite any of it and the experimenter of course did not mention it. At the age of eight years and six months the experiment on relearning began. For this purpose the 7 selections noted in Table I—one from each age level—were used and three new ones of the same average length and meter and presumably of approximately the same difficulty. The nature of the experiment was explained to the subject and his cooperation was adequate. He was not told, however, which passages were new and which were old, so that there would be no difference in motivation. He did not have any correct suspicion on the matter as evinced by the fact that when the experiment was over and the results were explained he showed considerable surprise at the information as to which passages were new and which were old.

Table I

Age in Months for Original Reading	Selection	Repetitions till All Words Anticipated	Repetitions till Recited Entire
15–18 III		361	382
18–21 VI		250	253
21–24 IX		376	385
24–27 XII		355	379
27–30 XV		304	328
30–33 XVIII		217	226
33–36 XXI		259	265
Av. of all		303	317
Av. of 3 early		329	340
Av. of 4 later		284	299
Control .... A		409	409
	B	445	451
	C	436	445
Av. control		430	435

The order of presenting the 10 selections in each trial was varied systematically. The first trial was in the order A, B, C, XXI, XVIII, XV, XII, IX, VI, III. The next was B, C, XXI, XVIII, XV, XII, IX, VI, III, A. The next was C, XXI, XVIII, XV, XII, IX, VI, III, A, B, and so on. Thus, in each succeeding trial the selection which had been at the first of the preceding list was now at the last of the new list. Ten trials completed this cycle whereupon it was repeated and this procedure gave each selection an even chance of any advantages which might be due to primacy or recency or any disadvantages of retroactive inhibition or similar processes. The trials were not run on an absolutely regular schedule. It was desired, as far as possible, to have them once daily but there were unavoidable interruptions. On occasion two trials would be given daily when time was available, but on every trial the 10 selections were always given with the usual 15-second pause between them.

For the first 17 trials the experimenter merely read the selections in the same fashion they had been read at the outset. Beginning with the eighteenth trial the prompting method was adopted as follows: The selection was read very slowly and the subject supplied any words which he could at the proper point. As the experiment progressed the subject would be reciting more and more words and phrases and the experimenter would merely be supplying the missing parts. On the nineteenth trial it was realized that a tremendous amount of time would be consumed if the prompting method was used on every individual trial and that probably very slight differences would be found from one trial to the next anyway. Consequently, the procedure was modified so that the experimenter read all the selections for two trials at the standard rate of 2 seconds per line and then the third trial was devoted to the prompting method. This arrangement was maintained until the end of the experiment so that trials 19, 22, 25, 28, etc., were prompting trials and the learning data were tabulated on the basis of these trials.

As the words were learned they were underlined in the book and the date noted on which they had been anticipated correctly. This procedure was continued until every word in the selection, with the exception of the initial cue words, had been anticipated. A record was made of the number of repetitions necessary up to this point. In most cases the subject was not at this time able to recite the entire selection without prompting and further repetition on the same schedule was made until he recited the selection from beginning to end with no prompting. This number of trials then was recorded as the final score. Due to the way the repetitions were distributed it was about 11 months until the first selection had been completely learned. It was then dropped from the schedule. It was about 16 months before the last selection had been perfected. It was possible that there was a little greater incentive toward the end of the experiment as the subject realized he was getting some of the selections out of the way. The effect of this greater incentive would be, if anything, to complete the more difficult selections earlier than they normally should have been. If any correction were to be made for this it would probably take the form of delaying the correct scores in the later trials so that the results hereinafter reported might perhaps be more significant even than they appear.

The principal results are summarized in Table I. The first two columns have already been explained. The third column gives for each selection the number of repetitions that were necessary until all the words had been correctly anticipated. As explained above, the subject might not be able to recite the passage entirely at that time. The figures in the last column give the number of repetitions necessary before he recited the entire selection without prompting. The upper block of the table with the Roman numerals involves the selections which had been presented in infancy or childhood, while the lower block gives the three new selections, A, B, and C, which were learned *de novo*.

Perhaps the clearest way to note the general tendency is to average the results of each block of the table. The results are rather striking, with 430 repetitions necessary for the new material as against 303 for the old from the first standpoint, and 435 and 317, respectively, from the second. These differences are 42 per cent and 37 per cent. It may be noted that there is no overlapping of the two distributions. The most rapid learning is for selection 18 with repetitions of 217 and 226 by the two criteria of learning. The values contributing to the averages in the upper part of the table are naturally rather scattered because different amounts of memory might be expected due to the varying lapse of time since the original presentation and the age of the subject at that presentation. Nevertheless, if we disregard this fact and average the memory scores for the original selections, it appears that we do have real differences between such scores and the memory for new selections. With small samples of this sort the accepted procedure is to use Fisher's *t*-function. For the averages of 303 and 430 repetitions necessary until all the words had been anticipated the value of *t* is 3.34 which gives almost exactly 99 chances out of a 100 that the difference between the averages is a real one. For the averages in the last column, *t* is 2.86 which gives a probability of about 98 out of a 100 that the difference is real. As mentioned above, the high variability of the relearning data is to be expected anyway, because of the different conditions of the original learning. Even so, the differences between the averages are significant.

It is interesting to divide the upper portion of the table into two parts—the three selections presented earliest of all, III, VI, IX, and the remaining four. Averages of these are given. All of them, of course, are smaller than the corresponding average for the new selections, A, B, and C. The earliest selections, III, VI, IX, required more repetitions than the later ones. All four averages differ significantly from the A, B, C averages with the possible exception of the difference between 340 and 435 in the last column, when the probability is only .90 that the difference is real. The difference between the averages for earlier and later selections, 329-284 and 340-299, are of somewhat doubtful statistical significance.

Again, if we consider the individual scores, there appears somewhat of a trend for the selections which had been presented originally at a later age to be remembered better than those presented at an earlier age. Selection VI is a definite exception to this trend but otherwise we note a general decrease in the magnitude of the entries in the table as we go down the column. If we simply rank the seven values in either column and compare those ranks with the actual order in which the rows are listed, that is, the original order of presentation, we get a correlation by rank difference squared formula of .50±.19. Again if we simply correlate the values in a given column with the age and month in which the original reading was begun, namely, 15, 18, 21, and so on, in the second column, we get a correlation of .55±.18 for repetition until all words are anticipated and a correlation of .52±.19 for repetition until the entire selection is recited. This trend conforms to what we might expect—that the selections which had been presented at the earliest age were retained least effectively.

LEARNING AT FOURTEEN YEARS

The eight-year experiment utilized only one-third (seven selections) of the available material which had been presented in infancy plus three new selections. The fourteen-year experiment employed another third of this original material plus three other new selections, and makes possible a comparison of the "saving" at these two ages.

The procedure at fourteen years was practically identical with that at eight and a half, except that the distribution of trials was a trifle more uniform. Two trials were given daily for the most part. One interruption of five days occurred at about the one hundred and fiftieth trial after several of the selections were already completed and out of the way. The entire 10 selections under comparison were always given in a trial, and their order from trial to trial was rotated systematically. For instance, if one trial was II, V, VIII, XI, XIV, XVII, XX, D, E, F, and next would be V, VIII, XI, XIV, XVII, XX, D, E, F, II. As in the earlier experiment, the 10 selections were merely read to the subject for the first 18 trials. Beginning with the nineteenth, every third trial used the prompting method in which the selection was read slowly and the subject anticipated any words or syllables which he could. These words were underlined in the text and the date noted at which they had first been anticipated correctly. This procedure was continued until every word in the selection, with the exception of the initial cue words, had been anticipated and the requisite number of trials constituted one item of score. The repetitions were continued if necessary until the subject could recite the entire selection without prompting, and the number of trials up to this point constituted the second item of score. The attitude of the subject in the present case was somewhat superior to that in the earlier experiment because he understood the scientific importance to a greater extent. Motivation seemed entirely adequate throughout. Toward the end there was a little unavoidable further motivation as certain selections were learned and dropped from further consideration and effort was made to get still others out of the way.

A variable which could not be controlled was the occasional tendency for the subject to think of words or phrases between trials. A little beyond 100 trials he began to recite phrases spontaneously when riding, walking, or swimming. According to his report at the end of the experiment, he seldom did this except when in the company of the experimenter. On this basis the occasions were not very numerous. The experimenter made no comment on such occasions. After trial 118 the subject remarked that some of the selections were nearly learned, and quoted part of selection XX to illustrate his point. A few days later he realized that XX was complete except for one group of words and he tried to quote it between trials in order to determine where he was "stuck." Subsequently, he listened intently to that part of the selection. The above is the only instance that the experimenter observed in which the conduct of the subject gave any selection an undue advantage. It is probable that this consideration between trials affected the selections about equally. When questioned at the conclusion of the experiment, the subject reported that no selections had been particularly impressive and he had no notion as to which ones were being relearned and which ones learned *de novo*.

The main results, together with some data from the eight-year experiment, by way of comparison, appear in Table II. The first column gives

Table II

Age in Mos. at Original Reading	Eight-year Experiment			Fourteen-year Experiment		
		Repetitions			Repetitions	
	Selec-tion	Anticipate Each Word	Recite Entire	Selec-tion	Anticipate Each word	Recite Entire
15–18 III	361	382	II	142	142
18–21 VI	250	253	V	133	139
21–24 IX	376	385	VIII	148	169
24–27 XII	355	379	XI	148	151
27–30 XV	304	328	XIV	145	145
30–33 XVIII	217	226	XVII	169	169
33–36 XXI	259	265	XX	127	127
Av. of all	303	317	....	145	149
Av. 3 early	329	340	....	141	150
Av. 4 later	284	299	....	147	148
Control .... A	409	409	D	163	169
B	445	451	E	145	151
C	436	445	F	163	166
Av. control	430	435	....	157	162

the age at which the original reading took place. The Roman numerals in the second column indicate the arbitrary designation of the selections that were used in the eight-year experiment. The two following columns give the number of repetitions as necessary before the subject had anticipated each word in the selection and also the repetitions required in order to recite it verbatim without prompting. The remaining columns give similar data for the fourteen-year experiment. The two selections involved in a row of the table had been presented in infancy under identical conditions. The averages for certain groups of selections are given in the rows indicated. The lower portion of the table gives the data for selections which were learned *de novo*—A, B, and C for the eight-year experiment and D, E, and F for the fourteen-year experiment.

The most general notion of the results may be obtained from the averages. It requires 145 repetitions before each word or syllable in the selection is anticipated in the relearning experiment, while with entirely new selections of comparable difficulty 157 repetitions are necessary. The corresponding averages, when it is a matter of actually reciting the selection without prompting, are 149 and 162. A considerable overlapping of the distributions is apparent, as some of the new selections require less repetition than some of those which are relearned. The saving averages about 8 per cent. As a small number of items contribute to each average, it is necessary to analyze the difference between averages according to the small sample theory (Fisher). In both of the above cases the probability, by this method of computation, is about 0.8 that the difference is real. Thus, from a statistical standpoint the differences cannot be considered entirely significant. It is interesting to compare the present experiment with the earlier one. In that case the saving was about 30 per cent as contrasted with the present 8 per cent, and the differences were of undoubted statistical significance. The intervening six years produced a considerable loss in retention for the material presented in infancy.

Continuing the analysis in the same way that it was made with the first set of data, the relearning is divided into two portions—Selections II, V, and VIII which were originally presented when the subject was youngest, and Selections XI, XIV, XVII, and XX which were given later in infancy. The averages appear in the rows of the table labelled "Av. three early" and "Av. four later," respectively. In the eight-year experiment the selections presented later in infancy actually required less repetition for relearning on the average. In the present instance this tendency has disappeared. Again, the seven figures in a given column may be ranked in order of magnitude and those ranks correlated with the order in which the selections were presented originally in order to discover any tendency for the later selections to be learned more readily than the earlier ones. In the eight-year experiment a correlation of .50 was obtained in this way. In the present case the correlation is zero.

Learning curves are shown in Figure 1. The abscissa indicates the trial and the ordinate the cumulative number of syllables correctly anticipated up to and inclusive of the trial. The solid curves are for eight and a half

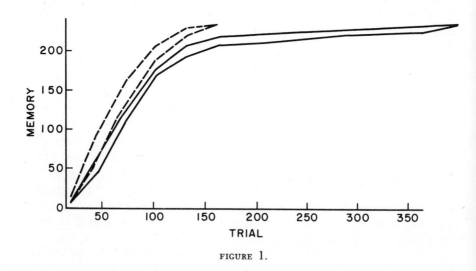

FIGURE 1.

years and the dotted ones for fourteen. The upper curve in each instance is for relearning and the lower for learning *de novo*. The separation of the curves was scrutinized for its statistical significance. Typical ordinates were taken at intervals of 21 trials and the significance of the difference between the ordinates for two curves computed in accordance with small sample theory. In the fourteen-year curves, after the first few trials, these differences have probabilities greater than .99 that the difference is real. This condition exists until near the eightieth trial when the probability becomes approximately .98. Thereafter the significance of the differences decreases as the curves approach one another. In the above respect the present experiment differs from the earlier. In that case, practically none of the differences between ordinates was significant. The result is perhaps attributable to the slightly greater homogeneity of data in the present case. It appears that the selections came along together to a greater extent than they did in the original experiment.

Another difference between the present and the earlier study is the much smaller number of repetitions necessary for both relearning and learning. For example, the three new selections required 162 repetitions for a complete recital in the present case, whereas in the earlier study they required 435. This difference is due partially to the greater maturity of the subject and to better motivation. He appreciated the scientific importance of the experiment and was also aware of the fact that when he had learned a selection he would be through with it. The main interest of the study, however, was in the comparative saving rather than the absolute scores.

LEARNING AT EIGHTEEN YEARS

The procedure in the present case was practically identical with that in the previous experiments. Two trials were given daily and this schedule was maintained with very little variation. A minor difference was the relearning of two selections which had served as controls in the two previous series. The 12 selections under comparison were always given in one trial and their order from trial to trial was rotated systematically. Motivation in the present instance was apparently about the same as in the second experiment. A variable which could not be controlled, of course, was the occasional tendency to think of words or phrases between trials. This was marked with reference to Selection D (infra) but otherwise the tendency was negligible. In a few instances while listening to a selection when he was not supposed to recite, the subject did speak it softly to himself. On the occasions when there was an apparent tendency to depart from the regular program in the way of reciting between trials, no comment was made and the practice seldom persisted. With the exception of Selections A and D, which had served as controls in the two earlier series, the subject apparently had no notion as to which were original and which were control selections.

The main results together with some data from the earlier experiment by way of comparison are given in Table III. The first column gives the age

Table III

Trials Necessary for Correct Recitation

Age in Mos. at Original Reading	Eight-year		Fourteen-year		Eighteen-year	
	Selection	Trials	Selection	Trials	Selection	Trials
15–18 III		382	II	142	I	202
18–21 VI		253	V	139	IV	190
21–24 IX		385	VIII	169	VII	181
24–27 XII		379	XI	151	X	220
27–30 XV		328	XIV	145	XIII	160
30–33 XVIII		226	XVII	169	XVI	175
33–36 XXI		265	XX	127	XIX	193
Av. of all		317		149		189
Av. 3 early		340		150		191
Av. 4 later		299		148		187
Control .... A		409	D	169	G	205
B		451	E	151	H	193
C		445	F	166	J	175
Av. Control		435		162		191
					A	112
					D	37

at which the original reading took place. The Roman numerals in the next column are the arbitrary designations of the selections used in the eight-year experiment. The next column gives the number of repetitions necessary before the subject recited the selection verbatim without prompting. The data were analyzed from two standpoints, the number of repetitions necessary before each word in the selection had been anticipated and the number of repetitions required for reciting it verbatim without prompting. Previous analysis indicated, however, that there was little choice between these two methods of scoring and for the remainder of the discussion the data will be confined to the last method—the number of trials necessary for a complete verbatim recital without prompting. Such scores for the eight-year experiment occur in the third column. The next two columns give similar data for the fourteen-year experiment and the last two columns for the third experiment. The lower portion of the table gives data for the control selections, that is, those which were learned *de novo*. These were arbitrarily designated by letters rather than by Roman numerals. In the last two columns Selections A and D appear a second time. They were included at the eighteen-year level to determine the difficulty of relearning a selection of this type which had been mastered 10 or 4 years previously.

The most general notion of the results may be obtained from the averages. It required 189 repetitions for a correct recital of the average selection in the present relearning experiment whereas for the corresponding control selections the average is 191. The difference obviously is negligible and of no statistical significance. By the other method of scoring (not shown in table) the corresponding averages are 172 and 175. The absence of any saving in the present case may be compared with the 27 per cent at eight years (30 per cent by the other method of scoring) and 8 per cent at fourteen years by either scoring method. Apparently the last four years were sufficient to eradicate completely any trace of the original stimulation in infancy.

As in the previous experiments, the selections were grouped and averaged so that the three which were presented earliest in infancy constituted one group and the four in later infancy a second group. The difference between these averages obviously is not significant in the present series.

Learning curves were plotted as in the previous series. The two curves for average relearning selection and average control selection are practically indistinguishable and not worth presenting here.

The gross number of repetitions necessary in the present study was much less than in the eight-year but slightly greater than in the fourteen-year experiment. The former difference is presumably due to greater maturity, better motivation, and an appreciation of the scientific importance of the experiment. The reason for the latter is less clear. It cannot be attributed to the mere lapse of time since the reading in infancy, because it characterized control as well as experimental selections. The subject reported occasional confusion of groups of syllables with similar groups which he remembered vaguely. It is quite possible that such similar groups were carried over from the fourteen-year experiment and caused this confusion. Indications of this carryover may be seen in the fact that Selection *D* which had been learned to the point of complete recitation at age fourteen was relearned at age eighteen in 37 repetitions, and on the nineteenth trial which was the first one on which he was allowed to attempt recitation the subject repeated 182 out of the 240 syllables. Incidentally on the second trial with that selection the subject stated that it sounded familiar and thereafter was suspicious that he had experienced it more recently than infancy. However quite early with Selection *G* (control) he stated that some words were vaguely familiar.

On the whole the experiment suggests that the effect of presenting nonsense material in infancy was very clearly manifest in relearning experiments at the age of eight and a half, traces were still apparent at the age of fourteen, but by the age of eighteen the effect had completely disappeared.

SUMMARY

Meaningless material (20-line selections of Greek drama) was read aloud to the subject daily beginning at the age of 15 months. Every three months a different set of similar selections was used as material and this procedure was continued till the age of three. When the subject was eight and a half years old he learned some of the original material by a modified prompting method in comparison with other material which he learned *de novo*. Similar experiments were conducted with still other material from the original selections and further controls at ages of fourteen and eighteen.

At the age of eight and a half the relearning required on the average 27 or 30 per cent (depending on the method of scoring) fewer repetitions than were needed to learn new (control) material. At the age of fourteen the corresponding saving was 8 per cent. At the age of eighteen there was no saving at all. At the age of eight and a half the original selections which had been presented later in infancy were relearned more readily than those presented earlier in infancy. No tendency of this sort was manifest in the two later series. Learning curves for experimental and for control selections were appreciably discrete in the first two series with the experimental curves rising more rapidly than their controls. In the eighteen-year series the curves were indistinguishable. The effect of the presentation in infancy was clearly manifest at the age of eight and a half, was still present but markedly less at the age of fourteen, and was completely gone at the age of eighteen.

4 · Visual Experience and Visual Imagery

T. F. SCHLAEGEL, JR.

Abridged from an article in the *Journal of Genetic Psychology*, 83 (1953), 265-277, by permission of the author and publisher.

From various causes, some children are born blind or partially blind and others incur blindness or deficiencies of vision at various times after birth. Most kinds of visual loss are not remediable. Therefore at any period of life there are blind persons, some of whom have had no visual experience at all, some with visual experience during only the first year of life, some with visual experience during only the first two years of life, etc. It is possible therefore, in the case of blind subjects, to study the later effects of having various amounts of visual experience. The present study is concerned only with the effects of early visual experience upon subsequent visual imagery.

THE PROBLEM

There are various kinds of imagery. For example, if several people are asked for their mental image of a "crying baby" there will be differences in the images they experience. Some will see the baby; others will hear it; some individuals will smell the baby or feel the touch of its skin, or will notice whether it is hot or cold; whereas others will notice their muscles work to pick it up. Usually more than one method is employed. The modalities considered in this study are: visual, auditory, kinesthetic, tactile-temperature, and olfactory-gustatory.

Heermann (1838) and Jastrow (1888) ascertained by statical inquiry among the totally blind that if their blindness occurred before a period embraced between the fifth and seventh years visual dreams were gradually outgrown. If sight was lost after the seventh year, visual dreams were found to survive throughout life.

The purpose of the present imagery study of blind school subjects was to determine the role of two factors: (1) visual acuity, (2) age of onset of incapacitating visual loss. Both of these factors proved to play an important role in the imagery employed.

MATERIALS AND METHODS

To determine the dominant method of imagery, a modification of Griffitt's test (1924) of "concrete imagery" was used. As adapted to this purpose, the test consisted of 125 words or phrases to which the subject responded with his *initial* mental image. Samples of the test words used are dog, street-car, George Washington. Samples of the test phrases used are: a girl talking on a telephone; a train pulling out of station; the driver whipping the horses. This test was given to blind school students and to a sighted group.

Blind Group

At the Indiana School for the Blind, 67 pupils ranging in age from 12 through 24 years with an average of 16.2 years were assembled and supplied with braille writing equipment. The author explained the test and made sure the subjects understood it by the use of trial samples. They were asked to write down one of the following words as an answer: see, hear, muscle, touch, temperature, smell, or taste. After questions were answered and it was felt that the test was understood, the examiner called out the words and phrases one at a time and the subjects wrote their first mental image in braille. These braille answers were translated by the faculty of the Blind School.

At a separate period, each of the Blind School subjects was interviewed concerning the date of onset of his significant visual loss.

The 67 Blind School subjects represent a heterogeneous group, not only in regard to age of onset but also in regard to the degree of vision. The visual acuity of the Blind School subjects was determined. On the basis of present vision, they were divided into three groups: (a) 0 vision: absolute blindness up to light perception only; (b) $\pm$ vision: the ability to detect any movement or objects to counting fingers at 5 feet; (c) $+$ vision: vision better than 5/200.

Control (Sighted) Group

At Shortridge High School, Indianapolis, 78 high school students, with ages ranging from 14 through 18 years and an average age of 15.4, were assembled. They were supplied with one sheet of paper numbered from 1 to 125. The test was given to this control group by the same examiner, and an attempt was made to duplicate the conditions of the test as given to the blind subjects. The test was explained, examples tried, and the test words and phrases called out while the subjects wrote down one of the following seven answers: see, hear, muscle, touch, temp., smell, or taste.

DATA AND RESULTS

The Dominant Method of Imagery

Definitions of dominance that could be used are: (a) A majority of responses of one type (63 or more). (b) One-third, or more, responses of one type (42+). (c) The type of imagery used most frequently.

Calculations comparing these three methods of defining dominance showed that the last definition gave the best spread of cases and that the other definitions did not add to the understanding of the problem.

When the averages of the blind and sighted groups are considered *as a whole* the relative dominance is the same for both groups in the following decreasing order: visual, auditory, kinesthetic, tactile-temperature, and olfactory-gustatory.

The Role of Present Visual Acuity in the Imagery Employed

Table I illustrates that there were significant differences between the three groups divided on the basis of present vision. (a) The Blind School subjects with the best vision (+) rated significantly higher in the percentage of responses of the visual type. Fifty-eight per cent of their imagery responses were of the visual type as compared with 41 per cent for the sighted and 42 per cent for all blind school subjects. (b) The average number of responses of those subjects with intermediate vision (±) did not differ significantly from those of the control group or from those of the entire Blind School group. (c) Those subjects with the poorest vision (0) had the lowest average number of visual responses and the highest average number of auditory responses. This group alone had auditory dominance.

Table II depicts this information in a slightly different form. Instead of comparing the average percentage scores, the dominant modality for each individual is considered. Each score in the table represents the number of subjects using that modality as their dominant method. Again, the importance of audition in those with 0 vision is seen in the fact that 70 per cent (16 of 23) had auditory imagery as their dominant method.

Table I

The Average Percentage of Visual, Auditory, Kinesthetic, Tactile-Temperature, Olfactory-Gustatory, and Unknown Imagery Responses for 67 Blind School Subjects Divided According to Their Degree of Vision and Compared with the Sighted Control

Type of imagery	Sighted control	0 Vision (No L.P. to L.P.)	± Vision (H.M. to CF at 5 gt.)	+ Vision better than 5/200
Vis.	41.7	27.9	42.4	58.6
Aud.	30.8	36.4	29.8	25.8
Kin.	10.2	15.3	8.9	5.8
T-T	9.8	11.9	9.0	3.7
O-G	7.1	6.2	5.2	3.8
Unk.	0.4	2.3	4.7	2.3
Total %	100.0	100.0	100.0	100.0

Table II

The Dominant Method of Imagery of Each of the 67 Blind School Subjects Scored Under the Various Methods of Imagery and Classed According to the Degree of Vision

Type of imagery	0 Vision (No L.P. to L.P.)	± Vision (H.M. to C.F. at 5 ft.)	+ Vision (from 5/200 up)
Vis.	6	13	20
Aud.	16	7	2
Kin.	1	0	0
T-T	0	1	0
Unk.	0	1	0
Total	23	22	22

P < .05—distribution significant.

The Role of the Age of Onset of Incapacitating Visual Loss

Figure 1 illustrates that the age of onset played the greatest role in the amount of visual imagery employed in those Blind School subjects with 0 vision, but as the degree of vision increased, the age of onset was less important. In Table III it is seen that none of the 0-vision students who lost

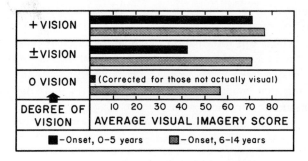

FIGURE 1. *Average visual imagery scores in blind school subjects as affected by vision and age of onset of "blindness."*

Table III

The Dominant Method of Imagery of Each of 23 Blind School Subjects with 0-Vision Grouped According to Whether the Onset of Their Incapacitating Visual Loss was before or After 6 Years of age

Age of onset of blindness	Number of subjects	Dominant method of imagery		
		Visual	Auditory	Kinesthetic
0-5 years	13	0	12	1
6-14 years	10	6	4	0

P < .01—distribution significant.

their sight before the age of 6 had visual imagery dominant (only three had *any* visual imagery): whereas among those who lost their vision later, 60 per cent (6 of 10) had vision as their dominant method of imagery.

COMMENT

"Visual Imagery" in the Sighted

Galton (1883) asked various sighted persons to describe the vividness of their mental picture when calling to mind the morning's breakfast table. To some the mental scene was as clear and natural as reality; to others the resulting mental image was tolerably distinct, with the prevailing features well brought out, but the rest dim and vague; and a third group could piece together only a vague, fragmentary, and unreliable series of images with no distinct or constant picture. Thus Galton described three degrees of sharpness of visual imagery in normal people.

The clarity of mental imagery played no role in this study, since the test requested only the first mental image no matter what its degree of clarity. In the interviews, however, it was found that vividness of visual imagery did not necessarily decrease with visual acuity. In the partially sighted, visual imagery may actually be clearer than present vision. This was true especially if vision in the past had been relatively good.

"Visual Imagery" in Those Blind Since Birth

An unexpected finding was the number of visual answers in those blind since birth. Because of this result, the students were interviewed. In talking with them, it was decided that what they meant by "see" was not a visual image but that they thought of the characteristics of the object named. For example, in response to the test words "George Washington" they thought to themselves, "He is tall with a large frame, has gray hair, and a large nose." Of course, it is impossible to prove that these subjects blind since birth did not construct a visual image out of their knowledge, but this seems improbable. The examiner and the subjects decided that what they did was "think of the object" rather than perceive a visual image. This impression is confirmed by the work of Librachowa (1934) who obtained introspective descriptions and analyzed the mental "products" from 600 subjects plus 20 blind persons. In the blind she frequently encountered the purely verbal type of statements. Because of the lack of the visual factor the content of the idea appeared exclusively.

These responses which were apparently not visual were left under the visual column, however, since calculating them separately produced no change in the significance of the results. Two of the 10 subjects blind since birth actually had some meager visual imagery. It will be remembered that under the 0 class of vision were included those with light perception. One person has one visual response which consisted of colors only. The other person had two visual responses in which she noted lights flashing.

The Role of Vision in the Choice of the Dominant Method of Imagery

Although the averages of the Blind School group compare closely with those of the sighted group, there is a greater variability among the children at the Blind School. This is seen in the wider range of responses (Figure 1). Since the Blind School subjects are not homogeneous with respect to vision, it was postulated that this variability of vision might explain the wider range of responses.

Both from common sense and the work of others we would have expected that visual imagery would not be dominant among the truly blind. The one unexpected result of this study was the high percentage of visual imagery in the semi-blind (+ and ± vision). Those with ± vision had visual imagery scores equal to the sighted and those with + vision had scores significantly higher. Why did these semi-blind subjects have more than the expected amount of visual imagery? Because of the importance of vision, the child may respond to the pressure of this importance by compensatory visual imagery. This question requires further investigation. It would be interesting to extend this study of imagery to cover the complete range of visual acuity from absolute blindness to 20/10 vision. Because of individual variation a large number of subjects would be needed.

The Role of the Age of Onset of Incapacitating
Visual Loss on Visual Imagery

Heermann (1838) and Jastrow (1888) found in studying visual dreams in the blind that the age of onset of blindness was important. The critical years were from 5 to 7. Those who lost their vision before these ages had no visual dreams. When blindness had occurred between the age of 5 and 7, some did and some did not experience visual dreams. In this study we have taken the age of 6 as the dividing line, but our data more closely support the idea of a transition zone. Of the 13 subjects with 0 vision blinded before the age of 6, only three had any visual imagery. Two of these had had light perception since birth. One had one visual response of colors only and the other subject had two visual responses of lights flashing. The third case with visual imagery in this group had had his onset at the age of 5 and scored 34 visual responses. There was one subject with loss of vision at the age of 6 who had 37 visual imagery responses. Another one, a girl completely blind since the age of 8, had no visual responses. Thus our results indicate a transition zone from 5 through 8 years of age, since when blindness had occurred during this period, some did and some did not possess visual imagery. An interesting question is why those who lose their sight before this transition period lose their ability for visual imagery and dreams. Is it disuse from lack of reinforcement or is it due to repression? An answer to this question might be obtained by regression under hypnosis to check for the presence or absence of visual imagery at an early age.

SUMMARY

An imagery test was given to 67 Blind School, and to 78 sighted, adolescents. When the average of the blind and sighted were considered as a whole they were essentially equal and the relative dominance was the same for both in the following decreasing order: visual, auditory, kinesthetic, tactile-temperature, and olfactory-gustatory. However, when the Blind School subjects were divided on the basis of present vision into three groups, significant differences in their imagery were found. When each of these three groups was divided into two subgroups on the basis of whether the age of onset of incapacitating visual loss was before or after 6 years of age, further differences were found.

It was thus found that the imagery of Blind School subjects was significantly affected by two factors.

1. *Present visual acuity.* Those subjects with the poorest vision had the least number of visual, and the greatest number of auditory, responses. As the visual acuity (at Blind School levels) increased, there was an average increase in visual imagery responses to an extent even greater than that of normal controls.

2. *Age of onset of incapacitating loss of vision.* If the onset was before the age of six, visual imagery tended to disappear, the loss being most pronounced in those subjects with the poorest vision.

References

Galton, F., *Inquiries into Human Faculty.* London: Macmillan & Co., Ltd., 1883.

Griffitts, C. H., *Fundamentals of Vocational Psychology.* New York: The Macmillan Company, 1924.

Heermann, G., "Beobachtungen und Betrachtungen über die Träume der Blinden, ein Beitrag zur Physiologie der Sinne," *Monatlich Medizinische Augenheilkunde,* 3 (1838), 116-180.

Jastrow, J., "The Dreams of the Blind," *New Princeton Review,* 5 (1888), 18-34.

Librachowa, M., "Structure of Individual (Specific) Reproductive Images and Generic Images," *Kwart. Psychology,* 5 (1934), 124.

5 · The Later Language Development of Twins

EDITH A. DAVIS

Abridged from *The Development of Linguistic Skill in Twins, Singletons with Siblings, and Only Children from Age Five to Ten Years*, by Edith A. Davis. Child Welfare Monograph No. 14. University of Minnesota Press, Minneapolis. Copyright 1937 by the University of Minnesota.

In selection, IV-4, it was found that up to age five twins in general are considerably retarded in linguistic development relative to singletons. The present study, using the same methods as the earlier study and comparable groups of subjects, investigates whether or not the early retardation of twins continues through the school years.

I. INTRODUCTION AND REVIEW OF RECENT STUDIES

Purpose of the Investigation

When Day found that the language performance of her eighty sets of preschool twins fell far below the norms set up by McCarthy, further research into the comparative linguistic development of twins and singletons became imperative. Since both the Day and McCarthy studies stopped just before the age at which school experience usually begins, a supplementary investigation would logically start where the earlier ones left off. To avoid the complications which must result if school as a factor were ignored, it was decided for the present study to capitalize the common factor of school experience and carry on the research entirely in school buildings and during school hours, thus saving much time and securing better standardized working conditions than could be had in the home.

To obviate the possibility of the personal equation operating to intensify or obscure obtained differences between the groups to be compared, it was decided that the entire problem should be handled by a single investigator. The study was undertaken with the knowledge that the results might be entirely negative as concerns differences between twins and singletons, but with the conviction that in any case worthwhile returns were assured from intensive investigation into phases of the use of language by school children that have been largely neglected in the past. To carry a little further the history of language development in twins and other children is the purpose of this investigation.

360

II. METHOD OF INVESTIGATION

Selection of Cases

It was apparent from the start that if this investigation were to yield results at all conclusive, a large number of cases would be necessary. Both twins and singletons must be representative of the Minneapolis and St. Paul population in socio-economic status; there must be equal numbers of boys and girls; and enough age levels must be studied to show development. Furthermore, since McCarthy found superior language development in preschool children who spent much time with adults, and since the inclusion of such children in her study might have accounted in part for the difference between her subjects and those of Day, it was decided to select a group of only children at each age to compare with the twins and with the ordinary singletons with siblings.* The twins studied must not only be equally divided between the two sexes, but must approximate the occurrence in the general population of fraternal and identical like-sex pairs and of unlike-sex pairs.

Because the method devised by McCarthy and employed by Day had to be gradually extended for use with older children, and because a difference between twins and other children at the age of 4½ years had been established, the logical age at which to begin the collection of data seemed to be 5½ years. Most children in Minneapolis enter kindergarten soon after the fifth birthday, and by the age of 5½ have had time to become adjusted to the change from home to school. Nevertheless, early in the investigation it became apparent that in at least one phase of the problem of language development, that of articulation, the kindergarten year is extremely critical. Such wide variation in speech ability occurred among kindergarten children that only a very large group could be depended upon to give a sampling adequate for all the contemplated intergroup comparisons.

The final procedure was to concentrate the study at the 5½-year level. Since the transition from kindergarten to first grade, although less of an ordeal now than formerly, is still a milestone in the child's life, a small group of cases at 6½ were selected, but no further study of yearly changes was attempted. The final group was 9½ years old, at which age most children are to be found in the second half of the fourth grade. By this time they have had a considerable amount of training and practice in oral expression yet remain cooperative and easily interested in a simple experimental situation.

The location of suitable sets of twins was greatly facilitated by the use of school registration cards, which give exact age, school history, and

* For purposes of convenience, singletons with siblings have been referred to simply as "singletons" throughout the study, while singletons without siblings have been called "only children."

Table I

Table I

Distribution of Cases by Age, Sex, and Sibling Relationship

Age in Years	Twins			Singletons			Only Children			All		
	Boys	Girls	Both	Boys	Girls	Both	Boys	Girls	Both	Boys	Girls	Both
5½......	48	48	96	49	50	99	27	26	53	124	124	248
6½......	11	11	22	11	11	22	10	9	19	32	31	63
9½......	24	24	48	26	26	52	12	13	25	62	63	125
Total....	83	83	166	86	87	173	49	48	97	218	218	436

paternal occupation. Information as to the presence of other children in the home was obtained from teachers, nurses' records, the children themselves, and when necessary by home visits. There were non-only singletons galore from all occupational groups, but only children from the lower occupational groups proved surprisingly difficult to find. Since the study of only children was subsidiary to the main problem, the number of only children was finally made approximately equal to half the number of twins and of singletons with siblings. This proportion will be found except in the 6½-year group, in which nearly the full quota of only children had been obtained before the change in procedure was decided upon. The distribution of cases is given in Table I.

The distribution of the 83 sets of twins by like- and unlike-sex pairs at each age level is given in Table II. The 1:1:1 ratio found in the general population is closely approximated except in the 5½-year group.

Table II

Distribution of Sets of Twins by Age and Sex

Age in Years	Both Boys	Both Girls	Unlike Sex
5½	18	18	12
6½	4	4	3
9½	8	8	8
Total	30	30	23

In studies of only children there has been little uniformity in defining what constitutes an only child. Some investigators have considered a child "only" if there was more than four years difference between him and the next older or younger sibling; others have made his status at the time of the investigation the only criterion. Thus a child who had lived for the greater part of his life with siblings or in an orphanage or boarding home, but had recently gone to live in a family of adults, would be listed as an only child. For the purposes of this study, which is interested primarily only in the language development of the only child, the following arbitrary rules were adopted:

1. An only child has no living brothers or sisters within nine years of his own age who are members of the same household.

2. A child who had siblings during the age of most rapid acquisition of language, but who had no siblings after the age of four years, is not an only child.

3. A child who has been a permanent resident in a home where other children within nine years of his age were found is not an only child.

Of the 97 only children included in the study, all but three would have qualified for the group under a much more rigid definition. One girl and one boy of 5½ and one boy of 9½ had only grown siblings. There were a few instances of two small families living together because of the depression but a child coming from a home where this was a permanent arrangement was not classified as an only child. Such questions as the effect of losing a child on the parental relation to the surviving child, or the influence on a child of living alone with two or more generations of adults, are beyond the scope of this study.

To make the cases representative of the total population of Minneapolis, each group was selected according to the cross-section method of occupational sampling customarily employed at the Institute of Child Welfare of the University of Minnesota. Although most of the data used in the study were collected subsequent to the 1930 census, the new census figures were unfortunately not available in time to base the selection of cases on the latest findings. Between 1920 and 1930 there was a decrease in the percentage of the Minneapolis population whose employment placed them in the three upper occupational groups, and an increase in those falling in the three lower classes. The experimental group therefore has too high a percentage of children drawn from the upper occupational classes to be satisfactorily representative of the 1930 population.

Experimental Situation and Procedure

All data were obtained in the school buildings and during school hours, thereby saving time and facilitating the work by better control of conditions than is usually possible in the home. An unused room of some sort could always be found, and a low table and chairs installed. Since in the modern school, children are from the beginning accustomed to association with a series of teachers, nurses, and examiners, a statement by the teacher or principal that some of the children were to go with Mrs. Davis to the nurse's room (dining room, library, speech room, or what not) was enough to start the procedure, and thereafter each child, having learned the way, considered it a privilege to escort his successor to the proper place.

Usually rapport was established by a few casual remarks on the way to the examining room or before the toys were produced. If the child did not begin talking freely of his own accord, the examiner framed her remarks in such a way as to stimulate conversation, saying, "I wonder what you play with at home," or "Here are some animals that not many children know," or "Now I'm going to show you something funny." If, after ten minutes with the toys, the child volunteered no remarks, and could not be induced to enter into conversation, the examiner said: "Now we're going to look at some books. I want you to tell me about the pictures."

This procedure may account in part for the fact that the mean length of time needed to obtain fifty responses was somewhat less than in the Mc-Carthy and Day studies. Some such expedient was essential with the occasional child who apparently was accustomed to playing in absolute silence, and certain concessions had to be made to the exigencies of school routine. Young children cannot be detained after the regular time for dismissal because they are expected home on schedule and many mothers cannot be reached by telephone.

With the two younger groups no explanation was given beyond the presentation of the toys and the direction that the child was to play with them. If conversation or questions on the part of the examiner were necessary, the child seemed to get the impression that he was expected to name and discuss the various objects, but spontaneous conversation usually took the same direction. Perhaps because of their longer school experience the 9½-year-olds proved almost certain to play in silence. This group were therefore instructed thus: "I want you to take these toys out of the boxes and play with them any way you like, just as you would if you were at home by yourself. But you must tell me just what you are doing while you play, so I will know."

Teachers reported that subjects of this age came back to the classroom beaming and gave such glowing accounts of their experience that those not included in the group were disappointed. "Why is it that some from our room can go downstairs and play cowboy when the rest of us can't?" they would ask. Even at this age, and with the more definite instructions which they were given, the general impression seemed to be that the examiner was interested in what was done rather than in what was said. The writing, they seemed to think, was a description of the situation. Many subjects of their own accord halted in their talk for the writer to catch up. In some instances of torrential talk it was necessary to request the child not to "tell me quite so fast," and occasionally a remark was lost. The procedure in such cases was to omit the remark entirely and go on to the next one. This accounts for some gaps in what would otherwise have been a connected narrative, and possibly tends to lower slightly the total percentage of spontaneous remarks. Sometimes the flood would cease and it would be necessary to interject a question, the answer to which would have to be recorded in place of the omitted spontaneous remark, but such instances were rare, and the writer is convinced that on the whole the records are as exact as though taken in shorthand and transcribed.

General Summary

The analysis of fifty remarks obtained under a standardized situation from each of 436 children between the ages of 5½ and 9½ years has made possible a number of group comparisons and the tracing of several developmental trends. Three discrete age groups of twins, singletons with siblings, and only children have been selected on the basis of paternal occupation to be representative of the Minneapolis—St. Paul population. For the most part, the methodology, both in the conduct of the investigation and in types of analysis, has been that devised by McCarthy and followed by Day, and whenever possible direct comparison has been made with the findings of the two earlier studies. Nevertheless this investigation in no sense duplicates the former ones. The greater chronological age of the subjects and the inclusion of only children necessitated a shift of emphasis to certain phases of language development which were not significant during the preschool period. It has been assumed that the reliability of the method has been satisfactorily demonstrated not only by McCarthy and Day but by the subsequent work of McConnon.

Language Usage by Twins, Singletons, and Only Children

Twins of 5½ years are decidedly inferior to other children in articulation. More defects were found in boys than in girls, and more in like-sex boy

Table III

Summary of Differences between Twins, Singletons, and Only Children in Linguistic Skill

Measure	Twins	Singletons	Only Children
Minutes required	13.7	14.5	13.1
Percentage having perfect articulation at 5½	46	76	79
Percentage having perfect articulation at 9½	87	90	100
Mean number of words per remark	5.07	5.12	5.73
Mean individual SD of sentence length	3.08	3.20	3.74
Percentage of single-word responses	17.8	20.2	16.8
Percentage of answers	23.7	28.6	18.3
Percentage of questions	9.7	8.4	10.3
Percentage of emotionally toned remarks	3.3	3.0	4.7
Percentage of elaborated sentences	5.3	5.8	8.8
Mean number of subordinate clauses per 1000 words	20	21.6	27.5
Subordination index	0.11	0.12	0.16
Mean number of auxiliary verbs per 1000 words	59	61	62
Mean number of different words	98.5	105.6	114.1
Pronoun index	0.37	0.41	0.49
Possessive pronoun index	0.14	0.12	0.10

pairs than in either boys or girls in unlike-sex pairs. The inferiority is especially marked in twins from the lower occupational groups. In other phases of language development the performance of twins from the upper occupational groups is very similar to that of other children, but in twins from the lower occupational groups the inferiority to other children is in some instances greater at 9½ than at 5½ years. This indicates that twins who enjoy a favorable environment tend to overcome the language handicap which is characteristic of the preschool period, but that in underprivileged twins the handicap persists at least up to the age of 9½ years. In most of the quantitative findings given in Table III the differences between twins and other children would be considerably greater if the comparisons were made only for subjects drawn from the lower occupational groups.

Except in articulatory difficulty, singletons with siblings appear to resemble twins in language ability more closely than they resemble only children. Apparently the presence of siblings, irrespective of twinship, operates so as to impede maximum progress toward adult command of language. The relative standing of twins, singletons, and only children in those phases of language development which seem to indicate possible differences is given in Table III. The singletons more than twins or only children lacked spontaneity of speech.

In Figures 1 and 2 the findings of the present study have been integrated with those of Day and McCarthy for two highly objective measures of language development—mean length of remark and mean number of different words. For this presentation the only children and singletons with

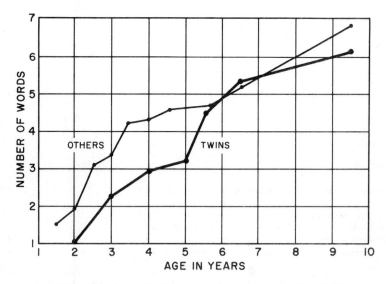

FIGURE 1. *Mean length of response for twins and other children.*

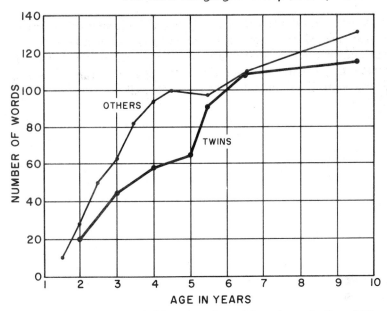

FIGURE 2. *Mean number of different words used by twins and other children.*

siblings have been grouped, as was done in the McCarthy study, and compared with twins. The curve representing this combined group is labeled "others." The difference between twins and singletons ("others") is slight at 5½ years and the curves come together at 6½ years, but at 9½ years there is again a small difference. There is a decided spurt in twins between the ages of 5 and 5½ years, for which the most logical explanation is the stimulation of the enriched linguistic environment which they have enjoyed during their six months of kindergarten experience.

Conclusions

The findings of this study seem to warrant the following general conclusions:

1. Only children are definitely superior to children with siblings in every phase of linguistic skill.

2. Singletons with siblings are in turn somewhat superior to twins.

3. Twins from the upper occupational groups by 9½ years have practically overcome their language handicap, but twins from the lower occupational groups have made relatively little progress. This finding necessitates careful control of the socio-economic factor in subsequent studies dealing with language development in twins.

4. Twins of the ages studied in this investigation are especially retarded in perfection of articulation. The inferiority is marked during the kindergarten period, particularly in twins from the lower occupational groups.

368 · EDITH A. DAVIS

5. At least during the kindergarten year, a child's mastery of articulation is closely related to other phases of language development. There are indications in the data that faulty articulation, if unduly prolonged, may become a major handicap preventing both adequate command of language and wholesome development of the personality.

6 · The Effects of Early Musical Training

ARTHUR T. JERSILD

Reprinted from pages 49-61 of *Training and Growth in the Development of Children*. New York: Bureau of Publications, Teachers College, Columbia University, 1932, by permission of the author.

This study describes one type of early training that is retained for some months and possibly is retained for years. This is training to produce vocally musical notes and intervals. Although much more research is needed, it would appear that some types of vocal training can profitably be begun at three years of age. It would seem that notes and intervals become relatively permanent items in the child's vocal repertoire.

The purpose in this experiment was to find the extent to which three-year-old children could be taught to sing tones and intervals not already included within their vocal range. Practice and control groups were employed. The experiment as a whole included a study of such varied factors as ability to sing tones, intervals, and songs, the effect of training on this ability, and the range and content of children's spontaneous vocalizations during their free play. In the present connection only the effects of training on ability to reproduce tones and intervals will be discussed.

PROCEDURES

The first step in the study was to test each child's ability to reproduce pitch, that is, to sing separate tones, such as middle C, D, E, and so on, and his ability to reproduce intervals, that is, to sing a unit of two successive tones of different pitch. Initial tests of this sort were given to 48 children, from thirty-one to forty-eight months of age at the beginning of the study. The subjects were members of a nursery school and three day nurseries.

The initial pitch tests consisted of the following 11 notes, beginning with middle C: C D E F G A B C D E F. The initial interval test included 12 intervals as follows: Ascending and descending major and minor seconds and thirds, perfect fourths, and perfect fifths.

The procedure during the tests was briefly as follows: The experimenter had at hand a pitch pipe, a small xylophone, and a psaltery. A given note was sung by the experimenter and sounded on one of the instruments. The child in turn was directed to reproduce the tone while it was being sounded. Various techniques were used to acquaint the child with what was expected of him and to induce him to sing. The children soon learned to respond in the desired manner.

In the pitch tests each tone was presented separately. The experimenter kept singing and sounding the tone to prompt the child's efforts. If the child reproduced the tone correctly, another item was presented. If he made no response or made an unsuccessful attempt, he was given a maximum of eight additional presentations of the same item or as many as could be given without provoking loss of interest and attention. If the child reproduced the tone, he was credited with a "hit"; if he tried and failed, with an "attempt"; if he made no response, with a "no attempt." The number of presentations of each tone was also recorded. Each of the 11 notes of the pitch test was presented in this manner.

The pitch test, covering all 11 notes, was given three times on three different days. After the conclusion of this test the interval test was administered. In this test the procedure was similar to that just described. The two notes constituting each interval were presented and a record was made of the child's response. The interval test was given twice on different days. To complete the initial tests accordingly, it was necessary to visit each child on five separate days.

The need of a valid means of scoring the child's response presented an immediate problem. The use of a tonoscope or other form of mechanical device entails practical difficulties in work with children so young, while any other procedure is open to subjective errors. After much preliminary work, however, it was decided to try the method of having the experimenter judge whether or not the child's vocalization correctly reproduced the tone which was being sounded. With the use of this method no response was put down as correct unless in the experimenter's judgment the child gave a clear-cut reproduction of the required tone. A description of the methods employed to determine the reliability of the experimenter's judgments follows:

The experimenter was first tested by another accredited musician. The tester sang notes at random, taking her cue from a piano beyond the hearing of the experimenter. The experimenter, in turn, was required to identify, with the aid of a pitch pipe, and to record in writing, each note that was being sung. When the test was completed, an item by item comparison was made of the tester's record of the tones which had been sung (in the exact order) and the record of the experimenter's judgments. On three repetitions of this test the experimenter made a perfect score each time.

To obtain an even more significant test of the experimenter's judgments two other musically trained observers were introduced on two occasions during actual tests of the children. The experimenter and the persons thus introduced took simultaneous but independent records of each child's performance. On one occasion the performance of 20 children who were given the entire pitch and interval tests was thus judged by the experimenter and a second examiner. An item by item comparison of the records showed an agreement of over 96 per cent in the case of pitch (in the total of 220 notes to be judged when each of 20 children was tested on 11 notes there was disagreement on only 7 notes). The two examiners showed an agreement of 95 per cent in their judgments on the interval tests of the 20 children. On a later occasion another musician, who, like the examiner mentioned above, possessed what is known as "absolute pitch," took independent records during the pitch tests of 10 children. An item by item comparison of recorded judgments in this case showed an agreement of 96 per cent. Out of a total of 110 responses, two were credited as correct reproductions by the experimenter, and as incorrect by the second examiner; the examiner, on the other hand, had given credit for two responses which were judged incorrect by the experimenter.

The results obtained in the projects above indicate that the testing method used in this experiment yielded a high degree of reliability within the limits of the procedure employed, though it must be said that unanimity among judges is not a substitute for mechanical recording. On the other hand, it can be seen that the procedure here used corresponds to the practical test which an individual must face either in connection with vocal training at school or in auditions of a professional character.

The coefficients of reliability of the tests, as measured by correlating the scores in successive tests at the beginning of the experiment and at later stages, ranged from $.54 \pm .11$ to $.95 \pm .02$, with a median of $.80 \pm .06$.

Separate records were kept of each child's performance on each item of the pitch and interval tests on each occasion that they were administered. In computing the initial scores, the child was given one credit for each item correctly sung during one or all of the repetitions of the test. This permitted a maximum score of 11 and 12 respectively on the pitch and interval tests. Nineteen children enrolled in a nursery school were designated as the practice group. The records of 29 additional children who were given the initial tests were examined to find control subjects as nearly equivalent as possible to the practice group with respect to scores in pitch, intervals, and age.

Following the initial tests, training of the practice group was begun. The training consisted of drill in the singing of songs containing notes within and beyond the child's pitch range, and periodic repetition of the pitch and interval tests with emphasis on items which the child had hitherto failed to reproduce. The children were given training in groups of two and sometimes three. The policy of grouping a relatively superior with a less competent child was used during training. The children were rotated so that the same two children did not sing together on successive days. Each training period was designed to last 10 minutes; at the beginning of the study a shorter period was usually found to be expedient, while during later stages a lengthened period was employed to compensate for earlier abbreviated sessions and to bring the average time to approximately 10 minutes. The experimenter worked with the children four mornings each week. Each child received two or, when time would permit, three training periods on different days each week. If a child was absent from school, his training was brought up to date by extra practice periods on his return.

Training was continued over a period of approximately six months, with loss of time during vacations and holidays, and with some slowing up of the procedure to make room for periodic retests. Since the tests, the training series in reproduction of tones and intervals, and drill in the singing of songs all provided exercise in the singing of tones and intervals, each session devoted to the child was counted as a training period. During the course of the experiment each child received 40 training periods, with an average duration of 10 minutes.

After training had been in progress for some time it became apparent that the range of tones and intervals included in the initial tests could not accommodate the effects of practice. Several children soon learned to sing all the items of the initial tests. To provide for this condition additional tones and intervals were introduced. The pitch test was augmented to include the 11 original notes plus G, A, B below middle C, and G, A, B, and C two octaves above middle C, a total of 18 notes. To the intervals' test was added the following intervals: ascending and descending major and minor sixths and sevenths, and octave, thus providing a total of 22 intervals.

The response of the children to the tests and to the training was decidedly favorable. This held true in the case of both the practice group and the controls. After the first session of the initial tests the children responded readily to another invitation to "come and have music." On only a few occasions would a child appear reluctant to leave the activity in which he was engaged when the invitation was given. Requests for another turn or for a prolongation of the music period were heard more frequently than requests to be relieved. At no time was a child induced to participate against his apparent wishes.

The initial tests of the practice group were completed in December 1930. Tests of control subjects were begun in December but were not completed until early in 1931. To compensate, in part, for this discrepancy in the time of completion of the initial tests of practice and control groups, the latter group was not given the end tests (after training) until after the tests of the practice group had been completed.

The first retest during training occurred in January, immediately after the Christmas holidays and before practice had been given other than that entailed by the initial tests. Retests were made again in February and in March. At the latter time the additional notes and intervals of the extended test (described above) were first introduced. Training came to an end in May. At this time each child of the practice group was tested twice on reproduction of pitch, twice on reproduction of intervals. The retests of the control subjects followed. The entire pitch test was administered to the controls on three separate occasions. The intervals' test was likewise administered three times. The provision of three separate tests of pitch and intervals in the case of the controls as compared with two in the case of the practice group gave the former children the advantage of an extra opportunity to reaccustom themselves to the procedure and also gave the experimenter additional time to reestablish rapport with the subjects. In scoring the final tests the procedure followed in scoring the initial tests was used.

Each item correctly reproduced, whether on each test or only once during the test series, was given a count of one. The maximum score on the final performance, including the items of the extended tests was, accordingly, 18 in the case of pitch, 22 in the case of intervals.

The summer vacation immediately followed the completion of the retests at the end of training. When the schools reopened again in the fall, the children of the two groups were once more tested. These tests were applied during the month of October, more than 10 months after the beginning of the investigation and 4 months after the end of the training period. On this occasion the pitch and interval tests were repeated three times with each subject and were scored as before.

As was mentioned above, the practice group originally included 19 children. One child was withdrawn from school during the course of training. The remaining 18 children completed the training series. Before the completion of the study several children originally included in the control group had become unavailable through illness and removal. The losses occurring in this way disturbed the original alignment of controls matched with practice subjects. As is shown in Table I, the control subjects who could be located for retests had an average age of about two months above the practice group average. Retests were made of children who had initial pitch records sufficiently similar to the practice group to serve as control subjects. Owing to unavoidable circumstances, the interval tests of two of these control children could not be completed; as a result only 16 pairs of children are indicated in the table of results of the interval tests. When the final retests were made after the summer vacation, it was possible to obtain records of 15 of the original members of the practice group and 14 of the members of the control group in the case of pitch, 13 in the case of intervals.

RESULTS

Table I gives the average scores of the practice and control groups when measured at the beginning of the study, at the end of training, and again after the elapse of a further period without training. Separate entries are made of performance on the original tests and on the augmented tests which were introduced after it became apparent during the course of training that the practice group could master more than was originally assigned.

· As was previously mentioned, all the subjects were not available for the retests given in October following a period of no training for either group. In view of this condition, two presentations of the results are given: First, the scores of all the children who were included in the experiment, with a parenthetic notation of the number of subjects included in the final retests; and second, a separate statement of the averages obtained when the 14 control subjects who were available for the final pitch retests and the 13 available for the interval retests are paired, as nearly as possible, on the basis of initial records, with a similar number of children of the practice group. The two entries are based on identical data, save that the first includes the records of a greater number of subjects.

The results shown in Table I indicate a substantial and statistically reliable advantage in favor of the practice group at the end of training. When retests were made after four months of no training the practice group was still well in the lead, both in pitch and intervals.

The periodic tests which were made during training present a general picture of the rate of improvement even though tests were not given at equal intervals. Table II shows the average scores obtained at various stages of practice. In the case of the interval tests, averages are given for 18 subjects, as compared with only 16 in Table I; the presentation of results of only 16 cases in the former case, as is previously explained, is due to lack of a sufficient number of control subjects.

The results in Table II show a steady increase in performance. As the average score increases, the relative variability tends to decline. This decline in variability, which was particularly marked on the final tests, largely results from the fact that the tests limited the maximum score that could be obtained. Several children correctly reproduced all the 18 notes and 22 intervals that were presented. (It is of interest, incidentally, that when 29 parents of the children here represented, 15 mothers and 14 fathers, were tested for pitch with no limit to the score, the 29 parents sang an average of about 20 notes as compared with an average of 15.5 notes sung by the three-year-old children when tested on a limited range of 18 notes.)

The benefit derived from training in this experiment was more pronounced and decidedly more permanent, relative to the performance of

Table I

Practice and Control Group Scores in Pitch and Intervals. Separate Entries of Average Scores (Number of Items Reproduced) of Original Tests and of Extended Tests Introduced During Course of Training. Age in Months as of January 1, 1931.

A second entry shows the average of 14 practice children matched as nearly as possible with the 14 controls who were available for the final pitch retests, and 13 similar pairs in the case of the interval tests. Average deviations are given in parentheses.

PITCH: ALL SUBJECTS

	N	C.A.	Initial Tests 11 notes (Dec. to Jan. '31)	Retest after 40 10-minute Practice Periods (May '31) Initial (11)	Extended (18)	N	After Period of No Training (Oct. '31) Initial	Extended
Practice Group	18	38.2 (3.7)	4.22 (2.44)	10.72 (0.11)	15.5 (1.78)	15	10.26 (0.76)	16.86 (1.0)
Control Group	18	40.1 (3.9)	4.22 (2.7)	6.44 (2.89)	8.0 (3.22)	14	7.0 (3.71)	10.21 (4.8)

INTERVALS: ALL SUBJECTS

	N	C.A.	Initial Tests (12 intervals) (Dec. to Jan. '31)	Retests after Training Initial (12)	Extended (22)	N	After Period of No Training, as Above Initial (12)	Extended (22)
Practice Group	16	38.7 (2.9)	4.25 (3.03)	11.5 (0.67)	17.0 (4.25)	15	11.4 (0.96)	19.0 (3.6)
Control Group	16	40.6 (3.7)	4.31 (2.89)	8.0 (2.5)	10.18 (4.26)	13	7.38 (3.59)	9.84 (3.8)

PITCH (14 Pairs)

	N	C.A.						
Practice Group	14	39.14 (3.2)	4.7 (3.0)	10.8 (2.5)	16.0 (1.6)		10.9 (.15)	16.8 (1.5)
Control Group	14	40.14 (4.0)	4.5 (3.2)	6.21 (2.8)	7.9 (3.2)		7.0 (3.4)	10.2 (4.8)

INTERVALS (13 Pairs)

	N	C.A.						
Practice Group	13	39.5 (3.1)	4.38 (3.5)	11.76 (0.48)	19.0 (2.9)		11.3 (1.1)	18.69 (3.9)
Control Group	13	42.0 (3.7)	4.46 (3.1)	7.61 (2.8)	9.0 (3.5)		7.4 (3.6)	9.8 (6.26)

the controls, than was anticipated by the investigator at the beginning of the study.

It is possible that the average would be different if mechanical devices rather than personal judgments had been used in the administration of the

Table II

Average Scores (and Average Deviations in Parentheses) on the Pitch and Interval Tests When Repeated at Various Times During Training

Separate averages are given for the extended tests used during the later stages of training.

PITCH

11 ascending notes from middle C to F			18 notes from G (below middle C) to C (2 octaves above middle C)		
Time of Test	N	Average No. of Notes Cor- rectly Sung	Time of Test	N	Average No. of Notes Cor- rectly Sung
December 1930 18		4.22 (2.44)			
January 1931 18		4.56 (2.90)			
February 1931 18		6.50 (3.33)			
March 1931 18		8.78 (2.00)	March	18	10.67 (2.78)
May 1931 18		10.72 (0.11)	May	18	15.50 (1.78)
October* 1931 15		10.26 (0.76)	October*	16	16.86 (1.00)

* After no training since May.

INTERVALS

Ascending and descending major and minor seconds and thirds, perfect fourths and fifths. Total: 12 intervals			12 intervals in left column plus major and minor sevenths and octaves. Total: 22 intervals		
Time of Test	N	Average No. Intervals Cor- rectly Sung	Time of Test	N	Average No. Intervals Cor- rectly Sung
December 1930 18		3.94 (3.05)			
January 1931 18		4.33 (2.89)			
February 1931 18		8.05 (2.61)			
March 1931 18		9.33 (2.33)	March	18	11.11 (3.44)
May 1931 18		11.56 (1.00)	May	18	17.44 (4.0)
October* 1931 15		11.4 (0.96)	October*	15	19.0 (3.6)

* After no training since May.

tests. The investigator is convinced, however, that even though different testing methods might have modified the averages, the general results would have been the same. This view is supported both by the measures of reliability which were obtained by the use of additional observers in this and a later study and by observations of the changes in individual children. Children who at the beginning of the study were unmistakably limited in their vocal range later essayed high and low tones quite beyond their original performance.

The results of a subsequent study in which the present experimenter's judgments were checked by three additional judges, all of whom took simultaneous and independent records during tests of 23 children, further strengthen the view that the results here set forth represent in general an authoritative and practical evaluation of the conditions which were being studied.

The figures in Table I show that during the summer vacation the discrepancy between the scores of the practice and control children was reduced to some extent. The former group maintained its score pretty well, while the latter improved upon some previous averages. The leveling tendency is rather slight, however, and the practice children still retain a distinct advantage.

There arises the question whether the improvement represents a fundamental change or merely the accelerated appearance of abilities which normally would develop at a later time. It is undoubtedly true that sooner or later, in the course of further experience and growth, most of the group would be able to achieve the average scores shown in the present results. Whether continued intensive training at this time might eventually raise the child's performance beyond anything that could be attained if training were postponed until later years, the data do not tell. Some observations made during the study do, however, offer certain suggestions.

The singing of some children at the beginning of the study was definitely confined to a restricted tonal area. One child's voice, for instance, was placed so low, both in singing and in daily speech, as to cause her mother some concern. As training progressed this child (as well as others similarly situated at the start) was able not only to essay the higher pitch range but also to reproduce specific high tones. During the course of training it sometimes happened that a child was able to sing a group of low notes and a group of high notes without being able to manage the notes between. The child's behavior had many of the earmarks of trial-and-error behavior. Through encouragement and example he was led to attempt tonal areas quite beyond his original repertory. Further vocal manipulation was necessary before he could reproduce a particular tone in this area. With additional exercise he was able to sing the particular tone without making a sliding approach. Still more vocal experimentation and exercise were required to bridge the gap between the high and low tones.

Observations of individual children indicated that the particular pitch range to which a child confined his singing and his speech may sometimes be largely a fortuitous matter rather than an expression of native capacity; further, that a child whose voice is persistently low or high or, to all appearances, capable only of monotones, may show radical improvement when patient training is given. It is possible that an early tendency to use only a limited tonal repertory may become intrenched as a fixed habit. If this is true, the value of early training is clear. According to this hypothesis, any attempt to increase the pitch range in later years may be rendered difficult because of a persistent habit of using only certain tones, somewhat in the same way that old speech habits interfere with the mastery of the accents of a foreign language.

The above statements do not imply that training at an early age increases capacity, on the one hand, or that lack of exercise causes deterioration of capacity through disuse. The view here set forth, partly on the basis of the quantitative results and of observations of individual children and partly on the basis of speculative premises, may be rephrased and summarized as follows: A child's tonal range often represents only a part of what he actually can produce, the particular tones which he employs may reflect the beginnings of vocal habit, originating in a more or less fortuitous manner; the development of proficiency in the use of a wide tonal range is similar in many ways to the acquisition of a new skill, requiring vocal manipulation and a trial-and-error approach to the production of new tones; by means of early training a child may be enabled to sing tones quite beyond his accustomed range; it is possible that early training may give the child a lasting advantage over other children, with similar original endowments, whose efforts to improve upon their accustomed ranges are not begun until a later age when old habits interfere with the establishment of new skill in the use of the voice.

VIII—BIOLOGICAL INFLUENCES UPON DEVELOPMENT

1 · Influence of Cortical Development Upon Early Behavior Patterns

MYRTLE MCGRAW

Reprinted from pages 27-36 of *The Neuro-muscular Maturation of the Human Infant*. New York: Columbia University Press, 1943, by permission of the publisher.

We are likely to think of growth as implying a progressive improvement in coordination or strength. The contribution of the following studies by McGraw lies in showing that certain early coordinations of infants, specifically suspending the body by the hands and engaging in swimming-like movements, actually deteriorate with age. Presumably this deterioration is due to the growth of the cerebral cortex, which inhibits some of the activities of the lower brain centers.

SUSPENSION GRASP BEHAVIOR

The ability to suspend the body weight by the force of hand grip on a rod is an infantile reaction which lends itself readily to numerical determinations. Simple stop-watch determinations of the time suspended provide values adequate to demonstrate the general course of development. This method was used in making 5,138 determinations on a group of children over a period of several years. The data were averaged over 10- or 20-day intervals during the first 300 days and over 200-day intervals thereafter. The trend of development during the first 300 days is shown by curves A in Figure 1. From these curves it is clear that the intensity of response tends to increase during the first 30 days, after which there is a gradual decline. Single-hand suspension is suppressed. Curves B in Figure 1 illustrate the course of development after the first 300 days. In general, suspension time is steadily increased. It might be said that the first 30 days represent an expansion in the development of nuclear centers governing this function. The subsequent decline probably corresponds to the onset of some inhibitory influence of cortical centers upon the activity of subcortical nuclei. Late, as illustrated in curves B, the ability recurs, but at this time under the dominance of the cerebral cortex. The general course of development is even more graphically illustrated by the logarithmic curve in Figure 2, which covers a period of eight years. The phenomenon manifests an in-

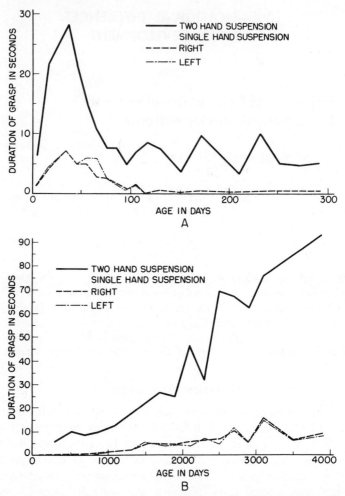

FIGURE 1. *The suspension time for the group of children: (A) suspension time averaged over 10-day intervals during the first four months and over 20-day intervals thereafter; (B) suspension time averaged over 200-day intervals after the age of three hundred days.*

crease in intensity during the first few weeks, followed by a period of progressive diminution in intensity of response. It reasserts itself as an activity under cortical control. The reflex phase is controlled by nuclear or subcortical centers; the decline or extinction of the powers of suspension is interpreted as an indication of development in cortical cells which exercise an inhibitory influence on subcortical functioning. The recurrence or re-enforcement of the ability to suspend the body is regarded as evidence of maturation in those cells which activate or control neuromuscular movements and of their integration with neural centers which govern other factors involved in deliberate performances.

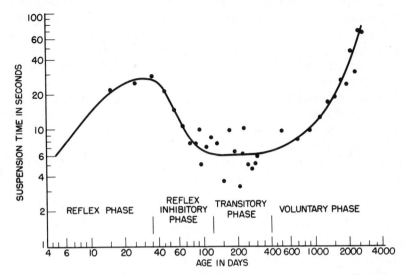

FIGURE 2. *Suspension time for the group of children plotted on a logarithmic scale against chronological age, showing the trend of suspension behavior for all ages to eight years.*

PROCEDURES WITH OTHER ACTIVITIES

Observations upon other neuromuscular functions of the infant were not so easily reduced to numerical values. However, observations were made and records were kept. It can be seen from the following accounts that the course of development of these more complex functions is not theoretically incompatible with the interpretations given to these simpler phenomena.

The procedure followed in studying other neuromuscular activities was fundamentally the same for each function. Observations were initiated immediately after birth of the baby or at the time of functional inception. Activities which were not a part of the newborn behavior repertoire could not be observed until some evidence of their emergence was indicated. Observations of each function in a number of children were made repeatedly until the activity attained a relative state of stability. Records were made on 16 mm. motion picture film or in protocols. Written descriptions were restricted to observable phenomena, with no attempt to inject interpretations. In addition to the sequential observations upon the group of children over a period of years, daily records were made of most of the performances of several babies in order to provide adequate longitudinal data of individual growth.

After the mass of data was accumulated, both the film and written records were analyzed for the purpose of selecting significant phases in the development of each function. In formulating the criteria for each phase of an activity it was realized that verbal descriptions of overt behavior only are not always adequate to differentiate voluntary from involuntary movements. That is, a report to the effect that an infant supported in an upright position engaged in progressive stepping movements does not distinguish stepping movements of the newborn infant from those which appear just prior to independent walking. Yet any moderately experienced observer can recognize the qualitative differences in such stepping. Furthermore, it was recognized that two babies may adopt movements which in pattern appear to be different but in fact reflect the same level of neural organization. For that reason a rationale based upon a theoretical interpretation of neural maturation was incorporated into the criteria formulated for appraising development in overt behavior.

Once the criteria were formulated for the phases of each function, it was possible to rate the many individual observations in accordance with developmental sequence. These ratings converted the descriptive data into a symbolic system so that the mass of data could be more easily manipulated. In making the ratings attention was focused upon those features common to the development of each function without specific regard for individual peculiarities. The method of rating was simple. A plus sign was ascribed to the phase most representative of the behavior as described or recorded on the film, and minus signs were assigned to other phases of the function. Because of the gradual process of growth a plus rating was on some occasions assigned to more than one phase in order to represent transitional periods more accurately. The number of phases in each function varied, as did also the number of observations, since some activities may attain relative stability within a few months, whereas the development of others extends over a period of years. A data sheet, after the ratings had been made on the observations of a particular child in a given function, is illustrated in Figure 3. Such a system of rating lends itself to the comparison of rates of development of different functions and also to an appraisal of an individual against a group of his contemporaries. However, our first concerns are the delineation of significant phases in the development of each function and a theoretical interpretation of the neural reorganization reflected in overt behavior. More specific correlation between structural and functional development must await further studies in neuroanatomy and neurophysiology; until these facts are available the organization of behavior data into a theoretical framework seems justifiable.

SWIMMING

After 445 observations of the aquatic behavior of 42 infants, ranging in age from eleven days to two and a half years, it became apparent that the significant developmental changes in such behavior could be conveniently classified into three phases, as follows:

Phase A, Reflex Swimming. When the newborn infant is submerged in

	AGE IN DAYS		PHASE								
NAME	OBSERVATION	MOVIES	A	B	C	D	E	F	G	H	I
BRIGGS, JAMES		2	+	−	−	−	−	−	−	−	−
	11		+	−	−	−	−	−	−	−	−
	18		+	−	−	−	−	−	−	−	−
	24		+	−	−	−	−	−	−	−	−
		30	+	+	−	−	−	−	−	−	−
	38		+	−	−	−	−	−	−	−	−
	44		+	−	−	−	−	−	−	−	−
	52		+	−	−	−	−	−	−	−	−
		62	+	+	−	−	−	−	−	−	−
	65		+	+	−	−	−	−	−	−	−
	74		−	+	−	−	−	−	−	−	−
	81		−	+	−	−	−	−	−	−	−
	89		+	+	−	−	−	−	−	−	−
		95	−	+	+	−	−	−	−	−	−
	102		−	+	−	−	−	−	−	−	−
	107		−	−	+	−	−	−	−	−	−
	118		−	+	+	+	−	−	−	−	−
		124	−	−	+	−	−	−	−	−	−
	128		−	−	+	−	−	−	−	−	−
	135		−	−	+	−	−	−	−	−	−
	142		−	−	+	−	−	−	−	−	−
	153		−	−	+	−	+	−	−	−	−
		156	−	−	−	+	−	−	−	−	−
	167		−	−	+	−	+	−	−	−	−
	170		−	−	+	−	+	−	−	−	−
	177		−	−	+	−	+	−	−	−	−
		186	−	−	−	+	+	+	−	−	−
	191		−	−	−	+	+	−	+	−	−
	193		−	−	−	−	−	+	−	−	−
	199		−	−	−	+	+	−	+	−	−
		202	−	−	−	+	+	+	−	−	−
		205	−	−	−	−	−	+	−	−	−
	213		−	−	−	−	−	+	+	−	−
	220		−	−	−	−	−	+	+	+	−
		221	−	−	−	−	−	+	+	−	−
	227		−	−	−	−	−	−	−	+	−
		229	−	−	−	−	−	−	+	−	−
		230	−	−	−	−	−	−	−	+	−
	235		−	−	−	−	−	−	+	+	−
		237	−	−	−	−	−	−	−	+	−
		243	−	−	−	−	−	−	−	+	−
		250	−	−	−	−	−	−	−	+	−

(table header spanning "PRONE PROGRESSION")

FIGURE 3. *Typical data sheet showing the ratings on one child in one activity during the first 250 days of life.*

a prone position the organization of neuromuscular activity is striking. The baby usually remains in the prone position; and definite rhythmical associated flexor-extensor movements in upper and lower extremities, together with a lateral flexion of the trunk corresponding to the flexor phase of the lower extremity, are usually manifested. These movements are ordinarily sufficiently forceful to propel the baby a short distance through the water. The movements involve the total musculature and are usually better organized than newborn crawling or stepping movements. Ingestion of water and coughing after removal from the water are less common among the reactions of the newborn than in older infants. Apparently some reflex still functions during the early weeks of life sufficiently to inhibit breathing efforts on the part of the submerged newborn infant. Line drawings A of Figure 4 illustrate the character and rhythmicity of reflex swimming movements. Since the cerebral cortex is not functioning appreciably at this time, it is reasonable to assume that these movements are under the control of subcortical nuclei.

Phase B, Disorganized Activity. After the first few months the rhythmicity and organization of pattern become somewhat dissipated when the infant is submerged in water. There follows a period when the baby tends to rotate from a prone to a dorsal position and movements of the extremities are of a struggling order. It may be that some awareness of the environment is expressed by the infant's bringing his hands to the water line on his face. Less control over the respiratory mechanisms is evidenced by coughing and the ingestion of water. Line drawings B of Figure 4 represent the character of movements commonly exhibited during this phase. This change in aquatic behavior seems to reflect the development of some neural mechanism which serves to disrupt the organization of reflex activity. During this period neither cortex nor subcortical nuclei function for the optimum benefit of the baby. It is a period of transition from reflex to a more voluntary type of activity.

FIGURE 4. *Three phases in the development of aquatic behavior of the human infant: (A) reflex swimming movements; (B) disorganized behavior; (C) voluntary or deliberate movements. These drawings were obtained by tracing successive frames of 16 mm. movie film illustrating the quality of consecutive movements made at different chronological or developmental stages.*

Phase C, Deliberate or Voluntary Movements. At about the time when independent walking develops, another change is exhibited in the aquatic behavior of the child. Again the baby tends to remain submerged in the prone position, to engage in flexor-extensor movements of the extremities, especially the lower extremities, and to propel the body through the water. The quality of these movements differs from the rhythmical movements of the newborn; they are more deliberate and apparently voluntary. The child is not merely fighting; he is making purposeful movements, fairly well organized, but less automatic than the reflex movements, in order to reach the edge of the pool. The nature of neuromuscular movements of this order are illustrated by line drawings C of Figure 4. The quality of the movements and the child's awareness of his environment indicate that the cerebral cortex is participating in the activity. It is not until much later that the child gains the ability to raise his head above the water level in order to breathe. There is reason to believe that unless swimming experience is continued at this time, these deliberate movements characteristic of the ambulatory child will be abandoned as the horizon for sensory experience and judgment expands.

After the observations were rated in accordance with the above criteria,

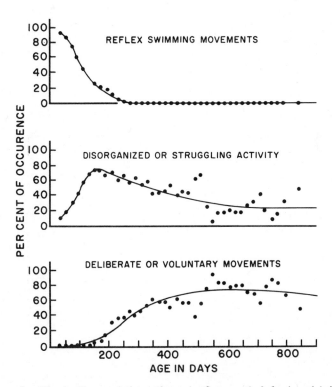

FIGURE 5. *The incidence of three phases in the aquatic behavior of infants.*

it was possible to calculate the developmental trend of each phase as demonstrated by the curves in Figure 5. Plus-minus ratings are too gross to demonstrate the rise in specificity of the reflex movements which occurs during the first three weeks or so of life. However, a greater variety of response becomes available as the cortex comes into play. To some extent it can be assumed that this variability of response is shown on the curve by the increase in scatter during the later age periods.

2 · Psychological Resemblances Between Identical Twins

ARNOLD GESELL AND HELEN THOMPSON

Reprinted from *Genetic Psychology Monographs*, 24 (1941), 7, 8, 31, 38, 47, 81, 82, and 89, by permission of The Journal Press.

No two human beings are more similar than a pair of identical twins. Dr. Arnold Gesell and his co-workers at Yale University studied a pair of twin girls for a period of fourteen years. They determined carefully their differences and identities, and, in addition, introduced experiments with one twin, using the other twin as a control for measuring the effects of the experiments. The excerpts quoted below are only a small sample from extensive reports of Dr. Gesell and his collaborators.

Twins *T* and *C* have several times appeared in the literature of child development as subjects of experimental study by the method of co-twin control. This is a method of comparative investigation in which one of two highly identical twins is used to define the differential effects of specified factors confined to the co-twin. In fact, *T* owes her pseudonym to the fact that she has served as the primarily trained or stimulated subject in the experimental studies, while *C* has served as the comparative control. She continues to serve as the basic twin for control reference even when she is secondarily or differentially trained for purposes of comparative investigation.

Through an exceptionally fortunate convergence of circumstances it has been possible to follow the development of these self-same twins from early infancy to puberty. The twins have remained ideal subjects for comparative study because their developmental opportunities have not been interrupted or distorted by any extreme illnesses or unusual events confined to one twin. For five years, while in the first to fifth grades, they attended different classrooms and came under the influence of different teachers, but otherwise their educational opportunities and avocational activities have remained substantially alike. During all these years they have maintained a friendly, interested, and cooperative relationship with the Yale Clinic of Child Development. This circumstance has facilitated detailed and intimate comparative estimates and has also enabled us to document their behavior with abundant motion picture records.

Emotional factors, which are extremely important in a long continuing biogenetic study, were kept under favorable control, due to the amiable temperament of the twins, their enjoyment of the experiences at the clinic, and the excellent cooperation of the parents, who appreciated the incidental guidance which was rendered. As already indicated, throughout these studies Twin T usually served as the primary trained twin. The circumstances and arrangements of the studies did not however result in any adverse kind of isolation of twin C. The social and personality factors surrounding the whole series of studies were kept in a natural equipoise.

In physical appearance the twins have been extremely similar from infancy to adolescence. Even persons who have had long contact with them occasionally mistake one for the other. It is hazardous to attempt to distinguish the twins on the basis of general appearance or even of general demeanor. It is safer to place reliance on a slight but discernible difference in a chin dimple or a tilt of the head, or a hair ribbon!

MOTOR TONICITY

In infancy T was slightly more advanced in postural activity than C. T was the first to roll over, to stand, to walk (13 days sooner), and to stand on one foot. In spite of this discrepancy, differences in postural attitudes were virtually indistinguishable. Similarity of facial expression appears repeatedly in the early photographic records.

As the twins grew older, a few differences in postural attitudes which are still characteristic became evident. C's face is the more relaxed; she has a dimple in her chin deeper than T's. T puckers her chin when smiling; and tends to hold her mouth slightly open while C holds hers closed. T tends to have a slightly more sober expression than C.

On the whole C maintains better and more symmetric body posture. T is likely to lower her head while C holds hers more erect.

In general T shows more body tension when posing for pictures. She is more likely than C to clench her dress or to assume a slightly stilted pose and expression. When body length (total reclining length) was measured the assistant always found that it was harder to hold T's feet against the anthropometric board.

In general T's nervous tension is more evident in the skeletal musculature, while C's nervous tension may express itself in the smooth muscle system. T is posturally more alert than C. C is more prone to gastric upset and had more difficulty than T in acquiring bowel and bladder control.

STAIR CLIMBING

The cinema records of stair-climbing performance proved to be well adapted for comparisons of motor tempo and speed. An experimental staircase of four treads was placed beside a crib, the platform of which formed a fifth tread. The staircase and a lure on the platform constituted an adequate stimulus for climbing behavior. The twins were tested both singly and together.

The comparative study of this behavior was begun at the age of 46 weeks when both twins were at a nascent stage for climbing. Prior to this time the development of postural behavior was very similar, with slight evidences of relative acceleration in Twin T. At 6 and 8 weeks, T was more active; at 36 weeks she wavered less in free sitting and showed a trifle more tendency to progress when prone; at 38 weeks she strained forward more in sitting and gave slightly more support when held standing; and at 40, 42, and 44 weeks T's performance in standing was a shade better than C's in self-support and balance. At 46 weeks there were no discernible differences. Each pulled herself to standing, stepped forward when both hands were held, and lifted one foot when placed before the staircase; but neither twin was able to place a foot or a knee on the first tread.

At this point in the twins' development, an experimental study was begun. Twin T was given a daily 10-minute practice period in stair climbing. At the end of six weeks, T could climb the steps in a little over 25 seconds while C did not yet progress further than putting the left knee on the first tread. T's training was discontinued at this time (age 52 weeks) and a week later C was given similar training. On the very first day of her training C scaled the steps seven times, a performance only approximated by T after three weeks of training and not surpassed until five and a half weeks of training. C's added seven weeks of maturity at the time of her training

Table I

Comparative Time in Terms of Cinema Frames Required to Climb Staircase

(Age 56 Weeks)

	T		C	
	1	2	1	2
Left foot on tread one	0	0	0	0
Right foot on tread one	23	23	24	24
Left foot on tread two	18	41	23	47
Right foot on tread two	17	58	23	70
Left foot on tread three	19	77	56	126
Right foot on tread three	19	96	26	152
Left foot on tread four	15	111	20	172
Right foot on tread four	17	128	11	183
Left knee on crib (five)	81	209	16	199
Right knee on crib (five)	13	222	24	223
Total time in seconds	13.8		13.9	

1. Number of frames from time one foot is in contact with step until other foot makes contact.
2. Frames from beginning of ascent until foot is in contact with tread.

was sufficient to offset T's slightly better postural control plus three weeks of practice. C's training continued for only two weeks.

At the end of this two-weeks training period, C (age 55 weeks) scaled the steps in 10.3 seconds; while T, age 52 weeks, at the end of six-weeks training, took 25.8 seconds, or twice as long. The average time to completely scale each tread was .84 seconds longer for T. One week later, when T and C were 56 weeks old, their performance on the experimental steps was remarkably alike.

RATE OF DEVELOPMENT

The comparative rate of mental growth in Twins T and C is reflected in the maturity ratings which were made on the basis of age norms. In infancy an allowance of two weeks was made for prematurity. Twenty-two developmental examinations and intelligence tests were made between the ages of 24 weeks and 13 years. The results are summarized in Table II.

A descriptive development quotient based on the adaptive behavior rating of the Yale schedules was assigned after each of the 14 examinations prior to six years. After this age a psychometric quotient was derived on the basis of the Stanford-Binet (1916 Revision).

Table II

Age of Twins	Twin T Approximate D.Q.	Twin C
24 weeks	75	75
28 weeks	75	75
32 weeks	75	75
36 weeks	75	75
40 weeks	80	80
44 weeks	75	75
48 weeks	80	80
52 weeks	80	80
62 weeks	80	80
80 weeks	80	80
2 years	85	85
3 years	90	85
4 years	90	90
5 years	95	95
	I.Q.	
6 years	103	100
7 years	100	97
8 years	104	97
9 years	101	97
10 years	87	88
11 years	92	92
12 years	90	90
13 years	89	85

There is a rather wide range of variations from D.Q. 80 at one year to a maximum of I.Q. 104 at eight years, with a recession to 85-90 at 13 years. The quotient range 85-90 is fairly descriptive of the intellectual level of the twins. The fluctuations in the quotients were closely parallel at all ages. The divergence never exceeded seven quotient points. On 16 examinations the quotient ratings were identical.

RESPONSE TO TRAINING AND HOME ENVIRONMENT

T and C received no consistently different treatment up to the age of 46 weeks. They were first in a hospital and then in a child care institution. As normal, healthy, attractive twins they were each given more than ordinary attention, but neither appeared to be favored. In fact, as infants they were so easily confused that if we had not had their palm prints we fear that in some unguarded moment they might have been confused. The nursery used adhesive tape encircling the wrist of Twin T for identification purposes.

Just prior to 46 weeks of age, T and C were both isolated from their ward mates due to a mild infection. T was released sooner than C. While C continued her solitary isolation for a brief period, T was returned to the nursery. T, moreover, daily received 20 minutes of individual attention while she was trained (by H.T.) in stair climbing and cube play, an arrangement which continued for six weeks. That T responded to this special attention was shown by the fact that T's responses to H.T. became so vivid that it was possible to distinguish T from her co-twin "by the outgoing gestures of social greeting." (Although H.T. has been deliberately impartial to the twins, T still elects H.T. when choosing a partner.)

C's delayed training at the age of 53 weeks was only 10 minutes in length as opposed to 20; and was continued for only two weeks. However, even during this short period C became socially so responsive that on occasion T and C were mistaken for one another. During this experiment although the twins were at times equally responsive, T continued to be more outgoing, more vivid and more reactive in social situations than C, particularly with reference to H.T.

At the age of 26 months the twins were taken home, where their newly acquired stepmother, unfamiliar with small children, had difficulty with discipline. T became prankish and received more punishment while C was favored and pointed to as the model. C was talked to more and was also held more often in the lap. On advice, the mother became less discriminating but has continued to favor C.

When T and C were eight years old, a half-sister was born. Neither child showed any evidence of jealousy. C was more communicative about the sister and referred to her accomplishments as she developed more than did T. It is C to whom the sister goes when in trouble and it is C who can more easily quiet her. As the twins grew older, it was T who preferred to stay overnight or spend the weekend with her grandmother or aunt, while C preferred to stay at home and help care for the young sister.

While it is C who talks about her sister, and tells of their grandmother's illness and death, it is T who answers factual questions.

A recent report of the twins' home behavior was given as follows by the stepmother: C has more patience than T with their younger sister. The sister will always go to C rather than to T. In the home C is the more sympathetic, more affectionate, and more obedient. C made a crocheted lace cover for the table; T started to crochet a wool afghan but tired of making it and showed her mother how it could be finished. At home T spends more time reading than does C. T appropriates the Sunday paper.

Both twins belong to the 4-H Club and are equally proficient at their dressmaking and cooking tests, but it C who helps T with an intricate or dextrous bit of sewing. Clearly it is C who fits into the home better than T, while it is T who finds her greater interest outside the home.

INTER-TWIN DOMINANCE

Whenever two or more are gathered together, the problem of rivalry and dominance emerges. This is true even of twins as alike as T and C. In this pair the similarity is so thoroughgoing that the equipoise is almost perfectly symmetrical. Rivalry and dominance are lost in reciprocal imitativeness and mutual adaptation. Dominance is subtle and inconspicuous. Even persons well acquainted with the twins arrive at their judgment reflectively and not very emphatically. A table of judgment as to dominance follows (Table III).

Table III

Age of Twins in years	Judgment by	Comment
2½	M.P.	"C's attitude more dominating."
3	G.H.	"C is the more aggressive and the more talkative; domineering would not be the word for she is too quietly dictatorial in her manner."
4⅔	Mother	"C dominates T."
6	A.G.	"If anything C was the dominant twin."
8	Teacher	"C is the leader."
10	M.M.	"If either twin takes the lead I would be inclined to say it was C."
12	O.	"C is the dominant twin."
12½	Mother	"T always waits for C to start."
13	H.T.	"C presents herself for measurement first."

Although the degree of dominance is very slight, it is significant that all judgments without exception point to C as the dominant twin. There is, actually, a great deal of "give and take" between T and C. It should be noted that it is T, not C, who gives the cue in tap dancing, and it is T who manages their community purse, and it is T who is less confused about directions. Yet in spite of this it is C, the more social child, who appears to dominate her otherwise more able twin.

3 · Resemblances Between Identical Twins Reared Apart

ROBERT S. WOODWORTH

Reprinted from pages 1, 3, 4, 21-26, and 29-30 of *Heredity and Environment*. New York: Social Science Research Council, 1941, by permission of the author and the publisher.

Identical twins have identical genes. Therefore, any differences between two identical twins are due to environmental influences such as birth injury and disease, or to differences in education and social environment. It is of particular interest, therefore, to study identical twins who have been reared in different environments. They show us, in effect, how the same individual develops under two sets of circumstances. No other situation can provide such information.

Nothing is more certain, after a little consideration, than the statement that heredity and environment are co-acting factors in the development of any living individual and that both are absolutely essential. If the individual's hereditary potencies could somehow be annulled he would immediately lose all physiological and mental characteristics and would remain simply a mass of dead matter. If he were somehow deprived of all environment, his heredity potencies would have no scope for their activity and, once more, he would cease to live. To ask whether heredity or environment is more important to life is like asking whether fuel or oxygen is more necessary for making a fire. But when we ask whether the *differences* between human individuals or groups are due to their differing heredity or to differences in their present and previous environments, we have a genuine question and one of great social importance. In a broad sense both heredity and environment must be concerned in causing individuals to be different in ability and personality, but it is a real question whether to attach more importance to the one or the other and whether to look to eugenics or euthenics for aid in maintaining and improving the quality of the population.

TWINS

Though the investigation of human heredity is beset with difficulties, due in part to the long interval between generations and in part to the lack of well-controlled matings such as are used by the geneticist in his experi-

394

ments on plants and animals, enough is known to justify the carrying over of certain fundamental laws and concepts. We know that certain human traits are dominant, and certain others recessive. We know that certain triats are genetically simple, and many others complex. We know, too, that in any mixed population—and every human population is decidedly mixed in comparison with the "pure lines" of the geneticist—it is practically impossible for two matings of the same parents, even, to result in offspring having the same heredity. The chromosomes of the parents are combined differently in their several children. The same parents can produce a considerable variety of children. though the variety is not so great as it is in the population as a whole.

But it sometimes happens that a pair of twins comes from a single fertilized ovum, that is, from a single ovum fertilized by a single spermatazoon. The embryo in this case, after starting life as a single individual, divides at a very early stage of development and gives rise to two individuals. Now as all daughter cells derived from the same fertilized ovum have exactly the same assortment of genes, the two (or sometimes more) individuals derived from the same fertilized ovum are exactly alike in genic constitution. They are truly identical as far as heredity is concerned. They are often indistinguishable in appearance. They are necessarily of the same sex. These "identical" or monozygotic twins thus afford perfect material for the study of the differentiating effects of environment. Since they are genetically identical any difference which develops between them must be due to some sort of environmental factor.

The remaining twins, called fraternal or dizygotic, are derived from two different eggs or ova, fertilized by two different spermatozoa. Genetically they are no more alike than other siblings. Being conceived and born at the same time does not make them any more alike in heredity. But their environment, both prenatal and postnatal, must on the whole be more alike than that of other siblings.

IDENTICAL TWINS REARED APART

The first pair of separated identicals to be tested and carefully studied was that reported by H. J. Muller (1925). The principal series of such pairs was gathered with much labor over a period of years by the Chicago group, Newman, Freeman and Holzinger, and reported in their book on *Twins* (1937). They discovered, measured, and tested 19 pairs of identicals who had been separated in infancy or early childhood and reared in different families and communities. Another pair has been added by Gardner and Newman (1940). And a British pair, reared apart up to the age of nearly ten years, has been studied by Saudek (1934). Diagnosis of monozygosity was carefully made in all these cases.

Table I presents certain data for each of the separated identicals. With regard to prenatal and natal environment, the case histories of the pairs numbered 1 and 8 suggest the possibility that the twin with lower IQ in each of these pairs got a poor start and perhaps suffered a slight but permanent handicap.

For the most part the environment in which the twins of the same pair were brought up did not differ extremely—not more than would be true of children brought up in the same community. In a few instances the difference was rather large. The greatest difference in education occurred

Table I

Some Data from Identical Twins Reared Apart (Newman, Freeman and Holzinger; Muller; Gardener and Newman; Saudek)

Case Number	Sex	Age at Separation	Age at Testing	Environmental Differences			IQ Difference
				in Years of Schooling	in Estimated Educational Advantages	in Estimated Social Advantages	
11	f	18 mos.	35	14	37	25	24
2	f	18 mos.	27	10	32	14	12
18	m	1 yr.	27	4	28	31	19
4	f	5 mos.	29	4	22	15	17
12	f	18 mos.	29	5	19	13	7
1	f	18 mos.	19	1	15	27	12
17	m	2 yrs.	14	0	15	15	10
8	f	3 mos.	15	1	14	32	15
3	m	2 mos.	23	1	12	15	− 2
14	f	6 mos.	39	0	12	15	− 1
5	f	14 mos.	38	1	11	26	4
13	m	1 mo.	19	0	11	13	1
10	f	1 yr.	12	1	10	15	5
15	m	1 yr.	26	2	9	7	1
7	m	1 mo.	13	0	9	27	− 1
19	f	6 yrs.	41	0	9	14	− 9
16	f	2 yrs.	11	0	8	12	2
6	f	3 yrs.	59	0	7	10	8
9	m	1 mo.	19	0	7	14	6
Muller	f	1 mo.	30	9	?	?	− 1
Gardner and Newman ..	f	1 mo.	19	0	2	?	− 3
Saudek	m	1 mo.	20	0	?	?	± 4

The estimated differences in educational and social advantages are in "points" with a maximum possible of 50. From the case material, each of five judges rated the environmental differences between every pair of twins on a scale of 10 points, and the figure given in the table is the sum of these five ratings. A minus sign before an IQ difference means that the twin who received the higher rating for educational advantages obtained the lower IQ.

in the case of two girls, one of whom was reared in a good farming region and who went through college and became a school teacher, while her twin grew up largely in the backwoods and had only two years of regular schooling. This girl however obtained employment later in a large city and became a general assistant in a small printing office where she performed a variety of duties including typesetting and proofreading. On being tested her IQ came out at 92, while that of her college-educated twin sister was 116. This difference of 24 points in IQ was the largest found in any case.

Another pair of young women had been separated in infancy and one had been reared on a good farm and had gone to school only for the eight grades, while the other had lived in a small town, gone through high school, studied music, and engaged in clerical work. The town girl's IQ as determined by the test was 106 while the farm girl made only 89. In spite of this large difference in the tests the country girl gave the impression of being fully as intelligent, or competent, as her twin sister.

A pair of young men from Tennessee had been brought up, the one in a small town where he went through high school and engaged in business, the other back in the mountains with irregular schooling amounting to eight grades at the most. Tested at the age of twenty-five, the mountain boy obtained an IQ of 77, the town boy of 96.

TREATMENT OF DATA

There are two main ways of treating the data from separated identicals. The more obvious way is to compare them with identical twins reared together, as can be done either by comparing the mean difference between twins in the one class with the corresponding difference in the other class, or by comparing the correlation between the paired individuals in the two classes. Either method is essentially a study of intrapair variance. The difference has to be taken without plus or minus sign, because in the identicals reared together there is no known differentiating factor to give either twin a distinctive place in the pair. Because the intrapair difference is taken without sign, it needs to be corrected for the chance error of observation.

The other way of treating the data is to look for environmental factors that might differentiate the members of a separated pair and to determine whether a given factor has produced a significant difference between the favored and the disfavored twins taken as a group. For example, if it can be seen that one twin has received better educational advantages than the other, in each pair we can determine whether there is a significant difference in IQ in favor of the better educated twins. Here each difference has a sign, plus or minus, and the average difference (account being taken of the signs) does not need to be corrected for chance errors of observation. It is important to notice this distinction between the two methods of treatment. Suppose the mean difference between identicals to be 5 points

IQ; this difference does not exceed the error of observation and therefore does not indicate any true difference. But suppose, in a sample of identicals reared apart, the better educated twin averages 5 points higher in IQ than the other. This may be a significant difference (given an adequate sample), for the chance errors of observation would not favor either class of twins as against the other class.

Taken without regard to sign, the average IQ difference between separated identicals is 7.6 points. Correction for chance errors of observation would bring this difference down to 6 points net, a figure to be compared with the estimated net difference of 3 points between identicals reared together, and of 15 points or more between children paired at random from the same community. It is probable, then, that environment did make these separated twins differ in tested intelligence, though not to any such extent as obtains among the children of a community.

When the IQ differences are averaged with account taken of sign, the twin having the advantage in educational opportunities usually surpasses the other. On the average the IQ was 6.0 points higher for the better educated twin. This difference is statistically reliable, being over three times its standard error. It seems safe to conclude that when one of a pair of identicals has been afforded better educational advantages than the other, the better educated one will on the whole do better in the intelligence tests.

However, there were only six pairs differing very much in the amount of formal schooling received. These six show an average difference of 13 points in IQ. The remaining pairs show only a small and unreliable IQ superiority for the better educated twin (3 points on the average, and only 1 point when the two cases of possible prenatal handicap are omitted). It appears, then, that rather a large educational advantage is required to give any dependable superiority in tested intelligence.

Years of schooling are of course not an adequate measure of educational advantages. Newman (1937) and his colleagues endeavored to do a little better by going over the case histories of their 19 pairs and estimating the educational difference between the twins by aid of a rating scale. The ratings are given in our table. There is a correlation of + .79 between the estimated educational difference and the obtained difference in IQ. This substantial correlation depends largely but not wholly upon the few pairs whose education was very unequal.

CONCLUSIONS FROM THE TWIN STUDIES

If we consider the results on the intelligence of identical twins reared apart, two conclusions seem probable even though the sample is still far too small to make either conclusion sure. In the first place, radical differences in education can create substantial differences in intelligence, so far as intelligence is measured by our tests. Differences in IQ as great as the standard deviation of the population have been found in several instances, corresponding to large differences in educational advantages. We can conclude that the educational environment, taken in a broad sense, has a marked effect on such intelligence as we are now able to measure.

In the second place, however, the differences between identical twins reared apart are remarkably small except in those cases where the contrast of educational advantages was very great. For the majority of the separated identicals the IQ difference was no greater than for identicals reared together. When individuals of identical heredity are subjected to environments differing about as much as those of the children in an ordinary community, such identical twins differ much less than the children of such a community. Therefore the differences found among the children of an ordinary community are not accounted for, except in small measure, by differences in homes and schooling. To repeat—if the differences in intelligence found among the children of a community were mostly due to differences in home and school environment, these differences would remain almost in full force even if the heredity of all the children were made identical. But when a trial is made of this hypothesis by placing identical twins in different families not too different in environment, the twins show only a small fraction of the difference found in the community at large.

These two statements—(1) that differences in environment can produce substantial differences in intelligence, and (2) that the differences actually present in a community are *not* due mostly to differences in environment—may appear mutually contradictory. That they are not contradictory has been emphatically pointed out by several students of the nature-nurture problem.

References

Gardner, I. C., and H. H. Newman, "Mental and Physical Traits of Identical Twins Reared Apart, Case XX," *Journal of Heredity*, 31 (1940), 119-126.

Muller, H. J., "Mental Traits and Heredity," *Journal of Heredity*, 16 (1925), 433-448.

Newman, H. H., F. N. Freeman, and K. J. Holzinger, *Twins: a Study of Heredity and Environment*, pp. 369. Chicago: University of Chicago Press, 1937.

Saudek, R., "A British Pair of Identical Twins Reared Apart," *Character & Personality*, 3 (1934), 17-39.

4 · The Nature of Improvement Resulting from Practice

A. I. GATES AND G. A. TAYLOR

Abridged from the *Journal of Educational Psychology*, 16 (1925), 583-593, by permission of the authors and the publisher.

Most performances of the child "improve" as he becomes older. Is this because of increasing age or because of practice? It can readily be shown that practice improves performance, but does this practice result in any permanent advantage? This is the problem of the present study.

THE PLAN OF THE EXPERIMENT

The present experiment was designed to test, in some measure, the nature of improvement in a mental function. For this purpose, it seemed advisable to use as subjects persons in whom growth was by no means completed and in whom growth was going on, presumably, with great rapidity and a mental function which had been little practiced and in which, presumably, the acquisition of technique would be of rather small amount. After some preliminary study, we selected as subjects a group of children, ages four years to five years, eight months, from the kindergarten of the Horace Mann School and as a function, memory for series of digits presented orally. Since this function constitutes one of the recurring tests in the Stanford-Binet scale, the results should throw some light upon the nature of the functions which are accepted as criteria of intelligence.

The experimental procedure called for two groups of subjects equivalent in abilities related to memory for digits, one of which was to be trained intensively and the other tested only at the beginning and end of the practice period. From a larger group of children, two groups were made up by matching each child in one group with a child in the other as nearly as possible the same in each of the following traits:

1. Sex
2. Age
3. Mental age on the Stanford-Binet test
4. Intelligence Quotient
5. Scholastic maturity as judged by teachers
6. Memory for digits, presented orally
7. Memory for letters, series presented orally

8. Memory for series of unrelated words, presented orally

9. Memory for series of related words, presented orally

10. Memory for a series of 10 geometrical figures, each presented visually for 5 seconds. After all were presented, a test of the recognition type—originals mixed with new designs—was given. Tests were given to pupils individually.

11. Memory for seven pictures—boy, hat, cap, and so on presented visually on a card strip for 15 seconds. Test by recognition method. All tests given individually.

12. Memory for picture "names." A series of 10 drawings of common objects with its common name under it in type. Task is to learn the "name" of each picture. Each card is presented 5 seconds: test by selecting words studied from a group including the old and new ones. Individual tests.

Two groups of 16 pupils, approximately matched in these traits and abilities, completed the experiment. The averages of these groups in the measurable traits are shown in Table I. It may be seen in the table that, in

Table I

Showing Average Scores of Practice and Control Groups in the Initial Test

Traits	Age* Oct. 1	MA* Oct. 1	IQ	Memory Digits	Memory Letters	Memory Unrelated Words	Memory Related Words	Geometrical Figures	Pictures	Picture Names
Practice group	5.1	6.31	122	4.33	3.64	3.86	14.0	4.3	5.3	7.5
Control group	5.1	6.35	123	4.33	3.71	4.07	13.7	4.0	5.7	7.0

* Age and mental age as of October 1, two months before the study was begun.

the averages, the two groups are substantially equivalent at the beginning of the experiment in the important traits taken into consideration.

THE RESULTS OF SPECIFIC PRACTICE IN MEMORY FOR DIGITS

Beginning shortly after the completion of the initial tests, the pupils in one group were given, individually, on each available school day, practice in immediate memory for digits. A large number of series of digits, arranged by chance, were prepared and presented according to the method prescribed in the Stanford-Binet scale. Each day, the pupil began with a series shorter than the largest one on which he had succeeded in two out of three trials on the preceding day. Each child, then, on each day was tested on three series of each length from a short series to a series on which he failed in two out of three attempts. The results are based on the number of digits in the largest series in which the subject was successful in two out of three attempts. In the group of 16 from which the averages were computed, all attended fairly regularly. In the case of absences, the pupil was given the score earned on the preceding test. The training was continued until May 20, the end of the school year, 78 days of practice.

The trained group progressed steadily from an initial score of 4.33 to a final average score of 6.40 digits—a gain of 2.07 digits. In the Stanford-Binet scale, 4 digits is placed at year four, and 6 at year ten. The practice group, then, advanced during a period of 4.5 months during which they practiced on 78 days, an amount equal to that which the average untrained child advances in approximately six years.

The control group was given the test on the first and last of the 78 days. The average score on the first test was 4.33 and on the last, 5.06, a gain of 0.73 digits. The gain of the practice group is appreciably greater than that of the untrained group.

THE INFLUENCE OF DISUSE ON IMPROVEMENTS

The problem, now, is to determine whether the improvement in the case of the trained group is due entirely to acquired techniques in handling digits and adjusting to the test conditions, or partly or wholly due either to the improvement of capacities underlying immediate memory for digits by some direct means or to capacities improved indirectly by a stimulation of growth, or to both. We therefore decided to apply, as one means of discovering the character of the improvement, a test of the influence of disuse.

One October 10, 1924, approximately four and a half months after the final practice day in May—a period approximately equal in length to the practice period—14 pairs of the original group of 16 pairs were found and tested. The results for the two groups were as follows:

Table II

	Practice Group	Control Group
Average score, initial tests, 12/20/23	4.36	4.41
Average score, final test, 5/20/24	6.36	5.08
Gain, during period of practice	2.00	0.67
Average score, test after disuse, 10/10/24	4.71	4.77
Gain over initial test	0.35	0.36

This result is most significant. While the practice group at the end of four and a half months of training excelled the control group by an appreciable amount—an amount equal to about six years of average growth according to the Stanford scale—after four and a half months of disuse, the advantage has been lost completely, the two groups were as nearly equal as they were at the beginning of the study.

As we see it, the experiment indicates that in the case of memory for oral digits among these children, at least, improvement brought about by four and a half months of practice, while appreciable, is due not to capacity increased directly or indirectly by means of accelerated growth but exclusively to the acquisition of technique. What constitutes technique, the experiment does not disclose. The factors may be better habits of attention under test condition, adaptation to the examiner's signals and voice, the elimination of strain or anxiety, or more subtle devices utilized in keeping the digits in mind, in seeing relations among them, in visualizing them or whatnot. Whatever they may be, the study indicates that they are rather unstable at least in the sense that all the skills and mnemonic devices acquired were lost during an equal period of disuse.

Another fact also suggests that the techniques were unstable. The tests in October 1924 were given by a different—but skillful—experimenter from the one who gave the earlier tests. As shown in Table II, the average scores of both groups in the last test were smaller than those obtained four and a half months before although somewhat better than those of the initial tests ten months earlier. The suggestion is that improvement brought about by practice consists in part of adaptations to the voice, mannerisms, and features of the test technique of the examiner.

RESULTS FROM THE SERIES OF TRANSFER TESTS

As a further check upon the nature of improvement, the series of memory tests, given before practice in digits was begun, were repeated in October 1924. The results of these tests are shown in Table III.

Table III

Showing the Initial (I) and Final (F) Scores and Gains (G) in Several Tests of Memory for the Practice and Control Groups

	Letters	Unrelated Words	Related Words	Geometrical Figures	Pictures	Picture Names
Practice I	3.64	3.86	14.0	4.3	5.3	7.5
Group F	4.11	3.86	16.2	4.9	6.8	9.0
G	0.47	0	2.2	0.6	1.5	1.5
Control I	3.71	4.07	13.7	4.0	5.7	7.0
Group F	4.28	3.93	17.2	5.2	6.7	8.8
G	0.57	0.14	3.5	1.2	1.0	1.8
Difference in favor of practice group	—0.10	0.14	—1.2	—0.6	0.5	0.3
PE difference	0.30	0.25	1.8	0.4	0.6	0.7

The differences in gain between the two groups are inappreciable; each group shows in about half of the tests a slight but really unreliable superiority such as should occur if the groups were substantially equal. There is, in other words, no evidence that the prolonged training with digits has brought about any permanent improvement in immediate memory for other materials.

RESULTS FROM A SECOND PERIOD OF PRACTICE

After reviewing the results of the "retention tests," that is, those given after the interval of disuse, the fact that they were not extensive led us to decide to give a longer series, a series which really amounted to another practice or "relearning" period.

Eleven of the originally trained pupils, all that were available, were matched as nearly as possible in sex, age, mental age, intelligence quotient, and memory for digits, with 12 others, 8 of whom were members of the original control squad. A comparison of the two groups is given in Table IV.

Table IV

Averages for the Two Groups in January 1925

	Age	MA	IQ	Digits
Original practice group	6.34	8.1	128	4.73
Unpracticed group	6.46	8.2	126	4.83

Beginning January 27, 1925—13½ months after the beginning of the study, 8 months after the end of the practice period, and 3½ months after the "retention" tests—both squads of children were given 22 days of practice in memory for digits somewhat more intensive than before. Each child was given three series of digits from lengths well within his grasp to a length of which he missed two or three times in three trials. This procedure was repeated three times on each day, that is, nine series of each length. The scores used for securing the averages were the number of digits in the longest series on which the subject succeeded in two-thirds or more of the trials. These exercises were conducted by two experienced examiners —each taking half of each group—who had given none of the earlier tests to these pupils.

The results, in terms of the average daily scores for the 22 practice days are shown in Table V.

Table V shows essentially equal improvement for the two groups. There is no evidence that the 78 days of training which ended 8 months earlier had brought about any improvement in the fundamental capacity underlying memory for digits either in some direct way or, indirectly, by the stimulation of growth of these capacities.

Table V

Average Daily Scores in Memory for Digits

Day	1	2	3	4	5	6	7	8	9
Practice group	4.73	4.82	5.00	4.82	4.73	4.82	4.91	5.09	4.82
Unpracticed group	4.83	4.83	4.93	4.93	4.93	5.00	4.93	5.17	5.00

Day	10	11	12	13	14	15	16	17	18
Practice group	5.27	5.27	5.18	5.36	5.27	5.45	5.18	5.36	5.54
Unpracticed group	5.25	5.33	5.33	5.25	5.42	5.50	5.58	5.66	5.66

Day	19	20	21	22	Day 22–Day 1
Practice group	5.54	5.73	5.63	5.73	1.00
Unpracticed group	5.75	5.83	5.92	5.92	1.09

SUMMARY

The main facts produced by the experiment are as follows:

1. Practice in immediate memory for digits on each of 78 days during a period of four and a half months by young children results in a marked gain in ability.

2. A group of children of equal ability in memory for digits and in sex, age, mental age, IQ, and in other forms of memory who were given no practice were, when tested at the end of the practice period, better than at the beginning but clearly inferior to the practice group.

3. After four and a half months of no practice, the two groups were again equal—the practice group had entirely lost its advantage. They were also equal in tests of immediate memory for other materials.

4. After three and a half more months without practice, both groups were given 22 days of intensive training at the end of which the two groups were still approximately equal. There was no evidence of any permanent effects of the 78 days of practice found.

The facts, we interpret as follows: The improvement brought about by specific practice is due to the acquisition of special and subtle techniques of work, to adjustments to the test conditions, familiarity with digits—to acquired information and specific methods of attack. These special techniques and mnemonic aids seem to be unstable and transitory inasmuch as after four and a half months of disuse they had disappeared.

Since the effects of the intensive training are so evanescent and since no permanent results of any kind favoring the practice group were found, the conclusion suggested is that training, under the conditions of the study, produced no increase in the capacities which underlie the function either in some direct way, or indirectly, by means of the stimulation of growth. The improvement brought about by practice seemed to be wholly in the form of devices, information, adjustments to the test conditions, "tricks of the task."

The demonstrated unstable and transitory character of improvement in memory for digits indicates the desirability of obtaining, in other studies of similar skills, a measure of the permanence of the improvement brought about by practice. Are the well-known increases in efficiency in memorizing poetry and prose, in solving verbal and mechanical problems, in rate of reading of several types which are usually rapidly produced by specific practice as evanescent as the improvement secured in this study? Or, is such instability peculiar to but few functions or is it a unique characteristic of the learning of very young children? The present material, so far as we know, gives no satisfactory answers to these questions.

5 · Physical Maturity of Boys as Related to Behavior

MARY COVER JONES AND NANCY BAYLEY

Abridged from the *Journal of Educational Psychology*, 41 (1950), 129-148, by permission of the senior author and the publisher; and *Child Development*, 28 (1957), 113-128, by permission of Dr. Jones and the Society for Research in Child Development.

Some of the most striking differences among individuals arise from their reaching physical maturity at different ages. At each age between eleven and eighteen years some boys may be small, underdeveloped, and sexually immature, whereas others may be fully grown, deep-voiced, and sexually mature. As the later-developing boys achieve maturity, these differences tend to disappear. The two studies which comprise this section follow some very early maturing and some very late maturing individuals over a considerable period of time. Psychological differences in adolescence (Part I) and in adulthood (Part II) are assessed. As the present section shows, there are differences in behavior between very early maturing and very late maturing boys. However, the interpretation of this finding is complicated by the fact that not only do they differ biologically, but the treatment accorded to them by their peers, their parents, and others also depends upon their physical appearance.

PART I

The problems of adjustment which are usually attributed to the adolescent period center around the youth's need to develop heterosexual interests, to select a vocation, and, in general, to acquire the status of adulthood in the eyes of his peers and of his elders. The impetus for the attainment of independent and mature status is undoubtedly related to the adolescent's physical changes, but the process of growing up is so complex and so interwoven with cultural factors that we have not yet been able to demonstrate more than a rather general relationship between physical and psychological phases of development.

It is well known that children mature at different rates, and reach the period of pubescence at different chronological ages. The present report deals with two groups of boys who fall at opposite ends of a normal sample distributed on the basis of one developmental characteristic (skeletal age). In an attempt to find differentiating behavior characteristics, statistical comparisons of the two groups have been made.

There are several ways in which children's physical maturity status may be expressed. One of the most commonly used for girls, is the age of menarche. As a possibly comparable measure for boys, some investigators have used the age of appearance of pubic or of axillary hair. Height and weight have also been used as an index of physical maturity, although maturity differences may be obscured by genetic differences in measurements of gross body dimensions. This difficulty is avoided by the use of skeletal age norms, from x-rays of the long bones of the hand and knee. Skeletal age has the advantage of being a stable and reliably assessed indicator of physical maturity, closely related to other aspects of physical maturing, and applicable at all ages from birth to young adulthood.

Physical Characteristics of the Early- and Late-Maturing Groups

The selection of contrasting extreme groups for the present study was on the basis of physical maturity assessments by the Todd standards for hand and knee. The groups included sixteen boys who were most consistently accelerated and sixteen who were most consistently retarded during the four and a half years for which we had cumulative skeletal x-rays, beginning at an average age of fourteen years. The total distribution from which these extremes were truncated consisted of ninety cases, a normal sample of boys in an urban public school system.

Figure I presents the comparative maturity assessments of the two groups at two age levels; each dot or circle indicates the skeletal age for an individual case.

On the average, the physically accelerated and the physically retarded

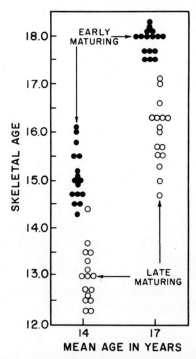

FIGURE 1. *Skeletal maturity assessments of early- and late-maturing individuals, at ages 14 and 17.*

boys are of the same age, but are separated by about two years in skeletal age (the criterion variable). Although some overlapping can be noted in the height of individual children at each age, the means of the groups are widely different. Even as early as eleven years all of the late-maturing are shorter than the mean for the early-maturing.

The boys who matured late were relatively very small from thirteen to fifteen years. In agreement with Bayley's study of body build in relation to skeletal maturing, they were characteristically slender built and long legged at all ages. Furthermore, their strength tests show them to have been relatively weak at the ages when they were lagging in size, and their scores in the tests of athletic ability were in most instances below average. The early-maturing boys, on the other hand, were usually large, broad-built and strong, and tended to show good athletic skill throughout the period of our records. Their superiority in strength and physical skills was greatest at ages thirteen to fifteen, when their early growth spurt accentuated their differences in size as compared with the slower-growing average and late-maturing boys.

Social Behavior in Boys' Groups

The psychological records examined in connection with the present study include both observational measures and reputation scores. We shall present first the ratings made independently by three staff members when the boys were in small groups (usually six) in a same-sex "free play" situation. These will be referred to as ICW (Institute of Child Welfare) ratings. The observations and ratings were concerned, in general, with social behavior and personal attributes which are important in social relationships.

The ratings have been converted into standard scores in which 50 represents the mean of the total group, with an SD of ten points. The direction and the degree of a child's deviation from the mean of his group are thus expressed in such a way that comparisons can readily be made between accelerated and retarded subgroups.

Figures 2, 3, and 4 present cumulative standard score curves, from ages twelve to seventeen, for a series of traits involving personal appearance, expressiveness, attention-seeking, and emotional patterns. As shown in Figure 2, the early-maturing are consistently rated as superior in physical attractiveness, with average scores which reach their highest value at age fifteen. The late-maturing fall somewhat below the group mean, increasingly so from age twelve to age fifteen or sixteen. These differences in attractiveness of physique are complexly influenced by factors of size and of body build. Early maturing is not only associated with a more rapid growth in height, but also with mesomorphy. The boys in this group tend to be "well-built," muscular, and athletic. By contrast, the more slender, poorly-muscled build of the late-maturers was rated as relatively "unattractive" by the adult observers.

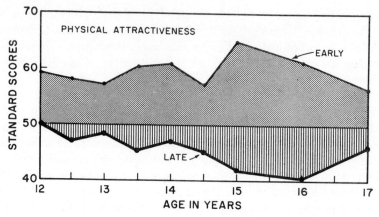

FIGURE 2. *Mean standard scores for early- and late-maturing groups, in physical appearance.*

Another group of traits which may have developmental significance are those related to expressiveness. Ratings of "animation" and "eagerness" are presented in Figure 3. In these characteristics the early-maturing are close to the group average, but the late-maturing are consistently above

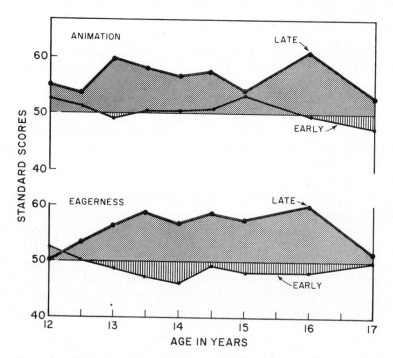

FIGURE 3. *Mean standard scores for early- and late-maturing groups, in expressive traits.*

the average. Similar differences were found for other traits involving expressiveness; comparisons were made for behavior defined, at contrasting extremes, as talkative-silent, active-stationary, busy-idle, peppy-indifferent, and laughing-sober. In each of these the early-maturing boys were distributed similarly to the total sample of boys, the late-maturing were consistently on the "expressive" side of the scale.

At least two factors are probably involved in determining this deviate position of the late-maturing. The first is a persistence of a childish activity pattern. A busy scurrying about and noisy interchange of shouts and comments is more characteristic of pre-adolescence than of later years; the adolescent often looks down upon such behavior as undignified, and adopts instead the role of a lounger, observing with tolerant superiority the childish antics of those younger than himself. A second factor is a reaction formation to inferiority. The "active small boy" may be expressing through his activity not merely a survival of an immature culture pattern, but may also use this, as the only technique he knows, to hold the attention of others and to compensate for a physically less favored status.

In this connection, it is instructive to consider the evidence concerning attention-seeking behavior, as presented in Figure 4. In the upper half of

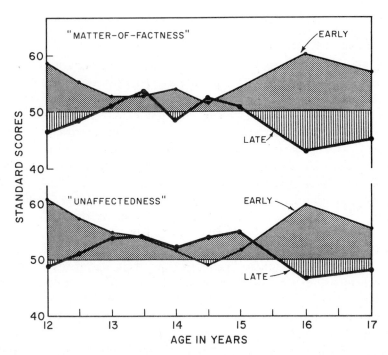

FIGURE 4. *Mean standard scores of early- and late-maturing groups, in attention-seeking behavior.*

this figure, the late-maturing boys tend to vary around the average in the trait "matter-of-factness." Their lowest score is at age sixteen, when they fall on the "show-off" side of the scale. Although the differences are small, this would be consistent with an interpretation emphasizing a "natural" or "childish" expressiveness in the earlier years of adolescence, and a more compensatory attention-seeking expressiveness in the later years. In contrast, the early-maturing are at these ages judged to be relatively nonattention-seeking: unaffected and matter-of-fact.

It may be noted that the two maturational groups show similar rather than different records in a number of traits of social importance. Thus, they present no marked nor consistent differences in observed popularity, leadership, prestige, poise, assurance, cheerfulness, or social effect on the group.

In view of the relation of maturing to physical abilities, and of the high valuation placed upon athletic performance in the adolescent culture, it is perhaps surprising that differences in maturing are not reflected in such traits as popularity, leadership, or prestige. On the average, the late-maturing boy succeeds in maintaining a fairly adequate status among his age-mates; very likely he is helped in this by his activity and other compensations, and it is also probable that some of the early-maturing are handicapped at times by the fact that they have outgrown their age group.

Reputation with Classmates

Another source of evidence concerning adolescent behavior and status is from the Reputation Test. Data are available from a series of tests in which classmates were asked to write down the name of anyone in the class conforming to certain descriptions. For example, "Here is someone who finds it hard to sit still in class," or at the other extreme, "Here is someone who can work quietly without moving around in his seat." Scores were obtained by determining the percentage of times a person was mentioned on a given trait description, and these measures were then transformed into standard scores in which 50 represented the "indifference point" (indicating no mentions at either extreme of the trait). Reputation scores are less differentiating than ratings; they tend to identify outstanding individuals, but may fail to distribute the middle range of cases who receive few or no mentions from their classmates. As a result differences between early- and late-maturing in average reputation scores are less marked than in average ratings by adults. However, a number of traits show differences which occur in the same direction on six testings and are significant.

The late-maturing are consistently more "attention-getting," more "restless," more "assured in class," more "talkative," less "grown-up," and less likely to have older friends. On five out of six tests they are more "bossy," and less "good-looking."

Less consistency is found for traits which have been established as especially important for adolescent prestige. On judgments "popular," "leader," "friendly," "daring," "active in games," and "humor aboout self," the late-maturing stand relatively well until the middle period of junior high school, and then tend to drop to lower status.

Table I presents a comparison of average standard scores for the two groups. The differences are not statistically significant but they present a picture which is in general similar to that already found in the observations by adults: the late-maturing appear as assertive (in a small-boy extroverted way) but at this age are somewhat lower in prestige traits.

Table I

Mean Standard Scores for Reputation Traits

	Early-maturing	Late-maturing
Attention-getting	48.1	52.2
Restlessness	45.3	52.9
Talkativeness	47.9	53.0
Bossiness	47.1	52.6
Assurance in class	45.6	50.0
Popularity	54.0	50.7
Leadership	51.3	47.5
Humor (about self)	53.5	48.7
Having older friends	56.2	42.3
Good appearance	54.4	49.3

At the earlier ages the more active and energetic of those in the late-maturing group were not unsuccessful in winning social recognition. But the early-maturing were much more likely to get and maintain the kind of prestige accorded to athletes and officeholders. Two of the sixteen early-maturing boys became student body presidents, one was president of the boys' club (a position next in importance to that of student body president), several were elected to committee chairmanships, and four attained outstanding reputations as athletes. The sixteen late-maturing boys produced only one somewhat "important" officeholder (a class vice-president), and one athlete.

Conclusions

A general picture emerges from the various ratings and characterizations of these two contrasting groups of boys. Those who are physically accelerated are usually accepted and treated by adults and other children as more mature. They appear to have relatively little need to strive for status. From their ranks come the outstanding student body leaders in senior high school. In contrast, the physically retarded boys exhibit many forms of relatively immature behavior: this may be in part because others tend to treat them as the little boys they appear to be. Furthermore, a fair proportion of these boys give evidence of needing to counteract their physical disadvantage in some way—usually by greater activity and striving for attention, although in some cases by withdrawal.

It is not surprising that those who are retarded in skeletal development should often be directly aware of other aspects of physical retardation, and it is not surprising that this should lead to anxiety. We have seen, however, that there are many complicating factors, which make it difficult to predict the course which any individual adjustment will take. Some of our late-maturing boys enjoyed a degree of personal security, and status in other areas, which helped to balance their temporary physical inadequacies. Some of the early-maturing boys with fine physiques, nevertheless had disturbing accompaniments of rapid growth (such as severe acne), which tended to offset other advantages.

Our findings give clear evidence of the effect of physical maturing upon behavior. Perhaps of greater importance, however, is the repeated demonstration of the multiplicity of factors, psychological and cultural as well as physical, which contribute to the formation of basic personality patterns.

PART II

A previous study (Part I) compared two groups of boys who had been classified as physically accelerated or retarded, in terms of skeletal age. These groups represented approximately the 20 per cent at each extreme of a normal public school sample. The comparison showed differences in physical growth, sexual maturing, and in a number of psychological measures, and led to the conclusion that ". . . those who are physically accelerated are usually accepted and treated by adults and other children as more mature. They appear to have relatively little need to strive for status. From their ranks come the outstanding student body leaders in senior high school. In contrast, the physically retarded boys exhibit many forms of relatively immature behavior: this may be in part because others tend to treat them as the little boys they appear to be. Furthermore, a fair proportion of these give evidence of needing to counteract their physical disadvantages in some way—usually by greater activity and striving for attention, although in some cases by withdrawal."

It is clear that early- or late-maturing may have a considerable bearing upon the social life and personal adjustment of some individuals during the middle years of their adolescence. Perhaps of greater importance, however, is the inquiry as to longer-term effects or relationships in adult life, and on this point no evidence has previously been offered.

The subjects who participated in the original study are now in their early thirties. Contacts have been maintained with many of the group during the intervening years; in a systematic follow-up study beginning in 1954 current data have been obtained for 20 of the early- and late-maturing boys, out of an original sample of 32. These constituted 11 early- and 9 late-maturing boys.

Adult Differences

We shall now consider the adult characteristics of the early- and late-maturing, as observed at an average age of 33 years. As was predicted at age 17, the differences in gross size tend to disappear. The early-maturing average only half an inch taller, at 5 feet 10 inches; and 7 pounds heavier, at 172 pounds. These differences are not significant. In body build, the prediction is that the early-maturing would be more mesomorphic. The tendency is in this direction, but the differences are not significant. The chief thing to note is the wide range of physiques within each group (both in adolescence and in adulthood) and the marked consistency over the years. A slight change is apparent in the direction of greater mesomorphy in eight of the nine late-maturing and they now present a somewhat more developed and sturdy appearance.

Some differences would be expected in constitutional indices of masculinity. Among the late-maturing, the majority of the original study and of those included in the follow-up were rated as having a deficiency in masculine development, at age 17. At age 33, however, ratings of gynandromorphy in the two groups showed considerable overlap and only a small and non-significant difference in favor of the early-maturing.

Personality differences in adult life have been examined with reference to a number of criteria. Two sources of data to be considered here are Gough's California Psychological Inventory and the Edwards Personal Preference Schedule. The first of these, the C. P. I., attempts to appraise aspects of character and temperament which are significant for social living and interpersonal behavior and which are related to personal maturity and creative achievement. Eighteen scales are available which describe individuals in terms of social responsibility, tolerance, flexibility, academic motivation, self-control and the like.

Most of the above scales did not show significant differences between the groups. One outstanding exception is the scale entitled "good impression," (interest in, and capacity for, creating a "good impression" on others). Differences here favored the early-maturing with a significance at the .006 level.

Some of the interpretative phrases associated with high scores on this scale include: "is turned to for advice and reassurance; fatherly; is concerned with making a good impression; is persistent in working toward his goal." High scorers on this "Gi" scale are also designated as responsible, cooperative, enterprising, sociable, and warm.

In our groups the early-maturing tend in addition to obtain higher scores on the C. P. I. scales for socialization, dominance, self-control, and responsibility. Although none of these shows differences at a significance level better than .07, it is true that the early-maturing have high average scores and present a consistently favorable personality picture with regard to these important social variables.

The phrases and adjectives associated with high scores on these five scales (good impression, socialization, dominance, self-control, and responsibility) remind us strikingly of the social behavior and personal traits attributed, by their peers and by adults, to the early-maturing boys in adolescence. For the total group of 43 boys thus far included in the follow-up, a correlation of .50 (significant at the .01 level) was found between the "good impression" score on the C. P. I., and their level of skeletal maturity 18 years earlier. The corresponding Pearson r for the socialization score at age 33, and skeletal maturity at age 15, was .40, significant at the .01 level.

One other scale yields an interesting difference, significant at the .05 level. This is the scale for what has been termed "flexibility." Those who score high on this scale are described by Gough as tending to be rebellious, touchy, impulsive, self-indulgent, assertive, and also insightful. Low scorers are described as deliberate, methodical, industrious, rigid, mannerly, overly controlling of impulses, complaint. In these terms, the late-maturers tend to be more "flexible" than the early-maturers.

We might hazard the guess that some of the little boy behavior—the impulsiveness, playfulness, and also the "touchiness" repeatedly noted in late-maturing adolescents is mirrored in the description of high scorers on this scale. We might speculate further that in the course of having to adapt to difficult status problems, the late-maturers have gained some insights and are indeed more flexible, while the early-maturing, capitalizing on their ability to make a good impression, may have clung to their earlier success pattern to the extent of becoming somewhat rigid or over-controlled.

The Edwards Personal Preference test shows relatively few significant differences between the two groups. This is a self-report device which measures 15 variables named from Murray's list of needs.

On the Edwards test, two of the scales are discriminating for our groups at the 4 and 5 per cent levels respectively. The early-maturing group scores high on the *dominance* scale: "to be a leader, persuade, argue for a point of view," while the late-maturing score high in *succorance:* "to seek encouragement, to be helped by others, to have a fuss made over one when hurt." For the total group of 40 who took the Edwards test at around age 33, skeletal maturing at age 17 correlated .40 with dominance, and —.48 with succorance (both significant at the .01 level).

To those of us who have known these young men for over 20 years, some of the most interesting questions remain to be answered. What have been their successes and failures in achieving occupational and personal goals? All are married, and in each group the present number of children averages 2.3. Socio-economic ratings, based on homes and neighborhoods, show no differences for the two groups. There are no significant differences in average educational level, although a slightly higher proportion of the later-maturing have college degrees and the only college teacher is in this group.

There is some indication that more of the early-maturing have attained vocational goals which are satisfying and status-conferring. Among this group five are in professional careers; four are executives; one is a skilled mechanic and one in a clerical position. Of the executives, three are in positions of somewhat impressive status.

Among the late-maturing, four are in professions, two are still university students, two are salesmen, and one is a carpenter. None has attained an important managerial position and several, by their own account and the nature of their work, seem somewhat precariously unsettled.

SUMMARY AND CONCLUSION

Boys who had been classified as physically accelerated or retarded in terms of skeletal age during adolescence were compared as young adults at age 33, to determine the long-term effects of rate of maturing upon personality.

Analysis of ratings by adults and classmates indicated that the early-maturing boys were significantly more attractive in physique, more relaxed, poised, and matter-of-fact. Consistent differences in other characteristics, such as interest in the opposite sex and "good-naturedness," were obtained over nine semesters of observation. Late- maturing boys were described as more expressive, active, talkative, eager, attention-getting.

The physical differences noted for these boys at adolescence have tended to disappear in adulthood. Personality characteristics as appraised by the California Psychological Inventory and the Edwards Personal Preference Schedule have shown a number of significant differences on the various scales for which the tests are scored (e.g., higher scores for the early-maturing on measures of "good impression" and "socialization.") Where such differences were found, they tended to describe the young adults much as they had been described in adolescence.

No differences were found between the early- and late-maturing in present marital status, family size, or educational level. A few of the early-maturing have made exceptionally rapid progress as junior executives and a few of the late-maturing are still somewhat unsettled, vocationally.

The foregoing presentation of data and the case summaries remind us again of the conclusions to the original study which stressed individual differences within each group, resulting from the complex interplay of factors. During the adolescent period late-maturing is a handicap for many boys and can rarely be found to offer special advantages. Early-maturing carries both advantages and disadvantages. In our culture it frequently gives competitive status, but sometimes also involves handicaps in the necessity for rapid readjustments and in requiring the adolescent to meet adult expectations which are more appropriate to size and appearance than to other aspects of maturing. The adolescent handicaps and advantages associated with late- or early-maturing appear to carry over into adulthood to some extent, and perhaps to a greater extent in psychological than in physical characteristics.

1 · Pictorial Depth Perception in
African Groups

W. HUDSON

Abridged from the *Journal of Social Psychology*, 52 (1960), 183-208, by permission of the author and The Journal Press.

Persons who are familiar from an early age with photographs and with realistic art are likely to assume that the interpretation of pictures offers no difficulty. The present study serves to disabuse us of this naive belief.

Western culture is book-learned, characterized by dependence upon the written word, illustration, diagram, photograph. Visual presentation is a common mode in the classroom. Educational and training programes, advertisements, safety, and health propaganda, and much current didactic literature make use of pictorial material. Certain characteristic perceptual habits have become normal for Western culture, and for the groups professing it. Pictorial representation of a three-dimensional scene requires the observance and acceptance of certain artistic or graphic conventions. Pictorial depth perception depends upon response to these conventional cues in the two-dimensional representation. There are three such cues concerned with form only, viz., object size, object superimposition or overlap, perspective. In the visual world, of two objects of equal size, that object nearer the observer is larger. When one object overlaps another the superimposed object is nearer to the observer. Parallel lines tend to converge with distance from the observer. In the two-dimensional representation of the three-dimensional scene, foreground objects are depicted larger than background items. Superimposed objects are perceived as nearer. Pictorial structuring by perspective technique is accepted as a convention for depicting distance. The incidental evidence furnished by African samples indicates that these pictorial conventions are not familiar to such subcultural groups. The present investigation is limited to the study of the perception of three dimensions in pictorial material by subcultural groups in southern Africa.

METHOD

Test Material

Test material was constructed to isolate the pictorial depth cues of object size, object superimposition and perspective. Six outline drawings and one photograph were constructed. The experimental situation is simple to

419

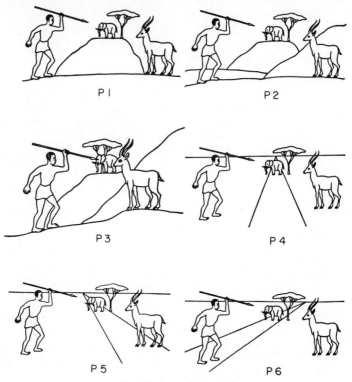

FIGURE 1. *Horizontal pictorial space.*

construct. Pictures 1-6 were designed to obtain the responses of observers to depth cues of size, overlap, and perspective in horizontal pictorial space. Each picture is similarly structured. The elephant is positioned centrally between a human figure and an antelope. In this "hunting scene," the elephant is depicted smaller than the antelope. This object size depth cue occurs in each of the six pictures. Pictures 2 and 3 carry the additional depth cue of overlapping. Pictures 4, 5 and 6 have perspective lines representing a road vanishing in a horizon. In all pictures the hunter's assegai is aligned on both elephant and antelope.

A similar picture was made using modeled objects. Human figure, elephant, and antelope were modeled to scale and subsequently photographed to reproduce a scene similar to Picture 1.

Testing Procedure

Pictures were presented separately to individual candidates in the given order. Questioning was done orally in whatever tongue was mutually intelligible to both candidate and tester. Where this practice was not feasible (with illiterate samples from different territories in southern

Africa), an interpreter was used. Answers were recorded seriatim. Complete picture sets were not administered to the first four samples.

Candidates were asked the following questions while viewing each picture:

1. What do you see?
2. What is the man doing?
3. Which is nearer to the man, the elephant or the antelope?

In addition candidates were required to identify each object in each picture, viz., man, assegai, elephant, tree, hill, antelope.

If a candidate reported that the man was aiming or throwing the spear without specifying his quarry, an additional question was asked to clarify whether he was aiming at elephant or antelope. In the majority of cases, this additional question was unnecessary.

Scoring Method

For reasons to be discussed later, responses to Question 3 were taken as indicative of the type of dimensional pictorial perception possessed by a candidate. If candidates reported the antelope in the "hunting scene" to be nearer the man than the elephant, their responses were classified as three-dimensional (3D). Similarly, for Question 2, if candidates reported the hunter to be aiming at the antelope, these responses were classified as three-dimensional. All other responses in the scenes were characterized as two-dimensional (2D).

Samples

The test was administered to 11 samples. Characteristics of these samples are given in Table I. Samples fell into two main types, a nonschool-attending group (Sample *a-e*) and a school-attending group (Sample *f-k*). The nonschool-attending group contained no children and consisted of four black and one white sample. The school-going group consisted of children mainly except for one sample of adult teachers. Three of the samples in this group were black, and three white. All samples were tested in the Union of South Africa, Samples *a-d* contain candidates whose territorial origins cover the Union of South Africa, South West Africa, High Commission territories, Federation of Rhodesias and Nyasaland, East Africa, Mozambique, and Angola. Age and educational data are lacking for two cases in Sample *e*.

RESULTS

Intersample Difference in Depth Perception for Outline Drawings

For each of the 11 samples the percentage number of candidates giving 3D responses are listed in Table II. 3D responses are fairly consistent per sample over the pictures.

Table I

Characteristics of Samples

		Age				Education			
	n	Under 14	14-20	21-40	Over 40	Illit-erate	Pri-mary	High-er	Grad-uate
a. Mine laborers (Illiterate) (Black)	57	—	36	19	2	57	—	—	—
b. Mine laborers (Primary) (Black)	54	—	23	29	2	—	54	—	—
c. Mine clerks (High School) (Black)	48	—	3	34	11	—	—	48	—
d. Mine laborers (Illiterate) (Black)	45	—	12	29	4	45	—	—	—
e. White laborers	60	—	2	29	27	10	46	2	—
f. School children (Grades & Std. 1) (White)	42	42	—	—	—	—	42	—	—
g. School children (Grade 1—Std. 6) (White)	113	113	—	—	—	—	113	—	—
h. School children (Std. 6) (Black)	34	—	34	—	—	—	34	—	—
i. Teachers (Graduate) (Black)	25	—	—	22	3	—	—	—	25
j. School Children (Stds. 8 & 10) (Black)	52	—	47	5	—	—	—	52	—
k. School children (Stds. 5 & 6) (White)	32	32	—	—	—	—	32	—	—

Table II

Percentage Candidates With 3D Responses

					Horizontal space		
Samples	n	Size P_1	Super-imposi-tion P_2	Super-imposi-tion P_3	Perspec-tive P_4	Perspec-tive P_5	Perspec-tive P_6
a	57	0	0	—	0	0	0
b	54	0	0	—	2	0	2
c	48	23	40	—	31	17	20
d	45	—	—	2	—	—	—
e	60	13	20	23	8	15	13
f	42	26	31	69	29	33	26
g	113	47	57	93	57	63	51
h	34	50	68	76	53	50	65
i	25	56	76	80	60	68	60
j	52	69	69	94	62	73	63
k	32	75	88	100	81	97	78

Intersample Differences in Depth Perception for Photographs

Percentage number giving 3D responses to Question 3 with respect to the photograph are listed for samples taking this test (Table III).

Illiterate mine workers do not see the photograph three-dimensionally.

Table III

Percentage Candidates With 3D Responses

Samples	n	Percentage
d	45	0
f	42	72
g	113	85
h	34	76
i	25	92
j	52	81
k	32	100

The remaining samples, where a high proportion of candidates perceive three-dimensionally, are all school-going samples, both black and white. There are minor differences within this second group. White school beginners and black pupils at the end of their primary course perceive the photograph three-dimensionally less frequently than do white pupils at the end of their primary course. But the main intersample difference in depth perception in photographs lies between the illiterate black sample and the school-going group, both black and white.

Object Identification as a Factor in Dimensional Perception

Since pictorial depth perception depends upon the perception of the appropriate cues there must be a direct relationship between object identification and dimensional perception.

In all pictures, except Picture 3, the man and the animals were correctly identified. In Picture 3, the depth cue of overlap was introduced and as can be seen from Figure 1, objects were superimposed over the central figure of the elephant in order to enhance the perception of depth. With the illiterate Sample *d*, this technique defeats its own object by complicating the representation of the elephant to such an extent as to render it unrecognisable to the candidates. This finding does not apply to Picture 2 where overlap is also used. In this instance superimposition is restricted to contour lines, so that the animals and objects retain their definition.

DISCUSSION

White and black school-going samples perceive depth more frequently in pictorial material than do illiterate black samples, and samples, both black and white, which have terminated their school course and live in isolation from the dominant cultural norm. As expected there is a direct relationship between incorrect identification of items, in the drawings and two-dimensional perception, but correct identification does not predicate three-dimensional perception. Outline drawings making use of perspective depth cues are less frequently seen three-dimensionally than those using overlap or size depth cues. This finding holds particularly in the case of white primary school pupils. School-going samples perceive three-dimensions in a photograph more readily than in an outline drawing, but this finding does not apply to illiterate samples. Intersample differences are less pronounced with photographic material than with outline drawings.

There are three hypotheses which can be set up on these results: (1) that the results are artifacts of the test, (2) that the results are culturally determined, (3) that the results are genetically determined.

Test Artifacts in Dimensional Pictorial Perception

This hypothesis has two aspects to it: (a) How far has the perceptual structure of the test influenced results? (b) How far has the semantic structure of the test influenced results?

Outline drawings were used to provide the simplest and least graphically contaminated medium for the representation of the appropriate depth cues in a standard scene. Such drawings have representational drawbacks. Perspective cues in particular tend to become symbolic and unrealistic, and the high proportion of incorrect identifications, particularly in the illiterate samples, lends support to this view. But responses to the photographic reproduction of the same pictorial scene modeled show that with that form of two-dimensional representation, which is least symbolic and most realistic of three-dimensions, the illiterate sample continues to perceive two-dimensionally. Work by Smith *et al.* (1958) on perceived distance as a function of the method of representing perspective showed that judgments of distances in drawings do not vary with the amount of detail included. They also concluded that the perception of depth did not differ in perspective line drawings and in photographs. These findings corroborate the evidence in the present study and on these grounds the hypothesis that test results are an artifact of the perceptual structure of the test can be rejected.

What do candidates understand the tester to mean when he asks the question—Which is nearer to the man, elephant or antelope? There is evidence to show that 2D responses are not semantically dependent on the wording of the question. With all samples except high school pupils (black) and graduate teachers (black) responses, whether 3D or 2D, were immediate. With the two samples specified hesitation in responding was noticeable and was particularly pronounced with the graduate teachers, some of whom took as long as one hour per picture to respond. Part of this hesitation may be due to occupational cautiousness or insecurity, but part of it was exposed by introspection as a problem in perceptual organization. Candidates asked the tester for information on the mode of perception because there were to them two possibilities, viz., 2D or 3D, which means that to them "nearness" was semantically unstable in the questionnaire. For the less highly educated and illiterate samples which perceived the pictures two-dimensionally in a majority of cases, there is additional evidence. Following their identification of objects in the pictures candidates were asked what the hunter was aiming at in the "hunting scene," prior to being questioned on relative proximity of animals to hunter. Candidates in all samples, choosing the elephant as the hunter's quarry, were those who perceived the elephant as nearer the hunter than the antelope. This means that the whole manifest content of the picture tended to be perceived two-dimensionally, and appropriately interpreted. The occurrence of this phenomenon is considered to be a function of perceptual organisation and not merely a semantic evaluation. The hypothesis postulating the influence of the semantic structure of the test on candidates' responses is rejected.

Cultural Factors in Dimensional Pictorial Perception

There are two levels of cultural factors to be considered viz., (a) formal education, (b) informal training.

The white primary groups (Samples *f, g, k*) 3D perception is associated with educational level. The higher the educational standard, the more frequent is the occurrence of 3D pictorial perception.

This finding does not apply to black samples, otherwise markedly superior performances would be expected from black high school pupils (Sample *j*) and graduate teachers (Sample *i*). Candidates in Sample *b* (mine laborers) possess a primary school level of education, but their pictorial perception is entirely two-dimensional and does not differ from that of the illiterate mine workers. In addition the 3D perception of the white laborers (Sample *e*), the majority of whom have had primary schooling, is markedly inferior to that of the white school beginners (Sample *f*).

Training in pictorial perception is not included in the formal school curriculum. It is gradually acquired by white children between the ages of 6 and 12 years (Samples *f, j, k*). During that period, there is an informal process of almost continuous exposure to pictorial material in the school and in the home, so that by the age of 12 years, most white children have learned to perceive pictures three-dimensionally.

But pictorial depth perception is not learned by the white laborers in Sample *e*, although they attended school. Mundy-Castle and Nelson (1960) have described this subculture elsewhere. It is an isolated group living under conditions of sheltered employment, closely intermarried, and centripetal. Families are large, and homes are poorly supplied with pictures, books, magazines, and newspapers. Consequently school-going children are not exposed in the home to the informal training necessary for the three-dimensional perception of pictorial material. School is equally isolated, and, as an agency by which the outside world may attempt to invade the community, is resisted by the elders of the group. There is little opportunity for scholars, unstimulated perceptually in the home, to acquire new depth perceptual organization with respect to pictures.

The black samples are also isolated. This is particularly true of Samples *a-d*, which are migratory and rurally orientated. The black urban samples (*h*, *i*, *j*) are enthnocentrically isolated. They have been urbanised for one generation only. Homes, even of graduates, are poorly furnished with pictures and illustrated reading matter. The women-folk seldom read and then mainly literature in the vernacular. Most books owned by the men are of the nature of textbooks. Daily and monthly magazines are taken, but most of these are sparsely illustrated with photographs. During the early years, however, when the white child is obtaining his informal training in pictorial material, the black child, even in an urban home, suffers from lack of exposure to pictures. He may acquire the skill at a later stage, but there is little opportunity for stimulation, particularly where formal schooling is presided over by teachers, many of whom perceive pictorial material two-dimensionally. Hence it does occur that a black graduate of London University perceives a picture flat. It also happens that a black teacher sees a picture flat, and his pupil perceives it three-dimensionally.

Such results are not unexpected. African art is essentially volumetric. Where it is pictorial as in wall decorations or body tattooing, it is either diagrammatic or two-dimensional naturalistic. Haselberger (1957) reports on a long continuous history of two-dimensional mural art in Africa. Jeffreys (1957) describes tattooing in Nigeria as the African counterpart to abstract pictorial art in Europe and America. Such evidence emphasises that the critical feature for pictorial depth perception appears to be adequate exposure to the appropriate experience.

SUMMARY

Pictures constructed to provide self-evident responses of 2D or 3D perception on the depth cues of object size, superimposition, and perspective were given to 11 samples, six of them school-going (3 white, 3 black) and five of them nonschool-going (1 white, 4 black). School-going samples saw predominantly three-dimensionally, the others almost entirely two-dimensionally both in outline drawings and on a photograph. The hypothesis that their dimensional perception was an artifact of test construction was rejected. Formal schooling and informal training combined to supply an exposure necessary for the development of 3D perception. Cultural isolation was effective in preventing or retarding the process, even in candidates possessing formal education of an advanced level.

References

Haselberger, H., "Die Wandmalerei der afrikanischen Neger," *Zeitschrift für Ethnographie*, 82 (1957), 209-237.
Jeffreys, M. D. W., "Negro Abstract Art or Ibo Body Patterns," *South African Museums Association Bulletin*, 6 (1957), 219-229.

Mundy-Castle, A. C., and G. K. Nelson, "Brain Rhythms, Personality and Intelligence in a Socially Isolated Community," *Nature,* 1960.

Smith, O. W., P. C. Smith and D. Hubbard, "Perceived Distance as a Function of the Method of Representing Perspective," *American Journal of Psychology,* 71 (1958), 662-674.

2 · How Turkish Children Learn to Read

GERTRUDE HILDRETH

Reprinted from the *Elementary School Journal*, 61 (1960), 14-23, by permission of the author and the University of Chicago Press.

Much of the intellectual development of the child cannot take place without the contribution made by reading. For many children, learning to read is one of the most difficult academic tasks. The present selection is not alone in suggesting that for the English-speaking child much of this difficulty is not inherent but derives from the differences between spoken and written English.

It was my privilege during the 1959-60 school year to visit primary schools in Turkey. I wanted to observe the teaching of reading and the other language arts. During my stay I visited classrooms, talked with teachers, school administrators, and university faculty members, and I casually observed children at home and on the street.*

What I saw of the children's lives in and out of school gave me clues to the emotional setting in which children learn to read. Turkish children, like boys and girls the world over, are active, playful, curious, and busy. I was impressed with the warm affection between Turkish parents and their children, the ease with which parents seem to manage children, and the happy relationships among children in small groups.

As a rule, parents and children show marked respect toward teachers; parents have confidence that the teachers and the school are working in the child's best interests. In the classroom, children are ordinarily attentive and industrious, eager to please the teacher and to demonstrate their new achievements.

What are the classrooms like? In the more traditional schools the beginners, like the older children, sit two by two at wooden desks facing the teacher and the blackboard. In other schools the children may be seated in small groups around two tables pushed together to form a square.

Abacus and Spools

Primary classes do not have the wealth of instructional materials found in American schools, but crayons, pictures, and small toys are put to good use. In the front of the room there may be a large abacus and possibly

* I am indebted to Ahmet Atilgan, director of primary schools, Istanbul, for the privilege of visiting the schools and making the observations reported in this paper.

a long string of spools for counting. The beginner also has his own small abacus, purchased inexpensively at the corner shop, as well as a small sack of hard, white beans and some matchsticks. The teacher usually keeps a collection of story pamphlets and other reading material in a corner bookcase.

The primary schools follow a modern curriculum that reflects a sound psychology of education for young children. Bookwork is related to activities that include short trips away from school. Some use is made of filmstrips for information and language work. In all grades children are served hot milk and bread before the morning recess.

Although teachers find it difficult to give pupils sufficient individual attention in large classes, they succeed in keeping the children interested and in managing the class. The general atmosphere is one of praise and encouragement. In one room, the entire class clapped when several children in turn "got a word just right."

How well are Turkish children learning the skills of literacy? Judging by the outcomes, the program of instruction in reading and related language arts is psychologically sound and conspicuously effective.

Little Books in Corner Shops

Children who attend school regularly learn to read, write, and spell without difficulty in three or four years. Ten-year-olds read children's literature and their school textbooks fluently without vocalizing. Even eight-year-olds who have an ordinary background can be seen eagerly scanning the sports news in the paper as they go along the street. I saw a ten-year-old reading some exciting sports news aloud to a group of younger boys gathered about him, and I saw girls of about the same age sitting on their doorstep reading story books.

Inexpensive, well-illustrated little story pamphlets are to be had in small shops everywhere. Young children with a taste for reading run into corner shops to help themselves to these little story booklets as if they were candy. The smallest of these booklets measures about five inches by six inches, contains from twelve to twenty pages, and costs about six cents. Larger picture-story leaflets for older children cost a little more.

There are three children's encyclopedias in the Turkish language as well as Turkish dictionaries for children. Within recent years there has been a marked increase in children's libraries.

Since the founding of the Republic in 1923, Turkey has had a compulsory system of primary education. From the age of seven all children are required to attend school for a five-year period. The school term begins the first of October and continues till the end of June, with sessions six days a week.

Primary classes may have from thirty to fifty pupils, depending on the neighborhood and other factors. Some schools are on double sessions, with one group attending in the morning, the other in the afternoon. Few children who enter first grade at the age of seven have attended kindergarten; however, some children enter the primary school at the age of six.

A Look at the Turkish Language

To understand the methods of teaching reading and spelling in Turkish schools, it is necessary to know something about the children's native tongue. Turkish is an inflected language: word endings do the work that pronouns, articles, and verb forms do in English.

Before 1928 Turkish was written and printed in Arabic calligraphy employing thirty-three nonphonetic characters; but in 1928, at one bold stroke, the national government enforced the use of a new alphabet consisting of twenty-nine Roman characters. The characters are the same as those used in English, though in Turkish diacritical marks are used with some letters.

With few exceptions, every letter is pronounced, and each letter has only one sound. Turkish has no double or treble consonants to represent a single sound like *sh* or *sch*. There are no double letters, and only one letter is sometimes silent. Monstrosities like *one, once, laugh, now, know* are not found in Turkish. The language has several sounds not heard in English; some of our twenty-six letters have different sounds in Turkish than in English, and several are omitted.

A few English words that are now part of the Turkish language illustrate the phonetic spellings:

dance—dans
auto—oto
telephone—telefon
football—futbol
passage—pasaj
address—adres
block—blok
college—kolej

Although the techniques and the materials used in teaching beginners to read and write vary somewhat from school to school, the basic principles are the same. Lessons in reading and writing begin with meaningful words and simple sentences that express ideas familiar to the children.

Full use is made of action and oral expression in learning the vocabulary. One day I visited a class where children read aloud a very short sentence on the blackboard, "Ali, catch the ball," and then demonstrated to show that they understood what they had read. A school satchel at the front of the room was used to fix the meaning of the word *satchel*. A child opened and shut the door to illustrate the meaning of the words *open* and *shut*.

In beginning classes I saw labels attached to common objects in the room. Children were given sets of small word cards to use for review at their seats. The pupils were checked on their recognition and understanding of such words as *catch* and *throw*.

At first, very little is done in a single lesson. The children are given several words, a short sentence or two, and are asked to copy them into notebooks.

Economical Learning

There is no naming, sounding, or writing of isolated letters in reading lessons. All work with letters and their sounds is done with méaningful words. The children learn the trick of analyzing by working with letter sounds within words.

For example, the child might first meet the sound *o* as in *throw* in the word *TOP*, which is Turkish for "ball." Later the pupil learns to recognize the letter *o* in various positions in other words. In this way vowels are not pronounced apart from the adjoining consonants.

The children practice until they recognize the sound of any letter in common words. They do not first learn a series of separate sounds that must later be blended to form words; nor do they first memorize a stock of word patterns that must later be broken into separate sounds. Blending does not present much of a problem with a language in which each letter in a word is pronounced.

This type of intrinsic phonics drill gives the pupils the necessary tool for working out new words already in their oral vocabulary or easily inferred from the story text. The pupils acquire simultaneously a knowledge of all the letters and their sounds; a stock of frequently recurring words easily recognized at sight; and a stock of common "sight" syllables.

From the first lessons reading, spelling, handwriting, and written expression are practiced simultaneously. These skills are learned and used for purposes genuinely related to the children's interests and behavior. No material is used in beginning reading lessons that is not familiar to the pupils as oral expression; all words and phrases represent familiar ideas. In beginning lessons oral reading is the commonest response.

The Alphabet Books

The key textbook for beginning reading is the *Alfabe*, or alphabet book, which contains some sixty pages of text and illustrations. Several versions of the *Alfabe* are used in beginning classes. Although the books differ in size, number of pages, content, and illustrations, they are alike in general organization and are all used in the same way in reading instruction.

Prepared under the supervision of the Ministry of Education or some other government agency, the books are sold for very little. One of the most widely used versions sells for eleven cents.

American-type readiness workbooks are also used. In these books the children color pictures, do matching exercises, trace dotted-line words, numerals, and pictures.

The chief feature of the *Alfabe* is the systematic introduction of the twenty-nine letters of the Turkish alphabet, one by one, in meaningful words. For example, one book begins with A and AT ("horse"), a word interesting to children and easy to say. Then comes *TUT* ("catch") for the *u* sound. G (as in *girl*) first appears in GEL ("come"). Ç as in *chick* is introduced in ÇIK ("go out"), H in HOROZ ("cock") and in HOŞ ("pleasant"). Ğ, a less frequent letter, first appears in the word YAĞMUR ("rain"), illustrated with a good picture. Each new letter introduced appears in several different words.

The separate letters are not presented in alphabetical order, but according to ease of learning and frequency of use in the children's vocabulary, as well as usefulness in forming common words. All the vowel sounds are introduced early. The least commonly used letters are introduced last of all. Two-thirds of the way through the book, children have met all the letters and their sounds in common words.

Letter sounds are presented not only in initial position in words but in other positions as well. Usually not more than one or two new letters are introduced on a page. Sometimes several pages of pictures and text appear with no new letter sounds. After a letter appears, it is repeated frequently on subsequent pages in common words; and there is provision for review of all the letters previously introduced, always in the children's familiar vocabulary.

Some help is given through pictures for learning the separate letter sounds; for example, a little girl watching a cat chase a mouse says "Oh-oh-oh." The Ü sound is illustrated with a picture of a crowing rooster.

Two-thirds of the way through the book there is an ABC chart with the letters in dictionary order and illustrations of words beginning with each letter.

Most of the *Alfabe* consists of sentences and paragraphs that give beginners daily practice in "straight ahead" reading. Exercises to review words and check meanings are included in the latter part of the book.

The forepart is entirely in capital letter block print. From the middle of the book, small letters and capitals are used as in ordinary printing. Gradually the size of the print becomes smaller, and sentences become longer with more text to the page.

The *Alfabe* lacks systematic vocabulary control, which is an established feature of modern American primers. However, the vocabulary and the text express ideas familiar to children, and children get additional experience with the *Alfabe* vocabulary through work at the blackboard, through the reading of the easiest little story pamphlets, and through practice in writing words and sentences.

The Enjoyment of Reading

The stories in the *Alfabe* use the most common and most familiar child-life scenes and actions: the child's world, the family, animals, pets, toys, games, nature, and seasons, school, household activities. In the latter part of the book, several pages are devoted to national patriotism—the celebration of the birthday of the Republic and a tribute to Kemal Atatürk, founder of the Republic.

With this introduction to deciphering the printed word, beginners are soon able to enjoy the easiest little story pamphlets. What fun to try out their new skills on the new words and phrases in an easy story!

Groups of children may have copies of the same little book. For more advanced children the teacher may place a dozen different little story booklets at the center of the table and let the pupils help themselves. The children are permitted to reject their first selection and choose another book. The teacher reads aloud to the group from these little story books, asking questions to check the children's understanding.

After only five or six weeks, some beginners have caught on easily and are beginning to read sentences in the *Alfabe* with much interest, reading a word at a time, using the finger as a marker.

By second grade the children are reading a wide variety of story pamphlets and other books, each proceeding at his own rate. During silent-reading periods each child reads his own book; later the children take turns telling the story to the class. At other times, children at one table may be reading story books while children at another practice arithmetic. At the beginning of the year a few advanced children are able to do rapid silent reading in larger books. These boys and girls seem to accept reading as a challenge. Their attitude seems to say: This is fun! See if you can get it for yourself.

The second grade may have a current events session when the children report spontaneously on events of the day. During one news session a newspaper account of an earthquake in eastern Turkey was the chief news story. The place was located on the map, the mountainous region was described, and discussion followed. The current events reports gave the class a good illustration of learning through reading.

In third grade one notes a wide range of independent reading: history stories and poems, arithmetic problems, newspaper items. The typical third-grader reads silently in selected story books as well as in various textbooks supplied by the school board. The more advanced pupils read and study with marked absorption.

Writing with Beans and Sticks

The first writing experience in some classes I visited consisted of forming words with beans or matchsticks. The children copied from the board or from large cards such words as *KAPI* ("door") or sentences like "I have a satchel."

When inspection showed that the work had been done correctly, the pupils wrote the words and sentences with pencil in their notebooks. Several children wrote a sentence at the board while others worked at their seats.

The notebook used was standard size for all grades, ruled in spaces about a third of an inch apart. In first grade one space was used for small letters, two spaces for capitals. Each child had one of these inexpensive practice notebooks and a larger notebook with a homemade calico cover for a final permanent copy of his best work. The teacher inspected and marked each page. By this method, without formal handwriting lessons or the use of copy books, most children were soon writing with a clear, round, unjoined hand.

In second grade, as in the first grade, each child has a large notebook into which he copies his permanent work. The children take pride in decorating the pages of the book according to their own ideas.

In some beginning classes the first writing is all done in capital letters, patterned after the beginning pages of the *Alfabe*; in other beginning classes the children write in regular manuscript style with small letters and capitals in correct proportion. The teachers themselves use manuscript style as a basic tool in teaching reading, writing, and spelling. Manuscript style is continued through the second grade; during the third year the pupils are taught conventional longhand, and from that time on they use a running joined script.

Spelling Without Hardship

With a phonetically consistent alphabet, learning to spell presents little difficulty. Ordinarily, when the pupil knows the sounds of all the letters and the correct pronunciation of a word, he can spell the word.

A few months after entering school most of the beginners can write simple sentences from dictation. Five or six write at the board while others write in their notebooks.

The chief problem in Turkish spelling is not recalling the letters that match the sounds in words, but a difficulty in grammar—remembering the endings of the various declensions. All the reading exercises for learning letter sounds and pronouncing words in print are aids to spelling.

Teachers consider it a fairly simple task to teach Turkish children to read, write, and spell. In beginning lessons, the combining of reading, writing, and spelling through the use of manuscript style results in a unified method that not only economizes time and effort, but makes the learning of writing and spelling more meaningful. The children can scarcely fail to learn with understanding because the process in learning all these skills begins and ends with meaningful words and expressions.

From their first lessons the pupils practice all the skills of a mature reader—reading for meaning, reading orally, responding to printed directions, using the sounds of letters to catch the meanings of new words. The pupil's interest is held because he experiences immediate success in meaningful reading. Full use is made of the child's capacities to see, hear, and say the words at the same time that he acts out the meaning.

Understanding the Printed Word

Do the children read with full comprehension of meaning? Learning to pronounce Turkish words is so simple that there is danger that pupils may merely pronounce words and copy sentences mechanically without understanding. These tendencies are offset by the use of meaningful words and phrases from the beginning; the pupils learn at once that reading means "to tell a story" or "to understand directions." In every reading lesson the teacher checks comprehension by asking questions, by writing directions on the board, and by using various exercises that require thought. The *Alfabe* contains exercises in word- and picture-matching or sentence completion.

The early use of story reading on an individual basis also tends to insure meaningful reading. No child would be interested in reading a story to himself if he could not understand it. After reading their stories the children take turns telling the class what the story was about. There is no oral reading solely for the purpose of demonstrating how well a child can pronounce words. The wealth of easy, interesting story material children can buy everywhere inexpensively also encourages extensive meaningful reading.

Since Turkish can be read easily by naming words aloud, there is a danger that lip reading may be unduly prolonged or even become a fixed habit, retarding the reading rate. Although an occasional older child or even an occasional adult shows a tendency toward lip reading, the typical Turkish adult reader has completely suppressed the practice.

There are definite advantages in teaching beginners in typical school classes at age seven rather than at an earlier age. By this time speech and language comprehension are more mature. The added mental maturity facilitates the task of perceiving word and letter symbols, of discriminating among them and building meaningful associations between the printed symbols and the ideas they represent. The pupils are also further advanced in the capacity to generalize that is required to analyze words by sounds. Children of this age bring to the reading task a wide-awake, lively interest; they are more ready to give attention to school lessons involving work with symbols and abstractions.

Spotting the Difficulties

Individual differences in learning to read and write show up from the first day in every beginning class. A few children have learned to read before they enter first grade; typical children make a good response to beginning lessons, while a few immature or handicapped children have difficulty in recognizing and copying a three-letter word or even one letter of a word. Children of the same age respond to reading lessons in various ways: what is hard for one is easy for another. The teacher must be continually on the alert to adapt methods to the aptitudes and responsiveness of the pupils.

In one class, slow beginners were identified at once through the simple blackboard and table exercises. One child was unable to copy the word *TUT* beneath the teacher's lettering on the blackboard. Another wrote a three-word sentence but copied it backwards. A slow second-grader sounded out letter by letter words that the other pupils quickly recognized at sight.

The teachers showed resourcefulness in adapting instruction in reading and writing to the individual requirements of the pupils so far as they were able to in large classes. By giving slow children easier tasks the teacher encouraged them to try again.

Does a Phonetic Alphabet Help?

The chief purpose of converting to a modern phonetic alphabet for the Turkish language was to promote universal literacy. Is learning to read and write and spell easier with a phonetic alphabet?

The teachers themselves consider the instruction a fairly simple task. Leading Turkish educators, some of whom learned both the older alphabet and the new, believe there is no question that a phonetic spelling system has distinct advantages for learning to read and write. People outside the teaching profession will tell you, "There's nothing to learning to read Turkish. Just say over the letters, and you have it."

The English-speaking person finds considerable truth in this statement, for as soon as he knows the sounds of the letters, street signs are easy to pronounce. He can easily be understood when he reads items from a menu card or when he uses other common words. If a person can pronounce a word accurately, he can usually spell it correctly.

Count Leo Tolstoi, writing in 1862, expressed the view that the Russian language had an advantage over all other European languages because each sound is pronounced as it is written (1905). John Carroll, an authority on the science of language, stated that English orthography seems to present special difficulties to the learner, both in reading and writing (1955). A Persian student at the University of Istanbul who had learned to read and write both the old style calligraphy and the modern Turkish system said that the latter was far easier to learn.

Self-Help for Beginners

Turkish children can help themselves more successfully in the early stages than children learning to read and write English. Guesses at Turkish words are more apt to be correct. By contrast, the beginner learning to read English is more dependent on the teacher or on another pupil to "tell him the words" in story reading and must have more instruction in inferring the meaning of words from the context. Furthermore, Turkish reading and spelling can be learned simultaneously without confusion. After the beginning stages, less teacher-supervised practice and less word drill is needed by typical pupils learning to read and write Turkish.

No one claims that the new alphabet has been the only factor in improving literacy rates in Turkey. Compulsory attendance regulations, new school buildings, better prepared teachers, children's libraries, the increased supply of inexpensive reading material for all ages, improved economic conditions, have all been contributing factors.

Unquestionably much of the difficulty young children in the English-speaking world experience in learning to read and write is due to the inconsistent spelling of the language. The beginners have to be taught that the sounds are not always represented by the same letters. They must try to guess at words from the sentence meaning. This requires more mental and linguistic maturity than many six-year-old beginners have. Many confusing words must be memorized as "sight" words if the child is to catch the meaning of the sentences. The child needs to learn several hundred words as a basis for learning to recognize recurring sounds within words.

A Simplified Alphabet for English?

Many linguists are of the opinion that these difficulties could be reduced by revising the English alphabet system. Revision would simplify the teaching of reading and spelling, and the children would have more interest in learning these skills. Certainly the current stir over phonics versus the whole-word method of teaching reading in our schools seems pointless with a language that "hasn't learned to spell."

So far, no strictly controlled experiment has been conducted to test the hypothesis that learning to read and spell is simpler and easier with a consistent system of orthography. Should the hypothesis prove true, it would furnish a strong argument for revising English spelling. Such a step might advance English to a leading place as a world language.

3 · Reactions to Finger Painting as a Function of Social Class

THELMA G. ALPER, HOWARD T. BLANE, AND BARBARA
K. ABRAMS

Reprinted from the *Journal of Social and Abnormal Psychology*,
51 (1955), 439-448, by permission of the senior author and the
American Psychological Association.

It is likely that the subjects of this study had never done finger painting prior to the time of the study and that they did not have specific attitudes toward finger pointing. The attitudes which they displayed must have been transferred from some general attitudes such as those toward "getting dirty" or "messing oneself." Opinions differ as to whether such attitudes are derived primarily from toilet training.

So far as social class differences are concerned, the student should be aware that traditions are transmitted downward in the social system. What is characteristic of a higher social class in one generation may be typical of a lower social group in the next generation.

During the past decade a new philosophy of child training has come into prominence. Variously termed "developmental," "permissive," "self-demand" or "child-centered," its two major tenets are (1) habit training should be started when the child is physiologically ready to comply, not before; and (2) the emotional climate in which the training takes place should be one of unconditional acceptance of the child, of tolerance for failure, not coercive adherence to rigid schedules. The first is consistent with the findings of a number of co-twin control experiments (see, e.g., Gesell and Thompson, 1929; McGraw, 1940). For the second there is some support from clinical studies (e.g., Huschka, 1947; Naumberg, 1947; Ribble, 1943) but the experimental evidence is still equivocal. The psychological advantages and disadvantages of permissive as compared with rigid child-training practices cannot, therefore, yet be clearly evaluated.

During this same period sociologists have been reporting striking social class differences in child-training practices (Davis and Havighurst, 1946; Ericson, 1947). Middle class parents, they find, are coercive, lower class, permissive. Middle class parents begin habit training earlier, set higher standards for achievement, and are less tolerant of failure. These studies, based only on what mothers say their practices are, include no data on how the children react to the parental demands. That class differences in training might result in class differences in personality development, however, is suggested by the sociologists. Davis and Havighurst (1946) generalize from their data, as follows: "We would say that middle class children are subjected earlier and more consistently to the influences which make a child an orderly, conscientious, responsible and tame person. In the course of this training, middle class children *probably* suffer more frustration of their impulses" (p. 707). Ericson's (1947) conclusions, based on the same population samples, are similar: "Middle class children are *probably* subjected to more frustrations in the process of achieving these learnings and are probably more anxious as a result of these pressures than are lower class children" (p. 501).

To test the validity of these generalizations, the reputed class differences in a specific area of habit training, namely bowel training, were selected as the focus of the present study. The rationale of the study was as follows: if the cleanliness standards of middle class parents are more rigid from infancy on, and if these standards are "frustrating," then an experimental task which requires the child to get dirty should elicit measurably different behaviors in middle and lower class children.

Three major differences in behavior were predicted:

1. Middle class children would more often try to avoid the task (refuse to enter into it, or be slower to accept it);

2. Middle class children would show more concern about getting dirty once in the task (maintain minimal contact with the materials);

3. Middle class children would show more concern about getting themselves cleaned up afterwards (go to the bathroom oftener).

Two experiments were designed to test these predictions. In the first, Experiment I, the child was required to use finger paints; in the second, Experiment II, a control experiment, crayons. It was predicted that the behavior of middle and lower class children would differ significantly in Experiment I, not in Experiment II.

EXPERIMENT I: THE FINGER-PAINTING STUDY METHOD

Subjects

Thirty-six four-year-old, white, nursery school children served as Ss. Eighteen were attending a university-sponsored nursery school in Cambridge, Massachusetts, the other 18 attended social-agency supported day nursery schools situated in lower class residential areas in Boston, Massachusetts.

Occupational, educational, residential, and other pertinent socio-economic data, as outlined by Warner, et al. (1949), obtained through parent interviews, teacher interviews, and school records, support the designation of the first group as middle class, the second as lower class. Both boys and girls were included, but not in equal numbers. All were within, or above, the normal IQ range.

As evidence of class differences in toilet training, parental time schedules, reported in median age in months for beginning and completing bowel training, are presented in Table I, along with the corresponding data from Davis and Havighurst (1946, p. 701). In both samples, middle class parents start training significantly earlier than do lower class parents. In the present sample, the middle class child achieves control significantly *later*; in the Davis and Havighurst sample, the two groups achieve control at about the same time. The first tenet of the new philosophy of permissiveness in child training, then, is seemingly more frequently violated by middle than by lower class parents in our sample since it is the former who start the training too early; *cf.* Spock (1948), and Gesell and Ilg (1943). The fact that middle class Ss achieve voluntary control later than do lower class Ss may be indirect evidence that the second tenet, a permissive emotional climate, is also being violated by our middle class parents.

Table I

Median Age in Months for Beginning and Completing Bowel Training in Lower and Middle Class White Children*

	Present Sample		Davis and Havighurst Data	
	Middle Class	Lower Class	Middle Class	Lower Class
Bowel Training Begun	9	11.2	7.5	10.2
Bowel Training Completed	27	18.0	18.4	18.8

* Present data compared with data from Davis and Havighurst (1946).

Materials

The Shaw (1934) finger paints, red, orange, yellow, green, blue, purple, brown, and black, were used. The paper was the usual 22- by 16-inch glazed paper recommended by Napoli (1946) for finger painting.

Procedure

Each S was tested individually in a small examining room where E had put out the materials in advance. These consisted of a sheet of dampened paper on the work table, the paints, in eight small jars, arranged in random order on a stand beside the table, and a smock, the latter being customary in these schools during painting sessions.

The E began the session by engaging S in conversation about finger paints: did he know what finger paints were, how to use them, etc. Regardless of *S*'s answers, *E* illustrated how both hands, both arms, and even the elbows could be used in this kind of painting.

To maximize contact with the paints, *S* was required to use his fingers for scooping the paints out of the jars.

The experimental task consisted of two finger paintings. For the first, the "free painting," the instructions were: "Paint anything you want to paint." For the second, the "family painting," the instructions were: "Paint a picture of your family—your brothers and sisters, mother and daddy." If *S* seemed uncertain of what was required of him, *E* asked: "Who are the people who live in your house?" *S* was then encouraged to enumerate these people and to draw them.

The *E* attempted to maintain an informal and permissive atmosphere during the experimental session.

Variables Measured

Sixteen formal variables were included for measurement. The list, including operational definitions, is given below.

1. Time to begin painting: measured from the moment *E* completes the instructions, to the time *S* begins actually to apply paint to paper; 10 sec. or less scored as "immediate," over 10 sec. as "delayed"; measured only for the "free painting."

2. Acceptance of task: scored as accepted if *S* does finger-paint; if refuses to paint, or, if in the second painting the content is something other than "a family," performance scored as "task not accepted."

3. Requests help: *S* asks *E* for help at some stage in the drawing.

4. Use of whole hand vs. finger-tip approach: *S* uses fingers and palm for smearing vs. only finger tips.

5. Use of both hands: *S* uses both hands in whole or part, simultaneously or successively.

6. Use of whole sheet vs. partial use of sheet: finished product covers whole sheet of papers vs. only a restricted portion.

7. Use of warm vs. cold colors: *S* makes more frequent use of red, orange, and yellow than of green, blue, and purple, as measured by a frequency count.

8. Use of monotones: *S* uses only one color.

9. Use of brown and/or black: *S* uses brown, black, or both.

10. Separate placement of colors: *S* applies paint in daubs, streaks, or patches, keeping each color separate against the white background of the paper.

11. Intermingling of colors: the colors border on each other, but each is retained in the finished product; overlapping of edges is included, "overlay," is not.

12. Indiscriminate mixing of colors: the identity of the separate colors is lost; the finished product characteristically looks "muddy."

13. Names "free drawing": S spontaneously announces what the drawing represents; scored only in the first painting.

14. Mutilation: S defaces finished product by smearing or overlay of fresh paint, original content unrecognizable in whole, or in part, by E; scored only in the second painting.

15. Asks to take paintings home: S asks permission to take his paintings home.

16. Washing-up behavior: S leaves task, goes to the bathroom, washes hands, face, etc., during or after task is completed.

For purposes of analysis and interpretation, the variables were grouped as follows: a. Measures of S's willingness to undertake the task: variables 1 and 2; b. Measures of S's willingness to remain in the situation: variables 3, 4, 5, and 6 in the free painting and 3, 4, and 5 in the family painting; c. Measures of color usage and color placement: variables 7, 8, 9, 10, 11, and 12; d. Measure of S's tolerance for an unstructured situation: variable 13; e. Measures of S's tolerance for the finished product: variables 14 and 15; f. Measure of S's tolerance for "the state of being dirty": variable 16.

RESULTS

The S was scored in terms of presence or absence of each variable. The scores are presented in Table II along with the probability values for significance of the differences between the two groups of Ss, computed by Fisher's (1950) exact test.

Free Painting Task

a. Willingness to undertake the task (variables 1 and 2). The behavior of the two groups differs significantly on one of these variables. Both groups comply with the instruction to paint a picture, but more lower class Ss accept the task immediately ($p = .001$).

b. Willingness to remain in the situation (variables 3, 4, 5, and 6). Three of the differences are significant in the expected direction. More lower class Ss use the whole hand for smearing ($p = .02$) and, indeed, smear with *both* hands ($p = .001$). More lower class Ss smear the paint over the *entire* surface of the paper ($p = .001$). Neither group requests help with the free painting.

The use of the finger tip, not the whole hand, and of a *different* finger tip for each separate color, is a middle, not a lower class behavior. Lower class Ss more often use a whole arm, "into-the-paints-to-the-elbow" technique. They apply the paints in wide swirling motions, using both hands, palms down, fingers spread, as contrasted with the constricted, small movements of middle class Ss.

c. Color usage and color placement.

Only one color usage variable yields a significant difference: lower class Ss more often use warm colors, red, orange, yellow; middle class Ss, cold colors, green, blue, purple ($p = .001$). The use of monotones is rare in both groups. Both groups use browns and blacks.

All of the color placement variables yield statistically significant differences. When clear separation of the colors occurs ($p = .05$), it does so only among middle class Ss. When the middle class S permits colors to come into contact he intermixes them in such manner that the colors lose their separate identity in the finished product ($p = .02$). The lower class S more often intermingles the colors ($p = .02$). As a consequence, the total effect of the two sets of paintings is strikingly different. The paintings of middle class Ss typically consist of daubs, streaks, or somewhat constricted wavy lines of paint widely separated from each other, or of dark, muddy-looking, formless masses with much overlay of one color on another, the original colors no longer being recognizable in the final product. The paintings of the lower class Ss, on the other hand, are more often warm and

Table II

Comparison of Middle and Lower Class Four-Year-Old Children on Two Finger-Painting Tasks

Variable	Free Painting Task			Family Painting Task		
	Middle Class Ss (N = 18)	Lower Class Ss (N = 18)	p^*	Middle Class Ss (N = 18)	Lower Class Ss (N = 18)	p^*
1. Begins to paint immediately	5	17	.001	—	—	—
2. Accepts task	18	18	1.000	4	12	.01
3. Requests help	0	0	1.000	8	3	.03
4. Use of whole hand	11	17	.02	12	17	.04
5. Use of both hands	8	17	.001	13	17	.09
6. Use of whole sheet	9	18	.001	—	—	—
7. Use of warm colors	1	10	.001	2	7	.06
8. Use of monotones	2	2	1.000	3	2	>.20
9. Use of brown and/or black	11	11	1.000	12	12	1.000
10. Separate placement of colors	4	0	.05	3	0	.11
11. Intermingles colors	2	13	.001	3	10	.02
12. Mixes colors indiscriminately	10	3	.02	8	5	>.20
13. Names free painting	14	7	.02	—	—	—
14. Mutilates painting	—	—	—	10	4	.04
15. Asks to take drawing home	—	—	—	18	1	<.001
16. Washing-up behavior	5	0	.02	18	18	1.000

* Computed by means of Fisher's (1950) exact test.

bright in color tone and the original colors are recognizable in the finished product.

d. The *S*'s tolerance for an unstructured situation.

Giving a name to the painting, is used as a measure of *S*'s intolerance for the unstructured situation. The difference between the two groups is statistically significant: more middle class Ss name the free painting (p = .02).

Sometimes the naming occurs right away, *S* announcing what he will paint. Sometimes it occurs only after the product is finished, when *E* routinely asked if the picture had a name.

e. The *S*'s tolerance for the finished product.

f. The *S*'s tolerance for the state of being dirty.

A frequency count of the number of Ss who left the task to go to the bathroom (variable 16) revealed a class difference. No lower class Ss went to the bathroom during, or at the end of the free painting task. Nor do they talk about wanting to go. This behavior occurs only among middle class Ss ($p = .02$).

Family Painting Task

a. Willingness to undertake the task (variables 1 and 2). As noted earlier, variable 1 was not measured here. Variable 2 did yield a significant difference in the expected direction: more lower class Ss comply with *E*'s instruction to paint a picture of the family ($p = .01$).

b. Willingness to remain in the situation. Two of these variables yield significant differences in the expected direction. As in the free painting, more lower class Ss use the whole hand for smearing ($p = .04$). Use of both hands for applying the paints, however, now only shows a tendency in favor of lower class Ss ($p = .09$).

c. Color usage and color placement.

None of the color usage variables yields a significant difference. One approaches significance: more lower class Ss tend to use warm colors ($p = .06$).

The direction of the differences for color placement variables remains the same in both paintings. But only intermingling ($p = .02$) reveals a significant between-class difference in the second painting.

d. The *S*'s tolerance for the finished product.

More middle class Ss mutilate the family painting ($p = .04$).

All middle class Ss asked for permission to take their paintings home. Only one lower class S made this request. The *p* here is beyond the .001 level of confidence.

e. The *S*'s tolerance for the state of being dirty.

After completing the second task, all Ss voluntarily entered the bathroom and washed up before returning to the classroom.

The results of Experiment I indicate, then, that the behavior of middle and lower class Ss does differ in the predicted ways: middle class Ss more often tried to avoid the finger-painting task and more often tried to avoid getting dirty while they were painting. They were apparently also more concerned than lower class Ss to get clean afterwards.

EXPERIMENT II: THE CRAYON STUDY METHOD

Subjects

Forty white, four-year-old, nursery school children served as S's. Twenty were enrolled in private schools in Worcester, Massachusetts, the other twenty in the social-agency-sponsored schools used in Experiment I. The sociological criteria for selecting the two groups, the one middle class, the other lower, were the same as in Experiment I.

The toilet-training time schedules are presented in Table III.

Table III

Mean Age in Months at Which Bowel Training Was Begun and Completed

	Middle Class		Lower Class			
	N	Ss	N	Ss	t	p
Bowel Training Begun	18	10	17	9	1.04	.30
Bowel Training Completed	18	25.9	16	17.4	4.49	<.01

Comparison of Tables I and III reveals some schedule differences. Experiment I was completed in 1948, Experiment II in 1951. In the 1948 sample (Table I), the middle class parent began the training earlier and completed it later than did the lower class parent. Both differences were significant. In 1951 (Table III), the middle class parent started and completed training later. But now only the completion data differ significantly for the two social classes. The reversal in starting-time, while not statistically significant, however, may have some importance.

In 1951, some middle class mothers volunteered during the interview that they had read "The Books" and that they were "following" them. By "The Books" they meant Gesell and Ilg (1943) and/or Spock (1948, 1946). In 1948, these books were not mentioned. Nor did lower class mothers mention them in 1951. Yet, if the attitudes of our 1951 middle class mothers were as consistently permissive as self-demand theory requires, and if the lower class mothers were continuing to be permissive, then logically, training should be completed approximately at the same time in the two social classes. But, as Table III shows, this is not the case. As in 1948, middle class Ss still achieve control significantly *later* ($p = .01$). What seems likely, therefore, is that the middle class delay in starting training may stand alone in "taking over" the new philosophy of child care. The attitudes and emotional climate may still be coercive. This will be considered again in a later section.

Materials

Milton-Bradley Trutone Crayons were used. The colors were the same as in Experiment I. The drawing paper was of the newsprint variety. The size of the paper corresponded to that customarily used in the given nursery school.

Procedure

The procedure was the same as in Experiment I, adjustments being made only for the difference in medium. For example, no demonstration of crayoning was given.

Variables Measured

1. Time to begin crayoning.
2. Acceptance of task.
3. Use of whole sheet vs. partial use of sheet.
4. Use of warm vs. cold colors.
5. Use of monotones.
6. Use of brown and/or black crayons.
7. Separate placement of colors.
8. Intermingling of colors.
9. Indiscriminate mixing of colors.
10. Names "free drawing."
11. Mutilation.
12. Takes initiative in cleaning-up: at end of session, S spontaneously offers to put away crayons and/or to clean the table.
13. Asks to take drawings home.
14. Asks to do an extra drawing: at end of session, S asks if he may make one more picture.

As in Experiment I, S was scored in terms of presence or absence of each variable.

These scores constitute the data for analysis.

RESULTS

Of the 24 differences analyzed, only two were statistically significant. Since this could occur by chance alone, no further discussion of these data will be presented.

The hypothesis Experiment II was designed to test is supported: middle and lower class S's behave in the same way when the drawing medium does not necessitate getting dirty.

DISCUSSION

As predicted, finger paints, not crayons, yielded statistically significant differences in the behavior of middle and lower class nursery school children. Middle class Ss do appear to be made anxious by the smearing requirement: they have a lower tolerance for getting dirty, for staying dirty, and for the products they produce while dirty. Among the more obvious variables to reveal these differences are the slower acceptance by middle class Ss of the finger-painting task, the maintenance of only minimal contact with the paints (e.g., a single finger tip, not a whole-hand approach), the substitution of a different content for the "family" painting and/or final mutilation of it. Differences yielded by other variables also support the thesis of tolerance differences, as can be seen by relating these variables to the empirical findings of other studies, as discussed below.

While investigators are not in complete accord about the psychological significance of color usage (Precker, 1950), many make a distinction between warm and cold colors. Cold colors in children's drawings have been associated with depression (Pfister, 1934), delinquency (Philips and Stromberg, 1948), poor adjustment (Waehner, 1946), and controlled reactions as opposed to free emotional expression (Alschuler and Hattwick, 1947); warm colors, with cheerfulness and good adjustment (Alschuler and Hattwick, 1947; Brick, 1944; Philips and Stromberg, 1948; Traube, 1937; Waehner, 1946; Wolff, 1946). The parsimonious application of these findings to our results is that middle class Ss by using more cold colors in Experiment I are attempting to control their feelings. The greater use of warm colors by lower class Ss is consistent with absence of situational anxiety.

Our color placement data fall into the three patterns previously noted by Alschuler and Hattwick (1947). One pattern, separate placement, they suggest, is the response of the emotionally more mature child who has an "extreme sense of order and cleanliness" and "repressed desires to smear and to soil" (p. 82). A second pattern, indiscriminate mixing, is the response of the emotionally immature child who is still functioning "on a manipulative, smearing level" (p. 47). Both the more controlled separate placement and the uncontrolled indiscriminate mixing occurred in middle, not lower class Ss in the present study. Lower class Ss more often resorted to a third pattern, the intermingling of colors. According to Alschuler and Hattwick (p. 47), intermingling is not associated with "strain or emotional tension."

Constricted use of the drawing paper has been found to characterize the behavior of the timid child (Lembke, 1930), the rejected and deprived child (Brick, 1944), the withdrawing, emotionally dependent child (Alschuler and Hattwick, 1946); use of the whole sheet, the "uninhibited" child (Wolff, 1946), the "relatively outgoing, assertive, self-reliant personality" (Alschuler and Hattwick, 1946). In our results, middle class Ss resort to the constricted pattern, lower class to the unconstricted.

The assigning of a name to the "free" painting, a variable which characterized middle class Ss, is reminiscent of Frenkel-Brunswick's (1949) concept of intolerance for ambiguity. The structuring of an unstructured situation by giving it a name may help S control or contain the anxieties aroused by smearing. By naming, S may be saying: "I have drawn *something*; I have not just been smearing."

The more frequent request of middle class Ss for help with the family painting suggests another mechanism of defense: only if the adult gets dirty, too, is it all right for the middle class S to get dirty!

The middle class S's lack of spontaneity about cleaning up the examining room would seem to be consistent with the rest of his behavior. It may mean that he wants to get away quickly from the scene of his smearing misdoings. Or, like the middle class child in the Fisher *et al.* (1941) balloon film, he departs without helping, knowing that "somebody else will clean up." Characteristically, for the middle class child, someone else does. Teachers in the lower class schools tell us that these children are taught to clean up after themselves. They appear here to do so willingly.

Two different explanations occur to us with respect to the middle class S's more frequent request to take his drawings home: (1) he may want to use his products as a gift to appease the parent who disapproves of his getting dirty; or (2) he may wish to destroy the evidence himself. To choose between these alternatives, we would have to know "the-take-home-policies" of these schools, as well as what, in fact, S would do with his products were he allowed to retain them.

Consistently, then, the finger-painting data support the thesis of social-class tolerance differences for getting and staying dirty. Middle class Ss are seemingly made more anxious by the smearing task. As predicted, however, behavioral differences break down when crayons are used as the drawing medium. Yet since some middle class mothers in the crayon study tell us that they are following "The Books," the argument could be made that the crayon study does not serve as an adequate control, that we are no longer dealing with coercively vs. permissively reared children. Indeed, there are no differences now in the parental time schedules for starting toilet training. Differences in time for completing training, however, persist. This latter fact, we feel, supports the argument that the emotional climate in which the training is taking place is different in the two social classes.

Middle class mothers, influenced by modern parent-oriented literature, may be *trying* to be more permissive. Yet if their attitudes toward dirt and messiness are still traditionally middle class, and Klatskin's (1952) study done during the same time interval suggests that they are, the likelihood is that these parents would resort either to inconsistent permissiveness or to a laissez-faire policy. In either case, we would expect control to be delayed since "the rules" for winning parental approval would not be clear to the child. Class differences in the atmosphere in which the training is taking place would thus still pertain. Exposure to a new philosophy of training, as Klatskin (1952) notes, does not insure the proper attitudes for applying it.

A recent study by Maccoby *et al.* (1954), however, raises some important questions. It overlaps in time, and to some extent in geographical sampling, our crayon experiment. On the basis of interviews with middle and lower class mothers, they report a shift "toward greater warmth and permissiveness, and less severity in socialization among upper-middle families with the more severe training occurring among the lower group" (p. 392). As in our crayon study, bowel training is started a little later by middle class mothers, but not significantly so. Unlike our study, training is completed by middle and lower class children at about the same time. This latter difference is an important one. Yet we cannot fully account for it.

In comparing their data with those of Davis and Havighurst (1946), Maccoby *et al.* (1954, p. 394) raise the question of sampling differences. Davis and Havighurst, they suggest, may have been dealing with a "lower" lower class sample. But Ericson (1947, p. 496) used the Davis and Havighurst sample and describes it as "for the most part, upper-lower class." Our lower class sample was primarily middle-lower. The linear relationship between severity of training and class membership, from lower-lower to upper-middle, as reported by Maccoby *et al.*, moreover, would fit neither the Davis and Havighurst data, nor ours. Sampling differences, therefore, would seem not to be the crucial factor.

A more promising lead is suggested by the Maccoby *et al.* question as to whether "upper-middle mothers were telling the interviewers not what they actually do but what they believe would be the right thing to say to the interviewer" (1954, p. 392). In telling us that they are following "The Books," our middle class mothers may also have been telling us "the right thing." Yet, since they report an even later age for completing bowel training, may this not mean that their standards for cleanliness are very high indeed?

We raise a final, and perhaps the most basic question for future research. Judging from recent, informal discussions with parents at PTA meetings, for example, middle class parents *are* reading "The Books." But they seem to be equating permissiveness and laissez faire. They mistake the "let the child do anything he wants to do, lest we frustrate him by imposing rules," for permissiveness. The consequences of permissiveness and laissez faire for personality development, however, theoretically should be quite different. Laissez faire, with its absence of rules, absence of any sort of guidance, should make for insecurity, indecisiveness, and feelings that the parents are not interested enough to help. Yet from the parents' point of view the training procedures might seem permissive because they are "lenient." Consistent with this possibility are the Maccoby *et al.* findings of statistically significant class differences in techniques of discipline. Upper-lower mothers more often use what Maccoby *et al.* describe as "negative techniques" (1954, p. 387): physical punishment, ridicule, and deprivation of privileges; upper-middle mothers more often use scolding statements involving withdrawal of love (1954, Table VI, p. 388). That the latter can make children very anxious indeed is clinically now well recognized.

To gain further insight into the problems raised by this discussion necessitates additional research. Among the studies which might profitably be undertaken are: (1) a repetition of the original finger-painting study in which the consequences of different parental attitudes as well as of different training procedures are investigated; (2) a study of the behavioral consequences of social class differences in habit training areas other than toilet training; and (3), a systematic study of the extent to which present-day parents are confusing permissiveness with laissez faire.

SUMMARY

Starting with the findings by sociologists that child-training practices differ markedly in middle and lower class families, two related experiments were designed to measure behavioral consequences of the reputedly coercive, rigid middle class procedures as contrasted with the more permissive lower class procedures. The conjectures of Davis and Havighurst (1946, p. 707) that middle class children "probably suffer more frustration of their impulses," and of Ericson (1947, p. 501) that middle class children "are probably more anxious as a result of these pressures," were tested, using class differences in toilet training procedures as the basis for the experimental design.

In the first experiment, eighteen middle and eighteen lower class white, nursery school children used finger paints for painting two pictures. The S chose his own content for the first picture. For the second, he was asked to paint a picture of his family. Quantitative analysis of the formal aspects of the paintings reveals statistically significant differences in the performance of the two groups of Ss. The middle class Ss show a lower tolerance for getting dirty, for staying dirty, and for the products they produce while dirty, as measured by such variables as time to begin painting, color usage, mutilation of the family painting, bathroom behavior, etc.

In the second experiment, crayons were used as the drawing medium. As predicted, the class differences obtained in the first experiment do not persist in the second experiment. The class differences in Experiment I, therefore, reflect differences in reactions "to getting dirty," not differences in drawing, as such.

The results are interpreted to mean that soiling and smearing behavior does arouse more anxiety in middle than in lower class children. The mechanisms used by the middle class child to handle this anxiety are discussed.

References

Alschuler, Rose H., and La Berta B. W. Hattwick, *Painting and Personality*, Vol. I, II. Chicago: University of Chicago Press, 1947.

Brick, N. "The Mental Hygiene Value of Children's Art Work," *American Journal of Orthopsychiatry*, 14 (1944), 136-146.

Davis, W. A., and R. J. Havighurst, "Social Class and Color Differences in Child-Rearing," *American Sociological Review*, 11 (1946), 698-710.

Ericson, Martha, "Child-Rearing and Social Status," In T. M. Newcomb, E. L. Hartley, and others, eds., *Readings in Social Psychology*. New York: Holt, Rinehart & Winston, Inc., 1947.

Fisher, M. S., L. J. Stone, and J. Backer, "Balloons: Demonstration of a Projective Technique for the Study of Aggression and Destruction in Young Children." New York: New York Film Library, 1941. (Film)

Fisher, R. A., *Statistical Methods for Research Workers*, (6th ed.) Edinburgh: Oliver and Boyd, 1936. Also in A. C. Edwards, *Experimental Design in Psychological Research*. New York: Holt, Rinehart & Winston, Inc., 1950, p. 84-85.

Frenkel-Brunswik, Else. "Intolerance of Ambiguity as an Emotional and Personality Variable," *Journal of Personality*, 18 (1949), 108-143.

Gesell, A., and Frances Ilg, *Infant and Child in the Culture of Today*. New York: Harper & Row, Publishers, 1943.

————, and Helen Thompson, "Learning and Growth in Identical Infant Twins, *Genetic Psychology Monographs*, 6 (1929), 1-124.

Huschka, Mabel, "The Child's Response to Coercive Bowel Training," in S. S. Tomkins, ed., *Contemporary Psychopathology*. Cambridge: Harvard University Press, 1947.

Klatskin, Ethelyn H., "Shifts in Child Care Practices in Three Social Classes Under an Infant Care Program of Flexible Methodology," *American Journal of Orthopsychiatry*, 22 (1952), 52-61.

Lembke, W., "Über zeichnungen von frechen und schuchteren kindern," *Zeitschrift für pod. Psychologie*, 31 (1930), 459-462.

Maccoby, Eleanor E., Patricia K. Gibbs, and others, "Methods of Child-Rearing in Two Social Classes," in W. E. Martin and Celia B. Stendler eds., *Readings in Child Development*. New York: Harcourt, Brace & World Inc., 1954.

McGraw, Myrtle B., "Neural Maturation as Exemplified in Achievement of Bladder Control," *Journal of Pediatrics*, 16 (1940), 580-590.

Napoli, P. J., "Finger-Painting and Personality Diagnosis," *Genetic Psychology Monographs*, 34 (1946), 129-230.

Naumberg, Margaret, "Studies of the Free Art Expression of Behavior Problem Children and Adolescents as a Means of Diagnosis and Therapy," *Nervous and Mental Disorders Monographs*, 71 (1947), 1-225.

Pfister, O., "Farbe unde Bewegung in der Zeichnung Geisteskranker," *Schweitzer Archiv für Neurologie und Psychiatrie*, 34 (1934), 325-365.

Philips, E., and E. A. Stromberg, "Comparative Study of Finger-Painting Performance in Detention Home and High School Pupils," *Journal of Psychology*, 26 (1948), 507-515.

Precker, J. A., "Painting and Drawing in Personality Assessment," *Journal of Projective Techniques*, 14 (1950), 262-286.

Ribble, Margaret A., *The Rights of Infants*. New York: Columbia University Press, 1943.

Shaw, Ruth F., *Finger-Painting*. Boston: Little, Brown and Co., 1934.

Spock, B., *Pocket Book of Baby and Child Care*. New York: Pocket Books, Inc., 1948.

————, *The Common Sense Book of Baby and Child Care*. New York: Duell, Sloan & Pearce, Inc., 1946.

Traube, T., "La valeur diagnostique des dessins des enfants difficiles," *Archives de Psychologie*, 26 (1937), 285-309.

Waehner, Trude S., "Interpretations of Spontaneous Drawings and Paintings," *Genetic Psychology Monographs*, 33 (1946), 1-70.

Warner, W. L., Marchia Meeker, and K. Eells, *Social Class in America*. Chicago: Science Research Associates, 1949.

Wolff, W., *Personality of the Preschool Child*. New York: Grune & Stratton, Inc., 1946.

4 · Intelligence Scores of Isolated Mountain Children

MANDEL SHERMAN AND CORA B. KEY

Abridged from the article in *Child Development*, 3 (1932), 279-290, by permission of the Society for Research in Child Development.

Every intelligence test that has been devised requires the subject to respond to test materials. Probably no set of test materials can be equally familiar to all children. What the child learns varies greatly from society to society, and it is difficult, if not impossible, to find test questions that do not penalize some groups.

Sherman and Key show that some American children are penalized by American intelligence tests because of the intellectual poverty of their environment.

This report of the results of intelligence tests made of mountain children is part of a larger study begun in the summer of 1929 to determine the cultural influences which affect intellectual, emotional, and personality development and the influences determining the attitudes of mountain people living in relative degrees of isolation.

The communities studied were four hollows located approximately 100 miles west of Washington, D.C., in the Blue Ridge Mountains and a small village at the base of the Blue Ridge about the same distance from Washington to the southwest. The Hollows were settled in the precolonial period by English and Scotch-Irish immigrants. When German immigrants were given most of the land in the Shenandoah valley surrounding these mountain ranges the English and Scotch-Irish people were forced up the mountainside. The topography of this region is such that the settlers were forced further within the mountains, settling in hollows surrounded by mountain ranges. There they built their log and mud cabins, many of which still remain and are inhabited. Each of the hollows selected for study, Colvin, Needles, Oakton, and Rigby are close to each other but are separated by comparatively high mountain ranges. Of these hollows, Colvin is at the lowest level in social development. This hollow is small, consisting of a small number of families living in scattered, mud-plastered log huts. There is no road, except for a trail to the outside world. One small log and mud cabin is rented by the county school board for a school.

There is no general meeting place and the church meetings which have been held in the past have been discontinued except for a very occasional revival meeting. With three exceptions, the adults are illiterate. They are descendents of the original settlers who married relatives and mixed very little with the people outside of the hollows. Colvin Hollow is so named because most of the inhabitants are Colvins. Many of the younger children do not know their last names. They identify themselves, for example, as Sadie's Bennie or Dicy's Willie.

Needles Hollow adjacent to Colvin Hollow, is next in the scale of social development. It is reached by a rocky road from a small hamlet at the base of the mountains. Its patches of ground, from two to five acres on the average, surrounding the cabins, approach the status of small farms. It is a more socialized community and many of the adults are literate. The children have had good school advantages compared to Colvin Hollow.

Oakton Hollow, next higher in the social scale, is separated from Colvin Hollow by a high mountain. The road to the valley is passable for old Fords and wagons most of the year. The hollow boasts of a combined general store and post office and many of the inhabitants receive mail and an occasional magazine. There exists a greater social consciousness than in Colvin or Needles Hollows. Oakton Hollow has had about four months of school each year for some time. The people are fairly prosperous although they have but little surplus farm products to sell in the valley.

Rigby Hollow, culturally further developed, can be reached from the valley much more easily than any of the other three hollows. The present school was established by missionaries about nine years ago and has been conducting regular school terms. Church and Sunday School services are held regularly. The farms are larger than those of the other hollows and there nearly always is a surplus which is sold in the valley. School terms have been about seven months each year for the past eight years and approximately 75 per cent of the inhabitants are literate.

For purposes of comparison a small farm and sawmill town, Briarsville, was chosen. It is located at the base of the mountains to the south of the Hollows. The town has a hard-surfaced road connecting it with the principal cities of Virginia. The school building is a modern structure with four classrooms, three of which are used regularly. The school board employs three well-trained teachers. The town has a good general store, telephones, and receives newspapers.

The comparison of the intelligence test results of the mountain children with those of the children of Briarsville is especially significant in view of the origin of many of the residents of this town. Many of the inhabitants migrated from the mountains in the past to obtain work on the adjacent farms and in the sawmill. At first socially isolated from the "first" families of this town, the children now mingle freely. It was thought that a comparison of intelligence test results of the mountain children with those of

Briarsville would be much more significant than with children of an average town or city.

Intelligence tests were given to more than half of the children of the four mountain hollows and Briarsville. Not every child was tested, for some of the younger children could not be taken to the place where the tests were given, and a few of the others refused to cooperate. Nine tests were used: the Stanford-Binet; The National Intelligence Test, Scale B, Form 2; Pintner-Cunningham Primary Mental Test. For performance tests the following were employed: Manikin, Seguin Form Board, Mare and Foal, Healy Puzzle "A," the Knox Cube Test from the Pintner-Patterson scale of performance tests, and Goodenough's Drawing of a Man.

A representative sample of the school population thus was tested. A total of 386 tests were given to the children in the mountain communities and 198 in Briarsville. The children in Briarsville were not given Stanford-Binet tests because of the difficulty in organizing the program there. One hundred and two children were examined in the mountain communities and 81 in Briarsville. In addition to an investigation of test scores and mental age results, a qualitative analysis of the responses was made.

Table I shows the length of the school term in five communities since 1918. The Colvin Hollow School has been the most irregular with the least number of months of schooling. Between 1918 and 1929 Colvin Hollow has had only 16 months of school at irregular intervals. It was impossible to find an exact record of the years in which school was held. Rigby Hollow has the most regular school term of the mountain communities.

The superiority of the Briarsville school system is shown not only in the greater number of months in which school was held in the past 11 years but also in the regularity of the school term.

Table I

Length of School Terms in Months in the Five Communities

Year	Colvin	Needles	Rigby	Oakton	Briarsville
1918-19		?	4	6	9
1919-20		2	4	6	9
1920-21		2	4	6	9
1921-22		0	4	6	9
1922-23	16 months	4	4	7	9
1923-24		2	4	5.5	9
1924-25		2	7	6	9
1925-26		2	7	4	9
1926-27		2	7	5	9
1927-28		2	7	3	9
1928-29		5	7	7	9
1929-30		7	7	7	9
Total months 1918-1930	16	30?	66	66.5	108

Table II shows the average intelligence quotient of the children in the four mountain communities and Briarsville. The average intelligence quotient of the Briarsville children was higher than that of the mountain chil-

Table II

Average Intelligence Quotients According to Various Tests

Tests	Mountain Communities			Briarsville		
	Number of cases	Average	S. D.	Number of cases	Average	S. D.
Stanford-Binet	32	61.5	11.2			
National	24	61.2	17.5	50	96.1	15.2
Pinter-Cunningham	42	75.9	17.1	31	87.6	13.0
Four performance tests:						
Year scale	54	83.9	24.8	10	118.6	17.1
Med. M.A. scale	54	79.1	23.8	10	95.6	16.3
Drawing of a Man	63	72.3	17.9	67	76.3	17

dren in every test, and had a smaller standard deviation. The results give further evidence of the effect of systematic training upon intelligence test ratings, a factor often slighted in comparative studies of intelligence test scores.

The dependence of the intelligence quotients on the kind of test used is shown in a comparison of the average IQ's of the mountain children on the different tests used. The highest average intelligence quotients are found in the test presumably most independent of language and of school training, and lowest in those utilizing language ability.

When we examine the results of the tests in Briarsville, on the other hand, we find that while the highest average IQ was obtained in the performance tests, the next highest was on the National Intelligence test—a test dependent upon language ability. This may be additional evidence that systematic and consistent training in a community of a comparatively high order or social organization is a stimulus to the development of the kind of intelligence we ordinarily measure by tests.

These mountain children are slow and cautious with a slow tempo of response. The way in which the environment influences a child's method of responding probably has not been studied sufficiently in intelligence test results. In scoring the results it was found that the children rated highest in those tests in which the tempo of the directions and the responses was slowest. It is not surprising to find that the children rated highest on tests which took into account least the factor of speed. The children in these mountains live in an environment which does not put a premium on speed and the problem of evaluation of their test scores thus is complicated further.

The Stanford-Binet test at once might be considered inadequate because of its evident dependence upon language and school training. Analysis of the successes and failures on this test further showed its unadaptability for studying this type of children. Failures were most evident on items involving abstract comprehension. This sort of failure differed in degree in the various communities. The Colvin Hollow children failed most frequently in tests involving calculation, in part because the terms used were foreign to them. The difficulty of evaluating failures on simple problems is due in part to the uncertainty of knowing whether the children failed because of insufficient language comprehension to understand the directions. Rote memory was found to be above the average of other test results, but the most common failure in Colvin Hollow was in the reversal of numbers. Following the giving and scoring of the tests, a number of children were given practice in the reversal of the number sequences 1-2-3. After it was thought that they could reverse this sequence other numbers containing four figures were given. As an example, the sequence of 6-5-2-8 was reversed by most of the children as 6-5-4-3-2-1.

The almost universal failure of the mountain children in the ball and field test indicates their lack of ability to comprehend and solve a simple problem involving foresight and planning ability. Few of the children appeared to have a plan for finding the ball in a circular field. Usually a line was drawn in the center of the diagram and in some cases this was varied by dots indicating trees. Many children of Colvin and Needles Hollows could not understand the directions of the ball and field test. They had little comprehension of the meaning of "field" and were astonished at a ball being lost. (Most of the children never had seen a ball.) One boy of thirteen made a curious effort. He drew a number of small rough circles in the enclosure which he explained as representing trees. Then he drew a line from one circle to the next connecting them. He then stated that he was hunting for the lost article under the trees. In this and other cases it was very difficult to assume, as one is forced to do in scoring the test, that the failure indicates a deficiency of innate intelligence even on that one test. Although it is not assumed that a child must have experience in the performance called for on a given test, and indeed such direct experience would mitigate the significance of the score, it can be assumed that a child must have had some approximate or similar experience. These mountain children live in an environment calling for little planning and ingenuity expected of an average child of not more than nine years.

Evidently space and form differentiation as employed in these tests are relatively foreign to these children. Only one of the younger children in Colvin Hollow correctly copied the drawing of a diamond.

The items which the children in all the hollows passed most consistently were the mutilated pictures, counting backwards from 20, arranging weights and comprehension of pictures. In two of the hollows most of the children

Table III

Average Intelligence Quotient on Five Tests According to Increasing Chronological Age*

Chronological Age	Number of Cases		Pintner-Cunningham		National Intelligence		Drawing of a Man		Performance Scale			
									Year Scale		Med M. A. Scale	
	Mountains	Briarsville	Mountains	Briarsville	Mountains	Briarsville	Mountains	Briarsville	Mountains	Briarsville	Mountains	Briarsville
6-8	12-13	8	84	94			80	93	91		89	
8-10	15-23	4-22	70	91		117	66	82	84	119	76	93
10-12	5-16	5-20	53	76	66	101	71	69	86	108	70	87
12-14	7-12	16			67	91	69	73	83		83	
14-16	8-15	14			52	87	49	70	75		73	

* The figures indicating the number of cases does not mean that every test was given to the numbers indicated. The minimum and maximum number of children given a test at the respective chronological ages is shown.

could not name the days of the week in correct sequence. This failure probably was due to the fact that they have no use for differentiation of days, since one day is like the next in its significance except for the days of going to school and staying at home.

Table III gives the average intelligence quotients on various tests according to increasing chronological age. It shows a decrease in intelligence quotients with increase in chronological age for every test except the National, applied to the mountain children. The decrease in the intelligence quotients in some of the tests is as great from the sixth to the tenth year as from the tenth to the sixteenth year. In some cases the decline in intelligence for children over ten is greater than for children between six and ten. An intelligence test is an indirect measure. An estimate of intelligence is based on the information the child has been able to obtain. In the mountain environment increments of information become less large with increases in age, and the seven-year-old has relatively more chance to gather information and to learn by experience than the twelve-year-old in the same environment.

SUMMARY

The results of the intelligence tests of mountain children living in varying degrees of isolation appear to corroborate the belief of many psychologists that the expression of intelligence, as measured by standardized tests, depends in a large measure upon the opportunities to gather information and upon the requirements made upon the individual by his environment. Since the ancestry of the children of all the Hollows came from the same stock, the claim cannot be made that some of these mountain people are "degenerate" and therefore their children are expected to be retarded intellectually, a claim too often advanced for the supposed inferiority of isolated mountain children. Furthermore, as has been shown in this paper, the young children of the various Hollows do not differ greatly in intelligence, whereas great differences are found between the older children of the different Hollows. The only plausible explanation of the increasing difference with increasing age is that children develop only as the environment demands development. The Colvin Hollow environment is as stimulating to the child of four or five as that of Oakton or Rigby, but Colvin Hollow requires relatively little more of its older children whereas Rigby Hollow requires an ability for social adjustment met only by a high order of intelligence.

5 · Independence in Swiss and American Children

LEONORE BOEHM

Reprinted from *Child Development*, 28 (1957), 85-92, by permission of the author and the Society for Research in Child Development.

That children of different countries develop differently scarcely any person would question. However, until recently, psychologists have had few ways of documenting this fact or of measuring national differences. Piaget's methods have provided an approach to this area of investigation. Dr. Boehm has used them for this purpose.

THE PROBLEM

The European who comes to the United States is surprised to find a more rapid social development in American children than he has been used to seeing in European children. In thought and action American children become independent of their elders at an earlier age than do European children. Not only do they depend less on adult guidance and judgment, but their consciences seem to mature earlier also.

Stendler (1954) has indicated that the American mother unwittingly transfers some of the child's dependency from herself to his peer group at the preschool age, while the Parisian mother still thinks of him as *"bébé,"* constantly needing her to teach him which kind of behavior she approves and which she disapproves. The American child learns to find satisfaction in the approval of his young playmates and strives to avoid their disapproval. Through parent interviews Stendler uncovered certain significant differences in educational goals between Parisian and American middle class mothers. The younger Parisian child is encouraged to be gentle, quiet, self-controlled; in other words, well-mannered and civilized; the older one to be self-sufficient, well-integrated, and an individualistic thinker, which prepares him to become a typical Frenchman (Stendler, 1954). Middle class American parents attempt to bring up children who will be independent of their parents, who will be accepted, practicing members of their own peer groups. [Note that this is achieved by substituting peer dependency for parent dependency (Mead, 1954).] Riesman (1950) explains this difference: In all "inner-directed societies" as in Europe's "old middle

460

class," parents try to bring about, through education, the internalization in their children of the parents' values and goals. The smaller child is pushed until he learns to "push himself to the limits of his talents and beyond," regardless of the possible conflict that his achievements might raise for him in his efforts to relate to his peers. Throughout childhood the parent remains the source of guidance. The child is brought up to believe in and respect the authority of his parents, teachers, and other surrounding adults who, as such, are held to be superior to him. The European parent remains omnipotent and omniscient. Thus Piaget (1929) received many answers from Swiss children who believed that it was their father or grandfather who had created the world, the rivers, the mountains. European parents think it is wrong to let children realize that they—the parents—do not know everything.

In all "other-directed societies," to which the upper middle class of our large cities belongs according to Riesman, parents are no longer sure of their own values and standards. Due to the rate of change of our society, to social mobility, to immigration, the new generation no longer follows in its parents' footsteps. On the contrary, children are supposed to surpass their parents. As Mead reminds us, many a mother dreams of her son's becoming President of the United States. No longer can the parent feel superior to the child, but suffering from a lack of self-assurance, he does not wish to face the responsibility of directing the child. He believes that the child's contemporaries can advise better than his parents, that they know better what standards are important, what ideals and goals a youngster should have. Thus it is the peer group that has become the individual's source of direction, whose reactions have become important, whose approval must be obtained. Being popular with one's age group is a primary value. It is even more to be sought after than fame achieved through competitive activity. Social security has become one aim of education. The child, of course, senses the lack of self-confidence in his parents, he senses that the parents see in him at least a potential equal, if not a future superior. He realizes that the parents' knowledge is limited and that they, too, make mistakes. As a matter of fact, American parents, teachers, and other authorities feel that this realization is necessary for the sake of the children's feelings of security and early adult independence. Instead of learning to obey blindly, without questioning the adult's judgment, as one does in Europe, the child here is encouraged to use critical thinking in the hopes that his reasoning will become "autonomous" or "interiorized" as Piaget (1926) calls this quality of objective, independent thinking.

Many an incident could be told by a person who has lived both in Europe and in the United States to give evidence of the differences in child development and behavior resulting from the respective differences in objectives and modes of training. A European child is a guest of his parents: a permanent guest, it is true, but one who will be asked to leave the dinner table if his behavior is not quiet and respectful. A European school child told this investigator that his father made the best pancakes when the fact was that the father, a scholar who was all thumbs in the kitchen or shop, would have difficulty boiling water. Constrast this with the American father who said that he believed he should treat his child as a potential equal (if not superior), and that their home belonged to children and parents together; or the director of a Congregational church school in Illinois, who, when asked by his five-year-old son if there was a God, though a firm believer himself, answered that some people believed in God, while others did not. He wanted his boy to decide independently in all matters possible, rather than to assume that his father was always right.

Good preschools in this country are geared toward an education for independent thinking as well as for group living. Perhaps because of the marked difference in educational aims, there are but few preschools in Europe. There the *bébé* is expected to look to his mother for guidance. It is held that he does not need to start his social education at such an early age. In our preschools children are encouraged to find their own solutions whenever they are able to, even if these are not as perfect as adults'. At a young age this is possible mainly in concrete, practical matters, be it in regards to their work or to social living. In most preschools there are fewer rules and regulations for the older than for the younger group. The older ones are supposed to make their own decisions. To give an example: There is usually a rule for the younger group, that rubbers or boots have to be worn outdoors on days when there are puddles on the playground. There often is no such rule for the older children. They have become old enough to realize that they must put boots on only if they want to play in puddles. They may choose to play where it is wet or where it is dry. Thus they may decide whether to wear boots or not.

Whereas the European school is concerned mostly with academic learning and little with cooperation or "character education"—the latter being the home's responsibility, a principal at an elementary school in Winnetka, Illinois, stated to the author that the school's primary functions are to teach children independent thinking and the skills necessary for living together. The teacher's role in this country is then, according to this informant, different from that of the European teacher. His obligation is to make the children realize that they are his potential equals. Children owe less respect merely to the teacher's role. They should be discerning enough to respect only a person who merits respect. Children should be made aware of the fact that their teachers sometimes err, and that their teacher's judgment is not always better than their own. Quite in contrast to the powerful European teacher, the more informal American teacher does not need to be feared and hated. He has become, in Riesman's words, a "peer-group facilitator and mediator."

Many observations in European and American schools give evidence of an earlier cooperation among children here. In Europe the child is often told to work individually; here, the children are encouraged to help each other, be it directly or by constructive suggestions and criticism. At an age when the European kindergartner uses "egocentric" speech, according to Piaget (1924), the American one needs speech mainly for real peer communication.

A question which comes to the fore when studying differing rates of social development is whether, in a culture which values cooperation among children more than dependence upon adults, *social conscience* matures earlier due to stress on skills necessary for group life. Does the child's conscience remain "egocentric" longer in an inner-directed society than it does in an other-directed society? It is quite possible that the relatively early independence of the American child causes his conscience to develop not only from identification and interiorization of the ethical values of his parents, but also from the values of those of his peers to whom he has, in part, transferred his dependence. Is this "inner-directed child" older than his "other-directed" opposite number before he stops basing his moral judgments on the outcome of the subject's actions alone? As Piaget states, the young child is anxious to "*expier par sanction*" (to unburden his conscience of its sense of guilt by undergoing punishment). This atonement is relevant to his own needs only and is entirely unconnected with those of the victim. It is a childish expiation chosen in order to re-establish the offender's inner balance because his deed has "destroyed the equilibrium of the world." The worse the deed then, even though it be an accident and possibly due to excellent intentions, the more disagreeable must the punishment be to absolve the child's conscience. The question which we are raising here would also suggest that an "inner-directed child" must be older than an "other-directed child" before he bases his moral judgments not only on the effects of the deed but also on the feelings of the victim and on the offender's intentions.

One wonders whether these findings of Piaget are true for all children in the civilized world. There might be a difference in the rate of formation of the conscience as well as in its content when one compares children in the United States with those in Calvinist Switzerland. One might expect a different type of conscience here where education is directed outwardly rather than inwardly, where ideals, goals, and values are geared primarily toward social adjustment and not toward character improvement or toward perfection of the soul for the sake of salvation. Possibly the values of an outer-directed conscience are easier for a human being to achieve than are those of an inner-directed conscience. Perhaps this is another reason why the American child's conscience may become autonomous earlier. It requires less introspection. It is less inwardly turned in its self-evaluation, less self-concerned, less perfectionistic. Thus it becomes less destructive to his self-confidence, less guilt- and shame-ridden than is the conscience of the

Swiss child who has been taught to struggle continually against his own tendencies toward wrongdoing. According to Riesman, however, Americans replace the inner-directed person's specific guilt feelings with diffuse anxiety, which he maintains is necessary to build up in the individual that emotional sensitivity to the feelings of others which will serve as a much needed facilitator of social adjustment.

PROCEDURE

This investigation grew out of an earlier study of the author's in which we used Piaget's *"méthode clinique"*—talking to individual children, telling stories, and asking questions designed to reveal their reasoning at different age levels. The original purpose of the research was quite different in nature from the study reported in this paper. At no time during the original investigation was it meant to be a comparative one. When the European data were gathered the author knew very little about the United States, its people, its culture, and its education. However, when gathering the American data in Winnetka, it became clear that significant comparisons could be made between children of the two cultures. The investigator has interviewed 261 children from kindergarten through high school, 80 Europeans and 181 Americans. In all, 12 stories have been used. This paper, however, reports on just two stories, used in elementary schools only.

Subjects

Europe: Twenty-nine French-speaking Swiss children, attending elementary school, which goes to tenth grade, in a rather run-down neighborhood in Geneva. United States: Forty American children, attending elementary school in Winnetka, a well-to-do suburb of Chicago.

One might wonder whether the results of this study were influenced by the difference in socio-economic background between the children living in the United States and those in Geneva. However, results obtained, with the same stories, from 10 upper middle class German children living in Berlin were quite similar to those obtained from the Swiss children. This would seem to indicate that the phenomenon we are studying here is due more to the cultural structure of the society in which a child grows than it is to his socioeconomic class.

First Story—The Scoutleader's Birthday Party

"A group of children X years old (the subject's own age) want to give a surprise birthday party to their scoutleader. One boy has accepted the responsibility of decorating the room. He wonders whom he could ask for advice." (The questions which follow are illustrative of the type used. Actually, in the *méthode clinique*, the investigator probes and probes, formulating each question on the basis of the answer the subject has given to the preceding one; thus a uniform questionnaire is not employed. In the course of this probing the experimenter asks a large number of questions. The few here quoted are deemed sufficient to indicate the nature of the questions used.)

1. "Whom do you think he might ask?"
2. "He had thought of asking his home-room teacher, a whiz in English, history, and arithmetic, who knows nothing of art, or to ask another student who is so artistic that he has won a scholarship to the museum's art classes. Whom do you think he decided to ask?"
3. "He did ask both, and their advice differed. Whose advice do you think he followed?"
4. "He thought both ideas were equally good. Which one do you think he followed?"
5. "If he chooses the student's idea, will he be very embarrassed toward the teacher whose advice he did not follow?"

Second Story—Fight

"Two boys had a fight before school to see who was stronger. Louis hit Marc's nose which started bleeding profusely."

1. "How do you think Louis felt about it?"
2. "Louis felt guilty and wanted to get rid of his bad conscience. He knew that if he asked his teacher what to do the teacher would tell him to write one hundred times: 'I should not fight before school,' whereas another friend would advise him to give his favorite toy to Marc. Do you think he asked the teacher or the friend?"
3. "Why?"
4. "Louis went to Marc and Marc told him to forget the incident: 'In a fight one child is apt to get hurt,' he said, 'I might have hurt you just as easily.' When do you think that Louis no longer felt guilty, when Marc had told him that he had forgiven him, when he had written the pages for the teacher, or when he had given his toy to Marc?"

RESULTS

First Story

Sixteen (or 69.5 per cent) of the 23 Swiss children, with whom the story was used in the above given form, all of them at least 10.3 years old, insisted that teachers and parents always give the best advice, even in matters of talent. Upon further insistence by the experimenter that it is the child who has the training particularly helpful for the scout, the Swiss children explained that adults know better because they have more experience. In the United States only three out of 40 children (7.5 per cent) preferred the teacher's advice to that of the gifted child and all three of these were six years of age. Whereas all but two Swiss children (91 per cent) imagined that the teacher would be angry if his advice was not followed, only six children in the United States (15 per cent) believed so—three were six years, two were seven, and one was nine years of age. Most American children felt certain that the teacher would want the scout to follow the best advice, not necessarily the teacher's. The answers seem to show that Swiss children have less confidence in their peers than do children in America, that Swiss children continue, until a later age, to believe in the omniscience of adult authorities and to rely on their judgment, and that they are afraid of their teachers.

Second Story

Only seven out of the 40 American children (17.5 per cent) showed "egocentricity" of conscience as compared to 20 out of 29 Swiss children (69 per cent). Whereas in America only two six-year-olds (5 per cent) at first thought about their expiation through punishment (though afterwards they did consider the whole situation), there were 13 Swiss children (45 per cent), distributed through the whole range of age, who remained solely concerned about their own atonement; another seven (24 per cent) were in a stage of transition. For many Swiss children the teacher's punishment alone re-established the equilibrium of the world, which was destroyed by their deed. In contrast to children in America, most Swiss children do not doubt the wisdom of their teacher's choice of punishment. When the investigator put these children on "the spot," questioning the teacher's judgment, a number of them became ill at ease and rationalized the teacher's action, finding some reason to justify his advice.

Rather than give up his favorite toy one American boy (2.5 per cent) and seven Swiss children (24 per cent) chose the written work. Others hated writing so much that they preferred giving away the toy. Thirteen Swiss children (45 per cent) wanted to undergo both punishments or at least the one they disliked the most to be sure of expiation. Several of these children were 14 years of age or older. In contrast, not a single American child expressed such a wish. Many Swiss children were of the conviction that some adult ought to be told of the accident even though the boys could take care of it very well themselves. One American boy thought that Louis should feel guilty, because he had not reported his misbehavior.

Being told that Marc has forgiven Louis hardly changed the Swiss children's position on needing punishment to be relieved from guilt feelings. These children again thought of the accident only from the point of view of their own expiation. None of the American children saw a need for punishment in this case.

Obviously the American children show an earlier independence from the teacher and his judgment than do the Swiss children; rather than assent to his wisdom they see the accident with more objectivity and accept the idea either that Marc is right and no guilt feelings are necessary, or that relief from guilt should come by giving pleasure to the child whom they have hurt. Thus they can conform with peer judgment. Their conscience becomes interiorized and autonomous at an earlier age than does that of the Swiss children. It is also a different type of conscience as pointed out before.

SUMMARY AND CONCLUSIONS

Twenty-nine Swiss children and 40 American children from 6 to 15 years of age were studied by the *méthode clinique* to determine the differences in rate of social development and in content of conscience. The study appears to have uncovered evidence that, in certain areas of social development, the American child matures earlier than does the Swiss child. The American child seems to transfer his parent dependence to a peer dependence at an earlier age. One result of this earlier transferring appears to be that the American child's conscience becomes less egocentric and interiorizes earlier than does that of the Swiss child. There is, however, some indication that the content of conscience differs in these two types of societies. Whereas the American child's conscience is turned, primarily, toward social adjustment, the Swiss child's is geared toward character improvement.

Within the age range studied, this study seems to support the following conclusions: (1) American children are emancipated from their own adults at an earlier age than are their Swiss counterparts. (2) They are less subjugated to adults. (3) They are, rather, more dependent on their peers. (4) They enjoy freedom of thought and independence of judgment at an earlier age. (5) They develop earlier a more highly autonomous, though less complex, conscience.

References

Mead, Margaret, "Social Change and Cultural Surrogates," in C. Kluckhohn and H. A. Murray, eds., *Personality in Nature, Society, and Culture*, 2nd ed. New York: Alfred A. Knopf, Inc., 1954, pp. 651-662.

Piaget, J., *The Moral Judgment of the Child*. New York: Harcourt, Brace & World, Inc., 1924.

——, *The Language and Thought of the Child*. New York: Harcourt, Brace & World, Inc., 1926.

——, *The Child's Conception of the World*. New York: Harcourt Brace & World, Inc., 1929.

Riesman, D., N. Glazer, and R. Denney, *The Lonely Crowd*. New Haven, Conn.: Yale University Press, 1950.

Stendler, Celia B., "The Learning of Certain Secondary Drives by Parisian and American Middle Class Children," *Marriage and Family Living*, 16 (1954), 195-200.

6 · The Effects of Social Climates

KURT LEWIN

Reprinted from an article entitled "Experiments in Social Space," *Harvard Educational Review*, 9 (1939), 21-32, by permission of the publisher.

The student may already have heard of the studies of social climates conducted by Lippitt and others under the direction of Lewin. The following is a nontechnical summary prepared by the director of these studies.

The psychologist of today recognizes that there are few problems more important for the development of the child and the problem of adolescence than a study of the processes by which a child takes over or becomes opposed to the ideology and the style of living predominant in his social climate, the forces which make him belong to certain groups, or which determine his social status and his security within those groups.

A genuine attempt to approach these problems experimentally—for instance, that of social status or leadership—implies technically that one has to create different types of groups and to set up experimentally a variety of social factors which might shift this status. The experimental social psychologist will have to acquaint himself with the task of experimentally creating groups, creating a social climate or style of living. The sociologist I hope will therefore forgive him when he cannot avoid handling also the so-called sociological problems of groups and group life. Perhaps the social psychologist might prove to be even of considerable help to the sociologist. Frequently the investigation on the border line between two sciences has proved to be particularly fruitful for the progress of both of them.

Take, for instance, the concept "social group." There has been much discussion about how to define a group. The group often has been considered as something more than the sum of the individuals, something better and higher. One has attributed to it a "group mind." The opponents of this opinion have declared the concept of "group mind" to be mere metaphysics and that in reality the group is nothing other than the sum of the individuals.

To one who has watched the development of the concept of organism, whole, or Gestalt, in psychology this argumentation sounds strangely familiar. In the beginning of Gestalt theory, at the time of Ehrenfels, one attributed to a psychological whole, such as a melody, a so-called Gestalt quality—that is, an additional entity like a group mind, which the whole was supposed to have in addition to the sum of its parts. Today we know that we do not need to assume a mystical Gestalt quality, but that any dynamical whole has properties of its own. The whole might be symmetric in spite of its parts being asymmetric, a whole might be unstable in spite of its parts being stable in themselves.

As far as I can see, the discussion regarding group versus individual in sociology follows a similar trend. Groups are sociological wholes; the unity of these sociological wholes can be defined operationally in the same way as a unity of any other dynamic whole, namely, by the interdependence of its parts. Such a definition takes mysticism out of the group conception and brings the problem down to a thoroughly empirical and testable basis. At the same time it means a full recognition of the fact that properties of a social group, such as its organization, its stability, its goals, are something different from the organization, the stability, and the goals of the individuals in it.

How, then, should one describe a group? Let us discuss the effect of democratic, autocratic, and laissez-faire atmospheres or clubs which have been experimentally created by Lippitt (1940a, 1940b, 1939), and Lippitt and White (1939), at the Iowa Child Welfare Research Station. Let us assume the club had five members and five observers were available. It might seem the simplest way always to assign one observer to one member of the club. However, the result at best would be five parallel microbiographies of five individuals. This procedure would not yield a satisfactory record even of such simple facts of the group life as its organization, its subgroups, and its leader-member relationship, not to speak of such important facts as the general atmosphere. Therefore, instead of assigning every observer to one individual, one observer was assigned to record from minute to minute the organization of the group into subgroups, another the social interactions, and so on. In other words, instead of observing the properties of individuals, the properties of the group as such were observed.

It is well known that the amount of success a teacher has in the classroom depends not only on her skill but to a great extent on the atmosphere she creates. This atmosphere is something intangible; it is a property of the social situation as a whole, and might be measured scientifically if approached from this angle. As a beginning, therefore, Lippitt selected a comparison between a democratic and an autocratic atmosphere for his study. The purpose of his experiment was not to duplicate any given autocracy or democracy or to study an "ideal" autocracy or democracy, but to create setups which would give insight into the underlying group dynamics. Two groups of boys and girls, ten and eleven years of age, were chosen for a mask-making club from a group of eager volunteers of two different school classes. With the help of the Moreno test both groups were equated as much as possible on such qualities as leadership and interpersonal relations. There were 11 meetings of the groups, the democratic group meeting always two days ahead of the autocratic one. The democratic group chose its activities freely. Whatever they chose the autocratic group was then ordered to do. In this way the activities of the group were equated. On the whole, then, everything was kept constant except the group atmosphere.

The leader in both groups was an adult student. He tried to create the different atmospheres by using the following technique:

Democratic	Authoritarian
1. All policies a matter of group determination, encouraged and drawn out by the leader.	1. All determination of policy by the strongest person (leader).
2. Activity perspective given by an explanation of the general steps of the process during discussion at first meeting (clay mold, plaster of Paris, papier-mâche, etc.). Where technical advice was needed, the leader tried to point out two or three alternative procedures from which choice could be made.	2. Techniques and steps of attaining the goal (completed mask) dictated by the authority, one at a time, so that future direction was always uncertain to a large degree.
3. The members were free to work with whomever they chose and the division of tasks was left up to the group.	3. The authority usually determined autocratically what each member should do and with whom he should work.
4. The leader attempted to be a group member in spirit and in discussion but not to perform much of the actual work. He gave objective praise and criticism.	4. The dominator criticized and praised individual's activities without giving objective reasons and remained aloof from active group participation. He was always impersonal rather than outwardly hostile or friendly (a necessary concession in method).

During the meetings of the two groups, the observers noted the number of incidents and actions per unit of time. It was observed that the autocratic leader put forth about twice as much action toward the members as the democratic leader, namely, 8.4 actions as against 4.5. This difference is even greater if one takes into account only the initiated social approach, namely, 5.2 as against 2.1. Still greater is this difference in relation to ascendant or initiated ascendant behavior: The ascendant actions of the autocratic leader were nearly three times as frequent as those of the democratic leader.

In regard to submissive actions, the proportion was opposite, namely, more frequent by the democratic leader, although in both groups submissive actions of the leader were relatively rare. A similar relation held for the objective, matter-of-fact actions. Here too the democratic leader showed a higher frequency.

On the whole, then, there existed a much greater impact on the members of the group by the leader in autocracy than in democracy, and the approach was much more ascendant and less matter of fact.

When we attempt to answer the question "How does the leader compare with the ordinary member in an autocracy and a democracy?" we must refer to an ideal average member who is a statistical representation of what would happen if all activities were distributed equally among the members of the group, including the leader. In Lippitt's experiment the figures showed two facts clearly: In both groups the leader was really leading. The autocratic leader showed 118 per cent more initiated ascendant acts than the average ideal member, and the democratic leader 41 per cent more. Both leaders were less submissive than the average member, namely, the autocrat 78 per cent, the democrat 53 per cent. It was interesting to note that both showed also more matter-of-fact action than the average ideal member.

However, the difference between the ordinary member and the leader was much less pronounced in democracy than in autocracy, both in ascendant and submissive action. The democratic leader distinguished himself, also relatively, more by his greater matter-of-factness.

What do these figures indicate about the situation in which the autocratic and democratic group members find themselves? I can only mention a few aspects: In the autocratic group it is the leader who sets the policy. For instance, a child says: "I thought we decided to do the other mask." The leader answers: "No, *this* is the one *I* decided last time would be the best one." In dynamical terms such an incident means that the child would have been able to reach his own goal but the leader puts up a barrier against this locomotion. Instead he induces another goal for the child and a force in this direction. We are calling such goals set up by the power of another person, an *induced* goal.

A parallel example in the democratic group might be this: A child asks, "How big will we make the mask? Are they out of clay or what?" The leader answers: "Would you like me to give you a little idea of how people generally make masks?" In other words, the leader in the democratic group, instead of hindering the children in getting to their own goal, bridges over whatever regions of difficulty that might exist. For the democratic group, many paths are open; for the autocratic only one, namely, that determined by the leader. In an autocracy the leader determines not only the kind of activity but also who should work with whom. In our experimental democracy all work cooperation was the result of spontaneous subgrouping of the children. In the autocracy 32 per cent of the work groups were initiated by the leader, as against no per cent in the democracy.

On the whole, then, the autocratic atmosphere gives a much greater and more aggressive dominance of the leader, and a narrowing down of the free movement of the members, together with a weakening of their power fields.

What is the effect of this atmosphere on the group life of the children? As measured by the observers the child-to-child relationship was rather different in the two atmospheres. There was about 30 times as much hostile domination in the autocracy as in the democracy, more demands for attention and much more hostile criticism; whereas in the democratic atmosphere cooperation and praise of the other fellow was much more frequent. In the democracy more constructive suggestions were made and a matter-of-fact or submissive behavior of member to member was more frequent.

In interpreting these data, we might say that the "style of living and thinking" initiated by the leader dominated the relations between the children. In the autocracy instead of a cooperative attitude, a hostile and highly personal attitude became prevalent. This was strikingly brought out by the amount of group or "we" feeling as against "I" feeling: Statements which were "We-centered" occurred twice as often in the democracy as in the autocracy, whereas far more statements in the autocracy were "I-centered" than in the democracy.

So far as the relation of the children toward the leader was concerned, the statistical analysis revealed that the children in the autocratic group who were *less submissive* to each other were about *twice* as submissive to their leader, as the children in the democratic group. Initiated approaches to the leader in the democratic group were less frequent than in the autocratic group. In autocracy the action by the member toward the leader had more the character of a response to an approach of the leader. The approach to the leader in the autocracy was more submissive, or kept at least on a matter-of-fact basis.

On the whole, then, the style of living in both atmospheres governed the child-child relation as well as the child-leader relation. In the autocratic group the children were less matter of fact, less cooperative, and submissive toward their equals, but more submissive to their superior than in the democracy.

Behind this difference of behavior lie a number of factors. The tension is greater in the autocratic atmosphere, and the dynamic structure of both groups is rather different. In an autocratic group there are two clearly distinguished levels of social status: The leader is the only one having higher status, the others being on an equally low level. A strong barrier kept up by the leader prevents anyone from increasing his status by acquiring leadership. In a democratic atmosphere the difference in social status is slight and there exists no barrier against acquiring leadership.

This has a rather clear effect on the amount of individuality. In our experiment every individual in the democracy showed a relatively greater individuality, having some field of his own in spite of the greater "we" feeling among them, or perhaps because of it. In the autocratic group on the contrary the children all had a low status without much individuality. The type of subgrouping showed this difference even more clearly. In the autocracy, there was little "we" feeling and relatively little spontaneous subgrouping among the children. If the work required the cooperation of four or five members, it was the leader who had to order the members to get together. In the democracy those groups came together spontaneously and they kept together about twice as long as in the autocracy. In the autocracy these larger units disintegrated much faster when left to themselves.

These group structures, in combination with the high tension in the autocracy, led in Lippitt's experiments to a *scapegoat* situation. The children in the autocratic group ganged together not against their leader, but against one of the children and treated him so badly that he ceased coming to the club. This happened to two different children during 12 sessions. Under autocratic rule any increase in status through leadership was blocked and the attempt to dominate was dictated by the style of living. In other words, every child became a potential enemy of every other one and the power fields of the children weakened each other, instead of strengthening each other by cooperation. Through combining in an attack against one individual the members who otherwise could not gain higher status were able to do so by violent suppression of one of their fellows.

One may ask whether these results are not due merely to individual differences. A number of facts rule out this explanation, although of course individual differences always play a role. Of particular interest was the transfer of one of the children from the autocratic to the democratic group, and of another from the democratic to the autocratic one. Before the transfer the difference between the two children was the same as between the two groups they belonged to, namely, the autocratic child was more dominating and less friendly and objective than the democratic one. However, after the transfer the behavior changed so that the previously autocratic child now became the less dominating and more friendly and objective child. In other words, the behavior of the children mirrored very quickly the atmosphere of the group in which they moved.

Later Lippitt and White studied four new clubs with other leaders. They included a third atmosphere, namely that of laissez-faire, and exposed the same children successively to a number of atmospheres. On the whole, the results bear out those of Lippitt. They show a striking difference between laissez-faire and democracy very much in favor of democracy. They show further two types of reaction in the autocratic groups, one characterized by aggression, the second by apathy.

On the whole, I think there is ample proof that the difference in behavior in autocratic, democratic, and laissez-faire situations is not a result of individual differences. There have been few experiences for me as impressive as seeing the expression in children's faces change during the first day of autocracy. The friendly, open, and cooperative group, full of life, became within a short half-hour a rather apathetic-looking gathering without initiative. The change from autocracy to democracy seemed to take somewhat more time than from democracy to autocracy. Autocracy is imposed upon the individual. Democracy he has to learn.

These experiments as a whole, then, bear out the observations of cultural anthropology and are well in line with other experiments on the effect of the situation as a whole. The social climate in which a child lives is for the child as important as the air it breathes. The group to which a child belongs is the ground on which he stands. His relation to this group and his status in it are the most important factors for his feeling of security or insecurity. No wonder that the group the person is a part of, and the culture in which he lives, determine to a very high degree his behavior and character. These social factors determine what space of free movement he has, and how far he can look ahead with some clarity into the future. In other words, they determine to a large degree his personal style of living and the direction and productivity of his planning.

References

Lewin, K., R. Lippitt, and R. K. White, "Patterns of Aggressive Behavior in Experimentally Created Social Climates," *Journal of Social Psychology*, 10 (1939), 271-299.

Lippitt, R., "An Experimental Study of the Effect of Democratic and Authoritarian Group Atmospheres," *University of Iowa Studies in Child Welfare*, Vol. 16, No. 3 (1940a), 43-195.

———, *An Analysis of Group Reaction to Three Types of Experimentally Created Social Climate*, Ph. D. thesis. Iowa City: University of Iowa, 1940b.

———, "Field Theory Experiment in Social Psychology: Autocratic and Democratic Group Atmospheres," *American Journal of Sociology*, 45 (1939), 26-49.

X—THE DEVELOPMENT OF STABILITY IN BEHAVIOR

1 · Shirley's Babies After Fifteen Years

PATRICIA NEILON

Reprinted from the article in *Journal of Genetic Psychology*, 73 (1948), 175-186, by permission of The Journal Press.

In Selection II-4, some account was given of Shirley's study of 25 children during the first two years. Neilon, who studied the same individuals at the age of seventeen, has made a unique contribution to the study of constancy of personality.

The matching technique that she used does not show what aspects of personality remain constant but shows that there is enough in common between two personality descriptions of each of a series of persons to permit correct matchings at better than a chance level.

Although mothers, nurses, and other observers of children have often been convinced that there is some continuity of "characteristicness," or general personality pattern in developing individuals, this continuity has been elusive of objective psychological measurement. That individuality exists in early infancy has been demonstrated by several investigators. That it also exists in adulthood is, of course, accepted, and differences are measured. That the pattern of personality shown in infancy continues through life, or that it changes its form of expression as growth and development proceed has, however, never been established. Just as manifestations of intelligence change with age, manifestations of individuality might change with development, while leaving the child in the same relative place in his group at successive measurements. Even assuming continuity of personality patterns, the individual who cries a great deal as an infant would not necessarily be expected to cry a great deal as an adult. The personality characteristic which caused the excessive crying in infancy might persist though, and be expressed in a different manner in adulthood. We do not know merely from the infant's crying, however, what form of expression this characteristic might take later. The infant who cries a great deal might babble a great deal as a toddler, and be talkative as an adult. Or, the same infant who cries a great deal might be subject to severe temper tantrums at preschool age, and have an inclination to impulsiveness or emotionality in adulthood. The entire personality pattern, including emphases and details might continue from infancy with changes in expression to adulthood. Or, perhaps, some elements of individuality might be retained while others disappeared with development and experience. Or, there is a third possibility that differences which existed in infancy were perhaps due to differences in age at birth, and to physical and physiological conditions. Although these and other more complex possibilities unquestionably exist, they have not been investigated. In part this is due to the difficulties of measurement in the field of personality, and in part to the lack of attempts at measurement of the same individuals after long intervals of time have elapsed. Moreover, measurements which are suitable for infants or children are inapplicable to adults and *vice versa*, so that continuity of measurements is impossible. As a result, most students of child personality have used the cross-sectional approach to investigate age and sex differences in a certain trait, or to produce experimental modifications. Rarely have they attempted to measure continuity in the natural environment.

PREVIOUS STUDIES

Early biographers seem to have believed in the emergence of individuality in infancy. Shinn (1900), for example, says: "Our baby showed temperament and luckily of the easy-going and cheerful kind from her first day (though we could hardly see this except by looking back afterward)." Hogan (1900) refers to the child's "early inclination to know what was going on about him," which continued, as did his seeming "happiest when he was let alone."

In the more recent writings, evidence concerning continuity of individuality is given firstly in studies of certain personality traits, secondly in studies using personality tests and rating scales, and thirdly in studies which aim at total personality investigation, usually by use of a descriptive technique. The individual's characteristic modes of response have tended to persist in the areas of perseveration, which was investigated by Cushing (1929), laughter, which was investigated by Brackett (1933), and crying, which was investigated by Bayley (1932). After studying "problem" behavior in a large and representative sample, however, Macfarlane (1939) concluded that "transitoriness" tended to be the rule rather than "persistence." Using time sampling techniques in studying preschool children, individual consistency has been found by Green (1933) in "frequency of group play," by Loomis (Jones and Burks, 1936) in the ratio of number of contacts initiated to those received, and by Jersild and Markey (1942) in conflict behavior in two observation periods separated by a year's time interval. Because they demonstrate some degree of stability in personality, reports of continuity of such traits or behavior items are valuable. The question of the continuity of total personality pattern, however, is far more complex. While the above reports are objective, they are, for our purposes, limited in scope. Attempts to investigate "total personality," on the other hand, often sacrifice objectivity to completeness.

Halfway between studies of single traits and studies using descriptive methods to investigate total personality are studies of the continuity of individuality which use standard personality tests and rating scales as measuring devices. Test-retest techniques used by Jones and Burks (1936) have shown that children tend to say the same sorts of things about themselves on two tests separated in time. While personality tests are the most objective of the measures available, such studies cannot adequately demonstrate the continuity or lack of continuity of individuality. In the first place, test-retest reliability, deliberately made a part of the test, might insure measured continuity. To many, in the second place, a person's impression of himself is not so important an aspect of personality as is the impression of him gained by others, which is not measured by a personality test. Finally, a test is also limiting, and totality is again sacrificed to objectivity. The rating scale, which is a semiobjective measure, has also been applied to this problem. Bonham and Sargent (Murphy and others, 1937) used the method on 38 children from birth to two and one-half years finding no consistently positive relationships in ratings except for good looks. In *Biographies of Child Development*, Gesell and others (1939) conclude:

> Our data [from 10 years of study at the Yale clinic] do not lend support to the concept of a relatively standard pattern of infancy. Nor are the findings of embryology in harmony with such a concept. From the standpoint of embryology the infant is already far advanced in the cycle of life. He is already stamped with individuality rather than with a standard pattern. . . . This perpetuation of characteristicness is not incompatible with morphogenesis and maturing. It is, however, inconsistent with the idea that individual differences at birth are slight and increase with age, or that the period of infancy is in any sense neutral or generic when compared with later periods of the life cycle.

There seemed to have been persistent temperamental differences in twins *T* and *C* (Gesell and Thompson, 1941), and Johnny and Jimmy (McGraw, 1939). After a series of studies of the same group of children for five years at Columbia University (Jersild, 1933; McKinnon, 1942), "consistency," it was concluded, "rather than inconsistency is characteristic of development." Also using a descriptive technique, Allport (1937) studied his own son. Here personality predictions made by the parents when the boy was four months old were compared with records of parents at two later ages and with records of four different teachers at succeeding age levels. "The prognosis at the age of four months," Allport declares, "is borne out in most respects . . . two of the initially dominant characteristics have shifted their emphasis. . . . But on the whole the schedule is consistent throughout." From this material, Allport advances the hypothesis that "from early infancy there is a consistency in the development of personality." Roberts and Fleming (1943), with data from 25 women at precollege, college, and postcollege levels found that the ratio of persisting to fluctuating traits was 3:2.

Elimination of the experimenter's bias, which is a factor in all biographical studies, is achieved by Gesell (1939). Movies of five children at ages one and five were used. From the movies, a trained observer who was unacquainted with the children ranked them on 15 behavior traits including energy, demeanor, dependence, social responsiveness, and the like. Out of 75 rankings, 48 coincided, 21 were displaced by one rank order, 5 were displaced by two rank orders, and 1 was displaced by three rank orders. "Our periodic cinema records," Gesell writes, "clearly show prophetic characters in behavior traits in the first year."

In the investigation of continuity of individuality, in summary, positive findings are more conclusive than negative ones. An impression of continuity was reported by early biographers. Continuity is likewise found in certain separate traits and behavior items. Investigators of "total personality" have been unable to retain both completeness and objectivity, between which a balance must be struck. Since a breaking down of "totality" has usually given negative results, it would seem that strict quantitative measurement of behavior must be discarded in this area. The method of the Gesell study (1939) provides another sort of objectivity. The matching method advocated by Vernon (1935, 1936a, 1936b) allows the use of total personality, but eliminates the strong effect which the bias of the single experimenter exerts upon the results in the case study or descriptive method. In one study reported by Vernon (1935), character sketches of 25 subjects were written by each of 3 experimenters on the basis of the behavior of the subjects during performance tests. Each experimenter then tried to identify the sketches of the other two. This method applied to growing children should provide evidence about the continuity of individuality.

THE PRESENT METHOD

This is essentially the method adopted in this study. Extensive personality data on infants were presented by Dr. Mary Shirley in her *The First Two Years: a Study of Twenty-five Babies* (1933). After two years of standardized observations of the children as well as two years' acquaintance with them and their families, Dr. Shirley wrote personality sketches. These sketches and later sketches of the same children prepared by the writer were used in a matching procedure to investigate the continuity of individuality.

The plan for the personality follow-up of the 25 babies, which was begun 15 years after the original study, included the objective measurements of the subjects who would be available for study, and the writing of new personality sketches which were to be matched with the original sketches written by Dr. Shirley. The writer did not consult the Shirley sketches after the study was begun, and did not know the pseudonyms used by Shirley until the follow-up sketches were completed. Two formal personality tests were used in the follow-up, the Goodenough (1942) *Speed of Association Test* and the Rundquist-Sletto (1936) *Minnesota Survey of Opinions.* In addition to these formally developed scales of personality measurement, a 5-point rating scale of 23 traits, and a scale of 6 special abilities were also used. *The Speed of Association Test, The Minnesota Survey of Opinions,* and the scale for self-rating were administered to the subject in this order. Following this was a more or less standardized interview concerning the subject's interests, in which a general impression of his personality picture could be gained. An interview was also held with each of the mothers. During this interview, the mother rated her child on the 23 traits and 6 special abilities. She was also encouraged to talk about the child, and to state why she placed him in each of the rating categories. Many anecdotes illustrating the various characteristics of the child were related, and his place in the family group was estimated. Each mother was also asked whether or not she believed the child to have changed in such respects as were referred to on the rating scale or in his general behavior pattern. Rating scales and special ability scales were mailed to the fathers. All of the objective data were interpreted in the light of the short interviews with the subjects and mothers, and personality sketches were written of the children as they seemed to be at the age of seventeen.

The original group of 25 babies was above average in socio-economic status, education, and intelligence. Such a superior sample was originally chosen by Dr. Shirley because it was felt that better cooperation of parents could be obtained than would have been the case if a sample more representative of the population at large had been chosen. At the end of two years, Shirley had 19 of her original 25 subjects. Fifteen years later, it was possible to gather partial data on all of these, and full data on 16.

The finished adolescent sketches were two to four typewritten pages in length. To the Shirley infant sketches proper, material was added from her sections of "Incidental Reactions" and "Personality as Revealed in Speech." This made the infant sketches comparable in length to the adolescent sketches. Since sex was readily determined in all sketches, the sexes were separated for the matching procedure. There were 5 sketches of adolescent girls to be matched with 6 infant sketches, and 10 sketches of adolescent boys to be matched with 13 infant sketches. One of the adolescent boy sketches had to be thrown out because there was no comparable infant sketch. Keeping the extra infant sketches made matching more difficult by eliminating the possibility of automatically matching the last sketch in either series. Because of the length of the sketches, the matching task was a difficult one. It was performed by graduate students and staff members at the Institute of Child Welfare, University of Minnesota, who carefully read and reread the material, weighed and re-evaluated the evidence. Ten judges matched the sketches of girls (5 versus 6 cases), and five judges matched the sketches of boys (10 versus 13 cases). Although statistically the chances for success are approximately equal for both tasks, the matching of 10 versus 13 cases is psychologically far more difficult. The greater number of cases necessitated more than twice the amount of reading, and made an almost impossible demand upon the memories of the judges. With 10 personality sketches and 10 pictures Vernon (1936b) found matching "almost impossible" for judges, even though this would involve less reading than the matching of two sets of sketches.

Chances of successful choice are both reduced and increased by the limitations of the matching process. Taking the simpler five versus six matching as an example, the chances that the first adolescent girl's sketch would be correctly matched would be one in six. Assuming this first match to be correct, the chances that the second sketch would be correctly matched would be reduced to one in five. And assuming the first two to be correctly matched, there would be one chance in four that a third would also be successfully matched, and so on, the task being made easier by process of elimination after every successful matching. The chances of matching all sketches successfully, therefore, would be $\frac{1}{6}$! When there are incorrect matches, however, the problem becomes more complex. If the first adolescent girl's sketch were incorrectly matched, it might be matched with either the sixth infant sketch, which has no mate, or with any of the four others. In the latter case, two incorrect matches would automatically come about. If the first two adolescent girls' sketches were incorrectly matched, there would automatically be at least three, and quite possibly four errors.

Chapman (1935, 1936) has given formulae for the solution of this rather complex problem which are based on the possible permutations of the cases. In matching five versus six sketches, a total of 720 permutations are possible, but only one of these arrangements allows for the correct matching of all sketches. When there are four correct matches, and one error, there are five possible permutations, that is the sixth or extra infant sketch might be matched with any one of the five adolescent sketches. The chances of making one error, then, would be $\frac{5}{720}$. Other probabilities can be worked out by Chapman's formula. Table I shows the probabilities of the chance success of one judge in matching 5 versus 6 and 10 versus 13 cases worked out by this formula. It must be emphasized that these figures

Table I

Probabilities of the Chance Success of One Judge in Matching Personality Sketches

Number of Successes	Probable Chances in 100	
	5 vs. 6 cases	10 vs. 13 cases
0	43	46
1	37	36
2	15	14
3	4	3
4	0.07	0.06
5	0.01	0.008

apply only to the chances of successful matching by one judge. The highest number of successful matchings obtained by any judge for the 5 versus 6 cases was four, and for the 10 versus 13 cases, five.

RESULTS

The results of 10 judges in matching the 5 adolescent sketches and 6 infant sketches of girls are shown in Table II. The majority of the judges succeeded at the 4 per cent level of probability, three succeeded at the .07 per cent level, and one at the 15 per cent level. The mean number of successes for all of the judges is 3.2. The significance of this figure can be calculated by another special method. According to Chapman (1935), the mean of random matchings is, by sampling theory, $\frac{t}{u}$ ($t =$ the smaller number of items to be matched; $u =$ the larger number of items to be matched). This agrees with Zubin's (1933) discussion of the problem of matching equal numbers of items, in which the mean of random matchings is one, and the standard deviation is also one. For the more general case, which can apply with either equal or unequal numbers, Chapman gives

Table II

Successes of Ten Judges in Matching Personality Sketches of Girls (5 vs. 6 Cases)

Number of Correct Judgments	Probability Level	Numbers of Judges
0	43%	0
1	37	0
2	15	1
3	4	6
4	0.07	3
5	0.01	0
		10 Total

the formula for the standard deviation. He gives also a formula for calculating the skewness of the distribution of random matchings which becomes more leptokurtic and more skewed as the difference between the numbers to be matched increases. The distribution takes the shape of Pearson's Type III Curve. Tables, which are correct to six places, have been worked out by Salvosa (1930) for this function. Area under the Type III curve above the obtained mean value in terms of the standard deviation can be determined from these tables. Using this procedure, it was found that there is less than one chance in 1,000,000 that the mean of 10 judges in matching 5 versus 6 cases would equal or exceed 3.2.

The results of 5 judges in matching the 10 adolescent sketches of boys with 13 infant sketches, which are less clear cut, are shown in Table III. These results are less clear cut probably because of the difficulty of the task, and the difficulty of obtaining judges for the task. One judge did succeed, however, at the .008 per cent level. The mean number of successes for all of the judges in this case is 2.6. Applying Chapman's formula to this figure, there are only 25 chances in 100,000 than the mean of five judges in matching 10 versus 13 cases would equal or exceed 2.6.

Table III

Successes of Five Judges in Matching Personality Sketches of Boys (10 vs. 13 Cases)

Number of Correct Judgments	Probability Level	Numbers of Judges
0	46%	0
1	36	1
2	14	2
3	3	1
4	0.06	0
5	0.008	1
		5 Total

The successes of individual judges as well as the high mean numbers of successes for both tasks as compared to chance demonstrate some common element in the sketches at both levels. Since the writer was not familiar with the earlier sketches nor with the pseudonyms used for the children at the time of preparing the later sketches, and since similarity existed in the sketches of the two-year-olds which were based on subjective thorough acquaintance, and the sketches of the same children at seventeen which were based on objective tests and rating material, we conclude that personality similarities exist.

Taking the subject rather than the judge as the unit may shed more light on the results. Table IV shows that one of the girls, Winnie, was always matched correctly by the 10 judges, while Judy was never matched correctly. It seems possible, in other words, to rank the subjects according

Table IV

Distribution of Ten Matchings of Infant and Adolescent Personality Sketches of Girls

| Adolescent Sketch | Winnie | Times Out of 10 Matched with Following Infant Sketch | | | | Carol |
		Va. Ruth	Sibyl	Judy	Patty	
Winnie	10					
Va. Ruth		9				1
Sibyl			7	3		
Judy			2		3	5
Patty				3	6	

to ease of matching: Winnie, whom 10 out of 10 judges matched correctly; Virginia Ruth, matched correctly by 9 judges; Sibyl by 7; Patty by 6; and Judy who was never matched correctly. In considering the problem of the probability of repeated successes in matching the same adolescent sketch, the only method of attack seems to be in considering the matching of each adolescent sketch as a separate task independent of other matching. This, of course, is not the case. As stated above, the chances of matching the first case are one in six, while after one sketch is correctly matched, the probability that a second will be correctly matched is one in five and so on. Considering each matching as a simple choice of one of six sketches also ignores the fact that the correct match for any given sketch may already be incorrectly matched elsewhere. For calculating the probability of repeated successes, nevertheless, the simplest method is one in which each adolescent sketch is considered separately, or as if it were the first to be matched. The probability that one sketch would be matched correctly by all judges, using this line of reasoning, is $\frac{1}{6_n}$ while other probabilities are worked out through use of the binominal expansion. This trend of difference between subjects in matchability was less definite for the boys on account of the small number of judges used. Fred and Harvey seemed to be most frequently matched, however. It is possible to interpret

Table V

Probability of Repeated Successes in Ten Matchings of Personality Sketches

Adolescent Sketch	Number of Correct Matches	Probability Level
Winnie	10	0.00000165%
Virginia Ruth	9	0.0000828
Sibyl	7	0.00217
Judy	0	0.1615
Patty	6	0.000248

the trend in three ways. Ease of matching could be attributable, firstly, to the greater degree of similarity in personality in some cases. Perhaps, secondly, it might be due to more adequate description of some cases, at one or both levels. Allied with this is the third possibility that some individuals are more outstanding, and therefore can be matched more successfully than the generality even though the degree of similarity or dissimilarity between early and later status is similar for all.

SUMMARY

Personality sketches of 19 children written by Shirley (1933) on the basis of observations during the first two years of life were matched with personality sketches of 15 of the same children prepared by the writer on the basis of test and rating material. Later sketches were prepared without acquaintance with the earlier ones. Five judges matched 10 sketches of adolescent boys, and 10 judges matched 5 sketches of adolescent girls. Both the results of the individual judges and the mean scores of all judges in matching were significant as compared to chance. Following are the conclusions of the investigation.

1. Personality similarities in an individual persist over a period of time.

2. Some individuals are more readily indentifiable after a period of time, presumably due to greater uniqueness of personality pattern.

3. The matching technique, utilizing total impression, allows for the demonstration of similarities in personality pattern in the same individual over a period of time.

References

Allport, G. W., *Personality: A Psychological Interpretation.* New York: Holt, Rinehart & Winston, Inc., 1937.

Bayley, N., "A Study of the Crying of Infants During Mental and Physical Tests," *Journal of Genetic Psychology,* 40 (1932), 306-329.

Brackett, C. W., "Laughing and Crying of Preschool Children," *Journal of Experimental Education,* 2 (1933), 119-126.

Chapman, D. W., "The Generalized Problem of Correct Matchings," *Annals of Mathematical Statistics,* 6 (1935), 85-95.

———, "The Significance of Matching with Unequal Series," *American Journal of Psychology,* 48 (1936), 167-169.

Cushing, H. M., "A Perseverative Tendency in Preschool Children: A Study of Personality Differences," *Archives of Psychology,* No. 108 (1929).

Gesell, A., and others, *Biographies of Child Development.* New York: Harper & Row, Publishers, 1939.

———, and H. Thompson, "Twins T and C from Infancy to Adolescence," *Genetic Psychology Monographs,* Vol. 25. No. 1 (1941), 3-121.

Goodenough, F. L., "The Use of Free Association in the Objective Measurement of personality," in Q. McNemar and M. A. Merrill, eds., *Studies in Personality.* New York: McGraw-Hill Book Company, Inc., 1942.

Green, E. H., "Friendships and Quarrels Among Preschool Children," *Child Development*, 4 (1933), 237-252.

Hogan, L., *A Study of a Child*. New York: Harper & Row, Publishers, 1900.

Jersild, A. T., "The Constancy of Certain Behavior Patterns in Young Children," *American Journal of Psychology*, 45 (1933) 125-129.

———, *Child Psychology*, rev. ed. Englewood Cliffs, N. J.: Prentice-Hall, Inc., 1942.

Jones, M. C., and B. S. Burks, "Personality Development in Childhood: A Survey of Problems, Methods, and Experimental Findings," *Monographs of the Society for Research in Child Development*, Vol. 1, No. 4 (1936).

Macfarlane, J. W., "The Guidance Study," *Sociometry*, 2 (1939), 1-23.

McGraw, M. B., "Later Development of Children Specially Trained," *Child Development*, 10 (1939), 1-19.

McKinnon, K. M., *Consistency and Changes in Behavior Manifestations*. Child Development Monographs, No. 30. New York: Bureau of Publications, Teachers College, Columbia University, 1942.

Murphy, G., L. B. Murphy, and T. M. Newcomb, *Experimental Social Psychology*. New York: Harper & Row, Publishers, 1937.

Roberts, K. E., and V. V. Fleming, "Persistence and Change in Personality Patterns," *Monograph for the Society for Research in Child Development*, Vol. 8, No. 3 (1943).

Rundquist, E. A., and R. E. Sletto, *Personality in the Depression: A Study in the Measurement of Attitudes*. Minneapolis: University of Minnesota Press, 1936.

Salvosa, L. R., "Tables of Pearson's Type III Function," *Annals of Mathematical Statistics*, 1 (1930), 191-198.

Shinn, M. W., *The Biography of a Baby*. Boston: Houghton Mifflin Company, 1900.

Shirley, M. M., *The First Two Years: A Study of Twenty-five Babies*. Vol. I. *Locomotor and Postural Development*. Minneapolis: University of Minnesota Press, 1931.

———, *The First Two Years: A Study of Twenty-five Babies*. Vol. III. *Personality Manifestations*. Minneapolis: University of Minnesota Press, 1933.

Vernon, P. E., "Can Total Personality Be Studied Objectively?" *Character and Personality*, 4 (1935), 1-10.

———, "The Evaluation of Matching Methods," *Journal of Educational Psychology*, 27 (1936a), 1-17.

———, "The Matching Method Applied to Investigation of Personality," *Psychological Bulletin*, 33 (1936b), 149-177.

Zubin, J., "The Chance Element in Matching," *Journal of Educational Psychology*, 24 (1933), 674-681.

2 · Stability of Passive and Dependent Behavior from Childhood to Adulthood

JEROME KAGAN AND HOWARD A. MOSS

Abridged from *Child Development*, 31 (1960), 577-591, by permission of the authors and the Society for Research in Child Development.

Several long-term longitudinal studies of human development began about 1930, or slightly before. Only through such studies can the relationship between child behavior and adult behavior be investigated. The first longitudinal studies are now beginning to yield data which have never before been available. Presented here is one of the first long-term research reports from the Fels Research Institute, located at Antioch, Ohio.

A basic assumption of developmental theory is that adult behaviors are often established in early childhood. Although retrospective reports obtained from the verbal protocols of adults support this assumption, it has been difficult to produce a more objective demonstration of the long-term stability of childhood behavior patterns. This unhappy state of affairs is a consequence of the expense and difficulty associated with collecting long-term longitudinal information on a large sample of children. Only extensive, longitudinal research programs, as exemplified by the Berkeley Growth Study or the Fels Research Institute, can furnish the answers to this developmental problem.

This paper presents one set of results which have emerged from a recent study of a group of "normal" adults from the Fels longitudinal research population for whom extensive information was available from birth through adolescence. The findings deal specifically with the long-term stability of passive and dependent behavior in the face of situations which are frustrating and/or demand problem solving activity. This particular behavioral variable was chosen for initial analysis because theoretical essays on personality development emphasize that the early dependence of the child on the parent is of the utmost importance in shaping his future personality. That is, the development of a variety of adult motives and behaviors are based on the quality and intensity of the dependent relationship with the mother and mother-substitute figures. Further, psychological symptoms are theoretically attributed to inconsistency in the gratification of the child's dependent overtures and/or to denial or inhibition of dependent motives or behavior.

In addition to the longitudinal material, each subject was recently assessed during early adulthood by means of both interview and test procedures. The adult assessment was focused on the behavioral variables of dependency, aggression, achievement, and sexuality and on the degree of conflict and type of defensive responses associated with behavioral strivings in these areas. It was anticipated that there might be important sex differences with respect to occurrence of these behaviors, and the assessment procedures were designed to detect these potential sex differences.

METHOD

The Sample

The subjects (Ss) in this analysis were 27 male and 27 female Caucasian adults born between 1930 and 1939 who had recently been through a comprehensive assessment program which included an average of five hours of tape recorded interview and a variety of test procedures. The Ss were between 20 and 29 years of age at the time of the assessment. In addition, these Ss had fairly complete longitudinal records from 3 to 10 years of age. The Ss were predominantly middle class but came from a variety of vocational backgrounds including agricultural, skilled labor, tradesmen, and professional groups. The religious affiliations of the group included 43 Protestants, 10 Catholics, and 1 Jewish subject. The mean Wechsler-Bellevue IQ of the group was 120 with an IQ range of 97 to 142.

Interview Variables: Adult Assessment

Each S was interviewed by the senior author for approximately five hours over two to three sessions. *The interviewer had absolutely no knowledge of any of the longitudinal information on the Ss.* Since these Ss had been studied by psychologists for over 20 years, rapport was usually excellent, and defensive and evasive answers were infrequent. Following the interviews, each S was rated (7-point scale) on 59 variables. Six of these adult interview variables dealt specifically with passive and dependent behavior; abridged definitions of these variables follow:

> *Degree to which dependent gratifications were sought in choice of vocation.* This variable assessed the degree to which security was an important aspect of job choice, the degree to which the subject looked to his employer for gratification of his dependent needs, reluctance to shift jobs because of temporary loss of security. For nonworking women, emphasis was placed on her attitudes about the importance of security in her husband's job.
> *Degree of dependent behavior toward a love object.* This variable assessed the degree to which the subject sought advice and emotional support from a love object (sweetheart, husband, wife), degree to which the subject looked for stability and wisdom in a love object, degree to which responsibility for decision making was given to love object.

Degree of dependent behavior with parents. This variable assessed the degree to which the subject looked for advice, support, emotional encouragement, and nurturance from one or both parents.

Degree of dependent behavior toward nonparental figures. This variable assessed the degree to which the subject sought advice, emotional support, and nurturance from nonparental figures who were not love objects, e.g., friends, relatives, and teachers.

Tendency to display behavioral withdrawal in the face of anticipated failure. This variable assessed the frequency and consistency with which S tended to withdraw from tasks and situations which he thought were difficult to master and in which failure was anticipated.

Degree of conflict over dependent behavior. This variable assessed the degree to which the subject avoided placing himself in dependent positions, his derogation of dependent behavior in self and others, and his emphasis on the value and importance of independent behavior.

A random sample of 32 taped interviews were independently studied and rated. The interrater reliabilities for the six dependency variables ranged from .63 to .82 with an average coefficient of .74.

Procedure for Evaluation of Childhood Behavior

The junior author, who had no knowledge of the adult psychological status of the Ss, evaluated narrative reports based on direct observation of the child in a variety of situations. Summaries of interviews with the child and the mothers were also available. The observation reports were based on (1) semiannual visits to the home in which a staff member observed the child interact with mother and siblings for a two to four hour period, (2) semiannual or annual observations of the child in the Fels experimental nursery school and day camp settings, (3) interviews with the child, and (4) observations of the child in the classroom. After studying this material, the psychologist rated each child for a comprehensive set of variables (7-point scale). The rater studied the material for each S for ages 3 to 6 and made his ratings. Following a period of interpolated work, he then studied all the material for each S for ages 6 to 10 and again made the ratings. A period of approximately six months intervened between the evaluation of the material for any one child for ages 3 to 6 and 6 to 10. The rater felt that retroactive inhibition was sufficiently intense to mask any halo effect of the preschool ratings upon the later ratings made for 6 to 10 years of age. That is, the amount of material studied and the large number of variables rated militated against the recall of specific ratings over such a long period of time. In addition, the high degree of interrater reliability for these ratings supports the above statement. Independent ratings of the four childhood dependency variables by a second psychologist produced satisfactory interrater reliabilities. The product-moment correlations for each variable were all in the .80's with an average reliability of .86. The four childhood variables which involved passive and dependent behavior were defined as follows:

Tendency to behave in a passive manner when faced with environmental obstacles or stress (rated for ages 3 to 6 and 6 to 10). This variable assessed the degree to which the child was behaviorally passive in the face of external frustrations and failed to make any active mastery attempts to obtain desired goal objects following frustration. The rating of a passive behavioral reaction emphasized withdrawal from the frustration but included whining, crying, and soliciting help.

Tendency to seek support, nurturance, and assistance from female adults when under stress: general dependence (rated for age 3 to 6). This variable assessed the S's behavioral tendency to obtain assistance, nurturance, or affection from mother and other female adults when confronted with a threat to his well-being, a problem, or loss of a desired goal object. Dependent behavior included seeking out adults when faced with a problem or personal injury, reluctance to start a task without help or encouragement, seeking assistance of others, seeking affection from and close contact with female adults.

Tendency to seek affection and emotional support from female adults (rated for ages 6 to 10). This variable assessed the degree to which the child sought affection or emotional encouragement from mother or mother substitute figures. Evidence included kissing, holding hands, clinging, seeking encouragement, or proximity to female adults.

Tendency to seek instrumental assistance from female adults (rated for ages 6 to 10). This variable assessed the degree to which the child sought instrumental help with specific problems from mother, teachers, or other female authority figures. Instrumental dependent acts included seeking help with tasks, seeking help when physically threatened.

As mentioned above the average interrater reliability for these four variables was +.86.

The distributions for both the childhood and interview variables were normal. Product-moment correlations were computed between each of the childhood variables and the six interview based dependency variables obtained in adulthood with separate analyses for males and females.

RESULTS

Stability of Dependent Behavior

Table I presents the product-moment correlations between the childhood and adult ratings of passive and dependent behavior.

The major result is that passive and dependent behaviors were fairly stable for females but not for males. For girls the ratings of passivity during ages 6 to 10 correlated significantly with the adult ratings of a dependent orientation in vocational choice, dependency on love object, dependency on parents, and withdrawal to failure. Childhood passivity was inversely correlated with adult conflict over dependent behavior. That is, females who were passive as children were apt to accept their dependent behavior in adulthood and show minimal anxiety over their dependent motives. Only dependent behavior toward nonparental figures failed to show a significant, positive correlation with the childhood ratings of passivity. Simi-

Table I

Correlations Between Passive-Dependent Behavior in Childhood and Adulthood

Childhood Variables	Dependency in Vocation		Dependency on Love Object		Dependency on Parents		Dependency on Others		Withdrawal to Failure		Dependency Conflict	
	M	F	M	F	M	F	M	F	M	F	M	F
Passivity (Ages 3 to 6)	−.07	.24	.10	.23	−.28	.25	.04	.19	.06	.26	.03	.01
Passivity (Ages 6 to 10)	.11	.73**	.25	.36*	−.20	.54**	.04	.06	.21	.52**	−.26	−.63**
General Dependence (Ages 3 to 6)	−.06	.21	.13	.20	−.07	.07	.11	−.06	.12	.00	.05	.26
Emotional Dependence (Ages 6 to 10)	.21	.08	.18	.37*	.02	.51**	−.02	.06	.35*	.37*	−.12	−.31
Instrumental Dependence (Ages 6 to 10)	.19	.39*	.06	.58**	.14	.32	.37*	.01	.09	.39*	−.04	−.17

$* p < .05.$
$** p < .01.$

larly, the childhood ratings of both instrumental and emotional dependency on female adults, for girls aged 6-10, predicted adult ratings of dependency on love object, dependency on parents, and withdrawal to anticipated failure situations.

For the men there were only two significant correlations between the childhood dependency ratings and those based on the adult interview. Boys who were high on instrumental dependency for ages 6 to 10 were high on dependent behavior towards nonparental figures in adulthood. Second, emotional dependence during ages 6 to 10 was positively correlated with adult withdrawal to failure.

Of the 18 correlations between each of the three childhood variables for ages 6 to 10 and the six adult variables, 60 per cent were significant in the expected direction for females, while only 9 per cent were significant for the men.

Tables II and III present the intercorrelations among the childhood and adult interview variables respectively.

The correlations among the passive and dependency variables between ages 3 to 6 and 6 to 10 were generally more consistent for girls than for boys. That is, for girls the correlations among passivity and general dependence for ages 3 to 6 and the three variables for ages 6 to 10 were all consistently high. For boys the stability of the passivity rating for ages 3 to 6 and 6 to 10 was quite high. However, the relationships between passivity for 3 to 6 and the two dependency behaviors for 6 to 10 were not as high as they were for girls. This finding suggests that overt seeking

Table II

Intercorrelations Among Childhood Dependency Variables

	Passivity (6 to 10)		Gen. Dep. (3 to 6)		Emot. Dep. (6 to 10)		Instr. Dep. (6 to 10)	
	M	F	M	F	M	F	M	F
Passivity (3 to 6)	.82**	.76**	.74**	.83**	.26	.80**	.38	.79**
Passivity (6 to 10)	..	..	.40*	.63**	.43*	.65**	.53**	.61**
General Dependence (3 to 6)	..	..	..	..	.37	.61**	.38*	.63**
Emotional Dependence (6 to 10)	..	..	..	..	..	..	.60**	.79**
Instrumental Dependence (6 to 10)	..	..	..	..	..	..	..	..

* $p < .05$.
** $p < .01$.

of affection and/or instrumental aid in school age boys begins to be dissociated from a passive withdrawal reaction to problem situations.

The intercorrelations among the adult dependency variables were generally positive for both sexes. Dependency on parents and dependency on love objects were each associated with withdrawal to failure and negatively related to conflict over dependency. It is interesting to note that women who are dependent on their parents tended to be dependent on their love object but not on friends or authority figures. Men, on the other hand, who were dependent on their parents tended to be dependent on friends and authority figures rather than on a love object. Dependency on parents and friends usually involves instrumental aid with problems, while dependency on a love object more often included the soliciting of emotional support and affection. It will be recalled that one of the two significant correlations for males between childhood and adult dependency involved instrumental dependency for ages 6 to 10 with adult dependency on nonparental authority figures. Emotional dependency for boys age 6 to 10 showed no correlations with the adult dependency variables. Thus, male dependent behavior is apt to emphasize the seeking of instrumental as-

Table III

Intercorrelations Among Adult Dependency Variables

	Dependence Love Object		Dependence Parents		Dependence Others		Withdrawal		Dependence Conflict	
	M	F	M	F	M	F	M	F	M	F
Dep. Vocation ...	.61**	.42*	.53**	.49**	.12	−.10	.41*	.50**	−.61**	−.56**
Dep. Love Object .	..	..	.24	.54**	.48**	.16	.49**	.54**	−.66**	−.50**
Dep. Parents	..	..	..	..	.39*	.03	.44**	.57**	−.59**	−.71**
Dep. Others	..	..	..	..	..	..	.38*	−.15	−.46**	.15
Withdrawal	..	..	..	..	..	..	..	..	−.57**	−.70**
Dep. Conflict	..	..	..	..	..	..	..	..	..	..

* $p < .05$.
** $p < .01$.

sistance with problems, while females are likely to seek affection and emotional support in addition to instrumental aid.

It is important to note that passive and dependent behavior for ages 6 to 10 showed a better relation to adult dependent behavior than the ratings for 3 to 6 years of age. This finding indicates that important age changes occur between ages 3 and 10 and that behavior displayed during the first few years of school is a better index of adult functioning than the earlier preschool behavior patterns.

DISCUSSION

The results support a basic hypothesis of developmental theory which states that the acquisition of certain adult response patterns begins in early childhood. The differential stability of passive-dependent behavior for men and women is probably the result of several factors. However, one set of processes which may contribute to this phenomenon is derived from the commonly accepted hypothesis that passive and dependent behavior is less punished in females than in males. Further, females are often encouraged to be passive while men are expected to be independent and autonomous in the face of frustration. Parental and peer group punishment for passive and dependent behavior should result in some inhibition of this behavior in males. Thus, we would not expect this class of behavior to be as stable for men as for women. Studies of both overt behavior and fantasy (Hattwick, 1937; Kagan, 1959; Sanford et al., 1943; Watson, 1959; Whitehouse, 1949) all indicate that dependent responses are more frequent for girls than for boys. Further, the sex stereotypes presented by communication media fit this description. The analysis of children's books by Child, Potter, and Levine (1946) indicated that girls are portrayed as passive while boys are presented as independent and heroic. Finally, a study of the likes and dislikes of 10-year-old children (Tyler, 1955) confirms the belief that girls accept passive behavior as more appropriate for their sex role than do boys.

Detailed analysis of the 54 cases indicates that there was a greater proportion of men, than women, who shifted from high dependency during childhood to independent behavior as adults. The women tended to be either dependent or independent for both childhood and adulthood. For example, in comparing emotional dependence for ages 6 to 10 with adult dependency on parents, not one female showed a major shift from high dependency in childhood to low dependency in adulthood. For the men, however, 20 per cent were rated very dependent during the ages 6 to 10 and very independent in adulthood.

The authors do not suggest that passive and dependent behavior in girls is rigidly fixed at school age and that change is a rare or unusual phenomenon. It must be kept in mind that the social milieu of these particular subjects remained rather constant throughout their lives. Their familial and extrafamilial environments were not disrupted to any marked degree. The parents and peers of these Ss retained their same values, their reference groups remained constant, and, in most cases, their geographical travel was limited. Thus, the degree of behavioral stability obtained for these females might not hold for populations that are more mobile or transient, for different ethnic or class samples, or for people subjected to major traumata during adolescence and early adulthood.

Implicit in these results is a strategy for certain research problems in developmental psychology. It would appear that a select group of theoretically relevant behaviors become clearly established as preferential response tendencies as early as 6 to 10 years of age. This means that one can study the child longitudinally without having to wait 15 to 20 years before asking important questions of the data. Since the current philosophy of financial support for research allows an investigator to chart a 5 to 10 year program, it is now feasible for one investigator to see the products of a longitudinally oriented project in a reasonable length of time.

SUMMARY

This paper summarized some results from a larger investigation of the stability of behavior in a group of subjects who were part of the Fels Research Institute's longitudinal population. This report dealt specifically with the long term stability of passive and dependent behavior from childhood through adulthood.

The Ss were 27 males and 27 females for whom extensive longitudinal information was available from birth through adolescence. One psychologist studied narrative reports based on observations of the child in various settings and rated each child on four variables describing types of passive and dependent behavior for ages 3 to 6 and ages 6 to 10. A second psychologist, who had no knowledge of the childhood data, interviewed each S in adulthood and rated each S on six variables related to aspects of adult passive and dependent behavior.

The results revealed that passive and dependent behaviors were quite stable for women, but minimally stable for men. Over 60 per cent of the correlations between the childhood (ages 6 to 10) and adult ratings of dependency were statistically significant for females, while only 9 per cent were significant for men. For example, the correlation between passive withdrawal from problem situations for ages 6 to 10 and adulthood was .52 ($p < .01$) for women and .21 for men. Similarly, the correlation between emotional dependence for ages 6 to 10 and adult dependency on parents was .51 ($p < .01$) for women and .02 for men. The correlations between the ratings for ages 3 to 6 and adulthood were considerably lower and not statistically significant.

It was suggested that environmental disapproval and punishment of dependent behavior in young males led to inhibition of and conflict over dependency in the growing boy. The social acceptance of passive and dependent behavior in females would be expected to result in greater stability for this class of responses for women than for men.

References

Child, I. L., E. H. Potter, and Estelle M. Levine, "Children's Textbooks and Personality Development: An Exploration in the Social Psychology of Education," *Psychological Monographs*, Vol. 60, No. 279 (1946).

Hattwick, Bertha, "Sex Differences in Behavior of Nursery School Children," *Child Development*, 8 (1937), 323-355.

Kagan, J., "The Stability of TAT Fantasy and Stimulus Ambiguity," *Journal of Consulting Psychology*, 23 (1959), 266-271.

Sanford, R. N., M. M. Adkins, R. B. Miller, and E. N. Cobb, "Physique, Personality and Scholarship: A Comprehensive Study of School Children," *Monographs of Social Research in Child Development*, Vol. 8, No. 1 (1943).

Tyler, Leona E., "The Development of Vocational Interests. I. The Organization of Likes and Dislikes in Ten Year Old Children," *Journal of Genetic Psychology*, 86 (1955), 33-44.

Watson, R. I., *Psychology of the Child*. New York: John Wiley & Sons, Inc., 1959.

Whitehouse, Elizabeth, "Norms for Certain Aspects of the Thematic Apperception Test on a Group of Nine and Ten Year Old Children," *Journal of Personality*, 1 (1949), 12-15.

3 · Predictions of Later Behavior from Childhood Evaluations

EMMY WERNER AND ELIZABETH GALLISTEL

Reprinted from *Child Development*, 32 (1961), 255-260, by permission of the authors and the Society for Research in Child Development.

This investigation extends over a time span of only eight years, but it is remarkable in respect to the number of subjects who were studied—over 3000. Groups of this size must be studied if one is attempting to predict relatively infrequent forms of behavior.

This study of special outcomes presents one way of evaluating the predictive effectiveness of pupil responses to inventories and of teacher's ratings in an eight-year study of children's adjustment in a rural county in southwestern Minnesota (Anderson *et al.*, 1959).

PROCEDURE

In 1950 a large number of tests were given to over three thousand school children in this county, all those from grade 4 through grade 12. Inventories to which the pupils responded covered family attitudes, social responsibility, social maturity, home chores performed, range of leisure time activities, pleasant-unpleasant orientation, and psychoneurotic symptoms. In addition, the teachers rated each pupil on 20 personality characteristics (Personality Profile) and on the Havighurst check list of responsible behaviors (Teacher Check List). On the basis of internal consistency, items from these measures were then selected to form a shorter instrument, the Adjustment Inventory. A new responsibility measure was developed from items of the 1950 measure of social responsibility and the Teacher Check List which discriminated between young people nominated as very responsible and others thought of as irresponsible. The sentence completion measure, the chores liked, and the Personality Profile were also shortened by including only items which had discriminated in an item analysis.

These revised measures, together with a new Family Attitude scale used by the University of Minnesota's Rural Sociology Department, were given in 1954 to all school children ($N = 3,500$) in grades 4 through 12 in the same county.

495

In 1958 all youngsters from this population who had become delinquent (146) and all who had received public recognition, special positions, or honors (136) were identified. In addition, social workers, school nurses, the probate judge, and the medical clinic provided the names of 18 young people, 13 girls and 5 boys, who had become emotionally disturbed.

RESULTS

The tentative base rates estimated from these referrals and nominations within the county are low. They are, however, based only on young people in their teens and early twenties. For outstanding performance, they are 32 per 1,000 for females, 28 per 1,000 for males. For delinquency based on the number of *individuals*, *not* on the number of offenses, they are 15 per 1,000 for females, 85 per 1,000 for males, 20 per 1,000 of these for repeated major delinquencies. For those diagnosed as emotionally disturbed, they are 6 per 1,000 for females and 2 per 1,000 for males. There are two reasons for the small size of the emotionally disturbed group: first, it was impossible to determine how many had sought help through a private physician and/or hospital outside the county; second, most of the young people in our study are still below the age at which severe emotional disorders and the major psychoses commonly have their onset.

The mean scores for each of the special groups on the predictor variables are shown in Table I. They are stanines or standard scores which permit the comparison of a given youngster in a special group with the average for all pupils in the county of his age and sex. The population mean is 5, and the standard deviation, 2.

Both the outstanding boys and the outstanding girls are differentiated by the largest number of predictors. These young people scored significantly higher than their agemates on measures of intelligence and socio-economic status, on Family Attitudes, Responsibility, Social Maturity, and the Adjustment Inventory. Their teachers rated them above the average on the Personality Profile and the Teacher Check List.

In contrast, boys and girls in the group who later encountered trouble were differentiated by fewer predictor variables. Those who were to become delinquents, both boys and girls, had significantly lower than average scores on measures of socio-economic status and on the 1954 Responsibility measure. Delinquent *boys* had, in addition, below average ratings on *all* our teacher instruments and on the 1954 Adjustment Inventory. Boys with a record of repeated major delinquencies (rape, burglary, bodily assault with knife, etc.) had considerably lower scores on more predictors than the other delinquent groups. The teachers' evaluations of the *girls* who became delinquent, though low, were not significant for this size sample. These girls, however, did score significantly lower on the 1950 Family

Table I

Mean Stanine Scores of Outstanding, Delinquent, and Emotionally Disturbed Groups on Predictor Variables (Means of All Members of Sample = 5)

Predictor Measures	Outstanding		Delinquent		Emotionally Disturbed
	Boys	Girls	Boys	Girls	Girls
IQ (1950)	6.9*	7.2*	5.2	5.3	4.7
SES Measures					
Sewell (1950 SES)	6.7*	6.7*	4.2*	4.3	4.0*
Personal Data (1954 SES) ..	7.3*	7.1*	4.1*	3.3*	4.5
Father's Education	6.6*	6.2*	5.1	3.9*	4.9
Mother's Education	6.6*	6.6*	4.9	3.9*	5.0
Teacher Ratings					
Personality Profile (1950) ..	5.9*	5.9*	3.8*	4.4	3.9*
Teacher Check List (1950) ..	5.8*	6.0*	4.0*	4.2	5.0
Personality Profile (1954) ..	6.6*	6.2*	3.8*	4.3	3.4*
Pupil Inventories					
Family (1950)	6.6*	6.2*	4.7	4.1*	5.6
Social Responsibility (1950) .	6.0*	5.4	4.5	3.8*	4.8
Responsibility (1954)	6.2*	5.8*	4.2*	4.1*	4.1*
Social Maturity (1950)	5.6*	5.8*	4.8	4.8	4.0*
Adjustment Inventory (1954)	6.2*	6.0*	4.0*	4.6	4.2
Not Significant					
Leisure Time Activities (1950)	4.7	5.0	4.9	5.8	4.9
Psychoneurotic Indicators ...	5.1	5.2	4.9	5.0	5.6
Home Chores (1950)	4.7	4.5	5.1	4.8	4.6
Sentence Completion (1954)	5.2	4.8	4.9	4.4	4.4
Likes (1954)	4.5	4.4	4.8	4.8	5.4
Family Attitudes (1954)	5.0	5.1	4.7	5.3	5.1

Note.—The number of cases varies as follows: outstanding boys 40-61, girls 45-69; delinquent boys 80-97, girls 13-18; emotionally disturbed girls 7-16. There were not enough disturbed boys to test for significance of differences.
* Significant at the .05 level or better.

measure describing home practices having to do with trust, sharing decisions, and closeness.

The emotionally disturbed on whom we have information have significantly lower scores on a measure of rural socio-economic status. This might, however, have been an artifact of our sampling since we used agency referrals and the county clinic. Table I shows only the scores for the girls since the boys' group was not large enough to constitute a sample adequate for statistical analysis. The disturbed girls scored low on the 1954 Responsibility measure and a measure of personal habits, reflecting social maturity. Their teachers rated them significantly lower than their classmates on the Personality Profile, both in 1950 and in 1954.

None of the special groups differed significantly from the population average in the number of chores performed at home and the number of leisure time activities. Fears and worries from the Psychoneurotic Inventory did not predict membership in any of the special groups, not even the emotionally disturbed. We should remember, however, that these tests were taken in middle childhood or early adolescence and that much research needs still to be done to isolate the signs predictive of psychoneurotic behavior in children in contrast with those known of adults.

The 1954 Family Attitude measure did not significantly differentiate any of the special groups, though the 1950 Family measure did. The 1950 Havighurst instrument contained many items of a *specific* nature covering home practices while the 1954 Family measure asked for a *general* expression of positive or negative attitudes toward family members. This evaluation might be more strongly influenced by the temporary emotional state of the youngster, especially an adolescent trying to liberate himself from home.

The differences in the results of these measures point up some of the problems in the evaluation of the relation between certain areas of early adjustment and later outcome. It may be, for example, that there are a number of psychoneurotic signs which can be reliably pinpointed in childhood, but that the form or content of our questions in this area were inadequate. Similarly, it may be that some way of measuring the affect tone of children's responses to a sentence completion measure could be found which would be significantly related to later adjustment, but, though a great deal of research effort was devoted to developing the scoring procedure used for this semiprojective measure, no significant differences were found in these scores for special group members. Both the Sentence Completion and the Likes measures had been found to have diagnostic value, but they had no significant relation to later outcome. There is some indication that they might be unduly influenced by temporary emotions.

Since IQ and SES had differentiated the special groups from the population average, we wondered whether the other measures were significant only because of their relation to those two variables or whether some of the predictors would differentiate members of a special group from agemates of the *same* intelligence and socio-economic status. Consequently, we tested for significance of difference on all predictors after control for SES and IQ by careful matching and analysis of variance (Table II).

The Personality Profile proved to be the instrument which most consistently predicted members of special groups after control for IQ and SES, differentiating outstanding members of both sexes, emotionally disturbed girls (no sample for boys), and delinquent boys. It failed to differentiate the delinquent girls whose sample was quite small. The 1954 Responsibility measure differentiated both boy and girl delinquents. A few other variables (parents' education, social maturity) were occasionally significant.

Finally, we sought to discover whether these instruments singly or in combination constituted an adequate screening instrument around which

Table II

Predictor Variables Which Differentiated Special Groups After Control of Intelligence and Socio-Economic Status by Matching and Analysis of Covariance

Variables	Outstanding		Delinquent		Disturbed
	Boys	Girls	Boys	Girls	Girls
Personality Profile (1950)	0	0	—	0	—
Personality Profile (1954)	+	+	—	0	—
Teacher Check List (1950)	0	0	—	0	0
Responsibility (1954)	0	0	—	—	0
My Jobs MI (Maturity Index)	0	0	—	0	0
Father's Education	+	0	0	—	0
Mother's Education	0	0	—	0	0

+, significant at .05 level or better above the mean of control group.
—, significant at .05 level or better below the mean of control group.
0, not significantly different from control group.

a preventive program might be built. Frequency distributions by outcome for all individuals in each stanine on the significant predictors were obtained for the follow-up group graduating in .1957 where we had information for every child. These indicated that combinations of IQ, SES, teacher ratings, and significant pupil measures were not sufficiently discriminating to serve as a screening instrument for each individual child. Though there were no outstanding youngsters in the lower three stanines and no delinquents in the upper three stanines, there were enough of *both* groups in the middle stanines to reduce the predictive accuracy beyond the point of usefulness as an independent screening instrument. This was true for the boys more so than the girls. Both positive and negative outcomes were more clearly separated for the girls.

SUMMARY AND CONCLUSIONS

1. Scores on a number of pupil inventories and teacher ratings of groups of school children later recognized as outstanding, delinquent, or emotionally disturbed were significantly different from the norms for their age and sex. Singly or in combination, however, they did not prove adequate for predicting outcomes for a particular individual. The best predictor instruments would seem more valuable as supplements to IQ and SES information available in school records than as independent screening instruments.

2. A sizeable proportion of the relation between adjustment measures and later outcomes can be accounted for by intelligence and socio-economic status.

3. After control for IQ and SES, the single predictor which most consistently differentiated special group members from their agemates was a teacher rating scale, requiring ratings of personality characteristics on a

five-point scale. As raters, the teachers had the opportunity to compare characteristic behavior of individual children with their agemates and to sample it in different situations over longer periods of time. The personality dimensions covered by the scale were broad enough to characterize both outstanding, disturbed, and delinquent groups and to be meaningful at each developmental stage—late childhood, adolescence, and adulthood.

4. The measure which most effectively differentiated delinquents of both sexes was a pupil instrument measuring social responsibility. It consisted of short descriptive phrases which had been validated empirically against groups known to be high or low on this specific criterion.

5. Measures reporting the range of recreational activities, the number of chores performed at home, the number of experiences liked, the general "affect" as determined from sentence completion tests, and the number of psychoneurotic symptoms all failed to predict membership in any of the special groups.

Reference

Anderson, J. E., D. B. Harris, E. Werner, and E. Gallistel, "A Survey of Children's Adjustment Over Time. A Report to the People of Nobles County," Institute of Child Development and Welfare, University of Minnesota, 1959.

4 · Stability in Ascendance-Submission

LELAND H. STOTT

Reprinted from the *Merrill-Palmer Quarterly*, 3 (1957), 145-159, by permission of the author and the publisher.

Dr. Stott stresses the number of factors which may influence a specific individual in respect to the stability or variability of his behavior.

INTRODUCTION

The general problem with which this paper deals is that of personality formation, change, and stability. Everyone recognizes that there are in every individual attributes that seem to set him apart from others, certain qualities of his general functioning that persist through time and give him individuality. However much some of his traits, his attitudes, his behavior patterns may change with age as he develops and has experience, there remain certain basic and pervasive qualities about him that persist and remain as the core of his personality—his individuality. What are the origin and bases of individuality? What facets of a personality persist through time and in what ways may we expect a child to change in the process of socialization? These are important and intriguing questions for which we have only partial and tentative answers.

As a basis for consideration of material relevant to this problem herein to be presented, I wish to take the following theoretical position regarding the nature of growth and development:

Development in all its aspects is a function of the processes of interchange between the living organism and its environment. For the developing human individual other human beings are the most important features of the environment. These "significant others" are those who care for, protect, comfort or abuse, and generally "handle" the child. Thus the interaction (interchange) that takes place very early in the child's life between him and these significant others is of prime importance. Certain developmental trends are set in motion and these trends tend to persist. The character of this development, of course, depends upon the kind and quality of interchange that takes place, and this obviously is determined, not alone by the nature of the environment but also, and very importantly, by the inherent constitutional nature of the child himself. Thus the child's basic per-

501

sonality "structure"—his individuality—very early begins to form as he, with his particular inherent temperamental nature interacts with the particular environment into which he is born.

PURPOSES AND PROCEDURES

The nature of this early established personality pattern soon manifests itself as the child begins to interact with his peers in the free play situation. Our present purpose is to present data and other material from the behavioral and developmental records of children in the peer group situation which is pertinent to this problem of early personality development. These children were among those studied intensively at The Merrill-Palmer School in Detroit and on whom long term developmental and behavioral records were kept beginning at birth.

Prior to the enrollment of these children in the project several lists of statements descriptive of the social behavior and other aspects of personality and conduct readily observable in young children had been prepared. The procedure in using these lists was for the teachers and other adults dealing with the children when young, in nursery school, and later in the recreational clubs, to check for each child those items which they felt were truly descriptive of him and his behavior. One of these lists was concerned with the ascendance-submissiveness aspect of peer group interaction.

During a period of approximately 12 years these sheets were checked by a number of different observers for more than 100 children. Concurrently, physical growth records were kept, the children were tested periodically, and many observational reports and other kinds of recorded material about the children and their families were gathered.

In analysis of the check list material we were particularly interested in the *quality* of the behavior of each child and in noting possible factors related to the development of different qualities of interaction. One of the prior steps therefore was to examine the items of the check list and attempt to classify them in terms of the quality of behavior described. The 30 items used in the study, classified in terms of the five* qualities which seemed to be involved, are:

I. Domination (bossiness)—ascendant behavior with definite tendencies toward the use of force or coercion
    4. Submits to a leader only after a struggle to dominate
    8. Directs all activity about him
    15. Definitely schemes to get others to carry out his plans
    16. Gives commands with an air of finality
    26. Fights for his place as a leader

* The six items of grouping III, describing behavior which is definitely "ascendant" seemed not to discriminate between domineering "bossiness" and the "natural leadership" category but seemed to be consistent with either category. Category III, therefore, does not identify a separate behavior "quality."

27. Opposition spurs him on to greater activity
28. Insists that other children do as he wishes

II. Natural Leadership—ascendant over other children because of personal resourcefulness and attractiveness

10. Other children make many appeals to him for information
12. Other children appeal to him to make decisions for the group
13. Dominates others through their love or admiration for him
14. Dominates other children through his wealth of ideas
30. Gets willing cooperation easily

III. Ascendance—behavior which might relate to either authoritarian "domination" or "natural leadership" patterns.

3. Dominates children more mature than himself
5. Usually leads a small group
6. Decides who shall participate in the group activities
7. Is a leader in any group
11. Dominates other children through his ability to talk effectively
22. Usually takes the initiative

IV. Timid Conforming Behavior—related to politeness and a need to please others

18. Hesitates to initiate activity
19. Hesitates to make suggestions to other children
23. Seeks approval of the leader before he acts
24. Does not push the issue when opposed

V. Dependent Ineffective Submissiveness—behavior showing inadequacy and immaturity

1. Submits to any child who takes the initiative
2. Even submits to younger children
17. Helpless unless someone organizes activity for him
20. Usually follows the ideas of others for activity
29. Does not defend his own rights with other children

VI. Individualistic Tendency—withdrawal, not necessarily related to either ascendance or submissiveness

9. Neither leads nor follows; plays alone
21. Can take the initiative if it is absolutely necessary
25. Stands aside to let others participate

These qualitative categories are regarded merely as behavior classifications without any implication that they represent types of children. One might reasonably expect that many children during the course of a few weeks of experience in a situation like The Merrill-Palmer Nursery School or one of its Recreation Clubs might exhibit a range and variety of behavior which would represent most, if not all, of the five categories, their behavior in each case being quite appropriate to the situation. On the other hand, one might also expect to find children whose characteristic interactive behavior patterns corresponded fairly closely to one or another of the categories.

In order to discover to what extent the actual recorded behavior of the individual members of our group patterned itself in terms of our five behavior qualities, the individual check list records were retabulated on an ascendance-submission behavior pattern form. Figures 1 and 2 are examples of these individual patterns.

On this pattern sheet the three item groupings denoting ascendence are placed together on the left portion and the submission categories are on the right. Age "levels," or ranges, in years and months during which the checkings were made for a given child are indicated at the left of each row. Thus a longitudinal picture of the child's behavior in relation to his playmates as checked by competent and interested observers was obtained. Each of these profiles shows the characteristic patterning, or the lack of consistent patterning, of the child's behavior and the extent to which the pattern persists or changes during the period of observation.

RESULTS

An examination of 106 such individual records revealed that persistence of pattern was far more frequent than change. Table I presents the breakdown of these 106 tabulations in terms of predominant pattern, and persistence and change.

Table I

Summary of the Classification of 106 Children in Terms of Predominant Pattern of Interactive Behavior (Ascendance-Submission) Indicating Persistence, and Frequency and Direction of Change

Nature of Pattern	Frequency	Per cent
Mainly ascendant throughout	23	22
Natural leadership throughout	14	13
Mainly submissive throughout	24	23
Wide range (mixed) throughout	25	24
Increase in ascendance with age	11	10
Decrease in ascendance with age	9	8
	106	100

Table I shows that 86, or 82 per cent, of the 109 children showed no consistent direction of change during their periods of contact with the School's services. There were four main pattern categories into which these 86 children fell:

Twenty-two per cent showed a "mainly ascendant" pattern in which the child displayed both "domineering bossiness" and "natural leadership," the checks spreading through the first three item categories.

Another 13 per cent showed a clear and consistent pattern of natural leadership with relatively little tendency to be forcefully domineering.

A "mainly submissive" pattern, spreading through the two categories on the submissive side, characterized 23 per cent of the cases.

The other common pattern was one showing a wide range of checkings spreading across the whole profile form thus indicating a tendency to be domineering, to show natural leadership qualities, to be submissive or isolated depending upon the situation in which the child found himself.

Only about 18 per cent of the total showed a change in pattern with age, either an increase or a decrease in the tendency to be ascendant.

In other words, so far as the quality of the child's behavior in relation to his peers is concerned our results show a strong tendency in most instances for the pattern the child started out with to *persist* at least through the age range covered by our data and that where changes did occur they were most frequently temporary with subsequent return to his original pattern.

THE CASE OF A. J.

In an effort to investigate further this tendency, a number of cases were selected for more intensive study. Two of these, contrasting in pattern and quality of interactive behavior but alike in that the pattern persisted, may now be examined in greater detail. Figure 1 shows the pattern of checked ascendance-submission items for child A. J. during the period of his attendance in the School's services. A cross (X) under a particular item indicates that, at least during the age range indicated at the left, that statement was judged to characterize this child's behavior.

It will be noted that during a period of more than 10 years (ages 2½ to 13 years) this child's general pattern of behavior changed very little. He was observed to exhibit certain qualities of constructive leadership, especially during the nursery school period (to age 5). Some of the most consistently checked items indicate that he was usually able to take the initiative and tended to dominate but that he was able, when he wished, to effect this dominance through his wealth of ideas and his ability to talk effectively.

However, along with these more admirable leadership qualities, and perhaps more consistently characteristic of him, A. J. was strongly inclined to be forcefully domineering. He was likely to try to direct all activity about him and he would submit to another leader only "after a struggle to dominate" being always ready to "fight for his place as a leader." Opposition to his efforts to dominate in a situation "spurs him on to greater activity" and he would scheme "to get others to carry out his plans."

The pattern suggests also that perhaps as a reaction to the refusal of others to submit to his domineering behavior, he would isolate himself. The item "neither leads nor follows; plays alone" was one of the most frequently checked items.

FIGURE 1. *Ascendance-submission check list pattern.*

Column groupings:
- **Domination (Bossiness):** 4, 8, 15, 16, 26, 27, 28
- **Ascendance (Undifferentiated):** 3, 5, 6, 7, 11, 22
- **Natural Leadership:** 10, 12, 13, 14, 30
- **Individualistic Tendency:** 9, 21, 25
- **Polite, Timid, Conforming:** 18, 19, 23, 24
- **Dependent Submissiveness:** 1, 2, 17, 20, 29

Item descriptions:
4. Submits to a leader only after a struggle to dominate.
8. Directs all activity about him.
15. Definitely schemes to get others to carry out his plans.
16. Gives commands with an air of finality.
26. Fights for his place as leader.
27. Opposition spurs him on to greater activity.
28. Insists that other children do as he wishes.
3. Dominates children more mature than himself.
5. Usually leads a small group.
6. Decides who shall participate in the group activities.
7. Is a leader in any group.
11. Dominates other children through his ability to talk effectively.
22. Usually takes the initiative.
10. Other children make many appeals to him for information.
12. Other children appeal to him to make decisions for the group.
13. Dominates other children through their love or admiration for him.
14. Dominates other children through his wealth of ideas.
30. Gets willing cooperation easily.
9. Neither leads nor follows; plays alone.
21. Can take the initiative if it is absolutely necessary.
25. Stands aside to let others participate.
18. Hesitates to initiate activity.
19. Hesitates to make suggestions to other children
23. Seeks the approval of the leader before he acts.
24. Does not push the issue in case of opposition.
1. Submits to any child who takes the initiative.
2. Even submits to younger children.
17. Helpless unless someone organizes activity for him.
20. Usually follows the ideas of others for activity.
29. Does not defend his own rights with other children.

Age in Years and Months	4	8	15	16	26	27	28	3	5	6	7	11	22	10	12	13	14	30	9	21	25	18	19	23	24	1	2	17	20	29
2–7	X						X	X					X						X											X
3–1			X		X	X		X				X	X						X											
3–7	X	X			X	X	X	X		X	X	X	X	X	X	X	X	X	X	X	X									
4–1			X	X	X	X	X	X	X				X	X	X	X	X	X	X					X						
4–7		X			X			X	X	X	X	X	X	X	X	X	X	X	X											
5–1			X	X	X	X	X	X		X	X	X							X											
6–1																														
7–1	X		X	X	X	X				X	X		X			X			X											
8–1																														
9–1	X		X		X	X							X			X			X											
10–1																														
11–1																														
12–1	X	X		X				X			X	X	X	X		X	X													

In addition to the formal recording of behavior tendencies on the check lists, there are many comments and more individualized descriptions of the child and his behavior in the files. Many of these comments are interesting in connection with the more rigid check list pattern. They indicate that from the very beginning of his nursery school experience A. gave evidence of his tendency not only to force his will on others but also to vent considerable hostility in acts of aggression upon them. "A. is very rough with the other children, slaps them hard. He is also a very determined child" was one of the first comments regarding him by his nursery school teacher. A month later (age 2 years 7 months) he continued "to slap the children and he has twice been removed from the playground because of this." During this early period other comments were: "A. has really very little respect for adults, particularly the students, but as soon as he understands you mean business he is most cooperative." "A. is an outcast from the group. He interferes quite often with the play of the other children." He was reported to push children off their tricycles, grab their caps off, tear down their "houses." It is quite clear that during this period before he reached the age of 3 he was expressing in his behavior something more than a healthy urge to lead or to be constructively dominant in interesting group activities.

During A.'s second year in Nursery School (age 3-6 to 4-3) there was only one mention by the staff of overly hostile behavior: "When A. becomes very angry with the other children in order to have his own way he sometimes bites." There was repeated reference to his tendency to play alone, and to his close association with one other boy. There was evidence that A. was the dominant one in this duo.

During his third nursery school year, however, A.'s tendencies toward hostility and aggression in his attempts to dominate was even more strongly evident. This is indicated in the following entries in the record:

> A.'s ego is getting the better of him. Wants to always do just the opposite to what the other children are doing. Attacks the other children in a vicious manner if they are not doing what he would have them do. One day recently J. had marks on his face from an attack by A.
>
> A. is very tense and definitely unstable. When he does something which he knows ought not to be done he accuses another child of the wrong doing. Seems to definitely try to be annoying.
>
> A. is scratching the other children if they interfere with his way of thinking. Let another child try to assert himself against A.'s will and he is sure to be scratched.

There were, however, in the record of this period references to many desirable qualities in A. He was obviously a very bright child. He was described as alert, with very quick comprehension and an excellent memory for past events. He was "very quick to sense any uncertainty in an adult's dealing with a situation." He characteristically contributed many suggestions as to how to do things or what to do for group activity. He was very adept at organizing group play and was "always the center of attention in things he organized himself." Thus it is evident that A. possessed the qualities and personal resources which make for what we have called "natural leadership." However, the predominant note throughout the record of A.'s last nursery school year is "domineering bossiness" expressing itself in a forceful and hostile manner.

There are, however, evidences in the record of fluctuations or temporary breaks in the pattern which seem to be characteristic of the tense, insecure child. One comment was as follows: "A. is much improved since spring vacation. He now makes an effort to please. His manner and speech are much improved." But at the end of that same month the comments were concerned with hostile "scratching" of other children indicating a complete return to his former aggressive pattern.

During A.'s five years in the Recreational Clubs much the same pattern persisted. During the first club year, however, there was generally less aggressive behavior of a hostile or teasing nature and he tended somewhat more strongly to pursue his own individual interests and activities. He continued to show lively interest in activities of his own choosing.

When A. was between 8½ and 9 years of age and during his third year in the clubs program, staff comments concerning his interactive behavior with peers became more frequent. These comments ran as follows:

> A. came in feeling very mean and threw his coat up on top of the rack. I told him he was crushing C.'s hat. He said, "Well, that's my sister's hat anyway so what do I care." While I went after him to see that he hung his coat up another boy left his on the radiator. I asked A. whose coat it was and he said, "What do I care, that isn't my business. I'd like to sock that guy anyway." Then he rushed towards some little fat fellow with glasses and began to strike him.
>
> We had a problem this evening with A. He was very uncooperative and a poor sport at the games. We continually had to reprove him until finally he became sulky.
>
> A. jumps on the other children. He is rough and often hurts them. Students cannot manage him. He is quiet for a little while, then he will suddenly jump up and go wild. He is not accepted by the group. He is not able to play the organized games. He prefers . . . individual pastimes. Students observed that the uncooperative things he does are to attract attention. He hates to be criticized and will get mad and leave the game. He starts fights with smaller boys and girls.

During his tenth year of life, A. continued to present much the same pattern of behavior in relation to his peers that was characteristic of him as a preschool child. A written staff summary of the child's behavior through the years of the School's contact with him states that "all past records show that A. was determined and resistant. They indicate that this behavior was not a 'passing phase' that will be easily outgrown. He has always shown that only the firmest authority could manage him." However, he often accepted and used correction constructively. He was also responsive to approval.

> In the Brownies (Club) he was creative, original, more so than almost any other child. If he could be kept busy and could talk to an appreciative and interested adult, he was good. Otherwise he became destructive, wild, uncontrollable.
>
> One cannot get away from the fact that A. is of a definite constitutional type, highly excitable, seemingly overactive, never being able to delay action, nor to act if it does not suit him. He is emotionally unstable with a tendency to be dishonest.

A.'s Environment

A. evidently had a normal birth. He was breast fed with afternoon supplementary feedings for the first 3½ months. He was weaned from the bottle at about one year. Before he was one year old he was bothered with eczema. With the elimination of wheat from his diet this condition was soon alleviated. His development during infancy appears to have been quite normal. On the whole he had a generally healthy, normal babyhood.

A. began to suck his thumb, however, shortly after he was born and this apparently was a disturbing matter for the parents. Thumb guards were placed on him which he "seemed not to mind" particularly. He would then suck a finger "but not with so much gusto."

By the time A. was 2½ he had developed "negativism" to a point where his mother sought help from the Merrill-Palmer staff regarding it. The child "absolutely refuses to do as directed and this is occurring very often of late." In the interviews with the mother at this time certain inconsistencies in parental handling became apparent. "Mr. J. is apparently somewhat of a martinet in his ideas of discipline and does not wish to wait long for the obedient response of the child." Mr. J. was said to adore the baby sister who was described as "a lovely doll-like little creature," and he was always on the alert lest A. hurt the baby. He, therefore, was constantly cautioning A., telling what he must and must not do in relation to the baby. It was also reported that except for disciplinary measures, the baby was receiving all the attention at home. Mrs. J. realized that A. was beginning to play for attention at home.

At this time the J.'s were living with Mrs. J.'s parents. Sometimes the grandmother would call for A. at the end of the Nursery School day. On one such occasion the grandmother said, "I've been telling A. that if he did not stop sucking his thumb he would have to have his teeth pulled like I had mine." Mrs. J. reported that both grandparents were "after him every minute in regard to his thumb sucking. They expected 'immediate response to discipline' and they are constantly saying 'don't do this—don't do that.'"

The grandmother was said to have been "very nervous and fussy about her things and utterly unable to cope with such a lively child as A." Neither the parents nor the grandparents had ever been around little boys before and "they apparently in many instances are setting standards of behavior which are utterly beyond possibility. Mrs. J. seems to realize this fact to a certain extent but she has not enough knowledge to cope with it successfully." The grandmother would take it upon herself to punish the child against her daughter's wishes, criticizing her for being "too easy going." The J.'s apparently realized that the situation was not good for the children but under the economic situation that existed at the time they were unable to maintain a home of their own.

When A. was 6 years 10 months of age the mother in an interview reported that A. was quite irresponsible in the neighborhood and that he could not be depended upon not to destroy other people's property. As a result he had been excluded from many of the homes of the neighborhood. This naturally was a matter of much concern to the parents.

In interviews, Mrs. J. referred several times to tension between herself and her husband, saying that they often argued at the table seriously enough so that their voices were raised in anger. They had stopped arguing about the children and how to handle them in their presence but they "constantly argued about other things." There were indications during the conversation that an active antagonism existed between mother and father.

On the whole, A. was said to obey his father who was quite severe in his discipline. It was not uncommon for him to spank A. three or four times in the course of a Sunday afternoon for various kinds of misdemeanors.

In A., then, we have a case in which the interchange between a highly excitable, overactive, emotionally unstable constitutional temperament, and a restrictive, somewhat punitive, and inconsistent environment resulted in a particular pattern of interactive behavior—one aspect of his "personality structure"—which was highly resistant to change. According to this interpretation "home influences" were extremely important in the child's development, but the effects of those influences were probably specific to the child's inherent "constitutional type."

THE CASE OF B. R.

The checked behavior pattern of B. R. stands in contrast to that of A. J. With only a few scattered exceptions, all of his checks are on the submissive side of the pattern sheet (Figure 2). This pattern, however, is similar to that of A. and consistent with the large majority of the 109 patterns (Table I), in that it did not change significantly during the nine years of observation. The picture of B. is predominantly one of polite,

Case: B. R.

Column descriptions (keyed by item number):

- **Domination (Bossiness)**
  - 4 — Submits to a leader only after a struggle to dominate.
  - 8 — Directs all activity about him.
  - 15 — Definitely schemes to get others to carry out his plans.
  - 16 — Gives commands with an air of finality.
  - 26 — Fights for his place as leader.
  - 27 — Opposition spurs him on to greater activity.
  - 28 — Insists that other children do as he wishes.
- **Ascendance (Undifferentiated)**
  - 3 — Dominates children more mature than himself.
  - 5 — Usually leads a small group.
  - 6 — Decides who shall participate in the group activities.
  - 7 — Is a leader in any group.
  - 11 — Dominates other children through his ability to talk effectively.
  - 22 — Usually takes the initiative.
- **Natural Leadership**
  - 10 — Other children make many appeals to him for information.
  - 12 — Other children appeal to him to make decisions for the group.
  - 13 — Dominates other children through their love or admiration for him.
  - 14 — Dominates other children through his wealth of ideas.
  - 30 — Gets willing cooperation easily.
- **Individualistic Tendency**
  - 9 — Neither leads nor follows; plays alone.
  - 21 — Can take the initiative if it is absolutely necessary.
  - 25 — Stands aside to let others participate.
- **Polite, Timid, Conforming**
  - 18 — Hesitates to initiate activity.
  - 19 — Hesitates to make suggestions to other children.
  - 23 — Seeks the approval of the leader before he acts.
  - 24 — Does not push the issue in case of opposition.
- **Dependent Submissiveness**
  - 1 — Submits to any child who takes the initiative.
  - 2 — Even submits to younger children.
  - 17 — Helpless unless someone organizes activity for him.
  - 20 — Usually follows the ideas of others for activity.
  - 29 — Does not defend his own rights with other children.

Age in Years and Months	Domination (Bossiness)							Ascendance (Undifferentiated)						Natural Leadership					Individualistic Tendency			Polite, Timid, Conforming				Dependent Submissiveness				
	4	8	15	16	26	27	28	3	5	6	7	11	22	10	12	13	14	30	9	21	25	18	19	23	24	1	2	17	20	29
2–7													X						X		X	X	X			X	X	X	X	X
3–1																														
3–7																				X	X	X		X	X	X		X	X	X
4–1																				X		X	X	X	X	X	X	X	X	X
4–7																				X								X	X	
5–1												X	X						X	X	X	X	X	X	X	X	X		X	X
6–1		X											X						X		X	X	X			X	X	X		X
7–1													X						X	X		X	X	X	X	X		X		
8–1																														
9–1																			X	X	X	X	X			X	X		X	X
10–1																			X	X	X	X				X		X		

FIGURE 2. *Ascendance-submission check list pattern.*

511

timid conformity. He commonly "stood aside to let others participate" in activities where "taking turns" was the rule. He "hesitated" to intiate group activity or to make suggestions to others and willingly submitted to any child who would take the initiative. He would even submit to children younger than himself. He would not "defend his own rights with other children" and would rarely "push the issue in case of opposition." He was also dependently submissive in the sense of being "helpless unless someone organizes activity for him" and in being inclined to "follow the ideas of others for activity." Rather consistent with this picture of timid submissiveness was his tendency to play by himself.

A suggestion that this rather extreme shyness and submissiveness probably was not due to any lack of innate ability or potential for leadership is found in the fact that five of the six other items checked for B. were in, or consistent with, the "natural leadership" category. He was checked twice as being able to get "willing cooperation easily" and once each as "dominating other children through his wealth of ideas" and for the fact that "other children make appeals to him for information."

The comments and observational reports of staff and students generally support the view of B. presented in the check list pattern of Figure 2. At age 18 months the Merril-Palmer Test of Mental Ability was administered to him. The results of this test were not too satisfactory due to "very poor cooperation," probably a result of his timidity. "B. insisted that both parents sit very close to him" during the test.

At age 2 years, at the beginning of his nursery school experience B. was described as quite dependent and strongly attached to his mother. However, he accepted the routine procedures of the Nursery School as a matter of course, accepted authority, and was responsive to requests made of him. He played almost entirely by himself but he watched the other children a great deal. He showed, even that early, an inclination to keep in the background. He habitually sucked his thumb but he would remove his thumb from his mouth willingly when such a suggestion was made.

Four months later B. was referred to as "a passive, rather timid child inclined to withdraw from other children." However, he was judged to be "a stable child with good self-control. He showed no signs of over-stimulation." He was deliberate in his movements, slow in manner of walking. He ate his lunch in the same manner—"slowly matter of fact and deliberate." One comment was that he likes "slyly to take toys from others but if there is resistance he gives up immediately."

At 2½ he was "quite babyish" when his father visited the Nursery School. He pretended he could not climb the slide. He was very timid and attached himself to his father. He continued to suck his thumb but would cooperate by removing his thumb when reminded to do so. He was described as "cooperative but not self-reliant in routine."

The comments continued to describe this general pattern of shyness, self-consciousness, and compliance throughout the whole nursery school period. At age 3½ B. underwent an appendectomy after which he showed even more shyness and also a tendency to react negatively to the attention of others. At around 4 years of age, however, a somewhat new pattern was reported. He was said at this time to be very independent and self-reliant—"he does not want to be helped in any way." He also began playing more with bigger boys, entering into the activities and even "holding his own" with the others. But this promise of a new trend in development toward more self-assertiveness seems not to have materialized.

When he was approaching five, one staff comment was that the School had been trying to help him overcome his introvertive, withdrawing tendencies by putting him in situations that would force him to participate in group activity. However, these efforts apparently had little lasting effect. At age 11 years when a Stanford-Binet test was administered he "submitted to the test willingly" and was "very attentive to instructions." Again at 12½ he was described as "very serious and business like" in his approach to the test. Always the impression was that he did what he did because it was expected of him—to be compliant with the wishes of someone else.

Even with B.'s apparent lack of drive to assert himself and his slow and deliberate manner of approach he did well on intelligence tests. At 4½ his Binet I.Q. was 127. At 6 years 3 months it was 115, and at 11 years 4 months it was 140. As his check list profile suggested he possessed the necessary intellectual potential for real leadership.

B.'s Original Constitutional Nature

In the records of B.'s early infancy there is very little information regarding his original temperamental nature. As we have seen during his attendance in the School services his behavior was repeatedly described as slow, deliberate, careful, and compliant. This suggests a rather "low activity type" of constitution, with low sensitivity to the environment. On the other hand his shyness and social apprehensiveness suggests a basically keen sensitivity to other persons, and that his response system early became one of apprehension and withdrawal rather than one of pell-mell approach activity. The probability that B.'s low activity-shyness-withdrawing pattern was not, as such, identical with his original constitutional nature, but rather was of psychogenic origin—a result of early interchange between his original nature and his effective environment—is suggested by comments of Mrs. R. in a staff interview when B. was almost 2 years old. In describing B.'s "disposition" as a baby the mother said he was "happy, very determined." She said she had had "quite a hard time getting him *not* to do the things he wanted to do." For a time he had temper tantrums "but he doesn't try that now." She also described him as "very active." She stated that "recently B. has been biting his finger nails when at all excited." Thus it would seem probable that by original constitutional nature B. was highly sensitive to his environment and even of a fairly high "activity type." His high sensitivity rendered him readily susceptible to early conditioning.

Home Influences

Mrs. R. was well above the average in educational status, having obtained an M.A. degree. She had taught in an institution of higher learning. During the early years of B.'s life, however, she was judged as being "not as stable as she should be." She was inclined to feel "pushed by the pressure of work." Her high standards of housekeeping she found difficult to maintain.

She habitually "bit her nails" until she was 20 years of age. Her responses to the Bernreuter Personality Inventory, when B. was about 4, gave her a percentile score of 68 in "neuroticism" and 69 in "introversion." She said the main thing she worried about was "sin" and that she feared being alone, mice, snakes, and deep water.

Mrs. R. felt that her relationship with her husband was "good," that they have similar interests, and that disagreements between them were rare. She characterized her husband as kind, nervous, a plodder, a procrastinator, worrisome, gentle, self-reliant, and dependable.

Mr. R. was described by a staff member as having a "good disposition," even tempered, and "easy going." He was judged to have more patience with B. than did Mrs. R. He felt that his wife tended to "expect too much" of the child.

It would seem that on the whole the R. family situation, judged by ordinary standards, would have been rated as "favorable" as an environment for children. It is quite possible, however, that B.'s persistent pattern of shy, submissive, compliant interaction with others had its basis established at a very early age through the interchange between a very sensitive, responsive, and rather active tempermental nature, and the most effective aspect of his environment, viz., a rather repressive, somewhat harassed mother with, perhaps, a "pressure-y", somewhat punitive, rather than a completely accepting, attitude toward her young children. This interpretation is in line with the view of Karen Horney (1939) regarding the nature and origin of extreme submissiveness which she refers to as a form of masochism. This quality of interaction, she says, arises from "certain conflicts in interpersonal relations" in "the attempt to gain safety and satisfaction in life through inconspicuousness and dependency." (p. 113)

DISCUSSION

The cases of A. and B. are merely illustrative of the large majority of case records under study in which the quality of social interaction which the child displayed in the beginning of his nursery school experience continued to be characteristic of him, in many instances, in spite of considerable effort on the part of the service staff to bring about the desired change. Each case, of course, is unique. The pattern of behavior varied as did the individuality of the child and the environmental situation. Furthermore, many aspects of each child's personality did change in the sense of becoming more mature, and marked changes in over-all social behavior occurred. But even with these changes in capacity to function and modifications of patterns of functioning, the fundamental qualities of his person and of his functioning remained to give him uniqueness and individuality among his play peers.

Cases A. and B. by themselves prove nothing. But they, along with many others in our group, at least strongly suggest that these pervasive. persisting qualities of personality with which we are dealing are not inherited, as such, in the biological sense, nor are they traits that parents and teachers deliberately set about to inculcate in the young. Rather, they are psychogenic in origin. As Burgess and Locke (1956) maintain, these qualities "develop in the interpersonal relations of the family. They arise more or less spontaneously in the social interaction of the child with parents. The earliest distinctive responses of the child to persons in his social environment may be said to be a resultant (1) of his genic traits, (2) of parental responses to him, and (3) of special factors in the situation, such as illness. The theory of psychogenic reaction patterns assumes that one fixed they are not subject to any great modification." (p. 244)

The different qualities of ascendance and of submissiveness in children's peer interactions, in view of the evidence at hand, seem to fall in the category of "psychogenic reaction patterns" resulting from the early interchange between the child with his individual constitutional nature, and his "environment."

References

Burgess, E. W. and H. J. Locke, *The Family*. New York: American Book Company, 1956.

Horney, Karen, *New Ways in Psychoanalysis*. New York: W. W. Norton & Co., 1939.

5 · A Thirty-five Year Follow-up of Intellectually Superior Children

LEWIS M. TERMAN AND MELITA H. ODEN

Reprinted from *The Gifted Group at Mid-Life*, with the permission of the publishers, Stanford University Press. © Copyright 1959 by the Board of Trustees of the Leland Stanford Junior University.

Do highly intelligent children become highly intelligent adults? What are highly intelligent persons like as children? as adults? These are the questions to which Lewis M. Terman and his collaborators have addressed themselves for many years.

EARLY HISTORY OF THE TERMAN STUDY OF GIFTED CHILDREN

Many philosophers and scientists from Plato and Aristotle to the present day have recognized that a nation's resources of superior talent are the most precious it can have. A number of factors, however, have operated to postpone until recent years the inauguration of research in this field. Among these are: (1) the influence of long-current beliefs regarding the essential nature of the genius, long regarded as qualitatively set off from the rest of mankind and not to be explained by the natural laws of human behavior; (2) the widespread superstition that intellectual precocity is pathological; and (3) the growth of pseudo-democratic sentiments that have tended to encourage attitudes unfavorable to a just appreciation of individual differences in human endowment.

The senior author's first exploration into the problems posed by intellectual differences occurred over a half-century ago when, as a graduate student, he made an experimental study of two small contrasting groups of bright and dull children. His interest was heightened a few years later when, in standardizing the 1916 Stanford-Binet Intelligence Scale, he located and studied about a hundred children whose IQ's were above 130. He then decided to launch, at the first opportunity, a large-scale investigation of the physical, mental, and personality traits of a large group of exceptionally gifted children and, by follow-up studies, to find out what kind of adults such children tend to become. It was obvious that no intelligent program for training the gifted child could be laid down until the answers to these questions had been found.

In 1921 a generous grant from the Commonwealth Fund of New York

City made possible the realization of this ambition. The project as outlined called for the sifting of a school population of a quarter-million in order to locate a thousand or more of highest I.Q. The subjects thus selected were to be given a variety of psychological, physical, and scholastic tests and were then to be followed as far as possible into adult life. The investigation was expected to tell us (1) what intellectually superior children are like as children; (2) how well they turn out; and (3) what are some of the factors that influence their later achievement.

The Selection of Subjects

The problem was to discover in the schools of California a thousand or more subjects with IQ's that would place them well within the highest one per cent of the school population. For financial reasons it was not possible to give mental tests to the entire school population. Instead, the search was limited chiefly to the larger and medium-sized urban areas. The following procedures were used to identify the children of highest IQ in the areas surveyed.

In grades three to eight each classroom teacher filled out a blank which called for the name of the brightest child in the room, the second brightest, the third brightest, and the youngest. The children thus nominated in a particular school building were then brought together and given a group intelligence test (National Intelligence Test, Scale B). Those who scored promisingly high on the group test were given an individual examination on the Stanford-Binet test. In grades below the third, only the Stanford-Binet test was given to those nominated by the teacher, since no suitable group test was available at that time for younger children. In high schools the selection of subjects was based on the Terman Group Test scores of students nominated by the teachers as being among the brightest in their respective classes.

Checks made on the method of selection indicated that the method used was identifying close to 90 per cent of all who could have qualified. The proportion was high enough to insure that the group selected for study constituted a reasonably unbiased sampling and that whatever traits were typical of these children would be reasonably typical of gifted children in any comparable school population. The original criterion for inclusion for the Binet-tested subjects was an IQ of 140 or above, but for various reasons sixty-five subjects were included in the IQ range of 135 to 139. Most of those below 140 IQ were either siblings of subjects already admitted to the group or were older subjects whose scores were deemed to be spuriously low because of insufficient top in the 1916 Stanford-Binet. The standard set was purely arbitrary and was intended to insure that the subjects included for study should be in the highest 1 per cent of the school population in general intelligence as measured by the test used. Its choice was not based on any assumption that children above this IQ level are potential geniuses. The standards for admission on the Terman Group Test and other group tests also required the subject to score within the top 1 per cent of the general school population on which the norms were established.

The nature and results of the early stages of the investigation have been fully described in an earlier publication and will be summarized in the following pages.

Composition of the Group

The gifted subjects whose careers we have followed number, in all, 1,528 (857 males and 671 females). This figure includes a few who were selected before 1921, and 58 who were not selected until the field study of 1927-28. These 58 were siblings of previously selected subjects who were too young to test at the time of the main search for subjects in 1921-22.

The Binet-tested group made up more than two-thirds of the total and included 1,070 subjects (577 boys and 493 girls). Selected by the Terman Group Test given in high schools were 428 subjects (265 boys and 163 girls). The remaining 30 subjects were chosen on the basis of scores on the National Intelligence Test or the Army Alpha Test. The average age of the total group at the time of selection was 11 years; the Binet-tested subjects averaged 9.7 years and those qualifying on a group test, 15.2 years.

The mean IQ of subjects who were given the Stanford-Binet was 151.5 for the boys, 150.4 for the girls, and 151.0 for the sexes combined. The IQ range was from 135 to 200 with 77 subjects scoring at IQ 170 or higher. The mean IQ of high-school subjects tested by the Terman Group Test was 142.6 and the range of IQ was from 135 to 169. These figures, however, were estimates based upon norms which were inadequate and were perhaps 8 or 10 IQ points too low. Later follow-up of the high-school subjects indicated that they were as highly selected as the Binet-tested group.

The sex ratio among the Binet-tested subjects was approximately 116 boys to 100 girls. The much higher sex ratio for the high-school subjects— roughly 160 boys to 100 girls—is probably due to the less systematic procedures used in locating gifted subjects in the high schools. A sex ratio of 116 males to 100 females may be fully accounted for by the greater variability of males. McNemar and Terman, in a survey of sex differences on variability in such tests as the Stanford-Binet, the National Intelligence Tests, the Pressey Group Test, and Thorndike's CAVD test, found that 29 of 33 sex comparisons based on age groupings showed greater variability of boys. In Scotland, 874 of 875 children who were born on four particular days of the calendar year 1926, and were still living in 1936, were given a Stanford-Binet test at the age of ten years. The S.D. of the IQ distribution for this perfect sample was 15.9 for boys and 15.2 for girls—a difference sufficient to give a sex ratio of 134 boys to 100 girls scoring as high as 140 IQ.

Kinds of Information Obtained

Besides the intelligence test scores on which the selection of subjects was based, information of many different kinds was obtained. The chief sources were as follows.

1. A twelve-page Home Information Blank was filled out by the child's parents. This called for information on developmental case history, circumstances of birth, early feeding, ages of walking and talking, illnesses, nervous symptoms, home training, indications of intelligence, age of learning to read, reading habits, educational and occupational achievement of parents, genealogical records, and ratings on twenty-five traits.

2. An eight-page School Information Blank was filled out by the child's teacher. The blank called for information on school health records, quality of school work in each separate subject, evidence of superior ability, amount and kinds of reading, nervous symptoms, social adjustment, and ratings on the same twenty-five traits that were rated by the parents. This information was also obtained for a control group of 527 unselected school children.

3. A one-hour medical examination was given to 783 gifted subjects. The examination covered vision, hearing, nutrition, posture, teeth, heart, lungs, genitals, glandular disorders, blood pressure and hemoglobin tests, pulse and respiration rates, urine tests, and neurological conditions.

4. Thirty-seven anthropometrical measurements were made of nearly 600 gifted subjects.

5. A three-hour battery of achievement tests was given to 550 gifted subjects in grades two to eight. The battery covered reading, arithmetical computation, arithmetical reasoning, language usage, spelling, science information, language and literature information, history and civics information, and art information. The same tests were given to a large control group of unselected subjects.

6. A four-page Interest Blank was filled out by all the gifted subjects who were able to read and write and by a large control group of unselected subjects. The blank called for information on occupational preferences, reading interests, school-subject interests, relative difficulty of school subjects, number and size of collections, and various activities and accomplishments.

7. A record of all books read over a period of two months was obtained from some 550 gifted subjects and from a control group of 808 unselected children. Each book read was rated by the child for degree of interest.

8. A test of play interest, play practice, and play information was given to all the gifted subjects above grade two, and to a control group of nearly 500 unselected children. This test yielded scores on masculinity, maturity, and sociability of interests, and a play information quotient.

9. A battery of seven character tests was given to 550 gifted subjects and

533 unselected children of a control group. These included two tests of overstatement; three tests of questionable interests, preferences, and attitudes; a test of trustworthiness under temptation to cheat; and a test of emotional stability.

Summary Portrait of the Typical Gifted Child

Although there are many exceptions to the rule, the typical gifted child is the product of superior parentage—superior not only in cultural and educational background, but apparently also in heredity. As a result of the combined influence of heredity and environment, such children are superior physically to the average child of the general population.

Educationally, the typical gifted child is accelerated in grade placement about 14 per cent of his age; but in mastery of the subject matter taught, he is accelerated about 44 per cent of his age. The net result is that during the elementary-school period a majority of gifted children are kept at school tasks two or three full grades below the level of achievement they have already reached.

The interests of gifted children are many-sided and spontaneous. The members of our group learned to read easily and read many more and also better books than the average child. At the same time, they engaged in a wide range of childhood activities and acquired far more knowledge of plays and games than the average child of their years. Their preferences among plays and games closely follow the normal sex trends with regard to masculinity and femininity of interests, although gifted girls tend to be somewhat more masculine in their play life than the average girls. Both sexes show a degree of interest maturity two or three years beyond the age norm.

A battery of seven character tests showed gifted children above average on every one. On the total score of the character tests the typical gifted child at age 9 tests as high as the average child at age 12.

Ratings on 25 traits by parents and teachers confirm the evidence from tests and case histories. The proportion of gifted subjects rated superior to unselected children of corresponding age averaged 89 per cent for four intellectual traits, 82 per cent for four volitional traits, 67 per cent for three emotional traits, 65 per cent for two aesthetic traits, 64 per cent for four moral traits, 61 per cent for two physical traits, and 57 per cent for five social traits. Only on mechanical ingenuity were they rated as low as unselected children, and this verdict is contradicted by tests of mechanical aptitude.

Three facts stand out clearly in this composite portrait: (1) The deviation of gifted children from the generality is in the upward direction for nearly all traits; there is no law of compensation whereby the intellectual superiority of the gifted is offset by inferiorities along nonintellectual lines. (2) The amount of upward deviation of the gifted is not the same for all traits. (3) This unevenness of abilities is no greater for gifted than for average children, but it is different in direction; whereas the gifted are at their best in the "thought" subjects, average children are at their best in subjects that make the least demands upon the formation and manipulation of concepts.

Finally, the reader should bear in mind that there is a wide range of variability within our gifted group on every trait we have investigated. Descriptions of the gifted in terms of what is typical are useful as a basis for generalization, but emphasis on central tendencies should not blind us to the fact that gifted children, far from falling into a single pattern, represent an almost infinite variety of patterns.

Six Years Later: The Promise of Youth

The six-year interval between the original research and the follow-up investigation of 1927-28 was in a number of respects favorable as to length; it was great enough to make a comparison between earlier and later findings significant and interesting, but not so long as to make it impossible to use any of the kinds of tests employed in the original study.

At the time of the follow-up (1927-28) the average age of the subjects was between 16 and 17 years and the majority were in high school. The data secured for the subjects included intelligence tests, school achievement tests, personality tests, and interest tests. Other types of data obtained were as follows: a Home Information Blank of four pages was filled out by parents of subjects up to and including age nineteen. A two-page Interest Blank was filled out by the subjects under twenty, and a two-page Information Blank by those twenty or over. A School Information Blank of two pages was filled out by the teachers of the children who were still in elementary or high school. A Trait Rating Blank provided ratings by parents and teachers on 12 traits selected from the 25 on which ratings were secured in 1921-22. Finally, blanks were provided for the field workers' reports on home visits and on conferences with the children themselves and their teachers. It was not possible, unfortunately, to repeat the medical examinations and physical measurements of the original study, but considerable information on physical development and health history was secured from parents and teachers.

Perhaps the most important outcome of the 1927-28 follow-up was the fact that the composite portrait of the group had changed only in minor respects in six years. As a whole, the group was still highly superior intellectually, for the most part within the top 1 or 2 per cent of the generality. There was some evidence that the boys had dropped slightly in IQ and that the girls had dropped somewhat more. This conclusion, however, needs to be qualified in two respects: For one thing, the intelligence tests used in the follow-up lacked sufficient top to yield IQ's strictly comparable with those of 1921-22; for another, it should be pointed out that some regression toward the mean is to be expected from purely statistical considerations.

The showing in school achievement was in line with that for intelligence. There was less skipping of school grades after the age of eleven or twelve years, but the quality of work for the group in general remained at an exceedingly high level. For example, nearly two-thirds of the high-school grades of the girls and more than one-half of the high-school grades of the boys were A's. The significance of this is accentuated by the fact that the gifted group in the high-school period averaged considerably younger than the generality of high-school students. In evaluating school achievement at the high-school or college level, it is also necessary to bear in mind that the higher the grade the more highly selected is the school population with whom the gifted subjects are compared.

The composite-portrait method is useful, just as concepts and generalizations are useful in the shorthand of thinking. Nevertheless, the composite portrait, like any other kind of average, fails to convey any sense of the uniqueness of the individual subjects who compose the group. Although deviations below average intelligence were not found in the 1927-28 follow-up, extreme deviations both from the group average and from the generality were found in almost every physical, mental, and personality trait, including size, athletic ability, health, scientific ability, literary ability, masculinity, social and activity interests, vocational aptitude, social intelligence, leadership, ambition, and moral dependability. It is true that on all of these traits the mean for the gifted group tends to be higher than for unselected children of corresponding age, but the range of variability in these and other traits was if anything greater in mid-youth than it had been in mid-childhood.

Eighteen Years Later: The Gifted Child Grows Up

For eight years after the follow-up described in the preceding section there was no systematic attempt to contact all the members of the gifted group. During that period, however, considerable correspondence was carried on with the parents and occasionally with the individual subjects of the group. Many wrote about their activities, or came to Stanford University for personal interviews. From the majority of the group, however, little information was secured during this period.

In 1936 plans were laid for an extensive field study to be made as soon as funds become available. First, however, it seemed desirable to get in touch with as many as possible of the original group by mail, and to secure certain information that would aid in planning for the projected field study. Accordingly, a letter was sent out detailing the study and its purposes, and asking for the address of the subject, of his parents, and of a relative or friend through whom the subject might be located in later years. The letter was usually sent to the parents, although occasionally it went to the subject himself at the most recent address in our files. When the addresses had been received, a four-page Information Blank was sent to each subject, and a four-page Home Information Blank to the parents or, if both parents were deceased, to a near relative. The blank was accompanied by a letter emphasizing our continued interest in the subject, and the value both to science and to education of exact knowledge regarding the adult careers of persons who had tested high in intelligence during childhood.

The subject's Information Blank called for detailed information regarding educational history, occupations since leaving school, avocational interests and activities, general health, marital status, and deaths among relatives since 1928. The Home Information Blank called for information on the subject's physical and mental health, indications of special abilities, personality and character traits, education and occupations of siblings, and the accomplishments and activities of the subject's parents. Both blanks gave ample space for "additional information" not called for by specific questions and this brought, in many cases, extremely valuable and detailed replies.

In 1939-41 four field workers spent the year interviewing the subjects and, wherever possible, their parents also. Intelligence tests were administered to the subjects, their spouses, and their offspring and extensive questionnaire data were collected from the subjects, the spouses, and the parents of the subjects. In addition, the Strong Vocational Interest Blank was filled out by the men of the group. The study was highly successful with some information secured either directly or indirectly for nearly 98 per cent of the living subjects, and fairly complete data were furnished by the 96 per cent who cooperated actively.

So great was the amount of material on hand at the close of the field study that the punched card technique was used to analyze and correlate the data more efficiently. Not only the 1940 information but also the extensive case history data accumulated since the inception of this research were coded and transferred to punched cards. This method of handling the data made possible a very detailed study of the gifted child grown up, which has been fully reported in the preceding volume of this series. This earlier volume includes also the results of a supplementary survey conducted by means of a questionnaire mailed in 1945-46, which brought up to date the records on the main events in the lives of the subjects between 1940 and 1946—close to 25 years after they had been selected for study.

In addition to the reports on mortality, general health and physique, mental health and general adjustment, intellectual status, educational histories, occupational status and income, vocational interest tests, avocational interests, political and social attitudes, marriage and offspring, and marital adjustment, Volume IV includes several special studies based on an analysis of total case history. The studies included subjects of IQ 170 and above, subjects of Jewish descent, factors in the achievement of gifted men, and the effects of school acceleration. Among the conclusions reached were the following:

That to near mid-life, such a group may be expected to show a normal or below-normal incidence of serious personality maladjustment, insanity, delinquency, alcoholism, and homosexuality.

That, as a rule, those who as children tested above 170 IQ were more often accelerated in school, got better grades, and received more schooling than lower-testing members of the group; that they are not appreciably more prone to serious maladjustment; and that vocationally they are more successful.

That gifted children who have been promoted more rapidly than is customary are as a group equal or superior to gifted nonaccelerates in health and general adjustment, do better school work, continue their education further, and are more successful in their later careers.

That the intellectual status of the average member of the group at the mean age of thirty years was close to the 98th or 99th percentile of the general adult population, and was far above the average level of ability of graduates from superior colleges and universities.

That in vocational achievement the gifted group rates well above the average of college graduates and, as compared with the general population, is represented in the higher professions by eight or nine times its proportionate share.

That the vocational success of subjects, all of whom as children tested in the top 1 per cent of the child population is, as one would expect, greatly influenced by motivational factors and personality adjustment.

That the incidence of marriage in the group to 1945 is above that for the generality of college graduates of comparable age in the United States, and about equal to that in the general population.

That marital adjustment of the gifted, as measured by the marital happiness test, is equal or superior to that found in groups less highly selected for intelligence, and that the divorce rate is no higher than that of the generality of comparable age.

That the sexual adjustment of these subjects in marriage is in all respects as normal as that found in a less gifted and less educated group of 792 married couples.

That the test of marital aptitude predicts later marital success or failure in this group a little better than the test of marital happiness, much better than the index of sexual adjustment, and almost as well as scholastic aptitude tests predict success or failure in college.

That offspring of gifted subjects show almost exactly the same degree of filial regression as is predicated by Galton's Law.

That the fertility of the group to 1945 is probably below that necesssary for the continuation of the stock from which the subjects come, and that this stock is greatly superior to the generality.

That Jewish subjects in the group differ very little from the non-Jewish in ability, character, and personality traits, as measured either by tests or by ratings, but that they display somewhat stronger drive to achieve, form more stable marriages, and are a little less conservative in their political and social attitudes.

THE GROUP REACHES MID-LIFE

The third field follow-up of the gifted subjects was made in 1950-52. In order to pave the way for the field worker contacts, a General Information Blank was mailed in the spring of 1950, and had been returned by the majority of the subjects by the fall of that year. The field work got under way in late 1950 and was completed about mid-1952.

The preliminary blank called for some twenty kinds of information that would furnish a profile of the gifted subjects at mid-life. Other blanks and tests used in gathering follow-up data included the following: a highly difficult test of intelligence (Concept Mastery test) comparable to that used in 1939-40 but with certain improvements; an abbreviated form of the 1939-40 marital happiness test; a four-page questionnaire calling for information on factors that had influenced rate of reproduction; an eight-page questionnaire designed to throw light on factors relating to childhood and family background that might have influenced personality development, motivation, or life success; a four-page blank relating to the development, health history, and personality characteristics of each child born to members of the group.

The field work program included personal interviews with as many of the subjects as possible (and usually the spouses also) who were living in California, the administration of the Concept Mastery test and the various supplementary questionnaires to the subject and the spouse, and the testing of offspring of appropriate age with the Stanford-Binet test. In the case of those subjects living at a distance (about 18% of the total), funds were not sufficient to provide for visits by field workers. Except for the personal interview and the intelligence tests, however, the same data were collected by mail for these subjects as for the in-state group seen personally.

The statistical treatment and analysis of the information collected in the follow-up was such an enormous and time-consuming task that it was decided in 1955 to bring the demographic information up to date for inclusion in the published report of the status of the gifted group at mid-life. Accordingly a two-page Information Blank was mailed to the subjects in the spring of 1955, calling for the latest information on the main items of basic data.

Table I

Data Secured for Subjects and Spouses, 1950–1955

	N	
I. *1950–52 Follow-up*	**Subjects**	**Spouses**
General Information (for subjects)	1,268	...
Supplementary Biographical Data (for subjects and spouses)	1,119	...
Data on Rate of Reproduction and Happiness of Marriage (for subjects)	972	...
Happiness of Your Marriage (for spouses)	...	565
Concept Mastery Test (subjects and spouses)	1,004	690
II. *1955 Follow-up*		
Information Blank (for subjects)	1,288	...

In addition to the data blanks for the subjects and spouses, Stanford-Binet tests have been given to a total of 1,525 offspring of the gifted subjects. For a large proportion of these children a record of developmental history (Information About Child) was filled out by a parent, usually the mother, at the time of testing. The data from this blank will be reported in a separate publication at a later date.

Status of the Gifted Study 1950–1955

When the follow-up data of 1950-52 were gathered, the subjects had been under observation for approximately 30 years, and at the time of the 1955 survey the time had extended to about 34 years. Of the original group of 1,528 subjects, 91 had died by 1950 and an additional 13 deaths by 1955 brought the total number of deceased subjects to 104. During the course of study we have completely lost track of only 28 subjects (11 men and 17 women).

SUMMARY

In the past 35 years we have watched the gifted child advance through adolescence and youth into young manhood and womanhood and on into the fuller maturity of mid-life. The follow-up for three and one-half decades has shown that the superior child, with few exceptions, becomes the able adult, superior in nearly every aspect to the generality. But, as in childhood, this superiority is not equally great in all areas.

The superiority of the group is greatest in intellectual ability, in scholastic accomplishment, and in vocational achievements. Physically the gifted subjects continue to be above average as shown in their lower mortality record and in the health ratings. While personal adjustment and emotional stability are more difficult to evaluate, the indications are that the group does not differ greatly from the generality in the extent of personality and adjustment problems as shown by mental breakdowns, suicide, and marital failures. The incidence of such other problems as excessive use of liquor (alcoholism) and homosexuality is below that found in the total population, and the delinquency rate is but a small fraction of that in the generality. Clearly, desirable traits tend to go together. No negative correlations were found between intelligence and size, strength, physical well-being, or emotional stability. Rather, where correlations occur, they tend to be positive.

INDEX